Martin Sludsky

With great respect
for your dedication when we
worked together creating the
great grey Tka. And Evanlyn Martin
for your friendship over ten years.
It is deeply appreciated.

Geoffrey S. Cowie
March 1983

THE
GOLF
COURSE

THE GOLF COURSE

Geoffrey S. Cornish and Ronald E. Whitten

Foreword by Robert Trent Jones

Special Photography by Brian D. Morgan

The Rutledge Press
New York, New York

The authors gratefully acknowledge permission to quote from:

T. C. Simpson and others, *The Game of Golf* (London: The Lonsdale Library, Seeley Service and Co., Ltd., 1931).

Herbert Warren Wind, "Understanding Golf Course Architecture" from *Golf Digest Magazine,* November 1966. Copyright © 1981 by Golf Digest/Tennis Inc.

Bernard Darwin, *James Braid* (London: Hodder & Stoughton, 1952). Reprinted with the permission of A. P. Watt, Ltd.

Walter Travis, "Merits and Demerits of the Garden City Links" from *Country Life Magazine,* February 1906. Reprinted with the permission of Doubleday & Co., Garden City, New York.

Charles Blair Macdonald, *Scotland's Gift: Golf* (New York: Charles Scribner's Sons, 1928). Reprinted with the permission of Charles Scribner's Sons.

H. J. Whigham, "The Ideal Golf Links" from *Scribner's Magazine,* May 1909. Copyright © 1909 by Charles Scribner's Sons; copyright renewed. Reprinted with the permission of Charles Scribner's Sons.

W. C. Fownes, "Oakmont—Where You Must Play Every Shot" from *The Golf Journal,* May 1973. Reprinted with the permission of the United States Golf Association.

Robert Trent Jones, "The Common Interests of the Golf Architect and the Greenkeeper" from *The Greenkeeper's Reporter,* February 1935. Reprinted with the permission of the Golf Course Superintendents Association of America.

Horace G. Hutchinson, *Fifty Years of Golf* (New York: Charles Scribner's Sons, 1919). Reprinted with the permission of Charles Scribner's Sons.

William S. Flynn, "Golf Course Architecture and Construction — Analysis of Layout" from *Bulletin of the Green Section of the USGA,* October 1927. Reprinted with the permission of the United States Golf Association.

James Braid, *Advanced Golf* (London: Methuen and Co., Ltd., 1908).

Robert Trent Jones, "Design with Respect to Play" from *The Golf Journal,* June 1959. Reprinted with the permission of the United States Golf Association.

Published by The Rutledge Press
A Division of W. H. Smith Publishers Inc., 112 Madison Avenue, New York, New York 10016

Second Printing 1982
Printed in the United States of America
Designed by Allan Mogel

Library of Congress Cataloging in Publication Data

Cornish, Geoffrey S.,
  The golf course.

  Bibliography: p.
  Includes index.
    1. Golf Courses — History. 2. Golf courses —
Designs and plans. 3. Architects — Biography.
4. Golf courses — Great Britain. 5. Golf courses —
United States. I. Whitten, Ronald E. II. Title.
GV975.C65   796.352′068   81-10627
ISBN 0-8317-3947-9

Title Page: *Cape Cod, Massachusetts. As the ocean receded, sandy fields formed. Golf evolved over five centuries in Scotland, on these fields or links along the estuaries of the rivers Eden, Tay and Forth, endowing the game with a mystical link to sand.*

Contents

Foreword

Until now, the hundreds of books and the millions of words that have been written about the great game of golf have been conspicuously deficient in detailing the men who have been responsible for providing the very cornerstone of the game—the golf course architects.

With few exceptions they have suffered an undeserved anonymity. This despite the fact they have created an art form on one of the broadest canvases available to man and despite the fact their work has been admired and enjoyed for centuries. It has been their unwarranted fate to have left the mark of their genius without true recognition.

The Golf Course will right a wrong that has been more than 200 years in persisting. Geoffrey S. Cornish and Ronald E. Whitten finally have set the record straight. This book is a monumental achievement, one that adds a previously missing and vital chapter to the history of golf. It is an accomplishment I know was years in compiling and one for which golfers the world over and especially golf course architects ever will be indebted.

Besides serving to identify the practitioners of our profession from the past as well as those presently actively engaged, this book also gives credit to those who were responsible for innovations that not only changed the appearance of golf courses, but that materially affected the method of play. Golf today, in all honesty, is what the golf course architects have made it—a game of relaxed recreation and limitless enjoyment for millions and a demanding examination of exacting standards for those few who would seek to excel—depending on the requirements of the moment.

I found *The Golf Course* to be fascinating and, to a certain degree, not unlike viewing a long-forgotten movie on television. It revived memories of "giants" I had known in the past: Stanley Thompson, with whom I was associated early in my career; Albert W. Tillinghast, who told me of his work as we walked the fairways during the playing of the 1934 U.S. Open at Merion; and Donald Ross at Pinehurst during the founding of the American Society of Golf Course Architects in 1948.

One of the outstanding accomplishments of the book is the tracing of the "lineage" of many who started their careers as golf course construction workers or as assistants to other architects and who went on to become golf course architects in their own right. Also identified are the sons of architects who have continued and perpetuated the names of their fathers in the profession.

I would be remiss if I did not acknowledge the role credited to me and to my sons, Bob, Jr., and Rees, in the profession. It is most gratifying to know my work has been recognized and appreciated by my peers.

Geoff Cornish and Ron Whitten are to be complimented for a job well done. They have written a long-overdue book that has done a great service to the game and to the men who have made it possible.

Robert Trent Jones

P. 6-7: *Links holes at Spyglass Hill GC, Ca., by Jones. The natural links of Scotland form the foundation for the practice of course architecture.*

Preface

Golf is one of those few games played on a field with virtually no rigid dimensions. Why? Obviously, size has something to do with it. An eighteen-hole course typically requires well over a hundred acres, and such a large area is far more difficult to standardize than the relatively small space of a football field or a tennis court. Geographic variation is another factor. The game has been played in many different locales, on widely differing terrains. It has proved impossible, even if it were desirable, to create a standard playing field adaptable to all sites.

But these facts alone do not provide a complete explanation. Even courses of the same acreage, situated side by side on similar terrains, can look and play quite differently. So there must be a more fundamental reason for all the variety found on golf layouts. And, indeed, there is. The fact is that every individual who has ever laid out a course has had his own particular ideas as to how it should be done.

Golfers should cherish that fact, for the endless variety of golf layouts has added much to the charm and interest of the sport, and even more to the challenge of mastering it. Yet the men responsible for this endless variety, the golf course architects, have been largely forgotten by the golfing public. The aim of this book is to reintroduce them.

Not all golf architects were masters of the art, by any means. Some, indeed, were amazingly casual in the creation of their designs. Nevertheless, almost all of them influenced, to a greater or lesser degree, the development of the game. As a collective discipline, the practice of golf course architecture has had an impact reaching beyond golf itself, into such realms as concern for the environment and the aesthetics of our landscape.

Herb Graffis, longtime close observer of the golf scene, once compared the efforts of course designers with those of the artists who planned the gardens of the French chateaux and stately English country homes of earlier centuries. The comparison was apt. Golf architecture has indeed become an art, with each course a small collection of eighteen unique compositions.

This book is a history of the men who practiced the art of golf design. The subject has not been examined to any great degree before. Previous books on golf design, especially those by H. S. Colt, Alister Mackenzie, George C. Thomas, Jr., and Robert Hunter, were superior treatises on the philosophy of course architecture; but none documented the evolution of courses nor the persons contributing to it. In contrast, this book touches only briefly upon philosophy of design, for it is so comprehensive a topic as to warrant a separate volume of its own.

This book is not a history of the game itself, its championships or its great champions. Those topics have been covered elsewhere many times, and exceedingly well, by such writers as Bernard Darwin and Herbert Warren Wind. In addition, such events had only indirect bearing on course design.

Nor is the book a history of the implements and rules of the game. These have affected golf course architecture, but limitations of space have necessitated brevity in their treatment here.

Finally, this is not a book on the history of course maintenance. Certainly the course superintendent has been the single most important figure in maintaining and embellishing the designer's creation, and it was with difficulty that we refrained from devoting a major portion of the text to the development of turfgrass science and course maintenance. But, as with other topics, these are of collateral interest, and so discussion of them has been limited.

What is contained in this book is a comprehensive history of the men who practiced golf course architecture and the way in which their art evolved. The narrative portion of the text traces the development of the profession from its early days in Scotland to achievements of the very recent past. It focuses upon many of the architects who had an impact, favorable or otherwise, on golf courses through the years, and concludes with an analysis of their accomplishments.

The second portion of the book profiles several hundred men who made important contributions to the his-

P. 9: *Hole #15, Cypress Point GC, California, by Mackenzie. Britishers carried links traditions around the world. Alister Mackenzie, the first international designer, established his reputation here. Of the architects active between the Wars, his philosophy most influenced post-War design.*

tory of course design. A perusal of the profiles reveals some fascinating sidelights of this history. One is the fact that for many, many years, golf course architects came from other vocations. There were golf professionals, superintendents, engineers and agronomists, of course; but there were also bankers, lawyers, professors, physicians and even a socialist politician. Clearly the lure of golf design extended to men from all walks of life, at least until contemporary demand for specialization established landscape architecture as the preferred academic background.

Another significant fact revealed by the profiles is the striking continuity between generations of designers. Perhaps no other art has displayed it on quite such a scale. Dozens of father-and-son or designer-and-apprentice combinations are evident, reaching beyond a single generation and sometimes into several. Indeed, if all architects were plotted on a graph, very few would be unconnected with at least one other designer. The profile section also contains the most comprehensive listings of architects' works ever compiled, followed by an outline of miscellaneous matters related to this history. Another section contains a master list of golf courses cross referenced to their designers, both those profiled and others.

The major goals of this book are to provide an awareness to the golfing public of the many factors and influences that affect golf courses, and to promote a better understanding of the one that affects them most—the golf course architect. At one point in the text we have broadly categorized designers, but final judgment of their worth must rest with the individual golfer. It might be pointed out, however, that if one characteristic separated the successful from the unsuccessful designer, it was tenacity. Former USGA President Frank Tatum, Jr., put it best: "The ones whose work has survived are those who have had the wit and guts to get it right regardless." [1]

In the pages that follow, we believe you will discover that many tenacious golf architects did "get it right regardless." The world of golf is better because of them, and perhaps the world at large is a little better because of what they wrought.

[1] Paper presented to the American Society of Golf Course Architects, Pebble Beach, California, April 1976.

P. 10–11: *Hole #7, Shoal Creek GC, by Nicklaus. The challenge of golf course design has lured persons from all walks of life, including a number of the greatest golfers of all time.*

10

PART ONE

P. 19: (Top) *Linksland far from the ocean in Nebraska.*
P. 19: (Bottom) *Machrie Hotel GC, Scotland,*
by Willie Campbell. Built around 1890 and remodeled
by Steel in the 1970s, Machrie is one of the scores
of true links scattered along the British and Irish coastlines.
Campbell, like many fellow Scots, emigrated to
America in the late nineteenth century, carrying the traditions
of his native links across the ocean to the New World.

P. 20: *The earliest Scottish links were designed entirely by nature and consisted of high, windswept sand dunes and hollows where grass grew if the soil was reasonably substantial. P. 21: (Top) The routing outline at St. Andrews resembles a shepherd's crook. Finalized in the 19th century, it was primitively in existence in the 15th. P. 21:(bottom) Widening the Old Course around 1848 introduced strategy. Previously, play across hazards had been mandatory (above). Wider fairways (below) provided long, safe routes for the prudent, with direct routes available to reward success by more daring golfers. The Old Course thus exemplified, in different periods, two competing philosophies of design, namely penal and strategic.*

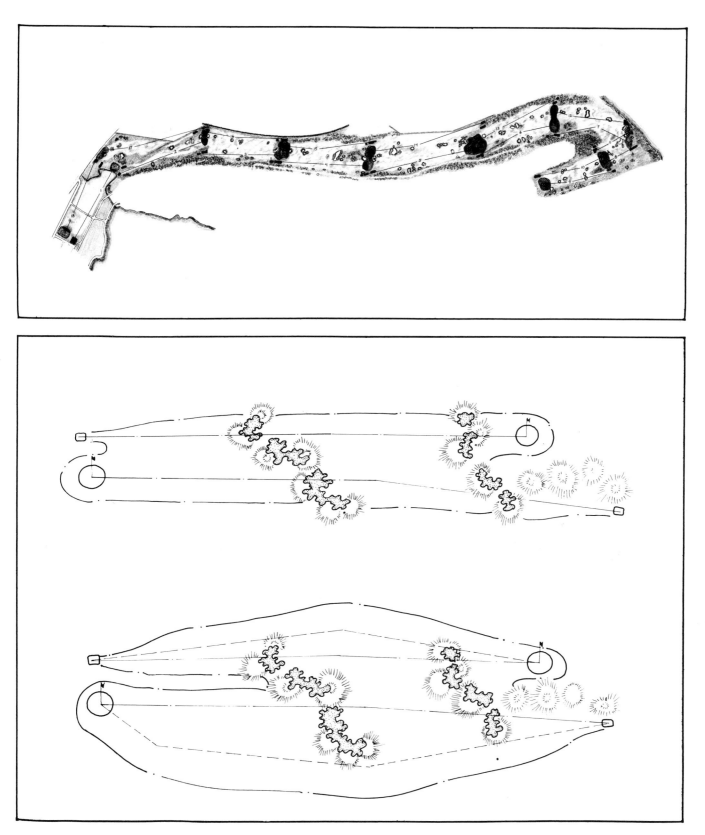

21

consolidated them into two long holes in order to maintain the integrity of the Old Course. This eliminated two greens and four holes, as each hole was played twice in a round, and thus reduced a round of golf at St. Andrews to eighteen holes. (Legend has a more romantic explanation for this change. A bottle of Scotch contained eighteen jiggers. The consumption rate was a jigger per hole. St. Andrews golfers felt the round should conclude with the bottle.)

In 1832 the practice began of cutting two cups into each of the common greens, creating eight "double greens" on which two matches, one heading out and one heading in, could be played at once.

Two years later King William IV was induced to recognize the St. Andrews links to be "Royal and Ancient." The Society of St. Andrews Golfers seized the opportunity to proclaim St. Andrews the official "Home of Golf" and the Society the foremost authority on the game. Prior to this, the Links of Leith had generally been considered the Home of Golf, but the Honourable Company of Edin-

burgh Golfers, the true patriarch of private clubs, had disbanded at Leith in 1831. (The Honourable Company reestablished at Musselburgh in 1836 and again at Muirfield in 1891.) Left without its strongest promoter and patron, the Links of Leith soon deteriorated and in 1834 could muster little to dispute St. Andrews's claim to its title.

St. Andrews thus became "The Royal and Ancient Golf Club of St. Andrews," and the golfing community afforded it the respect due royalty. Eighteen holes became the standard for any new course because St. Andrews had eighteen holes. Nearly every new course would be compared with St. Andrews to determine its merits and faults. Purists felt it near blasphemy to refer to anything but a linksland course, like St. Andrews, as a links. New terms were invented to describe inland and, by implication, inferior golfing grounds. The first term used was "green," which led to such derivatives as "greenkeeper," "green fee" and "green committee." Later, "golfing-course" became popular, and finally "golf course."

22

P. 22: Troia GC built in 1978 on true linksland in Portugal.
P. 23: (Top) The approach to the 17th green at St. Andrews, perhaps the first golf green planned by man.
P. 23: (Bottom) Turnberry, located on the western coast of Scotland, provided ideal links conditions.

Its lofty title, however, did not prevent the links at St. Andrews from being further altered. As a public course, in a town devoted to the game, St. Andrews had always seen considerable play. The narrow strip of playable grass was only some forty yards wide; and despite the use of double greens, play became increasingly congested and hazardous. Between 1848 and 1850, the course was widened by replacing the closest crops of heather with turf and by expanding the double greens into huge hundred-yard-wide surfaces. The widened course and huge double greens offered a unique feature: The holes could be played either as the "right-hand" course or in reverse as the "left-hand" course. During the same period of alteration, a new seventeenth green was also built. And in the first recorded instance of such a practice, some artificially created hazards were added to the Old Course.

An accidental but far-reaching result of the course widening was the introduction of the element of strategy into the game of golf. A player was no longer compelled to carry every hazard. He could, if he preferred, play a longer but safer route around a hazard at some sacrifice but without suffering an undue penalty. Previously, St. Andrews, like most links, not only required compulsory carries over most hazards but also penalized with whins, heather, sandy lies or lost balls any shot that strayed off line.

Thus, St. Andrews exemplified, in different periods, the two major, competing schools of thought in golf architecture. Originally it was an example of what in modern times is labeled "penal design." But after 1850 the Old Course, despite its blind hazards and fearsome bunkers with equally fearsome names, advanced the theory of "strategic design" by providing direct routes with substantial rewards to the bold player while offering safer but longer routes, at the cost of a stroke or part of one, to the less daring.

The original natural links of Scotland, especially St. Andrews, form the foundation for the practice of golf course architecture today. Their impressive settings and true golf values have exerted a profound influence on golf architecture to the present time and no doubt will do so forever. In the early development of the game of golf, its players, its rules and its implements all had to adapt to fit the existing conditions of nature as found on the links. As man began laying out and building golf courses, however, the opposite soon resulted. While the avowed purpose of course designers throughout history has been to imitate nature, the actual practice of golf architecture has demanded modifications of existing terrain and soil to create conditions resembling those found on the links.

SHOTS SUBSEQUENT TO THE TEE-SHOT
FURTHEST FROM THE HOLE
AS THE CROW FLIES
PLAYS FIRST
13Th

P. 24: *A form of pot bunker by the Dyes peppers the landscape at La Quinta Hotel GC in Ca.*
P. 25: *(Top) Royal Dublin, opened in 1885, was one of Ireland's first formal courses.*
P. 25: *(Bottom) Courses at Killarney in Ireland were planned first by the Parks and later by Guy Campbell and F. W. Hawtree.*

2.

Golf Spreads to England and Beyond

Wherever Scots went, they carried their national pastime and the lore of their links with them. The game of golf was introduced sporadically over a number of decades to distant outposts of the British Empire and other parts of the world, first by Scotsmen and later by Englishmen.

It had first spread to England, where a band of Scots played over a seven-hole course at Blackheath in 1608. By 1758 Molesey Hurst at Hampton was played regularly by the actor David Garrick and was praised as a "very good" golfing ground by a party of his Scottish friends. Another early formal layout was Old Manchester on Kersal Moor, opened around 1818.

Golf was known in America as early as 1779, and a golf club was founded in Charleston, South Carolina, in 1786. A club was formed in Calcutta, India, in 1829 and another at Bombay in 1842. Scottish officers convalescing near the Pyrenees introduced the game to France and built the Continent's oldest course, the Pau Golf Club, in 1856. It was also played in Hong Kong and on the Cape of Good Hope in South Africa by Scottish soldiers and engineers. By the 1870s courses had appeared in Australia and New Zealand, and by 1876 there were five in Canada: at Montreal, Quebec, Toronto, Brantford and Niagara-on-the-Lake.

Most of this early golf was played on rudimentary courses consisting of only a few holes. As golf spread far from Scotland, courses were laid out informally under widely different climatic conditions and on innumerable soil types and varying terrains. It was soon observed that blind shots, steep climbs, sharp drop offs, very flat terrain and a superabundance of natural problems including water and heavy underbrush did not contribute to pleasurable golf. Moreover, none of these early layouts achieved anything near the golfing satisfaction of the Scottish links, and few lasted beyond their initial season.

Despite its far-ranging introduction, golf was still not widely known or played as late as the first half of the nineteenth century, even in Scotland. But by the mid-1800s several events combined to capture the attention of the public in England and Scotland.

A number of widely publicized golf matches were held on the finest of the Scottish links, including St. Andrews and Musselburgh, in the 1840s. The expanding British railway system made it possible for large crowds to travel to and watch such exhibitions. The more venturesome of these spectators soon tried the links themselves.

Then, in 1848, the gutta-percha golf ball was invented. The introduction of this rubber-covered ball revolutionized golf. The cost of the old featherie was about four shillings; the new "gutty" cost only a single shilling. In addition, the gutty was much more durable. The featherie would more often than not split open when struck incorrectly; the new gutta-percha would merely dent under the same inexpert blow. Golf thus became a less frustrating and more affordable game.

The gutty led in turn to a revolution in golf club making, for its durability permitted far greater use of iron-headed clubs. Increasing use of irons resulted in the unintentional widening of fairways as the irons beat down the heather and bentgrass grew up in its place.

These several factors brought golf an increasing popularity through the last half of the nineteenth century. Yet its spread was not nearly as rapid as one might expect. By 1857 there were only seventeen golf clubs in Scotland, most of them playing over a handful of ancient, hallowed links. The growth of golf in other parts of Great Britain was even slower. By 1888 there were seventy-three golf courses in Scotland, fifty-seven in England, six in Ireland and two in Wales. More would come in the next decade. The first formal courses in England after the introduction of the gutty were Westward Ho! (1864), Wimbledon (1865) and Hoylake (1869). Early formal courses in Ireland included Royal Belfast (1881), Royal Dublin (1885), Portrush (1888), Lahinch (1892), Portmarnock (1894) and Sligo (1894).

The earliest records of golf course designers and their works date from this period of growth in the latter part of the nineteenth century. The first recognized designer was Allan Robertson, the long-time professional and club-maker of St. Andrews, who died in 1859. Robertson is

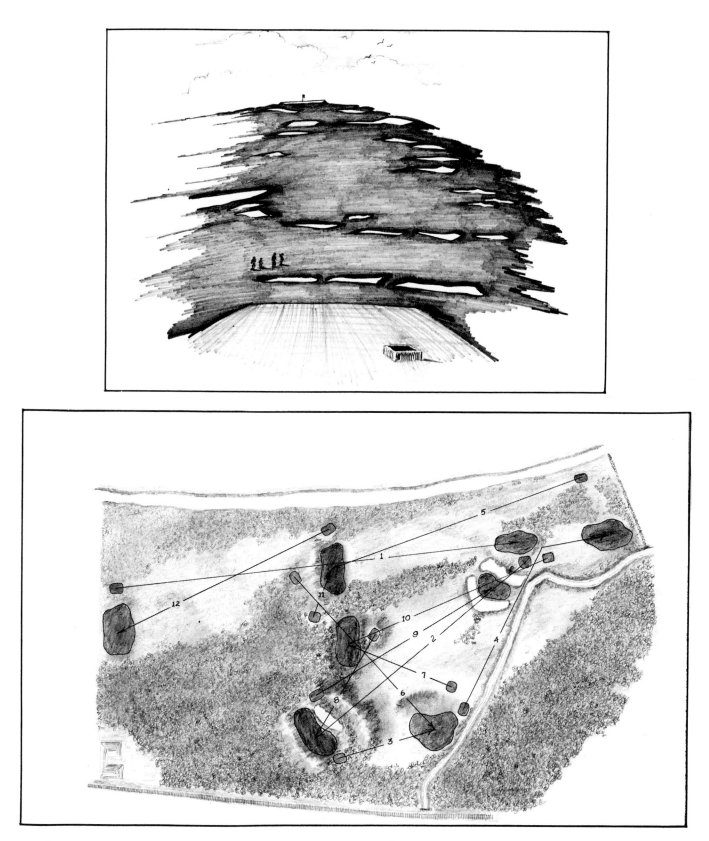

P. 26–27: *St. Georges (now Royal), Sandwich, by Purves (1877), one of many links laid out along English coasts in the half of the 19th century.*
P. 29: (Top) *The geometric design of inland England, with square bunkers in procession down the fairway to square greens.* P. 29: (Bottom) *Prestwick, site of the first Open in 1860, was cross routed from 1851 to 1882.*

usually credited with supervising the widening of the Old Course and with creation of its seventeenth green. He also did a ten-hole course at Barry, Angus, Scotland, in 1842, which forms the basis for the present championship course known as Carnoustie; and he laid out links in other parts of Scotland.[1] Allan Robertson's brother, David, emigrated to Australia in 1848 and introduced golf to that continent. It is quite likely that in so doing he planned one or more of Australia's earliest courses.

Old records indicate that most people turned to professionals like Allan Robertson to provide them with new golfing grounds. It seemed natural that the men who taught the game, made the implements and were the most proficient players should also lay out the courses. In the 1850s several clubs hired individuals to maintain the turf of their existing links and greens. These "greenkeepers" were soon called upon to help establish new golf courses. More often than not, the professional and the greenkeeper at a course were one and the same person. This person sometimes took on a third hat as a course designer.

Among the greenkeepers and professionals who laid out courses in the British Isles during the last third of the nineteenth century were the twins Willie and Jamie Dunn (of Musselburgh and Royal Blackheath), Willie's son Tom (of Musselburgh and later Wimbledon), Charles Hunter (of Prestwick), George Lowe (of St. Anne's-on-the-Sea), the brothers Tom and George Morris (of St. Andrews), the brothers Willie and Mungo Park (of Musselburgh), Douglas Rolland (of Elie and later Malvern), Archie Simpson (of Royal Aberdeen) and David Strath (of North Berwick).

These early course planners did their work on the spot, never resorting to a drawing board, with most courses laid out in a few days or less. They selected natural greensites, plotted holes to these sites and then arranged the holes into a circuit. Little construction was undertaken, for the natural contours of the land were seldom altered. Existing hazards, including roads, hedgerows and even stone walls, were incorporated; and existing turf was utilized. Except for assuring that a supply of sand for top-dressing the putting greens was close at hand, these designers rarely considered future maintenance.

P. 30–31: *A stabilized bunker on hole #4 at Royal St. Georges, Sandwich. The numerous courses established along the coasts of England in the latter part of the nineteenth century retained the styles of the Scottish links, in stark contrast to most inland courses of the same period with their artificially geometric features.*

Most of these same men were active in modifying existing courses, both the famous links and rudimentary layouts where golf had been played informally for centuries. Modifications to the hallowed links became necessary for a variety of reasons. They could not accommodate the increasing crowds as golf gained in popularity and thus became dangerous. Alterations to many were required when the eighteen-hole course became standard. Greater length was also required, because the new gutty nearly always outflew the old featherie. The planning and execution of changes to the ancient links by particular individuals were important to the future of golf architecture, for they established a tradition whereby clubs sought out recognized designers.

Sometimes the professional acted as a consultant, recommending modifications to existing courses or changes and adjustments to new ones already thought out by club members. Despite the knowledge that these greenkeepers, professionals and others possessed, and the fact that most of them learned the game on the ancient Scottish links, some of their courses are at best termed "dismal." Tom Simpson, himself an architect and student of course architecture, was prompted to christen the years from 1885 to 1900 the "Dark Ages of Golf Architecture." Simpson wrote:

> They failed to reproduce any of the features of the courses on which they were bred and born, or to realize the principles on which they had been made. Their imagination took them no farther than the conception of flat gun-platform greens, invariably oblong, round or square, supported by railway embankment sides or batters. . . . The bunkers that were constructed on the fairways may be described as rectangular ramparts of a peculiarly obnoxious type, stretching at regular intervals across the course, and having no architectural value whatever . . .[2]

Even the work of Old Tom Morris, called "Old Tom" to distinguish him from his famous son "Young Tom," was sometimes disappointing. A native of St. Andrews, Old Tom apprenticed under Allan Robertson and then served as greenkeeper and professional at the Prestwick links before returning, after Robertson's death, to serve in the same capacity at the Old Course. The most prominent name in the world of golf in the late 1800s, Old Tom Morris was called upon to modify a number of the ancient links. He also created new courses on superb linksland. But his results were sometimes curious. For example, his layout at Westward Ho! (Royal North Devon) originally had twelve holes that crossed one another.

In defense of Old Tom, he probably did as much as was required of any golf course designer of that time; and he produced layouts that were functional for the game he knew so well. The statement of Horace Hutchinson in 1898 that "the laying out of a golf course is a wonderfully easy business, needing very little special training . . ."[3] was not naive. It reflected the prevailing attitude of the time.

Old Tom Morris did make lasting contributions to the development of golf course architecture. He was apparently the first to ignore the traditional "loop" routing of nine holes out and nine back. For example, his routing of the course at Muirfield, which opened in 1891, utilized two nines with each starting and finishing at the clubhouse. Moreover, Muirfield's nines ran in different directions: the front nine clockwise, the back counter-clockwise. And only once did three successive holes play in the same direction. Such sophisticated routing took maximum advantage of wind conditions, forcing the player during a round to confront it from all angles. Morris's layout at Royal County Down in Northern Ireland, which opened about the same time as Muirfield, featured a similar routing plan.

It is quite possible that Old Tom has been blamed for changes that others made in his courses after they were opened for play. The "gun-platform" greens mentioned by Simpson may not have been Morris's creation; he was known to have utilized natural sites for his greens. The reputations of designers are plagued to this day by changes in their layouts made without their knowledge or consent, which upset strategy, balance and, in extreme cases, the continuity of the round.

Another of the early course designers, Tom Dunn, has been accused of lacking imagination. In retrospect, contemporary golf architects realize that Dunn strove for the functional in an age before funds and techniques were available for creating imaginative features. His great contribution was in designing inexpensive layouts for the multitudes who were taking up the game.

The latter half of the nineteenth century did see the introduction of a great many developments in turf maintenance. Foremost, of course, was the creation of the profession of greenkeeper, also called custodian or curator. The first turf cutter used to cut holes for putting cups was invented in 1849 at Royal Aberdeen. Lining the hole with a metal cup to prevent its being destroyed began about 1874 at the Crail Golf Club. The lawn mower was invented in 1830 but was not widely used on golf courses until decades later. Prior to its use, most inland courses in climates where bluegrasses predominated could only be played in autumn or winter, or during droughts, for at other times the turf was too lush. The practice of watering the putting surfaces originated in the 1880s, and by 1894

St. Andrews had sunk a well next to each of its massive greens to insure a steady source of water.

Despite the best efforts of greenkeepers, however, most of the inland golf courses created in this period suffered a common malady. Their turf was rock hard in summer and mushy in winter. Rolling of greens, a beneficial practice on the sandy links, proved disastrous on these clay soils. Except for those laid out in natural linksland, the courses of the late 1880s in the British Isles were built on land totally unsuited for playing the game of golf. And with agronomic knowledge, construction techniques and equipment so primitive, it was impossible to modify existing terrain and soil.

[1] Obituary, *Dundee Gazette*, September 1859, reprinted in an appendix in Clark, *Golf, A Royal and Ancient Game* (London: Macmillan, 1899).

[2] T. C. Simpson, *The Game of Golf*, IX New York: A. S. Barnes, (revised 1951), p. 162.

[3] Horace Hutchinson, "Concerning Golf Greens," *Harper's Weekly Magazine*, March 13, 1897, p. 274.

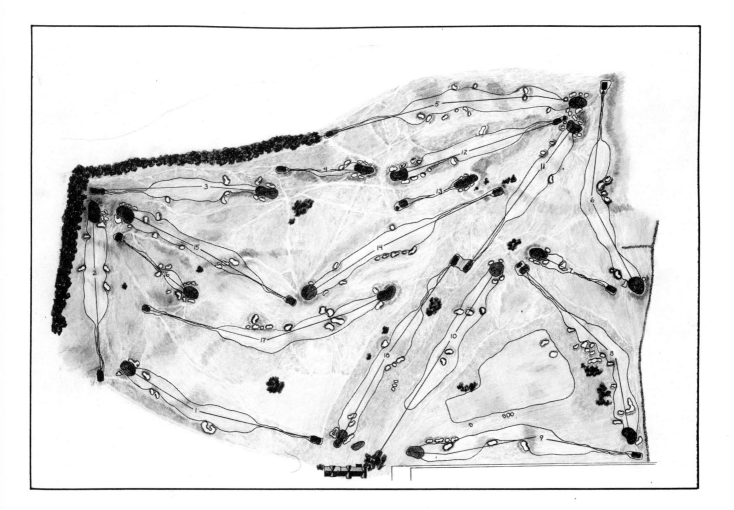

P. 33: *Outline of Muirfield GC, Scotland. Ignoring cross routing and the traditional single loop, Tom Morris, in 1891 produced a double loop of 2 nines with opposite rotations. Seldom did three successive holes play in the same direction and the wind was encountered in all quarters on early holes. Such sophisticated planning was a huge step in course design.*

3.

The Heathlands Era

Dozens of sorry inland courses built on impervious clay soils convinced most golf purists that only the ancient links could provide excellent golf. But a few golf course prospectors were unconvinced and kept searching for suitable inland terrain comparable to the best linksland. Their search was fruitful, for at the turn of the century they unearthed a mother lode of fine golfing land less than fifty miles south and west of London.

Here were the "heathlands," with well-drained, rock-free, sandy soil and a gently undulating terrain. This was true "golf country," and its discovery was a major step in the development of golf course architecture. Many of the world's greatest courses have since been created on land similar to that of the heaths, which, except for the presence of trees, is not unlike that of the links. The long delay in discovery of the heathlands, despite their proximity to London, is not difficult to understand. The heathlands were covered with undergrowth of heather, rhododendrons, Scotch fir and pines. Only a fool, it seemed, would spend time building a golf course in such a wasteland when vast meadows were available for the purpose.

The "fools" that did build courses in the heathlands became the most prominent golf architects of their day. Four names in particular stand out: Willie Park, Jr., J. F. Abercromby, H. S. Colt and W. Herbert Fowler. Their prominence was due in part to their vision in recognizing the true potential of this unlikely terrain and in part to their ability to shape the land into splendid golf holes.

And shape the land they did. Heather and other undergrowth had to be removed from most areas earmarked as playable. Many trees had to be felled, although all four architects integrated trees into their designs (a practice unknown before their time) and thus created a strategic and aesthetic asset not available to the old links. Earth had to be moved and contoured into green sites, tees and hazards. These men never moved earth when natural green sites and satisfactory contours could be found; but where nature was deficient, they were not reluctant to make alterations. The cleared areas had to be prepared

and seeded or sodded, and they took special interest in the types of grasses that would be planted.

All these tasks would seem to be modest undertakings in modern times, but in the early 1900s they called for new techniques in course construction. Considering the primitive state of available construction equipment, the results achieved by these designers and builders were extraordinary.

The first pioneering architect of this era was Willie Park, Jr. A superior golfer who won The Open twice, Park had been active in planning and modifying courses since 1890, first with his father, Willie Park, and then on his own. But it was not until 1901, when the original course at Sunningdale, Berkshire, England, in the heart of the heathlands, and the Huntercombe Golf Club, some fifteen miles northwest, were opened that Willie Park, Jr., demonstrated what revolutionary aspects of course design could be accomplished when new methods of course building were used. Here he proved what he had written in 1896:

> The laying out of a golf course is by no means a simple task . . . Great skill and judgement and a thorough acquaintance with the game are absolutely necessary to determine the best position for the respective holes and teeing grounds and the situation of the hazards.[1]

Sunningdale and Huntercombe stood in stark contrast to the countless geometric layouts with square greens, steep banks and stern cross bunkers previously built on whatever terrain existed. They featured tees and landing areas that were built up or lowered. Most of the greens were raised above the fairway level, had gentle shapes, were large and undulating. One green, the thirteenth at Huntercombe, was two-tiered. Both courses featured bold, manmade hazards, clearly visible to a golfer from the tee. Sunningdale even had an artificial pond.

The two courses made a reputation for Willie Park, Jr., and it has never diminished. Sir Guy Campbell, a fine mid-twentieth century designer, felt Park was the first really capable golf course architect, the man who set the

P. 34–35: *Utilizing British concepts, W. H. Fowler's fine American course Eastward Ho! on Cape Cod, combines the rolling terrain and ocean setting of a links with the tree-lined fairways and raised greens of the heaths.*
P. 37: *James Braid drew from his introduction to design on the heaths, as well as his links heritage, to create Gleneagles Hotel GC in Scotland.*

standard by which those who followed developed and amplified the art. Tom Simpson also gave Willie high marks, although he felt that Willie persisted throughout his career in placing bunkers only for the purpose of catching a poor shot. Herbert Warren Wind has written that Park had a sure touch for "devising golf holes that looked natural and played well." [2]

Park's later works continued to support his reputation. During his wide and active travels as a professional designer, Willie planned courses throughout the British Isles and Europe. He also laid out an estimated seventy courses in the United States and Canada, the best known being the North course at the Olympia Fields Country Club near Chicago, Woodway Country Club in Connecticut, and the Calgary Golf and Country Club in Alberta, Canada. Though at times ably assisted by his brothers, Willie was so busy as an architect that in the end, it is said, he literally worked himself to death. He died in 1925.

Willie Park, Jr., had done the preliminary routing on another early heathlands course, Worplesdon Golf Club in Surrey. But the course was completed by J. F. Abercromby, considered by mid-twentieth century course designer Frank Pennink and others to be one of the finest golf architects ever to practice in Britain. Like Park, Abercromby built his reputation on the heathlands. Unlike Park, "Aber" did very little work elsewhere.

Besides Worplesdon, Abercromby laid out several other courses in Surrey. Coombe Hill Golf Club, once considered "the finest and most artistic example of artificial construction work," [3] opened in 1908. He also did both the Old course and, after World War I, the New course at the Addington Golf Club. Abercromby spent most of his life as president of Addington and constantly sought to improve on his work there. He died just before World War II and, unfortunately, his New course was abandoned by the club just after the War. But Addington's Old course survived and has been highly regarded even in recent times.

H. S. Colt was the third of the revolutionaries who dared to carve golf courses out of the heather and pines of central England. Colt had his first design experience in 1894, when he laid out the Rye Golf Club on the southeast coast of England. But during the next half-dozen years, he was content to remain a solicitor and play a little competitive golf.

Upon the opening of Sunningdale in 1901, however, he became the club's secretary, and his interest in course design was soon renewed. Impressed with the basic design of Sunningdale, Colt supervised many changes during his twelve-year stint at the club. He replaced much of the heather that bounded the fairways with planted pines. He also altered and expanded the course to compensate for the greater distances golfers achieved with the rubber-cored golf ball. (This new ball was invented by Coburn Haskell of the United States in 1898 and gained acceptance in Great Britain in 1902 when Alex Herd used it in winning the Open. It flew some 15 to 20 percent farther than the gutty and thus necessitated lengthening and other alterations of existing courses.) In the process of expanding Sunningdale, Colt developed many of the exhilarating elevated tees that still exist on the older course today.

While serving at Sunningdale, Colt began planning courses in the surrounding heathlands for other clubs. Among them were Stoke Poges Golf Club (which opened in 1908), Swinley Forest Golf Club (1910) and thirty-six holes for St. George's Hill Golf Club (1913), of which eighteen survive. Swinley Forest, one of the first courses ever routed through a thick forest of trees, was considered by Colt himself to be his best design or, as he modestly put it, "the least bad course" he had ever done. He also experimented with the concept of integrating golf courses with housing and planned several such arrangements.

Colt was particularly adept at establishing turf in any environ. He could also be relied upon to make regular inspections of his work long after its completion to assist with the normal problems experienced by infant courses. He is said to have been the first to use a drawing board consistently to plan course designs, and he was apparently also the first to include tree-planting instructions. H. S. Colt was the first full-time golf course architect who had not previously been a professional golfer. He remained an amateur all his life, and he was a fine amateur competitor.

Colt, like Willie Park, Jr., did not always incorporate strategic concepts into his golf designs; but in his early British courses he did restore a strategic relationship between the placement of fairway and greenside bunkers, a "links" concept missing from most inland courses.

Colt also traveled far and wide to design courses. The majority of his work was done in the British Isles and Europe. Although the partners in his design firm, particularly Charles Alison, did most of the work that bears his name in North America, Colt did make at least two extended trips to the United States and Canada. He had a major part in planning courses for the Toronto Golf Club (1912) and the Hamilton Golf and Country Club (1914), both in Ontario, Canada; and the new course for the Country Club of Detroit, Michigan (1914). At home, his designs include a second eighteen, the New course, at Sunningdale; two courses for the Wentworth Golf Club;

and two remodeled courses for Royal Portrush in Northern Ireland. But perhaps a true measure of the respect in which he was held was his selection to design the third course, the Eden, at St. Andrews, which opened in 1912.

During this era, yet another Briton set out in the heathlands to build an ideal course. In 1902 W. Herbert Fowler, who had longed to design a golf course, was invited by his brother-in-law to do so on property at Tadsworth in Surrey. Fowler spent two years planning his course at a time when two days were still sufficient for many course builders, and initially rode through the heather on horseback, searching for proper greensites and then tracking each hole backward from there.

His creation, which opened in 1904, was called Walton Heath; it attracted even more attention than Park's Sunningdale had three years earlier. A special train brought dignitaries to the course; and the initial match was an exhibition by Vardon, Taylor and Braid, golf's "Great Triumvirate."

Fowler soon found his talents in sufficient demand to practice architecture full time. A somewhat despotic man, he quickly felt the need to put his hand to a traditional linksland course, and in 1908 his total redesign of the Royal North Devon Golf Club at Westward Ho! was completed. It, too, met with immediate acclaim.

Fowler remodeled the Saunton links, across the bay from North Devon, and laid out two more heathlands courses, the Red and the Blue, at the Berkshire Golf Club. All of these opened after the War, by which time Fowler was busy laying out courses on both coasts of the United States. One of his most impressive American works is Eastward Ho!, which one suspects he had a hand in naming, at Chatham, Massachusetts, on Cape Cod. Eastward Ho! combines the rolling terrain and ocean setting of a links with the tree-lined fairways and elevated greens of a heathlands course.

Herbert Fowler was perhaps the most naturally gifted architect of his time. "I never knew anyone who could more swiftly take in the possibilities of a piece of ground," Bernard Darwin once wrote, "and I think his clients thought, quite unjustly, that he had not taken sufficient pains, because he could see so clearly and work so fast." [4]

The original course at Walton Heath (Fowler built a second one there after the War) particularly impressed one of its first players, James Braid. Braid became the club's first professional upon its opening in 1904 and remained there the rest of his life. While Braid had no hand in changing the courses at Walton Heath, he was a five-time Open champion and thus received a great many requests to design courses. Though it was always an avocation with him, Braid took his designing seriously and stubbornly refused to change a design once it had been planned. He disliked even the suggestion that some hole be altered. In the beginning he did little more than stake out a rough layout and instruct a committee on how to properly construct and maintain the course. But he soon began conducting inspection trips to his courses, perhaps to insure that no one did change his designs. By the 1920s Braid was considered a most competent architect.

He was responsible for planning hundreds of courses, many of them on paper. His most prominent works, to which he paid personal attention, include the remodeled courses at Carnoustie Golf Club and Blairgowrie Golf Club, the East and West eighteens of Dalmahoy Golf Club, and the King's and Queen's courses at Gleneagles Hotel, all in Scotland.

Another of the Great Triumvirate, John Henry Taylor, also laid out a number of courses in the early 1900s. After the War, Taylor joined forces with Frederick G. Hawtree, a greenkeeper who had founded the British Golf Greenkeepers Association in 1912. The firm of Hawtree and Taylor designed some fifty-five courses in the British Isles and remodeled a similar number. They paid particular attention to the promotion of publicly owned courses, founding the Artisan Golfers Association and the National Association of Public Golf Courses, and they conceived and planned England's first municipal courses before World War I. Their most prominent work was the remodeling of the Royal Birkdale Golf Club into a championship course in 1931.

The third member of the Triumvirate, Harry Vardon, did a number of course designs but fewer than Braid or Taylor, partly because he spent many years before the War in ill health. Two other prominent architects, Alister Mackenzie and C. H. Alison, began their careers as assistants to H. S. Colt during the heathlands era. Their greatest creations would come after World War I.

Although this period lasted only fifteen years, from 1900 to 1914, it was a most important time in the history of golf course architecture. For the first time, golf architecture became a profession rather than simply a sideline for a club professional or greenkeeper.

Men like Park, Abercromby, Colt and Fowler proved on the heaths that exciting and pleasurable golf could be produced in any locale, so long as proper techniques in course building were used. These techniques included on-site study of the terrain, detailed plans developed on a drawing board, and on-site supervision or inspection once construction began.

They also realized that where a satisfactory natural

40

contour could be utilized in the design of a hole, it should be so used. But where none existed, natural-appearing sites for greens, tees, landing areas and even bunkers could be created by men.

The competent designers in this period recognized that aesthetics are an intrinsic part of the game of golf. When designing a course, these men subdued harsh natural features. They incorporated trees into the design of certain holes. They abhorred geometrically shaped greens and hazards and built theirs to blend into the surrounding terrain, although courses that were geometric and featured cross bunkers and artificial lines were still being created by others elsewhere in Britain.

Lastly, it was in this period that the strategic school of golf course design began to influence some people. Most of the courses built in the British Isles between 1900 and 1914, including those of Park, Abercromby, Colt and Fowler, were still of the penal variety. But particular holes on some of the more prominent courses could certainly have been classified as "strategic."

This is attributable in no small part to the enduring influence of the Old Course at St. Andrews. Park, Abercromby, Colt and Fowler all played much of their golf at the Old Course, as did many other designers in the British Isles. It was still the course to which every other course was compared. And its subtle strategies were only then beginning to be realized and appreciated.

The continuing significance of St. Andrews in this period was apparent in revisions of the golf course at Woking. One hole in particular, the fourth, had a considerable influence on at least one golf course architect and did a great deal to educate the golfing public in fundamental design principles.

The Woking Golf Club had been originally laid out by Tom Dunn in 1893 in Surrey, England. Ironically, it was right in the center of the heathlands; and had it shown any imaginative design at all, it would surely have attracted the attention that Sunningdale did years later. Instead, it was one of those functional but unexciting courses with square greens, giant cross bunkers bisecting many fairways and pot bunkers peppering the landscape.

P. 40: *Queen's (top) and King's (lower right) courses at Gleneagles show an English heathland influence in Scotland. P. 40: (Lower left) Possible playing routes on the Road Hole (#17) at St. Andrews. Principles of famous links holes were adapted to the heathlands by Colt and others. Paton and Low modeled their 4th at Woking near London after the 16th at St. Andrews.*

But in the early twentieth century, Woking was remodeled by two of the club's more domineering members, Stuart Paton and John L. Low. Neither had previously practiced architecture, but both were fine golfers, especially Low; both had a great interest in the game and were to write eloquently on it; and both had an abiding passion for St. Andrews. They set about to pattern Woking after the Old Course. They had sense enough not to try to imitate it but rather to recreate the playing strategies presented by the Old Course.

Paton paid particular attention to Woking's greens and over the years added various subtle slopes and mounds until finally not a single flat, square green remained. He and Low also did a great deal in rebunkering the course. It was one particular bunker, or pair of bunkers, that made such an impact upon club member Tom Simpson, who would later design many courses himself.

The fourth hole at Woking resembled the sixteenth at St. Andrews in that both were straightaway par-4s with a railline running along the right. Paton furthered the resemblance by placing a pair of bunkers in the center of the fourth fairway at the landing area in the manner of the "Principal's Nose" at the Old Course's sixteenth. Many years later Simpson recalled hearing the outrage and condemnation of the revised hole by his fellow members at Woking and wrote:

> . . . I went out, fully prepared to find myself in complete agreement with the views which had been so eloquently expressed. So far, however, from agreeing, I realised for the first time, as soon as I saw this much-maligned hazard, that the true line to the hole should not always be the centre of the fairway, and the placing of a bunker had a far more serious and useful purpose than merely the punishing of a bad shot. This led me to see the importance of golf architecture as an art as well as a science. . . .[5]

Paton and Low never designed or remodeled another course, although they spent years refining Woking. Yet they deserve mention in any history of golf course architecture, for they demonstrated, perhaps before anyone else, that it was possible on an inland course to challenge a golfer in more than one way, as did the links of Scotland.

[1] William Park, Jr., *The Game of Golf* (2nd ed.; 1896), p. 194.
[2] Herbert Warren Wind, "Understanding Golf Course Architecture," *Golf Digest Magazine*, November 1966, p. 25.
[3] T. C. Simpson, *The Game of Golf*, IX New York: A. S. Barnes (revised 1951), p. 170.
[4] Bernard Darwin, *James Braid*: London: Hodder and Stoughton (1952), p. 81.
[5] Simpson, *The Game of Golf*, p. 165.

Donald J. Ross and Tom Bendelow, deserve special mention. Ross, a one-time golf student of Old Tom Morris, hired on as professional of the Oakley Country Club in Boston in 1898, having been persuaded to emigrate by Professor Robert Wilson of Harvard who had met him while visiting Dornoch. James Tufts, of the American Soda Fountain Company, soon convinced Ross to work as winter professional at a new resort he was building in North Carolina. (Ross continued summer pro duties in the Boston area for several years.) The resort was named Pinehurst; once Ross arrived, he set about rebuilding and expanding the lackluster nine-hole layout that Tufts had installed. He subsequently built three additional courses at Pinehurst, #2 which opened in 1907, #3 (1910) and #4 (1919).

Despite their sand greens, the courses at Pinehurst impressed many affluent patrons from the north, and Donald Ross soon found his talents as a golf course designer in great demand. Ross is often said to have been the first full-time course designer in America, although he retained his position as professional and later golf manager at Pinehurst until his death in 1948. He was to become the most prominent golf architect of his day and one of the most respected.

Tom Bendelow, also from Scotland, quit a steady job with the *New York Herald* in 1895 to join the sporting goods firm of A. G. Spalding & Bros. as a "design consultant." In that capacity Bendelow claimed to have laid out hundreds of courses for clients who sought assistance from the huge sporting goods firm. He was, without doubt, the most prolific course builder in America in the early years of the century.

Tom was apparently a character, and quite a few colorful tales have developed concerning him. The most widely circulated but least embroidered concerned his method of design, which was dubbed "eighteen stakes on a Sunday afternoon." In fact, Bendelow did lay out a considerable number of courses somewhat in this manner, although he used more than eighteen stakes. He would stake out a first tee; pace off a hundred yards or so, stake out a cross bunker; pace on farther, stake out another bunker or some mounds; march on farther and stake out his green site. After doing this nine times, he would leave instructions with the club on how to properly build and maintain the course and then be on his way.

Golf historians have been aghast at such an operation, but it is an error to assume that Tom Bendelow was in any way a "con artist" in an era of otherwise competent, conscientious golf architects. In reality, Tom was widely respected as an architect in his later years, and

wrote and lectured on the subject at the University of Illinois. The fact is, in the late 1890s and very early 1900s, nearly all the golf courses in America were laid out in such a fashion. Designers of that time, like Alex Findlay, Robert White and even Donald Ross on occasion, practiced this method. It was all club members expected and all they were willing to pay for: The going rate was $25.00 per job, regardless of how long it took to stake the layout.

Few designers remained to supervise construction of their designs. The greenkeeper hired by the club, most often a Britisher, would actually build the course and over the years refine it, often changing even the designer's routing concept, which had been recorded only by stakes long since gone. Additional features were undoubtedly added to these courses by Scottish pro-greenkeepers after visits home to the links, for many an early northern professional spent a winter now and again in Scotland. Individual greenkeepers, therefore, had as much to do with this early American course design as did men credited with the "designing"; for if a designer was even brought in, he often did nothing more than route the layout with stakes.

Consequently, most American courses in this period were primitive compared with those in Britain and Scotland. Most were built quickly and inexpensively. In one of the numerous moves of the St. Andrews Golf Club, only two days were required to lay out and "build" a nine-hole course; and The Country Club (Brookline, Massachusetts) budgeted $50.00 to build its first six-hole course. Construction normally consisted of removing fences, clearing away surface stones and mowing the grass. The stones were often piled into mounds and when covered with dirt, were thought to make perfectly good hazards. These sharp mounds, nicknamed "chocolate drops," became the fashion for a time and were even added to courses which had no stones to cover. Little islands of unmowed vegetation were often left in the bunkers of these early courses. These "dragon's teeth" added nothing to the aesthetic values but did contribute to player frustration and to a high rate of lost balls.

Some early layouts had holes crossing one another. Nearly all greens were indistinguishable from fairways, and most natural obstructions were considered legitimate hazards. "Stone walls, trees, ploughed fields, fences, and chasms," wrote one golf enthusiast in 1895, "present excellent sporting requirements on a course, for variety is the spice of life."[1] In seeking the rationale for placement and style of manmade features and clearing lines at older clubs in the United States, golf architects of later eras were baffled. One explanation was provided by Elmer O. Cappers, historian at The Country Club (Brookline), who pointed out that the coexistence of golfers and horsemen in the early days at his club determined such matters.

For all their shortcomings, American courses at the turn of the century were functional. It is amazing that early greenkeepers were able to build and maintain their courses as well as they did with so little in the way of equipment, materials and skilled help available. These "sand lot" courses provided adequate training grounds for thousands of beginning golfers. But the expert golfers, or those who fancied themselves such, clamored for better courses on which to play their beloved game. It was this impetus that led to the advancement of course architecture in America in the early years of the twentieth century. Three courses created during that time—Myopia, north of Boston, the Garden City Golf Course on Long Island and the National Golf Links of America on Long Island—particularly influenced the state of the art.

[1] Henry E. Howland, "Golf," *Scribner's Magazine*, May 1895, p. 531.

P. 50: (Top) *Ekwanok GC, Vermont, Hole #10.* (Bottom) *CC of Lincoln, Nebraska, Hole #2 by W. H. Tucker, Sr., who came to the U.S. before the turn of the century at the behest of Willie Dunn and was active in course design until the 1950s.*

P. 50-51: Hole #12, Point Judith CC, Rhode Island.
*Clubs grew protective of their chocolate drops, steep
banks and sharp drop-offs. Acquiring a unique charm
as they mellowed into the landscape, such features
became traditional on some older courses in the East.*

5

5.

Landmark American Courses

Herbert C. Leeds was one of those dissatisfied with American golf courses at the turn of the century. But he was determined to do something about it. Well to do and a fine natural athlete, he had developed into a scratch player within two years of taking up the game and became one of the ruling fathers of the Myopia Hunt Club north of Boston shortly after joining in 1896. Leeds persuaded the membership to build a new course to replace the club's rudimentary nine holes; and soon after they consented, he was appointed to lay out the replacement.

Leeds took the task seriously. He visited Shinnecock Hills, which by then had a full eighteen holes, and came away convinced that he could build a comparable course. He started by locating his greensites in natural hollows and on natural plateaus, like those he had observed at Shinnecock. He then gave special attention to the construction of the greens. Not content to simply mow patches of grass, he had each green shaped into rolling surfaces; for he was determined that Myopia would not be cursed with a single flat, lifeless green.

Leeds routed his course to take advantage of the natural terrain. Stone walls, left over from the days when the land served as pastures and fields, were covered with soil and grassed to make them playable. Stone walls were not a legitimate golf hazard, Leeds felt, but mounds were. He later uncovered the walls, heaped the stones into mounds and re-covered them with soil to produce Myopia's giant "chocolate drops," still a feature of the course.

Finally, he had bunkers added: several on some short holes, almost none on the holes he felt to be challenging enough already. When his nine-hole layout was completed, it was selected to serve as the site for the 1898 U.S. Open.

The participants in that Open praised Leeds for his efforts and especially for the greens, which were unlike any in the country. But Leeds was not satisfied. He felt Myopia needed another nine to be a "proper links." The club soon purchased adjoining land, and Leeds laid out a second nine on decidedly hilly ground. Again paying particular attention to the greens, he took two years to con-

54

P. 52–53: *Sea Island, Georgia, Hole #7, Plantation Course by W. J. Travis, a major contributor to the landmark American courses created after 1900.*
P. 54: *Hole #13, The Mid Ocean Club, Bermuda, by C. B. Macdonald.*
P. 55: *The Chicago GC. Huge, deeply-creased greens and steep banks appear often on layouts by Macdonald and by his proteges, Raynor and Banks.*

The dream of having at least a few greens resemble some of the well-known ones in Great Britain is easily capable of realization. All that is necessary is to denude the present greens of their surface of turf, by means of a turf-cutting machine which peels it off in continuous rolls of even, uniform depth, arrange the undulations as desired, replace the sod, and fill in the interstices with fine, screened loam mixed with seed.[1]

Travis was able to convince his club to allow him to institute his suggestions; being a three-time U. S. Amateur and British Amateur champion no doubt helped. Over the next two years he reworked every green, carefully preserving the hallowed turf as he did so. He also built some new tees to extend the length of some holes and, in certain cases, to reroute play. He rebunkered each hole, digging some as deep as a man's height so that their faces had to be built up with layers of sod stacked like bricks, as at Muirfield and other courses in Scotland. In all, he added fifty new bunkers.

Garden City, as revised by Travis, hosted the 1908

U. S. Amateur and, just as six years previously, the participants were enthusiastic about the course. "The fairway and the boldly undulating putting-greens were even as velvet," wrote one onlooker, "but those hazards! . . . bunkers, traps and pots lurk on either side of the straight and narrow path, awaiting the pull or the slice of the unwary!"[2]

The "Grand Old Man," as Travis had come to be known, would design or remodel a good many courses in the next twenty years, including the East and West courses at the Westchester Country Club, Rye, New York; Yahnundasis at Utica, New York; and the original nine holes at the Sea Island Golf Club in Georgia. His true love, however, was the first course he ever had a hand in creating, Ekwanok in Manchester, Vermont. Ekwanok may have been the country's best golf course in the early 1900s, but it did not receive the early public attention of Myopia or Garden City. Travis touted its merits often, and by 1914 it was selected as the site for the National Amateur. Travis added a second course, Equinox, adjoining Ekwanok in the early twenties. At his death, in accordance with his wishes, Travis was buried near his beloved Vermont courses.

Walter Travis had a certain set of principles that he tried to instill in each of his courses. Hazards should be placed in relation to greens, he believed, so as to require "thinking" golf. Certain holes should necessitate deliberate slices, while others should require deliberate draws. One or two tee shots per round should call for an exceptionally fine carry, as should one or two approach shots. And greens should always be undulating, never flat.

Often, perhaps too often, Travis tried to institute his principles by means of a most effective weapon: the small, deep pot trap. He used the pot trap to such excess that critics of later years would label him a follower of the penal school of golf design, a master of the "God-fearing approach," a flamboyant but unimaginative architect. Certainly some of the criticism is justified, but Travis never deliberately set out to build a penal course. He had spent his entire golfing career as a notoriously short hitter. He had kept himself alive in countless matches by keeping himself in play and by mastering a deadly putting stroke. That philosophy carried over into his designs. His pot bunkers never hurt players, he said, so long as they stayed out of them.

One last note about Travis's redesign of the Garden City Golf Club: He remodeled the eighteenth hole, a par-3 across water, by building a severely tilting green and fronting it with a huge, deep bunker on the left and a smaller, steepfaced bunker on the right. Knowledgeable golfers quickly recognized the hole for what it was: Travis's version of the Eden, the eleventh hole at the Old Course at St. Andrews. It was not an imitation, Travis would point out, but an adaptation of that highly respected and highly feared par-3.

That idea was intriguing, modeling a hole on an American course after one from a famous old British links. But it was not originally Walter Travis's. It belonged to Charles Blair Macdonald.

Macdonald was the man who had designed and built America's first eighteen-hole course. He was a wealthy, intelligent man, devoted to the game of golf. He had been one of the founding fathers of the United States Golf Association, and was its first Amateur champion. But he was also, in the minds of some, stubborn, egotistical and autocratic.

Certainly Macdonald had the perfect personality to try something different and daring. In 1901, after reading a British magazine survey on the "best holes" in the United Kingdom, Macdonald resolved to build a "classical golf course in America, one which would eventually compare favorably with the championship links abroad, and serve as an incentive to the elevation of the game in America."[3]

Macdonald established a number of rules for this project. First, the course must be a links. He would only build it near the sea, on land as nearly comparable to the old linksland as could be found. After years of searching from Cape Cod to Cape May, he found two such sites, both on Long Island, New York. He eventually chose a site near Southampton and, coincidentally, adjacent to the Shinnecock Hills Golf Club.

Second, Macdonald's ideal course must contain a full eighteen holes of an exemplary nature. Not even St. Andrews, he felt, had eighteen first-class holes, but his course would. To this end, he solicited the opinions of many prominent golfers as to the ingredients of great golf holes. He personally made at least three trips to Great Britain, observing the most famous and many lesser-known courses. He surveyed and sketched dozens of holes, concentrating only on the features he considered distinctive. "I only approve of the Maiden at Royal St. Georges," he later wrote, "as a bunker, not a hole."[4] He would not be afraid to combine two or three features from different holes into a single hole on his ideal course, and, in the

end, more than half would be composites.

Third, he would spare no expense in making his course the best in the world. He spent a great deal of his own money on the project and also solicited subscriptions from seventy enthusiastic friends at an initial thousand dollars per membership.

Fourth, where nature was deficient, it would have to be improved upon. This was perhaps the most revolutionary action in course building in its time. When he examined the site, Macdonald was delighted to locate natural settings for several of his proposed holes, especially for his versions of Prestwick's Alps and the Redan at North Berwick. But he had a great deal of soil moved around to create "natural" settings for other holes. He also had some 10,000 loads of topsoil hauled in and spread around. He created a turf nursery, one of the first of its kind, and experimented with numerous varieties of grasses to transplant on his course. Since the site was in need of artificial watering, he had a complete irrigation system for greens installed. The greens themselves were built "scientifically," with strata of seaweed, loam and top-dressing to preserve moisture.

Fifth, Macdonald would obtain the assistance of the best experts in their respective fields, for mediocre talent could never result in an ideal course. He sought out Professor C. V. Piper of the United States Department of Agriculture for agronomic help and enlisted the aid of a local surveyor, Seth J. Raynor, to serve as his construction engineer. Raynor was to prove so invaluable that he would construct all the courses later laid out by Macdonald, as well as designing many of his own. In addition, Macdonald invited the opinions of such experienced golfers as Walter Travis, Devereux Emmet and his own son-in-law, H. J. Whigham.

Finally, Macdonald intended that each hole should make a golfer think before he swung. Naturally, the features of the best holes that Macdonald adapted had, for the most part, always required the golfer to place the ball rather than swing aimlessly. But Macdonald went further. Each of his holes provided for an alternative line of play. On each tee the player was called upon to exercise his judgment: Could he carry the bunker in front of the pin, or should he play to the right? Does it accomplish anything to drive over these bunkers, or should he place the drive down the intended fairway? Macdonald wanted long hitters and short hitters on equal terms when they played a match on his course.

C. B. Macdonald completed his course in 1909, after eight years of planning and two years of actual construction. It was named, somewhat immodestly, The National Golf Links of America. But the course lived up to its name as well as to its advance billing. It was like no other course in the country, and every player, every writer, every course designer who viewed it marveled at it. British observers, too, were astonished at what an ideal links creation Charlie Macdonald had wrought. Horace Hutchinson, Bernard Darwin and Ben Sayers, professional at North Berwick, all wrote laudatory articles about The National Golf Links in British publications between 1910 and 1913, the ultimate tribute to an American course.

Macdonald, who coined the title "golf architect" in 1902, would design fifteen other courses before his death in 1939, adhering to the same principles that made The National Golf Links so successful. But his clients would find his projects expensive. His Yale Golf Club, for instance, cost nearly half a million dollars, and his Lido Golf Club cost three quarters of a million. Macdonald never personally accepted a fee for any of his architectural work, however, with the exception of a lifetime membership in the club for which he was working.

All of Macdonald's later designs featured the same sort of adaptation of famous holes. He invariably built a "Redan" on each of his courses, and an "Eden." He also built a "Cape" hole on each layout, patterned after his fourteenth at The National. That hole, a dogleg par-4 across a bay with the green perched precariously close to the water, was truly a design original by Macdonald. The same hole can be found at the Yale Golf Club (the third), the St. Louis Country Club (the eighth) and, most dramatically, at the Mid-Ocean Club in Bermuda where it appears as the fifth hole.

Macdonald spent the majority of his time at The National Golf Links in his later years and forever tinkered with the bunkering on some holes and the slope of the greens on others. He was uncharacteristically hesitant to join in the acclaim for his magnificent creation; even as late as 1928 he wrote, "I am not confident the course is perfect and beyond criticism to-day." [5]

But Macdonald was a perfectionist. For the rest of the golfing world, The National was a course without peer. Its excellence would cause the rebuilding of many American golf courses, even some of the best, and would influence the quality of courses yet to be conceived.

Despite somewhat rigid classical lines, the work of Macdonald, as well as W. J. Travis and others, contributed great impressiveness to the style of American course architecture. Certainly Myopia and Garden City, and also Ekwanok, were fine American courses. At the same time, Sunningdale, Walton Heath and Woking, across the Atlantic, were also exceedingly well done. But The National was in a class by itself. It would be accurate to say that Charles Blair Macdonald and The National Golf Links of America revolutionized golf course architecture. Soon after it opened, H. J. Whigham wrote:

> There are many features about the National Links which will make the course famous; for example, the undulating putting greens, the absence of blind holes—nearly every tee commands a view of the entire length of the hole—and the size of the bunkers. But the main achievement is that a course has been produced where every hole is a good one and presents a new problem. That is something which has never yet been accomplished, even in Scotland; and in accomplishing it here, Mr. Macdonald has inaugurated a new era in golf. [6]

It is interesting to speculate on the influence that thoughts and trends from America may have had on British golf architecture in the years before World War I. America was preeminent in early earth-moving techniques, while turfgrass research was soon underway at a number of agricultural colleges. Several American architects were prolific writers, and many course planners from Britain and America were shuttling back and forth across the Atlantic. Doubtless an interchange of ideas among contemporaries occurred, and the highly laudatory articles describing The National Golf Links in British publications no doubt enhanced this influence.

[1] Walter J. Travis, "Merits and Demerits of the Garden City Links," *Country Life*, February 1906, p. 446.
[2] "The Amateur Golf Championship of 1908," *Harper's Weekly Magazine*, September 26, 1908, p. 10.
[3] C. B. Macdonald, *Scotland's Gift—Golf*, London: Charles Scribner's Sons, 1928, p. 173.
[4] Ibid., p. 182.
[5] Ibid., p. 193.
[6] H. J. Whigham, "The Ideal Golf Links," *Scribner's Magazine*, May 1909, p. 585.

6

6.

The Pennsylvanian Influence

Myopia in Massachusetts, Garden City and the National Golf Links on Long Island and Ekwanok in Vermont all contributed significantly to the advancement of American golf architecture in the early 1900s. By 1910 the scene of important activity had shifted to Pennsylvania. In the years before the first World War, that state was full of men who dreamed of building first-rate golf courses and did so. Their names are now familiar in golf design: Henry C. Fownes and his son, William C. Fownes; George C. Thomas, Jr.; A. W. Tillinghast; Hugh Wilson; William S. Flynn; and George Crump.

Henry C. Fownes's brainchild was the Oakmont Country Club. Fownes, son of a Pittsburgh steel tycoon, conceived the idea of building a links-type course on the plateau overlooking the Allegheny River northeast of the steel town. He organized a golf club in 1903 to fund his project, secured the property and drew the plans for his dream course. Then he set out with a crew of 150 men and two dozen mule teams and spent a year building it.

When Oakmont opened in 1904, it featured eight par-5's, one par-6 (the 560-yard twelfth hole) and a total par of 85 (this was bogey 85 corresponding to neither today's par nor today's bogey). It had no trees to speak of but did have huge, rolling greens; and its length reflected the acceptance of the Haskell ball.

Henry Fownes was satisfied with his course, but his son, William, was not. The younger Fownes, after he won the 1910 U. S. Amateur, appointed himself permanent course consultant to the Oakmont club and for the next thirty years continually made suggestions on how it could be improved. In summer he lived at the clubhouse and beginning in 1911, spent many an evening walking the course with its greenkeeper, deciding what changes were to be made.

Fownes was determined to make Oakmont the toughest course in the world. "A shot poorly played," he once remarked, "should be a shot irrevocably lost."[1] In order to implement this philosophy, Fownes sought the assistance of two greenkeepers, first John McGlynn and later Emil "Dutch" Loeffler. (Loeffler remained as green-keeper at Oakmont throughout his life, but during the 1920s, he and McGlynn maintained an active golf design and building practice on the side.)

The revisions made to the Oakmont course by Fownes and his assistants were numerous. Holes were lengthened and the par reduced. Ditches were dug in the rough to improve drainage and to create playing problems. The ditches were played as hazards and were, in fact, almost unplayable. Greens were canted in another effort to improve drainage, and kept cut very short. And a huge number of bunkers were added throughout the course.

Oakmont became the epitome of the penal style of golf course architecture. At one time, the course is said to have had 220 bunkers, an average of a dozen per hole. Since the heavy clay base upon which the course was built prevented the digging of all but a few deep bunkers, Fownes and Loeffler concocted a device to add to the difficulty of the otherwise flat, shallow bunkers. It was a special rake that, when dragged through the thick, brown river sand in Oakmont's bunkers, left deep grooves or furrows. Many felt it took two special talents to extract a ball from an Oakmont bunker—one if the ball sat on a ridge in the sand, another if it settled in a trough. Others believed that since a ball seldom stayed on the ridges in the sand, Oakmont's bunkers were easier to recover from than those raked in the conventional manner. Indeed, several neighboring courses adopted Oakmont's furrowed rake. In the 1960s, the river sand was replaced, the furrows eliminated and almost a quarter of the bunkers filled in. But that still left some 180 of them, which is sand enough for any challenge.

Oakmont's greens were always clipped exceedingly short, to approximately 3/32nds of an inch; and at Fownes's insistence, they were watered and rolled with a heavy roller before most golf events. Except for some modifications (most notably the relocation of number eight, an admittedly "awful" green), the club through the years has zealously preserved their greens basically as they were in the days of Fownes and Loeffler, and jealously protected their reputation as treacherous to putt.

P. 62-63: Merion GC, Hole #11, East Course by Hugh Wilson. In the years just before WWI, Pennsylvania was full of men who dreamed of building first-rate courses. Names like Fownes, Thomas, Tillinghast, Flynn, Crump and Wilson are now familiar. P. 65: Plantings in the bunkers at Merion leave the impression of British parkland and links courses.

William Fownes certainly achieved what he set out to accomplish. Oakmont has not been revered but feared. It is a decidedly homely course in appearance. Yet the club has wisely protected it from any massive facelifting. Oakmont remains as a classic example of the penal school of golf design.

At about the time Henry Fownes was opening Oakmont, George C. Thomas, Jr., was planning a course at the other end of Pennsylvania. Thomas was from one of the state's oldest and wealthiest families. He lived on the family estate, the Bloomfield Farm, in the Chestnut Hill area of Philadelphia. There he dabbled in landscaping and gardening, and even wrote a book about roses.

In 1905 a newly formed golf club offered to purchase the Bloomfield Farm as the site for their course. Thomas accepted, on condition that he be allowed to design the course. The club agreed, reasoning that Thomas had some previous course design experience, in Massachusetts and New Jersey; and, perhaps of greater importance, he didn't want to be paid for his services.

Thomas invited his close friend Samuel Heebner, then president of the Golf Association of Philadelphia, to assist him in the work. Together they routed the course, supervised its construction and refined it with the placement of traps and the planting of trees. The house in which Thomas was born and raised became the clubhouse, and in 1908 the Mount Airy Country Club was officially opened. Within a few years of its opening, the club changed its name to the Whitemarsh Valley Country Club. Ever since, the course has remained basically as Thomas and Heebner designed it, with small greens, liberal trapping and unusual balance. One of its par-3's was a monster at 235 yards. Another was a mere 125-yard pitch. Both were difficult to par.

Sam Heebner never designed another course; but Thomas, who moved to California after the War, did several more. To George Thomas, golf design was never really a profession, and often he did not accept a fee for his work. But he took his avocation seriously. He had very definite ideas about how a golf hole should challenge a golfer and how it should not, and he was not always tolerant of others' criticisms of his ideas.

Thomas was one of the few American golf course architects to record his philosophy in a book. That work, *Golf Architecture in America*, published in 1927, remains one of the finest in the literature of golf. In addition to his book, George C. Thomas, Jr., is best known for his marvelous work in California that includes the North and South courses for the Los Angeles Country Club (for

which Englishman Herbert Fowler did the preliminary plan), the Ojai Valley Golf Club, the Bel-Air Country Club and the Riviera Country Club.

Like Thomas, Albert W. Tillinghast was the son of a wealthy Philadelphian. The elder Tillinghast owned a rubber works, and for the first thirty years of his life Albert was a playboy. He was infatuated with the game of golf and made several trips to Scotland before the turn of the century, specifically to the shop of Old Tom Morris at St. Andrews, where he enjoyed discussions on design philosophy. Back home, "Tilly" belonged to Philadelphia's most fashionable clubs, and he competed in several national amateur championships.

In 1907 a close friend of the Tillinghast family, Charles Worthington (of pump fame and later to be the mower-equipment magnate), asked Albert to assist him in laying out a golf course. Worthington was building a resort on the Delaware River and reasoned that a "sporty links" would insure its success. Although he knew absolutely nothing about building a golf course, Tilly accepted the offer.

He soon took complete charge of the project, examining the site, drawing the plans and supervising the construction. The finished project, the Shawnee Country Club, was a remarkably fine first effort. Tilly had incorporated both the Delaware and Binnikill Rivers into his design and built some rather novel teeing areas on several holes. Shawnee quickly became the most popular resort in the Poconos. It remains in existence today, although the course has been radically redesigned and bears little resemblance to the original Tillinghast design.

Nevertheless, Albert Tillinghast, at the age of thirty-two, had discovered his calling. Tilly was determined to be the best in his new-found profession and with typical intensity, devoted all his energies to it. He established an office in Manhattan, gathered together a construction crew and advertised his availability. He was stubborn enough not to accept any design job unless his firm could also construct the course. This allowed him to insure that his plans would be carried out correctly. It also meant a bigger fee from each client.

There are those who say that, in his time, Albert W. Tillinghast was indeed the best. He was not as prolific as many of his contemporaries, they admit; nor did he ever build a breathtaking course on dramatic terrain. But, they argue, his courses have endured the test of time. A look at his list of accomplishments lends support to that view. Among his best-known works are the Upper and Lower courses at Baltusrol and the Ridgewood Country Club in

New Jersey, the East and West courses at Winged Foot and the Black course at Bethpage State Park in New York, the Five Farms course of the Baltimore Country Club in Maryland, the San Francisco Golf Club in California, the Brook Hollow Country Club in Texas and the Hermitage Country Club in Virginia. These courses, as well as most others Tilly designed, survived over the years, having been changed very little.

Sad to say, the memory of Albert Tillinghast did not last. By the late 1920s Tilly had made himself well over a million dollars. By the end of the Depression he had lost it all. And by 1937 Tilly had forsaken the game of golf entirely, and he spent his remaining years in obscurity running an antique shop in Beverly Hills, California. Indeed, so totally forgotten was Tilly that for years after his death, writers, when talking of his works, referred to him as "Arthur" or "Archie" Tillinghast. It was not until 1974, when someone noticed that four USGA championships were being held on courses of his design, that the public was reintroduced to Albert Tillinghast. That was accomplished by USGA official Frank Hannigan in a widely circulated magazine article that still stands as the most thorough profile of any American golf architect.

Another Philadelphian who entered golf course architecture by chance was Hugh Wilson. Wilson was a member of the Merion Cricket Club (renamed in 1942 the Merion Golf Club) and was on the committee appointed to plan a new course in 1909 when the club decided to move to new quarters. The committee decided a first-hand look at the famous courses of Britain was needed before any attempt to build a course was made. Hugh Wilson was given the honor of making the trip. It has been suggested that Wilson, who suffered with illness throughout his life, was sent to Britain in hopes it would restore his health. It's more likely that he was chosen because his business, insurance brokerage, allowed him an extended leave of absence, and because he was the best golfer of the group.

Before he left, Wilson paid a visit to the site of the National Golf Links of America in Southampton. He not only carefully examined the course under construction there but also discussed an itinerary with C. B. Macdonald, who had made many similar journeys years before.

Wilson spent seven months in England and Scotland, playing and studying courses and sketching the features that most impressed him. When he returned, the committee was content to let Hugh have at it. So, with the aid of committee member Richard Francis, who could read a

transit, Wilson plotted out an eighteen hole course on the L-shaped 127 acres Merion had purchased in Ardmore. C. B. Macdonald and H. J. Whigham both offered advice on the endeavor.

But when the new Merion course opened in 1912, it did not attract much public attention. Four of the holes, numbers 1, 10, 11 and 12, originally played across Ardmore Avenue. In the early 1920s Wilson redesigned these holes to eliminate the road crossings. Over the years, after the course was remodeled and refined, the golfing world came to recognize its virtues.

It started with two par-5's among the first four played and finished with three demanding holes routed around an abandoned stone quarry. There were no blind shots to any green. All its bunkers, which eventually numbered some 120, were also clearly visible. Legend has it that Joe Valentine, Merion's legendary greenkeeper, would spread bed sheets on the site of a proposed bunker while Wilson would assure himself, from some vantage point back down the fairway, that the hazard could be seen. Long ago these bunkers were dubbed the "White Faces of Merion."

It has been suggested that Hugh Wilson grasped the basic concepts of British golf design and conveyed them in his work, even better than Charles Blair Macdonald. It is not quite fair, however, to compare Merion and the National Golf Links. They are two fine courses born of different intentions. Hugh Wilson never meant to duplicate any British golf hole in his design of Merion. Rather, he had hoped to capture the flavor, beauty and playability of a British parkland course. Certain subtle touches at Merion, such as patches of Scotch broom in several bunkers, wicker-basket pins instead of the usual flagsticks and a wild swale in the seventeenth green reminiscent of the Valley of Sin at St. Andrews, leave that impression, as does the overall effect when playing the course. But Merion has always been an innovative, thoroughly American original.

Hugh Wilson was involved in the design of a few other courses. In 1914 he laid out a second course at Merion, the West Course located a few miles down the road, which has always suffered unduly by continual comparison with the original course. In 1925 he began a complete revision of the East Course's bunkering. But he died unexpectedly that year of pneumonia, at only forty-five years of age.

Another designer closely connected with Merion was William S. Flynn. Flynn had been lured from his home in Massachusetts to the construction site of Merion in 1911 with an offer to become its greenkeeper. He worked on

the construction crew and then did serve as greenkeeper for a very short time before leaving for war service. But Flynn made three enduring friendships in this short time at Merion. One was with Joe Valentine, the construction foreman who, on Flynn's recommendation, succeeded him as greenkeeper. Another was with Hugh Wilson himself. Flynn respected Wilson's knowledge, talent and experience in the British Isles and Wilson provided Flynn with practical suggestions that he was able to apply to his new courses.

Flynn's third friendship was with Howard C. Toomey, a civil engineer who worked on the construction of Merion East. When Flynn decided after the War to enter the profession of course architecture, he formed a partnership with Toomey. Howard handled bookkeeping and construction aspects; Bill took care of public relations and the actual designing.

The firm of Toomey and Flynn operated out of Philadelphia for over a dozen years. They created some magnificent layouts, including the Spring Mill course for the Philadelphia Country Club; the Cascades course for The Homestead in Hot Springs, Virginia; the James River course for the Country Club of Virginia in Richmond; and the Cherry Hills Country Club in Denver. They were also chosen to finish revising the bunkering at Merion East after Hugh Wilson's death.

One final Pennsylvania contribution to golf architecture in this period was by George A. Crump, although the course he built is actually in New Jersey, some twenty miles southeast of Philadelphia. Crump was the founder of the Pine Valley Golf Club in Clementon, New Jersey, generally considered the most difficult course in the world. Crump, the millionaire owner of the Colonnades Hotel in Philadelphia, conceived his idea to build a dream course in the sandy pine forest of New Jersey in 1912. Although he had the financial backing of many enthusiastic club members, including George C. Thomas, Jr., Crump spent over a quarter of a million dollars of his own money on the project.

Crump literally moved to the site and walked every foot of the property in an attempt to devise a basic layout. Finally, in 1913, he secured the services of H. S. Colt, who was touring the eastern seaboard, to help him route his

course. When Colt visited the site, he surely was struck by its similarity to the land around Sunningdale, the architect's home course in Britain. Indeed, countless British visitors to Pine Valley have remarked on the uncanny resemblance of the two settings.

Together Crump and Colt routed a preliminary layout that proved to be so sound that it was altered only twice during construction. Colt, on a later visit, convinced Crump to make the par-3 fifth into a long-iron shot rather than the short pitch originally planned. The fifteenth hole was extended from a par-4 to a par-5 when finally constructed.

In 1914 Crump and his crew began a long, tedious term of construction. Thousands of trees were felled and the stumps removed; they stopped counting at 22,000 stumps. The area was replete with natural springs, which provided much needed water. But it also necessitated the creation of several concrete dams to form spring-fed lakes. Soil was hauled in for tees, fairways and greens, for the existing land was primarily sand, although with modern irrigation systems the sand would have been ideal.

By the end of 1914 Crump had eleven holes ready for play, the original nine plus the present tenth and eighteenth holes. By 1917 all but four holes, numbers 12 through 15, were complete. But then, in January of 1918, George Crump died. The club raised sufficient funds to finish the eighteen holes, and Hugh Wilson of Merion, and his brother Alan, spent the remainder of 1918 completing Pine Valley. The Wilsons made a few alterations to the plans of Crump and Colt, most notably the aforementioned extension of the fifteenth hole.

Even before it formally opened as an eighteen-hole course in 1919, Pine Valley had earned a phenomenal reputation, not only among golfers but among golf architects. Travis, Tillinghast and Flynn all visited the course and were enthusiastic about its possibilities. Donald Ross and Charles Blair Macdonald both pronounced it the greatest course in the country.

What garnered Pine Valley such high praise from designers who were normally partial to their own works was perhaps the unique concept of the course. No other American course was like Pine Valley. Its fairways and greens were islands of playable turf, surrounded by natural sandy wastelands. Nearly every hole featured a forced

carry over unmaintained sand and brush to the fairway and another such carry to the green. While a great many trees had been removed in building Pine Valley, a great many remained, and over the years more grew back. By mid-century, few other courses in America were as thickly forested. The artificial lakes Crump built also came into play. Certain greens were precariously close to the water, like those of numbers 14 and 18.

Because it required such precise placement of each golf shot, Pine Valley was punishing to even the finest of players. Its introduction marked the zenith of the penal school of golf course architecture in America. No course quite like it has been built since, and no course has ever been as demanding of every stroke. Pine Valley remains today just as it did when it opened, a monument to its creator, George Crump, who never lived to see its fruition.

Emphasis on the Pennsylvanian influence on this period of golf design history is not intended to imply that other designers were not busy doing impressive things

elsewhere. Among the designs of John Duncan Dunn in this period was the Quaker Ridge Country Club in Mamaroneck, New York. C. B. Macdonald tackled a new challenge in 1914, the construction of a links entirely upon land reclaimed from the sea. This course, the Lido Golf Club in Long Beach, New York, opened after the War.

By 1911 Donald Ross had embraced the profession almost full time, although he was still professional at Pinehurst, North Carolina. While he continued to operate from there, his reputation had become such that he was called upon to design courses in many parts of the country. Among the dozens of Donald Ross courses that opened in this period before World War I were the Brae Burn Country Club in Massachusetts, the Wannamoisett Country Club in Rhode Island, the Oakland Hills Country Club in Michigan, the Scioto Country Club in Ohio, the Bob O'Link Golf Club in Illinois, the Broadmoor Golf Club in Colorado and the Atlanta Athletic Club (now the East Lake Country Club) in Georgia.

70

The British invasion of golf talent into the United States also continued in this era. Foremost among the second wave of emigrants who would have an impact on American course architecture were Herbert Strong and Norman Macbeth.

Strong, a professional from St. George's Golf Club in England, came to the United States with his brother Leonard in 1905 to compete in several golf events. Strong remained in the States and while serving as professional at the Inwood Country Club in New York, redesigned and rebuilt that club's course. He soon devoted a majority of his time to course design, and by the 1930s Herbert Strong would be responsible for some of the finest courses in North America: the Canterbury Country Club in Cleveland, Ohio; the Metropolis Golf Club in New York; Ponte Vedra Golf Club in Florida; Club Laval Sur Le Lac in Montreal; and Manoir Richelieu in Quebec.

Norman Macbeth, a tall, quiet Scot, ventured to America in 1901 and subsequently settled in Los Angeles. A fine player, who would win both the Southern and Northern California Amateur titles, Macbeth had his first design experience assisting in the layout of a new eighteen holes for the Los Angeles Country Club in 1911. He designed several southern California courses, including the San Gabriel Country Club, the Annandale Golf Club and his home course, the Wilshire Country Club.

And there were others who came in the early 1900s: Leslie Brownlee, a Scot who introduced the game to Oklahoma and built that territory's first courses; Grange "Sandy" Alves, who worked primarily as a greenkeeper in Cleveland but also designed several Ohio-area courses; Albert Murray, who moved with his brother Charles from England to Canada at an early age, won the Canadian Open at twenty and eventually designed several Canadian layouts; William Kinnear, a Scot who settled in Saskatoon in 1910 and did several early courses including Riverside Country Club in Saskatchewan; and Robert Johnstone, who served as professional at the Seattle Golf Club for many years and did a number of fine courses on the West Coast, including his own club's course.

A disturbing but temporary postscript to this period arose in 1916 when golf architects accepting fees for their services were stripped of their amateur status under the Amateur Rule. It was restored in 1921, however, when it was decided that the true definition of professionalism lay in making a profit from skill in playing the game.

---

[1] The Golf Journal, U.S.G.A. May 1973, p. 8.

P. 70: *Before and after the First World War, earth was moved by horses or mules pulling scrapers.*
P. 71: *Months were sometimes required to move the necessary earth and rough grade in a single green. Architects took advantage of the leisurely pace to alter their plans and add subtle touches as their features were executed on the ground.*

7.

The Roaring Twenties: The Golden Age of Course Design

When the Great War in Europe broke out in 1914, it found many Britons who relied upon golf for a livelihood in America. Some of those involved in golf course architecture returned to their native land, while others stayed on in their new homes. Around this time, Herbert Fowler set up offices in the United States; but by the early 1920s he moved back to Britain, where he designed, among other fine courses, thirty-six holes for The Berkshire. Willie Park, Jr., came to North America at about the same time Fowler did. But unlike Fowler, he remained in America until 1924, when he returned to Scotland because of serious illness. He died a year later.

Among other emigrants who, like Park, chose to stay in America after the War were:

• Wilfrid Reid, who had competed on several occasions in the United States. Reid settled as a club professional but designed over fifty courses and remodeled some forty others in a period of thirty years.

• Tom Winton, who came to America to work for Willie Park and then took a position with the Westchester County (New York) Park Commission. He built and maintained several public courses for that county.

• Harry Robb, of Montrose, Scotland, who built the Milburn Golf and Country Club in Kansas City, Kansas, and became its pro. He also laid out several other courses in Kansas.

• James Dalgleish, of Nairn, Scotland, who, like Robb, settled in Kansas City. Dalgleish designed courses all across the Midwest.

• David Hunter, the son of Charles Hunter of Prestwick, who did several courses in the New Jersey area while serving as professional at Baltusrol and Essex County (New Jersey) CC.

• David T. Millar, of Arbroath, Scotland, who settled in Detroit and was responsible for several courses in that area.

• Willard Wilkinson, who came from England and was associated with Tillinghast before starting a career that continued from the 1920s into the early 1960s.

H. S. Colt also practiced course architecture in America sporadically during the war years. Later he encouraged a new associate, Charles Hugh Alison, to join him. The two had met when Colt was laying out the Stoke Poges Golf Club in Britain where Alison was club secretary.

Perhaps because he had started in the same fashion, Colt was sympathetic to the young Alison's earnest desire to learn the trade. He gave Alison the chance to work with him, and Charles showed himself to be adept at supervising construction and equally talented at designing golf holes. By 1920 the two had formed a full partnership.

Alison was probably the first truly "worldwide" golf course architect. He was responsible for a majority of the work of the firm of Colt and Alison in the United States, including the North Shore and Knollwood Country Clubs near Chicago, Illinois; the Burning Tree Club near Washington, D.C.; and the complete rebuilding of nearby Chevy Chase. He also worked in Australia and Europe, and was the first architect to build first-rate courses in Japan. At the time of his death, in 1952, he was working on yet another course, this one in South Africa.

If Alison was not the first worldwide designer, then the title surely belongs to Alister Mackenzie. Mackenzie was a physician by profession; but he abandoned his medical practice in 1909 after assisting H. S. Colt with the design of his home club's course, Alwoodley, in Leeds. He worked with Colt on several other courses, most notably the Eden at St. Andrews, and for a time was a partner in the firm of Colt, Alison and Mackenzie. But by 1925 he was on his own and spent the remaining years of his life globetrotting, producing fine courses in such widespread locales as Ireland (where he remodeled the Lahinch Golf Club), Uruguay (the Golf Club de Uruguay), Australia (where he did several, including the West course of the Royal Melbourne Golf Club), Argentina (the Jockey Club at San Isidro) and Canada (the North course of the St. Charles Country Club in Winnipeg). Mackenzie finally settled in the United States where, as will be noted, he did perhaps his finest work.

74

P. 72-73: Hole # 17, Cypress Point by Mackenzie. Many of the fine American courses of the 1920s were planned by visiting or transplanted Britishers. P. 75: (Top) Sea Island, Georgia, Seaside 9 was originally the work of Colt and Alison. P. 75: (Bottom) Longmeadow CC, Massachusetts, was planned in 1922 by Donald Ross, soon to become the top name in American course design.

Tom Simpson, who had obtained a legal degree at Cambridge but found no need to practice law, joined Herbert Fowler's firm in 1910. After the War they were partners in a company that expanded in the 1920s to include J. F. Abercrombie and A. C. M. Croome.

Simpson was one of the great characters in the history of golf course architecture. He was a wealthy man and an accomplished writer and artist. He made a major contribution with *The Architectural Side of Golf*, which he authored in 1929 with H. N. Wethered. It featured numerous ink-and-wash sketches of golf holes, all by Simpson.

Simpson was, in fact, eccentric. He traveled from construction site to construction site in a silver, chauffeur-driven Rolls Royce, invariably dressed in cloak and beret with riding crop in hand. He once selected an assistant on the basis of the young man's suggestion as to how to mount a license plate attractively on a Rolls. Such an artistic eye, Simpson felt, would be valuable in course design. Eccentric or not, Tom Simpson's judgment was sound. The young assistant he hired was Philip Mackenzie Ross, who would prove himself after World War II to be one of Britain's finest designers.

Tom Simpson's abilities as a golf course architect were also sound. During the twenties in Britain, he did such fine work as the remodeled New Zealand Golf Club at Byfleet in England and the Cruden Bay course in Aberdeen. His finest efforts, however, were found on the Continent, at courses like Deauville (the New course), Chantilly and Morfontaine in France.

James Braid continued to produce fine layouts during the 1920s. He did, among others, a new course for Royal Musselburgh, and the East and West courses at Dalmahoy; and he remodeled the Carnoustie Golf Club into the severe test of golf we know today. His assistant at Carnoustie was John R. Stutt, a landscape contractor, who remained associated with Braid through the rest of the old man's design career and who became increasingly involved in the planning.

Another one-time Braid assistant was Cecil Hutchison, a former British Army officer and one of Scotland's finest amateurs. Hutchison learned a great deal from Braid and in the twenties began building courses of his own design. He worked on occasion with Guy Campbell, another ex-Army officer and a descendant of a golfing family.

Sir Guy Campbell was a successful amateur golfer and a superb writer. He worked with Bernard Darwin on the sports staff of the *London Times* until the mid-1920s when he resigned, unable to resist the lure of golf course design. His first work was the West Sussex Golf Club in England, done with the assistance of Hutchison. Guy Campbell maintained a steady design practice the rest of his life. Among his best works were the revisions of the Prince's Golf Club in England (with J. S. F. Morrison) and the Killarney Golf Club in Ireland. Sir Guy died in 1960 while laying out his only course in the United States, the Tides Inn in Virginia.

One other designer worked with Hutchison and Campbell at West Sussex. He was S. V. Hotchkin, also a former Army officer, who first became involved in course design in 1922 after purchasing and remodeling the Woodhall Spa Golf Club. For a time Hotchkin, Hutchison and Campbell were partners in an architectural firm. They later separated and Hotchkin moved to South Africa, ostensibly to retire. But he undertook to plan several of that country's finest courses, including the Humewood and Durban Country Clubs.

By the 1920s golf course architecture was also a full-time profession for a great many on the western side of the Atlantic. It was a special period of growing prosperity in America. Construction costs, real estate values and interest rates were low. Clients were willing and able to pay for the best and gave designers a free hand. Consequently, the twenties have been called the Golden Age of Golf Course Architecture in America, and these years saw the flair and style of golf courses enhanced immeasurably.

There had been some 742 courses in the United States in 1916. By 1923 there were 1,903. By 1929 there would be 5,648! That was an average increase of approximately 600 new courses per year from 1923 to 1929. Such a rapid growth rate would not be approached again until 1967.

It may seem impossible that a few dozen professional course architects could design so many courses in the United States and abroad, considering the fact that train rides between projects took days and boat trips required weeks. The truth is, professional designers did only a fraction of the courses built in the twenties. A good many courses, perhaps a majority, were still being laid out and built by locals or immigrants who remained indefinitely as pro-greenkeepers. Alex "Nipper" Campbell, for example, was a Scot who designed and built the Moraine Country Club in Dayton, Ohio, and then stayed on as its professional for decades. While men like this sometimes designed a few other courses in their locale, they never truly practiced course architecture.

There were also countless instances of "in-house" planning and design by a member or committee of a private club or by a city or county official for a new public layout. The Maidstone Golf Links, originally laid out by

William Tucker, was completely redesigned by club member C. Wheaton Vaughan.

Even in cases where a professional designer was hired, the architect sometimes provided the client with no more than one or two days at the actual site. In that time he would inspect the land, route the course, prepare an outline, sketches or diagrams of the holes and instruct the members on how to construct and maintain the course. This may have been a step above the practice of "eighteen stakes on a Sunday afternoon," but it was not a very big step. It left many clubs, or governing bodies in the case of public courses, to fend for themselves; and it is doubtful if such procedures ever produced a course as the architect had envisaged it. In some cases, the architect was not even present at the site. James Braid remodeled the St. Andrews Golf Club on Mt. Hope, New York, without ever setting foot on the property or even in the country. He recommended changes solely by examining topographical maps of the course at his home in England.

The preferable method involved an architect who, after inspecting the site and designing the basic course layout, would remain himself or leave an experienced superintendent to build the course, with the architect periodically visiting the site to inspect the evolution of his design and make adjustments and corrections as needed. A good number of these construction superintendents, men like Orrin Smith and James Harrison, later entered the field of golf course design.

Toomey and Flynn, Herbert Strong, Walter Travis, A. W. Tillinghast, Devereux Emmet, John D. Dunn and C. B. Macdonald were still very active along the east coast of the United States during the "Roaring Twenties." Macdonald was always assisted by his right-hand man, Seth Raynor, on the dozen or so courses he designed in these years.

Raynor not only constructed all of Macdonald's designs but did some sixty courses of his own. He had established his own practice in 1915 but was most prolific after the War. He played the main role in the remodeling of the Chicago Golf Club, which has been credited entirely, but incorrectly, to Macdonald. Other Raynor originals include the Country Club of Fairfield and the Greenwich Country Club, both in Connecticut, and the Yeaman's Hall Club in Charleston, South Carolina.

Raynor was responsible for luring two academicians into the field of golf design. The first was Charles H. Banks, an English professor at the Hotchkiss School of Salisbury, Connecticut, which hired Raynor to lay out its course. Banks served on the construction committee and worked closely with Raynor; when the latter moved on,

Banks resigned and went with him.

The other was Ralph M. Barton, a faculty member at the University of Minnesota. Raynor was hired to design a course for that institution, and Barton volunteered to supervise the construction. When this course was complete, Barton, like Banks, joined Raynor full time. (Ironically, at least one other math professor became a golf course architect, although in this case, Seth Raynor had nothing to do with the conversion. He was John Bredemus, a prominent Texas designer of the 1930s.)

The team of Raynor, Banks and Barton, along with C. B. Macdonald, went on to create another university course. In the mid-1920s they designed and built the excellent Yale University Golf Club. It was to be Raynor's last effort, for he died of pneumonia in 1926. Banks, who would die only five years later, finished several of Raynor's designs and did quite a few fine courses of his own in the East and Bermuda. Barton returned to his native New Hampshire and planned a number of courses in New England, including one nine of the Hanover Country Club owned by Dartmouth College. Macdonald did no more designing (except for endless tinkering with the National Golf Links), preferring to write his memoirs, which were published in 1928 as *Scotland's Gift—Golf*. This book contains several passages concerning his philosophy of golf course architecture.

Also active on the East Coast were: Maurice J. McCarthy, an Irish immigrant who is best known for the several courses he did at Hershey, Pennsylvania; Fred Findlay, Alexander's brother, who was hired from Australia by a Virginia seed firm and did most of his designing in that state; Orrin E. Smith, a former construction superintendent for both Donald Ross and Willie Park, Jr., who opened his own offices in Hartford, Connecticut, in 1924; Wayne E. Stiles, a landscape architect, and John R. Van Kleek, a landscape architect and civil engineer, who, as the Boston and Florida firm of Stiles and Van Kleek, did such notable courses as the Taconic Golf Club in Massachusetts; and Alfred H. Tull, a Walter Travis apprentice who became a partner of Devereux Emmet and his son in the firm of Emmet, Emmet and Tull.

In the Midwest, Chicago was a hotbed of golfing activity. Besides the old Scot Tom Bendelow, at least a dozen other full or part-time golf course architects could be found in that area. Among them were: Robert Bruce Harris, formally trained as a landscape architect; William B. Langford and Theodore Moreau, the firm of Langford and Moreau; C. D. Wagstaff; Leonard Macomber; Frank Macdonald and Charles Maddox, the firm of Macdonald and Maddox; Jack Daray; Harry Collis; Edward B. Dearie,

Jr.; Joseph A. Roseman; and George O'Neill. In Indianapolis, prominent amateur golfer William H. Diddel opened a practice.

On the West Coast, Willie Watson and William H. Tucker were busy during the 1920s. Tucker also had an active construction firm that built courses for a young Canadian designer, A. Vernon Macan. Macan laid out courses all along the West Coast, including the Broadmoor Country Club in Seattle, the Fircrest Country Club in Tacoma, the California Golf Club of San Francisco and a host of layouts in his home province of British Columbia.

Watson's construction superintendent for a time was William P. Bell, an easterner who came west in search of a fortune. Billy, who built most of the courses that George C. Thomas, Jr., designed in California in the 1920s, also had his own design firm. By the end of the decade, Billy Bell was one of the busiest architects of all. His early works include the Del Rio Golf and Country Club in Modesto, California, and the fine Stanford University Golf Club in Palo Alto.

Two nationally known amateur golfers became prominent golf designers in the Far West during the twenties. H. Chandler Egan, a two-time U.S. Amateur champion, moved from Chicago to Medford, Oregon, and laid out several courses in the Pacific Northwest, including the original Eugene Country Club in Oregon and the Indian Canyon Golf Course in Spokane, Washington. Max H. Behr, a U. S. Amateur runner-up, designed courses in southern California, including Rancho Santa Fe Golf Club and the Lakeside Golf Club of Hollywood.

One area on the West Coast, the Monterey Peninsula in California, was the location of two new courses that captured the attention of the golfing world in the 1920s. The courses, which were less than a mile apart, were the Pebble Beach Golf Links and the Cypress Point Club.

Pebble Beach opened for play in 1919. Its designers were two local men, Jack Neville and Douglas Grant. Neville was chosen because he was a fine golfer, several times a California Amateur champion, and because he was employed by the Pacific Improvement Company, the firm that owned the land and wisely chose to develop it into a golf course. Neville asked his friend, Douglas Grant, also a California Amateur champion, to assist him.

Neither man had any previous course design or construction experience. But like Hugh Wilson, George Crump and several other neophyte designers before them, Neville and Grant did an incredibly fine job. The course was adapted nicely into the existing terrain and very little earth was moved. The greens were deliberately kept small and were liberally contoured. Most importantly, they managed to build seven holes on which the ocean came into play.

Pebble Beach was not a links, for it was located on bluffs overlooking Carmel Bay. But it had a distinctive links feel about it, strung out in loop fashion and subject to the strong ocean winds. It was a resort course from the very start and was available for everyone to play. In fact, its official title for years was the Del Monte Golf and Country Club after the Del Monte Lodge located there.

Although Pebble Beach has been modified on some occasions, including very minor changes by Alister Mackenzie in collaboration with Robert Hunter, and by H. Chandler Egan, who revised the bunkering on several holes in 1928, the course remains as Neville and Grant devised it, a dramatic combination of inland and seaside golf. Grant was content to play the game after that and never worked on another course design. Neville worked with several professional architects on other projects and also experienced the termination before construction of numerous projects of his own design. He remained at Pebble Beach all his life, and even in the 1970s USGA officials consulted with him before tampering with the course.

Ten years after the opening of Pebble Beach, Cypress Point, the work of the Britisher Alister Mackenzie, was unveiled. Cypress Point did not have a long, exciting stretch of ocean frontage like its neighbor, but its three dramatic ocean holes more than sufficed. The sixteenth hole was the most breathtaking. It was a long, long par-3 over a bay to a green set on a peninsula. The sixteenth has become, over the years, the most photographed and perhaps the most recognizable golf hole in the country. It also graphically demonstrates the strategic philosophy of golf design at its heroic extreme. On the sixteenth the bold player shoots directly to the green, 220 yards away, across pounding surf some 100 feet below. The cautious golfer plays short to dry land on the left, and then pitches to the green with hope of putting for a par. Without the alternate route, Cypress Point's sixteenth would have been a terribly penal hole, unreachable to all but a few strong golfers; with it, the sixteenth requires a player to choose his route before swinging. (Despite considerable evidence to the contrary, some claim the sixteenth was first planned as a par-4 with the tee farther back.)

The fifteenth, which is a par-3 as well, also borders an ocean bay, but it is a short pitch with the green much closer to the precipice. The seventeenth is a dogleg par-4, with the tee shot across the water and the fairway split

P. 78: (Top) *The Donald Ross bunker style, preserved through several remodelings on Course #2 at Pinehurst.*

P. 78: (Bottom) *Typical Ross bunkers at Monroe CC, Pittsford, New York. By the mid-1920s, Ross was receiving more requests for his services than he could accept. Some 3,000 men were employed annually building his courses.*

into two by a stand of cypress trees. The course has several other masterful holes.

Cypress Point was possibly Alister Mackenzie's best course to that time. Ironically, the founders of Cypress Point had not originally retained Mackenzie as their architect. They had hired Seth Raynor, who had done the nearby Monterey Peninsula Country Club course. But Raynor died and although he had left preliminary plans for the course, they were never used.

Two of Mackenzie's assistants at Cypress Point deserve mention. Robert Hunter, who assisted on several of Mackenzie's California designs, is best known for his dissertation on golf course architecture entitled *The Links,* which was published in 1925. Jack Fleming, who served as construction foreman on many of Mackenzie's designs, was later active as a course architect on his own in the 1950s and 60's. Mackenzie himself did other courses in California during the 1920s, including the Pasatiempo Golf Club in Santa Cruz and the Haggin Oaks Municipal Golf Course in Sacramento.

Mackenzie, Thomas, Bell, Tillinghast and many others made major contributions to course design in the 1920s. But the outstanding figures in course design in this period were probably the veteran Scot, Donald Ross, and a Scottish-born Canadian, Stanley Thompson.

Donald Ross had been designing courses in the United States since the early 1900s. By 1920 he was probably the most active architect in the country. He had a nationwide reputation and was hired to build courses from coast to coast. Indeed, six of the eight National Opens between 1919 and 1926 were played on courses of his design. Each new course gained him more attention, and it became a symbol of status to have a Donald Ross layout. The Northland Country Club in Duluth, Minnesota, turned down a fine Willie Watson design, even after Ross himself had urged them to accept it. They wanted a Donald Ross course, which he reluctantly gave them.

Many of Ross's designs were simply built to his plans and instructions, without his personal supervision; and the architect often commiserated over the fact that layouts credited to him were not as he had intended. But he himself continually worked on at least eight courses at a time during the twenties and had a loyal crew of construction supervisors over the years, including Walter B. Hatch, Walter Johnston, James B. McGovern, James Harrison and Henry T. Hughes, who carried out his designs at other sites. The courses he did in this era were of a uniformly high standard. Among them were the Plainfield

P. 80–81: *La Quinta Hotel GC., Ca., by Dye (1980), where lines of bunkers and mounds are in harmony with natural land forms. Principles of art were first applied to golf design in the 1920s by Stanley Thompson and others.*

82

P. 82–83: *Elaborate Ross bunkers at Plainfield CC. P. 83: (Right)* Three
of the five principles of art include harmony *(Los Leones, Chile, top),*
emphasis *(Pebble Beach GC, center) and proportion (Banff Springs, bottom).*

Country Club in New Jersey; the Salem and Winchester Country Clubs in Massachusetts; the East and West courses at the Oak Hill Country Club and the Monroe Country Club, both near Rochester, New York; the East and West courses at the Country Club of Birmingham in Alabama; the Essex Golf and Country Club and Rosedale in Ontario; the Belle Meade Country Club in Tennessee; and the River Oaks Country Club in Texas.

In the late 1920s, Donald Ross, the architect with more offers than he could ever fulfill, actually pursued a contract to design a course. It is likely this was the only time in his long career that he did so, but he had seen the site for the intended course and was intrigued by its possibilities. Ross's proposal won. Perhaps because it had required an extra effort to get the job, he gave an unusual amount of personal attention to the course.

The result was the Seminole Golf Club in North Palm Beach, Florida, possibly Ross's finest creation. Laid out along two small ridges just off the Atlantic, Seminole was an exquisite job. It was heavily bunkered, 187 in all; but the bunkers were positioned and constructed to convey a sense of the nearby rolling surf.

The course was built to provide a challenge for every level of handicap. Each hole had multiple tees and alternate routes to the green, for by this time Ross was a confirmed advocate of strategic golf design. One hole, the fifteenth, featured alternate fairways: a shorter route with tempting water carries, and a longer but drier route for those content to play the par-5 in par. Seminole exists today with but one exception, just as it did when Donald Ross first opened it in 1929.

Another major force in the twenties was Stanley Thompson. One of a clan of Canadian tournament golfers, Thompson entered the design field following his return from France after the War. He soon became the most conspicuous course architect in Canada, and his reputation spilled over the border to the United States, into the Caribbean and on to South America. Part of his fame was certainly attributable to the magnificent Banff and Jasper courses he constructed in the rugged Rockies of Alberta. Built in high country devoid of topsoil along a rushing mountain river, Banff had the dubious distinction of being the first course in history to cost a million dollars to construct.

Thompson was most vocal in the 1920s in expounding the merits of strategic design, and his works reflected his philosophy. Besides Banff and Jasper, other impressive courses he did in those years included the Royal York Golf and Country Club in Ontario (now known as St.

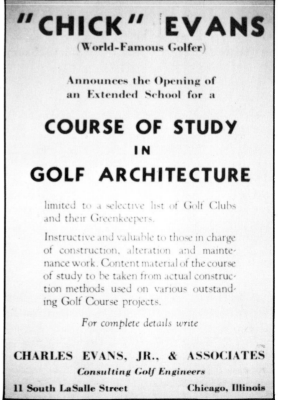

About GOLF COURSES Their Construction and Up-Keep

Stanley Thompson & Co. Limited
Toronto   Montreal
          Cleveland

George's) and the Ladies Golf Club of Toronto (probably the single "ladies only" golf club still in existence).

Stanley Thompson also launched the careers of several prominent contemporary designers. At one time or another, Geoffrey S. Cornish, Robert Moote, C. E. Robinson, Howard Watson and Norman Woods all worked for and with Thompson. And Robert Trent Jones, who, fresh out of Cornell, began assisting in the refining of Banff after it had opened, became Thompson's partner in 1930 and remained a lifelong friend even after he began his own illustrious career.

Important articles by American golf architects were appearing in periodicals of the twenties. Max Behr was a prolific writer, as were Walter Travis, founder and editor of *American Golfer*, and A. W. Tillinghast, who wrote for and later edited *Golf Illustrated*. The first years of the 1920s had also seen the publication in Great Britain of a book on course architecture by H. S. Colt assisted by C. H. Alison and A. Mackenzie, and another by Mackenzie on his own.

P. 84–85: *Memorabilia.* (Upper left) *Mackenzie in one of his own bunkers at Cypress Point. Resemblance of bunker shapes to the outline of nearby trees is in keeping with the art principle of harmony.* (Upper right) *Title page of Thompson's brochure.* (Lower left) *Evans was a strong advocate of formal training in golf design.* (Lower right) *Wee Burn CC., Conn. (1923) is a Dev Emmet masterpiece.*

8

8.

Golf Architecture in Depression and War

With readily available capital and an abundance of golf design talent, it seemed that the Golden Age of Golf Course Architecture would last forever. In reality, the era lasted only a scant ten years. The stock market crash of 1929, the bank closings of the early 1930s and the Great Depression brought an abrupt halt to course development in the United States.

The bank closings were especially harmful. Without financing, planned projects were shelved and existing projects abandoned. It was the rare club that had no members who lost fortunes.

Long-established clubs were able to weather the financial storm by implementing austerity measures. But the newer clubs, those born of the boom of the 1920s and patronized by younger men of new-found wealth, were vulnerable because they were overextended financially. Liberal lifetime or single-fee memberships had been handed out as promotional gimmicks. The remaining regular members could not meet the periodic dues. Such new clubs had operation and maintenance expenses to meet, as well as fees to course architects, contractors and subcontractors. With insufficient revenues, they were forced to disband.

In New York, the Midvale Golf and Country Club filed for bankruptcy soon after its new golf course was finished. Midvale was the first professional design of architect Robert Trent Jones, and it marked an inauspicious debut to what would be an illustrious career. In California, the Lake Norconian Club collapsed, taking with it the finely designed course of John Duncan Dunn, who had been promoting it as his masterpiece. Real estate development courses, like Norman Macbeth's Midwick Club near Pasadena and George C. Thomas, Jr.'s El Caballero in Tarzana, also closed and the land was sold.

Most public and municipal courses managed to stay open, but they were poorly funded and maintained. The feast of the 1920s and the famine that followed in the 1930s clearly demonstrated to architects that the most magnificently designed and built course would not remain magnificent for very long when adequate funds were not available for upkeep.

Golf course architecture did not become a lost art during the American thirties and the war that followed, but it did become a highly neglected one. In the twenty years between 1932 and 1952, a total of only 200 new courses opened for play. In the same span of time, some 600 courses closed forever.

Times were hard for men in the golf design profession. Full-time architects, especially those who also contracted the construction, were severely affected. With clients defaulting on huge sums of money, many of these architects lost fortunes while trying to settle their accounts honorably from their own resources. Mackenzie, Tillinghast and Strong, among others, were never able to recoup their losses, and all three died in straitened circumstances.

Part-time architects fared somewhat better. Some, like Fred Findlay and Edward Dearie, were able to make a living working as greenkeepers or club managers. Others, like Wilf Reid, Jack Daray and Harry Collis, served as club professionals. Some, like Alfred Tull, entered the maintenance equipment business; and many others practiced professions unrelated to golf, like Norman Macbeth, who operated a cement firm.

A number of America's most prominent architects would die during the thirties. Tom Bendelow, Charles Banks, H. Chandler Egan, Devereux Emmet, Charles Blair Macdonald, Alister Mackenzie, Maurice McCarthy and George C. Thomas, Jr., were among them.

But there were some bright spots on the bleak American landscape of the Depression. In 1932 the long-awaited "dream course" of golfing phenomenon Robert Tyre "Bobby" Jones, Jr., opened in Augusta, Georgia. Jones called it the Augusta National Golf Club, and from its beginning the course was something very special. Jones had asked the renowned Alister Mackenzie to help design his course, and together they routed a stunning layout through the grounds of an old arboretum.

Augusta National was specifically designed with spectator golf in mind. Several greens were situated to provide vantage points from nearby hillsides. Several mounds were created to serve as seats for viewers, and over the

88

P. 86–87: The Augusta National GC, Georgia, by Mackenzie. Although the Depression was worldwide, course construction outside the U.S. continued at a steady pace. Nationally there were a few bright spots, including "Bobby" Jones, Jr.'s "Dream course" at Augusta. P. 89: Prairie Dunes CC, Kansas, by Perry Maxwell, another bright spot on the bleak Depression landscape.

years many more would be added. But Augusta National was also a player's course. The fairways were broad, and little rough existed. Instead, Mackenzie and Jones utilized natural hazards of trees (there were thousands of tall Georgia pines lining the fairways) and water (two streams and a pond came into play on five holes on the front nine). The greens were large, with flowing contours. And the very few bunkers, only twenty-two at the beginning, were expertly placed.

Soon after Augusta opened, its nines were reversed, for it was felt that the water holes, including the now-famous Amen corner of eleven through thirteen, should be tackled later in the round. Augusta National was in some ways the first uniquely American golf course. It was a model of strategic design, reflecting the principles of Mackenzie and Jones. Mackenzie had codified his principles in his book, *Golf Architecture*, in 1920; and he was able to express all those "essentials of an ideal course" at Augusta National.

Jones, who, like Mackenzie, was a devout admirer of St. Andrews, strongly felt alternative routes should be provided for players of lesser ability. But he also felt there should be rewards, especially on par-5 holes, for those who took a chance and succeeded.

At Augusta every hole looked deceptively simple; and, indeed, a high handicap golfer could keep the ball in play for an enjoyable round. But every hole had a pre-ferred target, a spot from which it was most advantageous to play the next stroke. Augusta National could yield low rounds, but only to a golfer who thought his way around the course.

By the fifties Augusta National emerged as a standard for American golf course architecture. This was due in no small part to those progressive ideas of Alister Mackenzie and Bobby Jones.

Alister Mackenzie was responsible for other courses in the States during the 1930s, most of which were completed after his death. His associate on several projects was a former Oklahoma banker turned course designer, Perry Maxwell. Maxwell was probably the most prolific golf architect in America during the Depression.

This was ironic, for Maxwell did the bulk of his work in the so-called Dust Bowl area of Kansas, Oklahoma and Texas. But those very areas contained industries un-affected by the generally depressed economy of the United States. Oil interests in Tulsa hired Maxwell to build them a course, and in 1935 he gave them Southern Hills Country Club. The Carey Salt people of Hutchinson, Kansas, also hired Maxwell, and in 1937 he built the Prairie Dunes Country Club.

P. 90-91:
(Upper left and
bottom) *Scenes at
Augusta National.*
(Upper Right)
*Free-form style
of post-war architect
E.L. Packard was
probably influenced
by Mackenzie's.*

Prairie Dunes, featuring striking linkslike qualities, was originally planned as an eighteen-hole course. Only nine were built, however, and for twenty years the course had the reputation of being the best nine-hole course in the country. Perry's son, J. Press Maxwell, added nine more holes in 1957, following his father's routing plan and adding some touches of his own.

In 1936 Perry Maxwell lost the bid to lay out the Colonial Country Club for oilman Marvin Leonard in Fort Worth, Texas (architect John Bredemus was hired), but he was later retained to build three new holes at the course in preparation for the 1941 U. S. Open. Those holes are now perhaps the best at Colonial, the third, the fourth and the infamous fifth.

Perry Maxwell was especially noted for his severely contoured greens, which long ago were dubbed "the Maxwell Rolls." The most prominent example of the Maxwell Rolls is at Augusta National, which hired Perry in the late 1930s to rebuild some of its holes. Greens like the first, the tenth and the fourteenth are the result of Maxwell's handiwork. Among other very prominent courses on which Maxwell rebuilt the greens into rolling terrors were the Saucon Valley Country Club, the Pine Valley Golf Club (George Crump's masterpiece) and the Gulph Mills Golf Club, all three in the vicinity of Philadelphia.

The latter course was another of Donald Ross's great creations. Ross was still active in the 1930s, although the Depression curtailed his travels and he stayed closer to his home in Pinehurst, North Carolina. This allowed him to concentrate on his pet project, the Pinehurst courses.

By 1936 Ross had successfully converted the old sand greens of the three courses there to Bermuda grass and had sculptured them into visible, raised putting surfaces with undulating approaches, a style by that time widely recognized as his trademark. (Conversion to grass had been delayed because the high degree of perfection of the sand greens was felt to be superior to seeded Bermuda grass.)

Ross then set about rearranging the courses, re-bunkering nearly every hole and adding strategic mounds and hollows. The result when he finished, although truthfully he was never finished with Pinehurst and was forever refining the courses, was two pleasant resort courses, Pinehurst Numbers 1 and 3, and one long, deceptive, top-flight layout, Pinehurst Number 2, which was good enough to host the National PGA Championship a year after it opened.

At Pinehurst Number 2, Donald Ross demonstrated a brilliantly deceptive form of strategic design. The course appeared to be straightforward. Its fairways were not par-ticularly wide, but there was little rough. The greens were small and undulating, but very few of them were protected by more than a single bunker.

But the illusions soon vanished once a round at Pinehurst Number 2 was begun. A ball off the fairway was either in the pines on a mat of pine needles or on the soft, sandy soil cluttered with clumps of wiry "love" grass. An errant driver at Pinehurst seldom found a good lie.

And the tiny greens required a great deal of concentration. Some bunkers were well forward of the green, and the careless player could find his approach land over the bunker but short of the putting surface. Many holes had only one bunker at the corner or side of the green. Yet to follow one's natural inclination and play away from the bunker was often a mistake. Ross counterbalanced most bunkers with greenside mounds and hollows, most of which posed more difficult recovery problems than the sand.

Donald Ross considered his Pinehurst Number 2, with all its subtleties, to be his finest achievement.

Strangely enough, although the Great Depression was worldwide, golf course construction outside the United States continued at a steady pace. In the British Isles an average of forty new courses opened every year in the thirties, and professional architects were kept busy remodeling other British layouts into exciting tests of golf. In this period, Taylor and Hawtree rebuilt the Royal Birkdale Golf Club into such a fine course that it was proposed as the permanent site of The Open; C. K. Hutchison planned major changes to the thirty-six holes at the Turnberry Hotel to bring play closer to the nearby ocean; Guy Campbell revised the Killarney Golf Club of Ireland into a lovely lake-front course; and Tom Simpson remodeled the Ballybunion Golf Club into a dramatic oceanside test that was probably the best in Ireland.

New layouts were also appearing in other parts of the British Empire. In Canada the firm of Thompson and Jones kept busy, producing such solid courses as Digby Pines and Cape Breton Highlands (known also as the Keltic Lodge) in Nova Scotia, the Green Gables Golf Club on Prince Edward Island and Capilano in British Columbia. In Australia Alex Russell, who had assisted Alister Mackenzie in designing the Royal Melbourne course, laid out a second eighteen, the East course, for that club as well as many others throughout the country.

In Japan Kinya Fujita, who had attended college in America and had studied golf course architecture under Alison, was creating many fine layouts: the East and West courses at Kasumigaseki, the King's and Queen's courses at Narashino and the Nasu Golf Club. Hugh Alison was

also busy in Japan, creating such courses as Hirona and a new Tokyo Golf Club; and he inspected his pupil Fujita's work at Kasumigaseki. The deep bunkers he installed at those courses, including Kasumigaseki, with Fujita's blessing, so awed Japanese golfers that they derived from his name a word for them, "Arisons."

By the mid-1930s it appeared that golf course construction, both in the United States and abroad, might be on the rise again. In America, the federal WPA program allowed many municipalities to hire course architects to design and build public courses. Men like Robert Trent Jones, who had established a U. S. practice separate from Thompson's by the mid-1930s, Robert Bruce Harris, Perry Maxwell and Donald Ross took advantage of this program. Since the purpose of the WPA and similar programs in the United States and Canada was to create jobs, each course employed two hundred or more men during construction. Use of earth-moving equipment was limited, and these WPA courses were literally hand-built by men using only hand tools and wheelbarrows in most cases.

Actually, this method of construction was not entirely alien to the practices of the time. Although the bulldozer, which appeared in the 1920s, and the steam shovel,

P. 93: *Hole #2, Prairie Dunes CC, Hutchinson, Kansas, by Perry Maxwell. Natural plum thicket abounds in the rough at Prairie Dunes, enhancing the seaside impression of the course. Despite its location, far from the ocean deep in the American heartland, Prairie Dunes possesses striking links-like qualities.*

which was developed much earlier, had become major earth-moving tools, many architects before World War II preferred older methods, using horses, mules and scrapers for green and bunker construction, feeling that more natural lines could be achieved in this manner.

American architects also began to find employment remodeling existing courses. Many of the courses created in the boom of the 1920s were slapdash jobs, especially those laid out and built by organizations without professional design help. Little attention had been paid to strategy, balance and bunker placement. Some had pretentious features. Dozens of courses boasted a green with two large, symmetrical mounds, invariably dubbed "Mae West." Competent architects were hired to rectify the problems and eliminate such features.

Albert Tillinghast, who was hired in the 1930s by the PGA to advise member clubs on alterations, claimed to have eliminated some 7,427 useless bunkers in a two-year period. Many of these were penal fairway bunkers and others were obnoxious cross hazards. The effects of their elimination were dramatic, both in money saved and in enhanced player enjoyment.

But just as the profession seemed on the road to recovery, the second World War erupted in Europe in 1939. It abruptly altered the plans of those who thought a second golf boom was on the horizon. World War II put a great many men and women back to work, but it curtailed the golfing industry to an even greater degree than had the Great Depression.

Petroleum products became precious commodities. Courses outside metropolitan areas found themselves isolated and, without sufficient revenues, soon closed. The Maidstone Club on the far point of Long Island, summer playground of the very rich, and the Boca Raton Club near Palm Beach, Florida, winter playground of the same group, both folded for lack of patronage, closing four courses in the process. But so did Olympia Fields near Chicago with its self-contained community, including its own schools and fire department, and its four courses.

Even clubs without financial difficulties found it hard to maintain their courses without oil, fertilizer and manpower. Clubs like Augusta National, and Interlachen in Minneapolis, which was to have held the 1942 U. S. Open, closed for the duration and their fairways became pastures.

But the fate of North American courses was minor compared to the physical destruction inflicted upon European and Far Eastern countrysides. Some seaside courses, like Turnberry, were deliberately paved over and used as airfields, while others in Britain became training grounds for the British and the millions of American, Canadian, continental and overseas troops pouring into England. Other courses, from Prince's in England to Biarritz in France, from Oahu in Hawaii to Kawana Fuji in Japan, became pockmarked battlefields or bombed-out rubble. In a life-or-death struggle, the preservation of golfing grounds was of no importance.

The War would end, of course, and reconstruction begin once more. And by the late 1940s golf would again become one of the preferred pastimes of millions, and golf course design would reemerge as a vigorous profession. Among the prominent architects who would not live to see that day were Herbert Fowler, Cecil Hutchison, Norman Macbeth, William S. Flynn, Herbert Strong and Albert Tillinghast. And as was the case in the first World War, a number of promising but unknown associate architects would not survive combat and would never have the chance to prove their talents.

P. 94: *Waterville CC, Maine. Rigid lines testify to Orrin Smith's early use of steam shovels for final grading of greens and bunkers.* P. 95: (Top and bottom) *Undulations in greens dubbed "Maxwell Rolls," pot bunkers and other features at Prairie Dunes enhance the impression of Scottish links in the sand hills of Kansas.*

9.
The Age of Robert Trent Jones: Part I

A flurry of course reconstruction followed the second World War. In North America courses that had been left idle for as long as five years required extensive reconditioning before they could be reopened. Many clubs used this opportunity to remodel their layouts; and as a result, architectural business was fairly brisk. A brief recession in 1949–50 and the outbreak of the Korean Conflict slowed this activity for a time. But by 1953 course architecture was once again a healthy profession in the United States, with an average of one hundred new courses opened yearly in the last eight years of the decade, in addition to numerous remodeled or reconditioned layouts. By the 1960s, over 400 new courses were opening annually.

Up until the early sixties there were still many non-architect designed courses coming into play. But with more sophistication required in planning and construction, new clubs and course promoters turned to professional course designers. By the late 1960s, except for modest layouts, the majority of new courses in the United States were architect designed.

The era after World War II was one of transition. Golf course construction was revolutionized by modern earth-moving equipment. Where once it took up to 200 men, with horse-drawn scrapers, wheelbarrows and hand tools, two or three years to build an eighteen-hole course, by 1960 a dozen workers with modern equipment could construct a more elaborate eighteen in a few months.

The decade of the 1920s had seen the introduction of new techniques for the preparation and maintenance of golf courses. The practice of cultivating and carefully smoothing fairway seed beds became common. Prior to that time, pastures had often simply been mowed for use as fairways, and areas previously in other crops or cleared from forests were seeded with a minimum of fine grading. The greenkeeper then had to level these rough areas over a period of decades to achieve "billiard table" fairways. In the early twenties, gang units for mowing fairways had been developed, and horses to pull them were replaced by the golf course tractor. A mower with extra blades was used for putting greens, while quick coupling green, tee

courses in philosophy, history and the classics.

He also inspected as many golf courses as he could and sought out experts in the field. Even the great Tillinghast, after he had apparently lost much of his zest for golf architecture, found himself on more than one occasion confronted by the eager young Jones seeking an explanation or, some say, an argument. And Jones landed a position in 1929 working for Stanley Thompson on the refining of the magnificent Banff course in the Canadian Rockies.

As early as 1935 Trent Jones was writing about a third school of golf architecture. Besides the penal and strategic schools, Jones said, there existed a "heroic school" of course design. The heroic was a blend of the best of the penal and strategic schools. He explained:

> The trapping (in the heroic) is not as profuse as in the penal, nor as scarce as in the strategic. Traps vary from ugly, treacherous-looking ones to small, insignificant pot-bunkers. The line of flight is usually blocked by some formidable looking hazard placed at a diagonal and involving a carry of from 170 to 220 yards in which the player is allowed to bite off as much as he feels he can chew. If his game . . . is not equal to the task, a safe alternate route to play round it is provided. The same principle is used in the green design, in which the green is placed at an angle to the line of flight with an opening allowed for the cautious.[1]

In other words, as in strategic design, a heroic hole gives the golfer a choice of routes; but as in penal design, the player is punished if he gambles and fails by playing a poor shot. At first, the most common "diagonal hazard" Jones utilized for such purposes was the deep bunker, so steep-faced that a shot had to be wasted to get out. He was very fond of Tillinghast's bunkering at Winged Foot, two courses that the young designer cited as examples of heroic architecture. Over the years, Jones increasingly utilized water as the heroic hazard; and nearly every Trent Jones course would feature one or more greens perched ominously over a pond or creek, as well as other holes with similar water hazards.

But Jones was never an advocate of a strictly heroic or strategic or penal course. The trend, he felt, was to courses that featured all three philosophies blended into an appropriate combination depending on whether the course was intended as a municipal operation, a resort or a private layout to host tournaments. The course Jones always felt best reflected this trend was Jasper Park in Alberta, which was designed by Stanley Thompson and opened in 1925. In the forties and fifties, when Jones was on his own, he continued to popularize this blend or style

of architecture; and he felt Peachtree boasted holes of all three philosophies.

Jones has maintained that he absorbed much of his feeling for contemporary design from Thompson; but there is evidence, as well as the belief of other Thompson associates, that Trent Jones also exerted considerable influence on Thompson.

Robert Trent Jones produced in the 1950s such renowned courses as The Dunes in South Carolina (with its par-5 thirteenth that horseshoes around a lake as the ultimate heroic hole); Old Warson Country Club and Bellerive Country Club, both in St. Louis; Coral Ridge Country Club in Florida; Shady Oaks Golf Club and Houston Country Club, both in Texas; and Point O' Woods Golf and Country Club in Michigan. Abroad he created the Cotton Bay Club in the Bahamas, the original Dorado Beach course in Puerto Rico and the Brasilia Country Club for the new capital of Brazil.

Trent Jones's chief "rival" in the fifties, at least in terms of publicity, was Louis S. "Dick" Wilson, an associate of Toomey and Flynn in the late twenties and early thirties. Like many others, Dick Wilson abandoned design work during the Depression and managed a course in Florida until after the War. Then he formed his own firm and designed the West Palm Beach Country Club in 1949. This course, one of the first of what would be an explosion of courses in Florida, garnered fine reviews, and Wilson soon located other clients.

By the late 1950s Dick Wilson had created a small empire of courses in Florida, laying out such notable clubs as DeSoto Lakes, Tequesta and Cypress Lake. In the early sixties he created some of his best work in that state with the original thirty-six holes at Doral, the Bay Hill Club and Pine Tree. Wilson also presided over development of major golfing resorts in the Bahamas, at Arawak (now Paradise Island), Princess Hotel and Lucayan. Among his other clients was National Cash Register of Dayton, Ohio, for whom Wilson laid out two courses, the North and South, in the early fifties. Wilson also designed courses at new sites for the very old Meadow Brook Club and Deepdale Club, both on Long Island. Meadow Brook attracted special attention since its old course, forced to move due to rising taxes and encroaching suburbs, was so well respected. Wilson's Meadow Brook was greeted with immediate acclaim, and some went so far as to declare it the best course in the United States at the time.

Dick Wilson was not the student of classics and Cornell-trained designer that Robert Trent Jones was, but he was certainly talented. Having learned his craft through on-the-job training, Wilson was proud of the fact that he could personally build the courses he designed. Whether Jones and Wilson ever had a personal rivalry is conjecture now, although it was rumored that the very busy and selective Wilson accepted the commission to design Royal Montreal's forty-five new holes in 1958 partly because he had heard that Trent Jones was after it. In the fifties, countless comparisons were made of the two architects and their works. One article written during these years said they were producing the best courses ever built.

As it turned out, Dick Wilson shared the spotlight with Trent Jones for only fifteen years, for he died in 1965 at age sixty-one. Wilson died with half a dozen courses under construction and plans for many more at his office. He wrote very little about his profession and so left very little concerning his philosophy of design, except for his magnificent courses. They remain outstanding examples of the art. With the exceptions of Donald Ross and Robert Trent Jones, no architect has such an impressive list of consensus top-flight courses to his credit.

With Wilson's death, his associate, Joseph Lee, whom Wilson had recruited back in the National Cash Register days in Dayton, assumed the firm's practice. Two other Wilson-trained designers, Robert von Hagge and Robert A. Simmons, had already gone out on their own, with Wilson's blessing, before 1965.

Robert Trent Jones and Dick Wilson were not the only architects active in the fifties, of course. There were a great many others, and many of them created courses of substantial merit.

Besides Trent Jones, Stanley Thompson's stable turned out the following:

• Clinton E. Robinson, who established his practice in Canada after the War. Robinson designed the eighteen-hole addition for the Sunningdale Country Club in Ontario, the Brudenell Golf and Country Club on Prince Edward Island and the Upper Canada Village course in Ontario, among other magnificent layouts.

• Howard Watson, who began working for Thompson the very day that Clinton Robinson did. Watson started on his own in 1950, and much of his early solo work was in the Caribbean at courses like Caymanas Golf and Country Club in Jamaica and the Country Club de Medellin in Colombia. But Watson soon had excellent work in Canada to his credit, too, like the Pinegrove Country Club and Carling Lake Golf Club in Quebec, the Board of Trade Country Club in Ontario and many others. He also trained his son, John, who started his own practice in the 1970s.

• Geoffrey S. Cornish, who, after a stint as an instruc-

tor at the University of Massachusetts, set up a practice in the early fifties. By the late sixties Cornish, with his associate, William G. Robinson, a graduate landscape architect who joined him in 1964, had designed more courses in New England than any other person. Crestview Country Club in Massachusetts, two courses for Quechee Lakes Country Club in Vermont, the Eastman Lakes Golf Course in New Hampshire, the Stratton Mountain Club in Vermont, York Downs in Toronto, Cranberry Valley on Cape Cod, the new Ashburn Golf Club in Nova Scotia, the Porto Carras Links in Greece and two courses for the Summerlea Golf and Country Club near Montreal were among the 170 new courses designed by Cornish and Robinson and in play by the late seventies.

• Norman H. Woods, who based his practice in western Canada after Thompson's death. Woods designed many fine courses, including Kokanee Springs Golf Club in British Columbia, Rossmere Golf and Country Club in Manitoba, Lords Valley Country Club in Pennsylvania and the fine nine-hole Hilands Country Club in Montana.

Dick Wilson, of course, began with the old Pennsylvania firm of Toomey and Flynn. Among other assistants of that firm who established their own practices after the War were:

• William F. Gordon, who formed his company in 1941 to seed military installations and was very busy by the late 1940s. His son, David, a pilot in the War, finished college at Penn State and then joined the firm. By the fifties the two were full partners, and together they were responsible for such superior layouts as the Grace course at Saucon Valley Country Club in Pennsylvania, the Stanwich Club in Connecticut, Buena Vista Country Club in New Jersey and the Indian Spring Country Club in Maryland. William Gordon died in 1973 at age eighty, and David Gordon continued the work of the firm. Before entering the firm of Toomey and Flynn, Bill Gordon had supervised golf course construction for Willie Park, Jr., Leonard Macomber, Donald Ross and others. Probably no other architect in history received such broad practical experience before setting up his own practice, nor was any more imbued with the history of the art.

• Robert F. Lawrence, who had also worked for Walter Travis and who, like Dick Wilson, had settled as a course manager in Florida during the War. Lawrence produced such works as the Plantation Golf Club and the South course of the Fort Lauderdale Country Club while in that state but did his best-known designs after moving to the Southwest in the early sixties. There he did Desert Forest Golf Club and Camelback Country Club in Arizona, and

P. 106: (Top) *Timed automatic irrigation of courses led to uniform greenness throughout the golf season.* (Center) *R. B. Harris' bunkers are in proportion to one another and in harmony with the landscape.* (Bottom) *The Harris style as seen on the Brute Course at the Playboy CC, Wisconsin.*

111

10

10.
The Age of Robert Trent Jones: Part II

The history of golf course architecture since 1965 is difficult to discuss, for the events are so recent that any analysis of them can be fraught with misinterpretation. A few points, however, can be stated with some certainty.

Until the late 1960s, real estate, construction and financing costs were favorable, and golf course design and development was a thriving worldwide enterprise. But by the mid-1970s costs had skyrocketed and the picture changed.

Inflation took its toll, and the costs of building and maintaining a golf course multiplied drastically in a decade's time. New laws, including environmental regulations in America and land-use policies in Japan, further increased the expense; and quite often planned projects could not meet the regulations. High quality construction, including fully automated irrigation systems, special drainage systems and new formulas for building greens, also increased costs.

The price of an average course in this period came to at least a half million dollars for construction alone, with-

out any consideration for other development costs. Unfortunately, many golfers were unable or unwilling to pay fees commensurate with these higher costs. By 1974 tight money had greatly curtailed construction and forced a number of shakily financed golf developments into bankruptcy. But by the late seventies American course development had picked up somewhat, particularly in the Sun Belt. British architects, with their far-flung practices sometimes stretching over several continents, remained busy. In Canada golf construction kept a steady pace, particularly in the oil-rich west. It was also fairly brisk in Europe and the Far East.

But while many an American course architect found himself as busy as ever planning courses and preparing specifications, an astonishing number of projects fell victim to raging inflation or unyielding regulations. As a result, the number of courses actually built and opened for play in the United States annually was less than a quarter of what it had been in the sixties. Development of new, strictly private country clubs all but ceased, although

P. 112–113: *Green #16, Eagle Vail GC by Von Hagge and Devlin. P. 114: Mount Mitchell GC, by F. W. Hawtree. P. 115: (Top) Beau Desert GC, England, by W. H. Fowler. American style became the dominant influence on course design after World War II. P. 115: (Bottom) The Connecticut GC. Architects, builders and superintendents dealt with increasingly difficult properties.*

some existing clubs remodeled their layouts or added nines. But few courses could generate enough cash to cover expenses, let alone a profit, especially in regions with short playing seasons. Consequently, the majority of new courses in the late sixties and seventies were built either as municipally owned courses or as part of larger integrated real estate or resort developments. Courses at year-round resorts like Stratton Mountain in Vermont, which caters to golfers in summer and skiers in winter, became especially popular with investors.

Private clubs still in existence were sometimes forced by high taxes and reduced membership to move to new sites. Fortunately, sale of their valuable in-town land would normally pay for the development of a more elaborate facility on less expensive land farther out. The old Colonial Country Club in Memphis, Tennessee, for example, whose tight, 6,400-yard course had been the site of many tournaments, sold its prime location to developers. In exchange, it obtained sufficient land out in the country to build two courses. These were designed by Joseph Finger, a fine Houston, Texas-based architect who also did the Concord in New York and Pleasant Valley in Arkansas.

The ever-increasing value of land also affected the development of golf course architecture. Not only would dramatic, oceanfront courses become the exception in this period, but so too would courses on gently rolling, tree-lined terrains. Designers were increasingly confronted with the worst possible property, often the "left-over" land of a developer, on which to build their courses. Herbert Warren Wind once observed that had Pebble Beach been built in the contemporary era, there would be no holes on those magnificent seaside cliffs. Obviously, such land would be reserved by the developers for home sites, to be sectioned in parcels as narrow as possible to maximize profits. No doubt the less-expensive home sites would be those fronting the course. It should be noted, of course, that several homes do border the actual Pebble Beach Golf Links, but they share with the course the tremendous ocean views.

Yet any number of course architects rose to the challenge of less-than-desirable sites. Courses in this period were constructed on sanitary landfills (Mangrove Bay Municipal Golf Course, St. Petersburg, Florida, by William Amick, where marsh gas is piped off for city lighting), rocky, cactus-covered land (Baja Mar Country Club, Baja California, Mexico, by Percy Clifford), reclaimed lakes (the North course of the Firestone Country Club, by Robert Trent Jones), marsh lands (Hilton Head Golf Club by George W. Cobb), and in gravel pits and strip mines

(Laurel Green Country Club in western Pennsylvania, by Xen Hassenplug), slag heaps (Blyth Golf Club in England, by J. H. Stutt), and even on ledge rock (The Connecticut Golf Club, by Cornish and Robinson). Of all the traits necessary and desirable in a first-rate course architect, perhaps none was more important in this period than imagination. The ability to hew silken courses from sow's pens surely separated the poor designer from the successful one in the seventies.

The ranks of golf course designers had continued to expand in the late 1950s as more men felt the need to express themselves through molding of the landscape. Some new designers came directly from related professions, like Robert Muir Graves, a landscape architect; Ted G. Robinson, a land planner; Jack Kidwell, a pro-superintendent; and Jack Snyder, a landscape architect and second-generation superintendent. But most had worked for established architects, as had Francis J. Duane, who was with Robert Trent Jones from 1945 until 1963.

Prior to hiring Duane, Jones had worked almost alone; but from then on his office gradually expanded. In 1961 Yale engineering graduate Roger Rulewich entered the firm, taking over after Duane's departure as a major figure in the eastern office. Robert Trent Jones, Jr., joined his father in 1962 and was responsible for setting up a Pacific branch of the business, based in California. Jones's younger son, Rees, signed on with the organization in 1965. In 1968 graduate landscape architect Cabell Robinson started in the New Jersey office, establishing a permanent Jones branch in Spain in 1970 after Ronald Kirby (who had represented Jones in Europe from 1965 to 1969) formed his own design firm with touring professional Gary Player as a consultant.

By 1980 there were over 400 Trent Jones courses located in forty-two states and twenty-three countries. Robert Trent Jones, Jr., established his own practice in 1972 with ties to his father's. Rees Jones started his own entirely separate practice in 1974 and in the same year wrote an influential book on golf course developments, in collaboration with landscape architect Guy L. Rando. Both Robert Jr. and Rees developed individual styles unique from their famous father's, and each was the architect of top-flight layouts.

Although the fame of Robert Trent Jones had not abated nationally or internationally, other architects began to influence the field of course design. Three men in particular, Desmond Muirhead, Pete Dye and George Fazio, deserve special note because of their impact on course architecture and the national attention they have drawn to it in recent years.

Desmond Muirhead, a Scot who trained in Britain as a land planner, moved to the United States via Canada, where he attended the University of British Columbia and planned a golf course in Vancouver. In the early sixties he assisted in the development of the Sun City retirement village in Arizona and became intrigued with the relationship of its golf course to the housing plan.

By 1963 Muirhead had formed his own course design and construction firm, and the courses he developed attracted immediate attention. His distinctive style resembled that of few other architects. It could almost be said that Muirhead sculpted his courses from the terrain. His tees were parabolic, serpentine or pronged, and nearly always dozens of yards in length. Some of his greens appeared to flow into the horizon; others were so severely contoured as to resemble rolling surf. His water hazards, which were numerous, were free form in design; and he routed his holes around them in unique fashions. On one hole a green would be located on an island and on another, a fairway would be. Sometimes a tee, and sometimes a landing area, would be perched on a peninsula. Muirhead's bunkers resembled jigsaw pieces from a totally white puzzle.

Muirhead also prided himself on combining his courses into pleasing arrangements with the surrounding environment, be it a housing development or a desert wasteland. He abhorred architects who deliberately routed several holes in one direction so as to maximize the available frontage land for housing developers. He has also crusaded for more rational routing of courses to protect players from one another and adjoining landowners from errant shots.

Muirhead's critics argued that his style was really nothing more than contemporary landscape architecture and had been demonstrated in the mid-fifties by course architect Edward Lawrence Packard. They also claimed Muirhead's designs were sterile, well-manicured lawns devoid of any true golfing values. But the architect maintained his courses followed modern-day principles of strategic design and maximum flexibility. Among his creations are Mission Hills Golf and Country Club in Palm Springs, California; Baymeadows Country Club in Jacksonville, Florida; McCormick Ranch Golf Club in Scottsdale, Arizona; and Bent Tree Club in Dallas, Texas.

Paul "Pete" Dye entered the profession about the same time as Muirhead. An insurance salesman turned golf architect, Dye spent the first few years of his design career without conspicuous success. But in the mid-1960s,

after he made a tour of the grand old courses of Scotland, he began to develop his own style of design, a style as unique as Muirhead's but diametrically opposed to it.

Dye felt that graceful mounds and undulations on a golf course were artificial. True natural features, he observed, were characterized by abrupt change. These were the features that most impressed him on the Scottish links: the swales and hollows and pits around fairways and greens, the jagged sand hills and especially the steep bunker faces shored up by railroad "sleepers."

Respectful, too, of the works of many of the great early American architects, like Ross, Tillinghast and Macdonald, Pete Dye began to develop a philosophy that disdained the typical features of modern American golf courses, the same features, ironically, that British designers at this time were wholeheartedly embracing.

Dye's new courses sported tight, undulating fairways with small, wildly undulating greens surrounded by mounds, swales, hollows or pot bunkers, and roughs maintained in indigenous vegetation. Many of his tees, bunkers and even water hazards were lined with upright railroad ties, so many that the railroad tie came to be known as Dye's trademark. One Dye course, Oak Tree Golf Club near Edmond, Oklahoma, has some 8,000 ties running about it!

His courses were also shorter than most, often less than 6,200 yards from the regular tees and not over 6,500 from the back. Pete Dye prided himself on designing each hole with women players in mind, perhaps because his wife, Alice, was one of the country's premier amateur golfers. His placement of front tees was not an afterthought but rather the deliberate attempt to provide women with the opportunity to play each hole as designed but within their capabilities.

Dye's most prominent works include The Golf Club near Columbus, Ohio; Crooked Stick near Indianapolis, Indiana; the Harbour Town Golf Links on Hilton Head Island, South Carolina; and Cajuiles, a dramatic seaside layout in the Dominican Republic.

Dye's critics most often complained that his designs were exceedingly difficult to maintain. His severely contoured greens, small deep bunkers, huge wasteland bunkers and other novel features were not suited for modern maintenance equipment, they said. An elevated tee surrounded by a bank of railroad ties was charming, but it required daily hand mowing and the lifting and lowering of the mower at that.

In reality, few features on a Pete Dye layout were truly revolutionary, even in America. C. B. Macdonald, for instance, lined several of his bunkers with railway ties

at the National Golf Links. Perry Maxwell was notorious for his small, treacherous greens. Devereux Emmet had long experimented with mounds and hollows as substitutes for greenside bunkers, and Donald Ross did much the same at times. But in the late 1960s and early 1970s, no other golf course architect had the courage and the tenacity to try such different approaches to course design; his results caused immediate and widespread attention, probably because they were so opposite to the style ushered in by Robert Trent Jones in the 1950s and adopted and modified by nearly all contemporary American and British architects.

By the early seventies Pete's brother, Roy Dye, had joined him in the business and had been responsible for such typical "Dye designs" as the revised Country Club of Montreal and Waterwood National Golf Club in Texas. As contradictory as it might seem, the multitalented Jack Nicklaus worked at separate times with both Pete Dye and Desmond Muirhead. With Dye, he collaborated on Harbour Town; and with Muirhead, he assisted on several courses including Mayacoo Lakes in Florida. In the mid-1970s, Nicklaus formed a course design firm that planned,

P. 118: (Top) Hole #14, Stratton Mountain GC in Vermont ski country, by Cornish and Robinson.
P. 118: (Bottom) Hole #18, Wild Dunes GC on the coast of South Carolina, by George and Tom Fazio.
P. 119: Hole #3, Eagle Vail GC high in the Colorado Rockies, by Von Hagge and Devlin. Many new courses built after the late 1960s were integrated with housing, resorts or other forms of recreation.

among others, Muirfield Village in Ohio (with the advice and counsel of Muirhead), Glen Abbey in Toronto and Shoal Creek in Birmingham, Alabama.

George Fazio had been a successful club professional and competitive golfer in the 1940s and 50s. When he retired, he intended to operate a car dealership and a few daily fee golf courses in Pennsylvania; but friends lured him into designing a course. By the time he had completed it—the Atlantis Country Club in Tuckertown, New Jersey—Fazio was hooked on course design as a new career. His early works, like the Jackrabbit Road course of the Champions Golf Club in Texas and Moselem Springs Country Club in Pennsylvania, were warmly received. But it was not until the late 1960s that George Fazio was recognized as a major force in American course design.

By then it was apparent that Fazio had steadily, through a progression of works, developed into a fine classical course architect. His designs were not modernistic like Muirhead's, nor rugged like Dye's. They were, instead, reminiscent of the grand old courses of the Golden Era. Fazio's courses had a graceful and appealing appearance that belied their youthfulness. And they were challenging without being repetitive in the process. One Fazio hole might feature a huge bunker in the inside corner of a dogleg and a tightly bunkered green. The next might feature a trap on the outside of a dogleg and a green devoid of sand.

George Fazio certainly had a wealth of experience and observation upon which to draw. He learned the game in Philadelphia, amidst the bright collection of courses by Hugh Wilson, Donald Ross, William Flynn, William Gordon and others. Merion was a particular favorite of Fazio, and he nearly won a U. S. Open there. He also served as head professional for several years at Pine Valley, and he not only played the course on countless occasions but absorbed its nuances. With this background, Fazio was able to instill in his own works the distinctive qualities of many of the great American courses.

The works of George Fazio include Jupiter Hills in Florida, which contains a series of holes seemingly appropriated from Pine Valley; Butler National Golf Club in Chicago; Devil's Elbow Golf Club at Moss Creek; and the National Golf Club in Toronto.

Fazio also became a favorite architect of clubs hosting major tournaments in the seventies. In this capacity he made major revisions, including creation of several new holes at such hallowed courses as Oak Hill in New York and Inverness in Ohio. Fazio's nephew, Tom Fazio, ably assisted him on most of his works almost from the beginning, and became his partner in 1973.

P. 120-121: *Arrowhead GC, Colorado, by Robert Trent Jones, Jr. In
the 1970s Robert Trent Jones' sons, Robert, Jr. and Rees, developed unique
design philosophies and established private practices of their own. Bob
Jr.'s dramatic Arrowhead GC illustrates his personal concept of the golf
course as a work of art within the context of the surrounding environment.*

Muirhead, Dye and Fazio all left individual impressions on the history of golf course architecture in the sixties and seventies. Other designers may not have had the same impact but still produced impressive works. All too often, however, their creations have not been known outside their immediate communities, because they never hosted a major tournament; because their owners did not seek, or even shunned, publicity; or because prominent nearby courses overshadowed them. Such situations have never been conducive to widespread awareness of any course architect; and only time will determine whether a particular course, or a particular designer, attains the recognition deserved.

It is interesting to reflect upon the many decades of architects and their courses and to wonder which men will still be well regarded in fifty or one hundred years. Willie Park, Jr., and H. S. Colt certainly are two "pioneer" professional architects worth remembering. Donald Ross and Stanley Thompson did so many, many fine courses in the twenties and thirties that their reputations will surely not fade. Alister Mackenzie, one of the first to codify his aims and one of the few able to demonstrate them in layouts all over the globe, has had perhaps greater influence among newer generations of course architects than he had among his peers.

But the man who had the greatest impact on the profession of golf course architecture, and upon the game of golf itself, was Robert Trent Jones. This may seem a brash assertion, but an objective review of course design history supports it. It is possible that if the name of any golf course architect of the past or present is still well known in a hundred years, it will be that of Robert Trent Jones.

It is equally interesting to speculate on which contemporary courses will be highly considered in another century's time. Indeed, one must wonder whether any course will endure the test of time that the Old Course at St. Andrews has withstood.

But such speculation raises ominous thoughts. Will golf course architecture, and even golf courses themselves, still exist in fifty or one hundred years? The eloquent Alistair Cooke raised that point in his foreword to *The World Atlas of Golf,* and he was not optimistic. Cooke feared the last quarter of the twentieth century would be the twilight of golf design. Voracious governmental taxation and regulation, he felt, would eventually swallow up the glorious playing fields of the game.

The thought is sobering. It would be very sad for a marvelous layout to open one day and survive for only a short time because of active hostility or submissive apathy. And it would be tragic indeed should the day ever come when Merion is plowed under or St. Andrews paved over.

Let us hope such fears are groundless and that the powers that be will recognize the values, whether artistic, historical, ecological or simply recreational, of the golf courses within their domain. Surely the game that has been played for over half a millennium on the links of Scotland, and for a century in North America, is too durable to simply disappear.

P. 122-123: *Wild Dunes GC established Tom Fazio's reputation as a first-rate designer.* P. 124: (Top) *Double green, Eagle Vail GC by Von Hagge and Devlin.* P. 124: (Bottom) and 125: *Keystone Ranch GC by R. T. Jones, Jr., where design is related to environment.*

124

11

11.
Evolution of Golf Course Features

Nature and golf architects have shared in the evolution of course design. Each has influenced the style, shape, size and placement of greens, tees, fairways and hazards, although the dominance of each influence has varied in different periods. Thus, this evolution was not in a straight line. The trends have tended to proceed in a circular manner, in the form of an upward spiral.

P. 126–127: *Quechee Lakes, Vermont, #17, Highland Course. Holes which are initially controversial often achieve fame. P. 128: (Top) Form follows function. Shape, size and bunkers at green vary with type and length of approach shot. (Bottom) Forced carry over two hazards is penal and unfair.*

GEOFFREY S. CORNISH · WILLIAM G. ROBINSON
AMERICAN SOCIETY OF GOLF COURSE ARCHITECTS

P. 129: (Top) *Good strategic holes encourage advanced planning. Here, the tee shot must clear the fairway bunker or the second shot carry traps near the green. (Bottom) A "Cape"-type hole entices the player to cut as much corner as he dares. Such heroic holes bring out the gambler in a golfer.*

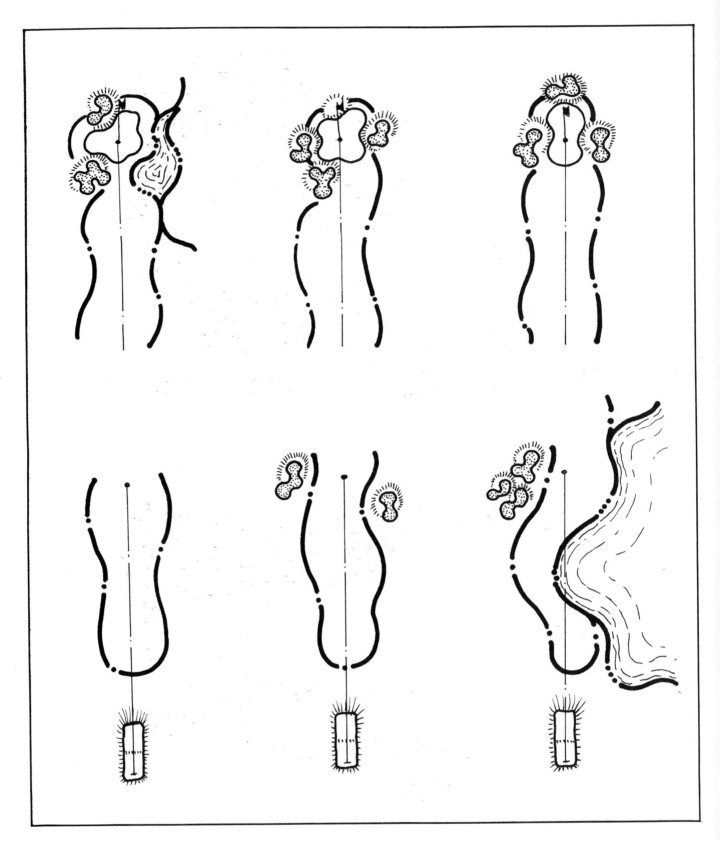

P. 130: *Good golf holes should balance shot values from stroke to stroke.*
Thus, combining the upper left approach with the lower right drive places
too much pressure on a player, while the lower left drive and upper right
green lacks challenge. Appropriate combinations of shot values are
crucial to integrity and playing interest of a layout.

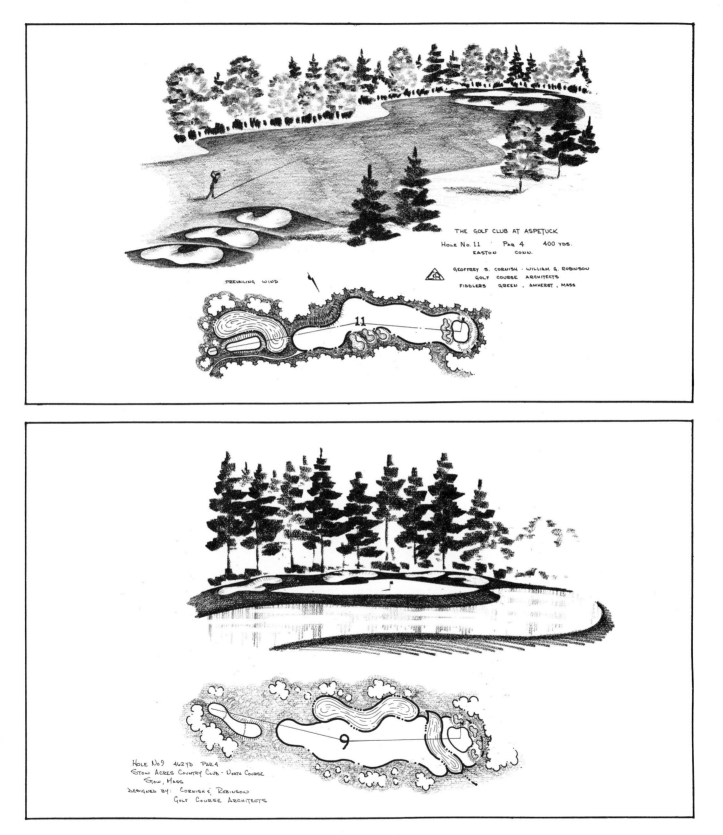

THE GOLF CLUB AT ASPETUCK
HOLE No. 11   PAR 4   400 YDS.
EASTON   CONN.

GEOFFREY S. CORNISH · WILLIAM G. ROBINSON
GOLF COURSE ARCHITECTS
FIDDLERS GREEN, AMHERST, MASS

PREVAILING WIND

11

HOLE No 9   462 YD   PAR 4
STOW ACRES COUNTRY CLUB - NORTH COURSE
STOW, MASS
DESIGNED BY: CORNISH & ROBINSON
GOLF COURSE ARCHITECTS

9

P. 131: *Tee shot values are similar on these par-4's, but approach shot values are not. (Top) The second shot must carry the deep front bunker, but with no trouble beyond the green, the shot value for a long or medium iron is fair. (Bottom) The shallow green is surrounded by trouble and is so severe for the long iron or fairway wood second that it may be unfair.*

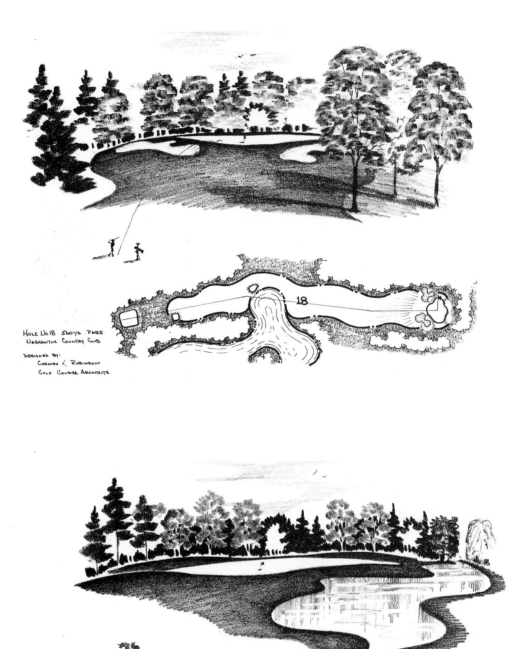

HOLE No 18 560 YD PAR 5
NASHAWTUC COUNTRY CLUB

DESIGNED BY:
CORNISH & ROBINSON
GOLF COURSE ARCHITECTS

P. 132: (Top) *This hole was considered unfair because a long hitter might reach the pond with his drive; yet the tee shot emphasizes accuracy while the second shot stresses length. The approach to the elevated green tests depth perception. (Bottom) Shot values increase as the golfer nears the green, but never become unfair. Both controversial par-5's were accepted.*

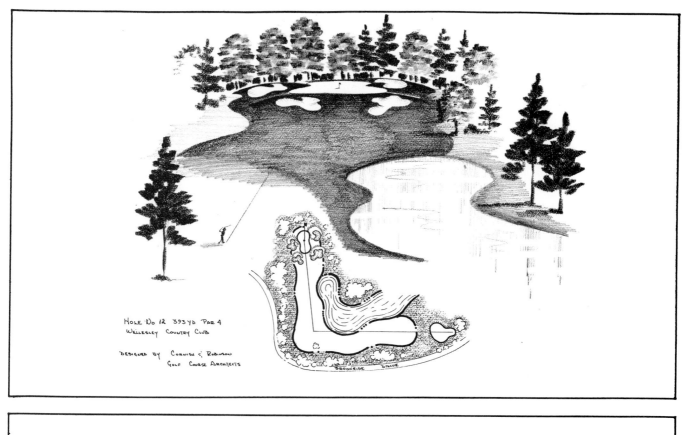

HOLE No 12 393 YD PAR 4
WELLESLEY COUNTRY CLUB

DESIGNED BY CORNISH & ROBINSON
GOLF COURSE ARCHITECTS

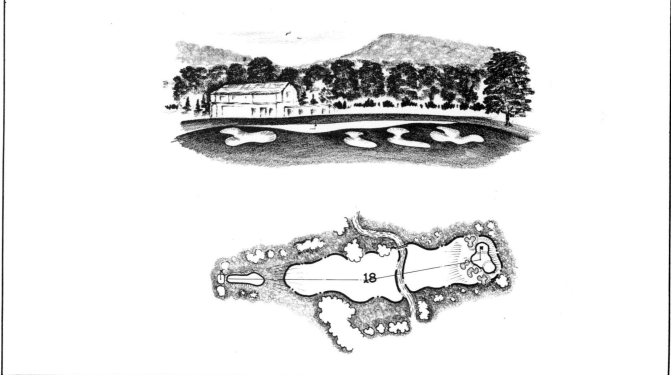

P. 133: *These par-4's have severe shot values for all but long, accurate hitters. (Top) The shot values of the tee and approach shots are determined by how close the golfer dares play to the pond. (Bottom) The value of a long, straight drive is great, because four deep bunkers guard the raised green.*

P. 134: *The par-5 fourth at Oakmont CC is a penal hole on a course that celebrates the penal philosophy. Yet the shot values are fair for all classes of players. The most timid golfer can reach the green in three adequate strokes, without encountering huge risk. The numerous bunkers are primarily a psychological hazard, although they will catch errant shots.*

P. 135: *In contrast, the par-5 thirteenth at Dorado Beach East has unfair shot values for the average golfer, though it is a sterling example of the heroic philosophy of Robert Trent Jones. A cautious player, driving clear of the first lake, must then hit a long, accurate wood or face a third over more water, palms and a trap. But the hole is a thriller for the daring.*

P. 136–137: *The par-5 fifteenth at Eastman GC tests golfers of all abilities on their own levels. At 480 yards, it can be reached in two long shots, or in three by short hitters. The average drive will find a level lie in the valley and an easy second to a landing area short of the green. The long hitter runs the risk of being caught by fairway and greenside bunkers.*

P. 138: (Top) "Greens" were born at St. Andrews in
the 1700s when attention was focused on keeping some
areas turfed. (Center) Following this example, other
courses nestled greens in hollows, sheltered from the
wind. (Bottom) By the late 1800s, greens were made
by leveling tops off natural plateaus. P. 139:
(Top) At Sunningdale in 1901, Willie Park first moved
earth to create raised, contoured putting surfaces.
(Bottom) This developed into the sculptured green of
contemporary design.

P. 140: (Top) *Until 1875 a player teed his ball on the green. Then level areas were provided off the green, though often too small to support grass.* (Center) *Artificial surfaces were tried, as were multiple tees. After WWII huge tees evolved, but their raised, square appearance proved monotonous.* (Bottom) *Free forms, introduced by Lawrence Packard, solved this problem.*

P. 141: (Top) "Bunkers" were originally scars on the links, resulting from
livestock sheltering behind hills or gardeners quarrying sea shells, and
later from golf balls rolling into hollows. (Center) Greenkeepers
began to modify and stabilize these scars, sometimes changing their shapes.
(Bottom) This practice led to the dramatic bunkering of today.

141

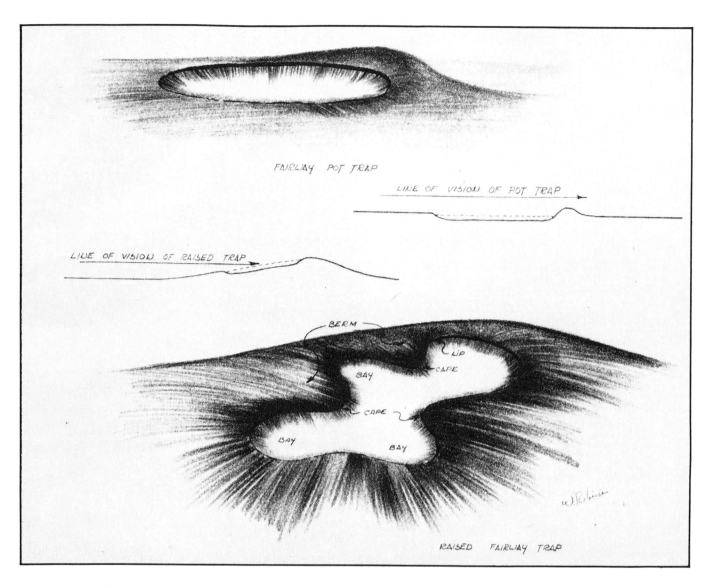

FAIRWAY POT TRAP

LINE OF VISION OF POT TRAP

LINE OF VISION OF RAISED TRAP

BERM

LIP

CAPE

BAY

CAPE

BAY

BAY

W. Robinson

RAISED FAIRWAY TRAP

P. 142: *Two bunker types arose from the links model,
the pit or pot (above) and the raised trap (below).*
P. 143: *Theories of bunker placement changed through
history. (Top) At first most were penal cross traps.
Later they became lateral and strategic. A modern
formula states that the further one hits, the more
accurate he must be; thus (far right) axes of bunkers
converge. (Bottom) Before WWII many bunkers adjoined
putting surfaces. Later placed far out, they caught
only high handicappers. A compromise was the result.*

142

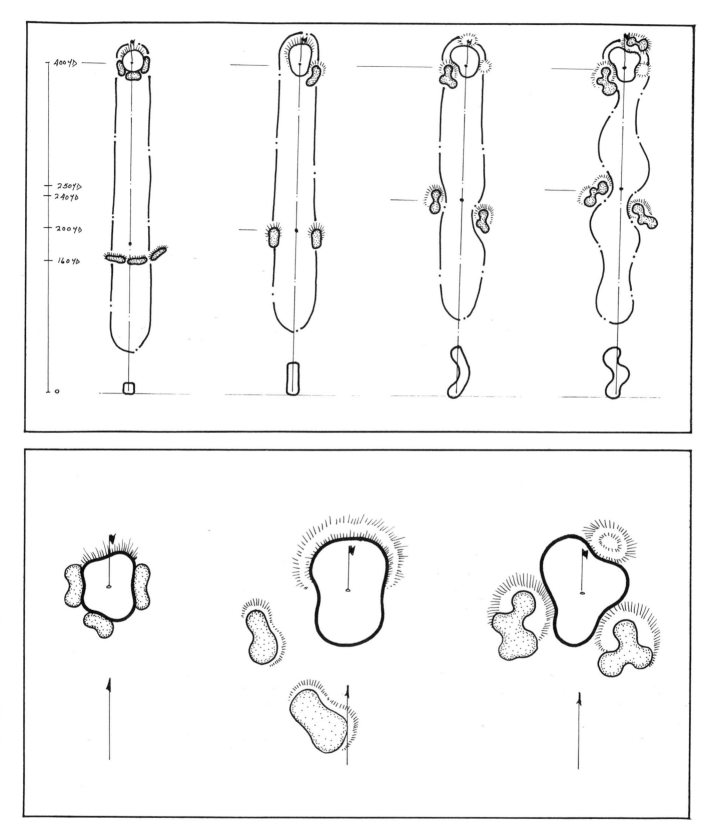

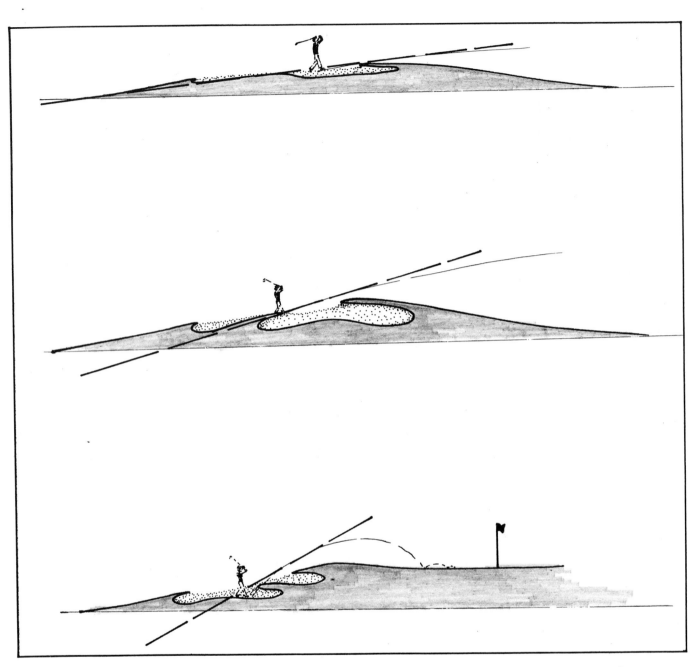

P. 144: *One aspect of contemporary bunker design is embodied in the concept that the closer a bunker is to the green, the greater should be its depth and the steeper its face. Thus, the distant trap (top) is shallow, while the one at greenside (bottom) is deep.*

P. 145: (Top) *Concentric mowing patterns around greens add the art principle of rhythm or radiation. (Bottom) Boundaries between fairway and rough can be straight or contoured. Wavy lines enhance target golf and eye appeal and help combat energy shortages.*

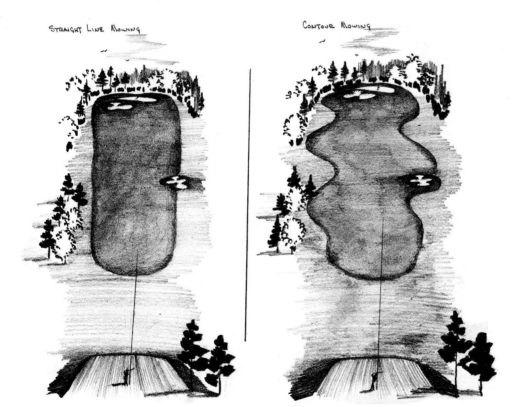

STRAIGHT LINE MOWING

CONTOUR MOWING

145

P. 146: *Golf architects have experimented endlessly, with varying degrees of success. One experiment which ended favorably was the introduction by Alister Mackenzie of a green with enormous undulations at Sitwell Park in England. The green first met with a storm of protest from the golfing public and was eventually accepted and later copied worldwide. A similar cycle of initial opposition, gradual acceptance and final endorsement has greeted many innovations in course design throughout its history.*

P. 147: *Not all experiments have been as successful as Mackenzie's, however. Some novel ideas have been tried and found wanting. Among the failures were (top) target areas requiring short irons from tees on dogleg par-four or -five holes; (lower left) extremely sharp doglegs; and (lower right) bunkers extending into putting surfaces, requiring putts around them. Innovations like these, which met with undiminished disfavor, have tended to be dropped or modified out of existence.*

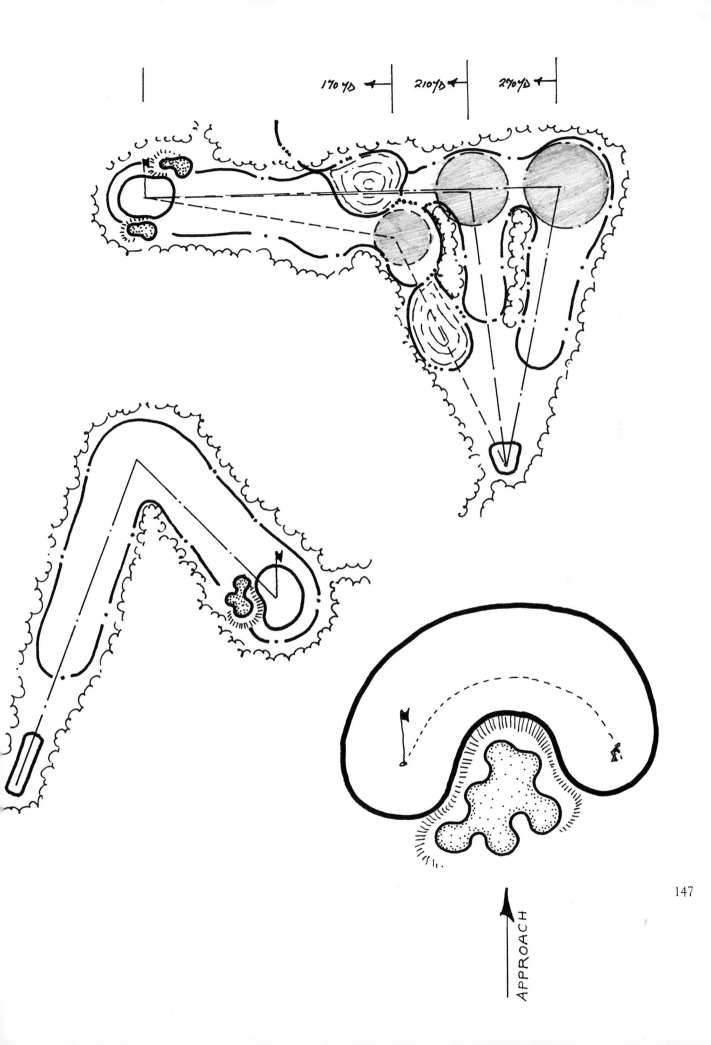

170 YD   210 YD   270 YD

APPROACH

147

PART TWO

Profiles

These biographical profiles of course designers include their courses through 1980. Several men other than course designers are profiled together with the genealogies of families that contributed to the art. Information in these profiles was gathered from a multitude of sources and from records of many people living and long gone.

Each course list following an architect's profile contains only works that the authors could verify. None of the course lists is intended to represent the complete work of any particular designer. In many cases architects, especially the pioneers, did many more than are listed, but the names of such courses are yet to be discovered. Also, as this book goes to press, many presently active architects have designs on their drawing boards which for a variety of reasons, are not listed.

Abbreviations used include:
ASGCA for the American Society of Golf Course Architects
BAGCA for the British Association of Golf Course Architects
a. for added holes. Example: a.9 indicates added 9 holes
c. for collaborated with
n.l.e. for no longer exists
r. for revision of an existing course. These range from minor changes to creation of almost a new layout.
RC for racquet club
TC for tennis club
YC for yacht club
(9), (27) etc. indicates number of holes. If no number is given it is thought to be 18

John Frederick Abercromby (1861–1935)
Born: Felixstowe, Suffolk, England. Died: Addington, Surrey, England, at age 74.

J. F. Abercromby, a doctor's son, took up golf in his youth and eventually became a scratch player, competing successfully in matches around London. At the turn of the century he was hired as private secretary to a financier at Bridley Manor, southwest of London. Impressed with three new golf courses in the area, Sunningdale, Walton Heath and Woking, his employer instructed Abercromby to provide him with a course.

Somewhat audaciously, "Aber" decided to lay out the course himself. He consulted with Willie Park, Jr., and Jack White during the initial stages; but the final product, Worplesdon GC opening in 1908, was basically Abercromby's design. Choosing to pursue a career in golf architecture, he soon landed the commission for the Coombe Hill GC and then laid out a course for the Addington GC, which was built just before the War. Abercromby settled at Addington, serving as its secretary and "beneficent despot" for the remainder of his life. He eventually built a second course there, and was constantly refining both.

In the 1920s Abercromby joined Herbert Fowler and Tom Simpson in the design firm of Fowler, Abercromby, Simpson and Croome. His work for the firm was done primarily in collaboration with Fowler in the London heathlands area. Abercromby was considered a totally free-hand artist, never measuring distances nor sketching designs, but laying out golf holes on site and supervising their creation. Contemporary critics felt he made the most natural-looking hazards of any architect of the day, and some considered him the finest British designer of the era before World War I.

Courses by John Frederick Abercromby:
ENGLAND: Addington GC, Surrey (Old course, 1914; New course, 1933,n.l.e.); Coombe Hill GC, Kingston Hill, Surrey (1909); Cowdray Park GC, Midhurst, Sussex (c.Fowler); Knole Park GC, Sevenoaks, Kent (c.Fowler); Manor House Hotel GC, Moretonhampstead, Devon (1930); West Went GC, Downe, Kent; Worplesdon GC, Woking, Surrey (1908).
NETHERLANDS: Haagsche GC, The Hague (a.2nd 9,1920,n.l.e.).

Charles Henry "Chic" Adams
"Chic" Adams began his golf career working for his father, who for many years held the position of course superintendent at the Cherokee (Iowa) CC. Turning professional in the 1940s, Adams served as pro-superintendent at the Sioux City (Iowa) CC for several years. A member of both the PGA of America and the GCSAA, he began designing courses as a sideline in the early 1950s but soon resigned his pro position to devote full time to golf architecture. In the late fifties he moved his design and construction business to Atlanta and concentrated on building courses in the Southeast. He retired in the late 1960s, taking a position as superintendent at a Florida course he had designed and built.

Courses by Charles Henry "Chic" Adams:
ALABAMA: Skyline CC, Mobile (1962).
FLORIDA: Airco GC, St. Petersburg (1962); Bay West Lodge & CC, Panama City Beach (1968); Diamond Hills G&CC, Pensacola (1959); Seminole Lake G&CC (1962); Turf and Surf GC, Tarpon Springs (9,1956); Yacht GC, Largo (1965).

GEORGIA: Castle View T&CC, Atlanta (1960); Dobbins AFB GC (9 par 3); Golfland GC, Marietta (par 3,1959); Monroe CC (9,1958); Pinetree CC [formerly O. B. Keeler Memorial GC], Kennesaw (1961); Riverside G&CC, Macon.
IOWA: American Legion GC, Marshalltown (9,1956); Ottumwa G&CC (1959).
KANSAS: Brookridge G&CC, Overland Park (27,1963).
KENTUCKY: Hurstborne CC, Louisville (27,1967).
MAINE: Fairlawn CC, East Poland.
TENNESSEE: Fox Meadows CC, Memphis (1957); Valleybrook G&CC, Hixson.
MEXICO: Club de Golf Monte Costello, Cuernavaca (1963).
Courses Remodeled by Charles Henry "Chic" Adams:
GEORGIA: East Lake CC, Atlanta (Course #2,1957,n.l.e.).
MISSOURI: North Shore CC (27).

Rokuro and Shiro Akaboshi
Rokuro and Shiro Akaboshi took up golf in their native Japan and were later educated in the United States, at Princeton University where Rokuro served as captain of the golf team. Returning to Japan after college, the brothers became pioneers of the game in that country. Rokuro was an accomplished competitor, winning the inaugural Japanese Open in 1927, and Shiro was highly regarded as a teacher.

The Akaboshi brothers collaborated on the design of many courses in the 1920s and 30s and are generally considered Japan's first native golf architects. It is estimated that they planned over sixty of the country's early courses, including the Hodogaya CC in Yokohama, the Naruo CC and the Abiko GC.

James Alexander
James Alexander, superintendent of British Transport Hotels, assisted golf architect Philip Mackenzie Ross with the replanning of the Ailsa course at Turnberry, Scotland, after World War II, and replanned the Arran course at Turnberry which reopened in 1954. He also planned major changes to the Queen's course at Gleneagles in the 1950s (in order to make it more equal to the King's course as a test of golf), and collaborated on the Prince's course at Gleneagles with I. Marchbanks and T. Telford. In addition, Alexander made extensive changes at the Manor House Hotel Course (Inland) in Devonshire, England.

Charles Hugh Alison (1882–1952)
Born: Preston, Lancashire, England. Died: Johannesburg, South Africa, at age 70.

Hugh Alison was educated at Malvern and Oxford University where he was an outstanding cricket player and golfer. He was the youngest member of the Oxford and Cambridge Golfing Society team, which toured the United States in 1903 and won every match he played during that tour.

After college Alison worked for a time as a journalist and then served as club secretary for the newly formed Stoke Poges GC near London. Here he met H. S. Colt, who was laying out the course. Intrigued by course design since his early golfing days, Alison assisted Colt with the completion of Stoke Poges and then with the construction of several other London-area courses including St. George's Hill.

After service with the British Army during World War I, Major Alison rejoined Colt. They formed a partnership that lasted twenty years and included, at different times, both J. S. F. Morrison and Alister Mackenzie. While Colt handled most of the design work in Britain and on the Continent, Alison worked extensively in North America and the Far East. Nearly all the courses built by the firm of Colt and Alison in the United States during the 1920s and 30s were designed by Hugh Alison. (Colt made only one short tour of North America in the late 1920s, although he had made two extensive visits before World War I.)

Alison was coauthor (with Colt) of Some Essays on Golf Course Architecture (1920) and contributed to Golf Courses: Design, Construction and Upkeep edited by M. A. F. Sutton (1933, rev. 1950).
Courses by Charles Hugh Alison:
(Most under the firm name of Colt and Alison)
GEORGIA: Sea Island GC (r.Plantation 9,a.Seaside 9, 1928).
ILLINOIS: Briarwood CC (formerly Briergate CC), Deerfield (1921); Knollwood Club, Lake Forest (1923); North Shore CC, Glenview (1924).
IOWA: Davenport CC (1924).
MARYLAND: Burning Tree Club, Bethesda (1924).
NEW JERSEY: Canoe Brook CC, Summit (South course).
NEW YORK: Century CC, White Plains; Colony CC, Algonac; Old Oaks CC (formerly Purchase CC), Purchase; Timber Point GC, Great River.
OHIO: Kirkland CC, Willoughby (1921); Westwood CC, Rocky River (1924).
WISCONSIN: Milwaukee CC (1929).
AUSTRALIA: Huntingdale GC, Melbourne, Victoria (1941).
CANADA: York Downs CC, Eglinton, Ontario (1921).
ENGLAND: Kingsthorpe, Northampton; Sunningdale CC, Berkshire (r.Old course,a.New course, 1922); Wentworth GC, Virginia Water (East and West courses, 1924).
HOLLAND: Haagsche G&CC, Wassenaar (1939); Utrecht GC (1929).
JAPAN: Fuji GC, Higashiyama; Hirona CC (1930); Kawana GC, Ito City (r.Oshima course,a.Fuji course, 1936); Tokyo CC, Hazayama City (New site, 1932).
SCOTLAND: Longniddry GC, East Lothian (1922).
SOUTH AFRICA: Bryanston CC, Johannesburg.
SPAIN: Real Club de la Puerto de Hierro, Madrid; Real GC, Santander.
Courses Remodeled by Charles Hugh Alison:
ILLINOIS: Bob O'Link GC, Highland Park (1924).
MARYLAND: Chevy Chase Club (1924).

162

Peter Alliss (1931–   )
Born: Berlin, Germany.

Peter Alliss, the son of famed British professional golfer Percy Alliss, has won numerous tournaments and written several books on golf. He became associated in a design-and-build firm with David C. Thomas, another well-known tournament player. At the time of the fall of the Shah (1979), the firm was engaged in planning a major golf complex on the shores of the Caspian Sea in Iran.

Courses by Peter Alliss and David Thomas:
ENGLAND: The Belfry GC, Sutton Coldfield (36,1979); Dewsbury District GC, West Yorks; Hessle GC; Hill Valley GC (1975); Kings Lynn GC (1975);Thorpe Wood Muni, Cambridge.
SCOTLAND: Blairgowrie (a.9).
Courses Remodeled by Peter Alliss and David Thomas:
FRANCE: La Baule.
SCOTLAND: Blairgowrie (a. 9); Haggs Castle GC.
ULSTER: Ballyclare GC.

Grange Gordon "Sandy" Alves (1885–1939)
Born: Aberdeen, Scotland. Died: Cleveland, Ohio, at age 54.

Grange Alves, called "Sandy" after his hair color, learned golf from his father and became a successful amateur player before emigrating to the United States at age nineteen. He worked as a stonemason's apprentice in Barre, Vermont, until 1909, when he landed a position as pro-greenkeeper at French Lick Springs, Indiana. While there, a flood ravaged the course and Alves supervised the reconstruction, redesigning several holes in the process.

Donald Ross was hired soon afterward to design a second course, and Alves constructed it. Impressed with his work, Ross recommended Alves to the Shaker Heights CC of Cleveland, Ohio. He was hired to supervised construction of its Donald Ross course, and stayed on in 1915 as the club's first professional. Eight years later he was chosen by fellow Masons to design and build a course for the Masonic organization in Cleveland. With Ross' help he created the Acacia CC which opened in 1923. Alves remained there as pro-greenkeeper until his death.

While at Acacia, Alves designed a number of Cleveland-area courses on the side. He was highly regarded as an instructor and continued to be a good player, winning the Ohio Open in 1922 and 1925. In addition, he served as vice president of both the National Association of Greenkeepers of America and the Professional Golfers Association of America.

Courses by Grange Gordon "Sandy" Alves:
OHIO: Acacia CC (c. D.J. Ross); Aurora CC; East Liverpool CC (1928); Highland Meadows CC, Toledo (1928); Highland Park GC, Shaker Heights (1927); Lyndhurst GC (1925); Madison CC, North Madison (27, 1926); Meadowlands GC, Willoughby (9,1930); Middle Bass Island GC, Sandusky (1930); Ridgewood Muni, Cleveland (1924); Twin Lakes CC, Kent (1925); University Heights GC, Cleveland (9,1929).
Courses Remodeled by Grange Gordon "Sandy" Alves:
INDIANA: French Lick CC (r.Valley course, 1911).
OHIO: Oakwood CC, Cleveland (5, 1928); Sylvania CC, Toledo (6, 1929).

William Walker Amick (1932–   ) ASGCA: President, 1977
Born: Scipio, Indiana.

William Amick received a B.A. degree from Ohio Wesleyan University where he played on the golf team and was then employed as a graduate assistant in Turf Management at Purdue University. He served for two years as an officer in the U. S. Air Force.

Amick trained under golf architects William H. Diddel and Charles "Chic" Adams, entering private practice on his own in 1959. He became known for his research on the conversion of sanitary land fills into golf courses and for his study of the future of executive layouts and other short courses.

Courses by William Walker Amick:
ALABAMA: Chattahoochee CC, Abbeville (9,1964); Cumberland Lake CC, Birmingham (1968).
FLORIDA: A. C. Read GC, Pensacola (a.Seaside, 1962); Alhambra G&CC, Orlando (1970); Beacon Woods CC, New Port Richey (1974); Crestview CC (9,1961); Eglin AFB GC (9,1976); Fairgreen CC, New Smyrna Beach (1977); Fairway GC, Orlando (9,1972); Fort George Island GC (9,1962); Fort Walton Beach Muni (1962); Havana CC (9,1963); Hollywood GC, Fort Walton Beach (9,1966); Inlet Beach GC. Jefferson CC, Monticello (9,1965); Killearn G&CC, Tallahassee (1967); Lake Lorraine CC, Shalimar (1968); Macclenny G&CC (1968); Mangrove Bay Muni, St. Petersburg (1977); Monsanto Employees GC, Pensacola (1961); Monticello CC (1977); Palm Coast GC, Flagler Beach (1973); Panama City Beach GC (now Hilton G&RC); Pelican Bay G&CC (1979); Perdido Bay CC, Pensacola (1963); Rocky Bayou CC, Niceville (1973); Santa Rosa Shores CC, Gulf Breeze (1964); Seminole GC, Tallahassee (r.3,a.9,1969); Seven Rivers CC, Crystal River (1968); Sherwood G&CC, Titusville (9,1966); St. Josephs Bay GC; Spruce Creek GC, Daytona Beach (1974); Thousand Oaks GC, Ponte Verda Beach (1972); Tiger Point G&RC, Gulf Breeze (1977); Pineview CC
GEORGIA: Briar Creek CC, Sylvania (9,1963); Donalsonville CC (9,1970); Green Meadows CC, Augusta (1962); Monroe CC (9,1971); Pineknoll CC, Sylvester (9,1968).
ILLINOIS: Chester CC (9,1969).
NORTH CAROLINA: Sky Lake GC, Highlands (9,1961).
OHIO: Homestead GC, Tipp City (1973).
SOUTH CAROLINA: Three Pines CC, Woodruff (1969).
TENNESSEE: Chestuee G&CC, Etowah (1971); WinDyke CC (West), Germantown (1963).
Courses Remodeled by William Walker Amick:
FLORIDA: A. C. Read GC, Pensacola Naval Air Station (r. Mainside course, 1962); Harbor City Muni, Eau Gallie (1970); Melbourne G&CC (1977).

R. Albert "Andy" Anderson (1918–   )
"Andy" Anderson, the son of a Racine, Wisconsin, golf professional, became a prolific course architect following the second World War. Settling in Florida, he founded World Wide Golf Enterprises, Inc. based in Sarasota. Among the numerous courses he designed and built were six that he operated for a time and later sold.

Courses by R. Albert Anderson:
ALABAMA: Rolling Green CC (formerly Prattville CC), Prattville.
FLORIDA: Cape Haze G&CC (1964); Capri Isle, Venice; Clewiston CC; Englewood GC; Florida State University, Tallahassee; Forest Lakes CC, Sarasota (1964); Futurama G, Sarasota (par 3, 1963); Harbor City CC, Eau Gallie (1963); Heather Lakes GC, Sarasota (exec., 1963); Lake Venice; Lehigh CC (formerly Lehigh Acres CC) (1960); Little Cypress G&CC, Wauchulla (1965); Palma Sola GC, Bradenton (1968); Rocket City GC; Rockledge CC, Cocoa; Rolling Green, Sarasota; Santa Rosa G&CC, Bradenton (exec., 1970); Seminole GC (Florida State Univ); Sorrento Shores, Nokomis; Starke G&CC; Sunny Breeze Palms CC; Sunrise National GC, Sarasota (1971); Tommy Bolt's Golden Tee, Sarasota; Venice East GC (exec., 1961); Whispering Hills, Titusville; Woodcrest Par 3 GC, Sarasota (1970).
GEORGIA: Cairo CC (1962); Four Seasons of Georgia, Newnan.
ILLINOIS: Shady Lawn GC, Beecher (1971).
INDIANA: Broadmoor CC, Shereville; Cedar Lake GC; Cary CC; Pheasant Valley GC, Crown Point; Hollow Acres CC.
MINNESOTA: Willmar CC (a.9,1960).
MISSOURI: Terre du Lac CC, Bonne Terre (1969); Tower Tee GC, St. Louis (par 3, 1969).
OHIO: Copeland Hills CC, Columbiana; Golden Tee GC, Cincinnati; Orchard Hills, Cleveland; Puckerbrush GC, Willoughby; Southern Hills CC, Youngstown.
TENNESSEE: Carrol Lake GC, McKenzie; Four Seasons of Tennessee, Smithville; McMinnville CC (1970); Shelbyville CC.
WISCONSIN: Oak Hills GC, Oak Creek (1962); Spring Valley GC, Union Center (1959).
Courses Remodeled by R. Albert Anderson:
FLORIDA: Bobby Jones Muni, Sarasota (36); Capitol City CC, Tallahassee (1960); Keystone Heights GC (1960); Palm Aire West CC [formerly DeSoto Lakes G&CC], Sarasota (1969); Punta Gorda CC (1966).

Charles F. Ankrom (1936–   ) ASGCA
Charles Ankrom attended West Virginia University and took additional courses in golf course turf and real estate at a community college of the University of Florida. He was employed as Director of Golf and in-house golf architect with the General Development Corporation.

From 1970 until 1972 Ankrom served as National Director of Golf Operations for the Boise Cascade Recreation Communities Group. In 1972 he founded Charles F. Ankrom Inc. to provide golf course design and consulting services.

Courses by Charles F. Ankrom:
(These are in addition to extensive design and operations work with General Development and Boise Cascade, and comprise a partial list only.)
FLORIDA; Crane Creek Road GC, Stuart (1977); Crystal Lakes GC, Okeechobee (9,1977); Indian River Plantation, Hutchinson Island (exec. 18,1978); Port Charlotte CC (r); Port Malabar GC; CC of North Port Charlotte, Port Charlotte (1970); Sandpiper Par 3 GC.

Javier Arana (1904–   )
Born: Bilbao, Vizcaya, Spain.

Renowned golfer Javier Arana began designing courses in 1936. Although his work has been confined to his native Spain, he is recognized as a leading contemporary golf course architect. His trademark has been an individual tree in one or more fairways. In their *Shell International Encyclopedia of Golf,* Steel and Ryde called Arana a "master in a specialized field."

Courses by Javier Arana:
SPAIN: Club de Campo; CdeG Cerdana; El Prat; El Saler; Golf Rio Real; Guadalmina; La Galea; Los Monteros; Real Automovil; Reina Cristina; Ulzama.

Rowland Armacost (1916–   )
A graduate of Western Maryland University with post graduate studies in art at North Carolina University, Rowland Armacost planned several golf courses for the U. S. military while serving as a pilot, stateside and overseas, during World War II. He then formed a landscape contracting firm in Berkshire County, Massachusetts, planning at least two courses.

Armacost became course superintendent in 1959 at Wahconah CC, Dalton, Massachusetts, where, in collaboration with Geoffrey Cornish, he planned and built a nine-hole addition. In the mid-1960s he designed and built Waubeeka Springs, an eighteen-hole layout in Williamstown, Massachusetts, where he became manager while continuing to design several courses as a sideline. These included the eighteen-hole Rolling Hills Par 3 (n.l.e.) at Lenox, General Electric's A. A. GC in Pittsfield, and the greens for the Skyline GC near Pittsfield, all in Massachusetts.

William Auchterlonie (1872–1963)
William Auchterlonie, who won the British Open in 1893, was a club maker by trade. In 1934 he became professional at the Royal and Ancient Golf Club of St. Andrews and during his tenure, planned the eighteen-hole Jubilee course, incorporating an existing short nine and an area of reclaimed land.

Brian T. Ault (1947–   ) ASGCA
Born: Washington, D.C.

Brian Ault earned an associate degree in civil engineering and for a short time served as an inspector for the Washington, D.C., Highway Department. In 1973 he became an associate architect in the firm of Edmund B. Ault, Ltd. where he had been personally tutored by his father.

Courses by Brian T. Ault: See Edmund B. Ault

Edmund B. Ault (1908–) ASGCA
Born: Washington, D.C.

Edmund Ault studied construction engineering at Columbia Technical Institute and for a time was employed in that field. He trained with golf architect Fred Findlay and then entered private practice as a course designer in 1946. For several years in the late 1950s he was associated with professional golfer Al Jamison.

At one time a scratch golfer, Ault played in the National Amateur on several occasions. He served in the Green Section of the USGA, was a past president of the Columbia Golf Association and was qualified by the U. S. Department of Justice as an expert witness in golf course architecture.

Courses by Edmund B. Ault:

ARKANSAS: Bella Vista CC (1977); Cherokee Village GC (1969); Coronado Exec. GC, Hot Springs (1980); Hot Springs Village CC (DeSoto and Cortez courses); Maumelle G&CC (1967); Mountain Ranch GC; Newport CC (a.9,1978).

DELAWARE: Delcastle Farms (1969); Dover AFB GC (9,1971); Garrison's Lake (1965); Pike Creek Valley GC; Shawnee CC (1964); Sussex Pines CC (1966).

FLORIDA: Carrollwood Village (1971); Coral Springs G&TC.

INDIANA: Lakeview West Boggs Muni, Loogootee (9,1978); Wesselman Park (9,1970).

IOWA: Sundown GC, Burlington (9 par 3,1978).

LOUISIANA: Eden Isles CC.

MARYLAND: Aberdeen Proving Ground (9,1965); All-View Public GC (1968); Aviation Y&CC (1962); Bay Hills (1968); Bethesda (1966); Bretton Woods (1968); Caroline CC (1963); Chartwell G&CC (1960); Chester River Y&CC, Chestertown (r.a.18,1977); Crofton GC (1966); Diamond Ridge CC; Eisenhower GC (1968); Falls Road Muni (1960); Five Farms—Baltimore (a.18,1960); Hawthorne GC (9,1960); Henson Creek Exec. GC; Hobbit's Glen GC, Columbia (1965); Hunt Valley CC (1966); Indian Head GC; Lakewood CC (1960); Maryland University GC (1958); Montgomery Village GC (1966); Northwest Park GC; Oakcrest GC (1969); Oakland GC (9,1965); Paint Branch GC; Piney Branch G&CC (1969); Ralph G. Cover GC (1962); River Road GC (c.A.Jameson); Sligo Creek GC (9,1965); Turf Valley CC (27,1962); Western Area GC (1968).

MISSOURI: Meadow Lake Acres (1960); Poplar Bluff Muni (1980); Smithville Lakes Muni, Smithville (1980).

NEVADA: Las Vegas CC (1965).

NEW JERSEY: Ramblewood (18,1961; 9,1964); Spooky Brook (1969).

NEW YORK: McGuire AFB GC (9,1967); Riverton GC, Henrietta.

NORTH CAROLINA: Etowah Valley CC (1965); Wedgewood CC.

OHIO: CC Villages of America (1972); Lakeside GC (9,1963); Mayfair CC (1968); Ravenna (1972); Town and Country (1968); Windmill GC.

PENNSYLVANIA: Belles Springs CC (1968); Bucknell University (9,1973); Center Square GC; Chambersburg GC, Scotland (a.9,1977); Charnita (1967); Clinton CC, Lockhaven (a.9,1976); Corry Muni (18,1964;18,1970); Great Cove (1968); Hidden Valley GC (1964); Honey Run (1970); Iron Master CC; Juaniata (1965); Lewistown CC (1973); Middleburg Recreation Area (1969); Monroe Creek GC (1967); Mountain View GC, Fairfield (9,1977); Northampton Valley CC; North Hills Muni; Oak Tree CC (1967); Olde Hickory (9,1966); Olmstead AFB GC; Pennsylvania National G&CC (1967); Pleasant View GC (1960); Sinking Valley CC; Summit GC (9,1967); Toftrees GC (1968); Tyoga CC, Wellsboro (a.9,1978); Tyrone CC (1962); V.F.W. GC; Waynesboro CC (9,1970).

SOUTH CAROLINA: Myrtle Beach Par 3 GC; Myrtlewood GC (27,1972).

TENNESSEE: Woodmont CC, Franklin (9,1977).

VIRGINIA: Bolling AFB (1960); Bryce Mountain GC; Bushfield CC (c.A.Jameson); Chantilly National (1959); CC of Virginia, James River (9,1968); Edwin R. Carr (1959); Forest Lake CC (c.A.Jameson); Hermitage CC (17,1971); Herndon Centennial Muni (1979); Holston Hills CC (9,1968); Lake Fairfax (1959); Langley AFB (9,1965); Leesburg CC (1968); Loudoun G&CC (9,1959); Mill Quarter Plantation (1974); Newport News Muni (9,1965); Penderbrook GC, Fairfax (1979); Petersburg CC (1968); Reston South GC (1969); River Bend CC (1960); Shannon Green (1970); Shenvallee CC (9,1968); Sheraton Motor Inn GC, Fredericksburg; South Wales G&RC; Spotswood GC (9,1960;9,1964); Springfield G&CC (c.A.Jameson); Sterling Park (1963); Stonehenge, Bon Air (1969); Winchester GC (1966); Winton CC (1969).

WEST VIRGINIA: Green Hills CC (1962); (The) Pines CC (1968); Preston CC (9,1965); Sandy Brae (1968).

WISCONSIN: Brighton Dale Muni (1971).

WEST INDIES: Belham River Valley GC, Montserrat (9,1968).

Courses Remodeled by Edmund B. Ault:

ARKANSAS: CC of Little Rock (1968); Fairfield Bay GC.

DELAWARE: Dover CC (9,1969); Green Hill Muni (1971).

FLORIDA: Broken Woods G&TC (1973); Miles Grant CC.

INDIANA: Fendrich GC (1972).

MARYLAND: Argyle CC, Silver Spring (1960); Bethesda CC; Bonnie View CC (1961); Burning Tree CC (1963); Elk Ridge CC; Fountainhead CC (1968); Hillendale CC (1962); Kenwood CC (1962); National Navy Medical (9,1961); Norbeck CC (1965); Silver Spring GC [formerly Indian Spring;]; Suburban CC (1964); Woodholme CC (1964).

MISSISSIPPI: Northwood CC, Meridian (1978).

MISSOURI: Hickory Hills CC.

NEW YORK: Blue Hill GC (1960), Hampshire CC (1962).

OHIO: Marietta CC (1970); Oakwood CC [now Oak Tree CC](1969).

PENNSYLVANIA: Butler CC; Conewango Valley CC (1972); Highland CC (1961); Indiana CC (1969); Nottingham CC (1962); South Hills CC (1973).

VIRGINIA: Army-Navy CC (1962); Belle Haven CC (1969); Eastern Shore Y&CC (1962); Fort Belvoir GC; Hampton GC; International Town & CC; Meadowbrook CC; Salisburg CC (1967).

WEST VIRGINIA: Clarksburg CC (1964); Parkersburg CC (1965).

PUERTO RICO: Dorado-Hilton (1973).

SWITZERLAND: Caslano (1966).

Russell D. Bailey

A landscape architect based in upstate New York, Russell Bailey planned a number of courses in the Syracuse and Utica areas from the 1950s through the 1970s. Two of his best known are the Beaver Meadow CC at Phoenix and the Skenandoa Club at Clinton.

Gary Roger Baird (1941–) ASGCA

Gary Baird received a B.Sc. degree in landscape architecture from California Polytechnic Institute in Pomona. In 1969 he joined the firm of Robert Trent Jones Inc. as a design associate, remaining until 1977 when he formed Gary Roger Baird Inc., Golf Course Design and Contract Planning. Courses of his design in play or under construction by early 1980 included a new 18 at Mountain Shadows GC at Rohnert Park, California, Roseburg CC (r.9,a.9) in Roseburg, Oregon, and Timber Creek CC at McKinney, Texas, with several more on the drawing board.

Robert Earl Baldock (1908–)
Born: Omaha, Nebraska

California-based golf architect Bob Baldock planned more than 300 courses in his career. A former professional golfer, he worked at one time for golf architect William P. Bell. His most active design period was in the 1950s and early 1960s; but with his son Robert L. Baldock, as partner, he continued in practice into the 1980s.

Courses by Robert E. Baldock, (All courses after 1969 with Robert L. Baldock)

ALABAMA: Skycenter (Jetport) CC, Huntsville (1968).

Arizona: Continental CC, Flagstaff (1960); General Blanchard GC, David-Monthan AFB (1961).

California: Alta Sierra CC, Grass Valley (1965); Antioch Muni (a.9, 1957); Azuza Greens GC (1965); Baywood G&CC, Arcata (1958); Bear Valley CC (1962); Bethel Island GC; Blue Lake Springs GC, Arnold (1966); Butte Creek G&CC, Chico (c.Baldock, 1965); Castle AFB GC (9,1955); Castle View Muni, Merced (1963); Chimney Rock GC, Napa (c.Baldock 1966); College of the Sequoias, Fresno (4,1953); Comstock CC, Davis (1965); Concord Muni (1963); Corral De Tierra CC, Salinas (1959); Delano Muni (9,1963); El Macero CC (1961); Eureka Muni (9,1957;a.9,1966); Exeter Muni (9,1963); Fairway Glen GC, Santa Clara (1961); George AFB GC, Victorville (1963); Gold Hills CC, Redding (c.Baldock, 1979); Hacienda Hotel Par 3 GC, Bakersfield (1957); Hacienda Hotel Par 3 GC's, Indio and San Luis Obispo (1955); Heather Farms GC, Walnut Creek (1966); Horse Thief G&CC, Tehachapi (1974); Intercity GC, Selma (c.Clark, 1969); Irwindale Muni (c.Baldock, 1965); Kings River G&CC, Kingsbury (1961); Lazy H GC; Leland Meadows Par 4 GC, Long Bain (1962); Lemoure Muni; Lew Galbraith Muni, Oakland (1966); Lindale Greens GC, Sacramento (1965); Lindsay Muni (9,1963); Los Banos CC (9,1955); Los Robles Green GC, Thousand Oaks (1964); Madera CC (1955); Mariposa Pines GC (1973); Merced G&CC, Slater (1961); Monterey Peninsula CC, Pebble Beach (Shore course, 1961); Mountain Shadow Muni (original 18, 1963, (Formerly Rohnert Park Muni); Mt. Whitney CC, Lone Pine (9,1959); Napa Muni (1958); Oakdale G&CC (9,1963); Paradise Pines GC (now Tall Pines) (1972); pariso Springs CC, Soledad (9,1955); Peachtree CC, Marysville (1960); Plumas Lake G&CC, Marysville (a.9); Ponderosa Muni; River Island GC, Porterville (1963); Rohert Park Muni (now Mountain Shades Muni, South course) (1963); San Joaquin CC, Fresno (1961); Selma Valley GC (1958); Sherwood Forest GC, Sanger (1968); Sierra Sky Ranch GC, Oakhurst (9,1954); Sierra View CC, Sacramento (a.9,1966); Skywest Public GC, Hayward (c.Baldock, 1964); Swallow's Nest Par 3 GC, Sacramento (1964); Teaford Lake GC, Bass Lake (1972); Tracy CC (9,1956); Tulare CC (1956); Turlock G&CC (c.Fleming); Valley Gardens CC, Santa Cruz (1971); Vandenburg AFB GC; West Winds GC (George AGB); Victorville (1964); Whitesbridge CC, Mendosa (1966); Willow Park GC, Castro Valley (1966); Yolo Fliers Club, Woodland (a.9,1957); Yosemite Lakes GC, Coarse Gold (1965).

COLORADO: Lowry AFB GC (1971).

FLORIDA: Tyndal AFB GC (1964).

HAWAII: Hickman AFB GC, Oahu (1966); Lakeside CC, Honolulu (27); Mililani GC, Mililana Town (1966); Olomana Golf Links, Waimanolo (1969); Pukalani CC (1979); Ted Makalena GC, Waipahu (1971).

IDAHO: Cherry Lane GC, Meridian (9,1979); Crane Creek CC, Boise (1962); Eagle Hills GC (a.9,1975;c.Fleming,Harmon); Lewiston CC (1974); Mountain Home AFB GC (9, 1956); University of Idaho GC, Moscow (1971).

KANSAS: Forbes AFB GC, Topeka (9,1962;a.9,1965,c.Baldock).

MASSACHUSETTS: Otis AFB GC (1972).

MICHIGAN: Sawyer AFB GC (1968).

MISSOURI: Richards-Gebauer AFB GC, Kansas City (1965).

MONTANA: Glacier View GC, West Glacier (1972); Glasgow AFB GC.

NEVADA: Alladdin Hotel GC, Las Vegas (9 par 3); Black Mountain G&CC, Henderson (1959); Brookside GC, Reno (1964); Camarlo GC, Henderson (1979); Carson City Muni (a.9,1956); Ely Muni (1956); Hacienda Hotel Par 3 GC, Las Vegas (1956); Henderson G&CC (1965); Soparovan CC, Fallon (9); Stead AFB GC (1965); White Pines GC, Ely (9,1957); Winnemucca Muni.

NEW MEXICO: Four Hills CC, Albuquerque (1961); Los Altos Muni, Albuquerque (1960).

OREGON: Bend CC (a.9,1972); Emerald Valley GC, Creswell (1966); Reames G&CC, Klamath Falls (a.9,1966,c.Baldock).

WASHINGTON: Hangman Valley Muni, Spokane (1968); Pasco Muni; Swallow's Nest GC, Clarkston (9,1964); Whispering Firs GC, McChord AFB (9,1961).

WYOMING: Casper GC (r.9,a.9,1960); Jackson Hole G&CC (1971); Olive Glenn GC, Cody (c.Capps,1970).

MEXICO: San Antonio Shores GC, Baja (1970).

PHILIPPINES: Manila G&CC, Makati (1961); Philippines CC (1961).

TAHITI: Golf D'Atimaona CC, Papeete.

Courses Remodeled by Robert E. Baldock.

CALIFORNIA: Belmont CC, Fresno (1956); Ft. Washington CC, Pinedale (1956); 1,001

164

Ranch GC, Riverside (1972); Santa Maria GC (1965).
HAWAII: Ala Wai GC, Honolulu (1962); Mid Pacific CC, Kalua (1968).
OREGON: Grant's Pass CC (r.,a.14).

Charles Henry Banks (1883–1931)
Born: Amenia, New York. Died: New York City, New York, at age 48. Interred: Salisbury, Connecticut.

Charles Banks graduated from Yale University in 1906. He then returned to his preparatory school, Hotchkiss, in Salisbury, Connecticut, where he served as English instructor and track coach for fifteen years. While a member of the school's construction committee, he met Seth J. Raynor, who had been hired to design and build a new golf course at Hotchkiss. He worked closely with Raynor on the job, and in 1921 resigned his teaching position to join Raynor's firm. "Josh" Banks stayed with Raynor until the latter's death in 1926, assisting him (and, on a few projects, C. B. Macdonald) in the design and construction of such courses as Fox Chapel in Pennsylvania and Yale University GC in Connecticut.

Banks finished ten of Raynor's projects and designed or remodeled over thirty other courses in the late 1920s. Nicknamed "Steam Shovel" Banks by his colleagues, he was an enthusiastic believer in massive earth moving to create the huge elevated greens and deep bunkers and ponds characteristic of his courses. Legend has it that at the Whippoorwill Club in Armonk, New York (a Ross course he completely redid, and claimed by many to be Banks's masterpiece), this enthusiasm for depth was dampened when a steam shovel excavating an exceptionally deep pond disappeared into the ooze. Fortunately the operator was rescued, but the steam shovel is said to still lie deep beneath the sixth fairway a half century later.

Banks also carried on C. B. Macdonald's tradition of including adaptations of famous golf holes. Invariably an "Eden," "Redan," "Alps," Macdonald's "Cape" or some other renowned hole can be found on a Banks layout, a fact intriguing to those golfers who may have played the course for decades without recognizing the holes.

Charles Banks died of a heart attack in 1931. His last project was the Castle Harbour GC in Bermuda, which abutted the famous Mid Ocean Club, a course he had helped to construct a decade earlier.
Courses by Charles Henry Banks:
CALIFORNIA: Monterey Peninsula CC, Pebble Beach (completed Dunes course after Raynor's death, 1926).
CONNECTICUT: Yale University GC, New Haven (c.Macdonald, after Raynor's death, 1926).
HAWAII: Waialae CC, Honolulu (completed after Raynor's death, 1927).
NEW JERSEY: Essex County CC, West Orange (West course); Forsgate CC, Jamesburg (East course, 1931); Hackensack GC, Orader (27,1930); Knoll GC, Boonton (1929); Montclair GC (a.9).
NEW YORK: Tamarack CC, Port Chester (1929); Westhampton CC, Westhampton Beach (1929).
BERMUDA: Castle Harbour GC, Southampton (Original 9, 1932).
COLOMBIA: The CC of Bogota (n.l.e.).
VENEZUELA: (The) Junko CC, Caracas.
Courses Remodeled by Charles Henry Banks:
CONNECTICUT: Hotchkiss School GC, Salisbury (1930).
NEW YORK: Knollwood CC, Elmsford (1927); Whippoorwill GC, Armonk (1930).

Herbert H. Barker
Herbert Barker served as head professional at the Garden City GC in New York from 1900 to 1911. He later held a similar position with the Roe Buck CC, in Alabama. Barker played in the 1913 U. S. Open.
Courses by Herbert H. Barker:
GEORGIA: Druid Hills CC.
MARYLAND: Columbia CC, Chevy Chase (1910).
OHIO: Mayfield CC (assisted Way).
VIRGINIA: CC of Virginia, Richmond (Westhampton course, 1908).

Ralph Martin Barton (1875–1941)
Born: Newport, New Hampshire. Died: New Hampshire, at age 66.

Ralph Barton attended Phillips Exeter Academy and Dartmouth College and also took courses at Harvard and the University of Chicago. From 1904 until the early 1920s he pursued a career in the academic world, teaching mathematics and holding administrative posts at Dartmouth College, the University of New Mexico, Lombard College and the University of Minnesota. While at Minnesota he undertook supervision of the University's golf course, designed by Seth Raynor.

This experience left Barton permanently enamored of golf architecture, and he subsequently trained under Raynor and C. B. Macdonald during the design and construction of the Yale Golf Club in Connecticut and the Mid Ocean Club in Bermuda. In 1923 he entered private practice, establishing a golf course architecture and engineering firm in New Hampshire, which he maintained until his death with the exception of a few months in 1941 spent working with the bridge division of the New Hampshire State Highway Department. For a short period he also had an office in Boston, Massachusetts.

Ralph Barton was a member of the American Mathematical Society and was listed in *Who's Who in America.*
Courses by Ralph Martin Barton:
CONNECTICUT: Sleeping Giant.
MASSACHUSETTS: Greenfield CC; Magnolia.
MINNESOTA: Midland Hills CC, St. Paul.
NEW HAMPSHIRE: Ammonoosuc Inn CC; Concord CC, Concord; Hanover CC, Dartmouth College (9); Laconia CC; Lakeport CC; Lancaster CC; Mackenzie GC; Mountain View CC;

North Conway CC; Peckets CC; Plymouth CC; Sugar Hill CC; Waumbek Village GC.
VERMONT: Newport CC (Original 9); Wilmington CC (n.l.e.).

Reginald Beale
An "in house" planner for Carter & Co. Seeds of London, England, in the 1930s, Reginald Beale designed Brockton Hill GC and revised Mid Surrey.

Robert D. Beard (1914–)
A native of Indiana, Robert Beard established the Fort Wayne design and build firm of Robert D. Beard, Inc. in 1959.
Courses by Robert D. Beard:
INDIANA: Big Pine GC, Attica; Canterbury Green GC, Fort Wayne; Cedar Creek GC, Leo; Crestview GC, Muncie (9); Havenhurst GC, New Haven (1967); Lake James CC, Angola (9); Lakeside GC, Fort Wayne (27); Pond A River GC, Woodburn (9); Tri-County GC, Muncie.
MICHIGAN: Cedar Creek GC, Battle Creek; Coldwater CC (9); Evergreen GC, Hudson (9); Katke GC, Ferris State College, Big Rapids (1974); Katke-Cousins, Oakland University, Rochester; Manley's GC, Albion; Maple Hill GC, Augusta (9); Neal Choate, Brooklyn (9); Stony Creek GC, Rochester (1978).
OHIO: Case Leasing GC, Celina (9); Marvin Rupp GC, Stryker.

Max Howell Behr (1884–1955)
Born: New York City, New York. Died: Los Angeles, California, at age 71.

Max Behr attended the Lawrenceville School in New Jersey and graduated in 1905 from Yale University, where he had been a member of the golf team coached by Robert Pryde. He had learned golf at the Morris County CC in New Jersey, and as a youth had competed in several father-son tournaments with his father, Herman.

Behr was a perennial bridesmaid in competition, losing the 1907 and 1908 New Jersey Amateurs and the 1908 U. S. Amateur, all to the same golfer, Jerome Travers. He finally won the New Jersey title in 1909 and successfully defended it in 1910, gaining his only victory over Travers in the final of the latter event.

In 1914 Behr became the first editor of the New York-based *Golf Illustrated* magazine. He resigned from the publication after the death of his first wife in 1918 and moved to California, where he continued to write on golf, especially on the design and construction of courses. He remained active as an author well into his sixties. In the early 1920s Behr also began designing and remodeling courses, but his business was curtailed during the Depression; and after World War II, when others resumed course design careers, Behr had lost interest.

Max Behr was something of a radical. In golf he was a strong advocate of the "floater" golf ball, petitioning the USGA for over fifteen years to adopt it. He didn't believe in rough on his course designs, preferring instead to defend his greens from every conceivable approach shot. He was outspoken on politics and religion, and late in his life developed his own religion based on his interpretation of numbers, although he disavowed any connection with Numerology, to which he was opposed.
Courses by Max Howell Behr:
CALIFORNIA: Hacienda CC, La Habra (1922); Lakeside GC of Hollywood, North Hollywood (1924); Montebello GC; Montecito CC, Santa Barbara (1922); Oakmont CC, Glendale (1924); Palos Verdes CC (1924); Pasadena CC; Rancho CC, Los Angeles (1922,n.l.e.); Rancho Santa Fe CC (1927); Victoria GC, Riverside (r.9,a.9,1923).
Courses Remodeled by Max Howell Behr:
CALIFORNIA: Brentwood CC.

Earl Lee "Smiley" Bell (1899–1955)
Born: Lenexa, Kansas. Died: Kansas City, Missouri, at age 56.

"Smiley" Bell began his career in golf running horse-drawn mowers for his father, Henry Bell, greenkeeper at Mission Hills CC in Kansas City, Kansas. He later worked as caddymaster at the club, and in the mid-twenties formed a course construction and management firm in Kansas City.

Bell opened his first commercial driving range, "Smiley's Sportland," the first operation of its kind in the Midwest, in 1928. He also worked on several Kansas and Missouri-area courses reconstructing greens, often converting them from sand to grass. In the mid-thirties he built Armour Fields GC, a daily fee course that he operated until it was subdivided in the early fifties. This led to other course design projects and until his death he was busy planning and constructing Midwestern courses with the avowed intent of bringing golf to as many communities as possible.
Courses by Earl Lee "Smiley" Bell:
KANSAS: Armour Fields GC, Kansas City (1937;n.l.e.); Coffeyville CC (9,1954); El Dorado CC (9,1950); Hillcrest Muni, Coffeyville (9,1923); Manhattan CC (1949); Smiley's Sportland GC, Kansas City (par3,1930,n.l.e.).
MISSOURI: Camp Crowder GC; Columbia Muni (9,1954); Shifferdecker CC, Joplin (r.9,a.9); Twin Hills CC, Joplin (original 9).
Courses Remodeled by Earl Lee "Smiley" Bell:
KANSAS: Garden City CC (r.,inst.grass greens); Independence CC; Park Hills CC, Pratt (r.,inst.grass greens,1953).
MISSOURI: Columbia CC (r.,inst.grass greens); Excelsior Springs CC (1951).

William Francis Bell (1918–) ASGCA: President, 1957
Born: Pasadena, California.

William F. Bell, son of William P. "Billy" Bell, trained under and worked with his father, after graduating from USC. He took over the practice upon the death of the senior Bell in 1953. He retained the firm name of William P. Bell and Son in honor of his father.
Courses by William Francis Bell:

ARIZONA: El Rio CC, Tucson; Encanto Muni, Phoenix; Forty Niners CC; Maryvalle GC, Phoenis; Papago Muni; Pima CC (Roadrunner Inn), Scottsdale; Randolf Park GC, Tucson (North course, 1960); Rolling Hills Exec. GC, Tucson; Yuma G&CC (c.W.P.Bell).

CALIFORNIA: Alameda Muni (South course); Almansor GC, Alhambra; Ancil Hoffman Muni; Antelope Valley GC; Apple Valley Inn & CC (2nd 9); Banning CC; Bermuda Dunes; Black Canyon CC; Blue Skies CC; Blythe Muni (1969); Bonita CC; California CC (New site); Canyon CC (North and South courses); Circle R Ranch GC, Escondido (c.W.P.Bell); Costa Mesa CC (36); Crown City Ranch GC, Alhambra; Crystalaire CC; DeBell GC, Burbank (c.W.H.Johnson); Diamond Bar Muni; Eaton Canyon GC (6); El Camino G&CC, Oceanside; Fullerton G&CC (27); Furnace Creek CC, Death Valley (a.9,1967); Grass Valley CC; Greentree G&TC (1978); Heinie Hills G&CC, Oceanside; Hidden Valley Lake CC, Middletown (1970); Industry Hills GC (1978); Jurupa Hills CC, Riverside; Kern County GC; Knollwood CC (c.Johnson); Lake Arrowhead CC (r.9,a.9); Lake Don Pedro G&CC, Sonora (1971); Lake Elsinore West CC; Lake Wildwood CC, Grass Valley (1971); La Mirada GC; Lomas Santa Fe (a.Exec.course); Long Beach Muni; Los Alamitos GC; Los Coyotes CC; Los Verdes G&CC, Palm Meadows GC; Palos Verdes; Malibu CC; Marina GC, San Leandro; Meadowvale GC, Lake Tahoe; Mesa Verde CC; Newporter Inn GC, Newport Beach; North Ridge CC, Fair Oakes (c.W.P.Bell); Olivas Park Muni, Ventura (1967); Oxnard Muni [now Silver K GC](1975); Palm Meadows GC; Palo Alto Muni; Pico Rivera Muni (1969); Pine Mountain Lake Club, Frazier Park (1971); Rancho Bernardo Inn & CC (West course); Rancho San Joaquin CC, Irving (1969); Randolph Muni (South course); Recreation Park GC; Riverside GC, Coyote (a.9); Salton City CC; San Clemente Muni (r.9,a.9); Sandpiper Golf Links, Santa Barbara (1972); San Luis Rey; Saticoy CC; Shoal Canyon Park Exec. GC, Glendale (9,1979); Skylinks GC, Long Beach (1972); Soule Park GC; Sunset Hills GC, Thousand Oakes; Torrey Pines Muni, La Jolla (36, C. W. P. Bell); Ventura Muni; Victoria GC, Carson; Whittier Narrows GC(27), Yucaipa Valley CC, Redlands.

COLORADO: Overland Park Muni, Denver (a.9); Valley CC.

HAWAII: Hawaii Kai CC, Oahu (r.18,a.18,1973); Keauhou Kona CC (1971); Keehi Muni, South Kona (1971); Makaha Inn & CC, Waianae (36,1968).

IDAHO: Idaho Falls CC (1970); Sand Creek Park GC, Idaho Falls (1974).

MONTANA: Bitterroot River CC, Missoula (1974).

NEVADA: Calvada Valley G&CC (a.9,1979); Dunes Hotel & CC; LaMancha GC, Boulder City (1974); Las Vegas Muni (a.9).

OREGON: Forest Hills GC, Cornelius (c.W.P.Bell); Illahee Hills CC.

UTAH: Bonneville Muni (a.9); Glendale Park Muni, Salt Lake City (1973); Hidden Valley CC (New site; 27); Hobble Creek CC, Springville (1973); Mountain Dell CC, Salt Lake City; Oakridge CC (c.W.H.Neff); Rose Park GC, Salt Lake City (a.9).

GUAM: Windward Hills G&CC.

Courses Remodeled by William Francis Bell:

CALIFORNIA: Coronado Muni; Del Paso GC; Irvine Coast CC, Newport Beach (1966); Montebello GC; Ojai Valley Inn & GC.

OREGON: Columbia-Edgewater CC, Portland (1970); Riverside CC, Portland (1970).

UTAH: Hidden Valley CC, Draper (36); Riverside CC, Provo (c.Neff).

William Park Bell (1886–1953) ASGCA: Charter Member; President, 1952

Born: Canonsburg, Pennsylvania. Died: Pasadena, California, at age 67.

"Billy" Bell studied agriculture at Duff's Business College in Pittsburgh, Pennsylvania. In 1911 he moved to California, where he became caddymaster at the Annandale Country Club in Pasadena and then superintendent at the Pasadena Golf Club.

Bell served as construction superintendent for golf architect Willie Watson on a number of southern California courses and then went into private practice as a course designer in 1920. In his early years he often collaborated with architect George C. Thomas, Jr.; and while Thomas is listed as architect of record and Bell as construction superintendent for these courses, Billy made major contributions to the designs.

By the 1930s Bell had earned a reputation as the most prolific architect in the West. During World War II, he served as a turf consultant to the U. S. Army Corps of Engineers, and in 1946 was awarded a commendation for his efforts in creating courses for wounded servicemen by the southern California chapter of the PGA. After the War, Billy was joined in practice by his son, William F. Bell.

Courses by William Park Bell:

ARIZONA: Arizona Biltmore GC, Phoenix (Original 18,1928); Encanto Muni, Phoenix (27,-1951); Mesa CC (1950); Randolph Muni, Tucson (North and South courses,1930); Tucson CC (1949); Wickenburg CC (1950); Yuma G&CC (1951).

CALIFORNIA: Alameda Muni (North 18,1927); Alondra Park GC, Lawndale (1950, c. W.H. Johnson); Altadena GC (9); Apple Valley Inn & GC (Original 9,1951); Arrowhead CC, San Bernardino; Bakersfield CC (1949); Balboa Park GC; Baldwin Hills CC, Culver City (c.Thomas, 1926,n.l.e.); Bayside CC, San Diego; Bel Air CC, Los Angeles (c.Thomas,1927); Brookside Muni, Pasadena (North course,1928;South course,1931); Castlewood CC, Pleasanton (Hill and Valley courses,1923); Circle J. GC, Newhall (1954); Circle R Ranch GC, Escondido (1953); Crown City Ranch GC, Alhambra (9,1954); Del Rio G&CC, Modesto (1926); Dryden Park Muni; El Caballero GC, Tarzana (c.Thomas,1926,n.l.e.); El Dorado Park GC, Long Beach (1932); Foothills G&CC, Pasadena (1954); Fox Hills CC, Culver City (c.Thomas,1926,n.l.e.); Furnace Creek CC, Death Valley (9,1939); Hesperia G&CC (1954); Hillcrest CC, Los Angeles (a.9 par 3); Irvine Coast CC, Newport Beach (1954); Kern River CC, Bakersfield (1953); La Cumbre G&CC, Santa Barbara (r.9,a.9,c.Thomas,1920,n.l.e.); Laguna Hills CC (1927); Lakewood GC (1933); Marine Memorial GC, Camp Pendleton; Marine Memorial GC, Santa Ana; Monterey Hills GC, Monterey Park (9 par 3,1949); Mountain Meadows G&CC, Pomona (1922,n.l.e.); Navajo Canyon CC, San Diego; North Ridge CC, Fairoaks (1953); Ojai Valley Inn & CC (c.Thomas,1925;r.1948); Pomona Valley CC (n.l.e.); Red Hill CC, Cucamonga (a.9,1947); Riviera CC, Pacific Palisades (c.Thomas,1927); San Clemente Muni (Original 9,1928); San Diego CC, Chula Vista (New site,1921); San Pedro CC; San Pedro Community Hotel GC (9 par 3); Santa Rosa Muni; Sepulveda GC, Encino (Balboa and Encino courses,c.Johnson,1953); Singing Hills CC, El Cajon (Original 18,c.Johnson,1953); South Hills CC, West Covina (1954); Stanford University GC, Palo Alto (1930); Sunnyside CC; Tamarisk CC, Palm Springs (1953); Torrey Pines

GC (North and South courses), LaJolla; Woodland Hills CC.

HAWAII: Kanehoe Marine GC (1947); Navy-Marine GC, Pearl Harbor (1947).

IDAHO: Sun Valley GC (Original 9,1938;a.9,1947).

NEVADA: Hidden Valley CC; Las Vegas Muni (Original 9).

OREGON: Forest Hills GC, Cornelius (1953).

UTAH: Bonneville Muni (Original 9); Hidden Valley CC, Salt Lake City (1928).

MEXICO: Agua Caliente GC, Aguascalieno [now Tijuana CC].

Courses Remodeled by William Park Bell:

CALIFORNIA: Annandale CC (r.2); Indian Hill GC, Claremont (1931); Pasadena GG, Altadena (1926); Riverside GC, Herndon (r.9,a.9,1939); San Gabriel CC (1930); Virginia CC, Long Beach (1939).

OREGON: Rogue Valley CC, Medford (r.9,a.9,1949).

UTAH: The CC of Salt Lake City.

Thomas M. Bendelow (1872–1936)

Born: Aberdeen, Scotland. Died: River Forest, Illinois, at age 64.

Tom Bendelow, one of America's pioneer golf course architects, came to the United States in the 1880s and went to work for the New York Herald. When public fervor for the game spread through New York in the 1890s, Bendelow staked out a rudimentary golf course in Van Cortlandt Park in the Bronx. This is generally considered the first municipal course in the United States and was the first of hundreds of courses to be laid out by Tom Bendelow.

Quitting his newspaper job in 1896, Bendelow toured the country building golf courses under the auspices of the Chicago Branch of A.G. Spalding & Bros. Of the more than 600 courses he is estimated to have planned, many were simple stake jobs. But later in his career, Bendelow began to refine his work, particularly after forming the Chicago-based firm of American Park Builders with Myron H. West in the 1920s.

Bendelow lectured on course design at the University of Illinois and wrote about it in national publications. He helped train, among others, Carl H. Anderson, Chick Evans and William B. Langford. He was always a strong advocate of publicly owned courses and his scores of modest layouts in and near cities contributed much to the growth of golf in America by giving beginners the chance to start inexpensively in the years before World War I.

Courses by Tom Bendelow:

CALIFORNIA: Griffith Park CC, Los Angeles (Wilson course,1914); Point Loma GC, San Diego (1912).

FLORIDA: Palma Ceia G&CC, Tampa (1917).

GEORGIA: Atlanta Athletic Club (now East Lake CC), Atlanta (1908).

ILLINOIS: Edgewater CC, Chicago (9); Elgin Wing Park GC (9); LaGrange CC (1913); Madison Park Muni, Peoria; Medinah CC (Course # 1, 1924; # 2,1926; # 3,1928); Marquette Park GC; Olympia Fields CC (Course # 1, 1916; # 3, 1920; n.l.e.); Rockford; Urbana CC; Ingersoll Muni.

INDIANA: Evansville Muni (1923); Hazelden CC, Brook (1915).

KANSAS: Topeka CC (9,1906).

NEBRASKA: Elmwood Park Muni, Omaha (1916).

NEW JERSEY: Essex County CC, West Orange (East course, 1898).

NEW YORK: Dyker Beach GC [formerly Marine & Field GC], Brooklyn (9,1897); Dyker Meadow GC, Brooklyn (9,1899,n.l.e.); Flushing GC (9,n.l.e.); Forest Park GC, Brooklyn (1910,n.l.e.); Fox Hills GC, Staten Island (1899); Huntington GC (9,1899,n.l.e.); Pelham Manor GC, Westchester (9,1898,n.l.e.); Rockaway Hunting Club, Cedarhurst (1900); Sunset Park GC, Brooklyn (n.l.e.); Van Cortlandt Park GC, Bronx (9,1895;9,1899).

PENNSYLVANIA: Allegheny CC, Sewickley (1902); Butler CC (9,1906); Grove City CC (1917); St. Clair CC, Pittsburgh (1916); Stanton Heights GC, Pittsburgh (1911).

WASHINGTON: Jefferson Park Muni, Seattle (1917).

WISCONSIN: Big Foot CC, Fontana; Washington Park Muni, Racine (9,1917).

CANADA: Calgary Muni, Alberta.

David W. Bennett (1935–   ) Born: Dallas, Texas ASGCA

A graduate of Texas Tech, Dave Bennett was employed as a landscape architect with the Texas Highway Department for seven years. In 1965 he joined the staff of golf architect Leon Howard, leaving in 1970 to form his own practice. At one time or another in the 1970s, Bennett had PGA tour golfers Terry Dill and Lee Trevino as consultants.

Courses by Dave Bennett:

ARIZONA: Arthur Pack GC, Tucson (1977); Desert Hills CC, Green Valley (1978).

ARKANSAS: Red Apple Inn & CC, Heber Springs (9).

COLORADO: Peaceful Valley CC, Colorado Springs.

FLORIDA: Hurlburt Field GC, Fort Walton Beach.

ILLINOIS: West Village GC, Aurora (1979).

KENTUCKY: Woodson Bend GC, Lake Cumberland.

MONTANA: Billings Muni (par 3,1978).

NEW MEXICO: Santa Teresa CC, Sunland (Spanish Dagger & Yucca courses,1976).

TEXAS: Grover Keaton Muni, Dallas (1978); Lost Creek GC, Austin; Maxwell Muni, Abilene (a.18,1979).

MEXICO: Taboada GC, Guanajuato.

VENEZUELA: Club de Golf, Caracas (1979).

Bradford L. Benz (1946–   ) ASGCA

Born: Olleivein, Iowa.

Bradford Benz attended Iowa State University, receiving a bachelor's degree in 1969 and a master's degree in 1970, both in landscape architecture. In 1973 he joined golf architect Richard M. Phelps in the course design firm of Phelps–Benz Associates.

Courses by Bradford L. Benz: See Richard M. Phelps

Charles R. "Buck" Blankenship (1906–   )

"Buck" Blankenship operated a dairy farm in Kentucky until retiring in the early 1950s. A fine golfer, he became a member of the PGA in 1955 and worked as pro-superintendent at several Kentucky courses. He also began designing and constructing golf courses on a part-time basis in the 1960s, and by the early 1970s estimated he had designed or remodeled some thirty-five layouts.

Courses by Charles R. "Buck" Blankenship:
INDIANA: Valley View GC, New Albany.
KANSAS: Village Greens GC, Ozaukie (original 9, 1968).
KENTUCKY: Bright Leaf GC, Harrodsburg (1963); Burlington GC (1960); Juniper Hills GC, Frankfort; Lakeshore CC, Madisonville (9,1971); Lone Oak CC, Micholasville (1969); New CC, Versailles (1969; Spring Valley CC, Lexington (now Spring Lake CC).

Frederick Bolton
Professional golfer Frederick Bolton planned several courses in the southern and south-western United States.
Courses by Frederick Bolton:
ARIZONA: Rio Verde, Scottsdale (c.M. Coggins, 1973) (orig.18).
FLORIDA: Blanding Boulevard GC, Jacksonville (1967); Ocean Palms CC (1966); Willow Lakes G&CC, Jacksonville (original course, 1967).
SOUTH CAROLINA: Persimmon Hill CC (1962); Spring Lake CC (orig.9); Spring Lake Par 3, Columbia (1963).

K. Warner Bowen (1935–   )
Born: Crystal, Michigan.
Following military service during the Korean War, Warner Bowen received an A.A. degree from Ferris State College and a B.A. degree from Michigan State University. He later did graduate work under Dr. James Beard, then head of Turfgrass Science at Michigan State. At his father's urging, Bowen entered private practice as a course architect and builder based in Sheridan, Michigan, in 1964.
Bowen's philosophy of golf design encompassed spending more hours on the job than others involved with the course, personally sculpting greens, tees and other features with large and small bulldozers, and exerting complete control over all phases of design and construction.
Courses by Warner Bowen:
ARIZONA: Yuma East.
FLORIDA: Jekyll, Hyde GC [formerly International Park Club], Lakeland.
MICHIGAN: Benona Shores GC, Shelby (1979); Centennial Farms GC, Sunfield; Country Creek GC, Elwell; Har-Lou GC, Gobles; Holland Lake GC, Sheridan; North Kent GC, Rockford (1979); Rogue River GC, Sparta; Rolling Hills Golf Estates, Ionia; Schuss Mountain GC, Mancelona (1977); Spring Valley GC, Reed City; Twin Oaks GC, St. John's.

James Braid (1870–1950)
Born: Earlsferry, Fife, Scotland. Died: London, England, at age 80.
James Braid learned golf at age four and won his first tournament at age eight, playing his early golf with such prodigies as Jack and Archie Simpson, and his cousin Douglas Rolland. He left school as a young teenager to pursue a golf career and by age nineteen had worked as an apprentice carpenter at St. Andrews, honing his golfing skills on the side. He played in his first professional tournament in 1894. In 1896 Braid became professional at the Romford GC in England and in 1904 moved to the newly opened Walton Heath GC, where he remained for the rest of his life as professional.
Braid, along with John Henry Taylor and Harry Vardon (the "Great Triumvirate"), dominated competitive golf during the first two decades of the twentieth century. He won most of his prestigious titles within a span of ten years: the British Open in 1901, 1905, 1906, 1908 and 1910; the *News-of-the-World* Matchplay Championship in 1903, 1905, 1907 and 1911; and the French Open in 1910.
Braid had worked on the design of a course or two as a young professional in Romford. He was called upon to design several courses soon after his initial victory in the British Open, and he wrote knowledgeable articles about course design as early as 1908. But it was not until after his active competitive days were over that Braid devoted much of his time to golf course architecture.
Fearing the ocean, he seldom ventured even as far as the Continent, and most of his work was done in the British Isles. He did design one course in America and one in Singapore, but both were done solely from topographic maps. Braid was greatly respected for accurate and detailed working drawings of the courses he laid out, both at home and abroad.
Many of Braid's designs were constructed by contractor John R. Stutt, and a nearly perfect accord was reached between the two. Subject to motion sickness, Braid dreaded travel by car, so Stutt's on-site work was invaluable to him. Braid also started C. K. Hutchison in design and collaborated with him on several projects.
Shortly before his death, James Braid was granted membership in the Royal and Ancient Golf Club, making him one of the first professional golfers ever to be so honored.
Courses by James Braid:
ENGLAND: Arcot Hall GC. Northumberland; Barnehurst GC, Kent; Basingstoke GC, Berkhamsted GC, Herts (r.12, a.6, 1927); Bognor Regis, Sussex; Brighton & Hove GC, Sussex; Bridport and West Dorset, Dorset; Buddock Vean, Cornwall; Charnwood Forest, Leicester; Church Stretton GC, Shropshire; Clitheroe, Lancs; Colchester, Essex; Croham Hurst GC, Surrey (1912); Dorking GC, Surrey; Drayton Park GC, Birmingham; Dunstable Downs GC, Bedfordshire; Eaglescliffe and District GC, County Durham; Enfield GC, Middlesex; Finchley GC, London; Fulford Heath; Hankley Common GC, Surrey (r.9, a.9, 1922); Henley, Oxon; Home Park GC, Surrey; Hoylake (Royal Liverpool); Ipswich GC; Kingswood GC, Surrey; Leamington and County GC, Warwickshire; Luffenham Heath, Lincs; Mere G&CC, Cheshire (1934); Middlesborough GC, Yorkshire; Newton Abbot GC, Devonshire; North Hants GC, Hampshire (1904); North Shore GC, Lincs; North Worcestershire; Orsett GC, Essex; Oswestry GC, Shropshire; Peel, Isle of Man; Perranporth, Cornwall; Petersborough Milton GC, Northamptonshire; Ramsey GC, Huntingdonshire; Romford, Essex; Royal Blackheath (new course), Royal Cromer, Norfolk; **St. Austell**, Cornwall; St. Enodoc GC, Cornwall (1907; r.1922 & 1936); Scarborough Southcliffe GC, Yorkshire; Sherborn, Dorset;

Stinchcombe, Gloucester; Swinton Park, Manchester; Theydon Bois, Essex (Original 9); Thorpeness GC, Suffolk; Tiverton GC, Devon; Torquay GC, Devonshire; Truro GC, Cornwall; Weir Park GC, Devonshire; West Hove, Sussex; Wildernesse GC, Kent; Workington, Cumbria.
IRELAND: Howth GC, Dublin; Limerick GC; Mullingar GC, Westmeath (1932); Newlands; Waterford GC, County Kilkenny.
NORTHERN IRELAND: Bangor GC, County Down; Carnalea; Kirkistown Castle.
SCOTLAND: Airdrie GC, Lanarkshire; Ayr Belleisle, Ayrshire; Ayr Seafield, Ayrshire; Blamore, Stirlingshire; Belle Isle GC, Ayshire; Blairgowrie GC, Perthshire (r.10, a.8, 1934); Blairmore and Strone, Argyll; Boat-of-Garten GC, Invernesshire; Brechin GC, Angus; Brora, Sutherland; Carnoustie GC, Angus (r.Medal course, a.Burnside course, 1926); Cawder GC, Glasgow (Cawder and Keir courses, 1933); Cowal GC, Argyll; Crow Wood, Glasgow; Dalmahoy GC, Midlothian (East and West courses, 1926); Deaconbank, Glasgow; Dullatur, Glasgow; Edzell GC, Forfar (1934); Forfar GC, Angus; Forres; Glenbervie GC, Stirlingshire; Glencruithen, Argyll; Gleneagles Hotel GC, Perthshire (Kings and Queens courses, c.Hutchison); Greenock GC, Renfrewshire (27); Hayston GC, near Glasgow; Hilton Park GC, Dunbartonshire; Kingsknowe, Edinburgh; Powfoot, Dumfrieshire; Rothesay GC, Island of Bute; Routenburn GC, Ayrshire; Royal Musselburgh GC, East Lothian (Preston Grange, 1925); Stranraer; Turnhouse GC; Welshpool GC, Montgomeryshire; Monkton Hall GC, Musselburgh (1937).
SINGAPORE: Singapore Island GC, Bukit Timah (Bukit course, 1924).
WALES: Holyhead; Monmouthshire GC; Portmadoc; Pwllheli (a.9); Rhyl GC, Flintshire (9); Royal Porthcawl; St. Delniol GC.
Courses Remodeled by James Braid:
ENGLAND: Berwick on Tweed; Bramley GC, Surrey; Denham GC, Middlesex; Ganton GC, Yorkshire; Hunstanton GC, Norfolk (r.bunkering, 1910); Littlestone GC, Kent; Northamptonshire County GC; Northumberland GC (1920); Parkstone GC, Dorset (1927); Sherwood Forest GC, Notts (1935); Southport and Ainsdale GC, Lancashire (1923); Wallasey GC, Cheshire (1929).
SCOTLAND: Bruntisfield Links; Crieff GC, Perthshire; Elie Golf House Club, Fife 1921. Murcar GC, Aberdeen; Nairn GC, Nairnshire; Prestwick GC, Ayrshire (r.bunkering, 1918); Queen's Park GC, Stirlingshire; Royal Burgess Golfing Society of Edinburgh; Troon GC, Ayrshire.
UNITED STATES: St. Andrews GC, Hastings-on-Hudson, New York (1930).
WALES: Aberdovey GC, Merionethshire.

Jeffrey D. Brauer (1955–   ) ASGCA
Born: Albany, New York.
Jeff Brauer graduated from the University of Illinois in 1977 with a B.L.A. degree and went to work immediately for the golf architectural firm of Killian and Nugent, Inc.

John Bredemus (1890–1946)
Born: St. Louis, Missouri. Died: Guadalajara, Mexico, at age 56.
John Bredemus attended Harvard University, where he established himself as a fine athlete. He participated in the 1904 Olympic Games. For a short time he taught college mathematics in the East before moving to Texas after the first World War. There he turned professional and played, without much success, in several professional tournaments. In 1922 he designed and built the Hermann Park GC for the city of Houston and remained as its professional.
Bredemus is one of several rather obscure figures in golf course architecture. Legend has it that he was an eccentric, hating shoes, refusing to play with new golf balls, and considering the tops of tall trees to be ideal vantage points for golf course planning. It is nevertheless a fact that he did some of the finest layouts in the state of Texas during the 1920s and 30s. Towards the end of his Texas career he was assisted by Ralph Plummer, a young professional golfer who went on to make a name for himself as a course architect following World War II.
In the late 1930s Bredemus moved to Mexico following a dispute with the U. S. government over income taxes. He continued to design golf courses and at his death had over a half dozen fine Mexican layouts to his credit.
Courses by John Bredemus:
TEXAS: Brae Burn CC (formerly Colonial GC), Bellaire; Colonial CC, Forth Worth (1935); Edinburg CC (9); Galveston CC (n.l.e.); Galveston Muni (1931); Hermann Park GC, Houston (1923); Memorial Park GC, Houston (1935); Mercedes GC; Oso Beach GC, Corpus Christie (1939); Ridglea CC, Fort Worth (1930); Rockwood Muni; Sequin GC (9); Tenison Park Muni, Dallas (West course, 1924); Z. Boaz GC.
MEXICO: Acapulco CC; Churubusco CC; Club de Golf Hermosillo (n.l.e.); Guadalajara CC (9,1942; 9,1948); Monterrey CC; Tampico CC.
Courses Remodeled by John Bredemus:
MEXICO: Mexico City CC (1939).

Russell F. Breeden (1917–   ) Born Alvamar County Virginia.
A native of Virginia, Russell Breeden entered private practice as a golf course designer in 1961 after training under golf architect Fred Findlay. By 1980 he had designed over seventy courses, supervising construction of many of them. Breeden's work included several collaborations in which he drew up route plans with George and Tom Fazio designing greens, tees and bunkers.
Courses by Russell F. Breeden   Among his best-known are:
NORTH CAROLINA: Pawtucket GC, Charlotte; Pine Tree GC, Asheboro; RainTree GC, Charlotte; Rock Barn GC, Conover; Scotch Meadow GC, Morganton.
SOUTH CAROLINA: Bay Tree GC (5A, Routed); Bonnie Brae CC; Chester CC; Chickasaw Point GC; Cypress Bay GC; Huntington Hills GC, Spartanburg; Kings Grant GC, Charleston; Lady's Island GC, Beauford; Lan-Yair GC, Spartanburg; Linrick GC; Mid Carolina CC, Prosperity; Newberry CC (a.9,1977); Ocean Isle Beach GC; Pineland Plantation G&Hunt Club, Mayesville; Pine Ridge CC; Possom Trot; Quaker Meadows GC (27); Robbers Roost; Shadow Moss G&TC; (The) Widow Maker (1979); Wildwood CC.
VIRGINIA: City of Halloud Muni (Back 9); Jordan Point CC (9); Sleepy Hole Muni, Portsmouth; Suffolk GC.
Courses Remodeled by Russell F. Breeden:

William P. Brinkworth

William Brinkworth served as pro-greenkeeper and manager at Jasper Park GC in Alberta, Canada, from 1920 until his retirement in 1959. He laid out the Edmonton CC with Duncan Sutherland in the 1920s, the Derrick Club (1959) and the Elk Island National Park GC, all near Edmonton, Alberta.

Ernest Brown

Canadian designer "Ernie" Brown planned several excellent courses in his home province of British Columbia in the 1960s and 70s. He emphasized the family aspect of the country club by providing some form of outdoor activity for every member of the family. He also experimented with the covering of a portion of each tee for play on rainy days. Two of his best-known courses were the McLeery Municipal GC in Vancouver and the Prince George (British Columbia) CC.

Leslie Brownlee

A native of Scotland, Leslie Brownlee emigrated to America, where he served for several years as professional at the Fort Smith (Arkansas) CC. He designed the first golf courses in Oklahoma, including the nine-hole Muskogee CC (1907) and the Lakeview CC in Oklahoma City (9 holes, 1907). Brownlee's stepbrother, Arthur Jackson, was also a pioneer golf architect in Oklahoma.

Cuthbert Strachan Butchart (1876–1955)

Born: Carnoustie, Scotland. Died: Ossining, New York at age 79.

Cuthbert Butchart, one of twin sons of golf club maker John Butchart, became a professional golfer in his teens and at age twenty-three took a position as professional at Royal County Down in Northern Ireland. He remained there for several years, staking out or reconstructing a number of Irish courses before returning to Scotland in 1904.

After working as a professional and laying out a few courses in Scotland, Butchart moved on to Germany. There he laid out and built the Berlin GC, served as its professional and became golf teacher to German royalty. A fine golfer, he also won the 1913 German PGA. Several courses of his design were under construction in Germany when the Great War broke out. Butchart was interned and spent the next few years in a German prisoner-of-war camp.

Upon his release, Butchart returned to Scotland but soon moved to the United States, where he became head professional at the newly opened Westchester Biltmore CC in New York. He lived in America for the remainder of his life, spending summers in New York and winters in Florida. As a sideline, he began marketing handmade woods bearing his famous club-making family name. He also designed and remodeled several American courses, many of them in Florida during the boom of the 1920s.

Courses by Cuthbert Strachan Butchart:
GERMANY: Berlin G&CC (1911); Oppersdorf Estate GC, Berlin.
FLORIDA: Eustis CC (n.l.e.); Mayfair CC, Sanford (1927).
Courses Remodeled by Cuthbert Strachan Butchart:
ENGLAND: Highgate GC, London (1904).

Willard C. Byrd (1919–) ASGCA

Born: Whiteville, North Carolina.

Following military service in the U. S. Navy during World War II, Willard Byrd attended North Carolina State College, receiving a B.S. degree in landscape architecture in 1948. He was employed in recreational site planning with the U. S. Army Corps of Engineers and later worked as a land planning consultant in North Carolina and Florida. He then served as assistant manager and designer in the Southeastern office of a large landscape architecture and city planning firm.

In 1956 he founded Willard C. Byrd and Associates, Landscape Architects, Town Planners and Golf Course Architects. By 1979 Byrd's Atlanta, Georgia, based firm had completed some 720 projects, including work on seventy-five golf courses. His professional staff in 1979 included Herbert Windom, environmental scientist; Kenneth F. P. Skodacek, land use designer; Clyde B. Johnston, landscape architect; and N. C. (Lee) Chang, city planner.

Courses by Willard C. Byrd:
ALABAMA: Indian Oaks CC, Phenix City (1976).
FLORIDA: Bay Isles, Sarasota (27); Bay Point G&CC, Panama City (18,1972; 9,1975); Boca Raton (9); Breakers West GC, West Palm Beach (36,1970); Lake City CC (1970); Ponce de Leon GC, Augustine (r. 18,a.9).
GEORGIA: Ansley CC, Atlanta; Atlanta CC; Cherokee Town & CC, Atlanta (r.9, a.9) Dunwoody CC, Atlanta (1966); Francis Lake GC, Valdosta (1973); Griffin CC; Howell Station, Gwinnett Co. (36); Northwoods, Gwinnett Col; Savannah Inn & CC; Spring Hill, Tifton; Thomas County CC, Thomasville; Treasure Lake, Carroll Co.; White Path, Ellijay; Wilson CC.
NORTH CAROLINA: Beech Mt., Banner Elk; Brook Green CC, Guilford Co. (9); Carolina Sands, White Lake; Catawba CC, Newton (27,1973); CC of North Carolina, Pinehurst (18,c. Ellis Maples; a.9); CC of North Carolina, Raleigh (a.9); Gates Four CC; Irongate GC, Fayetteville; Lake Hickory CC (27); MacGregor Downs, Raleigh; Willow Creek GC, High Point.
SOUTH CAROLINA: Callawassie Island, Beaufort Co.; Litchfield GC; Patriots Point, Charleston; Porches Bluff, Mt. Pleasant (36); River Hills Plantation GC, York Co.; Seabrook Island GC, Charleston (Original 18,1973); Soco Gap, Jackson Co.
TENNESSEE: Fox Den, Knox Co.
TEXAS: Sun Harbors, Brownsville.

Alexander "Nipper" Campbell

Scottish professional golfer "Nipper" Campbell emigrated to Massachusetts around the time of the first World War. He later moved to Dayton, Ohio, where he designed and built the Moraine CC, staying on as professional. He consulted on the design or redesign of several other courses in that area, and in 1927 laid out the original nine holes of the Basin Harbor Club near Vergennes, Vermont.

Sir Guy Colin Campbell (1885–1960)

Born: England. Died: Irvington, Virginia, at age 75. Interred: St. Andrews, Scotland.

Sir Guy Campbell, great-grandson of Robert Chambers, early British golf historian and codesigner of the original nine-hole course at Hoylake, was educated at Eton and at the University of St. Andrews. He was a fine oarsman and cricket player as well as a golfer, and he won several medals in competition at St. Andrews. In 1907 he was a semifinalist in the British Amateur Championship.

During World War I, Campbell served in the infantry and was wounded in action. He also served in World War II as a member of the Royal Rifle Corps, although he was in his late fifties at the time.

Campbell joined the staff of the London Times in 1920 as a special correspondent and later as subeditor of sports under the legendary Bernard Darwin. He also wrote countless magazine articles on golf, as well as several books. Most notable was his contribution to A History of Golf in Britain (1952) edited by Darwin, in which he outlined the history of course architecture in Britain.

Campbell began designing golf courses in the late 1920s, working in conjunction with Cecil K. Hutchison and S. V. Hotchkin on a series of layouts. He maintained a steady practice during the 1930s and resumed it after the second World War. He assumed the hereditary rank of baronet upon the death of his father, Sir Guy T. Campbell, in 1931.

Courses by Sir Guy Colin Campbell:
ENGLAND: Ashridge GC, Hertfordshire (c.Hutchison & Hotchkin); Leeds Castle GC, Kent (c.Hutchison & Hotchkin); Prince's GC, Kent (r.Blue course,a.Red course, 1951); Shoreham GC, Southdown (c.Hutchison & Hotchkin); Trevose G&CC, Cornwall (r.18,a.9) Warsash GC (c. Hutchison & Hotchkin); West Sussex GC, Sussex (c.Hutchison & Hotchkin).
IRELAND: Killarney G&FC, County Kerry (Mahony's Point course, 1939).
THE NETHERLANDS: The Haagsche GC, The Hague (New site, 1947).
UNITED STATES: Tides Inn CC, Irvington, Virginia (Original 9, Tartan course, 1960).
Courses Remodeled by Sir Guy Colin Campbell:
ENGLAND: Felixstowe GC, Suffolk (1949); Royal Cinque Ports GC, Kent; Rye GC, Sussex; Seacroft GC, Lincolnshire.
IRELAND: Royal Dublin GC, County Dublin.
SCOTLAND: North Berwick GC ("West Links"), East Lothian (1930).

William "Willie" Campbell

Born in Musselburgh, Scotland, Willie Campbell planned two courses in the British Isles before emigrating to the United States. In 1894 he became the first professional at The Country Club, Brookline, Massachusetts, where he presided over one of its expansions and later planned other courses in the Northeast. During his years at The Country Club, Willie also served as professional at the Essex County Club in the summer months of July, August and September.

Courses by William "Willie" Campbell:
PENNSYLVANIA: Toorresdale CC (original 18).
RHODE ISLAND: Wannamoiset CC (original course).
ENGLAND: Seascale GC, Cumberland (original 9).
SCOTLAND: Islay GC, Argylshire [now Machrie GC].
Courses Remodeled by William "Willie" Campbell:
MASSACHUSETTS: The Country Club, Brookline (expansion to 9, 1894–5); Franklin Park Muni, Boston (1900). (Both were new layouts on sites of existing courses.)

Warren David Cantrell (1905–1967)

Born: Hillsboro, Texas. Died: Irving, Texas at age 61.

Warren Cantrell attended Armour Institute of Technology, Chicago, and Texas A & M, earning degrees in engineering and architecture. Following graduation he formed a contracting business in Texas. It evolved into a large operation, headed by his brother, which handled such major projects as the roof for the Houston Astrodome.

Cantrell himself left the firm in 1940 because of ill health. A fine golfer, he turned professional and became a club pro in Lubbock, Texas. He soon became involved in local and sectional PGA activities and was eventually elected treasurer and later president (1964–65) of the PGA of America. He also served as the golf coach at Texas Tech University from 1953 to 1958.

Cantrell designed his first course after World War II and by the 1950s was busy planning on a part-time basis throughout West Texas and New Mexico. He had completed some thirty courses by the time of his death.

Courses by Warren David Cantrell:
NEW MEXICO: Colonial CC, Farmington CC (9); Hobbs CC (r.9,a. 9, 1957); Lovington Muni (9,1954); Ocotillo Park GC, Hobbs (9,1955).
TEXAS: Andrews Muni (1955); Big Springs CC (new site, 1960); Gaines County GC, Seminole (original 9,1958); Lake Waco CC (18 and par 3); Lubbock CC (r.9,a.9); Old Elm GC, Abilene (1964); Robstown GC (1960); San Angelo CC; Tascosa CC; Treasure Island GC, Lubbock (1964); Webb AFB GC, Big Springs.
Courses Remodeled by Warren David Cantrell:
NEW MEXICO: Albuquerque CC.
TEXAS: Amarillo CC (1960); Meadowbrook Muni, Lubbock (27,1955).

William Cantrell (1929–)

Born: Lubbock, Texas.

Bill Cantrell, son of professional golfer and course designer Warren Cantrell, attended Texas Tech University, where he earned a degree in architecture. For several years he operated his own architectural firm in Lubbock. Upon the death of his father in 1967, Bill completed construction of the courses Warren left pending. The experience persuaded him to branch out into golf course architecture; and his first solo course, the Sierra Blanca CC in Texas, was designed and built in the early 1970s.

Billy Casper

See Harry M. Rainville and Don Collett

Thomas E. Clark (1948–   ) ASGCA

Born: Pennsylvania.

Thomas Clark attended Pennsylvania State University, receiving a B.S. degree in landscape architecture in 1971. Since that time he has been employed with the firm of Edmund B. Ault, Ltd.

Courses by Thomas E. Clark: See Edmund B. Ault

Percy Clifford (1907–   ) ASGCA

Born: Mexico City, Mexico.

Percy Clifford, six times Mexican Amateur Champion, six times runner-up, and three times Open Champion, attended Beaumont College in England. His first experience in course design came in the late 1940s when he assisted golf architect Lawrence Hughes in planning the Club de Golf Mexico. Envisioning a top-flight course, Clifford did much to organize the club and spent months personally selecting the site and reviewing the plans.

By 1980 Clifford had designed nearly half of Mexico's golf courses. His quality layouts, comparable to the best in Britain and America, contributed significantly to the advance of golf in his native country. But throughout his career, Percy deplored extravagance in both construction and maintenance of North American courses, pointing out that golf had originated and flourished for centuries in Scotland, where thrift is considered a virtue.

Clifford's daughter, Sandra Fullmer, was formerly Women's Amateur Champion of Mexico, Spain and Germany. His son-in-law, Paul Fullmer, was the first executive secretary of the American Society of Golf Course Architects.

Courses by Percy Clifford:

COLOMBIA: Club de Golf Baru (1973).

MEXICO: Acapulco, Centro Deportivo (9,1947); Bahia de Banderas, Vallarta Jalisco (1974); Campestre de Lagunero; Chihuahua CC (1956); Club Campestre, Chihuahua (1951); CC Morelia, Michoacan (1960); CC, CD Obregon, Sonora (1953); CC, Queretaro (1951); CC Torreon, Ocahuila (1973); Club de Golf Avandara (1950); CdG Bajamar, Baja (1974); CdG Bellavista, Mexico City (1955); CdG Bugambilian, Guadalajara (1964); CdG Cerro Alto, Tepic, May (9,1963); CdG Dos Mares, Ensenada, B.C. (1962); CdG Erandeni, Michoacan (1975); CdG Hacienda, Mexico City (1956); CdG La Canada, Mexico City (36, 1972); CdG La Villa-Rica, Vera Cruz (1971); CdG Laguna, Atizapan (36, 1969); CdG Mexico, Mexico City (1949); CdG Montecastillo, Morellos (1963); CdG Pierre-Marques, Acapulco (27,1970); CdG Piramides, Teotihuacan (36,1966); CdG Ranchitos, Morelos (1967); CdG Rio Seco, Valles (9,1961); CdG San Carlos, Toluca (1968); CdG San Gaspar, Morelos (1972); CdG San Luis, San Luis Potosi (1958); CdG Tabachines, Morelos (1973); CdG Vallescondido, Mexico City (1974); Cocoyoc GC, Morelos (c.J.Finger,1973); Del Lago CC, Edo (1970); La Huertas, San Juan Del Rio (1965); Los Flamingos CC, Puerto Vallarta (1975); Queretaro CC (1955).

Courses Remodeled by Percy Clifford:

MEXICO: Chapultepec GC (1972).

Lloyd Clifton

Originally a golf course superintendent, Lloyd Clifton designed numerous courses in the state of Florida.

Courses by Lloyd Clifton:

FLORIDA: Cypress Creek, Orlando (1970) Highland Lakes GC; Indigo G&TC, Daytona Beach; Land of Lakes G&CC; Rosemont GC, Winter Park (1973); Silver Pines Exec GC (9); Sweetwater Oaks CC, Longwood (1976); Tomoka Inn, Daytona Beach (1970); West Orange GC (1967); Willow Lakes GC, Jacksonville (2nd 18, 1974); Winter Pines, Winter Park (1968).

Courses Remodelled by Lloyd Clifton:

FLORIDA: Dubs Dread GC.

Paul Coates

Paul Coates maintained a golf design practice from the 1930s into the 1960s in Minnesota and neighboring states.

Courses by Paul Coates:

IOWA: Waveland Muni, Des Moines (1937).

MINNESOTA: Bloomington CC; Cedarholm Muni (9); Gem Lake Public GC (9); Hastings CC; Highland Greens CC; Keller Muni, St. Paul (1929); Mendota Heights Par 3 GC; Stillwater CC

Courses Remodeled by Paul Coates:

MINNESOTA: Midland Hills CC.

George W. Cobb (1914–   ) ASGCA

Born: Savannah, Georgia.

George Cobb attended the University of Georgia, graduating in 1937 with a degree in landscape architecture. He was employed by the National Park Service as a landscape architect until 1941, when he entered the U. S. Marine Corps as an engineering officer.

The Marine Corps recognized in Cobb, a landscape architect and scratch golfer, the makings of a golf course architect and ordered him to design and build the Paradise Point GC at

Camp LeJeune. In his own words, "Not wanting to be court martialled I asked and got permission to retain Fred Findlay as course architect." Cobb acted as construction superintendent on this course and on a second built with Findlay at Camp LeJeune after opening of the first.

Cobb's first solo project was at the Cherry Point North Carolina Marine Corps Air Station in 1946. He entered private practice as a golf architect in 1947 but was recalled to active duty in 1951. Following his second tour of duty, Cobb reentered private practice as a golf architect and land planner, opening his office in Greenville, South Carolina, in 1956. Since the late 1950s he has served as design consultant to the Augusta National GC.

Courses by George W. Cobb:

ALABAMA: Burningtree CC, Decatur (1966); Ft. McClellan GC, Anniston (9,1971); Goose Pond Colony, Scottsboro (1970); Inverness CC, Birmingham (1973); Pine Tree CC, Birmingham (1969); Still Waters CC, Dadeville (1972).

FLORIDA: Beau Clerc CC, Jacksonville (9,1961); Deerwood CC, Jacksonville (1961); Gainesville CC (1963); Indian Lakes CC (r.9,a.9).

GEORGIA: Augusta National GC (9 par 3, 1959); Brookfield West, Atlanta (1972); Browns Mill Road GC, Atlanta (1970); Double Gate CC, Albany (1964); Dublin (r. 9,a.9); Forest Heights CC, Statesboro (1966); Green sland CC, Columbus (1960); Lakeside CC, Atlanta (1960); Mary Calder GC (9,1967); Milledgeville CC (1961); Sea Palms CC, St. Simons (1967); Waynesboro CC (9,1963); Windsor Forest CC, Savannah (9, 1962).

MARYLAND: Fort Eustis GC (1956); Fort Meade GC (1956); Laurel CC (1957); Prospect Hill CC, Bowie (1956); University of Maryland GC, College Park (1956).

NEW YORK: Eisenhower College, Seneca (exec. 9,1972).

NORTH CAROLINA: Bald Head Island CC, Southport (1972); Bryan Park, Greensboro (1973); Cabarrus CC, Concord (1966); Carmel CC, Charlotte (1950); Cherry Point GC (1946); Connestee Falls CC, Brevard (1972); Croasdaile CC, Durham (1965); Finley GC, University of North Carolina, Chapel Hill (1951); Green Valley GC, Greensboro (1947); High Meadows GC, North Wilkesboro (1964); Hounds Ear CC, Blowing Rock (1963); Jacksonville CC (1951); Cleghorn Plantation, Rutherfordton (1972); Mt. Valley CC, Waynesville (18 a par 3,1961); Mountain Glen, Newland (1963); North Hills CC, Raleigh (1967); Oak Island CC, Southport (1962); Paradise Point GC, Camp LeJeune (1945); Pope AFB, Fayetteville (9,1970; 9,1974); Quail Hollow CC, Charlotte (1961); Raleigh Golf Association (9,1958); Rolling Hills CC, Monroe (1964); Sapphire Valley CC (1958); Willow Haven CC, Durham (1958).

OHIO: Sharon Club, Akron (1965).

SOUTH CAROLINA: Adventure Inn GC, Hilton Head (9 par 3,1965); Berkeley CC, Moncks Corner (1961); Botany Woods CC, Greenville (9 par 3,1963); Charleston AFB (9,1966); Cobb's Glen, Anderson (1974); Fort Jackson GC, Columbia (1949); Fripp Island CC (18, 1964;18,1976); Green Valley CC, Greenville (1958); Greenwood CC (9,1950; 9,1958); Hilton Head GC (1969); Holly Tree CC, Greenville (1973); J. C. Long Estate, Mt. Pleasant (9,1957); Keowee, Seneca (1973); Myrtlewood GC, Myrtle Beach (1966); Port Royal GC, Hilton Head (36,1966;9,1974); Santee-Cooper Resort, Santee (1968); Sea Pines, Hilton Head (Ocean course, 1967; Sea Marsh crs, 1961); Snee Farm CC, Charleston (1970); Spanish Wells CC, Hilton Head (9,1970); Spartanburg CC (9,1959); Spring Valley CC, Columbia (1961); Springs Mill GC, Fort Mill (9,1960); Star Fort National GC, Ninety-Six (1969); Surf Club, Myrtle Beach (1960); Woodbranch CC.

TENNESSEE: Clarksville CC (1966); Stonebridge, Memphis (1974); Warriors Path GC, Kingsport (1970).

VIRGINIA: Greenbrier G&CC (27); Red Wing Lake GC, Virginia Beach (1971); Tides Inn, Irvington (a.9, Tartan, 1968; Golden Eagle Course 1975); New Quarter Park (1977); Pohick Bay (1978).

WEST VIRGINIA: CC of Charleston (1969); Glade Springs CC, Beckley (1971); Glade Springs #2, Daniels (1975); Twin Falls State Park (a.9).

THE BAHAMAS: Andros Island CC (9 par 3,1965).

Courses Remodeled by George W. Cobb:

ALABAMA: Birmingham CC (1964); Green Valley CC, Birmingham (1963); Mountain Brook CC, Birmingham (1968); Vestavia CC, Birmingham (1962).

FLORIDA: Timaquana GC, Jacksonville (1963).

GEORGIA: Capital City Club, Atlanta (1962); Coosa CC, Rome (1973); East Lake CC, Atlanta (1960); Fort McPherson GC, Atlanta (1965); Savannah GC (1963).

MARYLAND: Aviation Y&CC.

NORTH CAROLINA: Chapel Hill CC (1957); Greensboro CC (1968); High Hampton GC, Cashiers (1958); Hill and Dale CC, Durham (1960); Starmount Forest CC, Greensboro (1972); Wildcat Cliffs CC, Highlands (1963).

SOUTH CAROLINA: Greenville CC (1960).

VIRGINIA: Army-Navy GC, (Fairfax Course); Bellehaven CC, Alexandria (1959).

John N. Cochran

John Cochran received his undergraduate degree in engineering and did graduate study on turfgrasses at Abraham Baldwin College in Georgia and Pennsylvania State University. He turned professional in 1937, working at clubs in Georgia and Mississippi until the late 1950s. He then became professional at Columbine CC near Denver and later at the Denver CC.

In 1962 Cochran resigned to found "Golf Club Operations, Inc.," a turnkey organization that designed, built, operated and trained the club management for its new golf courses. J. P. Maxwell served as the firm's in-house architect, and Cochran worked with him on the design and construction of Hiwan GC and Boulder CC. When Maxwell left in the mid-1960s, the company discontinued some of its functions, but Cochran continued the business by taking on the full responsibilities of golf course architect.

Courses by John N. Cochran:

COLORADO: City Park GC, Pueblo (r.18,a.9,1966); Dos Rios CC, Gunnison (9,1966); Fox Acres CC, Red Feather Lakes (9); Snowmass CC, Snowmass-at-Aspen (a.9,1973).

IOWA: Crow Valley CC, Bettendorf (1970).

Courses Remodeled by John N. Cochran:

COLORADO: Denver CC (3,1966).

LOUISIANA: Bayou Desiard CC, Monroe (1973).

Milton Coggins (1902–   ) ASGCA
Born: Arizona.
   Milton Coggins studied economics at the University of Redlands in California, receiving a B.A. degree in 1926. Having played basketball, baseball, tennis and golf, he operated a sporting goods store in the 1930s and then played professional tennis for eleven years.
   In 1950 Coggins became sports director at Camelback Inn in Phoenix and served as golf professional at Encanto Municipal GC where he remained until 1961. While at Encanto, he designed his first course in 1955–56, and after 1961 practiced golf architecture on a full-time basis.
Courses by Milton Coggins:
   ARIZONA: Apache Wells GC, Mesa (9,1966); Camelot GC, Mesa (18,1967;9,1974); Chris Town GC, Phoenix (9,1962); Coronada GC, Scottsdale (9,1976); Fort Huachuca (9,1970); Glen Lakes GC, Glendale (9,1968); Kingman CC (9,1973); Overgaard GC (9,1970); Paradise GC, Phoenix (9,1972); Pinetop CC (1961); Pinetop GC (Lakes)(1973); Prescott CC (1971); Rio Verde, Scottsdale (routing plan only, 1972); Rolling Hills Exec GC, Tempe; Spook Hill [formerly Bush Highway GC], Mesa (1977); Sun City (North)(1960); Sun City (South)(1962); Sun City Lake West (1968); Sunland Village GC, Mesa (9,1974); Villa Monterey GC, Scottsdale (9,1965).
   CALIFORNIA: Sun City (1963).
   COLORADO: Roaring Fork Ranch, Carbondale (9,1973)(Exec).
   FLORIDA: Sun City GC, Ruskin (9,1961).
   NEW MEXICO: Riodoso Alto (9,1968).
   TEXAS: Clear Lake GC, Houston (1964).

Don Collett
   A partner for a short time with Ken Welton, Don Collett continued to practice golf design on his own after Welton's death. He later formed an association with William "Bill" Casper.
Courses by Don Collett:
   TEXAS: Inwood Forest CC, Houston (1969); Kerrville Hills CC (1971).
Courses Remodelled by Don Collett:
   NEVADA: Desert Inn & CC.

Harry J. Collis (–1938)
Born: England. Died: Flossmoor, Illinois.
   Harry Collis emigrated to America in the late 1890s and became greenkeeper at the Indianapolis CC. In 1906 he moved to the Chicago area, where he was hired as pro-greenkeeper at the Flossmoor CC. While at Flossmoor, Collis remodeled the course into a popular tournament site, developed a turf cutter that was eventually patented and created a strain of bentgrass named after the club.
   The remodeling at Flossmoor led to other course design jobs, and after World War I Collis worked steadily on a part-time basis planning courses all across the United States. On occasion he collaborated with his friend Jack Daray, professional at nearby Olympia Fields CC. Collis also operated the Flossmoor Turf Nurseries of Chicago, specializing in Flossmoor bentgrass.
   In the late 1920s Collis resigned from Flossmoor CC to pursue his own activities full time. But the Depression intervened, and he was never able to develop a prosperous business. He struggled through the 1930s to maintain his turf farm and other Chicago-area properties before ultimately losing them to bankers and tax men. Flossmoor CC then offered Collis the position of course superintendent, which he accepted; but he died in 1938 just before his scheduled return to the club.
Courses by Harry J. Collis:
   ARIZONA: La Palma CC; Phoenix CC (1919); San Marcos Hotel & CC, Chandler (1922).
   FLORIDA: Homosassa CC.
   ILLINOIS: Cherry Hills CC, Flossmoor (original 18; a.18,n.l.e.; both c.Daray); Dundee CC; Freeport CC; Glenwoodie GC (c.Daray); Harlem Hills CC, Rockford; Indian Woods CC, Matteson; Navajo Fields CC, Worth; Normandy CC, Flossmoor; Park Forest GC (n.l.e.); Pistaqua Hills CC, McHenry.
   INDIANA: Longwood CC [formerly Casa del Mar CC], Dyer (original 18;2nd 18, n.l.e.).
   IOWA: Newton CC (9).
   MARYLAND: Manor CC, Rockville.
   MICHIGAN: Chickaming GC, Lakeside; Meadowbrook CC, Northville (1921,c.Daray); Walled Lake CC.
   MISSISSIPPI: Edgewater CC, Gulfport (n.l.e.).
   WISCONSIN: Rhinelander CC (a.2nd 9).
Courses Remodeled by Harry J. Collis:
   ILLINOIS: Flossmoor CC; Medinah CC (r.a.5 course # 3).

Harry Shapland Colt (1869–1951)
Born: St. Amands, England. Died: St. Amands, England at age 82.
   H. S. Colt studied law at Cambridge University, where he became captain of golf. He continued to practice as a solicitor for a number of years, although he had laid out his first course, the Rye GC, in 1894. In 1901 he became secretary of the new Sunningdale Club, a position he occupied until 1913. It was during these years that Colt developed into one of the world's leading golf architects, designing courses in Great Britain, on the Continent, in the United States and Canada. He remained active on his own and with associates after World War I.
   One of Colt's greatest triumphs was the Eden Course at St. Andrews, which he completed in 1913. The fact that he was awarded this prestigious contract indicates the esteem in which he was held. Colt also trained a number of men who themselves became leading architects, including Mackenzie, Alison, J.S.F. Morrison and J. Harris, the son of Colt's construction engineer. All became widely known in the field. Most of Colt's American courses were planned by his associate C. H. Alison, although Colt made three visits to North America.

   Several "firsts" in course design are generally attributed to H. S. Colt: He was the first designer not to have been a professional golfer; he was the first real "international" designer, although Willie Park, Jr., rivalled him; he was the first to prepare tree-planting plans for his layouts; and he was the first to use the drawing board consistently. Colt was the author of *Golf Course Architecture*, published in 1920.
   Contemporaries described Colt as a great and wonderful personality.
Courses by Harry Shapland Colt:
   GEORGIA: Sea Island GC (r.Plantation 9, a.Seaside 9, 1928, c.Alison).
   ILLINOIS: Briarwood CC, Deerfield (c.Alison); Knollwood Club, Lake Forest (c.Alison).
   MARYLAND: Burning Tree Club, Bethesda (c.Alison & Mackenzie,1924).
   MICHIGAN: CC of Detroit, Grosse Pointe Farms (c.Alison,1914); Detroit GC (1906); Lochmoor Club, Grosse Pointe Woods (c.Alison).
   NEW JERSEY: Pine Valley GC, Clementon (assisted on route plan).
   NEW YORK: The Century GC, White Plains (c.Alison); Park CC, Buffalo; Timber Point GC, Great River (c.Alison).
   WISCONSIN: Milwaukee CC (c.Alison).
   BELGIUM: Knokke Sur Mer GC (36); Royal Waterloo GC (36); Royal Zoute GC.
   CANADA: Hamilton G&CC, Ontario (1919); Pine Ridge CC, Manitoba; St. George's G&CC, Ontario (1920); Toronto GC, Ontario.
   ENGLAND: Barton on Sea, Hants; Berkshire GC (c.Fowler,1926); Blackmon, Hants; Brancepeth Castle GC, Durham; Brokenhurst GC, Hants; Burrhill GC; Camberley Heath, Surrey; Churston, Devons; Copthorne GC, Sussex; Cuddington GC, Surrey; Denham GC; Edgbaston GC, Birmingham; Effingham GC, Guildford; Hendon GC, London; Hopwood; Leamington and County; Leckford GC, Hants (c.Morrison); Lilleshall Hill, Shropshire; Little Aston; Moor Park; Newquay, Devons; Northamptonshire County GC; Northumberland GC; Oxney; Robin Hood GC, Birmingham; Rowlands Castle, Hants; Rye GC; St. Georges Hill, Surrey; Sandy Lodge GC, Herfordshire; Southfields GC; Stoke Poges GC, Buckinghamshire; Sunningdale CC, Berkshire (r.Old course, a.New course,1922); Swinley Forest GC; Tandridge; Teignmouth; Trevose G&CC, Cornwall; Tyneside, Newcastle; Wentworth Club, Surrey (36,c.Alison & Morrison,1924); Worplesdon GC, Surrey; Worthing GC, Sussex (36,1906).
   FRANCE: Cannes CC; GC De St. Cloud, Garches (36); GC Du Touquet, Pas de Calais (45).
   GERMANY: Frankfurter GC (c.Alison); Hamburger GC (c.Alison & Morrison).
   HOLLAND: Haagsche CC, Wassenaar (c.Alison & Morrison).
   IRELAND: Castle GC; County Sligo GC; Rosapenna GC, County Donegal; Royal Portrush GC, County Antrim (36,1915).
   NORTHERN IRELAND: Belvoir Park; Royal Belfast GC.
   SCOTLAND: Longniddry GC, East Lothian; Royal & Ancient GC of St. Andrews (Eden course,1912).
   SPAIN: Madrid Royal CC (1932); Real Club De La Puerto De Hierro, Madrid (c.Alison,1914); Real Pedrena GC, Santander.
   TRINIDAD: Moca GC, Maraval Valley; St. Andrews GC, Port of Spain (1940;n.l.e.).
   WALES: Borth and Ynysias; Clyne GC; Prestbury GC (c.Morrison); St. Mellon GC (c.Morrison & Cotton); Southerndown GC.
Courses Remodeled by Harry Shapland Colt:
   ILLINOIS: Bob O'Link GC, Highland Park (c.Alison & Mackenzie,1924); Lochmoor Club; Old Elm Club Highland Park (1913).
   MARYLAND: Chevy Chase CC (c.Alison & Mackenzie).
   MICHIGAN: CC of Detroit, Cc. Alison, 1927).
   PENNSYLVANIA: Baederwood CC [formerly Huntingdon Valley].
   ENGLAND: Alwoodley GC (c.Mackenzie); Broadstone, Dorset; Formby GC; Ganton GC (4); Handsworth GC; Harborne GC; Northampton County GC; Royal Liverpool GC, Hoylake; Royal Lytham and St. Anne's; Royal Wimbledon GC, London (1908); Sandiway GC; Sandwell GC; Woodhall Spa (1912).
   FRANCE: Golf de Biarritz.
   IRELAND: Royal Dublin GC.
   MALAYSIA: Selangor GC (a.bunkers,1931).
   SCOTLAND: Muirfield.
   WALES: Aberdovey; Porthcawl (1913).

William Connellan
   William Connellan was associated with Wilfrid Reid in the golf design firm of Reid and Connellan, after working as a construction superintendent for Donald Ross.
   See Wilfrid Reid.

Graham Cooke
   Graham Cooke was born in Toronto, Ontario, and attended Michigan State University, receiving a degree in landscape architecture in 1971. Returning to Canada, he trained under Quebec golf architect Howard Watson for the next six years.
   Cooke entered private practice in the late 1970s and by 1980 had completed the thirty-six-hole Dorval (P.Q.) Muni as well as numerous alterations to existing courses. In addition, he was runner-up in the 1979 Canadian Amateur Championship.

Geoffrey S. Cornish (1914–   ) ASGCA; President, 1975; BAGCA, Honorary Member
Born: Winnipeg, Manitoba, Canada.
   Geoffrey Cornish received a bachelor's degree from the University of British Columbia and a master's degree from the University of Massachusetts, both in agronomy. His interest in golf course architecture was aroused upon graduation in 1935, when he was hired to evaluate soils and find topsoil on the Capilano GC under construction in West Vancouver, B.C., after two of his classmates had turned the job down in favor of graduate school. He then trained for four years with golf architect Stanley Thompson and was later employed for a short time as greenkeeping superintendent at the St. Charles CC, Winnipeg, Canada.

During World War II Cornish served with the Canadian Army Overseas, returning to become an associate of Stanley Thompson in 1946 and '47. This was followed by an association with Lawrence S. Dickinson, pioneer turfgrass scientist, at the University of Massachusetts until 1952, when he entered private practice as a golf architect.

By 1980 Cornish had planned more courses in the New England states than any other architect in history. He had also designed and remodeled layouts in other parts of the United States, in Canada and in Europe. He was the author of numerous articles on course design and turfgrass subjects. In 1981 he received The Golf Course Superintendents Association of America Distinguished Service Award and in 1982 The Donald Ross Award.

In 1964 Cornish was joined by William G. Robinson, who in 1977 established the firm of Cornish and Robinson, Golf Course Designers, Ltd. of Calgary, Alberta. Together they prepared the publication *Golf Course Design—An Introduction*, distributed by the National Golf Foundation. See William G. Robinson.

Courses by Geoffrey S. Cornish: (All courses after 1964 in collaboration with William G. Robinson)

CONNECTICUT: Avon CC (a.9,1967); Blackledge CC, Hebron (1966); Cedar Knob CC, Somers (1963); Century Hills CC, Rocky Hill (1974); Cliffside CC, Simsbury (1959); Clinton CC (1967); Connecticut GC [formerly GC at Aspetuck], Easton (1966); CC of Fairfield (a.1); Crestbrook CC, Watertown (9,1962); Ellington Ridge CC (1959); Fairfield Muni (9 par 3,1968); The Farms CC, Wallingford (1961); Hop Meadow CC, Simsbury (1961); Laurel View Muni, Hamden (1969); Millbrook GC, (original 9, 1963); Minnechaug GC, Glastonbury (planned greens, one 9,1959); Neipsic Par 3, Glastonbury (1974); Oak Lane CC, Woodbridge (1961); Orange Hills GC, Milford (a.9,1957); Patton Brook Exec, Southington (1967); Pautipaug CC, Norwich (1960); Pequabuck CC, Bristol (a.3); Portland GC :1974; Quinnatisset CC, Putnam (a.9,1967); Simsbury Farms Muni (1971); Sterling Farms Muni, Stamford (1971); Watertown CC (a.9,1970); Westwoods Exec. CC, Farmington (1964).

MAINE: Bangor Muni (1963); Brunswick CC (9,1964); Riverside Muni, Portland (a.9,1967); Running Hills CC, Frye Island; Waterville CC (a.9,1966).

MARYLAND: Towson G&CC (Eagles Nest 9) (1971).

MASSACHUSETTS: Allendale CC, New Bedford (9,1954;9,1961); Blue Rock, South Yarmouth (18 par 3,1961); Brewster Green CC (a.2,1979); Chicopee Muni (1964); Cranberry Valley GC, Harwich (1974); Crestview CC, Agawam (1957); Crestwood CC, Rehoboth (1959); Crystal Springs GC, Haverhill (1960); Duxbury Yacht Club (a.9,1969); Edgewood CC, Southwick (1963); Ellinwood CC, Athol (a.9,1969); Fall River CC (a.9,1975); Far Corner Farm GC, West Boxford (1967); Farm Neck GC on the Vineyard, Martha's Vineyard (9,1976); Foxborough CC (1955 & 1970); Grasmere, Falmouth (9 par 3); Greylock Glen CC, Adams (1973); Heritage Hills, Lakeville (18 par 3,1970); Hickory Ridge CC, Amherst (1969); Holly Ridge Par 3, South Sandwich (1966); Hyannis Par 3 (1966); Indian Meadow CC, Westboro (1960); Indian Ridge CC, Andover (1961); International CC, Bolton (1956); Iyanough Hills CC, Hyannis (1975); Juniper Hills GC, Northboro (a.9,1952); Marlborough CC (a.9,1969); Middleton GC (18 par 3,1965); Nashawtuc CC, Concord (1961); Pine Oaks GC, Easton (9,1966); Poquoy Brook GC, Lakeville (1963); Powder Horn, Lexington (18 par 3,1964); Rehoboth GC (1966); Ridders GC, Whitman (a.9,1963); Segregansett CC, Taunton (a.9,1976); Shaker Farms CC, Westfield (1954); Spring Valley CC, Sharon (1960); Stow Acres (a.9,1959; a.18,1965); Sun Valley CC, Seekonk (1956); Swansea GC (1962); The Thomson Club, North Reading (1963); Thunderbird, Tyngsboro (18 par 3,1963); Trull Brook GC, North Tewksbury (1962); Veteran's Memorial GC, Springfield (1960); Wahconah CC, Dalton (a.9,1959); Wampatuck CC, Canton (9,1957); Wareham CC (1963); Wellesley CC (9,1961); White Cliffs GC, Plymouth (9,1961).

NEW HAMPSHIRE: Beaver Meadows Muni, Concord (a.9,1968); Bretwood GC, Keene (1967); Eastman Lake GC, Grantham (1971 & 75); Sunningdale GC, Dover (9,1961); Westworth by the Sea, Portsmouth (a.9,1965); White Mountain CC [now Cold Spring GC], Ashland (1976).

NEW JERSEY: Bowling Green GC, Milton (1966); Packanack Lake CC (9,1963).

NEW YORK: Addison Pinnacle CC (9,1969); Colonie CC, near Albany (1963); CC of Ithaca (1958); Endwell Greens GC, Johnson City (1965); Grassy Brook GC, Alder Creek (9,1974); Heritage of Westchester, Somers (9,1974;18,1980); Higby Hills CC, Utica (1966); Highland Park CC, Auburn (a.9,1973); Honey Hill CC, Newport (1967); Ives Hill CC, Watertown (a.9,1974); Oswego CC (a.9,1971); Shepard Hill CC, Waverly (a.9,1970); Sodus Point GC (a.9;r.9,1966); St. Lawrence University GC, Canton (a.12,1971); Vesper Hills CC, Otisco; Vestal Hills CC. Binghamton (1957).

OHIO: Westfield CC (r.9,a.9,1967;a.18,1974); Zoar Village GC (1974).

PENNSYLVANIA: Concordville CC, Concord (a.4,1972); Hershey Poconos [formerly Le Chateau CC], White Haven (1970); Host Farms Exec. GC, Lancaster (9,1967); Mill Race GC, Benton (9,1973; a.9,1977); River Valley CC, Westfield (9,1962); Standing Stone GC, Huntingdon (1972); Sugarloaf GC (1966); Wilkes-Barre Muni (1967).

RHODE ISLAND: Alpine CC, Cranston (1960); Cranston CC (1974); Exeter CC (1964); Kirkbrae CC, Lincoln (1961); Quidnessett CC, East Greenwich (1959 & 1974); Valley Ledgemont, West Warwick (a.9,1963); Warwick CC (a.9,1953); Wimnisucket CC, Woonsocket (a.9,1961); Woodland CC, North Kingston (9,1963).

VERMONT: Farms Motel GC, Morrisville (18 par 3,1970); Manchester CC (1969); Montague GC (a.3); Mt. Snow GC (1970); Quechee Lakes CC (Highland & Lakeland,18,1970;18,1975); Stratton Mountain Golf Academy (1969); Stratton Mountain GC (1967).

WEST VIRGINIA: Canaan Valley State Park GC (1966); Pipestem State Park GC (18,1966;9 par 3,1966); Twin Falls State Park GC (9,1966).

CANADA: Campobello Provincial Park GC, New Brunswick (9,1974); Halifax G&CC (The New Ashburn), Nova Scotia (1969); Summerlea G&CC. Montreal, Quebec (Dorion and Cascades courses,1960); York Downs G&CC, Toronto, Ontario (27,1970).

GREECE: The Links at Porto Carras, New Marmoras (1975).

Courses Remodeled by Geoffrey S. Cornish: (All courses after 1964 in collaboration with William G. Robinson)

CONNECTICUT: Avon CC (1962–66); Fairfield CC (hole # 10,1960); Farmington CC (1); Glastonbury Hills GC (4); Hartford GC (2,1972); Keney Park Muni, Hartford (3); New London CC (5); Stanley Muni, New Britain (27,1973–75); Weeburn CC (3); Wethersfield CC (Hole

4); Woodway CC, Darien (4 and ponds).

DELAWARE: Dupont Golf Course, Dupont CC (Montchanin, Louviers and Nemours courses, 1979–80).

MAINE: Webhannet GC, Kennebunkport (4).

MASSACHUSETTS: Berkshire Hills CC (4 and lake); Braeburn CC, Newton (Holes # 11 & 12, 1970); The Country Club, Brookline (Holes # 1,4,17 & 18,1960, 63 & 69); Dedham Polo and Hunt Club (2); Framingham CC (2); Franconia Muni (6,1970–73); Fresh Pond GC, Cambridge (9,1967); Longmeadow CC (Hole # 11 and practice areas); Meadow Brook CC (9,1960–64); Myopia Hunt Club (Lake, bunkers & trees, 1960–62); Oakhill CC (5); Quabog GC, Monson (2); Tatnuck GC, Worcester (4); Weston GC (2); Woodland GC (18,1960–64); Worcester CC (2).

MINNESOTA: Somerset CC, St. Paul (Pond, trees & bunkers,1979); Woodhill CC, Minneapolis (1979).

NEW JERSEY: Knickerbocker CC, Tenafly (6).

NEW YORK: CC of Buffalo (Pond & trees,1965); Monroe CC, Rochester (Hole # 1,1965); Thendara GC (Hole # 12,1968); Westwood CC, Buffalo (Lakes,1959).

OHIO: Avon Oaks CC (Ponds, bunkers & trees,1978); Canterbury CC (Trees & bunkering,1978); Dayton CC (Hole # 18 and trees,1965); Miami Valley CC (Trees,1965); Portage CC (Trees, 1965); Youngstown CC (2).

RHODE ISLAND: Agawam Hunt Club (1963); Metacomet (Holes # 3 & 4,1957); Point Judith CC (9,1964); Rhode Island CC (Hole # 10,1960);

VERMONT: Ekwanok CC (8,1957–65).

CANADA: Breezy Bend CC, Winnipeg (18,1973); Elm Ridge CC, Winnipeg (2,1978); Fredericton GC, New Brunswick (2); Point Grey G&CC, Vancouver (18,1967–73); Quilchena GC, Vancouver (6).

Charles Kenneth Cotton (1887–1974) BAGCA: Founding Member; Chairman, 1971; President, 1974.
Born: England. Died: Reading, England.

C. K. Cotton graduated from Cambridge University, became a scratch golfer and served as secretary of several clubs. In 1946 he founded the golf architecture firm of Cotton (C.K.), Pennink, Lawrie and Partners, Ltd., whose associates have included John Harris, Frank Pennink, Charles Lawrie and D. M. A. Steel.

Courses by Charles Kenneth Cotton:

DENMARK: Randers GC (9); St. Knuds (c.Pennink).

ENGLAND: Brickendon on Grange, Heath; Castle Eden; Downfield GC; Frilford Heath, Berks (New course); Maisden Park, Lanc. (c.F.W.Hawtree); Peterlee; Ross on Wye; St. Pierre, Monmouthshire (36); Wentworth (Short course, 1948) (9).

ITALY: Olgiata GC, Rome; Venice GC (1958).

SINGAPORE: Singapore Islands Course (Island Course. 1927).

WALES: Brnyill GC; Royal Portcawl GC (1950); St. Pierre GC (36, C. Pennink).

Courses Remodeled by Charles Kenneth Cotton:

ENGLAND: Blackwell GC; Ganton GC; Hexham GC (1956); Royal Lytham and St. Anne's (1952); Saunton GC, Devonshire (1951); West Lancashire GC.

Thomas Henry Cotton (1907–   ) BAGCA (Honorary Member)
Born: Holmes Chapel, Cheshire, England.

Henry Cotton has been described as the greatest British golfer of his day. He was trained as a golf architect by Sir Guy Campbell, beginning with war damage appraisals following World War II and later worked with J. Hamilton Stutt. Cotton made a hobby of planning low-cost courses utilizing every natural feature, but also designed many lavish layouts in Britain, on the Continent and in the Madeira Islands. He worked with a variety of terrains ranging from swamps and rice fields to pine forests. His layout at Penina in Portugal involved the planting of tens of thousands of trees, many growing ten or more feet per year.

In the course of his nearly sixty-year career, Cotton wrote ten books and in his own words "contributed to golf journals and newspapers nonstop since 1931." He claimed never to have counted courses designed nor tournaments won but to remember each vividly. An excellent short account of his golfing career is contained in the *Shell International Encyclopedia of Golf* edited by Steel and Ryde.

Courses by Thomas Henry Cotton:

ENGLAND: Abridge GC; Ampfield (par-3 course); Canon's Brook GC (1962); Coventry GC; Ely City, Cambridge; Sene Valley GC; Windmill Hill, Bucks.

FRANCE: Mont D'Arbois GC (1968; New GC (a.9).

PORTUGAL: Monte Gordo GC; Vale do Lobo GC; Penina GC (27).

SCOTLAND: Gourock GC; Windy Hill GC.

SPAIN: Real Club at Puerto De Hierro, Madrid.

Courses Remodeled by Thomas Henry Cotton:

ENGLAND: Felixstowe Ferry GC; Temple GC; Wolverhampton GC; Eaglescliffe and District GC.

CHANNEL ISLANDS: La Moye GC.

SCOTLAND: Stirling GC.

Archibald "Pete" Craig
"Pete" Craig served as pro-superintendent at Penfield CC in New York until the late 1950s when he resigned to design and build golf courses on a full-time basis.

Courses by Archibald "Pete" Craig:

NEW YORK: Ballston Spa & CC (r.9,a.9,1965); Clifton Springs CC (new site, 1962); Craig Hill GC, Brockport (1966); Francourt Farms GC, Elmira (1963); Green Hills GC, Rochester; Island Valley GC, Rochester (1961); Northway Heights G&CC, Ballston Lake; Penfield CC; Sunnycrest, Rochester (27); Thunder Ridge CC, Rush (1973); Twin Hills GC, Spencerport (1970); Winged Pheasant GC, Farmington (1963); College GC, Delhi.

Arthur Capel Molyneux Croome (1866–1930)
Born: Stroud, Gloucestershire, England. Died: Maidenhead, Berkshire, England, at age 64.

Educated at Wellington and Oxford, A. C. M. Croome was one of Britain's great sportsmen, playing cricket, rugby and track at school, and golf, curling and billiards later. Following graduation, he accepted a post as schoolmaster, athletic coach and house parent at the Radley school where he remained until 1910. It was during this period that Croome took up golf, and he was soon competing in the British Amateur and other championships.

At the turn of the century, Croome founded the Oxford and Cambridge Golfing Society with his friends John L. Low and R. H. DeMontmorency. The group played exhibition matches on both sides of the Atlantic and numbered C. H. Alison among its early members. "Crumbo," as Croome was called by his friends, served as captain, and later president, of the Society.

Croome supplemented his income at Radley by writing articles on golf for London newspapers, notably the *Evening Standard* and *Morning Post*. Following his retirement from Radley, he turned to journalism full time, covering cricket for the *London Times* as well as continuing his golf columns.

While a newspaperman, Croome met and formed a lasting friendship with golf architect J. F. Abercromby. Fascinated by the design aspect of the sport, Croome assisted "Aber" on the design of several British courses and after World War I became a partner in the golf architectural firm of Fowler, Abercromby, Simpson and Croome. His role was primarily that of business manager and publicist for the company, but he was entirely responsible for the design of at least one course, the Liphook GC in the heathlands. Although the excellence of this course caused it to be considered a design milestone, Croome was prevented from further participation in the field of course design by the ill health that plagued the last years of his life.

George Arthur Crump (–1918)
Born: Philadelphia, Pennsylvania. Died: Merchantville, New Jersey. Interred: Philadelphia.

George Crump, the wealthy owner of the Hotel Colonnades in Philadelphia, was an avid hunter, fisherman and golfer, finishing as runner-up in the 1912 Philadelphia Amateur. He was among the founders of the Philadelphia CC before the turn of the century and played most of his golf there. But he harbored a dream of building his own golf course in the sand hills of New Jersey and in 1912 convinced a syndicate of friends to invest in the project.

Crump sold his hotel, purchased 184 acres of sand hills near Clementon, New Jersey, and moved to the site to create his dream. The Pine Valley GC became one of the world's toughest courses, one of its best and certainly the most ferociously penal. Crump spent the last six years of his life and over a quarter million of his own dollars in developing it. Many professional golf architects examined the work in progress, but only Britisher H. S. Colt was invited to make recommendations. Colt, impressed by Crump's basic design and carefully planned holes, suggested few major modifications. (On an earlier visit, Colt had helped with the route plan.)

George Crump died suddenly in January 1918. Fourteen holes at Pine Valley were completed at the time, but numbers 12 through 15 had only been roughed out. It took time to raise the necessary funds and four more years to complete construction, but under the guidance of Hugh Wilson, aided by his brother Alan and Britisher C. H. Alison, the full eighteen holes of the Pine Valley GC finally opened in 1922. George Crump's creation is a landmark in course architecture.

George Curtis
Formerly a course superintendent, George Curtis took up golf architecture in 1960.
Courses by George Curtis:
LOUISIANA: Pine Hills GC, West Mountain (1974).
MISSISSIPPI: Fernwood CC, McComb (1969); Liveoaks CC, Jackson; Pine Hills CC (1969); Rolling Hills CC.
TENNESSEE: Houston Levee CC, Memphis (1971); Milan CC (1960).

James Dalgleish (1865–1935)
Born: Berkshire, England. Died: Kansas City, Missouri, at age 70.

James Dalgleish was one of the many young British golfers who moved to America in the late 1890s. He landed a job managing the golf department for the A. G. Spalding & Bros. Sporting Goods Store in New York City, where he remained for five years. After brief stints at clubs in New York and Vermont, Dalgleish moved to Kansas City, Missouri, where he laid out and built the Evanston CC and remained as its pro/greenkeeper.

Dalgleish became the dean of golf professionals in the Kansas City area and was a charter member, in 1927, of the organization now known as the Golf Course Superintendents Association of America. He laid out a number of courses across the Midwest; but much of his work, done in the early days of American golf development, is now gone.
Courses by James Dalgleish:
KANSAS: Chevy Chase CC, Kansas City (1931,n.l.e.); Homestead CC, Prairie Village (n.l.e.); Victory Hills CC, Kansas City (1927). [Wichita CC, now MacDonald Park Muni].
MINNESOTA: Pine Beach East GC, Madden Beach (1926).
MISSOURI: Evanston GC, Kansas City (1903,n.l.e.); St. Andrews GC, Kansas City (n.l.e.); Swope Park GC, Kansas City (Course # 1, 1917).
NEBRASKA: Valley View GC, Omaha (1926,n.l.e.).

Jack L. Daray, Sr. (1881–1958)   ASGCA; Charter Member
Born: Louisiana. Died: Coronado, California, at age 76.

Jack Daray turned professional in 1901 and served as club pro at Highland CC, Grand Rapids, Michigan, and then at Olympia Fields CC near Chicago for many years. He also worked as winter pro at clubs along the Mississippi Gulf Coast. Among Daray's students were Princeton University president Woodrow Wilson (later president of the United States) and baseball great Ty Cobb.

Daray was one of a number of Chicago professionals who designed courses on the side during the 1920s. He kept active in the thirties and resumed his design work after World War

172

II. Although ill health necessitated his move to southern California in the early 1950s, he was still designing courses at the time of his death.

Jack Daray was a charter member of the PGA of America in 1916. His elder son, Captain Jack Daray, Jr., took up the practice of course architecture in the late 1970s after retiring from a naval career.
Courses by Jack L. Daray, Sr.:
ALABAMA: Old Spanish Fort CC, Mobile; Roebuck CC, Birmingham.
CALIFORNIA: Admiral Baker Memorial GC, U.S. Navy Base, San Diego (1956); Circle R. Ranch GC, Escondido; Coronado Muni GC (1957); North Island Naval Air Station GC, San Diego; Port Hueneme GC; Sail Ho! Par 3 GC; Sea and Air Exec. GC.
ILLINOIS: Cherry Hills CC, Flossmoor (original 18,c.Collis,1932); Glenwoodie GC, Chicago Heights (c.Collis); Melody Farms CC, Lake Forest; White Pines CC, Bensenville (1930).
LOUISIANA: Metairie CC, New Orleans (1925); Tchefuncta Park GC, Mandeville.
MICHIGAN: Big Rapids CC; Cascade Hills CC, Grand Rapids; Grand Rapids CC; Gull Lakeview GC, Richland ("West" course); Hastings CC (original 9,1922); Highland CC, Grand Rapids; Meadowbrook CC, Northville (c.Collis,1921).
MISSISSIPPI: Greenville CC (1950); Gulf Hills GC, Ocean Springs (1922); Edgewater GC, Biloxi (c.Collins) (n.l.e.).

John R. Darrah (–1971) ASGCA
Born: Chicago, Illinois.

John Darrah received a degree in engineering from Crane College in Chicago, worked as an engineer for a coal firm in Wyoming, and then returned to Illinois to work for the Union Fuel Company. Darrah resigned in 1931 due to ill health and after his recovery, took a position as greenkeeper at the Beverly CC near Chicago, where he remained until 1947. He then moved to the Olympia Fields CC, where he restored the two remaining courses after the complex had been almost abandoned during the war.

In 1949 Darrah left Olympia Fields to form a golf course construction business. After rebuilding and renovating many Chicago-area courses, he began designing as well as building. In the 1960s he planned several dozen courses in the Midwest.
Courses by John R. Darrah:
ILLINOIS: Arispie Lake CC, Princeton (9,1968); Kankakee CC (r.8,a.10,1963); Morris CC (new site,1970).
INDIANA: Arrowbrook CC, Chesterfield; Valparaiso CC (r.9,a.9,1962).
KENTUCKY: Hopkinsville G&CC (1971); London CC (new site,1969).
MISSISSIPPI: Back Acres CC, Senatobia (r.9,a.9,1967).

Arthur L. Davis (1939–   ) ASGCA
Born: Georgia.

Arthur Davis attended Abraham Baldwin College in Tifton, Georgia, where he worked part-time for Ray Jensen, owner of the Southern Turf Nurseries specializing in newly developed hybrid Bermuda grasses. In the course of his work, Davis met golf architects Robert Trent Jones, George Cobb, Dick Wilson, William Mitchell, Alfred Tull and others. The experience convinced him to change his major from agronomy to landscape architecture, and he received the B.L.A. degree from the University of Georgia in 1963.

Following graduation, Davis was employed with the firm of Willard C. Byrd and Associates until 1967, when he established his own practice in Atlanta. In 1970 he was joined by Ron Kirby in the firm of Davis, Player and Kirby, Inc., but in 1973 returned to private practice as a landscape and golf architect, Arthur L. Davis, inc., Rome, Georgia.

Davis felt that two experiences significantly influenced his own design techniques: an extended visit to the links and other British courses made in the early 1970s, and working with Jim Shirley, golf professional and construction superintendent who built several courses for Ellis Maples.
Courses by Arthur L. Davis: (D.P.K. indicates courses done by firm of Davis, Player and Kirby, Inc.)
FLORIDA: Pointe West GC, New Port Richey (9,1977).
GEORGIA: Arrowhead GC, Hasper (9,1968); Berkeley Hills GC, Norcross (9, 1971, D.P.K.); Cartersville CC (r.9,a.9,1972,D.P.K.); Cross Creek CC, Atlanta (c.J. Shirley, 1967); Dunwoody CC, Atlanta (c. W. Byrd, 1966); Green Acres GC, Dexter (9,1969); Old Town CC, Zebulon (9,1968); Pebble Brook CC, Manchester (9,1970); Pine Isle GC, Lake Lanier Island (1972, D.P.K.); River North CC, Macon (1973, D.P.K.); River Oaks GC, Cartersville (9,1971, D.P.K.); Twin Creek CC.
ILLINOIS: Holiday Inn GC, Crete (9,1970,D.P.K.).
NEW MEXICO: Alto Village CC (9,1973,D.P.K.).
SOUTH CAROLINA: Dolphin Head GC, Hilton Head (1973,D.P.K.).
TENNESSEE: Centennial Estates CC, Chattanooga (1977); Cobbly Nob GC, Gatlinburg (9,1971;9,1972;D.P.K.); Lawrenceburg CC (r.4,a.9,1976); Montclair CC, Chattanooga (r.9,a.9,1977).
AFRICA: Riviera Africaine GC, Abidjan, Ivory Coast (1972,D.P.K.).
JAPAN: Odawara CC (1973,D.P.K.).
PUERTO RICO: Palmas del Mar GC, Palmas (1973,D.P.K.).
SPAIN: El Paraiso GC, Marbella (1972,D.P.K.).
Courses Remodeled by Arthur L. Davis:
GEORGIA: Evan Heights GC, Claxton (9,1977); Little Mountain CC, McDonough (9,1970, D.P.K.); Robins AFB GC, Warner Robins (9 greens, 1970, D.P.K.); Standard Club, Atlanta (1971, D.P.K.).
TENNESSEE: Chattanooga G&CC (4,1975); Stones River CC, Murfreesboro (9,1977).

John Davis BAGCA
John Davis, a scratch golfer, holds the degree of B.Sc. He became a partner in the British golf design firm of Hawtree and Son in 1974. See F. W. Hawtree.

William F. Davis
William Davis left Hoylake, England, to take up duties as pro-greenkeeper at Royal Montreal around 1881. After a few years he moved on to the United States, where he designed the

Newport CC in Rhode Island. He is believed to have planned several other courses in New York and New England while serving as professional at Apawamis CC in New York. Because he was too busy to do so himself, he recommended the Canadian engineer Henry Hewett to plan the Tuxedo (N.Y.) CC.

Around 1889 Davis returned to Montreal for a few years and is thought to have laid out several courses in eastern Canada before settling as professional at the Newport CC in Rhode Island. Among his courses was the Ottawa (Ontario) CC, which no longer exists.

John Warren Dawson (1903–)
Born: Wheaton, Illinois.

The son of an Australian who emigrated to the Chicago area before the turn of the century, Johnny Dawson was one of four brothers who became prominent golfers. In his competitive career, Dawson was often a runner-up (in the 1928 North & South Amateur, the 1935 Mexican Amateur, the 1947 U. S. Amateur and the 1958 U. S. Senior Amateur), as well as winning several tournaments (including the 1936 Trans-Mississippi, and the California and Iowa Opens as an amateur).

After World War II Dawson became involved in the development of the desert regions of southern California and is generally considered to be the "Father of Palm Springs, California," It was through his efforts, beginning in the 1940s and continuing into the 1970s, that the area grew into a golfing oasis.

Dawson's first golf design experience came when he lured Lawrence Hughes from Colorado to design the Mission Valley CC in San Diego. Dawson soon arranged for Hughes to create the Thunderbird CC, which opened in 1947 and was probably the first of the post-war golf course housing developments.

Dawson served as a land planner, coordinating real estate efforts with golfing interests and acting as consultant to many golf architects on southern California projects. He worked with Lawrence Hughes on two other courses in Palm Springs, Eldorado (1958) and La Quinta (1959). He also assisted "Dick" Wilson with the Annenberg GC (and with the North Redoubt Club in New York) and Robert Trent Jones at Pauma Valley CC. In 1955 he collaborated with T. Ben Harmon on the Silverado CC at Napa, California, and in the 1970s worked with Ted Robinson on Westlake, Seven Lakes, Marrakesh and Desert Horizons, all in the Palm Springs area.

Edward B. Dearie, Jr. (1888–1952)
Born: Philadelphia, Pennsylvania. Died: Evanston, Illinois, at age 64.

Edward Dearie was a noted authority on golf course construction and maintenance. He began his career as greenkeeper at Wanango CC in Reno, Pennsylvania, and later spent several years building courses for golf architect Donald Ross in Pennsylvania and Illinois.

In 1921 Dearie settled at the Ridgemoor CC in Chicago. Ten years later he moved to the Oak Park CC, where he served as course superintendent until his retirement in 1951. During the 1920s and 30s he built a dozen new courses and remodeled an equal number in the greater Chicago area.

Dearie was a charter member of both the National Greenkeepers Association and the Midwest Association of Greenkeepers. He wrote extensively on the construction and upkeep of golf courses for national periodicals in the 1920s and 30s.
Courses by Edward B. Dearie, Jr.:
ILLINOIS: Big Oaks CC, Chicago; Lincoln Park Muni, Chicago; River Forest GC, Bensenville; Rob Roy GC, Chicago; Saint Andrews G&CC (36); Sportsman's G&CC, Northbrook (36).
Courses Remodeled by Edward B. Dearie, Jr.:
ILLINOIS: La Grange CC; Ridgemoor CC, Chicago; Oake Park CC; Twin Orchards CC (n.l.e.).

James Newton Demaret (1910–)
James Demaret, former night club singer and formidable golfer, was co-owner with Jack Burke of the Champions GC in Houston, Texas. He collaborated with several golf and landscape architects in planning courses and on his own designed the Onion Creek CC in Texas.

Bruce Devlin (1937–)
Born: Armidale, New South Wales, Australia.

Bruce Devlin took up golf at the age of thirteen. Although trained as a plumber by his father, eventually attaining the rank of master plumber, he also played a great deal of amateur golf. After winning the 1959 Australian Amateur and the 1960 Australian Open, he turned professional, moved to the United States and won nine tournaments on the PGA tour and many events around the world.

In 1966 Devlin was asked by members of the Lakes GC in New South Wales to recommend an architect to redesign their course. He had always admired the work of American "Dick" Wilson, who had died the previous year, so he suggested a Wilson trainee, Robert von Hagge. Devlin worked closely with von Hagge on remodeling of the Lakes, and the two soon formed a partnership in Australia. In 1969 they expanded into the United States as the firm of Von Hagge and Devlin.

From the beginning Devlin took an active role in the construction of the firm's courses; and as his professional career slowed, he assumed increased design responsibilities. Three of the firm's courses laid out primarily by Devlin were Crockett Springs National in Tennessee, Sheoah GC in Florida and Walden on Lake Conroe in Texas.
Courses by Bruce Devlin: See Robert von Hagge

Mark De Vries (1927–)
Mark De Vries attended Michigan State University, receiving a B.A. degree in landscape architecture in 1949. He was employed in that capacity with the Grand Rapids (Michigan) Department of Parks until 1963, when he entered private practice as a landscape architect.
Courses by Mark De Vries:
MICHIGAN: Alpine GC (1965); Broadmoor GC, Caledonia (1963); Chase Hammond GC, Muskegon (1969); Courtland Hills GC, Rockford (1979); English Hills GC, Walker (9,1973); Foremost Insurance Co. GC, Cascade Township (9,1973); Hickory Hills CC, Grand Rapids

(a.9,1979); Saskatoon GC, Alto (27,1963); Springfield Oaks GC, Pontiac (1974); Tyler's Creek GC; Western Greens GC, Wright Township (1963); Whispering Willows GC, Livonia (1966).

Gardiner Dickinson
Professional golfer Gardiner Dickinson designed two eighteen-hole courses at Frenchman Creek GC in Florida in 1975. He also planned revisions to Sawgrass, another Florida layout.

William H. Diddel (1884–) ASGCA: Charter Member; President, 1954, 1965.
Born: Indianapolis, Indiana.

Bill Diddel, who began playing golf before 1900, caddied for British Open Champion Alex Herd in 1902 when Herd was playing an exhibition match in Indiana. Diddel himself won the Indiana State Amateur in 1905, '06, '07, '10 and '12.

Diddel began designing golf courses in the 1920s and was active as a course architect through the 1960s. In the 1940s and 50s his firm was known as Diddel and Johnson.
Courses by William H. Diddel:
ARKANSAS: Hot Springs G&CC (courses 1 and 3) Arlington course,1932).
COLORADO: Denver CC (new site).
FLORIDA: Bardmoor CC, Largo (18,1970;a.18,1974); CC of Naples (1963); Jupiter Island Club, Hope Sound; Ormond Beach CC.
ILLINOIS: Edgewood Valley CC; Rolling Greens CC; Sunset Ridge CC, Northbrook (1924).
INDIANA: Beechwood GC; Benton County GC, Fowler; Brookshire GC, Carmel (1971); CC of Indianapolis; Crawfordsville Muni (1931); Elcona CC, Elkhart (1955); Ft. Harrison GC (1967); Fox Cliff CC, Martinsville (1970); Green Hills G&CC, Selma; Greentree CC, Carmel; Hawthorne Hills GC, Indianapolis (27,1963); Highland G&CC, Indianapolis (1921); Hilltop Farms GC, Martion (1957); HomeLawn Mineral Springs GC (1953); Martinsville CC (1925); Meridian Hills (1923); Oak Hill GC, Middlebury (1962); Park County GC (Purdue University (North course); Rozella Ford GC; Shady Hills GC; Speedway 500 GC, Indianapolis (1928); Tipton Muni (9,1936;a.9,1967); Walnut Grove GC, Albany (1969); Wawasee; Woodland GC, Carmel (1951).
KANSAS: Wichita CC (1950).
KENTUCKY: Highland CC; Wildwood CC, Louisville (1952).
MICHIGAN: Forest Lake CC, Bloomfield Hills (1926); Hidden Valley Club, Gaylord (1957); Shanty Creek Lodge GC.
OHIO: Fairborn CC; Hamilton Muni (1951); Kenwood CC, Cincinnati (36,1930); Meadowbrook CC, Dayton (2nd 9,1956); Miami View GC, Miamitown (1961); Sharon Woods CC; Swaim Fields GC, Cincinnati (1933); Twin Run GC; Wright Patterson AFB GC.
OKLAHOMA: Mohawk Park Muni, Tulsa (orig. 18, 1934).
TEXAS: Northwood Club, Dallas (1948).
Courses Remodeled by William H. Diddel:
ARKANSAS: Hot Springs G&CC (Course # 1, Now South).
ILLINOIS: Westmoreland CC, Wilmette (1963).
INDIANA: Evansville CC; Fort Wayne CC (1950).
KANSAS: Mission Hills CC, Shawnee Mission.
KENTUCKY: Big Spring CC, Louisville (1951).
MICHIGAN: Barton Hills CC, Ann Arbor; Black River CC, Port Huron (1956).
MONTANA: Harve Elks CC, Harve.
OHIO: Still Meadow CC (1965).
PENNSYLVANIA: Shawnee on Delaware, Stroudsburg.
CANADA: Hamilton G&CC, Ancaster, Ontario.

William H. Dietsch, Jr. (1928–)
Born: Atlanta, Georgia.

William Dietsch graduated from Staunton Military Academy in 1946 and attended the University of Pennsylvania, where he majored in mechanical engineering. He then served with the U. S. Army and was a witness to the first test of the hydrogen bomb in the South Pacific. Following military duty, Dietsch started in course maintenance in 1955 under superintendent Scott Tuppen. Shortly thereafter, Tuppen was hired to build courses for Robert Trent Jones, and he took his assistant with him. Dietsch worked for the Jones organization for twelve years, and for part of the time was closely associated with architect Francis Duane, then with the Jones firm.

Dietsch entered private practice as a course architect in 1967. His philosophy has demanded close involvement in the construction of all courses of his design.
Courses by William H. Dietsch, Jr.:
FLORIDA: CC of Miami (South); Development Corporation of America, Spring Tree Exec GC (9); Lakeview GC, Delray; Oriole Homes, Inc., Margate (18 championship & 9 exec.); Oriole Homes, Inc., Villages of Oriole, Delray; Rolling Hills CC, Davie (a.9); Southern International Corporation par 3, Miami; Spring Tree Exec GC (9); W.B. Homes, Inc., Sunrise (9 exec.).
Courses Remodeled by William H. Dietsch, Jr.:
FLORIDA: Pasadena GC, St. Petersburg.

Francis J. Duane (1921–) ASGCA; President, 1972
Born: Bronx, New York.

Francis Duane studied landscape architecture at the State University of New York, graduating in 1944. He was employed for a short time as a landscape architect with the New Hampshire Department of Forestry and Recreation.

In 1945 Duane became associated with the firm of Robert Trent Jones, where he remained until 1963 when he entered private practice as a golf course architect. He later formed an association with golfer Arnold Palmer and then returned to private practice on his own.
Courses by Francis J. Duane: (A number of these were in collaboration with Arnold Palmer.)
CALIFORNIA: Half Moon Bay CC (1972).
FLORIDA: Lake St. George CC [now Mariner Sands CC], Stuart (1973); The Meadows

CC, Sarasota (1976); Spring Lake G&CC.
  GEORGIA: The Landings at Skidaway Is. (original 18, c. Palmer,1973)
  HAWAII: Honolulu International CC (1976); Kapalua GC, Maui (1974).
  MONTANA: Big Sky Meadow Village GC, Gallatin County (1972).
  NEW JERSEY: Howell Park GC, Monmouth County (1971); Montammy CC, Alpine (1966); Pleasant Valley CC, West Orange (9,1964); Preakness Valley Park GC; Tamcrest CC, Cresskill(9,1970).
  NEW YORK: Bellevue CC, Syracuse (r.14,a.4,1972); Brae Burn CC, Purchase (1964); Golf Hill G&CC; Merrick Park GC (9,1967); North Shore Towers GC, Little Neck (1976); Osiris CC, Walden (9,1965); Pleasant View Lodge, Freehold (9,1968:9,1978); Rock Hill G&CC, Manorville (1966); Spook Rock GC, Ramapo (1969); The Sycamores, Coeymans (1972); Tall Timbers CC, Slingerlands (1967); Wildwood CC [formerly Hampton GC], Riverhead (1964); Sound Shore GC.
  NORTH CAROLINA: Sugar Hollow GC, Banner Elk (1974).
  SOUTH CAROLINA: Myrtle Beach National GC (54,1973 c. Palmer); Sea Pines Plantation, Hilton Head (Club course, 1973).
  VERMONT: Fox Run GC, Ludlow (9,1968); Sugarbush GC, Warren (c.R.T.Jones,1964).
  VIRGINIA: Massanutten GC (9,1975).
Courses Remodeled by Francis J. Duane:
  CONNECTICUT: Innis Arden GC, Old Greenwich (1964); Milbrook GC, Greenwich (3,1964); Patterson CC, Fairfield (1,1971).
  NEW JERSEY: Crestmont CC, West Orange (3,1963); Essex County CC, West Orange (9,1967).
  NEW YORK: Blue Hill GC, Orangetown (1970); Cherry Valley Club, Garden City (12,1978); Douglaston Park GC (5,1964); Elmwood CC, White Plains (1,1977); Engineers CC, Roslyn Harbor (3,1970;18,1977); Garden City CC (6,1970); Glen Oaks Club, Great Neck (1,1964); Hampshire CC, Mamaroneck (4,1964); IBM CC, Sands Point (1,1978); Inwood CC (1972); Latourette GC, Staten Island (4,1964); Mill River CC, Brookville (4,1971); Muttontown G&CC (1,1964); Nassau CC, Glen Cove (1970); Old Oaks CC, Purchase (6, 1968); Old Westbury CC (2, 1972); Quaker Ridge GC, Scarsdale (16,1964); Richmond County CC, Staten Island (4,1970); Ridgeway CC, White Plains (9,1976); Rockville CC (1,1965); Sands Point GC (1964); Scarsdale GC (4,1965); The Seawane Club, Hewlett Harbor (1964); South Forks CC, Amagansett (3,1974); Woodcrest CC, Muttontown (1976).
  VERMONT: Marble Island G&YC, Colchester (9,1964).

George Duncan (1893–1964)
Born: Aberdeen, Scotland.
  George Duncan won the British Open in 1920 and was runner-up in 1927. A member of the Ryder Cup team for several years, he served as its captain in 1929.
  Duncan laid out several courses on his own and in collaboration with his friends James Braid and Abe Mitchell. He was primarily responsible for restoring the course at Royal Dornoch to eighteen holes after World War II. Duncan added four new holes to replace four lost to the R.A.F. The tour "lost" holes were later returned to Royal Dornoch and made into the short, nine-hole Struie course.
Courses by George Duncan:
  ENGLAND: Hallowes, Yorkshire (c.Mitchell); Harrogate, Yorkshire; Mere G&CC (c.Braid); Tapton Park, Derby; Wheatley, Yorkshire.
  SCOTLAND: Royal Dornoch (a.4); Stonehaven GC.

William "Old Willie" Dunn (1821–1878)
Born: Musselburgh, Scotland.
  "Old" Willie Dunn was the patriarch of a distinguished line of professional golfers and course designers. He was born into a golfing family, although his father was a plasterer by trade. Conjecture has it that a Dunn was in part responsible for the interest of King James I in golf at Leith. Whether or not this is true, the name of Dunn has been renowned in the world of golf for centuries.
  "Old" Willie was partnered with his twin brother James in a famous challenge match played over St. Andrews, Musselburgh and North Berwick for the huge purse of 400 pounds. The "Twa (two) Dunn" were losers to the pair of Allan Robertson and "Old" Tom Morris.
  In 1850 Willie undertook the duties of greenkeeper and professional at Royal Blackheath in England where he was joined two years later by James. After twenty years they returned to Scotland, first to Leith, later to Musselburgh, and then to North Berwick. "Old" Willie is known to have rebuilt several holes at Royal Blackheath, to have designed the first Wimbledon course for the London Scottish Regiment in 1865 and to have planned a number of three-hole layouts on private estates.
  Four golf course designers who became famous on both sides of the Atlantic were sons or grandsons of "Old" Willie:

The Dunn Family

Several of Willie's other descendants became well-known professional or amateur golfers in Great Britain and the United States. Cameron and Robert Dunn, both sons of Seymour, became prominent American professionals, while Norman "Dick" Dunn, "Young" Willie's son, returned to England, served in the British Army during World War I and later became well known as an amateur golfer in Great Britain.

John Duncan Dunn (1874–1951)
Born: North Berwick, Scotland. Died: Los Angeles, California, at age 67.
  J. D. Dunn trained as a professional, greenkeeper and course builder under his father, Tom Dunn. After laying out a few courses in Britain and on the Continent, he followed his uncle "Young" Willie, only nine years his senior, to the United States in 1894. He worked briefly with Slazengers and Bridgeport Arms and then acquired the post of professional at the newly opened Ardsley-on-Hudson course designed by Willie.
  By 1900 J. D. was in charge of planning, building and operating golf courses for the Florida West Coast Railroad. Around the same time or earlier, he collaborated with Walter Travis on the design of several courses in the Northeast. Throughout these years he made numerous trips back to Britain and the Continent, on his own or in the company of his brother Seymour, who had joined him in America.
  J. D. settled in California after World War I, when he was hired as professional by the Los Angeles CC. He continued to reside in that state until his death. An excellent teacher of golf, J. D. was also a competent landscape artist and the author of numerous magazine articles and books on golf instruction.
Courses by John Duncan Dunn:
  CALIFORNIA: Atascadero CC; Avalon CC, Catalina Island [now Catalina GC]; Brockway CC, Lake Tahoe; Lake Elsinore GC (n.l.e.); Lake Norconian Club, Norco (1928,n.l.e.); Los Serranos Lake CC, Chino (1924); Peter Pan CC, Big Bear; Rio Hondo CC, Downey.
  FLORIDA: Bellair GC (9,1899); Gables GC (9,1898, n.l.e.); Oscala GC (9, n.l.e.); Tampa Bay GC (1898, n.l.e.); Winter Park GC (1900, n.l.e.).
  NEW YORK: Long Beach Hotel GC (1900,n.l.e.); Muifield Golf Links, Middle Bay (1931,n.l.e.); Quaker Ridge CC, Mamaroneck (1915).
  VERMONT: Ekwanok, Manchester (c.Travis, 1900).
  ENGLAND: Lee-on-Solent.
  FRANCE: Dinard GC.
  NETHERLANDS: Doorn GC; Haagsche GC, The Hague (n.l.e.).

Seymour Dunn (1882–1959)
Born: Prestwick, Scotland. Died: Lake Placid, New York, at age 77.
  Seymour Dunn traveled to America at age twelve to work as assistant to his brother, J. D. Dunn, at Ardsley-on-Hudson. He later held numerous professional and golf teaching positions on both sides of the Atlantic, among them the Griswold Hotel, New London, Connecticut (1896), Lawrenceville School (1898), Stevens Hotel, Lake Placid (1900) and later Ealing in England, La Boulie, France, and Royal County Down. According to his son, Cameron, Seymour settled down in 1906 at the Lake Placid CC to raise a family, but by the 1930s he was on the move again.
  Throughout his career, Seymour traveled back and forth to Great Britain on a number of business ventures, sometimes accompanied by J. D. Two of the brothers' most notable ventures were the establishment in 1900 of the first indoor golf school at Bournemouth, England, and the later founding of a similar school, the world's largest, in New York City.
  Seymour Dunn ranks among the great teachers of golfing fundamentals, numbering Jim Barnes, Walter Hagen, Gene Sarazen and Joe Kirkwood among his students. He was the author of *Golf Fundamentals, Elementary Golf Instruction, Standardized Golf Instruction* and *Golf Jokes.* The latter by Stravin Publishers, New York (1953), included an autobiography in its introduction.
Courses by Seymour Dunn:
  FLORIDA: Lake Placid Club, Sebring; Silver Spring, Oscala (n.l.e.).
  MISSISSIPPI: Laurel CC.
  NEW HAMPSHIRE: Ferncliffe CC.
  NEW JERSEY: Monmouth CC; Suneagles CC.
  NEW YORK: Ausable Club; Cazenovia CC (one 9); Chattaqua CC; Craig Wood CC (1st 9); The Fawn Club; Lafayette CC; Lake Placid CC (Lower course); Locust Hill CC, Pittsford (original 9,1928); Paul Smiths; Raquette Lake; Saranac Inn; Schroon Lake CC; Ticonderoga CC; Tuscarora CC.
  BELGIUM: Knock Sur Mer; Terverun; Private Course for King Leopold; Antwerp GC.
  ITALY: Florence; Private Course for King Emmanuel.
Courses Remodeled by Seymour Dunn:
  FRANCE: La Boulie.
  IRELAND: Royal County Down.

Tom Dunn (1849–1902)
Born: Royal Blackheath, England. Died: Blagdon, England, at age 52.
  Tom Dunn became professional at Wimbledon (London Scottish) in 1870. This course had originally been laid out by his father, "Old" Willie Dunn, with eighteen holes but over the years had been reduced to seven. In his first year, Tom redid the course, extending it again to eighteen holes. He later held the post of professional at North Berwick, Tooting Bec near London, Meyrich Park in Bournemouth and at other courses.
  Tom Dunn was the most prolific course designer of his day. He produced layouts that were inexpensive and serviceable, making it possible for increasing numbers of golfers from all social classes to take up the game, particularly in England. He is quoted as saying repeatedly: "God meant this site to· be a golf course." The first inland, as opposed to links, designer, he was a firm believer in a cross bunker requiring a carry from the tee, another for the approach and a third for a three-shot hole. Dunn himself considered Broadstone in England, where he was "not stinted for men, money or materials," to be one of his best efforts and Meyrich Park to be his greatest challenge because of its dense cover of heather, furze and pine forest.
  Tom was married to Isabel Gourlay, "the greatest woman golfer of her day" and a descendant of the Gourlays of Musselburgh, renowned as golf instructors to the kings of Scotland and later as ball makers to the Royal Family of Great Britain. Tom traveled to America on several occasions, visiting brother "Young" Willie, sons John Duncan and Seymour, and

174

daughter May, who was a pioneer woman professional golfer.

Despite his presence in the United States, it is doubtful that Tom ever laid out an American golf course. He is thought by his grandson Cameron Dunn to have planned a course at Palatka, Florida, that was never built, and is believed by some to have done the old Tampa Bay Hotel course. But while many a club in the United States claims to have a Tom Dunn course, these layouts were all designed by one of the other Dunns. Tom's work in Great Britain and on the Continent, however, is extensive, and he claimed to have some 137 courses to his credit.

An important account of Tom Dunn's career, prepared by Seymour's son Cameron from his grandfather's random notes, appeared in *The Professional Golfer* in April and May of 1969.

Courses by Tom Dunn were located at or may have borne these names:

CANARY ISLANDS: Ralara.
FRANCE: Coubert; Dinard.
GREAT BRITAIN: Ashley Park; Bath; Babraham; Balham; Bedstone Court; Beckenham; Brighton; Broadstone; Bromley; Brooke; Bulwell; Buscot; Chiselhurst; Deal; Deer Park at Richmond; Eltham; Enfield; Eridge Park; Fan Court; Forest Nottingham; Frinton-On-Sea; Frome; Furzedown; Ganton; Harold; Hempstead Park; Hinksen Marsh; Hurlingham; Kingsdown; Landsdown; Maidenhead; Meyrich Park, Dorset; Mid Surrey; Newmarket; Norbury; Petworth; Raynes Park; Richmond; Saham; Saunton; Seaford; Sevenoaks; Sheffield; Sheringham; Shireoaks; Seacroft; Slengingford; Stairmore, Northwood; Staunton; Surbriton; Tooting Bec; Ventnor; Waddesden Manor; Walton-On-Thames; Welbech Abbey; Weston Super; Mare; Wicham; Wimbledon (Royal); Woking; Worlingham; Worlington and Newmarket.

Courses Remodeled by Tom Dunn:
GREAT BRITAIN: Hastings (extended); Littlestone; Seaford; Wimbledon (London Scottish).

William "Young Willie" Dunn (1865–1952)
Born: Musselburgh, Scotland. Died: London, England, at age 87.

"Young" Willie Dunn trained as a professional, greenkeeper and course builder under his brother Tom, sixteen years his senior, who was then in England. According to Henderson and Stirk[1], Willie served as professional at Westward Ho! for a few months in 1886 or '87 and then laid out the Chingford course near London before moving on to Biarritz in France. While working as professional at this club, which he had helped his brother to build, Willie met W. K. Vanderbilt and was persuaded to try his hand at an American course.

Willie was the first Dunn to relocate to the New World, and the course he created for the Vanderbilt syndicate, Shinnecock Hills on Long Island, opened with twelve holes in 1891. To build it, he had employed a crew of 150 Indians, none of whom had ever seen a golf course, golf ball or club. Willie remained at Shinnecock for several years as pro-greenkeeper and won the unofficial U. S. Open in 1894. As a golfer, he was among the first to experiment with steel shafts and cardboard tees.

As a designer, Willie was ahead of the heathlands architects in utilizing an occasional lateral bunker in place of the traditional cross bunker. He was also the first of the colorful American designers of fluctuating fortune who experienced periods of great wealth followed by periods of near penury during which his family would be dispatched home to England to await improved circumstances. According to his son Norman William "Dick" Dunn, "Young" Willie numbered John D. Rockefeller, John L. Sullivan, "Buffalo Bill" and Zane Grey among his close friends.

Until 1910 Willie remained on the eastern seaboard, laying out courses and working as a pro-greenkeeper, making occasional trips back to Britain and the Continent. Later he was employed as a club designer with the firm of Crawford, MacGregor and Canby Company of Dayton, Ohio, according to nephew Cameron Dunn. In the early 1920s Willie was located in St. Louis and years later, in the Palo Alto–Menlo Park area of California. He returned to England in 1940 and remained there until his death in 1952.[1] Henderson and Stirk, *Golf in the Making*, p.107.

Courses by William "Young Willie" Dunn:
CALIFORNIA: Willie is believed to have collaborated on several courses in this state with J. D. Dunn.
CONNECTICUT: New Canaan CC (Original course, 1898).
GEORGIA: Jekyll Island CC.
IOWA: Algona CC (9,1920).
MARYLAND: Baltimore CC (Rolland Park course, n.l.e.).
NEW JERSEY: Lakewood CC; Lawrence Harbour CC.
NEW YORK: Ardsley on Hudson; Elmira CC (9); Shinnecock Hills (n.l.e.); Scarsdale CC (original 9); Westbrook CC, Great River.
PENNSYLVANIA: Philadelphia CC [now Bala CC].
ENGLAND: Chingford, near London (c.T.Dunn).
FRANCE: Biarritz (c.T.Dunn).
CANADA: Royal Montreal GC (at Dixie), near Montreal (18,1900;r.1903;n.l.e.).

Robert Charles Dunning (1901–1979)
Born: Kansas City, Kansas. Died: Emporia, Kansas, at age 78.

Bob Dunning attended military academies, where he excelled at all sports, and for a time played semi-pro baseball. He then attended Kansas University and Emporia State College, receiving a B.A. degree in 1921.

Following college, he turned professional and after apprenticing under Art Hall of Kansas City became pro-greenkeeper at McAlester (Oklahoma) CC. He worked on several course remodeling jobs while at McAlester and then in the mid-1930s attended the Massachusetts Turfgrass School, where he met Dr. John Monteith. He joined Monteith as an assistant in 1940.

Dunning spent World War II with the Army Corps of Engineers developing Bermuda grass runways in Texas. After the War he assisted Ralph Plummer in establishing several veterans' hospital courses in the South and then formed a successful turf equipment business based in Tulsa, Oklahoma. During the 1950s, Dunning was highly regarded as a turfgrass expert and greens consultant. His Texas experience had convinced him that golf greens could be built

on bases consisting almost entirely of sand, and he converted several sand green courses in Oklahoma to sand-base grass greens with great success.

Dunning retired from his equipment business in 1960 and with the assistance of his wife, Inez, devoted the next eighteen years to the full-time design and construction of golf courses. The death of his wife and his own health forced him to retire in 1978.

Courses by Robert Charles Dunning:
KANSAS: Alvamar Hills GC, Lawrence (Jayhawk 9 and Quail Creek 9,1968); Dub's Dread GC, Piper (1963); Happy Hunting CC, Lenexa; Leawood South CC (1969); Pawnee Prairie Muni, Wichita (1970).
MISSOURI: Blue Hills G&CC, Kansas City (1964); Excelsior Springs GC (a.par 3); Holiday Hills CC, Branson.
OKLAHOMA: Elk City G&CC (1953); Guymon CC; Hobart CC (9,1965); Pauls Valley G&CC; Pauls Valley Muni (9,1951); Sunset CC, Bartlesville; Woodward Muni (1954).

Courses Remodeled by Robert Charles Dunning:
KANSAS: Coffeyville CC (r.& rebuilt greens); Indian Hills CC, Prairie Village (rebuilt greens); Kansas City CC, Shawnee Mission (rebuilt greens); MacDonald Park Muni, Wichita (rebuilt greens); Meadowbrook CC, Prairie Village (rebuilt greens); Mission Hills CC, Shawnee Mission (rebuilt greens); Sim Park Muni, Wichita (rebuilt greens).
MISSOURI: Hickory Hills CC, Springfield; St. Joseph CC (rebuilt greens).
OKLAHOMA: McAlester CC (r.9,a.grass greens,1935).

Paul "Pete" Dye (1925–   ) ASGCA
Born: Urbana, Ohio.

After attending Rollins College and Stetson University in Florida, Pete Dye was employed as a life insurance salesman in Indianapolis. A fine amateur golfer, he won the Indiana Amateur in 1958 after being runner-up in 1954 and 1955. He also served as chairman of the Green Committee at the CC of Indianapolis, where he guided the club through a major replanting of its course. In 1959 Dye left the insurance business after becoming one of the youngest "life insurance millionaires" in his company. He laid out his first course the same year and was soon embarked on a career in course design, working for a short time with golf architect William Newcomb.

Dye had done a series of low-budget courses in the Midwest by 1963, when he and his wife toured the great courses of Scotland. When they returned, Dye began to incorporate several of the features he had observed in Scotland, including small greens, pot bunkers and railroad ties, into his own designs. The characteristic Dye style that evolved had considerable impact on late-twentieth century course architecture.

Throughout his career, Dye's wife, Alice, a top amateur golfer, was an invaluable source of advice. In addition, Dye was assisted on several projects in the late 1960s by tournament golfer Jack Nicklaus and in 1969 was joined in practice by his brother Roy Dye. Pete Dye was the subject of a superb two-part article by Herbert Warren Wind in *Golf Digest*, May and June 1978.

Courses by Paul "Pete" Dye:
ARIZONA: Paradise Village GC; Carefree Ranch Club.
CALIFORNIA: La Quinta Cove GC (27,1977); Carmel Valley Ranch GC (1980).
COLORADO: CC of Colorado, Colorado Springs (c.R.Dye,1973).
FLORIDA: Amelia Island Plantation, Fernadina Beach (27,1974); Delray Dunes G&CC, Delray Beach (1969); John's Island Club, Vero Beach (36,1974); The Moorings, Vero Beach (1972); Tournament Players Club, Ponte Vedra Beach (1979).
ILLINOIS: Bob Goalby/Yorktown Par 3 GC, Belleville (1963); Oakwood CC, Coal Valley (1964).
INDIANA: Crooked Stick GC, Carmel (1964); Eagle Creek Muni, Indianapolis (1974); El Dorado CC, Indianapolis; Elks Lodge #2186 GC, Plainfield; Harbour Trees GC, Noblesville; Heather Hills CC, Indianapolis; Monticello CC; North Eastway Muni, Castleton (1963).
IOWA: Des Moines G&CC (36,1968).
MARYLAND: Martingham G&TC, St. Michaels (c.R.Dye,1971).
MICHIGAN: Brandywine CC, Niles (1963); Radrick Farms GC, Ann Arbor; Wabeek CC, Bloomfield Hills (c.R.Dye,1971).
MISSISSIPPI: Marsh Island GC, Ocean Springs (1974) [now Pine Island GC].
NEW MEXICO: Alto Village GC (a.9);.
NORTH CAROLINA: The Cardinal GC, Greensboro (1975); Oak Hollow GC, High Point (1972).
OHIO: Avalon Lakes GC, Warren (1967); The Golf Club, New Albany (1967); J. D. Wright Recreation (T.R.W.), Chesterland (c.R.Dye,1972); Little Turtle Club, Granville (c.R.Dye,1973).
OKLAHOMA: Oak Tree CC, Edmond (18, 1976;a.9,1978); Oak Tree G&CC.
SOUTH CAROLINA: Harbour Town Golf Links, Hilton Head Island (1969); Long Cove GC, Hilton Head Plantation.
TEXAS: Waterwood National GC, Huntsville (c.R.Dye,1974).
VIRGINIA: Kingsmill GC, Williamsburg (1975).
WISCONSIN: Playboy Club & Hotel GC, Lake Geneva (Briarpatch course,1971).
DOMINICAN REPUBLIC: Campo de Golf Cajuiles, La Romana (Teeth of the Dog, 1971; Links, 1976).
MEXICO: El Palmar GC, Las Hadas (c.R.Dye,1974); San Carlos CC, Guayamas (1977); San Gil CC.

Courses Remodeled by Paul "Pete" Dye:
ARIZONA: Randolph Muni (North course).
FLORIDA: Marco Island CC.
INDIANA: The CC of Indianapolis.
NEBRASKA: The CC of Lincoln (3,1964).
CANADA: The CC of Montreal (c.R.Dye,1975).

Roy A. Dye (1929–   ) ASGCA
Born: Springfield, Ohio.

Roy Dye graduated from Yale University with a bachelor's degree in chemical engineering. Since 1969, he has practiced golf course design in association with brother Pete Dye.
Courses by Roy A. Dye: See Paul Dye.

Henry Chandler Egan (1884–1936)
Born: Chicago, Illinois. Died: Everett, Washington, at age 51. Interred: Medford, Oregon.
H. Chandler Egan graduated from Harvard in 1905. He was one of the top early college amateur golfers in America: NCAA Champion in 1902; U. S. Amateur Champion in 1904 and 1905 and runner-up in 1909; and Western Amateur Champion in 1902, 1904, 1905 and 1907.
In the early 1910s Egan retired from national competition and moved to an apple farm in Medford, Oregon. From it he introduced golf to southwestern Oregon and competed successfully along the West Coast, winning the Pacific Northwest Amateur title in 1915, 1920, 1923, 1925 and 1932. He is perhaps best known for his 1929 "comeback" on the national level, when he reached the semi-finals of the U. S. Amateur at the age of forty-five. He was selected as a member of the 1930 and 1934 Walker Cup teams.
Egan became involved in golf course design shortly after his move to Medford. He laid out his first course there in 1911 and subsequently designed and built several other Pacific Northwest courses. He revised the Pebble Beach Golf Links specifically for the 1929 Amateur, where he played such outstanding golf. Egan was constructing a course in Washington at the time of his unexpected death from pneumonia.
Courses by Henry Chandler Egan:
CALIFORNIA: Bayside Muni, Eureka (1933); Pacific Grove Golf Links (Original 9,1932).
OREGON: Bend G&CC (9,1926); Coos CC, Coos Bay (9); Eastmoreland GC, Portland (1921); Eugene CC (1926); Medford CC; Oswego Lake CC (1926); Rogue Valley CC, Medford (1911); West Hills Muni, Portland (1924;n.l.e.).
WASHINGTON: Indian Canyon GC, Spokane (1935); Legion Memorial GC, Everett (1937).
Courses Remodeled by Henry Chandler Egan:
CALIFORNIA: Pebble Beach Golf Links (1928).
OREGON: Waverley CC, Portland.

Devereux Emmet (1861–1934)
Born: New York. Died: Garden City, New York, at age 73.
Devereux Emmet was the son of a judge and a descendant of Thomas Addison Emmet, a founder of Tammany Hall. The Emmet family was listed in Ward McAllister's *First Forty Families in America*, and "Dev" and prominent architect Stanford White married sisters who were nieces of A. T. Steward.
Emmet was a golfer and huntsman. For two decades he routinely bought hunting dogs in the South in the spring, trained them on Long Island through the summer, took them to Ireland for sale in the autumn and then spent the winter hunting and golfing in the British Isles. One such winter was devoted to measuring British golf holes for his friend C. B. Macdonald, who was then planning the National Golf Links.
Emmet's earliest design work, including the Island Golf Links, Cherry Valley (built on property belonging to his father-in-law) and a few other layouts, was done at no charge. Later he turned "professional" and received a fee for his work. In 1930 he formed the partnership of Emmet, Emmet and Tull with his son, Devereux Emmet, Jr., and Alfred Tull, and continued with it until his death in 1934.
Courses by Devereux Emmet:
CONNECTICUT: Hob Nob Hill GC, Salisbury (1934;n.l.e.); I. Kent Fulton Estate GC, Salisbury (1933); Keney Park Muni, Hartford (9,1927;9,1930); Wee Burn CC, Darien (1923).
MARYLAND: Congressional CC, Bethesda (Original 18,1924).
MASSACHUSETTS: Coonamessett GC, North Falmouth (Original 9,1929) [Now Clauson's Inn GC].
NEW JERSEY: Cooper River CC, Camden (1929;n.l.e.); Greenacres CC, Trenton (1932).
NEW YORK: Broadmoor CC, New Rochelle (1929;n.l.e.); Cherry Valley GC, Garden City (1916); Edison CC, Rexford (1926); Eisenhower Park GC [formerly Salisbury Golf Links], East Meadow (Red course,1914); Garden City GC (1899); Glen Head CC [formerly Women's National](c.Tull,1923); Glenwood CC, Farmingdale; Hampshire CC, Mamaroneck (1927); Huntington CC (1911;r.1928); Huntington Crescent CC, Huntington (36,1931;2nd 18,n.l.e.); (The) Island Golf Links, Garden City (9,1899,n.l.e.); Leatherstocking CC, Cooperstown (1909); Manhasset CC (1917); Mayflower GC, New York City (1930); McGregor GC, Saratoga Spa (1921); Meadow Brook Club, Westbury (1914); Mohawk GC, Schenectady; Nassau CC, Glen Cove (New site); Pelham CC (New site,1921); Pomonok CC, Flushing (1921;n.l.e.); Queensboro Links, Astoria (1917); Rockwood Hall CC, Tarrytown (1929,n.l.e.); St. George's G&CC, Stony Brook; St. Lawrence University GC (Original 9); Schuyler Meadows Club, Loudonville (1928); (The) Seawane Club, Hewlett Harbor (1927); Vanderbilt Estate GC, Manhasset (9.1929;n.l.e.); Vernon Hills CC, Mt. Vernon (1928); Powelton GC (r.a.12).
NORTH CAROLINA: Hog Back Mountain GC, Tryon (9,1931;n.l.e.).
BAHAMAS: Bahamas CC, Nassau (1922;n.l.e.); Nassau CC (1927).
BERMUDA: Belmont Hotel & Club, Warwick (9,1924;9,1928); Castle Inn GC (9 par 3;n.l.e.); Hotel Frascate GC (9 par 3;n.l.e.); Riddell Bay G&CC, Warwick (1922).
Courses Remodeled by Devereux Emmet:
DELAWARE: DuPont Estate GC, Wilmington (9,1929).
NEW YORK: Bonnie Briar CC, Larchmont (1928); Engineers GC, Roslyn (1921); Old Country Club, Flushing (1928;n.l.e.); Wheatley Hills CC, East Williston (1929).
BERMUDA: St. George Hotel GC (1928).

Devereux Emmet, Jr.
The son of golf architect Devereux Emmet, Devereux Emmet, Jr., was a partner in the firm of Emmet, Emmet and Tull, founded in 1930 and dissolved on the death of Emmet, Sr. in 1934. Emmet Jr. is not known to have designed any courses after his father's death and, according to Tull, was never active in the design end of the firm.
See Devereux Emmet and Alfred Tull

176

Paul Erath (1905–   )
Paul Erath became a member of PGA in 1933 and served as pro-superintendent at several Pennsylvania clubs before joining the construction staff of golf architect "Dick" Wilson in the 1950s. After supervising Wilson's reconstruction of Dunedin in Florida, Erath returned to Pennsylvania to build the Laurel Valley CC to Wilson's plans. He remained at Laurel Valley as course superintendent, designing a number of local golf courses as a sideline.
Courses by Paul Erath:
PENNSYLVANIA: Canadian-American GC, Venago (1973); Champion Lakes CC, Bolivar (1965); Pleasant View CC, Norvelt (1967); Port Cherry Hills CC, McDonald (1966); Saranac GC, Stahlstown (9,1964).
Courses Remodeled by Paul Erath:
PENNSYLVANIA: Fox Chapel GC, Pittsburgh; Laurel Valley CC, Ligonier (1965).

Lindsay B. Ervin (1942–   ) ASGCA
Born: Brownwood, Texas.
Lindsay Ervin, a graduate landscape architect, trained under golf architect David Gill and then joined a landscape architecture firm. In 1976 he designed the twenty-seven-hole Hog Neck GC in Easton, Maryland. In 1979 he established his own practice and that year planned Cove Creek CC, Kent Island, Maryland and Birdwood GC, Charlottesville, Virginia.

Charles "Chick" Evans (1890–1979)
Born: Indianapolis, Indiana. Died: Chicago, Illinois, at age 89.
"Chick" Evans, winner of the 1916 U. S. Open and Amateur, wrote extensively about golf architecture for periodicals and laid out several courses on his own. For a short period in the 1920s he was associated with Tom Bendelow who instructed him in course design. In 1927 he was hired by the Cook County (Illinois) Board of Parks to "dot the forest preserves with golf," and it is thought that several of these courses were built. His best-known creation is Cutten Fields CC in Guelph, Ontario, Canada, designed and built in the late 1920s. Evans set up a design office in Chicago in the 1930s, but its output was severely curtailed by the Depression.

Keith E. Evans (1944–   ) ASGCA
Born: Plymouth, Michigan.
Keith Evans graduated from Michigan State University with a B.A. degree in business administration in 1966. Following military service, during which he was a member of the U. S. Army European Rifle Team, he was employed with Lever Brothers and Capital Irrigation.
In 1973 Evans returned to Michigan State University to study landscape architecture, receiving his degree in 1976. He was associated in course design with golf architects Joseph S. Finger (1977) and Richard Watson (1978) before joining the staff of Rees Jones Inc. in 1979.

Floyd Farley (1907–   ) ASGCA; President, 1966.
Born: Kansas City, Missouri.
Floyd Farley began his career in golf as a caddy in 1919. He was later employed as professional at Crestwood CC, Kansas City, Dundee GC, Omaha, and Twin Hills GC in Oklahoma City. He designed, built and operated the Woodlawn GC in Oklahoma City from 1932 to 1947 and during that period won the Oklahoma PGA Championship in 1936 and 1942 and the Oklahoma Match Play Open in 1937. In 1947 he designed and built the Meridian GC in Oklahoma City, which he owned until 1961.
Prior to 1947, Farley had helped many small Oklahoma communities obtain golf courses by means of the "eighteen stakes on a Sunday afternoon" method. After 1950 he devoted himself full time to golf course architecture and developed a decided preference for par-70 layouts, with three par-3 and two par-5 holes per nine. Farley felt his own style to have been most influenced by golf architects William P. Bell and Perry Maxwell.
Courses by Floyd Farley:
KANSAS: Clay Center CC (9,1964); Crestwood CC, Pittsburg (a.9,1977); Leroy King's Course, Hesston (9,1956); McConnell AFB, Wichita (9,1960); Overland Park Muni (27,1971); Riverview CC (now Hidden Lakes CC), Wichita (1954); Salina Muni (1970).
MISSOURI: A.L. Gustin, Jr. Memorial GC, U. of Mo., Columbia (1957); Ava CC (9,1965); Cabool-Mountain Grove CC (9,1969); Current River CC, Doniphan (9,1970); Fort Leonard Wood GC (1958); Greene Hills CC, Willard (9,1969); Jamestown CC, St. James (9,1969); Lake Valley CC, Camdenton (1969); Marceline CC (9,1970); Salem CC (9,1969); Twin Oaks CC, Springfield (c.Horton Smith,1956); Walnut Hills CC, Sedalia (1970); Willow Springs CC (9,1970).
NEBRASKA: Holmes Park Muni, Lincoln (1964); James H. Ager, Jr. GC, Lincoln (9 par 3,1964); The Knolls GC, Lincoln (9 par 3,1962); Mahoney Park Muni, Lincoln (1975); Maplewood Village, Omaha (9 par 3,1962); Meadowbrook GC, Omaha (9 par 3,1963); Miracle Hill GC, Omaha (1963).
NEW MEXICO: N.M. Military Institute GC, Roswell (1957); N.M. State University GC, Las Cruces (1962).
OKLAHOMA: Adams Park Muni (Sooner Park), Bartlesville (1962); Alva CC (9,1950); Arrowhead State Park GC, Eufaula (1960); Atoka Muni (9,1964); Beaver's Bend State Park GC, Broken Bow (9,1976); Brookside GC, Oklahoma City (9,1952); Cedar Valley GC, Guthrie (27,1974); Earlywine Park Muni, Oklahoma City (1974); El Reno CC (9,1948); Elks CC, Duncan (2nd 9,1962); Fort Cobb Lake State Park GC (1962); Fountainhead State Park GC, Checotah (1960); Franke CC [formerly Broadmoore CC], Moore (1962); Hillcrest CC, Oklahoma City (1950); Hook & Slice GC, Oklahoma City (9 par 3,1972); Kickingbird GC, Edmond (1971); LaFortune Park Muni, Tulsa (27,1960); Lake Hefner, Oklahoma City (South course,1962); Lake Texoma State Park GC, Kingston (9,1956;9,1958); Lawton CC (2nd 9,1957); Lew Wentz Memorial GC, Ponca City (2nd 9,1957); McAlester CC (9,1956); Meridian GC, Oklahoma City (1947); Midwest City Muni (9,1954); Mohawk Park Muni, Tulsa (2nd

18,1955); Osage Hills CC [now Sand Springs Muni], Sand Springs (1955); Quail Creek CC, Oklahoma City (1961); Recreation GC, Healdton (9,1951); Regional Park Muni, Midwest City (1972); Roman Nose State Park GC, Watonga (9,1960); Sequoyah State Park GC, Hulbert (1959); Seth Hughes Par 3, Tulsa (9,1959); Shattuck CC (9,1970); Sulphur Hills CC (9,1960); Surrey Hills GC; Tinker AFB (1957); Twin Lakes CC [now Norman CC], Norman (1st 9,1949); Western Village GC, Tulsa (1954); Westwood Muni, Norman (1966); Wewoka Muni (9,1949); Woodlawn GC, Oklahoma City (1932).

TEXAS: Tanglewood on Texoma GC.
Courses Remodeled by Floyd Farley:
KANSAS: Indian Hills CC, Prairie Village (1958); Kansas City CC, Shawnee Mission (r.2,1959); Lake Hefner (North Course,r.); Lake Quivira CC, Kansas City (1958); Milburn CC, Overland Park (1957); Mission Hills CC, Shawnee Mission (r.2,1959); Rolling Hills CC, Wichita (1963).
MISSOURI: Blue Hills CC, Kansas City (Old course,1958).
NEBRASKA: Norfolk CC (r.13,a.5).
OKLAHOMA: Hillcrest CC, Bartlesville (r.1st 9,1960); Lincoln Park Muni, Oklahoma City (36,1965); Mohawk Park Muni (1955); Rolling Hills CC, Tulsa (1957); Vinita GC.

George Fazio (1912–) ASGCA
Born: Norristown, Pennsylvania.

George Fazio played on the professional golf tour, tying with Hogan and Mangrum in the 1950 U. S. Open won by Hogan in the playoff, and placing fifth and fourth respectively in the 1952 and 1953 Opens. He also served as resident professional golfer at several clubs, including Pine Valley.

Fazio entered private practice as a course architect in 1959 and advanced rapidly in the profession to become one of the nation's leading designers. In 1962 he was joined by his nephew Tom, forming the respected firm of George Fazio–Tom Fazio, Golf Course Architects. The Fazios were consulting architects for a number of major golf tournaments, including the 1973 Masters Tournament at Augusta National; the 1974, '76, '77 and '79 U. S. Open Championships; the 1978 World Hall of Fame at Pinehurst; and the 1980 PGA Championship at the Oak Hill Country Club.
Courses by George Fazio–Tom Fazio:
ARIZONA: Sun City, Phoenix (Willowbrook and Willowcreek courses.)
CALIFORNIA: Desert Cove CC, Indian Wells (36,1979)[now Vintage CC].
CONNECTICUT: Ridgefield Muni (1973); Tumble Brook CC, Hartford (9).
FLORIDA: Alcoa's Jonathan Landing, Jupiter; Bluewater Bay CC, Ft. Walton Beach; East-pointe CC, Juno Beach; Innlet Harbour Par 3 GC; Jupiter Hills Club; Jonathan's Landing CC; Jupiter Hills Village Club; Ocean Trail GC, Jupiter; PGA Resort Community GC, Palm Beach Gardens (54); Palm-Aire CC, Pompano Beach (Cypress & Oaks courses); Palm Beach Polo & CC[formerly Wellington CC]; River Bend Club, Tequesta.
HAWAII: Kuilima Hotel GC, Oahu.
ILLINOIS: Butler National GC, Oakbrook; Lincolnshire Marriott Hotel & GC, Chicago.
MARYLAND: Congressional CC, Bethesda (9).
MASSACHUSETTS: Oakridge GC, Agawam; Presidents GC, Wollaston; Wollaston CC, Milton.
NEVADA: Edgewood Tahoe CC, Lake Tahoe.
NEW JERSEY: Atlantis GC; Playboy Club Hotel Course, Great Gorge (27).
NORTH CAROLINA: Pinehurst # 6, Pinehurst.
OHIO: Saw-Mill Creek Lodge GC, Cleveland.
OKLAHOMA: Indian Springs CC (Original 18,1964).
PENNSYLVANIA: Bristol Wood Par 3 GC; Chester Valley CC, Frazer; Downingtown Inn GC; Hershey East CC; Kimberton GC (1962); Langhorn CC; Moselem Springs CC, Reading; Pocono Manor (West course,1965); Silver Spring CC (1969); Squires GC, Ambler; Way-nesborough CC (1964).
SOUTH CAROLINA: Bay Tree Golf Plantation, Myrtle Beach (54); Isle of Palms GC, Charleston (now Wild Dunes GC); Moss Creek Plantation, Hilton Head Island (Devil's Elbow; North and South courses); Palmetto Dunes Resort, Hilton Head Island (Fazio course); Plantation Pines Par 3 GC, Johns Island (1980); Wild Dunes GC, Isle of Palms (1980).
TEXAS: Champions GC, Houston (Jackrabbit course); Eldorado CC (1964); Tennwood GC, Houston.
BAHAMAS: Coral Harbour GC, Nassau; Sand Cliff Club.
CANADA: The National GC, Toronto.
COSTA RICA: Cariari International CC, San Jose.
PANAMA: Coronado Beach CC.
PUERTO RICO: Rio-Mar GC, San Juan.
VIRGIN ISLANDS: Mahogany Run GC, St. Thomas.
Courses Remodeled by George Fazio–Tom Fazio:
FLORIDA: Everglades Club, Palm Beach; Jupiter Island Club, Hobe Sound.
GEORGIA: Atlanta Athletic Club (Highlands Course); Augusta National GC.
INDIANA: Meridian Hills CC, Indianapolis.
MARYLAND: Columbia CC, Bethesda.
NEW YORK: Apawamis CC, Westchester; Oak Hill CC, Rochester; Winged Foot GC, Mamaroneck.
OHIO: Inverness CC.
OKLAHOMA: Southern Hills CC, Tulsa.

Tom Fazio (1945–) ASGCA
Born: Norristown, Pennsylvania.

Tom Fazio entered private practice as a golf course architect in 1962, assisting his uncle George Fazio and continuing his studies in engineering, landscape design, soils, accounting and business wherever his career took him. The partnership of George Fazio–Tom Fazio became one of the nation's leading course design firms. Tom gradually took over from his uncle and by the late 1970's was doing most of the firms planning.
Courses by Tom Fazio: See George Fazio

Fred Federspiel
Fred Federspiel served for many years as superintendent at several courses, including the Oswego Lake CC in Oregon, where he was located in 1960. He laid out a number of courses in the Northwest in the 1950s and 60s.
Courses by Fred Federspiel:
OREGON: Agate Beach GC (9); Merriwether National GC; Salishan Golf Links; Santiam GC, Stayton; Sunriver CC (South course).
WASHINGTON: Briarcliff CC, Rainier (1969); Olympia G&CC (2nd 9,1959); Royal Oaks CC, Vancouver (1952); Vancouver Muni.

Arthur H. Fenn (1858–1925)
The United States' first native born professional golfer, Arthur H. Fenn laid out the Poland Springs CC in Maine.

Marvin H. Ferguson (1918–) ASGCA
Born: Texas.

Dr. Marvin Ferguson graduated from Texas A & M University and received a Ph.D. degree from the University of Maryland. From 1940 until 1969 he was engaged in turfgrass research with the USGA Green Section and Texas A & M. He then entered private practice as a golf course architect under the firm name of Agri-Systems of Texas and later under his own name.

Dr. Ferguson played a major role in developing the USGA method of green construction and wrote numerous papers on this and other turfgrass subjects.
Courses by Dr. Marvin H. Ferguson:
ARANSAS: Ben Geren GC, Ft. Smith (1970).
KANSAS: Wolf Creek GC, Olathe (1972).
LOUISIANA: Les Vieux Chenes Muni, Lafayette (1977).
MISSOURI: CC of Missouri, Columbia (1974); West Plains CC (12,1977).
NEW MEXICO: Ocotillo Park GC, Hobbs (1977).
TEXAS: Briarcrest CC, Bryan (1971); Cielo Vista Muni, El Paso (1977).
TENNESSEE: Holly Hills CC.
Courses Remodeled by Dr. Marvin H. Ferguson:
ARKANSAS: Hardscrabble CC, Ft. Smith (1970).
MISSOURI: Carrollton CC (9,1969); Hillcrest CC, Kansas City (4,1975); Westwood CC, St. Louis (1,1969).
TEXAS: Abilene CC (1,1975); Braeburn CC, Houston (4,1969); Bryan Muni (6,1971); Coronado CC, El Paso (1972); Northwood CC, Dallas (5,1974).

Robert Ferguson (1848–1915)
Robert Ferguson, British Open Champion in 1880, '81 and '82, built four or five golf courses on his own and assisted Peter McEwan, the club maker, in laying out Braid Hill in Edinburgh, Scotland.

S. Mure Ferguson (1855–)
Born: Perthshire, Scotland.

S. Mure Ferguson, who became captain of the Royal and Ancient Golf Club in 1910, planned the first version of the New Zealand GC in England in collaboration with Lock-King. This layout marked the first attempt to build a course through mature trees.

George and Willie Fernie
The Fernies, of Troon and Dumfries, were respected pro-greenkeepers in the latter half of the 1800s. After the turn of the century, George designed Hunstanton GC and Caldwell GC, Glasgow, Scotland. Willie planned Southendown, Troon, Troon Portland, Pitlochry and the original Ailsa and Arran courses at Turnberry, as well as Whitsand Bay, Cornwall, England and Cardross and Whitecraigs in Scotland. He also modified Felixstowe CC in England while serving as its professional.

Homer D. Fieldhouse
Based in Wisconsin, Homer Fieldhouse designed courses throughout the midwestern states from the mid-1950s through the 1970s.
Courses by Homer D. Fieldhouse:
ILLINOIS: Braidwood Recreation Center (9,1965); Gibson Woods Muni, Monmouth (1966).
IOWA: Lake Creek CC, Storm Lake (1972).
KANSAS: Sugar Hills GC, Goodland (9,1969).
MINNESOTA: Valley High Par 3 GC, Houston.
OHIO: Candywood GC, Vienna (1966); Ponderosa CC, Warren (1966).
SOUTH DAKOTA: Hillcrest G&CC, Yankton (2nd 9,1972).
WISCONSIN: Camelot CC, Lomira (1966); Clifton Highlands GC, Prescott (1972); Eagle Bluff CC, Hurley (1967); Fox Lake CC (a.9,1965); Golden Sands GC, Cecil (1970); Golf Village Executive GC, Neeyah (9); Rock River Hills GC, Horizon (1965).

Alexander H. Findlay
Born: Scotland.

Alex Findlay emigrated to the United States in the early 1880s to manage a ranch in Nebraska. Here he laid out a golf course around 1885. He was later in charge of planning, constructing and operating courses for the Florida East Coast Railroad, the same position as that held by J. D. Dunn with the Florida West Coast Railroad.

177

Findlay was for a time associated in course development with Wright and Ditson and later with Wannamakers. In addition, he continued to plan courses on his own and later in collaboration with his brother Fred. It has been claimed that Findlay laid out more than 500 courses in the United States, Mexico and Canada, many of them constructed by his sons, Norman, Ronald and Richard.

Courses by Alex Findlay: (Partial list only)

FLORIDA: Miami Golf Links; Ormond GC; Palm Beach CC; Ponce de Leon GC (original 9); St. Augustine CC.
NEW HAMPSHIRE: Maplewood GC; Mt. Pleasant CC.
NEW JERSEY: Newark Athletic Club; Pitman GC (1929); Tavistock CC.
NEW YORK: Lake Placid CC (Upper course).
NORTH CAROLINA: Esseeola Lodge (original 18,n.l.e.,1912).
PENNSYLVANIA: Aronomink CC (original course,n.l.e.,1913); Pittsburgh Field Club (original course).
BAHAMAS: A six-hole course in Nassau (1900).

Frederick A. Findlay (1872–1966)
Born: Scotland. Died: Charlottesville, Virginia, at age 94.

Fred Findlay, the son of a British Army officer, joined the Army at the age of fourteen and served for twenty-one years, most of them as a bandmaster. Upon retiring from the Army, he moved to Australia, where he spent thirteen years as a club professional and did his first golf design work.

After the first World War, Findlay moved to the United States, following older brother Alex who had emigrated there as a young man and become a pioneer golf promoter and course designer. Fred settled in Virginia, serving as professional and superintendent at various clubs and designing a number of courses over the next thirty years. In his later years he was partnered with his son-in-law, Raymond Loving, Sr., in a course design and construction firm that is now maintained by his grandson, Raymond "Buddy" Loving, Jr.

Findlay remained active as a golf architect into the early 1960s. A fine landscape artist and poet as well as golfer, he consistently shot his age during the last twenty years of his life. Although an artist, he detested blueprints and claimed that the land was his drawing board.

Courses by Frederick A. Findlay:

NORTH CAROLINA: Paradise Point CC, Camp LeJeune (1939); Chapel Hill CC.
PENNSYLVANIA: Phillipsburgh CC (1922); Reading CC (1923).
SOUTH CAROLINA: Parris Island GC (1951).
VIRGINIA: Augusta CC, Staunton (1927); Bide-A-Wee CC, Portsmouth (1955); Boonsboro CC, Lynchburg (1927); Crater CC (1934); Culpepper CC; Farmington CC, Charlottesville (1928); Glenwood CC, Richmond (1925); Hopewell CC (1940); Ingleside Augusta CC, Staunton (1926); James River CC, Newport News (1932); Keswick Club of Virginia (1938); Laurel GC (1926); Lawrenceville CC; Luray GC (1934,n.l.e.); McIntyre Park GC, Charlottesville (9,1952); Meadowbrook CC, Richmond (1959); Ole Monterey CC, Roanoke (1925); South Boston CC (1942); Spotswood CC. Harrisonburg (1935); Swannanoa GC, Waynesboro (1926); Williamsburg CC (9). Winchester CC; Wytheville CC (9).

Courses Remodeled by Frederick A. Findlay:
VIRGINIA: CC of Virginia, Richmond (James River and Westhampton courses).

Joseph S. Finger (1918–   )
Born: Houston, Texas.

Joseph Finger received a bachelor's degree in engineering in 1939 from Rice University, where he had been captain of the golf team under coach Jimmy Demaret. He continued his education at the Massachusetts Institute of Technology, receiving his master's degree in 1941.

Finger was employed for five years in oil refining and then became president of a plastics manufacturing company, where he developed a corrugated plastic building panel. During these years he also operated a dairy farm.

In 1956 Finger planned his first golf course, a nine-hole addition near Houston. His early work included a number of courses for the U. S. Air Force as well as several jobs, where he had received leads from former coach Demaret. In addition, Finger wrote the booklet "The Business End of Building or Rebuilding a Golf Course" distributed by the National Golf Foundation and several well-timed articles on course design and construction.

Courses by Joseph S. Finger:

ARKANSAS: Bella Vista CC (1966); Blytheville CC (r.9,a.9,1968); Burns Park Muni (27); Pine Bluff CC (r.9,a.9,1968); Pleasant Valley CC, Little Rock (27,1969).
CALIFORNIA: Travis AFB, Fairfield (1960) (Cypress Lakes CC).
GEORGIA: Atlanta Athletic Club (9,1971); Atlanta CC (Consulting architect,1965); Highland CC, LaGrange (9,1972); Moody AFB, Valdosta (9,1968).
LOUISIANA: Ellendale CC, Houma (1967).
MISSISSIPPI: Deerfield CC, Madison (1980); Keesler AFB, Gulfport (9,1962-4).
NEW MEXICO: Pichaco Hills CC, Las Cruces (1979).
NEW YORK: Concord Hotel, Kiamesha Lake (1964); Glen Oaks Club, Old Westbury (27, 1971); Grossinger GC (12,1968).
OKLAHOMA: Cedar Ridge CC, Tulsa (1970).
PENNSYLVANIA: Westmoreland CC, Export (12,1967).
TENNESSEE: Colonial CC, Memphis (36,1972).
TEXAS: Amarillo AFB (1962); Baywood CC (1962); Bayou Muni, Texas City (1973); Blue Lake Estates, Lake LBJ (9,1962); Golfcrest GC, Houston (1970); Grapevine Muni (1978); H and H Guest Ranch GC, Kingwood CC, Houston (1971); Las Colinas CC, Dallas (1964); Laughlin AFB, Del Rio (9,1960); Oak Hills CC, San Antonio (r.6,a.3,1961-9); Parrin AFB, Sherman (9,1962); Piney Point GC, Houston (9 par 3,1961); Randolph AFB, San Antonio (1958); Riverhill GC, Kerrville (1974); Star Hollow Club, Fort Worth (9,1967); Tejas GC, Houston (1966); Westwood CC, Houston (r.3,a.15,1963-70); Williamson Creek Muni, Austin (1973).
MEXICO: Bosques del Lago, Mexico City (36,1974); Club Atlas, Guadalajara (1970). Cocoyoc GC, Morales (c. Clifford 1973).

Courses Remodeled by Joseph S. Finger:
ARIZONA: Arizona CC, Phoenix (4,1960).
ARKANSAS: Little Rock CC (3,1965).
GEORGIA: Peachtree CC, Atlanta (18 greens,1973).
LOUISIANA: Baton Rouge CC (1973); Shreveport CC (9,1960).
NEW JERSEY: Montammy CC, Alpine (4,1971).
NEW YORK: Lawrence Park Village (1970); Westchester CC; Muttontown G&CC.
TENNESSEE: Richland CC, Nashville (9,1967).
TEXAS: Braeburn CC, Houston (4,1966); Columbian Club, Dallas (6,1971); Galveston CC (6,1972); Lackland A.F.B.GC; Lakeside CC, Houston (14 greens,1966-8); Prestonwood CC, Dallas (1978); River Oaks CC, Houston (12 greens, 1969); San Antonio CC (15,1959); Valley Inn & CC, Brownsville (1966); Willow Brook CC.

John Francis "Jack" Fleming (1896–   )
Born: Tuam, County Galway, Ireland.

Jack Fleming left his native Ireland at the age of eighteen bound for Manchester, England, in search of a position as gardener to some wealthy Briton. After classes in agriculture and a stint tending a soccer grounds, he landed a job as a "pick and shovel" man at a golf course being built by Dr. Alister Mackenzie.

Working his way through the ranks, Fleming became a construction foreman for Mackenzie in 1920. In 1926 he was sent to Marin County, California, where he supervised the building of the Meadow Club to a design by Mackenzie and Robert Hunter.

Mackenzie himself later moved to California and designed a number of layouts that Fleming built, among them the dramatic Cypress Point Club. Then the Depression hit and, at his mentor's urging, Fleming accepted a position as superintendent of grounds maintenance for the City and County of San Francisco. He remained in this position until his retirement in 1962, continuing his golf design practice on a part-time basis.

Following Mackenzie's death in 1934, Fleming completed some of his unfinished courses and then built a few of his own. In the late 1940s he designed and built a number of short courses in the San Francisco area, and by the late 1950s had developed a flourishing practice. He continued, until his retirement in 1975, to be an active course architect in northern California.

Courses by John Francis "Jack" Fleming:

CALIFORNIA: Adam Springs G&CC, Cobb (9); Almaden CC, San Jose (1955); Baymeadows GC, San Francisco (exec.9); Blue Rock Springs GC, Vallejo (Original 9,1941;a.9,1970); Boulder Creek CC; Calero Hills CC, San Jose; Cypress Hills GC, Colma (9 plus exec.9,1963); Dry Creek Ranch GC, Galt (1963); El Campo GC, Newark (1959); Glenhaven G&CC, Milditas (1961); Golden Gate GC, San Francisco (9 par 3,1950); Golden Gate Fields GC, Albany (9 par 3); Harding Park GC, San Francisco (r.1934;a.3,1960;a.9-hole "Fleming" course,1962); I.B.M. GC, San Jose (9 par 3); J.F.K. Memorial GC [formerly Napa Muni], Napa (c.B.Harmon & R.Baldock,1958); Lake Chabot Vallejo GC, Vallejo (exec. course, 1955); Lincoln Park GC, San Francisco (r); Mace Meadows GC, Jackson (9); Manteca Park GC (9,1966); Mather AFB GC, Sacramento (1963); McLaren Park Muni, Daly City (9,1962); Menlo Park (1962); Mount St. Helena GC, Calistoga (9); Pruneridge Farms GC, Santa Clara (exec.9); Roseville CC; Salinas Fairways GC (1957); Santa Rosa G&CC (1958); Sharon Heights G&CC, Menlo Park (1962); Sierra View CC, Roseville (Original 9,1956); Spring Creek G&CC, Ripon (Original 9); Swenson Park Muni, Stockton (1952); Tanforan GC, San Mateo (exec.9); Warm Springs GC, Fremont (9).
COLORADO: Centennial GC, Littleton (9 par 3).

William S. Flynn (1891–1945)
Born: Massachusetts. Died: Philadelphia, Pennsylvania, at age 54.

William Flynn graduated from Milton High School, where he had played interscholastic golf and competed against his friend Francis Ouimet. He laid out his first course at Heartwellville, Vermont, in 1909 and was then hired to assist Hugh Wilson with completion of the Merion East course at Merion GC in Pennsylvania.

Flynn found his services as a course architect much in demand as a result of his work at Merion. He and Wilson had hoped to form a design partnership, but Wilson's failing health prevented it. Instead, Flynn joined forces after World War I with Wilson's friend Howard Toomey, a prominent engineer. Flynn was responsible for design and construction, Toomey handled business and financial matters and Hugh Wilson continued to collaborate on courses until his death in 1925. In addition, golf architects William Gordon, Robert Lawrence and "Dick" Wilson all started out as assistants with the firm of Toomey and Flynn.

Flynn's "second love" was the art of greenkeeping, and he wrote many articles and pamphlets on the subject. He also started a number of men in the profession, among them the great Joe Valentine, long-time superintendent at Merion, whom he met when he himself was serving as greenkeeper at Merion prior to World War I.

Courses by William S. Flynn:

COLORADO: Cherry Hills CC, Denver (1923).
FLORIDA: Boca Raton (36); Cleveland Heights G&CC, Lakeland (c. Toomey); Indian Creek GC, Miami.
MASSACHUSETTS: The Country Club, Brookline (Primrose course,1927); Kittansett Club, Marion (route plan).
NEW JERSEY: Atlantic City CC; Seaview CC, Absecon (a.9,c.Toomey); Woodcrest, Haddonfield.
NEW YORK: Pocantico Hills GC [formerly J.D. Rockefeller Estate], Tarrytown; Rockwood Hall GC, Tarrytown; Shinnecock Hills GC, Southampton (c.Toomey,1930)
OHIO: The Country Club, Cleveland (1930); Elyria CC; Pepper Pike Club,Cleveland.
PENNSYLVANIA: Green Valley CC [formerly Marble Hall CC], Conshohocken (c.Toomey); Harrisburg CC (1916); Huntington Valley CC; Lancaster CC; Lehigh CC, Emmaus (c.Toomey,1926); Manufacturers G&CC, Oreland; Philadelphia CC, Gladwyne (Spring Mill course,c.Toomey,1927);Philmont CC(North Course,c.Toomey);Rolling Green CC,Springfield; York CC.

VERMONT: Hartwellville CC(1910,n.l.e.).
VIRGINIA: CC of Virginia (James River course; 1928); The Homestead, Hot Springs (Cascades course,1923).
Courses Remodeled by William S. Flynn:
COLORADO: Denver CC.
DELAWARE: Hercules Powder Club, Wilmington.
FLORIDA: Miami Beach Polo Club; Normandy Island GC [now Normandy Shore CC].
ILLINOIS: Glen View Club; Mill Road Farm GC.
MARYLAND: Naval Academy, Annapolis; Woodmont CC, Bethesda.
NEW JERSEY: Pine Valley GC; Springdale CC, Princeton.
NEW YORK: The Creek Club, Locust Valley; Tuxedo Park Club; Westchester Biltmore, Rye; Women's National GC, Locust Valley.
PENNSYLVANIA: Bala GC; Eaglesmere CC; Manor Club; Merion Cricket Club, Haverford; Plymouth CC, Norristown; Springhaven Club, Wallingford; Whitemarsh Valley CC.
VIRGINIA: CC. of Virginia, Richmond; Co.; Norfolk CC; Yorktown CC.
WASHINGTON, D.C.: Burning Tree Club; Columbia CC; East Potomac Park; Rock Creek Park.

James Foulis, Jr. (1870–1928)
Born: St. Andrews, Scotland. Died: Chicago, Illinois, at age 58. Interred: Wheaton, Illinois.
James Foulis and his brothers David, Robert, John and Simpson all grew up on the links at St. Andrews. Their father, James Sr., was foreman of Old Tom Morris's golf shop for some thirty-five years. Old Tom taught the game to each of the boys, and the three eldest helped him in constructing courses. All of the brothers except John were avid golfers, but James was the best, eventually winning the second U. S. Open in 1896.
Foulis emigrated to the United States in 1895 to serve as the first professional at C. B. Macdonald's Chicago Golf Club. He remained as club maker and professional until 1905, routing a number of midwestern courses during the period. His brother David joined him in the early 1900s and together they developed the first mashie-niblick club, which they patented in 1905. Marketing this and other clubs under the name D & D Foulis Company, they operated a highly successful club manufacturing firm until the 1920s.
After working at several clubs in Chicago and St. Louis, Foulis became pro-greenkeeper at Olympia Fields CC in 1917. He supervised construction of the four courses laid out there, then left in 1922 to pursue a golf design career. He worked part time as an architect until 1927, when he and engineer Ralph Wymer formed the short-lived pioneer Golf and Landscape Company, which disbanded with Foulis's death the following year.
Courses by James Foulis, Jr.:
COLORADO: Denver CC (9,1902,n.l.e.).
ILLINOIS: Bonnie Brook CC, Waukegan; Hickory Hills CC, Palos Park (1923); Hinsdale CC; Onwentsia Club, Lake Forest (9,1896;a.9,1898); Pipe O'Peace GC, Blue Island (1927).
MICHIGAN: Kent CC, Grand Rapids (original 9).
MISSOURI: Glen Echo CC, Normandy (1901); Hickory Hills CC; St. Louis CC (original course,n.l.e.).
TENNESSEE: Memphis CC (original 9,1905,n.l.e.)
WISCONSIN: Hillmoor CC, Lake Geneva (1924).

Robert Foulis (1873–1945)
Born: St. Andrews, Scotland. Died: Orlando, Florida, at age 71. Interred: Wheaton, Illinois.
Robert Foulis worked from an early age in Tom Morris's golf shop at St. Andrews, and assisted in the construction of a few Scottish courses of Morris's design. Though he had learned the game from Old Tom, Foulis never played much competitive golf, because his eyesight was poor as the result of two childhood accidents.
In 1895 Robert's brother James accepted a position in the United States that Robert himself had previously turned down. Following in 1896, Robert assisted James in laying out and building the Onwentsia Club in Lake Forest, Illinois, and stayed on as its first professional. Soon after the turn of the century, the remaining Foulis brothers, their sister and parents all moved to America and settled in Wheaton, Illinois. By this time James was a renowned competitive golfer and course designer; and Robert was well known, too, having toured the small towns of the Midwest teaching golf and staking out courses.
In 1902 James and Robert designed and built the Glen Echo CC in St. Louis, and Robert again stayed on as professional. He then created a number of St. Louis-area golf courses, including the Bellerive CC in 1910. Becoming Bellerive's first pro-greenkeeper upon its completion, Foulis remained there until his retirement in late 1942. He continued to practice course architecture on a part-time basis, as he had ever since moving to the United States. In addition, he was a member of the PGA and the National Association of Greenkeepers.
Courses by Robert Foulis:
ILLINOIS: Onwentsia Club, Lake Forest (c.J.Foulis,1896:a.9,1898,c.Whigham & Tweedie).
MINNESOTA: Minikahda Club, Minneapolis (original 9, c.W.Watson).
MISSOURI: Algonquin CC, Glendale (1904); Bellerive CC, Normandy (1910,n.l.e.); Bogey CC, St. Louis (1910); Forest Park Muni, St. Louis (1913); Glen Echo CC, Normandy (c.J.Foulis,1902;r.1904); Jefferson City CC (original 9,1922); Log Cabin Club, Clayton (1909); Meadow Brook CC [formerly Midland Valley CC], St. Louis (1911,n.l.e.); Normandie GC, St. Louis (1901); North Shore CC [formerly Riverview CC], St. Louis (original 18); Sunset CC, St. Louis (1910).
WISCONSIN: Lake Geneva CC (original 9,1897).
Courses Remodeled by Robert Foulis:
MINNESOTA: Minikahda Club, Minneapolis (original 9, c.W. Watson).
MISSOURI: Triple A CC, Forest Park.

William Herbert Fowler (1856–1941)
Born: Edmonton, England. Died: London, England, at age 85.
W. Herbert Fowler, born into an affluent family, was educated at Rottingdean and at Grove House School, Tottenham. He was an excellent cricket player in his youth, his size and stature making him an intimidating opponent.
Fowler took up golf at the age of thirty-five and was soon a successful scratch amateur. He was a member of both the Royal and Ancient Golf Club of St. Andrews and the Honourable Company of Edinburgh Golfers. His first course design opportunity came when a group headed by his brother-in-law agreed to finance construction of the Walton Heath Golf Club in the early 1900s.
Walton Heath opened to critical acclaim; and while Fowler remained a lifelong director of the club, he was soon busy with other courses. In the early 1910s he partnered with Tom Simpson in the firm of Fowler and Simpson. Simpson did most of the firm's work on the Continent, while Fowler concentrated on British courses. He also spent a considerable amount of time in the United States during World War I and designed several American courses. In the early 1920s the firm was briefly expanded to include J. F. Abercromby and Arthur Croome, with the latter partners acting primarily as consultants.
Courses by William Herbert Fowler:
CALIFORNIA: Ambassador Hotel GC, Los Angeles (1920;n.l.e.); Del Monte G&CC (r.9,a.9); Lake Merced G&CC, San Francisco (1922); Los Angeles CC (rt.South course,1911).
MASSACHUSETTS: Eastward Ho! CC, Chatham (1922).
ENGLAND: Abbeydale GC; Beaudesert GC, Staffs.; Berkshire GC, Ascot, Berks.(Blue and Red courses,1928); Blackwell GC, Worcestershire; Bradford GC; Delamere Forest GC, Northwich, Cheshire; Huddersfield GC; Kingsgate GC; Lord Mountbatten Estate GC; Mortimer Singer Estate GC; Royal Automobile Club; Saunton GC, North Devon (r.Old course,1921;a.New course,1915); Walton Heath GC, Tadworth Surrey (Old course, 1904; New course,1915); West Kent GC; West Surrey GC (1909); Yelverton, Devon.
SCOTLAND: Cruden Bay G&CC, Aberdeen (27).
WALES: Bullbay GC.
Courses Remodeled by William Herbert Fowler:
CALIFORNIA: Del Paso CC, Sacramento (1922).
PENNSYLVANIA: Allegheny CC, Sewickley (r.,a.3,1922).
ENGLAND: Broadstone GC, Dorset. (r.bunkering); Ganton GC, Scarborough, Yorks.; Royal Lytham and St. Annes GC, Lancs.; Royal North Devon GC, Westward Ho! (1908).
WALES: Aberdovey GC, Merioneth; Southerndown GC, Bridgend, Glamorgan.

The Fownes of Oakmont
Henry Clay Fownes (1856–1935)
Born: Pittsburgh, Pennsylvania. Died: Pittsburgh, Pennsylvania, at age 79.
H. C. Fownes began working in the iron manufacturing business with his brother-in-law, William Clark. He later formed the Carrie Furnace Company with his own brother, William C. Fownes, operating it until 1896, when it was bought out by the Carnegie Steel Corporation. By then Fownes was a wealthy man and was content to serve as director of several steel firms and two banks, and to play a great deal of golf. He was an accomplished golfer, qualifying at age forty-five for the 1901 U. S. Open with a score one stroke less than his son's.
In 1903 Fownes formed the Oakmont CC in a Pittsburgh suburb, laying out the original course. He participated actively in the refinement of the course in its early years, and it remains in its basic routing just as he planned it. H. C. Fownes served as president of Oakmont for over twenty years until his death from pneumonia in 1935.

William Clarke Fownes, Jr. (1878–1950)
Born: Chicago, Illinois. Died: Oakmont, Pennsylvania, at age 72.
William C. Fownes, Jr. (not II) was the son of Henry Clay Fownes, but he was named for his uncle. He followed in his father's footsteps in both business and pleasure, working in the steel business, taking up golf and assisting H. C. with the original design of the Oakmont CC. William became a premier golfer in the early 1900s, winning four Pennsylvania Amateurs and the 1910 U. S. Amateur. He was also selected as captain of the first American Walker Cup team in 1922 and served as president of the USGA in 1925 and '26.
William Fownes served for many years as chairman of the Green Committee at Oakmont, and in that capacity worked closely with legendary greenkeeper Emil "Dutch" Loeffler in turning Oakmont into an increasingly fearsome course. He created countless bunkers and a special rake to groom them, and experimented with the greens until they were lightning fast. Fownes tinkered and groomed and promoted the course all his life, becoming a leading turfgrass authority in the process. He was made an honorary member of the National Association of Greenkeepers in 1932 for his efforts at Oakmont, but he never showed an inclination to work on any other course.

Manuel L. Francis (1903–   )
Manuel Francis worked on construction crews building courses on Long Island for Donald Ross and other architects in the 1920s. He was promoted when it was discovered that he was the only man who could start the tractors recently introduced in course construction, and by the end of the decade was in charge of several crews. When the Depression made construction work scarce, Francis became greenkeeper at the South Portland (Maine) CC and later at the Haverhill (Massachusetts) CC.
Francis then moved on to the Vesper CC in Lowell, Massachusetts, where he served as superintendent from 1950 through the 1970s. During his tenure there, he developed "Vespers," a velvet bentgrass with special putting qualities, and became widely known in the United States and Mexico as a turfgrass consultant. He also designed or redesigned a number of golf courses on the side, including the Green Harbor CC at Marshfield, Massachusetts, which he operated, after his retirement, with his son Manuel, Jr. In 1980 Francis was presented with the Distinguished Service Award of the Golf Course Superintendents Association of America in recognition of his contributions to golf and turfgrass development.
Courses by Manuel L. Francis:
MASSACHUSETTS: Dun Roamin GC, Gilbertsville (9); Green Harbor CC, Marshfield; Hickory Hill GC, Lowell/Lawrence; Westminister GC (Original 9).
NEW HAMPSHIRE: Lake Tarleton Club (13,n.l.e.); Whippoorwill CC.

Courses Remodeled by Manuel L. Francis:
MASSACHUSETTS; Blue Hill CC, Canton (6); Framingham CC; Old Newberry CC; Vespers CC, Lowell(18).
NEW HAMPSHIRE: Abenaqui CC, Rye (3); Exeter CC; Keene CC; Rochester CC.
MEXICO: Churubusco, Mexico City; Club de Golf de Bellavista, Satillite.

Ronald W. Fream

Ronald Fream received a B.S. degree in 1964 from California State Polytechnic Institute, Pomona, and did graduate work at Washington State University. He was employed with Robert Trent Jones, Inc. from 1966 to 1969, worked as construction superintendent on a Robert F. Lawrence course in Arizona in 1970, and was associated with golf architect Robert Muir Graves until 1972. He then became a partner in the golf design firm of Fream/Storm Associates, Ltd.

More recently Fream took an active part in founding the firm of Thomson, Wolveridge, Fream and Associates of Los Gatos, California, and Melbourne, Australia. As managing partner, he had primary responsibility for projects in the United States, Africa, Europe and the ʹCaribbean. In 1980 he left this firm to operate alone.

Courses by Ronald W. Fream: (Partial list only)
CALIFORNIA; Bixby Village GC, Long Beach (9 exec,1979); Mint Valley Murii.
Washington; Canyon Lakes CC (c.Thomson and Wolveridge); Kayak Point Muni, Port Susan Bay (1977); Longview Muni; Zintel Canyon GC, Kennewick (1977).
Courses Remodeled by Ronald W. Fream:
CALIFORNIA: Santa Ana CC.
MONTANA: Glacier View.

Kinya Fujita (1889–1969)

Born: Tokyo, Japan. Died: Kasumigaseki, Japan, at age 80.

Kinya Fujita, son of a wealthy Japanese banking family, was educated at Waseda University, where he excelled at several sports. He worked for three years in the family bank and then traveled to the United States for graduate study, attending the University of Chicago, Miami of Ohio and Columbia University. For a time he worked for a silk importing firm in New York City, then returned to Tokyo to organize and operate an import-export firm with American backing.

Fujita might be called the Japanese version of Charles Blair Macdonald. His interest in golf course design was roused when he met C.H. Alison, who was laying out the Tokyo GC, in 1914. Fujita traveled to Britain in 1919 to meet again with Alison and to study his techniques. Returning to his own country, he organized the Kasumigaseki Country Club in the 1920s and built its first course, the East. He also served as the club's captain, its secretary and the chairman of its board of directors. For good measure Fujita was the club champion in 1929, 1933 and 1935. After laying out a second course at Kasumigaseki, Fujita invited Alison to inspect both courses and recommend changes. Alison made only slight alterations to either course, but he added the deep bunkers.

Fujita designed several courses before World War II, and his services were in demand during the reconstruction period after the War. He remained a lifelong patriarch at Kasumigaseki and died on its grounds while making plans to remodel the highly respected East course.

Courses by Kinya Fujita:
JAPAN: Chiba CC, Chiba Prefecture; Higashi Matsuyama GC, Saitama Prefecture; Ito International GC, Shizuoke Prefecture; Kasumigaseki GC, Saitama Prefecture (East course,1929; West course,1932); Narashino CC, Chiba Prefecture (King's & Queen's courses); Nasu GC, Tochiga Prefecture; Oarai GC, Ibaraki Prefecture; Sanrizuka GC; Shiun CC, Niigata Prefecture;Shizucke CC,Shizucke Prefecture; Yahata CC.
Courses Remodeled by Kinya Fujita:
JAPAN: Kawana GC, Shizuoka Prefecture (r.Fuji and Oshima courses).

Paul Fullmer (1934–) ASGCA

Born: Evanston, Illinois.

Paul Fullmer received his bachelor's degree in journalism from Notre Dame University in 1955. He worked for two years as a sports columnist with the *Aurora* (Illinois) *Beacon News* and then began a career in public relations with Selz, Seabolt and Associates. He became president of the firm in 1979.

Fullmer was the first executive secretary of the American Society of Golf Course Architects when it retained Selz, Seabolt in 1970. He assisted in executing numerous changes in Society policies. His wife, Sandra, daughter of golf architect Percy Clifford, is former Women's Amateur Champion of Mexico, Spain and Germany (in one year she won all three titles) and four times Chicago District Champion.

Jose "Pepe" Gancedo (1938–)

Spanish businessman "Pepe" Gancedo won the Spanish Amateur five times and was six times a member of Spain's World team. He entered the field of golf course architecture in 1971. Among his courses in Spain are the Club de Golf Poniente at Majorca, together with CdG Costalita and Torrequebrado CC, both in Costa del Sol. He also remodeled CdG Santo Ponsa.

James Peter Gannon

Based in Ireland in the 1920s, James Gannon designed Villa D'Este in Italy (1924), the original nine at Lenzerheide in Switzerland and the original nine at San Andres de Llavaneras, Barcelona, Spain.

Ferdinand Garbin (1928–) ASGCA: President, 1968
Born: Pennsylvania.

Ferdinand Garbin studied agronomy under H. Burton Musser at Pennsylvania State University, receiving a B.S. degree in turfgrass science in 1959. He was associated for a number of years, beginning in 1955, with golf architect James G. Harrison, to whose daughter, Joan, he was married. In the mid-1960s Garbin entered private practice on his own.

Courses by Ferdinand Garbin: (See James G. Harrison)
NEW YORK: Peek 'N Peak Resort, Clymer (1973).
OHIO: Birchwood CC, Sharon (r.9,a.9,1974); Chippewa GC, Barberton (9,1964;9,1967); Mohawk CC, Tiffon (9,1967); Pleasant Vue GC, Paris (9,1967); Steubenville CC (r.9,a.9,1967); Sunnyhill GC, Mogador (r.3,a.9,1967).
PENNSYLVANIA: Beaver Lakes CC, Aliquippa (1974); Blue Knob Resort, Claysburg (9,1974); Blueberry Hill GC, Warren (9,1969); Colonial GC, Uniontown (1973); Cross Creek Resort, Titusville (r.3,a.9,1971); Emporium CC (r.9,a.9,1970); Folmont Resort GC; Four Seasons, Boswell (Exec.9,1976); Four Seasons Resort, Jennerstown (1974); Greenville CC (r.9,a.9,1970); Lakelawn GC, Harrison City (1970); Lenape Heights GC, Ford City (9,1966); Logo de Vita GC; Meadow Link Farm GC, Murrysville (1969); Pennsylvania State University GC (1965); Rittswood GC, Butler (1965); Sewickley Heights GC; Silver Lake School GC; Valley Brook CC, McMurry (27,1966).
VIRGINIA: Beaver Hills CC, Martinsville (1972); Blacksburg CC (1968); Castle Rock GC, Pembroke (1971); Thorn Spring CC, Pulaski (r.9,a.9,1972).
WEST VIRGINIA: Skyline GC, Osage (r.18,a.9,1971).
PUERTO RICO: Dorado del Mar.
Courses Remodeled by Ferdinand Garbin:
NEW YORK: Elmira CC (7,1968).
PENNSYLVANIA: Blue Ridge CC, Harrisburg (3,1964,c.Harrison); Highland CC; Park Hills CC, Altoona (5,1973); Somerset CC (r.4,irrigation for 9,1974); Suncrest CC, Butler (7,1966); Westmoreland CC, Export (3,1974); Wildwood CC (2,1972).

Ronald M. Garl (1945–)

A native of Lakeland, Florida, Ronald Garl attended the University of Florida on the first scholarship ever granted by the Florida State Golf Association. He graduated in 1967 with a B.S.A. degree in turfgrass science and shortly thereafter entered private practice as a golf course architect based in Lakeland. Garl was elected president of the Florida State Golf Association in 1979.

Courses by Ronald M. Garl:
ALABAMA: Ozark G&CC, Ozark (9).
FLORIDA: Avila GC, Tampa; Babe Zaharias GC, Tampa (1972); Bird Bay G&CC, Venice (exec) Caloosa G&CC, Sun City Center; Centennial CC, Clearwater; Clearwater Golf Park (exec,1971) Continental CC, Wildwood (1972); Cypresswood CC, Winterhaven; Deer Run GC, Arcadia (9); Eagle Natural G&CC, Ocala; 400 Club, Stuart; Golf Hammock CC, Sebring (1976); Imperialakes CC, Mulberry (18,1976;a.18); Indian River Trails CC, Vero Beach; Junior Players Wee Links GC, Walt Disney World (exec); King Point West GC, Sun City (1980); Kingsway CC, Lake Suzy (1978); Marina G&CC, Punta Gorda; North Dale GC, Tampa (1978); Orange Blossom GC, Sebring; Plantation CC, Venice (a.18,1980) Punta Gorda Isles G&CC (1971;a.18,1980); Ravines GC, Middleburg (1979); Seven Springs G&CC, New Port Richey (a.18,1978); Sugarmill Woods G&CC, Homosassa (1975); Sweetwater Creek CC, Lakeland; Valle Oaks GC, Zephyr Hills (1979); Wildwood CC.
ILLINOIS: Lake Shore G&CC, Taylorville.
MICHIGAN: Timber Oaks GC, Grand Traverse.
NEW MEXICO: Angel Fire GC, Eagle Nest.
TEXAS: Fairway Oaks G&CC, Abilene.
Courses Remodeled by Ronald M. Garl:
FLORIDA: Martin County G&CC, Stuart; Rogers Park GC, Tampa; University of Florida GC, Gainesville.
NEVADA: Las Vegas CC (1979).

J. Porter Gibson (1931–) ASGCA
Born: Charlotte, North Carolina.

J. Porter Gibson attended Carlisle Military School (S.C.) and received B.S. and C.E. degrees from Belmont Abbey College (N.C.) and an additional C.E. from Clemson University. From 1958 to 1960 he designed golf courses for the Sam Snead Golf and Motor Lodge franchise, and over the next several years planned courses on his own or for the R & G Construction Company.

Between 1971 and 1974, Gibson was a partner in the firm of Tait-Toski-Gibson, Inc., involved in golf course and community planning and construction. This firm, which included well-known golfer and golf teacher Bobby Toski, was a pioneer in the use of waste water for irrigation. Gibson founded Roan High Golf Inc. in 1974.

Courses by J. Porter Gibson:
FLORIDA: Palm Beach National CC, West Palm Beach; Tomoka Oaks CC, Daytona Beach.
GEORGIA: Bacon Park GC, Savannah (a.3r.9).
MARYLAND: Breton Bay CC, Leonardtown; White Plains GC.
NORTH CAROLINA: Elizabeth City GC; Fairmont GC; Gastonia National GC; Kings Mountain GC; Mallard Head CC, Riedell County; Mooresville GC; Northgreen Village CC, Rocky Mount; Northmoore GC, Robbins; Pine Lake CC, Charlotte; Piney Point CC, Norwood; Seascape GC, Kitty Hawk; West Port CC, Denver; Woodbridge CC, Shelby.
SOUTH CAROLINA: Cherokee National GC, Gaffney; Deer Track I CC, Myrtle Beach; Deer Track II CC, Myrtle Beach; Island Green CC, Myrtle Beach (1980); Rock Hill CC; Wedgefield Plantation CC, Georgetown.
VIRGINIA: Ivy Hill CC, Forrest; Round Meadow CC, Christiansburg.

David Arthur Gill (1919–   ) Born: Keokuk, Iowa ASGCA

David Gill attended Iowa State University and obtained a degree in landscape architecture in 1942 from the University of Illinois. After service in the U. S. Army during World War II, he was licensed as an engineer in Illinois. He then went to work for golf architect Robert Bruce Harris, assisting in the design and construction of courses.

Gill opened his own office in Illinois in the 1950s and although struck with polio in 1953, made a remarkable recovery and continued to practice golf architecture on a full-time basis. He went to extraordinary lengths to train and assist young people interested in entering the profession.

Courses by David Gill:
ALABAMA: Decatur CC (9,1959).
ARIZONA: Royal Palms Club, Phoenix (9,1970); Valley CC, Scottsdale (1957).
FLORIDA: Tides CC, St. Petersburg (1972); Vinoy Park Club, St. Petersburg (9,1962).
GEORGIA: Cherokee Town & CC, Atlanta (1957).
ILLINOIS: Arlington CC; Arlington Lakes Muni, Arlington Heights (1976); Arlington Park GC, Arlington Heights (1966); Arrowhead GC, Wheaton (9,1969); Cherry Hills CC, Flossmoor (9,1966); Cress Creek CC, Naperville (1961); Jackson CC, Carbondale (9,1967); Kenlock GC, Lombard (9,1965); Kishwaukee CC, DeKalb (9,1964); Lakeshore CC (a.9); Links Muni at Jacksonville (1978); Nicholas Park Exec. GC; Rochelle CC (9,1965); Thunderbird CC, Barrington (1964); Village Links, Glen Ellyn.
INDIANA: (The) Hulman Links at Lost, Creek, Terre Haute (1977).
IOWA: Elks CC, Council Bluffs (9,1969) [Now Lakeshore CC]; Geneva G&CC; Green Valley Muni, Sioux City (1960); Highland Park GC, Mason City (9,1965); Spencer G&CC (1966); Westwood GC, Newton (9,1967).
MICHIGAN: Harbor Point GC, Harbor Springs (r.15,a.3,1972); Marquette CC (9,1967).
MINNESOTA: Bunker Hills Muni, Coon Rapids (1968); Dwan GC, Bloomington (1970).
MISSOURI: Cape Girardeau CC (9,1969).
NEBRASKA: Fremont GC (11,1961); Loahland CC, Hastings (1964).
NORTH DAKOTA: Heart River Muni, Mandan.
SOUTH DAKOTA: (The) Meadowbrook GC, Rapid City (1976;a.9,1977).
WISCONSIN: Cherokee Park CC, Madison (1964); Ives Groves GC, Racine (1971); North Shore CC, Mequon (27,1965); Parcwood CC, Mequon (1961); Riveroaks CC, Mequon (1961); Villa Du Parc CC [formerly Parewood CC, later Riveroaks CC]; West Bend CC (a.9,1959).
Courses Remodeled by David Gill:
IOWA: Dodge Park GC, Council Bluffs (1970); Duck Creek GC, Davenport (1969).
ILLINOIS: Apple Orchard CC, Bartlet (4,1960); (The) Arsenal Club, Rock Island (1966); Blue Mound CC, Wauwautosa (3,1960); Downer's Grove GC (3,1976); Glen Oak CC, Glen Ellyn (4,1965); Naperville CC (5,1969); Park Ridge CC (4,1964); Rock Island Arsenal GC; Rolling Green CC, Arlington Heights (6,1968); St. Charles CC (1967); Sandy Hollow Muni, Rockford (1973); Sunset CC, Mt. Morris (4,1963).
MICHIGAN: Cascade Hills CC.
MINNESOTA: Green Haven GC, Anoka (3,1971).
NEBRASKA: Happy Hollow GC, Omaha (9,1964); Highland CC, Omaha (1973).
WISCONSIN: Blue Mound CC, Wauwautosa (3,1960); Brown's Lake GC, Burlington (2,1963); Brynwood CC, Milwaukee (6,1964); Meadow Brook G&TC; Ozaukee CC, Mequon (3,1968); Racine GC; Westmoor GC, Brookfield (9,1973).

Garrett D. Gill (1953–   ) ASGCA
Born: Chicago, Illinois.

Garrett Gill received a bachelor's degree in landscape architecture from the University of Wisconsin, and earned a master's degree in the subject at Texas A & M. Throughout his school years, he also trained under his father, golf architect David Gill, and in the late 1970s joined the Gill firm full time. While at Texas A & M, he wrote a forty-page paper, *Golf Course Design and Construction Standards,* which soon entered selected golf course bibliographies.

John Hamilton Gillespie (–1923)

John Hamilton Gillespie, a transplanted Scot, was hitting golf balls around what is now downtown Sarasota, Florida, as early as 1885. Gillespie, who became mayor of Sarasota in the 1920s, is believed to have laid out several of Florida's earliest courses, including Kissamee GC and the Gillespie GC.

Frank Clark Glasson (1913–   )
Born: San Jose, California

The superintendent at Los Altos G&CC after World War II Glasson worked with retired professional Tom Nicoll in restoring the course. In 1950 Glasson formed a course construction firm and by the mid fifties was designing courses several of which he owned and operated.

Courses by Frank Clark Glasson:
CALIFORNIA: Deep Cliff GC, Cupertino; Emerald Hills Exec. GC, Redwood City (9); Fairway Glen GC, Santa Clara; Fall River Valley GC, Fall River Mills (a.9, 1980); Indian Pines G&TC, Mi-Wuk Village (9); Lake Arbor GC; Little Knoll Exec. GC, Napa; Los Gatos Exec. GC, San Jose (9); Palo Alto Hills GC; San Ramon CC (1962); Sunken Gardens Muni, Sunnyvale (9). Sunnyvale Muni; Sunol Valley GC (Cypress & Pines courses 1967; Twain Harte Exec. GC (9); Wakiup Exec. GC (9).
COLORADO: Lake Arbor GC, Arvada.
NEVADA: Paradise Valley CC, Las Vegas (1960).

Harold W. Glissmann (1909–   )
Born: Douglas County, Nebraska.

Harold Glissmann began his career in golf in the 1930s helping his father, Henry, and brother Hans to construct and operate three daily-fee courses near Omaha, Nebraska. When these courses closed during World War II, Glissmann became grounds superintendent at the famed Boys Town community near Omaha.

In the 1950s Glissmann formed a golf design and construction firm and built many small-town courses in Nebraska and Iowa. He also owned and operated daily-fee layouts in Omaha, including Miracle Hills GC. He retired from his design work in 1965 but continued to serve as a turfgrass consultant for clubs and businesses well into the 1970s.

Courses by Harold W. Glissmann:
IOWA: Emmettsburg CC (9,1951); Five-by-80 GC, Menlo (9,1965); Ida Grove G&CC (9).
NEBRASKA: Cedar Hills Executive GC, Omaha (9,1959); Central City CC; Harrison Heights GC, Omaha (c.Glissmanns,1933,n.l.e.); Indian Hills GC, Omaha (c.Glissmanns,1934,n.l.e.); Lakeview GC, Ralston (9,1966); Polk County GC, Osceola (1959); Seward CC (1964); Valley View GC, Fremont (9); Valley View CC, Fremont(9); Westwood GC, Omaha (9 par 3).
Courses Remodeled by Harold W. Glissmann:
IOWA: Council Bluffs CC (c.Glissmanns,1935,n.l.e.).
NEBRASKA: Kearney G&CC.

David W. Gordon: (1922–   ) ASGCA; President, 1959
Born: Mt. Vernon, New York.

David Gordon served as a pilot with the U. S. Army Air Force in World War II and then completed his education at Pennsylvania State University, receiving a B.S. degree in agronomy. From 1947 to 1952 he worked in the field as construction superintendent for his father's firm, the William F. Gordon Company.

Since 1952 he has been a partner in the Gordon firm, involved in the design aspects of the business, and he has continued to maintain the practice since his father's death in 1974.

Courses by David W. Gordon: See also William F. Gordon
FLORIDA: Hidden Hills CC, Jacksonville.
NEW JERSEY: Little Mill CC, Marlton (a.9); Princeton CC.
NEW YORK: Bay Park GC, Long Island; Finger Lakes GC, Ithaca; North Rockland GC; North Woodmere GC, Long Island (9); South Rockland CC.
OHIO: Browns Run CC, Middletown.
PENNSYLVANIA: Blue Mountain CC, Harrisburg; Frosty Valley CC, Danville; Glenhardie CC, Valley Forge (9); Hershey's Mill GC, Malvern; Manada Gap CC; Northampton County CC, Easton (r.12,a.6); Twin Lakes, Souderton (a.9); Warrington G&CC; Wedgewood GC, Allentown.
VIRGINIA: CC of Staunton; Hermitage CC, Richmond.
BERMUDA: Queens Park Exec GC (9).
Courses Remodeled by David W. Gordon:
CONNECTICUT: Hartford CC.
FLORIDA: Timuquana CC, Jacksonville.
NEW JERSEY: Raritan Valley CC, Sommerville.
NEW YORK: Hyde Park Muni, Niagara Falls (36,also a.18).
PENNSYLVANIA: Lehigh CC, Emmaus; Williamsport CC.

William F. Gordon (1893–1974) ASGCA: Charter Member; President, 1953, 1967
Born: Rhode Island, Died Abington, Pa., age 80.

William Gordon was an outstanding track star in his youth and served as an athletic instructor with the U. S. Navy during World War I. Upon discharge he took a job as salesman with the Peterson Seed Company and in 1920 joined the Carter's Tested Seed Company as superintendent of the golf course construction division. In this capacity he constructed courses for such well-known golf architects as Willie Park, Jr., Leonard Macomber, Donald Ross and Devereux Emmet.

In 1923 Gordon joined the firm of Toomey and Flynn, where he remained until 1941, becoming a partner in the late 1920s. During the Depression, he was also part owner and manager of Marble Hall GC in Philadelphia. Gordon founded the Pennsylvania Public Golfers Association and served as its first president from 1936 to 1940, and was also a member and president (1940) of the Philadelphia Public Golfers Association.

In 1941 Gordon formed his own corporation, which was involved until 1945 in the seeding of military installations. For the next five years the firm constructed golf courses for Donald Ross and J. B. McGovern. From 1950 to 1973 Gordon designed and built courses of his own under the incorporated name of William F. Gordon Company. Layouts planned after 1953 were done in collaboration with his son, David. William Gordon was a pioneer in the achievement of perfectly finished surfaces on greens, tees and fairways, and was chairman of the ASGCA's Historical Committee.

Courses by William F. Gordon:
FLORIDA: Ocala Muni.
MARYLAND: Hillendale CC, Townson; Indian Springs CC, Silver Spring (36).
NEW JERSEY: Medford Village GC [formerly Sunny Jim GC].
NEW YORK: Delhi Muni; Engineers CC, Roslyn; Irondequoit CC, Rochester.
PENNSYLVANIA: Bel Air CC, Philadelphia; Bon Air CC, Glen Rock; Brookside CC, Pottstown (r.9,a.9); Colonial CC, Harrisburg; Conestoga CC; Cornwells CC, Eddingston; Indian Valley CC, Telford; Lehigh CC, Allentown; Locust Valley CC, Coopersburg; South Hills GC, Pittsburgh; St. Clair CC, Pittsburgh; Upper Main Line CC, Philadelpha.
VIRGINIA: Goose Creek CC, Leesburg; Warwick CC, Newport News.
WASHINGTON, D.C.: Fairfax CC; Langston GC.
WEST VIRGINIA: Berry Hills CC, Charleston.
Courses Remodeled by William F. Gordon:
NEW JERSEY: Alpine CC; Canoe Brook CC; Green Acres CC, Lawrenceville; Lawrenceville School GC.
PENNSYLVANIA: Buck Hill Inn & CC, Buck Hill Falls; Chambersburg CC; Manufacturer's G&CC; Meadowlands CC, Ambler; Susquehanna Valley CC, Hummels Wharf; Wildwood CC, Allison Park.

181

WEST VIRGINIA: Southmore CC, Charleston.
Courses Planned Jointly by William F. Gordon and David W. Gordon:
CONNECTICUT: Stanwich Club, Greenwich.
DELAWARE: Du Pont, Wilmington (r. Du Pont and Nemours courses; a. Montchanin and Louvier courses).
MARYLAND: Bethlehem Steel Club (Sparrows Point CC; 27); Ocean City G&YC, Berlin.
NEW JERSEY: Buena Vista CC, Buena; Green Knoll GC, Sommerville; Indian Springs GC, Marlton; Newton CC (a.9); Oak Hill GC, Milford; Rochleigh-Bergen County GC, Hackensack; (r. Rockleigh course, a.9 Bergen course); Seaview CC, Absecon (r.18,a.9); Tall Pines Inn GC, Sewell; Willow Brook GC, Moorestown.
NEW YORK: Bethlehem Steel Club, Hamburg; Moonbrook CC, Jamestown (r.12,a.6).
PENNSYLVANIA: Bethlehem Muni; Bethlehem Steel Club, Bethlehem (r.18,a.9); Blackwood CC; Bucks County GC, Jamison; Fairways CC, Warrington; Hawk Valley GC, Bowmansville; Lancaster CC (r.18,a.6); Mahoning Valley CC, Lehighton; Radnor Valley CC, Villanova (r.4,a.14); Saucon Valley CC, Bethlehem (r.Old course; a.Grace, Junior & Weyhill courses); Sunnybrook CC, Plymouth Meeting; White Manor CC, Malvern; Whitford CC, Downington.
VIRGINIA: Ethelwood CC; Williamsburg CC; Willow Oaks CC, Richmond.
WEST VIRGINIA: Oglebay Park Par 3 GC.
CANADA: Elm Ridge CC, Montreal (36); Richelieu Valley CC, Montreal (36).
Courses Remodeled Jointly by William F. Gordon and David W. Gordon:
NEW YORK: Binghampton CC Engineers C, Roslyn; Yahnundasis CC, Utica.
PENNSYLVANIA: Galen Hall CC; Gulph Mills CC; Philmont CC (North course).

Roy L. Goss
iDr. Roy Goss, Washington State University turfgrass specialist, designed several courses in collaboration with Glen Proctor but was best known for turfgrass research and the assistance he gave course superintendents.
Courses by Roy L. Goss and Glen Proctor.
WASHINGTON: Alderbrook G&CC, Union (1970); Lake Padden, Bellingham (1970); Tumwater Valley, Olympia (1970).

Douglas Grant
California amateur champion Douglas Grant was invited by his friend Jack Neville to help design the course that became the famous Pebble Beach CC. Although he did no other design work, Grant was always consulted on changes at Pebble Beach.

Robert Muir Graves (1930–　) ASGCA: President, 1974
Born: Trenton, Michigan.
Robert Muir Graves attended Michigan State University and received a B.Sc. degree in landscape architecture from the University of California in 1953. He entered private practice as a licensed landscape architect in 1955 and gradually specialized in golf design over the next four years. After 1959 he was involved in designing, remodeling or consulting on some 300 golf courses throughout the United States and abroad, working in all major vegetative and climate zones.
Although he was not the first landscape architect to become a golf course planner, Graves is generally felt to have ushered in the era of landscape architecture as the preferred academic background for course designers. He wrote extensively on a number of topics relating to golf course architecture and lectured on the subject at the University of California and at Utah State University.
Courses by Robert Muir Graves:
CALIFORNIA: Big Canyon CC, Newport Beach (1971); Blackberry Farm GC, Monte Vista (9,1962); Carmel Valley G&CC (1964); Chalk Mountain Muni, Atascadero (1977); Cherry Chase GC, Sunnyvale City of San Jose Muni (1968); Diablo Hills GC, Walnut Creek (9,1974); Discovery Bay GC, Stockton El Cariso GC, Sylmar (1976); Franklin Canyon GC, Rodeo (1968); Las Positas Muni, Livermore (1967); Moffett Field GC (a.2nd 9,1968); Moraga CC (9,1974); Naval Postgraduate School, Monterey (9,1961;r.4,1963;a.9,1972); Northstar at Tahoe, Truckee (1980); Rio Bravo GC, Bakersfield Rossmoor Walnut Creek GC (a.9,1975); Royal Oaks GC, Clayton (9,1961); Saratoga CC; (The) Sea Ranch GC (9,1973); Stockdale CC, Bakersfield (9,1975); Swenson Park Muni, Stockton (a.9,1970); Van Buskirk Park Muni, Stockton (a.9,1970); (The) Villages G&CC, San Jose (27,1970); Walnut Creek Muni (1969).
IDAHO: Bigwood GC, Sun Valley (9,1971).
MONTANA: Bill Roberts Muni, Helena (9,1978); Buffalo Hill GC, Kalispell (r.18,a.9,1977); Green Meadow CC, Helena (1981).
NEVADA: Jackpot GC (9,1970).
OREGON: Black Butte Ranch GC (Big Meadows course, 1972), Sisters; Kelso Elks GC (r.9.a.18).
WASHINGTON: Meadow Springs GC, Richland (a.9,r.9,1973); Port Ludlow GC (1975); Washington State University, Pullman (9,1971).
EAST MALAYSIA: Labuan GC, Sabah (9,1975); Sabah G&CC, Kota Kinabula.
Courses Remodeled by Robert Muir Graves:
CALIFORNIA: Almaden CC, San Jose (1,1968); Concord Muni (5,1974); Diablo G&CC (2,1964); Green Hills G&CC, Millbrae (1965); Green Valley G&CC, Suisun (1965); Hillcrest CC, Los Angeles (6,1974); Lake Merced G&CC, Daly City (1965); Lakeside GC, North Hollywood (1972); Los Altos G&CC (9,1973;1,1975); Meadow Club, Fairfax (1964); Mira Vista G&CC, El Cerrito (1,1967); Pajaro Valley CC, Watsonville (1965); Palo Alto Hills G&CC (5,1968); Presidio Army GC, San Francisco (1964); Rancho San Joaquin CC; Round Hill G&CC, Alamo (1975); San Jose G&CC (1968); Sequoyah CC; Stockton G&CC (13,1968).
IDAHO: Hillcrest CC, Boise (6,1968); Plantation GC, Boise (1975).
NEVADA: Glenbrook CC, Lake Tahoe.
OREGON: Columbia Edgewater, Portland (1966); Oswego Lakes CC; Waverley CC (1).
WYOMING: Casper CC (1973); Casper Muni (1973).
WASHINGTON: Pasco Muni (r.a.12); Washington State University GC.

R. G. "Bob" Grimsdell
Based in South Africa before and after World War II, "Bob" Grimsdell designed the Royal Johannesburg (East course), the Swartkop CC in Pretoria, nine holes at Defence GC in Bloemfontein and other new courses in South Africa, as well as revising several of the country's existing layouts, including Durban CC.

E. D. "Sonny" Guy
A long-time Mississippi club professional, "Sonny" Guy served as a director of the Southern Turfgrass Association in the 1950s. Over the years he designed several golf courses within his home state.
Courses by E. D. "Sonny" Guy:
MISSISSIPPI: Grove Park GC, Jackson (9); Livingston Park GC, Jackson (1949); Robbinhead Lakes GC, Brandon (1977); University of Mississippi GC, Oxford; University of Southern Mississippi GC, Hattiesburg (1959).

Herman C. Hackbarth (1883–1974)
Born: Oconomowoc, Wisconsin. Died: Little Rock, Arkansas, at age 91.
Herman "Hack" Hackbarth began a career of nearly fifty years as professional and greenkeeper at the Little Rock CC in Arkansas in 1907. At that time the club had only a six-hole sand greens course, but over the years Hackbarth enlarged and remodeled it into one of the best in the state. He was a well-respected golf teacher; and although never successful competitively himself, several of his pupils won state titles.
Hackbarth was also prominent in the state of Arkansas, planning over forty courses, including such fine layouts as Hardscrabble CC and Pine Bluff CC. A turfgrass expert, he introduced bentgrass greens to Arkansas in 1939, when he installed them at Little Rock CC. He was also instrumental in organizing a state greenkeepers association.
Hackbarth remained at the Little Rock CC until 1956 and even after retirement, lived on the course and played it almost every day.
Courses by Herman C. Hackbarth:
ARKANSAS: Belvedere CC, Hot Springs (194); Carroll County GC(9); CC of Little Rock; Hardscrabble CC, Fort Smith (1926); Magnolia CC (9,1953); Pine Bluff CC (1936); Pla-Mor GC, Fort Smith (1933); Rebsamen Park Muni, Little Rock (17,1953); Riverdale GC, Little Rock (1932); Western Hills CC, Little Rock (1961).
MISSOURI: Dogwood Hills GC, Osage Beach (1963).

Eddie Hackett (1910–　) BAGCA
Eddie Hackett attended the Catholic University School in Dublin, Ireland, and then was a golf professional for nearly fifty years, beginning as an assistant at Royal Dublin. He also worked at the Johannesburg CC, Elm Park GC and Portmarnock GC. During these years, he worked closely with Henry Cotton in England and Belgium and with F. W. Hawtree, who was designing the second course at Killarney GC and the Westport course.
Hackett designed his first golf course in 1964. He was consulting golf architect to the Golfing Union of Ireland, Bord Failte and Great Southern Hotels.
Courses by Eddie Hackett:
IRELAND: Arklow (a.9); Ashford Castle (9); Bantry (9); Ballybofey (a.9); Ballybunion GC (a.2nd course); Bodenstown GC; Boyle (9); Cahir Park (9); Cavan GC (a.9); City of Derry GC (a.9); Clongowes Wood College (9); Clonmel (a.9); Connemara Golf Links; Donegal-Murvagh; Dublin Muni; Enniscrone (a.9); Ferriter's Cove; Golf Cursa Ceann Seibeal; Gweedore (a.9); Letterkenny; Longford GC (a.9); Mahon Muni; Nenagh (a.9); North West (a.9); Operman CC (now Dublin Sports Club); Oughterard (a.9); Rockwell College (9); Roscrea (a.9); Skerries (a.9); Strabane (a.9); Stranorlor (a.9); Trabolgan (9); Tuam; Waterville; County Longford.
Courses Remodeled by Eddie Hackett:
IRELAND: Ardee; Balbriggan; Ballina; Ballinasloe; Ballinrobe; Ballybunion; Baltinglas; Bandon; Birr; Blacklion; Borris; Cairndhu Larne; Callan; Carlow; Carrick-on-Shannon; Carrick-on-Suir; Castlebar; Castlerea; Castletroy; Charleville; Claremorris; Clontarf; Coollattin; Corballis; Courtown; Donabate; Dooks; Douglas; Dunhaoghaire; Dungarvan; East Cork; Edmonstown; Elm Park; Ennis; Enniscorthy; Enniskillen; Fermoy; Foxrock; Gort; Greenore; Greystones; Heath; Hermitage; The Island; Lismore; Loughrea; Lucan; Massereene; Milltown; Mitchelstown; Monkstown; Mountrath; Mullraney; Newcastlewest; Newlands; Nuremore; Omagh; Parknasilla; Portmarnock (8th hole in new 9); Portumna; Rathfarnham; Roscommon; Roscrea; Rossmore; Royal Tara; Rush; Slade Valley; St. Annes; Swinford; Thurles; Tralee; Trim Tullamore; Waterford; Wicklow.

Walter Hagen (1892–1969)
Famed professional golfer Walter Hagen was active as a consultant to the golf architectural firm of Stiles and Van Kleek in the 1920s. He later drew up on his own the plans for the Koganei CC near Tokyo, Japan, completed around 1937.

Robert Bernhardt Hagge
See Robert Von Hagge.

Eugene Hamm (1923–　)
Born: North Carolina.
After service in the U. S. Navy during World War II, Eugene Hamm trained in golf management at Pinehurst, North Carolina, under the GI Bill. Following admission to the PGA, he became assistant to Ellis Maples (later a golf course architect himself). In the mid-1950s Hamm left a head professional job to supervise construction of the Duke University GC, Durham, North Carolina, to the design of Robert Trent Jones.

182

In 1958, after assisting on a second Jones project, Hamm opened his own course design firm and was active in the Carolinas and Virginia for more than twenty years. Always a fine competitive golfer, he won both the 1978 and 1979 Carolinas Seniors on courses of his own design.

Courses by Eugene Hamm:
NORTH CAROLINA: Burlington GC, Greensboro (par 3,1961); Burning Ridge CC, Conway (1979); Chevoit Hills GC, Raleigh (1968); Colonial CC, Thomasville (1973); Echo Farms G&CC, Wilmington (1974); Fairfield Harbour G&CC, New Bern (1975); Falling Creek GC, Kinston (1970); Foxfire G&CC, Pinehurst (18,1968;9,1973;9,1980); Henderson CC (r.9,a.9,970); North Ridge CC, Raleigh (Lakes course,1968;Oaks course,1972); Pilot Knob Park GC, Pilot Mountain (1962); Pine Lake CC, Charlotte (1963); Pine Tree GC, Kernersville (1972); Royal Oaks CC, Chapel Hill (1971); Sippihaw CC, Fuquay-Varina (2nd 9,1968); Wake Forest CC (1967); Washington Y&CC (2nd 9,1973); Wildwood CC, Raleigh (1961); Williamston CC (9,1974); Yadkin CC, Yadkinville (1962).
SOUTH CAROLINA: Azalea Sands GC, North Myrtle Beach (1972); Beachwood GC, North Myrtle Beach (1968); Eagle's Nest GC, North Myrtle Beach (1972); Nicholes GC; Pineland GC, Mullins (1971); Quail Creek GC, Myrtle Beach (1970); Raccoon Run GC, Myrtle Beach (1976); Sea Gull GC, Pawley's Island (1970).
VIRGINIA: Chatham CC (9,1958); DuPont CC, Martinsville (r.9,a.9,1965); Floyd CC (9,1969); Forest Park CC, Martinsville (2nd 9,1964); Gay Hill CC, Galax (9,1963); South Boston CC (r.9,a.18,1963); Spooncreek GC, Stuart (9,1962); Tuscarora CC, Danville (1960).
Courses Remodeled by Eugene Hamm:
NORTH CAROLINA: Chapel Hill CC (1973); Chicorae CC, Dunn (1963); Danville CC (1958); Green Valley G&CC [formerly Cape Fear CC], Fayetteville (1960); Sedgefield CC, Greensboro (1961).
TENNESSEE: Cleveland CC (1968).

George Hansen (–1951)
George Hansen served as superintendent of the Milwaukee (Wisconsin) Park System and designed five of the city's municipal golf courses: Grant Park (1920), Greenfield (1923), Currie (1927), Brown Deer (1929) and Whitnall (1932).

Walter S. Harban (1857–   )
Dr. Walter S. Harban, dentist to several presidents of the United States, was a prominent member of the Green Section of the USGA. He planned the first version of the Columbia CC (n.l.e.) in Maryland and collaborated with golf architect W. H. Tucker on the design of the Bannockburn Club (n.l.e.) in Glen Echo, Maryland. Harban continued to dabble in course design and maintenance in the early 1920s and planned several changes at Columbia, his homecourse.

Jeff D. Hardin (1933–   )   ASGCA
Born: Tolleson, Arizona.
Jeff Hardin received a B.Sc. degree in civil engineering from the University of Arizona in 1959 and was employed for eleven years as a civil engineer, construction manager and golf course designer with the Del E. Webb Corporation in Arizona and California. In this capacity he collaborated on projects in Arizona, California, Hawaii and Spain with such well-known golf architects as Robert Lawrence, George and Tom Fazio, and Milt Coggins.
In 1972 Hardin formed his own engineering management company, Jeff. D. Hardin, Inc., with an engineering approach to integrated golf and housing to include detailed drainage of course and subdivision, grading plans, cost estimates and quantities checked by computer. Greg Nash became associated with Hardin shortly after the firm's establishment.
Courses by Jeff D. Hardin and Greg Nash:
ARIZONA: Belleair, Phoenix (c.Lawrence,1973); Continental CC, Flagstaff (3rd 9,1973;4th 9,1979–81); Continental GC, Schrader Ranch, Scottsdale (1978); Design Master, Peoria (9,1978); Dobson Ranch, Mesa (c.Lawrence, 1974); El Conquistador CC, Tucson (1980–81); El Conquistador Resort GC (9,1980–81); Leisure World GC (2nd 18,1979); Los Caballeros GC, Wickenburg (9,1979); Rio Verde CC (3rd 9,1978); Sun Lakes (lst 9,1972;2nd 9,1973,c.J.Winans; 3rd 9,1979); Sunland Village, Mesa (18,c.Coggins,1974;r.2nd 9,1975); Villa de Paz, Phoenix (a.9,1976); Wigwam West, Litchfield (c.Lawrence,1974).
Sun City, Arizona: Lakes East (c.Webb Staff,1970); Lakes West (c.Webb Staff & Coggins,1968); Palmbrook CC (c.Webb Staff,1971); Quail Run (9,c.Webb Staff,1977); Riverview (c.Webb Staff,1972); Sun City CC (c.Webb Staff,1966); Union Hills CC (c.Webb Staff,1974); Willowbrook (c.Webb Staff & G.&T.Fazio,1972); Willowcreek (c.Webb Staff & G.&T.Fazio,1972).
Sun City West, Arizona: Briarwood CC (c.Webb Staff, 1980-81); Hillcrest GC (c.Webb Staff, 1978); Pebblebrook GC (c.Webb Staff, 1979); Stardust GC (c.Webb Staff, 1980).
CALIFORNIA: Sun City Executive GC (c.Webb Staff,1967).
HAWAII: Kuilima Hotel, Kahuku, Oaju (c.Webb Staff & G.&T.Fazio,1971).
COLOMBIA: Club Campestrie La Colina, Bogota (1974).
Note: Del E. Webb courses Lakes West in Sun City, Arizona, and at Kuilima Hotel in Hawaii were designed by Hardin and the Webb planning staff in collaboration with consulting architects Milton Coggins and George and Tom Fazio as shown above. The rest of the Sun City and Sun City West courses were planned by Hardin and Nash plus the Webb Staff. The Del E. Webb planning staff included combinations of James Winans, John Meeker, and Thomas Ryan, together with Hardin and Nash, who were Webb employees until 1972, for eleven and two years respectively.

T. Benjamin Harmon (–1974)
Benjamin Harmon earned a degree in engineering at Washington State University and in 1952 was hired by Patrick Markovich to serve as his assistant professional at the Richmond (California) CC. A few years later, Markovich bought a large ranch and invited Harmon to lay

out and construct a golf course on it. The result was the original Silverado CC. Harmon later constructed a few courses for golf architect Lawrence Hughes and designed several projects of his own in California in the 1960s before his death in a fishing accident at sea.
Courses by T. Benjamin Harmon:
CALIFORNIA: Bennett Valley GC; Glen County G&CC, Willows (1960); Silverado CC, Napa (c.Dawson,1955); Watsonville CC (27); Wilcox Oaks CC, Red Bluff (1956).

Paul Harney (1929–   )
Four times winner of the Massachusetts Open, Worcester (Mass.) born Paul Harney became a distinguished touring professional. In the 1960s he operated a course design business based in New England and planned his own course, the Paul Harney GC, at Falmouth, Massachusetts.

Donald Harradine (1911–   )   BAGCA: Founding Member; Chairman, 1980
Born: Enfield, England.
Donald Harradine was educated at Woolwich Polytechnic and trained as a golf professional, greenkeeper and club maker under his stepfather, J. A. Hockey, who had himself designed three courses. Harradine's first golf design experience came in 1930, when he remodeled a course at Ragaz Spa, Switzerland. He then worked for and with British golf architects John Morrison, Sir Guy Campbell, C. K. Cotton and Fred Hawtree, and American Edmund Ault.
In his career, Harradine worked on some 300 courses in Angola, Austria, Cyprus, France, Germany, Greece, Italy, Liechtenstein, Poland, Portugal, Rumania, Spain, Canary Islands, Switzerland and Yugoslavia. He has also written numerous articles on course maintenance and with the assistance of his wife, founded the International Greenkeepers Association.
Courses by Donald Harradine:
AUSTRIA: Linz; Seefeld.
FRANCE: Chalampe; Chaumont en Vexin; Nimes; Rochefort en Yvelines; Strasbourg; Valbonne, Cannes.
GERMANY: Bad Pyrmont; Bad Woerishofen; Bielefeld; Erding, Muenchen; Goeppingen; Goettingen; Guenzburg; Heidelberg; Kassel; Oberau, Garmisch Partenkirchen; Prien; Recklinghausen; Regensburg; St. Eurach, Muenchen; Waldkirchen, Tegernsee GC.
GREECE: Corfu; Glyfada near Athens; Rhodes (Rodos) GC.
ITALY: Cervinia; Varese.
SWITZERLAND: Breitenloo; Davos; Lenzerheide; Montreux; Ragaz Spa; Schoenenberg; Zumikon-Zuerich.
YUGOSLAVIA: Bled.
Courses Remodeled by Donald Harradine:
SWITZERLAND: Lugano; Zumikon-Zuerich; Bad Ragaz.

William E. Harries
Between the wars, William Harries operated the firm of Harries and Hall, which was based in Buffalo, New York, and for a short time included a Toronto, Canada, branch office managed by W. Scruggs. After World War II Harries was associated with the firm of Tryon and Schwartz & Associates, Inc. of East Aurora, New York, landscape architects and golf course designers.
Courses by William E. Harries:
NEW YORK: Audubon GC; Beaver Island; Brighton GC, Tonawanda Township; Brookfield CC; Brooklea CC, Rochester; Byron Meadows CC, Batavia; Byrncliff, Varysburg; Elma Meadows, Erie County; Moonbrook CC, Jamestown (2nd 9); Niagara Falls Muni; Normanside CC, Albany; Oneida CC; Sheridan Park GC, Tonawanda Township; Shorewood CC, Dunkirk (9); Thendara CC (9); Turin Highland CC; Westwood CC.
Courses Remodeled by William E. Harries:
NEW YORK: East Aurora CC.

Robert Bruce Harris (1896–1976)   ASGCA: Charter Member; President, 1947, 1948
Born: Gilman, Illinois. Died: Chicago, Illinois, at age 80.
Following service in the U. S. Navy during World War I, Robert Harris attended the University of Illinois, earning a degree in landscape architecture. In 1919 he opened a landscape design business in Chicago and planned a number of school grounds and parks. An avid golfer, he laid out his first course, the Hubbard Trail CC, Hoopeston, Illinois, in 1927. Although his firm continued to specialize in landscape design in the 1930s, he did design and build several more courses during that period.
According to a protégé, Richard Nugent, Harris had faith in the future of golf even in the depth of the Depression. He and his brother purchased several defunct Chicago-area courses, both in the Depression and the post-war years, and successfully renovated and operated them as daily fee courses. Nugent felt that Harris's experiences as a course operator during the Depression and the labor and material shortages of the second World War were responsible for his emphasis on economical maintenance requirements in his designs, almost to a fault, according to his detractors.
Following World War II, Harris devoted virtually full time to golf architecture and rapidly became a leader in the profession. By the 1950s he was busy designing courses throughout the Midwest and the South, and estimated that he planned or remodeled over 150 during his career. Several of his projects featured integrated housing. He was also responsible for training a number of men who became successful course architects, including Lawrence Packard, David Gill, Richard Nugent, Kenneth Killian, Richard Phelps and William Spear.
According to Lawrence Packard, Harris and Stanley Thompson were the first to conceive of a professional society for golf architects, and Harris was a charter member and the first president (1947–48) of the American Society of Golf Course Architects. He was coauthor with Robert Trent Jones of the influential chapter on course design that appeared in the first edition (1950) of H. Burton Musser's *Turf Management*. He spent his final years in retirement at the CC of Florida, his personal favorite design.
Courses by Robert Bruce Harris   Among his best known are:

ALABAMA: Azalea City GC [formerly Spring Hill GC], Mobile (1957).
ARIZONA: Oro Valley G&CC, Tucson (1958); Tucson National GC (1963).
COLORADO: Flatirons CC [formerly Boulder CC], Boulder (1933).
FLORIDA: CC of Florida, Delray Beach (1957).
ILLINOIS: Bunn Park GC, Springfield (1949); Clinton Jaycees GC; Hillcrest CC, Long Grove (1964); Hubbard Trail CC, Hoopeston (1927); Illinois State University GC, Normal (1963); Indian Lakes CC, Bloomingdale (Iroquois & Sioux Trial courses,1965); Lake of the Woods GC, Mahomet (1954); Lincoln Greens Muni, Springfield (1957); Lockhaven CC, Alton (1955); Maplecrest GC, Downers Grove (1958;9 n.l.e.); Midlane CC, Wadsworth (1964); Midwest CC, Oakbrook (r.East course,r.9,a.9,West course;1954); Orchard Hills G&CC, Waukegan (1930); Parkview Muni, Pekin (r.9,a.9,1956); Sullivan CC (Timberlake GC) Sullivan (1954); Valley Green CC, North Aurora (9,1962); Western Illinois University GC, Macomb (9,1942).
INDIANA: Decatur GC (9).
IOWA: University of Iowa GC, Iowa City (Finkbine course,1953); Valley Oaks GC, Clinton (1965).
KENTUCKY: Iroquois Park Muni, Louisville (original 9,1949); The Standard CC, Louisville (original 9,1950).
LOUISIANA: Lakewood CC, New Orleans (1962).
MICHIGAN: Bay City CC (r.9,a.9,1951,n.l.e.); Holly Greens GC, Pontiac (27,1962); Signal Point Club, Niles (1964).
MINNESOTA: Wayzata CC (1958).
MISSOURI: Meadowbrook CC, Ballwin (new site,1961); Ruth Park GC, University City (9,1931;9,1952).
NORTH DAKOTA: Apple Creek G&CC [formerly Bismarck CC], Bismarck; Chakinkapa Park GC, Wahpeton; Grand Forks CC (new site,1964); Jamestown CC (9).
OHIO: Belmont CC, Perrysburg (1968); Glengarry CC, Toledo (r.9,a.9,1957); Kittyhawk Muni, Dayton (Kitty & Hawk courses, 1961); Eagle Course, 1962; Riverbend GC, Miamisburg (1962); Tall Oaks CC, Toledo.
SOUTH DAKOTA: Chamberlain CC (1952).
TENNESSEE: Bluegrass CC, Hendersonville.
WISCONSIN: Playboy Club/Hotel GC, Lake Geneva (Brute course,1968); Riverside Muni, Janesville.
Courses Remodeled by Robert Bruce Harris:
CALIFORNIA: Monterey Peninsula CC, Pebble Beach (r.Shore course,1962).
FLORIDA: Delray Beach G&CC (1949).
ILLINOIS: Acacia CC, Harlem (1951,n.l.e.); Briarwood CC [formerly Briergate CC], Deerfield (1958); Illini Hills CC, Illinois CC, Springfield (1950 & 1962); Itasca CC (1953); Thorngate CC [formerly Vernon Ridge CC], Deerfield (1951).
IOWA: Duck Creek Park GC, Davenport (1957).
NORTH DAKOTA: Edgewood Muni, Fargo (1951); Riverbend GC [formerly Grand Forks CC], Grand Forks (1951).
OHIO: Columbus CC (r.2,1960); Toledo CC (1960).

John Dering Harris (1912–1977)

Born: Chebham, Surrey, England. Died: Puttenham, Surrey, England, at age 64.

John Harris, a low-handicap golfer nearly all his life, was educated in civil engineering at Nautical College in Berkshire, England. His father and uncle operated a construction firm specializing in golf courses, Frank Harris Brothers. Joining the firm after college, Harris had the opportunity of working with most of the leading British golf architects. He became director of the business after his father's death in the 1930s but discontinued operations when war broke out.

Harris served with the Royal Navy during World War II, attaining the rank of Commander. He returned to golf design in the late 1940s, working with architect C. K. Cotton, with whom he formed a partnership in the 1950s. In 1960 Harris left to establish his own firm and begin worldwide operation. By the 1970s his associates included Bryan Griffiths and Michael Wolveridge of Great Britain, Peter W. Thomson (five times British Open Champ) of Australia and Ronald W. Fream of the United States.

Although many of the courses bearing Harris's name were designed and built by members of his staff, many were his own designs; and he traveled the globe to supervise their construction. It was noted after his death that he may have been better known abroad than in Great Britain, for he did relatively little work in his native land. Harris himself once estimated that, including his construction work with Frank Harris Brothers, he had participated in the design, remodeling or building of over 450 courses.

Courses by John Dering Harris: (partial list only)
AUSTRALIA: Royal Canberra GC, Yarralumia (1960); Southport GC, Queensland.
AUSTRIA: Enzesfeld G&CC.
BARBADOS: Barbados G&CC, Christchurch (1974).
DENMARK: Aalborg GC (9); Copenhagen GC.
ENGLAND: Cranbrook GC, Kent; Great Hay GC; Panshanger, Herts; Southwood GC, Hants.
FRANCE: D'uxelles GC (17); Ormesson, Paris.
HONG KONG: Royal Hong Kong CC, Fanling (Eden course,1963).
INDONESIA: Bali Handara CC (1975,c.Thomson,Wolveridge & Fream).
IRELAND: Courtown (c.Cotton); Fermoy GC; Lahinch GC, County Clare (a.3rd 9,1965).
ITALY: Alassio GC; Albarella GC, Venice; GC Garlenda; La Mandria GC, Turin (Original 9,1966); Menaggio E. Cadenabbia GC, Milan; GC Padova.
JAMAICA: Runaway Bay CC, St. Anns (1961).
JAPAN: Nambu Fuji GC, Iwate Prefecture.
NEW ZEALAND: Wairakei GC (1973).
NORTHERN IRELAND: Bushfoot Park.
PORTUGAL: Estoril Sol GC (1975).
ST. KITTS: Royal St. Kitts GC (1973).
SCOTLAND: Dougalston GC, Glasgow.
SINGAPORE: Singapore Island GC (New course,1963).

SPAIN: Club de Campo, Madrid; Campo de Golf Parcelas, Majorca; Campo de Golf Somosaguas, Madrid (1971); Punta Rojja GC, Majorca; Real Club de los Puerta de Hierro, Madrid (r.18,a.18,1962); Royal Madrid; Shangri-La Minorca GC (1977).
TOBAGO: Tobago GC, Mount Irvine (1969).
TRINIDAD: St. Andrews GC, Maravel (New site,1975).
Courses Remodeled by John Dering Harris:
NEW ZEALAND: Hutt GC, Wellington (1966).

James G. Harrison (1900–   ) ASGCA; President, 1955, 1969

Born: Pennsylvania.

James Harrison worked for golf architect Donald Ross, first as a teamster and later as a foreman, between 1921 and 1927. He was then associated for a short time with Hartford, Connecticut, based architect Orrin Smith. In the late 1920s Harrison entered private practice, first planning and building his own course, Pennhurst at Turtle Creek, Pennsylvania. Between 1955 and 1964 he was joined in practice by his son-in-law, Ferdinand Garbin.

Courses by James G. Harrison:
MARYLAND: Maplehurst CC, Frostburg (1955).
MICHIGAN: Warwick Hills CC, Grand Blanc (c.F.Garbin, 1956).
NEW YORK: Cragie Brae CC, Rochester (1962); Webster GC [now Happy Acres], Webster (c.F.Garbin,1957).
OHIO: Chippewa CC, Barberton (1963); Hidden Valley CC; Spring Hill CC, Richmond (1963); Tannenhauf GC, Alliance (1957); Walnut Hills CC, Columbus (1955).
PENNSYLVANIA: Beaumont CC, Hollidayburg (1967); Beaver Valley CC, Beaver Falls (r.9,a.9,c.F.Garbin,1958); Blairsville CC (1963); Bradford GC; Brookside CC, Pottstown (1956); Carradam CC, Irwin (1962); Cedar Brook CC, Bell Vernon (1963); Cumberland CC; Downing Muni; Erie MacCaune CC, Erie (1964); Foxburg CC (1968); Glen Oak CC, Waverly (1959); Harrisburg Sportsman CC (1963); Hidden Valley CC, Reading (1956); Hidden Valley GC, Pottsville (c.F.Garbin,1957); Indiana CC (1963); Lake View CC, North East (1957); Latrobe CC (a.9); Montaus CC, Pittsburgh (1960); Montour Heights CC (r.9,a.9); Mount Lebanon CC; North Fork CC, Altoona (1966); Park Hills CC, Altoona (1966); Penn State University GC (r.18,a.18,1965); Pine Acre CC, Bradford (1970); Punxsutawney CC (1969); Range End GC; Rittwood CC, Butler (1964); Rolling Acres CC, Beaver Falls (1960); Rolling Hills, Pittsburgh (1961); Scranton Muni [now Mt. Cobb Muni] (1958); Sewickley Heights GC; Sportsman GC; Sun Crest CC, Butler (1966); Tamarack CC; Valley Brook, Pittsburgh (1961); Venanco Trails GC; V.F.W. GC (9); Wave Oak CC; Willowbrook CC; Windber GC.
WEST VIRGINIA: Bridgeport GC (1956); Highland Spring CC, Wellsburg (1960); Lake View CC, Morgantown (1956).
PUERTO RICO: Dorado del Mar.
Courses Remodeled by James G. Harrison:
KENTUCKY: Bellefonte CC; Cedar Knoll GC.
NEW JERSEY: Tavistock CC.
OHIO: Geneva On The Lake GC; Lake Forest CC.
PENNSYLVANIA: Bedford Springs CC; Bloomsburg CC; Central Hills CC (r.Original 9); Chestnut Ridge CC; Churchill Valley CC; Conshohocken GC; Edgewood CC; Fox Chapel GC; Grandview GC; Highland CC; Hillcrest CC (r.;a.9); Irwin CC; Pike Run CC; St. Clair CC; Valley Heights GC.
WEST VIRGINIA: Cheat Lake GC; Tygart's Valley CC; Woodland CC.

Xenophon G. Hassenplug (1908–   ) ASGCA

Born: Bellevue, Ohio.

Xenophon Hassenplug attended Ohio Wesleyan University and Toledo University, majoring in civil engineering. His first experience in golf course construction came in 1946, when he was involved in planning irrigation and seeding of an eighteen-hole course being planned by J. B. McGovern at the Overbrook CC near Philadelphia. McGovern died during construction of the course, and Hassenplug went on to complete the eighteen holes and then to collaborate with golf architect ''Dick'' Wilson on two other Pennsylvania projects, Radnor Valley near Philadelphia and Westmoreland CC near Pittsburgh. Upon completion of these layouts, he entered private practice combining golf course design, land planning, irrigation and civil engineering.

Courses by Xenophon G. Hassenplug:
NEW YORK: Shelridge CC.
OHIO: Brookside Muni, Ashland (9,1969); Buckeye Hills CC, Washington Court House (197); Glenwood Muni (9).
PENNSYLVANIA: Indian Lake Lodge (c.A.Palmer); Lone Pine GC, Washington (1969); Mayfield GC, Clarion (1968); Mayview G&CC; Overbrook CC, Radnor (c.McGovern); Radnor Valley (c.Wilson,1947); Rivers Bend GC, Everett (1966); Seven Oaks GC, Beaver (1977); Seven Springs, Chamption (1968); Silver Springs Resort GC; Timberlink GC, Ligonier (1964); Valley Green GC, Greensburg (1964); Westmoreland CC, Export (c.Wilson,1948).
WEST VIRGINIA: Brooke Hills Park, Wellsburg (1977); Coonskin Park, Charleston (1970); Esquire CC, Huntington (1973); Grand Vue Park Par 3 GC; Huntington Elks CC; Marshall Park, Moundsville (1973); St. Marys GC (9,1968); Waterford Park, Chester (9,1967).
Courses Remodeled by Xenophon G. Hassenplug:
MARYLAND: Cumberland CC (r.11,1966).
OHIO: Bowling Green State University (r.9,1972).
PENNSYLVANIA: Chartiers CC, Pittsburgh (1969); DuBois CC (9,1968); Elk County CC, Ridgway (9,1966); Ligonier CC (9,1965); Mt. Odin Muni, Greensburg (9,1967); North Park GC and South Park GC, County of Allegheny (1969); Pittsburgh Field Club (1962–1970); Pleasant Valley CC, Mt. Pleasant (9,1968).
WEST VIRGINIA: Guyan G&CC, Huntington (3,1974).

Walter B. Hatch (1884–1960)

Born: Brockton, Massachusetts. Died: Amherst, Massachusetts, at age 75.

Walter Hatch graduated from the Massachusetts Agricultural College in 1905 and went to work for Donald Ross, later becoming his associate. He is said to have introduced Ross to the use of topographical plans in course design. Hatch traveled widely in the United States and Canada, supervising construction for Ross and sometimes entering into construction contracts. He also planned a number of layouts, although Ross was the architect of record for all except two: the Amherst GC and the Thomas Memorial GC at Turners Falls. These were both in the vicinity of Amherst, Massachusetts, where Hatch maintained an office in the Ross name.

Walter Hatch left the field of golf architecture during the Depression as a result of financial difficulties. He became collector of taxes in Amherst and later did research for local attorney Bruce Brown.

Frederick G. Hawtree (1883–1955)

Born: Ealing, Middlesex, England. Died: Hayes, Kent, England.

F. G. Hawtree, the first of three generations of British golf course architects, started out as a greenkeeper and began designing courses around 1912. Following service with the British Army during World War I, he practiced on his own until 1922, when he formed the partnership of Hawtree and Taylor with J. H. Taylor, one of British golf's "Great Triumvirate." The firm also included George Cann of Taylor's club-making firm as a shareholder and continued until World War II, when it was voluntarily liquidated.

As managing director of the firm, Hawtree was responsible for the day-to-day details and design work, while Taylor handled early interviews with clients and appeared at official openings. At one time, Hawtree had four highly regarded Irish foremen, Regan, Ryan, Brick and Ward, working under him. Each had a special flair for shaping golf courses, and they were widely known throughout the British Isles and on the Continent.

Hawtree and Taylor created some fifty new courses and remodeled another fifty, including the famous Birkdale (now Royal Birkdale) Golf Club. They also produced one of the world's first all-weather driving ranges in London. In 1931 Hawtree built twenty-seven holes for himself at Addington, Croydon, and thus established Britain's first privately owned "daily fee" course.

F. G. Hawtree was instrumental in founding the British Golf Greenkeepers Association and the National Association of Public Golf Courses, and served as president of both. He was also on the board of the Sports Turf Research Institute and on the council of the English Golf Union.

Courses by Frederick G. Hawtree:

ENGLAND: Addington Court Public GC (27); Addington Palace GC, Croydon; All Weather Golf Practice, Kensington; Birmingham Corporation, Marston Green Muni & Pype Hayes Muni; Brighton Corporation, Hollingbury Park and r. Dyke GC; Buckhurst Park (9); Caterham GC (9), Chigwell GC; Crohamhurst GC; Elfordleigh Hotel, Plympton, Devon (9); Enfield U.D.C., Whitewebbs Muni; Harpenden GC, Hammond End; Hartsbourne Manor GC; Heysham GC; High Port, Wilts.; Highwood GC, Bexhill; Holywell Park, Wrotham (9); Hull GC; Ifield GC, Crawley, Sussex; Ipswich GC, Purdis Heath; Knowle GC, Bristol; London County Council, Hainault Forest (a.9); Maxstoke Park, Castle Bromwich GC, Birmingham; Norwich Muni; Pinner Hill GC; Richmond Park GC, Prince's and Duke's courses; Rochford Hundred; Ruislip & Northwood Muni; St. Albans Corporation, Batchwood Hall Muni; Selsdon Park GC; Southampton Corporation Muni (27); Stockgrove GC (9); Swinton Park GC, Lancashire; Wallasey Corporation (18 pitch & putt); Wells-next-the-Sea (9 approach & putt); West Middlesex GC (9); Woodland Manor GC, Otford, Kent; Woolacombe Bay Hotel (9 approach & putt); Worthing Corporation, Hill Barn GC; Wyke Green GC, Osterley.

IRELAND: Arklow GC.

ITALY: Pallanza GC, Lake Maggiore.

PORTUGAL: Lisbon Sports Club (Original 9).

SCOTLAND: Hilton Park GC, Glasgow (c.Taylor); Williamwood GC, Glasgow.

SWEDEN: Bastad GC.

WALES: Rhuddlan GC.

Courses Remodeled by Frederick G. Hawtree:

GREAT BRITAIN: Ashburnam GC; Birkdale GC; Boyce Hill GC, Essex (9); Filton GC, Bristol (9); Freshwater Bay GC (9); Henbury GC; Littlehampton GC (9); Moor Park GC (r. to provide Rickmansworth Muni); Royal Birkdale GC (c. Taylor); Royal Porthcawl GC (4); Sonning GC (9).

IRELAND: Portmarnock GC.

MONTE CARLO: Monte Carlo GC.

Frederick W. Hawtree (1916–) BAGCA: Founding Member; Chairman, 1974; President, 1975

Born: Bromley, Kent, England.

F. W. Hawtree joined his father's firm, Hawtree & Taylor, upon graduation from Oxford in 1938. During World War II, he served with the Royal Artillery in the Far East, where he was taken a Japanese P.O.W. On his return to England he re-entered private practice with his father in the course architecture firm of Hawtree & Son.

After his father's death in 1955, Hawtree continued to maintain the firm and completed some seventy courses over the next twenty-five years. He was joined in 1969 by A. H. F. Jiggens and in 1974 by his son, Martin, the third generation of Hawtree golf architects. Hawtree & Son created courses in Britain, Ireland, France, Italy, Spain, Belgium, Holland, Germany, Switzerland, Iran, South Africa, El Salvador, Morocco and the United States.

F. W. Hawtree remained active in the golfing organizations founded by his father and was himself influential in forming the British Association of Golf Course Architects in 1970. He served as its president in 1978–80. He also participated from its beginnings in the Golf Development Council, for whom he wrote "Elements of Golf Course Layout and Design."

Hawtree summed up his own design philosophy as an attempt to "suit the golf course to the site, not the site to a preconceived notion of what a golf course should be."

Courses by Frederick W. Hawtree:

BELGIUM: Limburg GC, Hasselt; Royal Waterloo GC, Brussels (36).

ENGLAND: Addington Court GC, Croydon (a.18); Ashton-in-Makerfield, Lancashire (9); Bebington (a.9); Bedwell Park; Berwick-upon-Tweed (a.9); Bowring Park, Liverpool; Braintree, Essex; Broome Manor GC, Thamesdown; Burnham & Berrow (a.9); Cheshunt Park; Chipping Sodbury GC, Gloucestershire; Cold Norton, Essex; Deangate Ridge GC, Rochester; Downshire; Duxbury Park Muni; Easingwold, Yorkshire; Eastham Lodge, Merseyside; Easthampstead Park Muni; Eaton Hall, Chester; Enmore Park, Somerset (a.9); Fox Hills, Chertsey, Surrey (Chertsey and Longcross courses); Gog Magog, Cambridgeshire (a.9); Hatchford Brook Muni; Humberstone Muni, Leicester; Ingestre GC, Stafford; Ipswich GC (a.9); John O'Gaunt GC, Bedfordshire (a.18); King's Norton, Birmingham (27); Little Hay GC; Lullingstone Park GC (18;a.9); Lutterworth GC, Leicester; Malkins Bank, Cheshire; Malton & Norton GC, Yorkshire (a.9); Malvern, Worcestershire (a.9); Minchinhampton, Gloucester; Mowsbury Park Muni, Bedford; Nelson GC (a.9); Newcastle under Lyme; P.L. London, Herts; Port Sunlight GC, Eastham Lodge (9); Portsdown Hill, Portsmouth; Poult Wood Muni, Prenton; Risebridge GC, London; Scunthorpe (1979); Southcliffe and Canwick, Lincs; Theydon Bois, Essex (a.9); Tinsley Park, Sheffield; Wellingborough GC, Great Harrowden; Welwyn Garden City, Herts; Western Park Muni; Woodbridge GC, Suffolk (a.9); Worsley Muni (9).

FRANCE: Golf de Bondues, Roubaix (9); G de Cornauaille [formerly G de Quimper], Brittany (9); G de Domont, Paris; G de Lyon (27); G de Prieure, Paris (36); G de Rochefort, Paris; G de St. Metz (9); G de St. Toulouse (a.9,1980); G de Valcros, Hyeres (9); G de Vaudreuil, Normandy; La Herliere GC.

GERMANY: Dusseldorf (Hubbelrath) Land and GC.

HOLLAND: Wittem G&CC (9).

IRAN: Imperial Sports Club, Tehran.

IRELAND: Blainroe, County Wicklow; Corballis GC; Forest Little; Howth Castle, County Dublin (27); Killarney G&FC (Killeen course); Portmarnock (a.9); Westport, County Mayo; Woodbrook GC.

MOROCCO: Societe Africaine du Tourisme, Resort Development Cabo Negro (Original 9).

NORTHERN IRELAND: Killymoon; Lisburn, Belfast; Massereene, Antrim (a.9); Tandragee, County Armagh (a.9).

PORTUGAL: Lisbon Sports Club (a.9).

EL SALVADOR: Casino Club; Country Club, Cuzcatlan (9).

SCOTLAND: Balnagask, Aberdeen; East Kilbride GC, Lanarkshire; East Kilbride Muni; Grangemouth Muni; Torrance House.

SOUTH AFRICA: (The) Country Club, Johannesburg (18 & 9); Plettenberg Bay, Cape Province.

SPAIN: Golf de Pals, Gerona; Roca Llisa, Ibiza (9); Royal Aeroclub de Zaragoza (9); Sitges (a.9); Son Vida, Majorca; Terramar CdG (9); Vallromanas, Barcelona (9); Zaragoza.

SWITZERLAND: Bad Ragaz; Lenzerheide (a.9).

UNITED STATES: Mount Mitchell Lands GC, North Carolina.

WALES: Abergele and Pensam; Llandeilo, South Wales; Fairwood Park, Swansea; Glynhir GC.

Courses Remodeled by Frederick W. Hawtree:

ENGLAND: Delamere Forest GC (7,1979); Doncaster GC (3,1973); Finham Park, Coventry (3,1973); Hillside GC, Southport (1962–68); Lindrick GC (17th green,1968); Pyecombe, Sussex (4,1980); Royal Birkdale (1963 & 1967); Sandiway GC (3,1959); West Lancs GC.

BELGIUM: R. G. C., Les Buttes Blanches, Ghent (3).

FRANCE: Fontainebleau GC (4,1965).

RHODESIA: Royal Salisbury GC (2,1969)

SCOTLAND: Bruntisland Lings Golfing Society, Edinburgh (1972); Morton Hall GC, Edinburgh (r.9.a.5,1979); Western Gailes (4,1975).

SPAIN: San Andres de Llavaneras, Barcelona (9).

WALES: Nefyn GC, N. Wales (5); Royal St. David's GC, Harlech (r.bunkering,1960).

Martin Hawtree (1947–) BAGCA

Born: Beckenham, Kent.

After taking an arts degree at the University of East Anglia and a master's in civic design at the University of Liverpool, Martin Hawtree remained at Liverpool for three years doing research in the history of modern town planning for his doctorate. He joined his father's firm, Hawtree & Son, in 1973.

While families such as the Dunns and the Maples may have worked longer in the business world of golf in general, the Hawtree dynasty—F. G., F. W. and Martin—were probably involved in the longest continuous practice of golf course architecture on record, dating from 1912.

Courses by Martin Hawtree: (The following are his special designs)

ENGLAND: Bedwell Park; Farnham Park, Beaconsfield (a.9); Humberstone Heights Muni, Leicester; Little Hay, Hemel Hempstead (1981).

SCOTLAND: East Kilbridge Muni (Course #2).

See also F. W. Hawtree.

Alexander "Sandy" Herd (1868-1944)

Born: St. Andrews, Scotland. Died London, England.

Alexander Herd won numerous major golf tournaments, including the 1902 British Open in which he used the new rubber core ball. He designed several courses, on his own or in collaboration with others.

Courses by Alexander "Sandy" Herd:

ENGLAND: Aspley Guise & Woburn Sands, Bucks (c.Charles Wilmot); Heysham, Lancs; Lees Hall, Sheffield; Ulverston, Cumbia.

Donald Herfort, Jr. ASGCA

Donald Herfort was employed as senior accountant with the 3-M Corporation in St. Paul, Minnesota, when he was appointed to a committee in charge of building a company course. After consulting with two professional architects, the committee elected to design its own course, and Herfort was chosen to lay it out and to supervise construction. At about the same time, he was involved in the conversion of Lisbon Bissell GC in nearby North Dakota from sand to grass greens. With these experiences behind him and several other projects awaiting him, Herfort left 3-M to devote full time to course architecture.

Courses by Donald Herfort, Jr.:
IOWA: Oneota CC, Deborah (r.9,a.9).
MINNESOTA: Birnamwood GC, Burnsville (9,1969); Chromonix CC, Lino Lakes (9,1970); Cimarron GC, East Oakdale (9,1970); Country View GC, St. Paul (9,1970); Cuyana CC (r.9,a.9); Dellwood National GC (1969); Detroit Lakes CC, Detroit Lakes (9,1968); Edenvale, Eden Prairie (1971); Indian Hills CC, North St. Paul (1970); Interlaken GC, Fairmount (r.9,a.9,1968); Little Crow GC, Kandiyohi County (1968); New Prague GC (9,1967); New Ulm CC (9,1966); Northfield GC (r.9,a.9,1976); Purple Hawk CC, Cambridge (1969); Tartan Park GC, St. Paul (1965).
NORTH DAKOTA: Enderlin GC (9,1968).
SOUTH DAKOTA: Kuehen Park GC, Sioux Falls (9,1975).
WISCONSIN: Amery GC (r.9,a.9,1968); Hudson CC (r.9,a.9,1969); Merrill GC (r.a.9,1972); Royal Scot CC, Green Bay (1970).
Courses Remodeled by Donald Herfort, Jr.:
MINNESOTA: Galls GC, White Bear Lake (1978); Keller GC, St. Paul (1,1970); Minnetonka CC, Excelsior (3,1968); Northland CC, Duluth (1 hole plus all tees,1968); Phalen Park GC, St. Paul (1976); Red Wing CC (9,1967); Wadena GC (9,1977); White Bear Yacht Club (1,1971).
NORTH DAKOTA: Fargo CC (r.irrigation,18,1968); Lisbon Bissell GC, Lisbon (conversion to grass greens,9,1965).
SOUTH DAKOTA: Elmwood Park GC (r.9).

Homer G. Herpel (1906–1977)
Born: St. Louis, Missouri. Died: University City, Missouri, at age 71.
After working as a newspaper cartoonist in his youth, Homer Herpel turned to golf as a career. He became a member of the PGA in 1937 and served as professional at several St. Louis clubs. Retiring as a club professional in 1955, he began designing and supervising construction of courses in the St. Louis area. Herpel worked first in association with golf architect and contractor Chic Adams and later did over a dozen layouts of his own in greater St.Louis.
Courses by Homer G. Herpel:
MISSOURI: Fox Creek CC; North Shore CC (27); Paddock CC; Lodge of the Four Seasons Exec. GC; Teamsters GC, Revely.

Arthur Wright Hills (1930-   ) Born: Toledo, Ohio   ASGCA
Arthur Hills's interest in golf began as a youngster, when he worked on the maintenance crew at the Meadowbrook CC near Detroit. He later studied agronomy at Michigan State University, where he played on the golf team, and then earned a master's degree in landscape architecture at the University of Michigan. Hills was employed with a landscape design firm in Los Angeles for a short time before entering private practice as a golf course architect in 1967, based in Toledo, Ohio. For several years he was associated with British professional Tony Jacklin.
Courses by Arthur Wright Hills:
COLORADO: Tamarron CC, Durango (1974).
FLORIDA: The Club at Pelican Bay, Naples (1979); Estero Woods GC (1975); Imperial CC, Naples (1973); Lakewood GC, Nanles (18 par 3,1979); Myerlee CC, Ft. Myers (1972); Palmetto Pine CC, Cape Coral (1970); Pine Lakes CC (par 3), Naples (1980); San Carlos G&CC, Ft. Myers (a.18 exec,1979); Wilderness CC, Naples (1974); Wyndemere G&CC, Naples (18 par 3,1979); Vista Royale, Vero Beach.
INDIANA: Wabash CC (a.9,1979).
MICHIGAN: Giant Oak GC, Temperance (1970); Millrace CC, Jonesville (9,1971); The Moors, Portage (1979); Riverview Muni (a.9,1979); Wyndwyck CC, St. Joseph (1968).
OHIO: Byrnwych CC, Maumee (1967); Detwiler GC, Toledo (1969); Dunham Muni, Cincinnati (exec.9,1977); Elk Creek GC; Glenview Muni, Cincinnati (27,1974;a.9,1979); Orchard Hills CC, Bryan (r.9,a.9,1967); Shaker Run, Lebanon (1979); Weatherwax GC, Middletown (36,1971).
CANADA: Board of Trade GC, Toronto, Ontario (r.9,a.9,1975).
JAPAN: Higashi Ibaragi CC, Ibaragi (36,1974).
Courses Remodeled by Arthur Wright Hills:
FLORIDA: Dunedin CC (1974); Oxbow CC, Port Labelle (1973).
KENTUCKY: Ft. Mitchell CC (1971).
MICHIGAN: Meadowbrook CC, Northville (1974).
OHIO: Belmont CC, Rossford (1974); Bowling Green University GC (1968); Fairlawn CC, Akron (1973); Highland Meadows GC, Sylvania (1974); Inverness CC, Toledo (1970); Ottawa Park GC, Toledo (1974); Sycamore Creek CC (1969); Toledo CC (9,1974); Wildwood CC, Middletown (1970).
CANADA: Essex G&CC, Windsor, Ontario (1969).

Reuben P. Hines, Sr. (–1964)
Reuben Hines worked as a golf course superintendent for most of his life. He was a member of the Golf Course Superintendents Association. In the late 1940s and early 1950s he held the post of superintendent of Parks in Washington, D.C., and was in charge of five golf courses as well as numerous parklands. He also served as a turf consultant to several golf clubs.
Hines owned and operated a turf nursery in Maryland during the 1950s, and his close contact with golf course contractors and builders led to several remodeling jobs. By the late 1950s he had also designed a half-dozen courses.
Courses by Reuben P. Hines, Sr.:
MARYLAND: Beaver Creek CC, Hagerstown (1956).
VIRGINIA: Courthouse CC, Fairfax (1955); Oak Hills CC, Richmond (1959); Warrenton CC (1959).

WASHINGTON, D.C.: Oxon Run GC (9,1956).
Courses Remodeled by Reuben P. Hines, Sr.:
MARYLAND: Manor CC, Rockville.

Donald Hoenig
Donald Hoenig planned several courses in New England in the 1960s, on his own or in collaboration with his father. Among them are the widely known Pleasant Valley CC at Sutton, Massachusetts; his own course at Thompson, Connecticut; and a floodlit eighteen-hole executive course, the Firefly GC, in Seekonk, Massachusetts, for professional golfer Jo-Anne Gunderson Carner and her husband.

George A. Hoffman (1892-   )
Born: Hackensack, New Jersey.
George Hoffman moved with his parents to a ranch in west Texas at the turn of the century. He gained experience in golf course construction by helping to build a course in the Dominican Republic in 1919.
Returning to Texas in the 1920s, Hoffman entered private practice as a golf architect and designed numerous courses in the western part of the state. With a working knowledge of Spanish, he also landed jobs in Mexico and Central and South America. He remained active until his retirement in the 1970s.
Courses by George A. Hoffman:
TEXAS: Ascarte Park Muni, El Paso (27,1955); Johnson Park GC, Fredericksburg (1969); Riverside GC, San Antonio (1932;r.1962); Windcrest GC, San Antonio (1964); Victoria GC.
MEXICO: Juarez CC,

Karl Hoffman
Hoffman collaborated with German golf architect Bernhard von Limburger before World War II but died soon after the War. See Bernhard von Limburger.

Cecil B. Hollingsworth
A high school football and golf star in Los Angeles, Cecil Hollingsworth attended UCLA and was employed as assistant football coach and physical education instructor there in the early 1930s. He then owned and operated a daily fee golf course in the 1940s, and in the 50s began a large golf complex in El Cajon, the Singing Hills CC. Hollingsworth designed the courses he owned with the exception of the original eighteen holes at Singing Hills, which had been planned by William Johnson.
Courses by Cecil B. Hollingsworth:
ARKANSAS: Twin Lakes GC, Mountain Home (1978).
CALIFORNIA: Alondra Park CC, Lawndale (a.18 par 3,1947); Singing Hills CC, El Cajon (Oak Glen course & Pine Glen exec. course,1967).

Frederic Clark Hood (1866–1942)
Born: Chelsea, Massachusetts. Died: Boston, Massachusetts, at age 76.
Although A. C. M. Croome (Liphook), H. C. Leeds (Myopia), K. Fujita (Kasumigaseki) and Hugh I. Wilson (Merion) are often referred to as "one-time" architects, the truth is that each was an active designer at some time in his career, alone or in association with others. In contrast, F. C. Hood of Kittansett, like George Crump of Pine Valley, was truly a "one-timer", despite references sometimes made to his participation in planning major changes at The Country Club, Brookline, Massachusetts. (That Club's historian, Elmer O. Cappers, could find no evidence that Hood played a role in its planning, although the latter did hold vital acreage for the Club's future acquisition in his own name, at no cost to the Club, from 1916 to 1922.)
Founder and president of the Hood Rubber Company, F. C. Hood was responsible for planning The Kittansett Club at Marion, Massachusetts, built in 1922–23. While credit for the design is sometimes given to the firm of Toomey and Flynn and to Flynn's friend Hugh Wilson, and club records indicate that several experts, including Toomey and Flynn and Donald Ross, were consulted, no construction contract was ever awarded to Toomey and Flynn. Instead, Hood developed preliminary plans prepared by Flynn, completed specifications and acted as construction superintendent on a crew of local men with Kittansett's future greenkeeper, Elliot "Mike" Pierce, as foreman. Hood has given partial credit to Wilson and Flynn for creation of the famous third hole.
This account differs significantly from the often-repeated tale that Toomey and Flynn built the course with a star-studded team, including future design greats William Gordon, Robert Lawrence and L. S. "Dick" Wilson as foremen. The story of Kittansett exemplifies the confusion that sometimes surrounds the origin of a course as a result of popular legend. It is also proof that a talented amateur with a considerable knowledge of top American and British layouts could produce a great golf course.
The nature of course designers being what it is, F. C. Hood would no doubt feel complimented by the manner in which Elmer Cappers discovered who created Kittansett. Playing a round with Hood's son Donald, Cappers remarked, "The Devil himself must have laid out the third hole." "Yes," replied Hood, "it was my father."
F. C. Hood is not to be confused with F. G. Hood, who designed several courses in New Zealand.

Charles "Gus" Hook
"Gus" Hook was the director of Parks and Recreation for the city of Baltimore, Maryland. In this capacity he designed three new municipal courses and remodeled two others. They include Card Park, Clifton Park (r.), Forest Park (r.), Mt. Pleasant (1933) and Pine Ridge (1959).

186

Hugh Leon Howard (1928–)
Born: Graham, Texas.

Leon Howard studied agronomy at Texas A & M University, receiving a bachelor's degree in 1954 and a master's degree in 1959. While in school, he worked part time remodeling greens on local golf courses. The experience led to a master's thesis, "Compaction Problems in Putting Green Soils," which was later referred to by the USGA Green Section Committee in preparing their specifications for greens construction.

Howard designed and built his first original layout in 1958. The next year he formed his own Texas-based landscape architecture firm, concentrating on the design and construction of golf courses in the southwestern United States. Until 1965 he was assisted by Dave Bennett and in the mid-1970s was joined by his brother, Charles Howard.

Courses by Leon Howard:
ALABAMA: Willowbrook CC, Huntsville.
ARKANSAS: Fairfield Bay GC (1974); Hindman Park GC, Little Rock (1967).
COLORADO: Broomfield CC (1961).
KANSAS: Schilling AFB GC, Salina (1965,n.l.e.).
MISSISSIPPI: Fish Lake CC, Greenville (1968); Mississippi Valley College GC, Greenville (1973).
NEBRASKA: Applewood Muni, Omaha (1970).
NEW MEXICO: Gallup Muni (1965); White Sands GC.
OKLAHOMA: Durant CC; Page Belcher Muni, Tulsa (1977).
TENNESSEE: Mill Creek GC, Nashville (1973); Mountain Lake Resort GC, Fairfield Glade (1971); Temple Hills CC, Columbia (27,1973); Two River Muni, Nashville (1974).
TEXAS: Bar-K GC, Leander (1974); Camelot CC, Carrollton (1970); Casaview CC, Dallas; Chaparral CC, Sequin (1970); Clear Creek GC, Fort Hood (1970); Cleburne Muni; Columbian Club, Carrollton (a.9,1960); Corpus Christi Golf Center; DeCardova Bend GC; Diboll Muni (1968); Dyess AFB GC, Abilene (9); East Ranch GC, Austin (1974); Elm Fork Muni, Dallas (1969); Granbury GC; Harlingen CC (1968); Harker Heights Muni (1966); Hideaway-in-the-Pines GC, Bastrop (1971); Highland Lakes GC, Kingsland (1967); Hilltop Lakes CC, Normangee (a.9); Hollylake Ranch GC, Hawkins (1971); Hurricane Creek CC, Anna (1970); Lago Vista CC, Lake Travis (1971); Lakeway GC, Lake Travis (Live Oak course,1966; Yaupon course,1971); Lakewood Village GC, Lake Ray Hubbard (1973); Landa Park GC, New Braufells (1969); Laredo AFB GC (1967); L.B. Houston Muni, Dallas (1969) [formerly Elm Fork Muni]; M & W GC, Winnsboro (1970); Meadowlakes G&CC, Marble Falls (9,1972;n.l.e.); Mesquite Muni (1965); Morris Williams Muni, Austin (1965); New World of Resorts GC, Lago Vista (1976); Nocona Hills CC, Fort Worth (1971); Nolan River CC, Cleburne; North Lake Ranch GC, Georgetown (1973); Oak Hill GC, Austin (1969); Pecan Plantation GC, Granbury (1971); Pedernales GC, Spicewood (1967); Pinewood CC, Beaumont (1961); Red Oaks GC, Brownwood (1970); Rockdale GC (1965); Ross Rogers Muni, Amarillo; Shady Oaks GC, Baird (1967); Sherill Park Muni, Richardson (1973); Sotogrande CC, Fort Worth (1969); Spring Lake GC, Paris (1967); Van Zandt CC, Canton (1966); Webb Hill CC, Wolfe City (1968); Western Hills GC, Fort Worth (1969); White Bluffs of Whitney GC, Whitney Lake (1969); Wildwood CC, Beaumont (1966); Woodcreek Resort CC, Wimberly (a.18); Woodhaven CC, Fort Worth (1969); World of Resorts Inn, Lago Vista.
VIRGINIA: Burke Lake Park GC, Annandale (par 3,1970); Ross Hill Muni, Annandale (1973); Greendale Muni, Alexandria (1977).
Courses Remodeled by Leon Howard:
ARKANSAS: Texarkana CC (9,1958).
LOUISIANA: Shreveport CC.
NEW MEXICO: Albuquerque CC.
TEXAS: Iraan GC (1973); Lakewood CC, Dallas.

Stafford Vere Hotchkin (1876–1953)
Born: Woodhall Spa, Lincolnshire, England. Died: Woodhall Spa, Lincolnshire, England, at age 77.

S. V. Hotchkin served in the Leicestershire Yeomanry during World War I. An officer in the 17th Lancers, he attained the rank of colonel by the time of his retirement from the military. In 1922–23 he served as a conservative member of Parliament and for many years held the post of alderman in the Lincolnshire County Council.

Hotchkin's first golf design experience was the remodeling of his home course, Woodhall Spa, which he purchased in 1920. He then formed Ferigna, Ltd., a firm that dealt with all phases of the golf course business, including design, construction, maintenance, equipment and seed. In the mid-1920s he made an extended tour of South Africa, designing or remodeling a number of the nation's top courses, and many considered him the best architect to have worked there.

In 1930 Hotchkin was joined by fellow military officers Cecil Hutchison and Guy Campbell in a golf design partnership. After a few years, Hutchison and Campbell went into business for themselves, and Hotchkin continued designing on his own until World War II. He then retired to serve as secretary at Woodhall Spa, a position that was later held by his son Neil.

Courses by Stafford Vere Hotchkin:
ENGLAND: Ashridge GC, Hertfordshire (c.Campbell & Hutchinson); Grimsby GC, Lincolnshire; Leeds Castle GC, Kent (c.Campbell & Hutchison); Newmarket GC; Purley Downs GC, Surrey; R.A.F. Cranwell GC; Southdown at Shoreham GC (c.Campbell & Hutchison); Stoke Rochford GC, Lincolnshire; Sutton-on-Sea GC; Warsash CC (c.Campbell & Hutchison); West Sussex GC, Pulborough (1930; c.Campbell & Hutchison); Links, Suffolk.
SOUTH AFRICA: Humewood CC, Port Elizabeth (1929); Maccauvlei CC, Transvaal (1926); Port Elizabeth GC.
Courses Remodeled by Stafford Vere Hotchkin:
ENGLAND: Woodhall Spa GC, Lincolnshire (1922); Royal Worlington and Newmarket.
SOUTH AFRICA: Durban CC (1928); East London CC, Cape Province; Mobray CC, Cape Province; Royal Port Alfred GC, Port Elizabeth.

Henry Barry Hughes (1908–)
Born: Chillicothe, Missouri.

Henry B. Hughes was the son of Henry T. Hughes, a construction superintendent for Donald Ross at the Broadmoor GC in Colorado. While Henry was too young to join brothers Lawrence and Frank on their father's construction crew, he did herd sheep, used in those days to clip grass around the fairways.

In 1924 the senior Hughes moved his family to Denver, where he constructed the Cherry Hills CC for William S. Flynn and remained as greenkeeper at the club. While Lawrence and Frank went to work for Donald Ross, Henry served on his father's greenkeeping crew until 1933, when he took over the head greenkeeper position.

Hughes remained at Cherry Hills until 1947, and then traveled to Mexico City to construct the Club de Golf for brother Lawrence. He returned to Denver in 1950 and for the next thirteen years served as superintendent at the Green Gables GC and designed courses in the Rocky Mountain area. By the mid-1960s he was devoting full time to golf architecture, retaining an associate and later partner, Richard Watson.

Hughes retired from design work in 1970 but remains active in golf, operating and maintaining a course in Denver.

Courses by Henry Barry Hughes:
COLORADO: Adams County GC, Brighton (1965); Aurora Hills GC (1969); Bookcliff CC, Grand Junction (1956); Columbine CC, Littleton (1955;r.1966); CC of Fort Collins (9,1960;9,1969); Estes Park GC (1958); Glenwood Springs GC (9); Hyland Hills CC, Bloomfield (1959); John F. Kennedy Muni, Denver (27,1968); Lake Estes Executive GC, Estes Park (9); Limon GC (9,1967); Loveland Muni (1960); Meadow Hills CC, Denver (1957); Meeker CC (9,1971); Montrose GC (9,1961); Paradise Valley CC, Englewood (27); Sterling CC (1956); Twilight GC, Denver (9 par 3,1960); Valley Hi CC; Windsor Gardens GC.
KANSAS: Belleville CC (9,c.Watson); Scott County GC, Scott City (9).
NEBRASKA: Ashland CC (9,1968;c.Watson); Atkinson-Stuart GC (9 c.Watson); Bloomfield-Wausa GC (9,c.Watson); Colonial GC, Lincoln (9 par 3,1964;c.Watson;n.l.e.); Friend CC (9,1967;c.Watson); Mid-County GC, Arapahoe (9,c.Watson); Wayne CC (c.Watson).
TEXAS: Hunsley Hills CC, Canyon (1962); Sinton Muni (1968,c.Watson).
UTAH: Willow Springs G&CC, Sandy (1960); Willow Creek CC.
WYOMING: Midway GC, Greybull (9,c.Watson); Old Baldy Club, Saratoga (1964); Paradise Valley CC, Casper (1958); Rolling Green CC, Green River.
Courses Remodeled by Henry Barry Hughes:
COLORADO: Hillcrest CC, Durango (9,1954 & 1969).

Lawrence Marion Hughes (1897–1975)
Born: Missouri. Died: San Diego, California, at age 78.

Lawrence Hughes's father, Henry T. Hughes, was employed as construction supervisor for Donald Ross, and in his late teens Larry and brother Frank went to work for him on the Broadmoor GC. After discharge from the Army following World War I, Hughes returned to work for Donald Ross, building a number of courses before settling down upon completion of the Holston Hills CC in Knoxville, Tennessee, to serve as its manager and greenkeeper.

During the Depression, Hughes operated a garage in Denver, Colorado, and in the late thirties began to do a little course design work on the side; but it was not until after World War II that he was offered the opportunity to establish a full-time business. In 1946 he met Johnny Dawson, prominent amateur golfer, member of a golfing family and avid real estate promoter. Dawson was sure of the value of development in southern California and convinced Hughes that there were sufficient underground springs to support golf courses on the desertlike terrain. With Dawson raising the financial backing, Hughes began designing; and in 1947 his first course, the Mission Valley CC in San Diego (now the Stardust CC) opened for play. For the next two decades he continued to create courses in the Southwest and in Mexico, where he built the Club de Golf de Mexico with the help of Mexican golfer Percy Clifford in 1950. Hughes was assisted on many of his jobs by brothers Frank and Henry and by apprentice Harry Rainville. Henry Hughes and Harry Rainville both went on to form successful golf design businesses of their own.

Courses by Lawrence Marion Hughes:
ARIZONA: Antelope Hills GC, Prescott (1956); London Bridge GC, Lake Havasu City (1970); Orange Tree CC [formerly Century CC], Scottsdale (1958); Paradise Valley CC, Scottsdale (1957); Pinewood CC, Flagstaff (1958); Scottsdale CC (1954).
CALIFORNIA: Borrego Springs CC (9,1964); Candlewood CC [formerly Clock CC], Whittier (1954); Corona National GC [formerly Pepper Tree CC], Corona (1964); De Anza Desert CC, Borrego Springs (1959); Eldorado CC, Palm Desert (1958); Green River CC, Corona (1959); Indio Muni (18 par 3,1964); La Canada CC (1962); La Quinta CC (1959); Las Posas CC, Camarillo (1958); Marin CC, Novato (1957); Marine Corps GC, Nebo (Par 3,1952); Palm Springs CC (1958); Palm Springs Ranch GC (1960); Road Runner Dunes Muni; Round Hill G&CC, Alamo (1960); Santa Ana Canyon CC (1960); Santa Barbara Community GC (1955); Stardust CC [formerly Mission Valley CC], San Diego (1947); Thunderbird CC, Cathedral City (1951).
NEVADA: Desert Inn & CC, Las Vegas (1952); Reno CC (1958).
SOUTH DAKOTA: Tomahawk Lake GC [now Homestead Mine GC], Deadwood (9).
TEXAS: Coronado G&CC, El Paso (1961).
MEXICO: Bosques De San Isidro GC, Guadalajara (1973); Chiluca GC (1974); Club Campestre de Hermosillo (9); CC Jurica, Queretaro (1975); Club de Golf Acozac, Mexico City (1973); CdG Mexico, San Buenaventura (27,1949); CdG Santa Anita, Guadalajara (1969); Club Santiago, Manzanillo (1975); El Campestre Chiluca, Mexico City (1975); El Cid G&CC, Mazatlan (a.2nd 9,1971); Mexicali G&CC (1960); San Isidro GC; Valle Alto GC, Monterrey (1955).
Courses Remodeled by Lawrence Marion Hughes:
CALIFORNIA: Imperial G&CC [formerly Barbara Worth CC], El Centro (1955).
MEXICO: Guadalajara CC (1974).

T. Frank Hummel (1926–)
Born: La Junta, Colorado.

Frank Hummel attended Willamette University and Colorado University, receiving a B.S.

degree in engineering in 1948. During the early 1950s, he won many regional amateur golf titles while working as a combustion engineer in Pueblo, Colorado. Turning professional in 1956, he served as club pro in Fort Morgan and later in Greeley, Colorado.

In the early 1960s Hummel designed and built a second nine at the Highland Hills Muni in Greeley. After a few additional projects, he resigned his professional position in 1968 to form a course design firm with Theodore Rupel, superintendent of the famed Cherry Hills CC in Denver. In 1970 Hummel formed his own golf design and construction business with offices in Colorado and Arizona. A licensed pilot, he was active through the 1970s creating courses in some of the more remote areas of the Great Plains.

Courses by T. Frank Hummel:

COLORADO: Aspen Muni (1970); Collindale GC, Fort Collins (1970); Donala CC, Colorado Springs (1973); Durango Muni (9); Eisenhower GC, U.S. Air Force Academy ("Silver" course,1977); Four Lakes CC, Littleton; Foxhill CC, Longmont (1973); Highland Hills Muni, Greeley (a.2nd 9,1963); Louisville Muni; Loveland Muni (a.9); Riverview Muni, Sterling (9,1972); Twin Peaks Muni, Longmont (1978); Wray CC (9,1970).

KANSAS: Buffalo Dunes Muni, Garden City; Emporia Muni (1970); Great Bend Petroleum Club (a.2nd 9); Hesston Muni (1976); Mariah Hills Muni, Dodge City (1974); Prairie Dog GC, Norton (9,1969).

MONTANA: Ennis Muni (9); Jawbone Creek GC, Harlowton; Madison Valley Muni, Ennis; Powder River CC, Broadus; Roundup Muni (Pine Ridge 9).

NEBRASKA: Chadron CC (9); Chappell CC (9,1973); Grand Island Muni (1977); Scottsbluff CC (new site,1976).

WYOMING: Buffalo Muni (9); Gillette CC; Kendrick Muni, Sheridan (a.2nd 9); Niobrara CC, Lusk (9); Red Butte CC, Gillette; Westview Park GC, DuBois (9); Wheatland CC (9).

Charles Hunter (1836–1921)

Charles Hunter succeeded "Old" Tom Morris as greenkeeper and professional at Prestwick. He planned several Scottish courses, including the original Macrihanish, St. Nicholas Prestwick and the original five holes at Troon (1878).

David S. Hunter (1876–   )

The son of Charles Hunter, David emigrated to the United States, where he became professional at Baltusrol and later at Essex County, both in New Jersey. He was the author of *Golf Simplified,* published in 1921. He is known to have laid out the original Mountain Ridge CC (n.1.e.) in New Jersey in 1913 and to have remodeled the East course at Essex County CC in 1916.

Wiles Robert Hunter (1874–1942)

Born: Terre Haute, Indiana. Died: Santa Barbara, California, at age 68.

Robert Hunter attended Indiana University, receiving a B.A. degree in 1896. He was a world-renowned sociologist and author, writing such works as *Poverty* (1904), *Labor in Politics* (1915), *Why We Fail As Christians* (1919) and *Revolution* (1940); and he spent his life addressing and attempting to solve serious social problems. He was among the organizers of the Chicago Bureau of Charities in the late 1890s, and he lived for a time at Jane Addams's Hull House and later at Toynbee Hall in England.

In the early 1900s Hunter served as chairman of the New York Commission for the Abolition of Child Labor. He also participated in a campaign against tuberculosis. In 1910 he ran unsuccessfully for governor of Connecticut on the Socialist ticket. He later resigned from the party and in 1917 moved to California, where he taught and wrote for years at the University of California at Berkeley.

Ironically, Robert Hunter was also an avid enthusiast of golf, in those days considered an elitist sport. During his stays in Great Britain, he studied the great courses; and he had frequent contact in America with prominent course designers. He wrote one of the classic books in the literature of course architecture, *The Links* (1926), which is still considered one of the finest essays on the subject and which contains some remarkable illustrations of true links as well as early American courses.

Hunter was instrumental in luring Alister Mackenzie to California and shortly after publication of *The Links* began assisting the talented Britisher with most of the courses he did in that state. Although there is little evidence of a formal partnership, most club records list "Mackenzie and Hunter" as the architects of: the Cypress Point Club, Pebble Beach (1927); the Meadow GC, Fairfax (1928); the Monterey Peninsula CC, Pebble Beach (r. original course); the Northwood CC (1928); the Pebble Beach Golf Links (r. bunkering, 1927); and the Valley Club of Montecito, Santa Barbara (1928).

The only documented course that Robert Hunter designed on his own is the Berkeley CC which was reorganized after WWII and is now the Mira Vista CC, although some believe this layout was also the result of a collaboration, with architect William Watson.

Michael John Hurdzan (1943–   ) ASGCA

Born: Wheeling, West Virginia.

Michael Hurdzan graduated from Ohio State University in 1966 and then earned an M.S. in turfgrass physiology and a Ph.D in environmental plant physiology at the University of Vermont. From 1957 to 1966 he had worked sporadically for golf architect Jack Kidwell of Columbus, Ohio, and in the early 1970s began practicing with him on a full-time basis. In 1976 they formed the partnership of Kidwell and Hurdzan, Inc.

Although Hurdzan once stated in an article that the chances of becoming a golf course architect are about equal to those of being struck by lightning, the progress of his own career proved it could be done. During his years at the University of Vermont, he operated a ski and sports shop. He also established the University Tree Service, which engaged in course design and construction as well as other landscape services. The firm added new nines to the Barre (Vermont) CC and the Newport (Vermont) CC, and had twenty-eight employees by the time Dr. Hurdzan sold it to return to Ohio.

By the late 1970s Kidwell and Hurdzan was one of the most active course design firms in the nation. In addition to his practice, Hurdzan completed seventy-five hours toward a B.Sc. in landscape architecture at Ohio State University and taught an advanced turfgrass course there, became a captain in the Special Forces Reserves and wrote a monthly column for *Weeds, Trees and Turf* and another on course architecture for *Golf Business.* He also found time to work on a book on the history of golf course architecture and to establish an extensive library of golf books and a large collection of clubs and balls from past eras.

Courses by Michael John Hurdzan: See Jack Kidwell.

Horace G. Hutchinson (1859-1932) Born and died London, England

Horace Hutchinson, renowned British golfer, won the British Amateur in its first and second years of play, 1886 and 1887. He was a prolific golf writer whose numerous publications included the first instructional book on the game, *Hints On Golf* (1886), the *Badminton Book of Golf* (1886) and *Fifty Years of Golf* (1919). Passages in his books provide insight into the development of golf course design during the years when the game was spreading from Scotland to England, throughout the British Empire and finally to the United States. His references to the National Golf Links on Long Island and the Myopia Hunt Club at Hamilton, Massachusetts, were laudatory.

Around 1886 Hutchinson assisted the originator and owner of the Eastbourne GC, Mr. Mayhewe, in planning the course. This was the site of the notorious "Paradise Green," with contours so severe that if a player missed the hole on his first putt he could putt "forever." Hutchinson was also the designer of the Royal West Norfolk in England and a nine-hole course in the Scilly Isles (The Isles of Scilly GC).

Cecil Key Hutchison (1877–1941)

Born: East Lothian, Scotland. Died: London, England, at age 64.

C. K. Hutchison was educated at Eton College, Windsor, where he excelled at all sports, playing on the cricket team, winning the school mile and competing in golf and skating. The son of a locally prominent golfer, he had learned the game on the links at Muirfield. By the turn of the century he was one of the top amateurs in Britain, winning the St. George's Challenge Cup in 1903 and 1910, the "Golf Illustrated" Gold Vase in 1909 and representing Scotland in the annual England–Scotland matches each year from 1904 to 1912. Hutchison was also runner-up in the 1909 British Amateur Championship, where he tragically bogied the home hole at his own home course, Muirfield, to lose one down.

Hutchison joined the Coldstream Guards, fought in the Boer War and later joined the Royal Scots, attaining the rank of major. Captured by Germans during World War I, he was confined to a P.O.W. Camp for several years.

After the war, his competitive game having suffered, Hutchison turned instead to golf course design. He served as assistant to James Braid during the construction of Gleneagles and the reconstruction of Carnoustie in the mid-1920s, and then entered the firm of Colonel S. V. Hotchkin, who had assisted him with remodeling of the course the latter owned at Woodhall Spa. Guy Campbell, a former *Times* sportswriter whose background was remarkably similar to Hutchison's own, also joined the firm. Together the three designed and built many impressive courses in Great Britain during the period from the late twenties to mid-thirties, when golf development was at a near standstill in the United States.

Hutchison was highly regarded in his time for his refreshing approach to golf design and his eagerness to incorporate innovations in his works.

Courses by Cecil Key Hutchison: ("C&H" indicates collaboration with Campbell & Hotchkin)

ENGLAND: Ashridge GC, Berkhamsted, Hertfordshire (C&H); Leeds Castle GC, Kent Southdown at Shoreham GC (C&H); Tadmarton Heath GC, Banbury, Oxon; Warsash GC (C&H); West Sussex GC, Rulborogh, Sussex (C&H,1930); Kingston, Herefordshire.

Courses Remodeled by Cecil Key Hutchison:

ENGLAND: Ganton GC, Scarborough, Yorkshire; Prince's GC, Sandwich, Kent; Royal West Norfolk GC, Brancaster, Norfolk (1928); Woodhall Spa GC, Lincolnshire (1926).

SCOTLAND: Pitlochry GC, Perthshire; Turnberry Hotel GC, Ayshire (r.Arran & Ailsa courses,1938,work suspended at outbreak of war).

Seichi Inouye

One of Japan's leading golf course architects, Seichi Inouye had completed some twenty courses by the early 1960s. It is believed that he may have worked under Kinya Fujita as early as the 1930s.

Courses by Seichi Inouye:

JAPAN: Kasugai CC, Nagoya (East & West courses); Kyushu Shima CC (1964); Yomiuri CC, Nishinomiya (36); Yomiuri CC, Tokyo (1964).

PHILIPPINES: The Valley CC (1964).

Arthur J. Jackson (1894-1981). Died Oklahoma City.

Born in Scotland, Arthur Jackson traveled to America in the early 1900s to join his stepbrother, Leslie Brownlee, in the Oklahoma Territory. After constructing the first golf courses in Oklahoma to Brownlee's designs, Jackson served as professional at a succession of clubs. While at the Tulsa CC just before World War I, he laid out his first course on the Ponca City estate of E. W. Marland, oil magnate and later governor of Oklahoma.

In 1920 Jackson designed and built the Lincoln Park Municipal GC in Oklahoma City, remaining as its pro until his retirement in 1952. He continued to design courses throughout his tenure at Lincoln Park and even did a few in the Oklahoma City area after retirement.

Jackson organized the Oklahoma section of the PGA and served as its first secretary, and in the early 1950s was made a lifetime member of the PGA of America. He was an outstanding teacher and trainer of young professional golfers, and among his assistants at Lincoln Park were U. C. Ferguson (who succeeded him at the course), Ralph Hutchinson (who served for many years at Saucon Valley) and Ralph's brother, Willard Hutchinson.

Courses by Arthur J. Jackson:

OKLAHOMA: Airport GC, Oklahoma City (n.l.e.); Lincoln Park Muni, Oklahoma City (West

course,1921;East course,1932); Marland Estate GC, Ponca City (9,1915,n.l.e.); McAlester CC; Northwest Park Muni, Oklahoma City (1933,n.l.e.); Ponca City Muni (original 9,1951); Southwest Park Muni, Oklahoma City (1932,n.l.e.); Trosper Park GC, Oklahoma City (1958); Woodson Park GC, Oklahoma City (n.l.e.).
Courses Remodeled by Arthur J. Jackson:
  OKLAHOMA: Frederick GC (1949).

Thomas Ridgeway Jackson (1941–) Born: Kennet Sq. Pennsylvania.
  Thomas Jackson trained under and worked with golf architects George Cobb and Robert T. Jones. He entered private practice in 1973.
Courses by Thomas Jackson:
  ALABAMA: Terri Pines CC, Culman.
  FLORIDA: East Lake Woodlands G&CC (1974); Sandestin GC (Inn at Sandestin) (1976).
  GEORGIA: Sea Palms (1974).
  NORTH CAROLINA: Highshore Hills CC (1974); Hyland Hills GC, Southern Pines; High Vista CC; Carolina Shores CC; Granada Farms CC.
  SOUTH CAROLINA: Hickory Knob State Park GC; Oristo G&RC (1973); Pebble Creek CC (1976).
  Courses Remodeled by Thomas Jackson:
  NORTH CAROLINA: Quail Hollow CC (1974).

Al Jamison (1908–)
  Following a long career as a professional, Al Jamison was associated with golf architect Edward B. Ault in the 1950s. After the firm of Ault and Jamison was dissolved in the latter part of the decade, Jamison designed a few courses on his own before his retirement. These included Gordon Trent GC, Lake Wright GC in Norfolk and Pine Crest GC (course # 2) in Fairfax. All were in Virginia.

Don January (1929–)
  Well-known touring professional Don January collaborated with Billy Martindale on the planning of several courses in the Southwest.
Courses by Don January and Billy Martindale:
  OKLAHOMA: Westbury GC, Oklahoma City (1976).
  TEXAS: Brentwood CC; Great Hills GC; Lake County Estates (9,1975); Los Rios CC (1974); Royal Oaks CC, Dallas; Walnut Creek GC (1971); Woodland Hills; Woodcrest CC.

A. H. F. Jiggens   BAGCA
  A chartered surveyor and civil engineer, A. H. F. Jiggens retired from the local government service in England to become a partner in the British golf architecture firm of Hawtree and Son in 1969.
Courses by A. H. F. Jiggens: See Frederick W. Hawtree.

Leo I. Johnson (1918-)
  In 1935 Leo Johnson began working at the Sioux City (Iowa) CC, where he eventually became course superintendent. He designed, built, owned and operated a nine-hole par-3 course, the Sun Valley GC, in Sioux City in the 1950s. Johnson left the Sioux City CC in 1958 to pursue a career in course design and was still active in the 1970s based in the Phoenix– Tucson area.
Courses by Leo I. Johnson:
  IOWA: Ankeny G&CC; Brookside GC, Kingsley (1965); Emerald Hills GC, Arnolds Park (1973); Quail Creek GC, North Liberty (1970); Sun Valley Par 3 CC, Sioux City; Van Buren GC, Keosauqua (1970).
  KANSAS: Paganica G&CC, Hutchinson (1972).
  MINNESOTA: Brightwood Hills GC, New Brighton (1969).
  MONTANA: Cottonwood CC, Glendive (9,1962).
  NEBRASKA: Kearney CC (2nd 9,1972).
  NORTH DAKOTA: Cando GC (1968); Riverwood Mini, Bismarck (1969).
  Courses Remodeled by Leo I. Johnson:
  KANSAS: Council Grove CC (9,1970); Elkhart GC (r.9,add grass greens,1969); Eureka GC (r.9,add grass greens,1969).

Walter Johnson
  Walter Johnson was associated with golf architect Donald Ross until Ross's death. He then established his own practice on a part-time basis.
Courses by Walter Johnson:
  MASSACHUSETTS: Sun Valley GC (rt.); Fresh Pond Muni, Cambridge (9).
  RHODE ISLAND: Kingstown Muni [formerly Quonset Naval Air Station Course]; Potowomat CC (a.9).

William H. Johnson   (1898–1979)   ASGCA
  Born: Pittsburg, Kansas. Died: Los Angeles, California, at 80.
  Bill Johnson, who had worked on a number of railroad crews as a youth, hired onto Willie Watson's construction crew at Lake Arrowhead, California, in 1924. After working on other course construction projects for Watson and for William P. Bell, Johnson became superintendent of the Los Angeles County Parks System in 1931. He remained in that position until 1958, gaining a wide reputation as a turfgrass expert and designing his first golf course, a new "Roosevelt" nine at Griffith Park, where the original course had been taken over by the zoo.
  Johnson began designing courses steadily after World War II, working first on a series of collaborations with William P. Bell and later on his own. An honorary member of the Southern California PGA, Johnson belonged to the Golf Course Superintendents Association of America and served as its president in 1951.
Courses by William H. Johnson:
  CALIFORNIA: Alondro Park CC, Lawndale; Arroyo Seco Par 3 GC; Banning (9,1960); Big Tee Par 3 GC, Buena Park (9,1947); Compton Par 3 GC, Los Angeles (9,1952); DeBell GC, Burbank (1958); Devonshire, Chatsworth (27 par 3,1959); Donney Brook, San Bernardino (18 par 3,1961); El Caballero, San Fernando Valley (1955); El Camino, Ocean Side (1953); Griffith Park GC, Los Angeles (Roosevelt 9,1933;Coolidge 9 par 3,1941; Los Feliz 9 par 3,1944;r.Harding course,1948;r.Wilson course,1948); Harbor Park GC, Wilmington (9,1957); Knollwood, Granada Hills (c.Bell,1957); L & L GC, South Pasadena (18 par 3,1944); Massacre Canyon Inn & CC [formerly Gilman GC], Gilman Hot Springs (River 9,1958); Oceanside CC (1957); Pala Mesa, Fallbrook (1961); Pedley, Glen Avon (18 par 3,1959); Rancho Muni,Los Angeles (c.Bell,1947); Roy Rogers GC, Chatsworth (9 par 3,1956); San Gorgonio GC, Banning (9 par 3,1962); Sepulveda Muni, Encino (Balboa & Encino courses,1953); Silver Creek, San Bernardino (9,1960); Singing Hills, San Diego (1953); South Gate GC (9 par 3,1948); Squires, South of Fallbrook (9 par 3,1961); Twin Lakes, Industrial City (18 par 3,1954); U.S. Veterans Hospital GC, San Fernando (9); U.S. Veterans Hospital GC, Encino (9).
Courses Remodeled by William H. Johnson:
  CALIFORNIA: Bel-Air, Los Angeles (3,1958); Glendora CC (r.9); Victoria CC, Riverside (3,1958).

Robert Johnstone (–1937)
  Born: North Berwick, Scotland. Died: Seattle, Washington.
  In 1905 Robert Johnstone became professional at the Seattle GC, a position he held for the rest of his life. He laid out a new course for the club in 1907. He later designed several other courses in the Pacific Northwest, including Ingleside GC (1909) and Presidio GC (1914), both in San Francisco, California.

A. H. Jolly, Sr. (1882–1948)
  According to A. H. Jolly, Jr., the senior Jolly was one of six brothers, born and raised at St. Andrews, Scotland, who were active in the business world of golf in the United States and Canada between 1901 and 1965. A. H. Jolly, who designed several courses, stayed on for a time as full-time, summer or winter professional at each of them with the exception of the Oconto CC.
Courses by A. H. Jolly, Sr.:
  ARIZONA: Douglas CC (1947); Nogales GC (rebuilt 1945).
  MICHIGAN: Gladstone Community CC (1936); North Shore GC (1927–28); Oconto CC (1929); Riverside CC, Menominee (1920–23).

Rees Lee Jones (1941–)   ASGCA., President, 1978
  Rees Jones graduated from Yale University with a degree in history in 1963 and went on to study landscape architecture at Harvard University's graduate school of design. In 1964 he joined his father's firm, Robert Trent Jones, Inc., where he remained until 1974, when he entered private practice under the firm name of Rees Jones, Inc. While with his father's firm, he was involved in the design or supervision of over fifty golf courses and has since planned a number of notable layouts on his own.
  Jones coauthored the influential Urban Land Institute publication *Golf Course Development*, with landscape architect Guy L. Rando. Jones himself designed, collaborated on the design or supervised the construction of each of the developments described in the book.
  Rees Jones stated repeatedly that a golf course should provide a strong test from the back tees and a more comfortable challenge from the regular men's and women's tees. He played to a seven handicap.
Courses by Rees Lee Jones:
  CONNECTICUT: Redding CC (a.9,1980).
  KENTUCKY: Griffin Gate GC, Lexington (1980).
  SOUTH CAROLINA: Bear Creek GC, Hilton Head (1979); Gator Hole GC, North Myrtle Beach (1980); Oyster Reef GC, Hilton Head Island (1981).
  TENNESSEE: Graysburg Hills GC (1979).
  VIRGINIA: Virginia Beach GC, Virginia Beach.
  NAMIBIA (South West Africa): Swakopmund CC.
  Courses Remodeled by Rees Lee Jones:
  INDIANA: Fort Wayne CC (1978).
  MICHIGAN: Leland CC (1979).
  NEW JERSEY: Montclair GC, Verona (1977; Flanders Valley GC (a.9); Ridgewood CC.
  NORTH CAROLINA: (The) CC of North Carolina, Southern Pines (1977); Myers Park CC, Charlotte (1978).
  PENNSYLVANIA: Eagle Lodge GC, Lafayette Hill (1979).
  TENNESSEE: Meadowview GC, Kingsport (1978).
Courses by Rees Lee Jones in collaboration with Robert Trent Jones: *(partial list)*
  ALABAMA: Alabama International GC, Alpine (West course, 1973).
  FLORIDA: Inverrary CC, Lauderhill (East,West & South courses,1970); Turnberry Isle CC [formerly Aventura CC], North Miami (South course,1971;North course,1974).
  GEORGIA: Fairington G&TC, Decatur (1969); Gordon Lakes GC, Fort Gordon (1975).
  MARYLAND: Ocean Pines G&CC, Ocean City (1972).
  MASSACHUSETTS: Ferncroft CC, Danvers (1970).
  NEW JERSEY: Panther Valley CC, Allamuchy (1969).
  NEW YORK: Bristol Harbor Village GC, Canandaigua (1974); Ransom Oaks CC.
  SOUTH CAROLINA: Arcadian Shores G&HC, Myrtle Beach (1974); Skyway GC, Myrtle Beach (27,1975).
  TEXAS: Rayburn G&CC, Sam Rayburn (a.9,1973); Sugar Creek CC, Houston (Original 18,1970).

189

Robert Trent Jones (1906–   ) ASGCA: Charter Member; President, 1950
Born: Ince, England.

Robert Trent Jones moved with his parents to the United States in 1911. He became a scratch golfer while still a teenager and set a course record at the age of sixteen while playing in the Rochester City Golf Championship. He was low amateur in the 1927 Canadian Open. Jones attended Cornell University, where he followed a course of studies personally selected to prepare himself for a career in golf course architecture. Completing this program in 1930, he undertook additional courses in art. While still at Cornell, he had designed several greens at the Sodus Bay Heights Golf Club in New York. Two of these still exist and are maintained by the club as the earliest examples of Jones's work.

In 1930 Jones became a partner with Stanley Thompson in the firm of Thompson, Jones & Co. of Toronto and New York. These two architects were profoundly influential in the nearly universal acceptance of strategic design in North America. In addition, Jones, more than any other post-World War II golf architect, reversed the trend toward playing equipment becoming the determining factor in how a course should be played. Jones's philosophy was that the course itself should determine play and that every hole should be a difficult par but an easy bogey.

By the mid-1950s Robert Trent Jones had become the most widely known and probably the most influential course architect in history. By 1980 he had planned over 400 courses in play in forty-two states and twenty-three countries, and had remodeled many others. He logged an estimated 300,000 miles by air annually, and in 1974 was selected to design a course near Moscow, the first in Russia since those in the British Colony of czarist days. He also served as architectural consultant to numerous courses hosting major championship tournaments, many of them courses of his own design.

Jones was the author of many essays on golf course architecture, including contributions to Herbert Warren Wind's *The Complete Golfer* (1954), Will Grimsley's *Golf—Its History, Events and People* (1966) and Martin Sutton's *Golf Courses—Design, Construction and Upkeep* (2nd ed., 1950). The Sutton work featured several of Jones's freehand sketches of golf holes. Jones was also the subject of countless articles. The most significant of these to the profession of golf course architecture was Herbert Warren Wind's profile in the *New Yorker* magazine (August 4, 1951).

Robert Trent Jones was the first recipient of the ASGCA's Donald Ross Award for outstanding contributions to golf course architecture. He became an advisory member of the National Institute of Social Science, a member of the American Academy of Achievement and recipient of its 1972 Golden Plate Award, and a member of the Royal and Ancient Golf Club of St. Andrew. In 1981 Jones was given the William D. Richardson Award by the golf writers in recognition of consistent and outstanding contributions. He and his wife, the former Ione Tefft Davis of Montclair, New Jersey, have two sons, Robert Jr. and Rees, both of whom practice golf architecture.

Courses by Robert Trent Jones:

ALABAMA: Alabama International CC, Point Aquarius, Talladega (36); Turtle Point Y&CC, Florence.

ALASKA: Elmendorf AFB GC, Anchorage (1970).

ARIZONA: Goodyear G&CC, Litchfield Park (36); Rio Rico GC (1971); Village of Oak Creek CC, Sedona.

CALIFORNIA: Birnam Wood GC, Santa Barbara; Bodega Harbour GC (9,1974); Calabasas Park CC; Eldorado Hills West, Sacramento (Exec.); Forest Meadows Exec. GC (1974); Laguna Seca Golf Ranch, Monterey; Lake Shastina GC, Shasta; Mission Viejo GC, San Juan Capistrano; Murrieta GC (1970); Pauma Valley CC: Sam Snead All-American Exec. GC, Colton; Sam Snead All-American Exec. GC. San Diego (27); Silverado GC, Napa; Spring Valley Lake GC, Apple Valley; Spyglass Hill GC, Pebble Beach; Valencia Valley GC, Saugus (1965).

COLORADO: Broadmoor GC, Colorado Springs; Eisenhower GC, U. S. Air Force Academy, Colorado Springs; Roxborough Park GC, Denver; Steamboat Springs GC (1975).

CONNECTICUT: Black Hall Club, Old Lyme; Bruce Memorial GC, Greenwich; Fairview CC, Greenwich; Lyman Meadow GC, Middlefield; Patterson Club, Fairfield; Rock Rimmon CC, Stamford (Original 9).

DELAWARE: Wilmington CC South (1960).

FLORIDA: American Golfers Club Exec. GC (1958); Appollo Beach CC, Tampa: Beauclerc CC, Jacksonville; Coral Ridge CC, Ft. Lauderdale; CC of Miami, Hialeah (East & West courses); Inverray Exec. GC and Inverray G&CC (36), Ft. Lauderdale; Kings Point Par 3 GC, Delray Beach (1973); Kings Point West Exec. GC, Sun City (1974): Ponte Vedra Club (9); Royal Palm Y&CC, Boca Raton; Sam Snead All-American Exec. GC, Titusville; Turnberry Isle GC (formerly Aventura CC), Miami (36).

GEORGIA: Atlanta Athletic Club, Norcross (27); Chattahoochee GC, Gainesville; Fairington G&TC, Decatur; Fort Benning CC; Gordon Lakes GC, Augusta (1975); Peachtree GC, Atlanta (c."Bobby" Jones, Jr.); (The) Standard Club, Atlanta; Stone Mountain GC; Sunset Hills CC, Carrollton (9,1949); University of Georgia GC, Athens.

HAWAII: Hawaii Kai, Honolulu (Exec.); Mauna Kea Beach Hotel GC, Kameula; Princeville at Hanalei, Kauai (27); Royal Kaanapali GC, Lahaina, Maui; Waikoloa Village GC, Kameula.

IDAHO: Elkhorn GC, Sun Valley (1975).

ILLINOIS: Hilldale Village GC; (The) Rail, Springfield.

INDIANA: Otter Creek GC, Columbus.

KANSAS: Crestview CC, Wichita (27); Custer Hills GC, Fort Riley (Original 9,1960).

KENTUCKY: CC of Paducah (9,1965;18,1979).

LOUISIANA: Timberlane CC, Gretna.

MAINE: Evergreen Valley CC, Stoneham.

MARYLAND: Camp David GC (1,1954); Congressional CC, Bethesda (r.9,a.9); Golden Triangle CC, Anne Arundel City; Green Spring Valley Hunt Club, Garrison (r.9,a.9); Ocean Pines CC, Ocean City.

MASSACHUSETTS: Crumpin Fox GC, Bernardston (9); Ferncroft CC, Danvers.

MICHIGAN: Boyne Highlands GC, Harbor Springs; CC of Detroit (a.Short course,1966); Oakland Hills, CC, Birmingham (North course); Point O'Woods G&CC, Benton Harbor.

MINNESOTA: Hazeltine National CC, Chaska; Jonathon Par 30 GC, Chaska.

MISSOURI: Four Seasons GC; Bellerive CC, Creve Coeur; Old Warson CC, Ladue.

MONTANA: Yellowstone GC, Billings (1958).

NEBRASKA: Cape Hart GC, Offut AFB, Omaha.

NEVADA: Incline Village Exec. GC and Incline Village GC, Lake Tahoe; Lake Ridge Estates CC, Reno.

NEW HAMPSHIRE: Portsmouth CC (1956).

NEW JERSEY: Duke Estates, Somerville; Hominy Hill GC, Colt's Neck; Panther Valley CC, Allamuchy; Tammy Brook CC, Cresskill; U.S. Veterans Hospital, Lyons; Upper Montclair CC, Clifton (27); Wayne CC (n.l.e.); Willingboro CC.

NEW YORK: Albany CC, Vorheesville; Amsterdam Muni (1939); Baiting Hollow CC, Riverhead (1965); Bristol Harbour Village GC, Canadaigua; Colgate University GC [also known as Seven Oaks GC], Hamilton; Colonie Muni (a.9,1980); Cornell University GC, Ithaca; Cragburn Club, Elam; Durand-Eastman Park GC, Rochester; Eisenhower Park, East.[Meadow (Blue & White courses); Fallsview Hotel GC, Ellenville; Frear Park GC, Troy (9); Green Lakes State Park GC, Fayetteville; Hancock Muni (n.l.e.); IBM CC, Poughkeepsie; James Baird State Park GC, Poughkeepsie; Lido GC, Long Beach; Marine Park GC, New York City (27); Midvale G&CC, Penfield (1930); Montauk G&RC, Manhasset (1961); Pines Hotel GC, South Fallsburg; Quaker Hill CC, Pawling; Raddison Greens GC, Baldwinsville (1977); Ransom Oaks CC, Amherst; Tuxedo Club, Tuxedo Park; West Point (U.S. Military Academy) GC; Wiltwyck CC, Kingston.

NORTH CAROLINA: Carolina Trace G&CC, Sanford (18;a.9,1978); CC of North Carolina (a.9,1980); Duke University GC, Durham; Tanglewood Park GC, Clemmons (East & West courses).

NORTH DAKOTA: Oxbow CC, Fargo (1975).

OHIO: Arthur Raymond GC, Columbus; Firestone CC, Akron (r.South course;a.North course); Winding Hollow GC, Columbus.

OREGON: West Delta Park GC, Portland.

PENNSYLVANIA: Centre Hills CC, State College (a.9); Taminent-In-The-Poconos.

SOUTH CAROLINA: Arcadian Shores GC, Myrtle Beach; Dunes Golf & Beach Club, Myrtle Beach; Greenville CC (Chanticleer course); Palmetto Dunes GC, Hilton Head (Jones course); Skyway GC (27, 1975); Seabrook Island, Crooked Oaks Course.

TENNESSEE: Link Hills CC,Greenville; Scona Lodge GC, Alcoa.

TEXAS: Corpus Christi CC; Horseshoe Bay GC, Lake LBJ; Houston CC; Rayburn Country G&CC, Sam Rayburn; Shady Oaks CC, Fort Worth (1956); Sugar Creek CC, Ft. Bend County.

VERMONT: Sugarbush CC, Warren; Woodstock CC.

VIRGINIA : Fairfax CC; Fort Beloir GC; Golden Horseshoe GC, Williamsburg; Lower Cascades GC, Homestead Hotel, Hot Springs; Spotswood Exec. GC (9); Stumpy Lake GC, Norfolk.

WEST VIRGINIA: Bel-Meadow GC, Clarksburg; Cacapon Springs GC, Cacapon State Park; Speidel GC, Oglebay Park, Wheeling.

WISCONSIN: Madeline Island Golf Links, La Pointe; (The) Springs GC, Spring Green.

BAHAMAS: Cotton Bay Club, Eleuthera.

BELGIUM: Golf de Bercuit, Brussels.

BERMUDA: Port Royal GC, Southampton.

BRAZIL: Brasilia GC.

CANADA: Kananaskis GC, Alberta (36, 1982); London Hunt & CC, Ontario; River Shores G&CC, B.C.

COLOMBIA: "El Rincon" Club, Bogota.

DOMINICAN REPUBLIC: Playa Dorado GC, Puerta Plata (1979).

ENGLAND: Moor Allerton GC, Wike/Bardsey, Yorkshire (27).[

FIJI: Pacific Harbour GC, Deuba.

FRANCE: Bondues GC, Lille.

GUADELOUPE: Golf Internationale de St. Francoise (1978).

ITALY: I Roveri CC, Torino; Pevero GC, Costa Smeralda, Sardinia.

JAMAICA: Half Moon-Rose Hall GC, Montego Bay.

JAPAN: Karuizawa GC [also known as Golf 72](72).

MARTINIQUE: Golf de la Martinique.

MEXICO: Campo de Golf, Tres Vidas, Acapulco (36,1969); Cancun GC; Mazatlan GC (9); Palma Real GC.

MOROCCO: Dar Es Salaam, Rabat (Royal Golf Rabat; 45).

PHILIPPINES: Luisita GC, Tarlac.

PORTUGAL: Troia GC.

PUERTO RICO: Cerromar Beach GC, Dorado Beach (36); Dorado Beach G&TC (36).

SPAIN: Andalucia La Nueve GC, Marbella (Los Naranjas, Los Olivas & 18-hole Par 3 courses); El Bosque GC, Chiva (Valencia); Los Lagos C, Mijas, Milaga; Sotogrande GC (Old, New & 9-hole Par 3 courses).

SWITZERLAND: Golf Club de Geneve, Geneva.

THAILAND: Navatanee GC.

VIRGIN ISLANDS: Fountain Valley GC, St. Croix (1966).

U.S.S.R.: Tovarich Hills GC.

Courses Remodeled by Robert Trent Jones:

ALABAMA: CC of Birmingham (West course,1959); Lakewood CC, Point Clear (1949).

ARKANSAS: North Hills CC, North Little Rock (1979).

CALIFORNIA: Annandale CC, Pasadena (1970); Bel-Air CC, Los Angeles (1974); California GC of San Francisco (5,1967); El Caballero CC, Tarzana (1964); Glendora CC (1965); Hacienda CC, La Habra; Menlo CC, Redwood City; Olympic CC, San Francisco (Lakeside course, 1954); San Gabriel CC; Silverado CC, Napa (1965); Stanford University GC, Palo Alto (1966).

CONNECTICUT: CC of New Canaan (1960); Greenwich CC; Hartford CC, West Hartford; Innis Arden GC, Old Greenwich; Ridgewood CC, Danbury; Round Hill CC, Greenwich.

FLORIDA: Boca Raton Hotel & C (1963); CC of Orlando; LaGorce CC, Miami Beach (1953); Melreese GC [formerly LaJeune GC], Miami (r.,a.4,1966); Ponte Vedra CC, Ponte Vedra Beach (r.18,1954;a.9,1962).

GEORGIA: Augusta National GC (3,1947); Sea Island (Plantation & Seaside 9's).

190

ILLINOIS: St. Charles CC (1933).
MAINE: Portland CC, Falmouth (1951).
MARYLAND: Burning Tree Club, Bethesda (1963 & 1977); Chevy Chase CC (1948); Elkridge CC, Baltimore (1956); Suburban GC, Baltimore (1949).
MASSACHUSETTS: International GC, Bolton (1969).
MICHIGAN: Birmingham CC (1953); Bloomfield Hills CC; CC of Detroit, Grosse Pointe Farms (1952); Detroit GC (36); Oakland Hills CC, Birmingham (South course, 1950,'72 & '78).
MINNESOTA: Interlachen CC, Edina.
MISSOURI: St. Louis CC, Clayton.
NEW JERSEY: Arcola CC, Paramus (1956); Baltusrol GC, Springfield (Lower course, 1953); Canoe Brook CC, Summit (1974); Crestmont CC, West Orange (1978); Essex County CC, West Orange (36); Galloping Hills Park GC, Union; Glen Ridge CC; Green Brook CC, Caldwell; Montclair GC (first 9, 1959); North Jersey CC, Wayne (1979); Rockleigh GC; Tavistock CC, Haddonfield.
NEW YORK: Bartlett CC, Olean; Bellport GC (1965); Century CC, White Plains; Cherry Valley CC, Garden City; Cold Spring CC, Cold Spring Harbor; CC of Buffalo, Williamsville; CC of Rochester (3,1960); Dellwood CC, New City (1956); Garden City CC (1960); Huntington CC; IBM CC, Port Washington (1954); Ithaca CC (Former course,1939); Locust Hill CC, Rochester (1931); Moon Brook CC, Jamestown; Muttontown G&CC, East Norwich; National Golf Links of America, Southampton (1948 & 1969); Niagara Falls CC, Lewiston; North Hempstead CC, Port Washington; Oak Hill CC, Rochester (East course,1956 & 1967); Powelton CC, Newburgh; Sands Point GC, Port Washington; Scarsdale GC, Hartsdale; Siwanoy CC, Bronxville (1953); Sleepy Hollow CC, Tarrytown; Tam-O-Shanter GC, Brookville (1968); Valley View GC, Utica (1940); Vestal Hills CC, Binghamton (1938;n.l.e.); Winged Foot CC, Mamaroneck (West course,1958); Woodmere CC (1952).
NORTH CAROLINA: Charlotte CC (1962); CC of North Carolina, Pinehurst (1976); Linville GC (1965); Pinehurst CC (Courses # 4 & # 5); Tanglewood GC, Clemmons (West course, 1974).
OHIO: Firestone CC, Akron (South course,1960).
OKLAHOMA: Southern Hills CC, Tulsa (1957).
OREGON: Eugene CC (1965); Portland GC (1950).
PENNSYLVANIA: Gulph Mills GC, King of Prussia (4,1966); Oakmont CC (1964); Pittsburgh Field Club (1952); Valley Brook CC, McMurray (9,1979); Westmoreland CC, Export.
TENNESSEE: Belle Meade CC, Nashville (1957).
VIRGINIA: (The) Homestead, Virginia Hot Springs Upper Cascade course.

WISCONSIN: Milwaukee CC (1961 & 1975).
WYOMING: Jackson Hole G&TC (1967).
BERMUDA: Mid Ocean GC (1953).
BRAZIL: Itanhanga GC.
FRANCE: Chamonix GC (1980); Bondues GC, Lille (1967).
GERMANY: GC Hamburg-Ahrensburg, Hamburg (1978).
GREECE: Glyfada GC, Athens (1978).
JAPAN: Sobhu CC, Chiba (1971).

Robert Trent Jones, Jr., (1939–   ) ASGCA
Born: Montclair, New Jersey.

After receiving a B.A. degree from Yale University, Robert Trent Jones, Jr., joined his father's golf design firm in 1960. Eventually he took over the California office and acquired full responsibility for the firm's Western and Pacific Basin practice. He then formed and headed the Robert Trent Jones II Group, Golf Course Architecture and Recreational Planning, based in California with an overseas counterpart, Pacific Planners International, Ltd. He consistently sought staff members with exceptional academic and practical backgrounds.

Jones Jr. became interested in the concept of the golf course as a work of art that blends with its environment. He was the subject of an article in the August 22, 1977 issue of *People* magazine. This and other articles describing his courses indicated wide recognition of his work by the mid-1970s. By 1980 he had designed over sixty courses and remodeled many others, in addition to those he worked on with his father.

Courses by Robert Trent Jones, Jr.:
ALASKA: Elmendorf AFB, Anchorage.
ARIZONA: Houghton Road GC, Tucson; Oak Creek CC, Sedona; Rio Rico G&CC.
CALIFORNIA: Birnam Wood GC, Montecito; Bodega Harbors CC, Bodega Bay (1977); Calabasas Park CC; Forest Meadows GC, Calaveras County; Laguna Niguel GC; Laguna Seca Golf Ranch, Monterey; Lake Shastina Resort (2 courses); Murrieta GC, Murrieta Hot Springs; Shoreline Park Muni, Mountain View; Silverado CC, Napa; Spring Valley Lake CC, Apple Valley.
COLORADO: Arrowhead GC, Littleton (1979) [formerly Roxborough Park GC]; Beaver Creek GC, Avon; Keystone Resort GC; Steamboat Village GC, Steamboat Springs (1975).
HAWAII: Kiahuna Golf Village, Poipu Beach, Kauai; Makena GC, Maui; Maui Resort GC; Princeville Makai GC, Kauai (27); Waikoloa Village, Hawaii (2 courses).
IDAHO: Elkhorn at Sun Valley.
KANSAS: Crestview CC, Wichita (27).
NEVADA: Incline Village Course, Lake Tahoe (par 3); Lakeridge GC, Reno.
NEW MEXICO: Cochiti Lake GC.
NORTH DAKOTA: Oxbow CC, Fargo.
OKLAHOMA: Kaw Lake Golf Resort.
OREGON: Sunriver CC (Fairway Crest Course); West Delta Park GC, Portland.
TEXAS: Green Meadows Golf & Sports Club, Irving; Horseshoe Bay GC, Marble Falls (a.18,1979); Las Colinas G&CC, Irving (a.2nd 18); Mill Creek CC, Salado (a.13,r.5).
WISCONSIN: Madeline Island Golf Links, LaPointe; Sentry International Headquarters GC, Stevens Point.
AUSTRALIA: Mandurah Resort GC, Perth.

FIJI: Pacific Harbour GC, Deuba; Wakaya Island GC.
INDONESIA: Pondok Indah GC, Jakarta Selatan.
JAPAN: Fujikoshi CC, Shiba Prefecture; Golf '72, Karuizawa (5 courses);Ohnuma GC, Onuma, Hokkaido; Sapporo CC. Sapporo, Hokkaido (2 courses; Takakurayama GC, Mt. Takakura; Uenohara GC; Oak Hills CC, Tokyo.
MACAO: Coloane Island GC.
MALAYSIA: Bukit Jambul, Penang; Tanjong Penggerang GC, Johor; Desaru Resort GC.
MEXICO: Campo de Golf, Tres Vidas, Acapulco (East & West courses); Cancun Pok Ta-Pok Resort Course, Quintana Roo; Club Mazatlan Sur, Sinaloa; Mazatlan Resort; Palma Real GC [formerly Ixtapa-Zihuatanejo Resort Course], Guerrero.
PHILIPPINES: Alabang G&CC, Rizal; Calatagan G&CC, Rizal; Canlubang GC, Laguna (2 courses).
THAILAND: Navatanee GC, Bangkok.
Courses Remodeled by Robert Trent Jones, Jr.:
CALIFORNIA: Annandale CC, Pasadena; Bel-Air CC, Los Angeles; California GC, South San Francisco; Glendora CC; Hacienda CC, La Habra; Menlo CC, Woodside; Palo Alto Muni; Pruneridge Farms GC, Santa Clara; San Gabriel CC; Santa Rosa CC; Stanford University GC, Palo Alto.
HAWAII: Kuilima GC, Oahu; Mauna Kea Beach Hotel GC, Kamuela.
IDAHO: Sun Valley Resort.
OREGON: Eugene CC.
WYOMING: Jackson Hole G&TC (1967).
Several courses also appear under Robert Trent Jones, Sr. They were worked on jointly by father and son.

Robert Tyre "Bobby" Jones, Jr. (1902–1971)
Born: Atlanta, Georgia. Died: Atlanta, Georgia, at age 69.

"Bobby" Jones, Jr., was one of the greatest golfers of all time, winning fifteen of the major titles in the world of golf. While he never practiced course architecture himself, he worked with Alister Mackenzie on Augusta National in the early 1930s, with Robert Trent Jones on Peachtree in the early 1950s and with George Cobb on the par 3-course at Augusta National in 1959. All three courses were originally conceptualized by Jones. The first two exerted a profound influence on the golf design profession throughout North America, and the par-3 started a modest nationwide boom in par-3 courses.

In referring to his collaboration with Mackenzie at Augusta National, Jones insisted there was no question that Mackenzie was the architect while he himself was advisor and consultant. He pointed out that no one learns to design a golf course simply by playing golf, no matter how well. He also noted that both he and Mackenzie were great admirers of the Old Course, a remark not lost on golf architects throughout the world.

David W. Kent
A graduate civil engineer, David Kent worked with his father, who was a golf course contractor. In the mid-1950s Kent began designing courses on his own from a base in California, using scale models for his greens. He also set up a service to assist established clubs in maintaining their courses.

Courses by David W. Kent:
CALIFORNIA: Combat Center GC (9); El Niguel CC, South Laguna (1963); Penmar Exec. GC; Twenty Nine Palms Marine Base GC (1960); Valley Verde CC, Poway.
WASHINGTON: Bellevue Muni (1967).
Courses Remodeled by David W. Kent:
CALIFORNIA: Palos Verdes CC, Palos Verdes Estates (1971).

Gary Kern (1937–   ) ASGCA
Born: Indiana.

Gary Kern studied engineering at Texas A & M and Purdue Universities, becoming a licensed land surveyor in Indiana, Ohio and Kentucky. After college he was employed for a time with a civil engineering firm specializing in land planning for single and multi-family developments.

Kern was encouraged by golf architect William Diddel to enter the field in 1969. After assisting on the design of one course, Kern went on to plan a number of layouts on his own and after 1974 devoted full time to golf architecture.

Courses by Gary Kern:
ILLINOIS: Mt. Vernon GC (a.9,1979); Sycamore Hills CC, Paris (r.8,a.10,1976).
INDIANA: Brook Hill GC, Brookville (9,1973); El Dorado G, Greenwood (r.9,a.9,1976); Greenfield CC (r.9,a.9,1976); Greenfield Ramada Camp Inn (9,1974); Knightstown GC (9,1976); Milligan Park GC, Crawfordsville (9,1977); Mohawk Hills GC, Carmel (9,1972); Nappanee Muni (a.9,1979); Raintree Springs GC, Knightstown (1979); Tomahawk Hills GC, Jamestown (9,1971); Turkey Run GC, Waveland (1973).
Courses Remodeled by Gary Kern:
INDIANA: Sky Valley GC, Hillsboro (9,1972).

William H. Kidd, Sr. (1886–1967)
Born: Monteith, Scotland. Died: Minneapolis, Minnesota, at age 81.

William Kidd emigrated to the United States in the early 1900s, becoming professional at the Algonquin CC in St. Louis. He later moved to Interlachen CC in Minneapolis, remaining until his retirement in 1958, when he was succeeded by his son, Willy Jr. The senior Kidd was runner-up in the 1914 Western Open. He took up golf design upon his retirement from Interlachen.

Courses by William H. Kidd, Sr.:
MINNESOTA: Albany CC (a.9,1960); Elk River CC (1962); Faribault CC; Island View GC, Winona (9 & 9 par 3); Princeton CC (9).

Jack Kidwell (1918–) ASGCA: President, 1979
Born: Ohio.
 Jack Kidwell graduated from Columbus (Ohio) Central High School and received credits from the Utah State Agriculture College. In 1938 he and his father purchased a golf course, and Jack served there as a pro-superintendent for twenty-eight years. He became a class A PGA professional and a class A golf course superintendent. In 1936 he was runner-up in the Ohio High School State Golf Tournament to Paul F. "Pete" Dye, who also became well known as a golf course designer.
 Kidwell entered the field of course architecture on a full-time basis in 1957. In 1976 he and Dr. Michael Hurdzan founded the firm of Kidwell and Hurdzan, Golf Course Architects and Consultants.
Courses by Jack Kidwell: (All courses after 1975 in collaboration with Michael Hurdzan)
 FLORIDA: River Green South, Avon Park (a.9,1974).
 INDIANA: Hidden Valley GC, Lawrenceburg (9,1973;a.9,1976).
 KENTUCKY: Kenton County CC, Independence (a.9,1974;a.9,1979).
 OHIO: Airport GC, Columbus (now Port Columbus GC); (1960); Alum Creek Park GC, Gahanna (9,1975); Banks Exec. GC; (Exec 9-Recreation, Dublin (1965); Beckett Ridge G&CC, Cincinnati (1974); Black Hawk GC, Galena (1964); Blacklick Woods Met. Park, Reynoldsburg (r.5,a.18,1972); Blue Ash Muni (a.9,1979); Bolton Field GC, Columbus (1969); Broadview GC, Pataskala (9,1968); Brookside Park GC, Ashland (a.9,1977); Buttermilk Falls GC, Georgetown (9,1979); California GC, Cincinnati (a.4,1975); Cincinnati Muni (1978); Deer Creek State Park Muni, Mt. Sterling (1979); Fostoria GC (a.10,1970); Galion CC (a.9,1967); Groveport GC (a.9,1973;r.1977); HV-JAC GC, Delaware (9,1968); Hiawatha GC, Mt. Vernon (9,1961); Hickory Flat GC, West Lafayette (1968); Hickory Hills CC, Grove City (1979); Hueston Woods State Park, Oxford (1969); Kings Mill GC, Waldo (9,1960); Larch Tree CC, Trotwood (1971); Lakota Hills CC; Lee Win GC, Salem (1967); Licking Springs Golf & Trout Club, Newark (1960); Mohican Hills GC, Wooster (9,1972;a.9,1975); Nuemann Park GC, Cincinnati (3rd 9,1975); Oakhurst CC, Grove City (1958); Ohio University GC, Athens (a.9,1963); Oxbow Club, Belpre (1974); Pine Hills GC, Carrol (1962); Piqua CC (a.9,1974); Pleasant Hill GC, Monroe (1970); Pleasant Valley GC, Medina (1969); Punderson State Park, Cleveland (1969); Reeves GC, Cincinnati (9 par 3,1973); Reid Park, Springfield (North course,1965;South course,1966); River Green GC, West Lafayette (1967); Salt Fork State Park, Cambridge (1970); San Dar Acres GC, Bellville (1975); Shawnee Lookout GC, Cincinnati (1976); Shawnee State Park GC, Portsmouth (a.9,1979); Stoney Creek CC, Reynoldsburg (1964); Sugar Isle GC, New Carlisle (9,1972); Table Rock GC, Centerburg (9,1973;a.9,1976;a.9,1978); Tanglewood GC, Delaware (1968); Thornapple CC, Columbus (1966); Troy CC (a.9,1975); Twin Lakes GC, Mansfield (1959); Upper Landsdowne CC, Ashville (9,1962); Willow Run GC, Alexander (1963); Wilson GC, Columbus (9,1972); Woodland GC, Cable (a.9,1976).
 WEST VIRGINIA: Deerfield CC, Weston (9,1977).
Courses Remodeled by Jack Kidwell:
 OHIO: Brookside CC, Columbus (2,1977); Elyria CC (2,1975); Kenwood CC (36); Lakewood CC, Westlake (1,1975); Marion CC (1977); Miami Shores (1st 9,1977); Mt. Vernon CC (1977); Snyder Park CC, Springfield (4,1962); Wildwood GC, Fairfield (3,1977); Wright Patterson AFB, Dayton (4,1971); York Temple CC, Columbus (1,1975).

Kenneth Killian (1931–) ASGCA
Born: Chicago, Illinois.
 Kenneth Killian graduated in 1957 from the University of Illinois with a B.S. degree in landscape architecture. From 1957 to 1964 he was employed with golf architect Robert Bruce Harris. In 1964 he formed the partnership of Killian and Nugent, Inc. with Richard Nugent.
Courses by Kenneth Killian: (All in collaboration with Richard Nugent)
 ILLINOIS: Buffalo Grove GC (1968); Concord Green GC, Libertyville (9 par 3,1964); Edgebrook GC, Sandwich (1967); Greenshire GC, Waukegan (1964); Kemper Lakes GC, Long Grove (1978); Moon Lake GC; N.T.C. GC, Great Lakes (a.9,1971); River Oaks GC; Robert Black Exec. Muni (1979); Shelby Green GC, Libertyville (1964); Spring Creek GC (a.9,1966); Tinley Park Muni; Weber Park Par 3 GC (9); Western Illinois University GC, Macomb (r.9,a.9,1971); Cook County Forest Preserve GC.
 INDIANA: Notre Dame University, South Bend (1966); Oak Meadow GC, Evansville; Sand Creek GC.
 MICHIGAN: Barrien Hills CC, Benton Harbor (1965); Lost Lake Woods Club, Alpena (a.9,1968–74).
 OHIO: Sugar Creek G&CC.
 VIRGINIA: Poplar Forest GC (9,1980).
 WISCONSIN: Abbey Springs GC, Milwaukee (1972); Evergreen CC; Hartford CC (r.9,a.9,1967); Reedsburg CC (1978); Tuckaway CC, Milwaukee (1967) Yaharah Hills (36).
 Courses Remodeled by Kenneth Killian: (All in collaboration with Richard Nugent)
 ILLINOIS: Bob O'Link GC, Highland Park (1968); Deerpath GC, Lake Forest (1971); Elmhurst CC, Wooddale (1968–72); Evanston CC. Skokie (1968–72); Exmoor CC, Highland Park (1969); Fox Lake CC; Glencoe GC (1964); Joliet CC (1969-73); Lake Shore CC #3, Glencoe (1965–70); Lincolnshire CC, Crete (1964); Medinah GC (1970); Northmoor CC, Highland Park (1970); Onwentsia Club, Lake Forest (1964); Park Ridge CC (3,1966); Ridge CC, Chicago (1972); Skokie CC; Sportsman Muni, Northbrook (27,1978); Wilmette Park GC.
 MISSOURI: Algonquin GC, Glendale (1971).
 WISCONSIN: Brynwood CC, Milwaukee (1968); Butterfield CC, Hinsdale (1967–69); Maple Bluff CC.

William Kinnear (–1945) Born Leven, Scotland.
 A professional golfer from Scotland, William Kinnear designed several courses and revised a number of established layouts in western Canada between the Wars while serving as professional at Riverside CC in Saskatoon. His courses include the Saskatoon CC and Riverside CC as well as several others.

Ronald Kirby (1932–)
Born: Beverly, Massachusetts.
 Ronald Kirby, winner of the Massachusetts State High School Golf Team Championship in 1949 and runner-up in 1950, studied at the Boston Museum School of Fine Arts in 1946 and '47. He then attended the University of Massachusetts's Stockbridge School of Agriculture on a Francis Ouimet Scholarship, receiving an associate degree in agronomy in 1953.
 Kirby served as superintendent on a number of golf courses, including one in the Bahamas designed by "Dick" Wilson. He was then employed for several years with Robert Trent Jones, Inc. in the United States and England. Around 1970 he formed an association with touring professional Gary Player, which became the firm of Kirby, Player and Associates, Inc., Golf Course Architects. This firm, which has planned courses in many parts of the world, has included golf architect Arthur Davis (now in private practice), landscape architects Denis Griffiths and Rodney Wright, and biologist Randy Russell.
Courses by Ronald Kirby: (Kirby, Player & Associates, Inc.)
 ALABAMA: North River GC, Tuscaloosa.
 GEORGIA: Alpine Valley GC; Berkely Hills GC, Norcross (9); Cartersville CC (9); Cartersville Muni (9); Nob North GC, Dalton; Pine Isle, Buford; River North, Macon; Royal Oaks (c. Davis).
 NEW MEXICO: Alto Village (9).
 NORTH CAROLINA: Twin Valley CC, Wadesboro (9).
 SOUTH CAROLINA: Dolphin Head GC, Hilton Head Island; Kiawah Golf Links, Kiawah Beach.
 TEXAS: Fair Oaks CC, San Antonio (1979); Hogan Park, Midland (a.9,1978).
 VIRGINIA: Brandermill, Richmond.
 WEST VIRGINIA: Shawnee Muni, Institute (9,1979).
 JAPAN: Gary Player GC, Kumamota (27,1979); Niigata Forest, Toyoura Village (36); Nishi Nihon GC, Nogata; Odawara GC; Odawara Gotenba, Gotenba (1979).
 PHILIPPINES: Lake Paoay GC, Ilocos Norte (1979); Puerto Azul GC, Pasay City (1980).
 PUERTO RICO: Palmas Del Mar.
 SOUTH AFRICA: Letsatsing GC, Pilansburg (1979); Gary Player GC (Sun City).
 SPAIN: Almerimar, Almeria; Club de Golf Escorpion, Valencia (36); El Paraiso, Estepona, Malaga; Mas Palomas, Gran Canary Islands (North course).
Courses Remodeled by Ronald Kirby: (Kirby, Player & Associates, Inc.)
 GEORGIA: Dalton CC; Druid Hills GC, Atlanta.
 TEXAS: Oak Hills CC, San Antonio (2); Midland CC.
 PHILIPPINES: Wack Wack G&CC, Manila (East course,1979).
 SOUTH AFRICA: Kensington GC, Johannesburg (1980); Royal Johannesburg GC.

Ben Knight (1889–)
 Ben Knight emigrated from Scotland to Minnesota with Willie McFarlane in 1909. In 1919 he laid out the Winona GC in Minnesota, remaining as its professional until his retirement in 1952. At that time he stated he had designed thirty-two courses in Wisconsin and Minnesota during his career.

Donald Joseph Knott ASGCA
 Donald Knott attended the University of California at Berkeley, receiving a Bachelor of Landscape Architecture degree in 1969 and a Master of Architecture degree in 1973. He worked for Robert Trent Jones, Jr. in 1973–4 and again after three years with Trent Jones Sr. in Malaga, Spain. In 1979 he married Victoria Susan Graves, eldest daughter of golf architect Robert Graves.
 Knott participated actively in the design of several Trent Jones Sr. and Jr. courses, including: Coto de Caza in California; Beaver Creek and Keystone GC in Colorado; Makena In Hawaii; Sun River in Oregon; Calatagan in the Philippines; and the remodeling of Sun Valley in Idaho.

Richard La Conte
 Richard La Conte was associated for several years with golf architect William F. Mitchell. He then practiced on his own and later formed a partnership with Edward "Ted" McAnlis.
Courses by Richard La Conte:
 OHIO: Briardale Muni, Euclid; Briarwood GC, Cleveland; Dorlon Park GC; Leaning Tree, Richfield; Willard CC (9); Whetstone River GC.
 FLORIDA: Lone Pine GC, West Palm Beach (Executive 18,1977).

John B. LaFoy (1946–) ASGCA
Born: Forest Hills, New York.
 John LaFoy grew up in Greenville, South Carolina. He attended Clemson University, receiving a B.A. in architecture in 1968. He went to work the same year for golf architect George W. Cobb, later returning to the position after a three-year tour of duty with the U.S. Marine Corps. LaFoy's duties included accompanying Cobb on frequent consultations to Augusta National, an experience much envied by other course architects.
Courses by John B. LaFoy: (All in collaboration with George W. Cobb)
 NORTH CAROLINA: Bryan Park, Greensboro (1973; Grouse Moor, Linville (1978); Pope AFB, Fayetteville (9,1975).
 SOUTH CAROLINA: Clemson University (1976); Cobb's Glen, Anderson (1975); Holly Tree CC, Greenville (9,1974); Keowee Key, Walhalla (1973).
 VIRGINIA: Golden Eagle, Irvington (1976); New Quarter Park, York County (1977); Pohick Bay, Fairfax County (1978); Tides Inn CC (Golden Eagle course).
 WEST VIRGINIA: Glade Springs #2, Beckley (1976); Mountwood Park, Wood County (1977); Twin Falls State Park, Mullens (1978).
Courses Remodeled by John B. LaFoy: (All in collaboration with George W. Cobb)
 MINNESOTA: Somerset CC, St. Paul (9,1976).

Harold "Hal" Lamb

A professional golfer based in Salt Lake City, Utah, Harold Lamb won the 1922 Utah Open. He designed several of his home state's earliest courses, including the CC of Salt Lake City (1922) and Nibley Park Muni (1923).

William Boice Langford (1887–1977) ASGCA: Charter Member; President, 1951, 1963
Born: Austin, Illinois. Died: Sarasota, Florida, at age 89.

William Langford suffered from polio as a child and took up golf as part of a rehabilitation program. He developed into a fine amateur and was a member of three Yale University NCAA Championship teams between 1906 and 1908.

After earning a masters degree in mining engineering at Columbia University, Langford apprenticed with Chicago golf architect Tom Bendelow. He formed his own course design firm in 1915, but it was not until after World War I that he and another Bendelow trainee, Theodore J. Moreau, formed a partnership. Langford and Moreau were active in course design and construction throughout the Midwest in the 1920s.

The firm of Langford and Moreau was producing detailed engineering drawings and balanced cuts and fills for construction as early as the 1920s. Golf architect Samuel Mitchell, who worked for the firm, emphasized the thoroughness of its planning procedures, while E. Lawrence Packard was told by Langford that he had designed some 250 courses and had at one time employed eighty men, including three survey crews of four to six men preparing topos and setting grades.

Langford owned and operated several daily-fee courses in the Chicago area and was a strong promoter of public courses. He served for many years on the USGA Public Links Committee, as well as on local and regional public golf associations. During and after the depression, he wrote several articles advocating three- and six-hole courses with multiple tees.

The Langford and Moreau firm dissolved in the early 1940s, but after World War II Langford again developed a golf design business. In the 1960s, in semi-retirement, he served as consulting golf architect to the landscape architecture firm of McFadzean and Everly of Winnetka, Illinois.

William Langford retired to Florida in the late 1960s. He died there in 1977, just a few weeks short of his ninetieth birthday.

Courses by William Boice Langford:
ARKANSAS: Texarkana CC (c.Moreau).
FLORIDA: The Breakers GC [formerly Royal Poinciana CC], Palm Beach (r.9,a.9,c.Moreau;1926); Eglin AFB GC [formerly Chicago GC], Niceville (c.Moreau,1925;r.1952); Kelsey City GC, West Palm Beach (c.Moreau;n.l.e.); Key West GC (c.Moreau,1923); Martin County G&CC, Stuart (r.9,a.9,1951); Miami Beach CC (1916); St. Lucie River CC. Port Sewall (c.Moreau,n.l.e.); Valparaiso CC (c.Moreau,1927).
ILLINOIS: Acacia CC, Harlem (c.Moreau); Bryn Mawr GC, Lincolnwood (c.Moreau,1921;r.1951); Butterfield CC, Hinsdale (c.Moreau,1921); Fox Lake G&CC (c.Moreau); Franklin County CC, West Frankfort (c.Moreau,1922); Hickory Hills CC, Chicago (9 par 3,9 exec.,1954); Maple Crest GC, LaGrange (9 par 3,1951); Mid City GC, Chicago (c.Moreau,1924;n.l.e.); Morris CC (9,c.Moreau,1925); Oaklawn GC, Chicago (9 par 3,1952); Ravisloe CC, Homewood (c.Moreau); Ruth Lake CC, Hinsdale (c.Moreau); Twin Orchard CC, Bensenville (c.Moreau,1924;n.l.e.); Village Green CC, Mundelein (1955); Winnetka GC (a.9 par 3,1960).
INDIANA: Culver Academy GC (c.Moreau,1922); Gary CC (c.Moreau,1921); Harrison Hills CC, Attica (9,c.Moreau,1923); Maxwelton GC, Syracuse.
IOWA: Credit Island GC, Davenport (c.Moreau,1925); Duck Creek Park GC, Davenport (c.Moreau,1927); Wakonda Club, Des Moines (c.Moreau,1922).
KANSAS: Indian Hills CC, Prairie Village (c.Moreau,1921); Kansas City CC [formerly Indian Creek GC], Shawnee Mission (c.Moreau); Lake Quivira CC, Milburn G&CC, Overland Park (1917).
KENTUCKY: Bowling Green CC; Henderson G&CC.
MICHIGAN: CC of Lansing (c.Moreau); Iron River CC (c.Moreau,1932).
MINNESOTA: Mankato GC (a.2nd 9,a 1954).
NEBRASKA: Happy Hollow C. Omaha (New site,c.Moreau); Highland CC, Omaha (c.Moreau); Omaha CC (New site,c.Moreau,1927).
TENNESSEE: Colonial CC, Memphis (1916,n.l.e.); CC of Morristown (1957); Gatlinburg G&CC (1956); Green Meadow CC, Maryville (Original 9); Ridgeway CC, Memphis (Original 9,c.Moreau,1919;2nd 9, 1950;n.l.e.).
WISCONSIN: Lawsonia Links, Green Lake (c.Moreau,1929); Leatham Smith GC, Sturgeon Bay; West Bend CC (c.Moreau); North Shore CC (n.l.e.).
JAMAICA: St. James GC, Montego Bay (9).
Courses Remodeled by William Boice Langford:
FLORIDA: Coral Gables Biltmore CC; Everglades C, Palm Beach (c.Moreau,1937); Miami Biltmore CC, Coral Gables.
ILLINOIS: Fresh Meadow CC, Hillside; Glen Oak CC, Glen Ellyn; Idlewild CC, Flossmoor (c.Moreau); Riverside CC (1951); Skokie GC, Glencoe (c.Moreau,1938); Tam O'Shanter GC, Niles (1948,n.l.e.); Westmoreland CC, Wilmette (c.Moreau).
IOWA: Keokuk CC (1951).

Robert F. "Red" Lawrence (1893–1976) ASGCA: Charter Member; President, 1956, 1964
Born: White Plains, New York. Died: Tucson, Arizona, age 83.

Robert Lawrence got his first golf design experience working for Walter Travis on the construction of two courses at the Westchester Biltmore CC in 1919. From 1921 to 1932 he was employed with Toomey and Flynn, becoming a partner in the firm.

In the late 1920s Lawrence constructed several Toomey and Flynn designs in Florida,

including thirty-six holes at the Boca Raton Hotel, which he had helped to design. When the design firm was dissolved during the Depression, Lawrence became course superintendent at Boca Raton and remained for twenty years. While there he became friends with the club's teaching professional, Tommy Armour. As a joke, Lawrence once persuaded Armour to instruct a wealthy patron while sitting under a beach umbrella with drink in hand. This unorthodox method eventually became Armour's trademark!

In the late 1930s Lawrence designed a few courses in the Miami area, but most were not built until after World War II. As business improved after the War, Lawrence resigned from Boca Raton to devote full time to golf course architecture. He worked primarily in Florida until 1958 when he moved to Tucson, Arizona. Continuing his practice in the Southwest, Lawrence did some of his finest work, including Desert Forest CC and the University of New Mexico GC. In the 1970s he was assisted by civil engineer Jeff Hardin.

Courses by Robert F. "Red" Lawrence:
ARIZONA: Belleaire Executive GC, Glendale (1974); Boulders CC, Carefree; Camelback Inn & CC, Scottsdale (Camelback course,1970); CC of Green Valley (3rd 9,1973); Desert Forest GC, Carefree (1961); Dobson Ranch GC, Mesa (1975); Fountain of the Sun GC, Mesa (Exec. course,1971); Goodyear G&CC, Phoenix (West course,1974); Meadow Hills CC, Nogales (1960); Nautical Inn Executive GC [formerly Stone Bridge CC], Lake Havasu City; Santa Cruz CC [formerly Kino Springs GC], Nogales (1974); Sierra Estrella GC [formerly Estrella Mountain GC], Goodyear (9,1962;9,1967); Tubac Valley CC (1959–60); Tucson Estates CC (18 par 3,1960;a.18 Exec. 1972).
FLORIDA: Boca Raton Hotel & Club (1928); Dania CC (9,1951); Delray Beach CC (a.9,1962); Diplomat CC, Hollywood (1957); Ft. Lauderdale CC (South course,1951;r.North course); Miami Shores GC (1937); Orange Brook GC, Hollywood (r.,a.9); Plantation GC, Ft. Lauderdale (1951); Pompano Beach CC (Palms course,1954); Redlands G&CC, Homestead (1947); Sunset GC, Hollywood (9).
NEW MEXICO: Horizon CC, Belen (9,1972); Paradise Hills GC, Albuquerque (1960); Sunport CC, Albuquerque (18 par 3,1970); University of New Mexico GC, Albuquerque (South course,1966).
Courses Remodeled by Robert E. "Red" Lawrence:
ARIZONA: San Marcos Hotel & Club, Chandler; Tucson CC; Tucson National GC.

Charles Dundas Lawrie (1923–1976) BAGCA
Born: Edinburgh, Scotland. Died: Edinburgh, Scotland, at age 53.

Charles Lawrie was educated at Fettes and at Oxford, where he was a cricket star. After service with the Coldstream Guards during World War II, he was involved in sports administration and amateur golf. He reached the semi-finals of the 1955 Scottish Amateur and won thirty-two consecutive matches with partner Donald Steel in the annual Halford Hewitt tournament. He also served as honorary captain of the 1961 and 1963 Walker Cup teams.

Lawrie specialized in the administration of golf events, organizing many of the Open tournaments. His last was in 1972 at Muirfield. He served as chairman of the Royal and Ancient Selection Committee, choosing Walker Cup participants, from 1963 to 1967. In the late 1960s Lawrie became a partner in the golf design firm of Cotton (C.K.), Pennink, Lawrie and Partners Ltd., but he had completed only a handful of courses before his untimely death in 1976.

Courses by Charles Dundas Lawrie:
GREAT BRITAIN: Abbey Hill at Milton Keynes (c. Pennink); Carmoden near Edinburgh; Corhampton at Cookham (2nd 9); Fakenham (c. Pennink); Rookery Park at Lowestoft; The Short Course at Royal Lytham; Twickenham Park (c. Pennink); Westhill in Hampshire; Woburn Duke and Duchess.
Courses Remodeled by Charles Dundas Lawrie:
GREAT BRITAIN: Royal Wimbledon.

Joseph L. Lee (1922–   )
Born: Oviedo, Florida.

Joe Lee, an outstanding high school and college athlete, graduated from the University of Miami with a degree in education. He took golf while still in college and after teaching for a year at Delray Beach Jr. High School in Florida decided instead to pursue a professional golf career. Golf architect Dick Wilson, a Delray Beach acquaintance, helped Lee to land the job of assistant pro at Moraine CC, Dayton, Ohio, which Wilson was remodeling at the time.

Lee spent two years at Moraine and while Wilson was working on the neighboring National Cash Register CC courses, the two families lived together. In 1952 Lee left Moraine to assist the completion of NCR. He went on to supervise construction of several Wilson designs and in the mid-1950s was given major responsibility for design and construction of Villa Real GC in Havana, Cuba.

By 1959 Lee was a full partner with Wilson. He finished the four courses Wilson had been actively building at the time of his death in 1965 and then established his own practice with the assistance of many of the same crew that had been with Wilson for a decade or more. Concentrating mainly in the Sunbelt, Lee created some of America's top courses, including a collaboration in the mid-1970s with the legendary Ben Hogan on the thirty-six hole Trophy Club near Fort Worth, Texas, the only course design work ever actively undertaken by Hogan. "Joe Lee's Course Designs Are Challenging But Fun" by Ross Goodner, (Golf Digest, February 1981, p. 211) provides an account of Lee's accomplishments and philosophy.

Courses by Joseph L. Lee:
ALABAMA: Lakewood GC, Point Clear (a.Magnolia 9,1967); Riverchase CC, Birmingham (1975).
CALIFORNIA: La Costa CC, Carlsbad (a.3rd 9,1973).
FLORIDA: Banyan GC, West Palm Beach (1973); Barefoot Bay G&CC, Sebastian; Bent Pine GC, Vero Beach (1979); Boca Del Mar G&TC, Boca Raton (South course,1975); Boca Greens CC, Boca Raton (1979); Bonaventure CC, Ft. Lauderdale (East course,1970); Broken Sound GC, Boca Raton (1976); Canongate GC, Orlando (1968); Century GC, West Palm Beach (1969); Century Village GC, Deerfield Beach (1976); Charter World G&RC, Boynton Beach; Del-Aire CC, Delray Beach (27,1978); Errol Estates Inn & Apopka (27,1976); Feather Sound CC, St. Petersburg (a.South 9,1975); Fernandina Beach GC (a.South 9,1975); Gadsen CC, Quincy; Gator Creek GC, Sarasota (1976); (The) Hamlet of Delray Beach (1973); High Ridge GC, Boynton Beach (1979); J.D.M. CC, Palm Beach Gardens (a.2nd 9's,North and South

193

courses); Lake Buena Vista Club (1972); (The) Little Club, Delray Beach (18 Par 3,1969); Mid-Florida GC, Sanlando (1975); Ponte Vedra CC (a.9,Lagoon course); Quail Ridge CC, Delray Beach (North course,1974;South course,1977); Rainbow's End G&CC, Dunnellon (a.9,1978); River Ranch CC, Indian Lake; Sugar Mill CC, New Smyrna Beach (1970); Suwannee River Valley CC, Jasper (9); Turtle Creek Club, Jupiter (1969); Tuscawilla CC, Winter Springs (1973); Tyndall AFB GC, Panama City (a.2nd 9); Walt Disney World GC, Lake Buena Vista (Palm course,1969; Magnolia course,1970; Buena Vista course,1976); West Winds GC, Boynton Beach; Winter Springs CC, Orlando; Pipers Landing GC.
GEORGIA: Bent Tree CC, Jasper (1973); Big Canoe GC, Marble Hill (1974); Bull Creek GC, Columbus (1971); Callaway Gardens GC, Pine Mountain (Gardenview course, 1969; Skyview course,1969); Canongate-on-Lanier, Cummings (1970); Flat Creek CC, Peachtree City (1970); Hidden Hills CC, Stone Mountain (1974); Horseshoe Bend CC, Roswell (1975); Indian Hill CC, Marietta (1970); (The) Island Club, St. Simons Island (1975); Jekyll Island GC (Pine Lakes course,1967; Indian Mounds course,1975); Rivermont G&CC, Alpharetta (1975); Sea Island GC (a.Marshside 9, 1973); Snapfinger Woods GC, Decatur (17,1974); Tally Mountain Club, Tallapoosa; Valdosta CC (a.18).
ILLINOIS: Plum Tree National GC, Harvard (1970).
LOUISIANA: Beau Chene CC, Madisonville (1974); Beau Chene GC, Mandeville (a.9,1977); Tchefuncta CC, Covington (a.3rd 9).
NORTH CAROLINA: Crosscreek CC, Mt. Airy; Kenmore Estates, Flat Rock (1979).
PENNSYLVANIA: St. Clair CC, Pittsburgh (a.3rd 9,1971).
SOUTH CAROLINA: Houndslake CC, Aiken (1976).
TENNESSEE: Fall Creek Falls State Park GC, Pikesville (1972); Montclair CC, Chattanooga (9).
TEXAS: (The) Trophy Club, Roanoke (Creek and Oaks courses,1976); (The) Woodlands CC (West course, 1974).
VIRGINIA: Half Sink GC.
BAHAMAS: Bahamas Princess Hotel &CC, Freeport [formerly King's Inn G&CC]; Fortune Hills GC, Freeport (1972); Great Harbour Cay CC, Berry Island (1969); King's Inn G&CC, Freeport (Ruby course,1967); Lyford Cay (a.18); Shannon G&CC, Freeport (1970); South Ocean Beach Hotel GC, Nassau (1971).
COLOMBIA: Club Lagos De Caujarel, Barranquilla (1972).
GUAM: Anderson AFB GC.
ST. MAARTEN: Mullet Bay GC (1974).
VENEZUELA: Barquisimeto CC (1979).
Courses Remodeled by Joseph L. Lee:
FLORIDA: (The) Breakers GC, Palm Beach; Clearwater CC; Gulfstream GC, Palm Beach; Palm Beach National G&CC (r.;a.18); Sara Bay CC Seascape G&RC, Destin (1979).
GEORGIA: Green Island CC, Columbus (1978).
ILLINOIS: Cog Hill GC, Lemont (Course # 4,1977); Glenwoodie GC (1978); St. Andrews G&CC, West Chicago (Courses #1 & #2); Seminary GC, Mundelein.
KENTUCKY: Owensboro CC (18,1978).
LOUISIANA: Baton Rouge CC.
MICHIGAN: Warwick Hills Club, Grand Blanc (1967).
PENNSYLVANIA: Hidden Valley CC, Pittsburgh (1968).

Herbert Corey Leeds (1855–1930)
Born: Boston, Massachusetts. Died: Hamilton, Massachusetts, at age 75.
Herbert Leeds graduated from Harvard College in 1877 and was awarded a B.A. degree in 1891. A lifelong sportsman, he was an excellent baseball and football player while in college. He was also a yachting enthusiast and spent three years after graduation sailing in the Far East and the West Indies. As late as the turn of the century, Leeds was a crew member in several International Cup Races and his book *Log of the Columbia* (1899), related his experiences aboard a racing yacht. He was also an expert card player and wrote *The Laws of Bridge* and *The Laws of Euchre.*
Leeds took up golf when he was nearly forty but within two years was playing at scratch. Though beyond his prime when national amateur tournaments became prominent, he did win several club championships and invitation tournaments. He was a member of the USGA Executive Committee in 1905.
Leeds's first golf design experience was the creation of a new eighteen-hole course for the Myopia Hunt Club, replacing its rudimentary nine-hole layout, which had been built by R. M. Appleton, Master of the Fox Hounds. Leeds, who remained at Myopia all his life and served as captain of its Green Committee, built the front nine in 1896 and the back nine in 1901. The course exists today, with only minor changes, just as he created and, over the years, refined it.
Leeds's efforts at Myopia created a landmark course, the scene of many early matches, including four U. S. Opens. It was praised by leading American and British golfers and written about in publications on both sides of the Atlantic. Myopia's historian, Edward Weeks said of Leeds that:

> He never ceased digging new traps. It was his habit to carry small white chips in his pocket. . . . When the drive of a long hitter was sliced or hooked Leeds would place a marker on the spot and a new trap filled with soft white Ipswich sand would appear. This resulted in some holes being praised by British professionals as the most skillfully trapped in the United States.[2]

After a tour of the great links of Britain in 1902, Leeds returned to the United States to build several other courses. Although club champion at The Country Club, Brookline, Massachusetts, there is no evidence that he participated in any of its expansions. He did, however, create the original course at the Essex CC in Manchester, as well as the Bass Rocks GC in Gloucester. He also worked outside his native state, as far north as Maine (the original nine at the Kebo Valley Club in Bar Harbour)[3] and as far south as South Carolina (the original nine at Palmetto CC in Aiken).

[2]Letter, Edward Weeks to Geoffrey S. Cornish, August 2, 1979 (unpublished).
[3]with Andrew Liscomb.

Peter W. Lees (1868–1923)
Peter Lees, greenkeeper at Royal Mid Surrey, emigrated to the United States around 1910 to construct and maintain the proposed Lido GC on Long Island for architect Charles Blair Macdonald, on the recommendation of J. H. Taylor, one of the "Great Triumvirate" of British golf.
Lees was described in obituaries as a noted golf architect and is known to have designed the original nine at Hempstead CC on Long Island and to have revised Ives Hill CC at Watertown, New York. He was better known, however, as a constructor of courses for such architects as Macdonald, Tillinghast and others.

Stanley Leonard
A well-known professional golfer from Vancouver, British Columbia, Stanley Leonard won many tournaments in the United States and Canada. In 1974 he was appointed professional and director of golf at Desert Island CC in California.
Leonard assisted a number of golf architects in planning courses in the 1960s, and later did design work on his own and in collaboration with Philip Tattersfield of Tattersfield Associates Ltd, Land Design Group, Vancouver, B.C.
Courses by Stanley Leonard: (In collaboration with Philip Tattersfield)
ALBERTA: Redwood Meadows, Bragg Creek.
BRITISH COLUMBIA: 100 Mile House, Cariboo; Tall Timber CC, Langley.
Courses Remodeled by Stanley Leonard: (In collaboration with Philip Tattersfield)
CALIFORNIA: Desert Island CC, Rancho Mirage.
BRITISH COLUMBIA: Peace Portal GC, Douglas.

William B. Lewis, Jr.
Based in Sarasota, Florida, William Lewis planned numerous courses in the Southeast.
Courses by William B. Lewis, Jr:
FLORIDA: Bent Tree G&RC, Sarasota (1975); Ft. Myers Exec. GC (1972); Village Green Par 3 GC, Bradenton (9,1969); Village Green Par 3 GC, Sarasota (9); Whiskey Creek Exec. GC.
NORTH CAROLINA: Fairfield Mountains GC (1973); Glen Cannon CC, Breverd (1966); Great Smokies, Hilton (1975); Wolf Laurel GC, Mars Hill (1969).
SOUTH CAROLINA: Tega Cay CC (2 courses,1971).

Albert Linkogel
Albert Linkogel served as superintendent at Westwood CC, St. Louis, Missouri, from the 1930s until 1953, when he resigned to operate a turf nursery, lawn and garden supply business in St. Louis. In the 1950s he began converting sand green courses in Missouri and Illinois to grass. He also designed several original courses in those states.
Courses by Albert Linkogel:
ILLINOIS: Columbia GC (1960); Hillcrest GC, Washington (Par 3).
MISSOURI: Cape Girardeau GC (original 9,1955); St. Ann GC, St. Louis (9); St. Charles GC.

Edward G. "Ted" Lockie (1908–   )
A longtime PGA professional in East Moline, Illinois, Edward Lockie designed several courses in the Quad Cities area in the 1960s and 70s before his retirement to Palm Beach Gardens, Florida, in 1976.
Courses by Edward G. "Ted" Lockie:
ILLINOIS: Golfmohr GC, East Moline (1967); Pinecrest G&CC, Huntley (1972).
WISCONSIN: Grandview GC, Hortonville (1969).

Emil F. "Dutch" Loeffler (1894–1948)
Born: Pittsburgh, Pennsylvania. Died; Oakmont, Pennsylvania, at age 54.
"Dutch" Loeffler's entire career was spent at the Oakmont CC. He began as a caddy at the age of ten, became caddymaster in 1912, greenkeeper in 1913 (when John McGlynn vacated the position) and professional in 1930. He was a fine golfer, winning the 1920 and 1922 Pennsylvania Opens and qualifying for the 1920 and 1921 U. S. Opens. He was also a member of the National Association of Greenkeepers of America and served as its national treasurer in 1929.
Loeffler was best known for his work at Oakmont as course superintendent, a position he held, even while serving as club professional, until his retirement in 1947. He instituted the changes and maintenance practices suggested by William C. Fownes, Jr., to make Oakmont the world's toughest golf course. He also had several ideas of his own, and it was he who invented the weighted rake that formed the furrows in Oakmont's bunkers.
In the 1920s Loeffler was associated with John McGlynn in the design and build firm of Loeffler-McGlynn Co. of Oakmont, Pennsylvania. The firm constructed courses of its own design, did numerous reconstructions at established layouts and also contracted to execute the work of other architects.
Courses by Emil F. "Dutch" Loeffler:
MICHIGAN: Red Run CC.
PENNSYLVANIA: Alcoma CC; Ambridge CC; Beaver Valley CC, Beaver Falls (Original 9); Greene County GC; Highland CC; Hillcrest CC; Kittannine CC; Latrobe CC (Original 9); Monongahela Valley CC; Montour Heights CC (Original 9); Nemacolin CC; Pleasant Valley CC; Shannopin CC; Uniontown CC; Westmoreland CC, Verona (n.1.e.); Wildwood.
Courses Remodeled by Emil F. "Dutch" Loeffler:
PENNSYLVANIA: Butler CC; Chartiers CC; Edgewood CC.

Robert M. Lohmann (1952–   ) ASGCA

Robert Lohmann graduated from the University of Wisconsin with a B.S. degree in landscape architecture in 1974. The following year he joined the golf design firm of Killian and Nugent.

Raymond F. "Buddy" Loving, Jr. (1926–   ) ASGCA

Born: Richmond, Virginia.

"Buddy" Loving received a B.A. degree from the University of Virginia and an additional degree from Phillips College. He also took courses in landscape architecture, turfgrass science and financial management at Virginia Polytechnic Institute. He was trained in golf course architecture by his grandfather, Fred Findlay, for whom he began working part time in 1946, and by his father, Raymond, Sr., who also did some design work.

In 1968 Loving, along with A. M. Pulley and E. H. Coffey, contracted to build the Manchester (Vermont) CC to the plans of Cornish-Robinson in order to gain experience in another part of the country. The credit for the high quality of the finished layout was given to the contractor by the architects.

Courses by Raymond F. "Buddy" Loving, Jr.: In addition to collaboration on all Fred Findlay courses after 1950, Loving's designs include (several were with his father):

MARYLAND: Winters Run GC.

VIRGINIA: Boars Head Inn Par 3 GC; Confederate Hills CC (c. Pulley); Country Club Lake; Evergreen CC (c.Pulley); Farmington CC (a.9); Hunting Hill CC; Lake Monticello CC, Charlottesville (c.Pulley); Lakeview Exec. GC; Pen Park Muni; Retreat G&CC; Shenandoah Valley GC; V.P.I. GC; Williamsburg Colony Inn Par 3 GC.

Courses Remodeled by Raymond F. "Buddy" Loving, Jr:

VIRGINIA: Army-Navy CC (c.Pulley); Fairfax CC (c.Pulley); James River CC; Patuxent Naval Air Station.

George Low, Sr. (1874–1950)

Born: Clearwater, Florida. Died: Clearwater, Florida.

Pioneer American golfer George Low as joint runner-up in the 1899 U. S. Open and before World War I had worked as professional at Baltusrol in New Jersey, Ekwanok in Vermont, and Huntingdon Valley in Pennsylvania. He also served as golf instructor to U.S. presidents Taft and Harding.

Low designed several courses in the Northeast. In the 1920s he formed a short-lived partnership with golf architect Herbert Strong before moving to Clearwater, Florida. There he served as professional at the Belleview Biltmore until poor health necessitated his retirement in 1940. Low's son, George, Jr., was long associated with PGA tournaments and was a respected putting expert.

Courses by George Low, Sr.:

NEW JERSEY: Rockaway CC (1916); Weequahic GC, Newark (original 9, 1914); Echo Lake CC (c.Ross).

NEW YORK: Blind Brook CC, Portchester; Hotel Champlain, Lake Bluffs (1917).

John Laing Low (1869–1929)

Born: Fife, Scotland. Died: Woking, England, at age 59.

John Low learned golf at St. Andrews and was an avid competitor all his life. He reached the semi-finals at the British Amateur in 1897 and 1898, and was runner-up in 1901. He also won many tournaments at St. Andrews, including the Silver Cross in 1900 and 1909.

A graduate of Cambridge University, Low assisted in the creation of the Oxford and Cambridge Golfing Society in 1897 and served as its captain for twenty years. He organized the Society's first matches in America in 1903 and captained the team that included C. H. Alison. Low was also a respected authority on the rules of golf, serving as chairman of the Rules Committee of the Royal and Ancient until 1921.

John Low was on the staff of the *Pall Mall Gazette* and later the *Athletic News*, and wrote extensively about golf in those and other newspapers. He also wrote several books on golf, including *Concerning Golf* (1903), the first to codify the principles of golf course architecture.

In the early 1900s Low and fellow club member Stuart Paton worked together in remodeling the Woking GC course. Their efforts turned the staid Tom Dunn layout into a remarkably strategic course; and although they did no other design work, the discussion, publicity and controversy arising from their changes at Woking contributed greatly to the development of golf course architecture. According to Tom Simpson, both Low and Paton were elected Extraordinary and Honorary Members of the International Society of Golf Course Architects.

John Low's principles are summarized as follows:

1. A golf course should provide entertainment for the high and medium handicapper while presenting a test for the accomplished golfer.
2. The objective of inventors is to reduce skill required for golf. If it were not for the counter skill of golf architects, the game would be emasculated.
3. The shortest, most direct line to the hole, even if it be the center of the fairway, should be fraught with danger.
4. The architect must assure that the ground dictates play. He should see that there is a special interest for the accomplished golfer in each stroke, just as the billiard player always has in mind the next stroke or strokes.
5. The fairway must be oriented to tee and green so that placement of the tee shot determines the safety of the approach shot.
6. Bunkers should be used sparingly by the architect. Except on one-shot holes, they should never be placed within 200 yards of the tee. Elevations and depressions can also be used to contour the entrance to the green. Fairway bunkers 200 to 235 yards from the tee, placed five to ten yards off the accomplished player's line to the green, are the most effective.
7. Putting greens should be of the low, narrow, plateau type, with the plateaus tilting away, not toward, the player.
8. Because the element of chance is the essence of the game, a course should not be a test of skill alone.

9. All really great golf holes involve a contest of wits and risks. No one should attempt to copy a great hole because distant vistas may affect the play of the hole.
10. Contouring of putting surfaces should not be severe, and there should be a special position for the flag on important days.
11. Committees should leave "well enough alone."

Low's principles were discussed and illustrated by Tom Simpson in an article in the *Edinburgh Golf Monthly* that was reprinted in *Golfdom,* May 1955.

George Lowe

Originally from Carnoustie, George Lowe moved to England, where he became greenkeeper at St. Annes in the late 1800s. In England he planned Studeley Royal Park, Ripon; the first version of Royal Birkdale; the second nine at Seascale in Cumberland; and Windermere GC in Westmoreland. He also made extensive changes at his home course, Lytham and St. Annes.

A. Vernon Macan (1882–1964) ASGCA

Born: Dublin, Ireland. Died: Victoria, British Columbia, at age 82.

A. V. Macan attended Trinity College in Dublin and earned a degree in law at the University of London. He then emigrated to Vancouver, British Columbia, where he established a law practice and became one of the area's top amateur golfers. He won a number of regional events in Canada and across the border was victorious in the 1913 Washington State Amateur and the 1913 Pacific Northwest Amateur.

After World War I Macan decided to pursue a career in golf design. His fame as a player led to several projects, and by the 1920s he was the busiest architect in the Pacific Northwest. He continued to design courses until his death and was assisted on his last projects by civil engineer Donald Hogan.

Courses by A. Vernon Macan:

CALIFORNIA: California GC of San Francisco, South San Francisco (1926); San Geronimo National GC (1965).

IDAHO: Hillcrest CC, Boise (9,1940;9,1957); Purple Sage Muni, Caldwell (1963).

OREGON: Alderwood CC, Portland (n.1.e.).

WASHINGTON: Broadmoor GC, Seattle (1927); Edgewater Muni, Pasco (1954); Fircrest GC, Tacoma (1925); Overlake G&CC, Medina (1953); Sunland CC, Sequim (9,1964); Wenatchee CC (1958); Yakima CC.

CANADA: (British Columbia): Marine Drive GC, Vancouver (1923); Nanaimo CC, Vancouver; Penticton G&CC; Richmond CC; Shaughnessy GC, Vancouver (new site); Shaughnessy Heights Club, Vancouver (n.1.e.).

Courses Remodeled by A. Vernon Macan:

OREGON: Waverley CC, Portland.

WASHINGTON: Seattle GC (1950).

CANADA (British Columbia): Royal Colwood G&CC, Victoria; Victoria CC.

Norman Macbeth (1879–1940)

Born: Bolton, England. Died: Los Angeles, California, at age 61.

Norman Macbeth learned his golf at Lytham and St. Annes, and as a teenager lowered his handicap from 18 to 2 in the space of three seasons. He won Amateur titles in England and India before moving to the United States in 1903 and settling in Los Angeles in 1908. A businessman all his life, including many years as vice president of the Riverside Cement Company, Macbeth remained active in amateur golf, winning the Southern California Amateur on two occasions (1911 and 13) and the Northern California Amateur once.

In 1910 Macbeth assisted in the design of the old Los Angeles CC course. Following service with the American Red Cross in Europe during World War I, he designed and built a number of southern California courses, all too many of which later succumbed to the Depression, like the highly regarded Midwick CC of Monterey and the St. Andrews GC of Laguna Niguel. His most prominent surviving works include the Wilshire CC, Los Angeles (his lifelong home course built in 1919), the Annandale CC, Pasadena (redesigned in 1917) and the San Gabriel CC.

Charles Blair Macdonald (1856–1939)

Born: Niagara Falls, Ontario, Canada. Died: Southampton, Long Island, New York, at age 83. Interred; Southampton, Long Island.

Charles Blair Macdonald was the son of a Scottish father and a Canadian mother. His mother was a direct descendant of Sir William Johnson, owner of a huge tract of land in the Mohawk Valley in pre-Revolutionary New York. Macdonald himself grew up in Chicago but returned to his father's homeland in 1872 to attend the University of St. Andrews. Here he learned the game of golf under the tutelage of his grandfather and was able to watch matches involving "Old Tom" and "Young Tom" Morris, David Strath, Robert Clark (author of *Golf, A Royal and Ancient Game*), D. D. Whigham (whose son, H. J., later married Macdonald's daughter, Frances) and many other renowned golfers.

The game, the Old Course, the town of St. Andrews and "Old" Tom made a deep and lasting impression on Macdonald. Returning to Chicago in 1875, he described the next few years as the "dark ages" because of the virtual impossibility of playing golf. He ended up knocking balls around at deserted Civil War training camps. Then in 1892 he laid out the nine-hole Chicago Golf Club at Belmont. This was expanded to eighteen holes the next year, making it the first eighteen-hole course in the United States. In 1895 the Club moved to Wheaton, where Macdonald laid out a new eighteen holes.

Throughout his life, golf course design was an avocation for Macdonald, and he never accepted a fee for his services. During his years in Illinois he was with the Chicago Board of Trade. In 1884 he married Frances Porter of Chicago; they had two daughters, Janet and Frances. The family moved to New York in 1900, where Macdonald became a partner in the firm of C. D. Barney & Co., Stockbrokers.

But golf and golf design were abiding passions. Macdonald won the first U. S. Amateur Championship in 1895. He was a founder of the Amateur Golf Association of the United States, which evolved into the United States Golf Association. He conceived the Walker Cup Series, coined the title "golf architect" in 1902 and is known as the "Father of American Golf Course Architecture." His protégés in golf design included Seth Raynor, Charles Banks and Ralph Barton.

Robert Sommer's article "The National Golf Links," in *Golf Journal*, January/February 1977, provides a detailed account of Macdonald's monumental layout, which revolutionized course design in America and influenced the profession in Britain as well. Herbert Warren Wind, in his *Story of American Golf*, says of C. B. Macdonald that he "contributed more to the advancement of golf in America than any other person of his generation." A biography of Macdonald by John P. English is included in *The Dictionary of American Biography* (DNB supp 2:204; 1958).

Macdonald's own reminiscences, *Scotland's Gift—Golf*, contains passages describing his design philosophy. In particular Chapter XV of the book provides a detailed discussion of his principles of golf architecture. These may be briefly summarized as follows:

1. The aspiring golf architect should read and absorb the spirit of Humphrey Repton's *The Art of Landscape Architecture* (1797), especially the thought that "true taste in every art consists more in adapting tried expedients to peculiar circumstances than in that inordinate thirst after novelty . . ."
2. Putting greens are to the golf course what faces are to portraits.
3. A course should be so laid out that the golfer must contend with the wind from all directions.
4. Neither the character of a person nor that of a golf hole can be adequately judged at the first meeting.
5. No course laid out through trees can be ideal. This does not mean that a classical course cannot be laid out through trees, for there is a difference between an ideal and a classical course.
6. Variety is the foundation of golf course architecture. Ideal and classical courses demand variety, personality and romantic charm.
7. Hazards should be of great variety and always fair.
8. The science and beauty of golf is enhanced when the golfer is made to play the ball from any stance.
9. Sand mounds planted with sea bent are ideal. Pot bunkers are best placed on the side of a mound or hill. Deep ditch hazards are objectionable. Water hazards must be well defined. Beware of bunkers, paths and rough.
10. There should be two long two-shot holes with large cross bunkers guarding the greens. However, cross bunkers directly across the fairway are objectionable unless placed on a diagonal so the player can "bite off what he can chew."
11. Any bunker properly placed is excellent.
12. Long carries should not be made compulsory; but if attempted, there should be a premium for success.
13. Never sacrifice accuracy for length.
14. A course should be absorbing and challenging for all types of golfers.
15. Never construct a "trick green."
16. Ground sloping into a bunker increases its peril.
17. A bunker is fair if a player can get out of it in one stroke.
18. Three tees should be provided for men.
19. Macdonald ends his chapter by stating that he believed in the veneration of anything in life bearing the testimony of ages as being unexcelled, even a golf hole.
20. Finally, he quotes from another landscape architect, Prince Puckler: "Time is not able to bring forth new truths but only an unfolding of timely truths."

Courses by Charles Blair Macdonald:

CONNECTICUT: Yale University GC (1926).

ILLINOIS: Chicago GC at Belmont (1892–93); Chicago GC at Wheaton (1895; r.,c.Raynor,1923.).

MARYLAND: Gibson Island GC.

MISSOURI: St. Louis CC.

NEW YORK: The Creek Club; Deepdale GC (1925); Lido GC (1917); The Links GC (1919); Moore Estates GC; The National Golf Links of America (1911); Otto Kamns Estate Course, Manhasset; Piping Rock GC; Sleepy Hollow GC; Whitney Estates, Manhasset.

WEST VIRGINIA: The Greenbriar (1926); The Greenbriar Old White (1914).

BERMUDA: Mid-Ocean GC (1924).

Frank Macdonald

A native Scot, Frank Macdonald formed the firm of Macdonald and Maddox with Charles Maddox, Sr, in 1923.

Courses by Frank Macdonald: See Charles Eugene Maddox, Sr.

Alister (Alexander) Mackenzie, M.D. (1870–1934)

Born: Yorkshire, England. Died: California, at age 64.

Alister Mackenzie (his given name was possibly Alexander, but he always used "Alister" in the United States), the son of Highland parents, graduated from Cambridge University with degrees in medicine, natural science and chemistry. In the South African War he served as a surgeon with the Somerset Light Infantry, closely observing and analyzing the ability of Boer soldiers to hide effectively on the treeless veldt.

In 1907 golf architect H. S. Colt, on a visit to the Alwoodley GC near Leeds, stayed overnight at Mackenzie's home. Impressed with Mackenzie's models of greens and bunkers, Colt invited his collaboration on the revision of Alwoodley. Over the next few years Mackenzie gradually gave up his medical practice to devote full time to golf course architecture. In 1914 he won first prize in C. B. Macdonald's *Country Life* competition for the best two-shot hole for the proposed Lido GC on Long Island, New York. This competition, judged by Bernard Darwin, Horace Hutchinson and Herbert Fowler, brought Mackenzie considerable publicity on both sides of the Atlantic.

With the outbreak of war in Europe, Mackenzie returned to medicine as an army surgeon but soon transferred to the Royal Engineers to develop camouflage techniques based on the knowledge he had gained in South Africa. The art and science of camouflage as developed by Mackenzie is credited with saving thousands of lives in both world wars. Marshall Foch is said to have estimated that it reduced casualties on the Western Front by one third. Years later Mackenzie observed on several occasions that successful course design, like camouflage, arises from utilizing natural features to their fullest extent and creating artificial features by closely imitating nature.

Shortly after the Armistice in 1918, Mackenzie made his first trip to the United States, where he collaborated with Colt and Alison on the revision of Chevy Chase near Washington, D.C. He later designed a number of courses in the United States and Canada, on his own or in collaboration with other noted architects, including Colt, Alison, and Hunter. His Cypress Point in California finally established his reputation as a golf course architect. During the 1920s he also planned courses in the British Isles, Australia, New Zealand and the Argentine.

Of all the course architects of the late 1920s, Mackenzie probably exerted the greatest influence on contemporary design. Features he listed in 1920 as essential for an ideal golf course became standards for course architecture after World War II.

It was Mackenzie's philosophy, perhaps resulting from his medical training, that good health was of paramount importance and that a pastime such as golf, combining excitement with fresh air and exercise, could exert an extraordinary influence on human health and happiness. It has been said that this philosophy and Mackenzie's wide range of outdoor activities, as well as his academic background, prompted Bobby Jones to select him as the architect for Augusta National.

Alister Mackenzie was the author of *Golf Architecture*, published in 1920. His many accomplishments are outlined in R. Saltzstein's article "Letting Nature Make A Course" (*Golf Journal*, April 1977). In his last years he was partnered with Perry Maxwell.

Courses by Alister Mackenzie:

CALIFORNIA: Charlie Chaplin Estate GC, Beverly Hills (Short course); Cypress Point Club, Pebble Beach (c.Hunter, 1928); Green Hills CC, Millbrae (1932); Haggin Oaks Muni, Sacramento (1932); Harold Lloyd Estate GC, Beverly Hills (Short course); Meadow GC, Fairfax (c.Hunter,1927); Monterey Peninsula CC, Pebble Beach (r.Original course; a.Dunes course,c.Hunter,1925); Northwood GC (9,c.Hunter,1928); Pasatiempo GC, Santa Cruz (1929); Pittsburg G&CC; Sacramento GC (n.l.e.); Sharp Park Muni, San Francisco (c.Fleming,1931); Valley Club of Montecito, Santa Barbara (c.Hunter,1928); Union League G&CC, San Francisco, (n.l.e) Wawona Hotel GC, Yosemite (9,c.Fleming).

GEORGIA: Augusta National GC (c.Bobby Jones,1933).

ILLINOIS: North Shore CC, Glenview (c.Colt & Alison,1924).

MICHIGAN: Crystal Downs CC, Frankfort (r.9,a.9,c.Maxwell,1933); University of Michigan GC, Ann Arbor (c.Maxwell,1931).

OHIO: Ohio State University GC, Columbus (Grey and Scarlet courses, 1934).

ARGENTINA: Jockey Club of San Isidro, Buenos Aires (Red and Blue courses,1935).

AUSTRALIA: Australian GC, Kensington, New South Wales (27,1926); Flinders GC, Victoria; Lake Karrinyup CC, Balcutta (c.Russel, 1927); New South Wales GC, Sydney (1928); Royal Melbourne GC, Black Rock (West course, 1926); Sandringham GC, Melbourne; Victoria GC, Cheltenham (1927); Yarra Yarra GC, Melbourne (c.Russell, 1929). GC, Melbourne (c.Russell,1929).

CANADA: St. Charles CC, Winnipeg, Manitoba (North 9,1930).

ENGLAND: Alwoodley CC, Leeds (c.Colt,1907); Blackpool-Stanley Park; Buxton and High Peak GC, Derbyshire; Castletown GC, Isle of Man; Cavendish GC, Derby; City of Newcastle GC, Newcastle-on-Tyre; Darlington GC, Durham; Douglas Muni, Isle of Man; Felixstowe Ferry GC, East Anglia (n.l.e.); Fulford GC, Heslington, Yorks; Grange-Over-Sands GC; Hadley Wood, Herts; Harrogate GC, Yorkshire; Headingley GC, Adel, Leeds; Manchester GC, Lancashire; Moor Allerton GC, Leeds (1922,n.l.e.); Moor Park GC, Rickmansworth, Herts (Westcourse); Moortown GC, Leeds (1909); Oakdale GC, Yorkshire; Reddish Vale, Manchester; Sitwell Park GC; Walsall GC; Wheatley GC, Doncaster, Yorks; Worcester G&CC; Worcestershire GC.

IRELAND: Muskerry GC, County Cork.

NEW ZEALAND: Heretaunga GC, Wellington.

SCOTLAND: Blairgowrie GC, Rosemont, Perthshire (r.9,a.9 Rosemont course, plus 9-hole Short course, 1927); Duff House, Banff; Newtonmore (c.Braid); Royal and Ancient GC of St. Andrews, Fife (Eden course,c.Colt,1913); Troon GC (New course).

URUGUAY: GC de Uruguay, Montevideo.

Courses Remodeled by Alister Mackenzie:

CALIFORNIA: California GC of San Francisco; Claremont CC, Oakland; Lake Merced GC, San Francisco (1929); Pebble Beach GC (r.bunkering,c.Hunter,1928).

ILLINOIS: Bob O'Link GC, Highland Park (c.Colt & Alison,1924).

MARYLAND: Burning Tree Club, Bethesda (c.Colt & Alison,1924); Chevy Chase Club (c.Colt & Alison).

NEW YORK: Bayside Links, Queens; Lake Placid Club (1931).

SOUTH CAROLINA: Palmetto CC, Aiken (r.greens,1931).

ARGENTINA: Mar de Plata GC (1930).

AUSTRALIA: Kingston Heath GC, Cheltenham (1928); Royal Adelaide GC, Seaton (1926); Royal Queensland GC, Hamilton, Brisbane (1927); Royal Sidney GC, New South Wales (r.bunkering).

ENGLAND: Felixstowe; Harrogate GC, Yorkshire; Inillingdon GC, Sussex; Royal St. Georges GC, Sandwich, Kent; Timperley; West Herts GC, Watford (1922); Weston-Super-Mare GC, Somerset.

IRELAND: Lahinch GC, County Clare (1927).

NEW ZEALAND: Titirangi GC, Auckland (1926).

Dr. Alister Mackenzie codified the thirteen features of an ideal golf course as early as 1920. They include:

1. Two loops of nine holes.
2. A large proportion of good two-shot holes, two or three drive and pitch holes, and at least four one shotters.
3. Little walking between greens and tees with a slight walk forward from the green to the

next tee to provide additional length if needed in the future.
4. Undulating greens and fairways but no hill climbing.
5. Every hole possessing a different character.
6. A minimum of blindness for approach shots.
7. Beautiful surroundings with all artificial features appearing to be natural.
8. Sufficient heroic carries from the tee but with holes planned to provide alternate routes for the weaker player who is content to lose a stroke or a portion of one to avoid a hazard.
9. An infinite variety in the strokes so that the use of every club is required.
10. An absence of the need to look for lost balls.
11. A course so interesting that both low and high handicappers are stimulated to improve their games by attempting shots they have hitherto been unable to play.
12. A course arranged so that the high handicap player or even the beginner should enjoy his round regardless of his score.
13. A course equally good over the entire playing season with the texture of greens, approaches and fairways perfect.

Leonard Macomber (1885–1954)
Born: Brookline, Massachusetts. Died: Washington, D.C., at age 69.
Based in Chicago, Leonard Macomber planned courses from New York to Wisconsin in the 1920s. In 1937 he traveled to Russia hoping to interest that country in golf, but without success. His last course, the Bellhaven CC in Alexandria, Virginia, was designed in 1954.

Courses by Leonard Macomber:
ILLINOIS: Breakers Beach CC; Euclid Hills CC [now Silver Lake, North Course]; Libertyville CC; Mission Hills CC; Waukegan Willow CC.
NEW YORK: Drumlins GC.
OHIO: Poland CC; West Hills CC; Tam O'Shanter (Course #1 and #2).
PENNSYLVANIA: Butler CC (r.9.a.9).
VIRGINIA: Bellhaven CC, Alexandria (1954).
WISCONSIN: Maple Crest CC.

Charles Eugene Maddox, Sr. (1898–   )
Born: Centralia, Illinois.
Charles Maddox spent his early days honing his golf game on Chicago-area courses and working for his father in the Maddox Construction Company. The company had been formed in 1870 as a road grading firm by Asa Maddox, Charles's grandfather. Charles's father, Eugene Maddox, branched out into golf course construction when he took command of the firm in the early 1900s.
After the first World War Charles became head of the company, concentrating on golf development. In 1923 he joined forces with Frank Macdonald, a native Scot who had served as a course superintendent in Chicago. The firm of Macdonald and Maddox created a number of impressive Chicago-area courses, several of them owned and operated by Maddox, and all constructed by the Maddox Construction Company. Charles Maddox also constructed courses for other prominent architects in the twenties, including Langford and Moreau, Robert Bruce Harris and C. D. Wagstaff.
During the Depression, Maddox lost most of his course holdings. He was forced to work for a time as a course superintendent; and his construction company abandoned golf, instead building oil rigs and working on government projects. Following World War II, Maddox reorganized the construction outfit and soon found plenty of work restoring or reconstructing courses for other architects. In the 1950s, joined by sons Charles Jr. and William, he began designing courses again as well as building them.
While constructing some of the best works of architects like Edward Lawrence Packard and Robert Bruce Harris, Maddox has also created some notable layouts of his own, including one of America's few true linksland courses at Dauphin Island, Alabama.

Courses by Charles Eugene Maddox, Sr:
ALABAMA: Isle Dauphine CC, Dauphin Island (1962).
ILLINOIS: Atwood GC, Rockford (1971); Bartlett Hills G&CC (c.F. MacDonald); Blackhorse GC, Downers Grove (9 par 3,1966); Danville VA Hospital GC (9,1951); Downey VA Hospital GC, North Chicago (1978); DuWayne Motel GC, West Chicago (9 par 3,1960); Edgewood CC, Virden (9,1962); Ellwood Greens CC, DeKalb (1972); Forest Hills CC, Rockford (1976); Gleneagles GC, Lemont (Red and White courses, c.F.MacDonald,1924); Lakeview CC, Lodi (9,1957); Menard CC, Petersburge (9,1964); Old Wayne GC, West Chicago (1960); Parkview Muni., Pekin (original 9, c.F. MacDonald,1930); Silver Lake CC (South Course); Stonehenge GC, Barrington (1970); Sun and Fun GC, Decatur (9 par 3,1964).
INDIANA: Beverly Shores GC (c.F.MacDonald,1930); Frankfort GC (9,1965); The Golf Club of Indiana, Lebanon (1974); The Hoosier Links, New Palestine (1973); Lake Hills G&CC, St. John (27,c.F.MacDonald); Old Oakland GC, Oaklandon (1964); Orchard Ridge CC, Fort Wayne (r.); Turkey Creek GC, Gary (c.F.MacDonald); Vincennes GC (9,1974).
MICHIGAN: Elks CC, Benton Harbor (1967); Raisin River CC, Monroe (1963).
MINNESOTA: Brookview CC, Minneapolis (27,1968); Majestic Oaks CC, Blaine (27,1971); Olympic Hills GC, Eden Prairie (1971); Rolling Green CC, Hamel (1969).
MISSOURI: Crackerneck CC, Blue Springs (1964).
NORTH DAKOTA: Larrimore GC (9,1963).
SOUTH DAKOTA: Elmwood GC, Sioux Falls (a.9,1960); Pierre CC (1966); Prairiewood GC, Aberdeen (1969) [now Moccasin Creek GC].
WISCONSIN: Rhinelander CC (9,c.F.MacDonald); Trout Lake CC (c.F.MacDonald).

William E. Maddox (1925–   )
Born: Chicago, Illinois.
The son of golf architect and contractor Charles Maddox, William Maddox was associated for many years with his father and brother Charles, Jr. He then took to the drawing board on his own and has to his credit, among other courses, the Forest CC, Zellwood Station GC,

Spanish Wells CC and Alden Pines GC at Fort Myers, all in Florida, as well as the Pheasant Run Lodge GC in Illinois.

Charles Mahannah (1944–   ) ASGCA
Charles Mahannah, son of golf architect Mark Mahannah, worked for several years for his father before establishing his own practice. Among courses of Charles's design are Bonaventure CC (West course,1975); Miles Grant Course, Stuart; and Kendale Lakes G&CC in Miami.

Mark Mahannah, (1906–   ) ASGCA
Born: Miami, Florida.
Mark Mahannah was a member of the course maintenance crew at the Miami Biltmore GC (now the Coral Gables Biltmore) in the 1930s and in 1940 became head superintendent. The club was closed by World War II, and Mahannah spent the duration as a technical advisor on turf problems at an army post in Pinellas County, Florida. In the late 1940s he took the position of superintendent at the Riviera CC in Coral Gables.
Mahannah began designing and remodeling courses on a part-time basis in southern Florida in the early 1950s. Within a few years, he was busy enough to form a full-time course design and construction firm.

FLORIDA: Boca Grande CC; Boca Teeca CC, Boca Raton (27,1968); Bonaventure CC, Miami (2nd 18,c.C.Mahannah,1975); Calusa CC, Miami (1969); Cocoa Beach Recreation Club (1968); Diplomat Hotel & CC, Hallendale (Presidential course,1962); El Conquistador CC, Bradenton (1973); Fountainbleau CC, Miami (1971); Greynold Park GC, North Miami Beach (9,1964); Gulfstream GC (18 par 3,1960); Haulover Beach GC, Miami (18 par 3,1964); Hillcrest East G&CC, Hollywood (1974); Homestead AFB GC (1961); Honey Hill CC, Opalocka; Isle Del Sol G&RC, St. Petersburg (1977); Jacaranda CC, Miami (18,-1970;18,1975); Jacaranda West CC, Venice (1976); Key Biscayne Hotel GC, Miami Beach (18 par 3,1954); Key Colony GC, Key Biscayne (18 par 3,1962,n.1.e.); Kings Bay Yacht & CC, Miami (1959); Kings Inn G&CC, Tampa; La Mancha GC [formerly Royal Palm Beach G&CC], (La Mancha and Willows courses,1960); Lake Venice CC (1959); Lost Tree Club, Singer Island (1960); Miles Grant CC, Stuart (c.C.Mahannah,1972); Mirror Lakes CC, Lehigh Acres (1970); Ocean Reef Club, North Key Largo (Dolphin course,1951); Okeechobee G&CC (1966); Plantation Hotel CC [formerly Old Paradise CC]; Port Charlotte CC (c. Dave Wallace) Rio Pinar CC, Orlando (1958); Sandpiper Bay CC, Port St. Lucie (Sinners course,1961); Sun City GC (1967); Westview CC, Miami (1953;a.9,1955); Beach Club Hotel GC, Naples, Broward CC, Hollywood.
NORTH CAROLINA: Pine Island CC, Charlotte (1969).
BAHAMAS: Grand Bahama Hotel & CC, Freeport (27,1961).
COLOMBIA: Santa Marta GC (1972); Macarena GC; Club Campestre de Bucaramanga (c.Saenz).

Courses Remodeled by Mark Mahannah:
FLORIDA: Coral Gables Biltmore CC; Everglades GC, Palm Beach (1958); Hollywood Beach Hotel GC (1955); Naples Beach Hotel GC (1953); Normandy Shores GC, Miami Beach; Palma Ceia G&CC, Tampa Springs (1979); Crystal River (1958); Tarpon Springs CC (1957).
CUBA: Havana Biltmore GC (1957).

Piero Mancinelli
Born: Venice, Italy in the 1920s.
Schooled and trained as an architect and engineer in Italy and England, Piero Mancinelli worked on construction of the Olgiata CC near Rome under British golf architect C. K. Cotton. Encouraged by the Britisher, Mancinelli entered the field of course architecture, remodeling several courses in northern Italy and one on the island of Elba. After establishing his own architectural and engineering firm, he planned the Is Molas GC on Sardinia with assistance from British professional golfer Bert Williamson. Is Molas was opened in 1976 and that same year hosted the Italian Open.
An account of Mancinelli's background and accomplishments by Herbert Warren Wind can be found in *The New Yorker,* May 16, 1977, on page 108.

Theodore Manning (1944–   )
Theodore Manning graduated from the University of Massachusetts in 1967 with a degree in landscape architecture. He then worked successively for the golf design firms of Robert Trent Jones, Desmond Muirhead and Jack Nicklaus, and Joseph Finger. On his own he designed and supervised construction of the third nine at Heritage Village CC, Southbury, Connecticut, in 1972. By the late 1970s he was engaged as a contractor in the golf and turf construction field.

Maples Family of Pinehurst
The Maples family was associated with Donald Ross and with construction and maintenance at the Pinehurst CC in North Carolina for decades. It produced two full-time golf architects, Ellis and his son Dan, as well as several members who designed courses on a part-time basis.

The following family tree, prepared by Dan F. Maples and Palmer Maples, Jr., illustrates the role played by the Maples in the development of golf and golf course since the turn of the century. James Maples, Sr., was the first of the family to settle in the Pinehurst area, arriving from Pennsylvania in the 1840s. His son, James Jr., the father of Frank, Walter, Angus and six other children, was not himself involved in golf but is considered to be the patriarch of the Maples golfing dynasty.

Family Tree

James Maples, Jr. (1856–1909)

Frank Maples (1886–1949)
Construction Superintendent & Greenkeeper at Pinehurst for 48 years, he worked with Donald Ross in establishing the course

Henson Maples (1917–1980)
Golf Course Superintendent 30 years— Pinehurst CC, Pinehurst, N.C.

Gene Maples
Golf Course Superintendent

Wayne Maples
Golf Course Superintendent

Ellis Maples
Golf Course Architect
Golf Professional
Golf Course Superintendent

Joe Maples
Golf Professional
Golf Course Superintendent

Dan Maples
Golf Course Architect
Landscape Architect
Golf Professional

Walter Maples (1883–1970)
Carpenter and Builder

Gene Maples
Golf Professional

Angus Maples (1882–1958)
Golf Course Superintendent at Pine Needles GC, which he had helped to construct

Palmer Maples, Sr. (1906–1979)
Golf Professional

Palmer Maples, Jr.
Golf Course Superintendent
Director of Education,
GCSAA

Nancy Maples
Amateur Golfer

Willie Maples
Golf Professional

Dan Frank Maples (1947–) ASGCA

Dan Maples received an associate of science degree from Wingate Junior College in North Carolina and a bachelor's degree in landscape architecture from the University of Georgia in 1972. During the summers from 1964 to 1972, he worked in golf course construction and maintenance, specializing in fine grading.

In 1972 Maples joined his father's course design firm, Ellis Maples and Associates, which later became Ellis Maples–Dan F. Maples, Golf Course Architects. As a hobby, he researched the history of course construction at Pinehurst.

Courses by Dan Frank Maples: See Ellis Maples.

Ellis Maples (1909–) ASGCA: President, 1973

Born: Pinehurst, North Carolina.

Ellis Maples attended Lenior Rhyne College. During the summer months, beginning at age fourteen, he worked under his father, Frank Maples, on the golf course at Pinehurst. In 1929–30 he worked as an assistant in the Pinehurst golf shop and for the following seven years served as assistant greenkeeper under his father at Mid Pines and Pine Needles CC.

In 1937 Maples designed and built a nine-hole course at Plymouth, North Carolina, where he remained as pro-greenkeeper until 1942. He then entered war service as an agronomist involved with grassing military installations and later served as a technical advisor on types of mowing equipment to be used at army installations.

In 1946–47, while working as pro-manager at New Bern (N.C.) CC, Maples redesigned that course as well as two others and planned one new course. In 1948–49 he supervised construction of the last course of Donald Ross's design, the Raleigh (N.C.) CC. He stayed on as pro-superintendent at Raleigh until 1953 when, deciding against a career as a touring professional, he entered private practice as a course architect.

His firm was known as Ellis Maples and Associates until 1972, when he was joined by son Dan and the name was changed to Ellis Maples–Dan F. Maples. Edwin B. Seay, a Maples protégé who became a well-known course architect, often spoke of Ellis Maples's abiding interest in golf and of his uncanny ability to estimate by eye the cubic yardage of earth that would have to be moved to construct a hole.

Courses by Ellis Maples:

GEORGIA: Goshen Plantation CC, Augusta (1970); West Lake CC, Augusta (1968).

NORTH CAROLINA: Bermuda Run G&CC, Clemmons (1972); GC (1959); Brook Valley CC, Greenville (1966); Carmel CC, Charlotte (South course,1962;2nd 9,1970); Cedar Brook CC, Elkin (1968); Cedar Rock CC, Lenoir (1964); Cedarwood CC, Charlotte (1961); Chockoyette CC, Roanoke Rapids (1970); Coherie CC, Clinton (9,1948); CC of Johnston County, Smithfield (1967); CC of North Carolina, Pinehurst (Original 18,1963); Deep Springs CC, Madison (9,1969); Duck Woods GC Kitty Hawk (1969); Forest Oaks CC, Greensboro (1962); Gaston CC, Gastonia (1958); Grandfather G&CC, Linville (Carlson Farms course,1964); Indian Valley CC, Burlington (1969); Kinston CC (1955); Meadow Greens CC, Lakesville (1967); New Bern G&CC (1954); Piedmont Crescent CC, Swepson-

ville (1968); Pine Brook CC, Winston-Salem (1955); Pinehurst CC #5 (c.R.S.Tufts,1961); Red Fox CC, Tyron (1966); Roanoke CC, Williamston (9,1955); Roxboro CC (1969); Sapona CC, Lexington (1967); Silver City CC (9,1968); Smithfield CC (r.9,a.9,1963); Twin Oaks GC, Greensboro (18 par 3, 1957); Walnut Creek CC, Goldsboro (1968); Whispering Pines CC (East course,1959;West course,1968); Winston Lake Park GC, Winston-Salem (1964).

SOUTH CAROLINA: Calhoun Club, St. Matthews (9,1960); Columbia CC (New site,27,1962); CC of Orangeburg (New site,1960); CC of South Carolina, Florence (1969); Midland Valley CC, Aiken (1960); Wellman CC, Johnsonville (1965).

TENNESSEE: Ridgeway CC, Memphis (New Site,1971).

VIRGINIA: Chatmoss CC, Martinsville (1959); Countryside [formerly Arrow Wood CC], Roanoke (1967); Kempsville Meadows G&CC, Norfolk (1954); Lexington GC (1971); Olde Mill GC, Groundhog Mountain (1974); Roanoke CC (9,1966).

Courses Remodeled by Ellis Maples:

NORTH CAROLINA: Emerywood Club, High Point (9,1962); Myers Park CC, Charlotte (1962); Reynolds Park CC, Winston-Salem (1966); Stanley County CC, Badin (1966).

Courses by Ellis Maples and Dan Maples:

ALABAMA: Sehoy Plantation, Hurtsboro (9 with double tees,1973).

NORTH CAROLINA: Deep Springs CC, Madison (a.9,1978); Green Valley CC, Kings Mountain (a.9,1974); Keith Hills CC, Buies Creek, Campbell College (1975); Lake Surf CC, Lobelia (1973); Mountain Springs G&CC, Linville (Executive course,1978); Whispering Pines CC (South course, 1974); Elkin CC, Elkin; Stanley County CC.

SOUTH CAROLINA: Marsh Harbour Golf Links.

VIRGINIA: Devil's Knot-Wintergreen, Nellysford (1974); Middle Plantation CC, Williamsburg (1974); Tazewell County CC (9,1978).

Courses Remodeled by Ellis Maples and Dan Maples:

TENNESSEE: Gatlinburg CC (1974).

Lane L. Marshall (1937–) ASGCA.

Born: Rochester, N.Y.

A graduate landscape architect, Lane Marshall served as president of the American Society of Landscape Architects in 1977 and 1978. In addition to his landscape practice, he designed a number of golf courses.

Courses by Lane L. Marshall:

FLORIDA: Bobby Jones Muni (a.9 Exec); Capri Isles GC, Sarasota; Foxfire G&TC; Gasparilo Pines (1972); Manatee County GC, Braden; Myakka Pines GC; Sarasota Muni; Tarpon Lake Village GC (1975); Tarpon Woods GC (1975); Wildflower CC, Grove City.

Jerry Martin (1939–) ASGCA

Born: Phoenix, Arizona.

Jerry Martin grew up in Tucson, Arizona, and attended high school in Morocco. He returned to the United States to study fine arts at the University of Arizona. Following military service, he worked for a year on a surveying crew before returning to the university of Arizona, where he earned his degree in city planning in 1967.

Martin was employed for five years with a civil engineering firm and was associated with the firm of Robert Trent Jones, Inc. for another five . He then became golf course architect and manager of recreational planning with Jack G. Robb Engineering of Costa Mesa, California.

Billy Martindale

Billy Martindale and Don January designed several courses together in the early 1970's. January rejoined the P.G.A. tour in 1976, but Martindale continued design work, including Oak Forest CC, Longview; Pecan Hollow CC, Lancaster and Pine Forest CC, Bastrop, all in Texas.

See Don January.

Gerald H. Matthews (1934-   ) ASGCA. Born Grand Rapids, Michigan.

Gerald Matthews attended Michigan State University, receiving a B.S. degree in landscape architecture as well as B.S. and M.S. degrees in urban planning. During his schooling, he worked for ten summers at golf course maintenance and supervised the construction of one course.

In 1960 Matthews and his father established the golf architectural firm of Gerald H. Matthews and W. Bruce Matthews. Over the years, Gerald took on the active design work of the firm, with his father acting as consultant. Eventually, he formed Design Group, a firm based in Lansing, Michigan, involved in golf course and landscape architecture together with land planning.

Courses by Gerald H. Matthews: See W. Bruce Matthews.

W. Bruce Matthews (1904-   ) ASGCA. Born Hastings, Michigan.

Bruce Matthews received a B.S.L.A. degree from Michigan State College in 1925. His first course design experience was with the golf architecture firm of Stiles and Van Kleek of Boston, Massachusetts, and St. Petersburg, Florida. In 1929 he entered private practice in Michigan, designing his first original course at the Manistee CC.

When the Depression curtailed course construction in 1931, Matthews became manager and greenkeeper at Green Ridge CC in Grand Rapids. He remained in that position until 1959 but continued to design golf courses on the side. In 1959 he re-entered golf architecture on a full-time basis. He also owned and operated a course of his own design, the Grand Haven CC in Grand Rapids.

In 1960 he and his son formed the course architectural firm of Gerald H. Matthews and W. Bruce Matthews, in which the elder Matthews gradually took on the role of consultant.

Courses by W. Bruce Matthews: (All courses after 1959 in collaboration with Gerald H. Matthews)

INDIANA: Summertree GC, Crown Point (1974).

MICHIGAN: Antrim Dells GC, Atwood (9,1971;9,1976); Birchwood Farm G&CC, Harbor Springs (1974); Candlestone GC, Belding (1978); Crockery Hills GC, Nuncia (r.5,a.9,1976); Crystal Lake GC, Beulah (9,1970); El Dorado GC, Mason (9,1966;9,1978); Fellows GC, Wayne (1961); Godwin Glen GC, South Lyon (27,1972); Grand Blanc GC (1967); Grand Haven GC, Grand Rapids (1965); Highland Hills GC, DeWitt (1963); Independence Green GC, Farmington (1965); Indian Run GC, Kalamazoo (9,1972); Kalamazoo Elks CC (2,1976); Kaufman GC, Grand Rapids (1963); Lake Isabella GC, Weidman (1970); Lake o' the Hills GC, Haslett (9 par 3,1968); Lake of the North GC, Mancelona (9,1971); Lake Pointe CC, St. Clair Shores (6,1964); Lakewood Shores G&CC, Oscoda (1969); Lincoln Hills GC, Birmingham (9,1963); Ludington Hills GC (r.4,a.10,1975); Old Channel Trail GC, Montague (9,1966); Pine River CC, Alma (9,1961); Riverside GC, Battle Creek (9,1964); Royal Oak GC (9,1960); St. Clair Shores CC (1974); Salem Hills GC (1961); San Marino GC, Farmington (9,1965); Sandy Ridge GC, Midland (1966); Scott Lake CC, Comstock Park (1961); Shenandoah G&CC, Walled Lake (1964); Southmoor GC, Flint (1965); Sugar Springs GC, Gladwin (1978); University Park GC, Muskegon (9,1966); West Ottawa GC, Holland (1964); Wilderness Valley, Gaylord (1979); Winding Creek GC, Zeeland (9,1967); Wolverine GC, Mt. Clemens (1965); Mitchell Creek GC, Mitchell.

Courses Remodeled by W. Bruce Matthews: (All courses after 1959 in collaboration with Gerald H. Matthews)

INDIANA: Elcona CC. Elkhart (1969); Ft. Wayne CC (3,1968).

MICHIGAN: Birmingham CC (3,1963); Blythfield CC (5,1973); Bonnie View GC, Eaton Rapids (r.4,a.2); Brynwood CC (r.1,a.2,1979); Cascade Hills CC, Grand Rapids (1974-80); CC of Detroit (1962); Farmington CC (1962); Indian Hills GC, Okemos (1968); Knollwood CC, Birmingham (r.1,a.1,1969); Meadowbrook CC, Northville (1); Muskegon CC; Pine Lake CC, Orchard Lake (1972); Plum Hollow GC, Southfield (1,1966); Stonycroft Hills CC, Bloomfield Hills (5); Walnut Hills CC, East Landsing (2,1963); Washtenaw CC, Ypsilanti (1,1962); Winters Creek GC (9,1980).

CANADA: Essex G&CC, Windsor, Ontario (2,1967-76).

Courses by W. Bruce Matthews before 1960:

MICHIGAN: Blossom Trails GC, Benton Harbor (1952); Brook Hollow CC, Williamston (9,1955); Dun Rovin GC, Northville (1956); Flint Elks (1960,first collaboration with G. H. Matthews); Forest Akers GC, Michigan State University, East Lansing (1957); Manistee GC (1930); McGuires GC, Cadillac (1954); Sunnybrook CC, Grandville (1955); Tyrone Hills GC, Livingston County (1958); White Birch Hills GC, Bay City (1953).

Courses Remodeled by W. Bruce Matthews before 1959:

MICHIGAN: Green Ridge CC, Grand Rapids (1930-50); Midland CC; Traverse City CC.

James Press Maxwell (1916–   ) ASGCA: President, 1960
Born: Ardmore, Oklahoma.

The son of golf architect Perry Maxwell, Press Maxwell started in the business upon graduation from high school. His father put him to work running mule teams and fresno scrapers at such sites as Southern Hills and Augusta National.

After service as a pilot with the U. S. Air Force in World War II, Maxwell returned to his father's firm. By this time Perry Maxwell had lost a leg, and Press was responsible for much of the on-site supervision of their designs.

Continuing from the time after his father's death in 1952, Maxwell designed and built many courses along the Gulf Coast, flying from course to course in his own Cessna. In the early 1960s he moved his base to Colorado and in the early 1970s retired from full-time practice to maintain a ranch, although he continued to work on an occasional project.

Courses by James Press Maxwell:

CALIFORNIA: Huntington Sea Cliff GC, Huntington Beach.

COLORADO: Applewood GC [formerly Rolling Hills], Golden (9,1956;9,1961); Boulder CC (new site,1965); Cherry Hills CC, Englewood (r.1959;a.9 par 3,1961); Cimarron Hills GC, Colorado Springs (1974); Cortez Muni (9,1964;9,1974); Fairways GC, Boulder (1964); Greeley CC (1962); Hiwan GC, Evergreen (1965); Inverness GC, Englewood (1974); Kissing Camels GC, Colorado Springs (1961); Patty Jewett GC, Colorado Springs (a.18,1968); Pinehurst CC, Denver (27,1960); Rolling Hills CC, Golden (new site,1968); Snowmass at Aspen GC (original 9,1967); Vail GC (1966); Woodmoor CC, Monument (1965).

KANSAS: Prairie Dunes CC, Hutchinson (2nd 9,1956).

LOUISIANA: East Ridge CC, Shreveport (1957).

MISSISSIPPI: Hattiesburg CC (1962).

MISSOURI: Fremont Hills CC, Nixa (1971); Tri-way GC, Republic (1971).

OKLAHOMA: Meadowbrook CC, Tulsa (1954).

TENNESSEE: Farmington CC, Germantown (1968); Orgill CC, Millington (1970).

TEXAS: Brookhaven CC, Dallas (Championship,Master's and President's courses,1959); Camp Hood GC (1948); Canyon Creek CC, Richardson; Irving CC (9,1957); Oak Cliff CC, Dallas (1955); Pecan Valley CC, San Antonio (1963); Pinecrest CC, Longview (r.9,a.9,1959); Randolph Field GC (1948); Riverbend CC, Sugarland (1958); Riverlake CC, Dallas; Royal Oaks CC, Dallas (1970); Village CC, Dallas (1969).

UTAH: Park City GC (r.9,a.9,1972).

Courses Remodeled by James Press Maxwell:

COLORADO: Columbine CC, Littleton (1958); Denver CC (1964); Lakewood CC, Denver (1963).

OKLAHOMA: Oklahoma City G&CC (1952).

Courses Jointly Designed by James Press and Perry Duke Maxwell:

ALABAMA: Lakewood GC, Point Clear (1947).

LOUISIANA: Bayou DeSiard CC, Monroe (1949); Palmetto CC, Benton (1950).

OKLAHOMA: Oakwood CC, Enid (1947); University of Oklahoma GC (1950).

TEXAS: Camp Hood GC (9,1948); CC of Austin (1950); Knollwood CC, Irving (1952); Randolph Field GC, Randolph AFB (original 9,1948).

Perry Duke Maxwell (1879–1952) ASGCA: Charter Member

Born: Princeton, Kentucky. Died: Tulsa, Oklahoma, at age 73.

Perry Maxwell, of Scottish descent, was educated at the University of Kentucky. In 1897 he moved to Ardmore Indian Territory to recover from an attack of tuberculosis and eventually settled in what would become, in 1907, the state of Oklahoma. He was employed as a cashier and later as vice-president of the Ardmore National Bank, becoming one of the town's leading citizens. Around 1909 he took up the game of golf after reading an article by H. J. Whigham; and in 1913, with his wife's assistance, he laid out a rudimentary nine-hole course on their farm north of Ardmore. This course became the Dornick Hills G&CC.

Maxwell retired from banking soon after his wife's death in 1919 and spent the next several years touring America's most prominent southern and eastern golf courses. He added a second nine to Dornick Hills in 1923 and installed the first grass greens in the state of Oklahoma at the same time. Shortly thereafter he was hired to build courses in Tulsa and Oklahoma City and by 1925 was working full time as a golf architect. He partnered for three years in the early thirties with Britisher Alister Mackenzie and supervised completion of some of Mackenzie's work after his death.

Maxwell was best known for his wildly undulating greens, and his reputation was of such stature that he was hired to rebuild greens at Augusta National and Pine Valley, among others. His last designs, following the amputation of his right leg in 1946, were supervised by his son, J. Press Maxwell, who later became a golf architect himself. It is estimated that during his career Perry Maxwell designed some seventy courses and remodeled fifty others.

Courses by Perry Duke Maxwell:

ALABAMA: Lakewood GC, Point Clear (1947).

IOWA: Veenker Memorial GC, Iowa State University, Ames (1934).

KANSAS: Arkansas City CC (Original 9,1937); Prairie Dunes CC, Hutchinson (Original 9,1937); Topeka CC (r.9,a.9,1938).

LOUISIANA: Bayou DeSiard CC, Monroe (1949); Palmetto CC, Benton (1950).

MICHIGAN: Crystal Downs CC, Frankfort (r.9,a.9,1933,c.Mackenzie); University of Michigan GC, Ann Arbor (c.Mackenzie,1931).

MISSOURI: Excelsior Springs GC (a.Par 3 course); Grandview Muni, Springfield.

NORTH CAROLINA: Reynolds Park GC, Winston Salem (1944); Starmount Forest CC [formerly Starmount GC], Greensboro (1929).

OHIO: Ohio State University GC, Columbus (Scarlet and Grey courses,c.Mackenzie,1935).

OKLAHOMA: Dornick Hills G&CC, Ardmore (9,1913;9,1923); Lake Hefner Muni, Oklahoma City (North course,1951); Lawton CC (9,1948); Muskogee CC (1924); Oakwood CC, Enid (1948); Oklahoma City G&CC (1930); Ponca City CC; Rolling Hills CC [formerly Indian Hills CC]; Tulsa (1926); Southern Hills CC, Tulsa (1936); Twin Hills G&CC, Oklahoma City (1926); University of Oklahoma GC, Norman (1951).

PENNSYLVANIA: Eugene Grace Estate GC, Bethlehem; Melrose CC, Cheltenham (1927).

TEXAS: Colonial CC, Ft. Worth (a.holes 3–5,1940); (The) CC of Austin (1950); Knollwood CC [formerly River Hills CC], Irving (1952); Walnut Hills CC, Ft. Worth (n.l.e.).

Courses Remodeled by Perry Duke Maxwell:

GEORGIA: Augusta National GC (r.greens,1937).

199

KANSAS: Lawrence CC; Macdonald Park Muni (formerly Wichita CC), Mission Hills CC, Shawnee Mission.
NEBRASKA: Omaha CC (r.greens).
NEW JERSEY: Pine Valley GC, Clementon (r.several greens,1933).
NORTH CAROLINA: Hope Valley CC, Durham.
OKLAHOMA: Lincoln Park Muni, Oklahoma City (r.greens); Mohawk Park Muni, Tulsa (r.greens); Tulsa CC.
PENNSYLVANIA: Gulph Mills GC, King of Prussia (1934–37); Merion GC, Ardmore (r.greens,East and West courses,1939); Philadelphia CC, Gladwyne (Spring Mill course,1938); Saucon Valley CC, Bethlehem (Saucon course,1947); Sunnybrook CC, Philadelphia (n.l.e.).

Charles Maud

Englishman Charles Maud emigrated to California, where he laid out the state's first golf course in 1892. Known as Pedley Farms at Arlington (later Arlington GC and now Victoria GC), it was owned by Colonel W. E. Pedley, who is thought to have assisted Maud in laying out several other courses. Although Max Behr revised the original nine and added an additional nine, the present Victoria GC still contains several of Maud's holes.

Charles Maud was the winner of the first California Amateur in 1899, and served as the first president of the Southern California Golf Association in 1900.

Courses by Charles Maud:
CALIFORNIA: Del Monte GC, Monterey (original course); Delmar GC (original 9); Riverside Golf and Polo Club; Victoria GC [formerly Pedley Farms at Arlington] (original 9).

Edward "Ted" McAnlis

See Richard La Conte

Maurice J. McCarthy, Sr. (1875–1938)

Born: County Cork, Ireland. Died: Flushing, New York, at age 63.

Maurice McCarthy came to the United States at the age of fifteen and obtained a job as a teaching professional in Pittsfield, Massachusetts. A few years later he laid out his first course, the Jefferson County GC (now Ives Hill) in Watertown, New York. But throughout his life, course design remained a part-time endeavor for McCarthy. He was proudest of his accomplishments as a teacher. His son, Maurice Jr., was the 1928 NCAA Champion and a top-flight amateur in the 1930s.

McCarthy served as professional at several New York-area clubs but in his later years was employed exclusively by the A. G. Spalding Sporting Goods Company in New York City, where he gave lessons to all patrons of golf clubs.

It is estimated that Maurice McCarthy designed or remodeled about 125 courses during his lifetime, most of them in the Eastern and Middle Atlantic states. His most famous works are at Hershey, Pennsylvania, where he laid out four different courses over the years for his friend, Milton Hershey. These range from a short "beginner's course," Spring Creek, to a nationally recognized championship course, the Country Club's West Course.

Courses by Maurice J. McCarthy, Sr.:
CONNECTICUT: Hubbard Heights GC, Stamford.
MICHIGAN: Battle Creek CC.
NEW JERSEY: Knickerbocker CC, Tenafly (Original course).
NEW YORK: Green Meadow GC, Port Chester; Jefferson County GC [now Ives Hill], Watertown (1899); Nassau Shores CC, Amityville; Old Flatbush CC, Brooklyn (9,1925,n.l.e.).
PENNSYLVANIA: Hershey CC (West course,1930); Hotel Hershey GC (9); Mahoning Valley CC, Lansford (n.l.e.); Parkview Manor GC, Hershey (1927); Spring Creek GC, Hershey (9,1933).
SOUTH CAROLINA: Forest Lakes Club, Columbia.
TENNESSEE: Kingsport CC.

Thomas John Andrew McAuley (1930–   )   BAGCA

A graduate of Queens University, Ulster, Northern Ireland, and fellow of the Institution of Civil Engineers and the Institution of Structural Engineers, T. J. A. McAuley worked as an assistant to German golf architect Dr. Bernhard von Limburger from 1969 to 1973. During those years, he also collaborated with Peter Alliss and David Thomas in course design. He later combined his practice as a golf architect with partnership in a firm of consulting, civil and structural engineers located in Belfast, Northern Ireland.

Courses by Thomas John Andrew McAuley   In addition to courses planned but not built by 1979 in Brazil, Iran, Italy and Spain, his designs include:
ENGLAND: Birchwood GC, Cheshire; Locking Stumps, Warrington (1975); Welcombe, Stratford-upon-Avon (1978).
IRELAND: Fort Royal, Donegal (9,1974).
NORTHERN IRELAND: Clandehoye, Co. Down (1973) c. Alliss and Thomas.
SCOTLAND: Glendevon, Gleneagles (1977).
Courses Remodeled by Thomas John Andrew McAuley:
ENGLAND: Moretonhampstead, Devon, Grange Coventry (6,1981).
NORTHERN IRELAND: Ballyclare, Co. Antrim (9) c. Alliss and Thomas.

Peter McEwan (1834–1895)

Scottish club maker Peter McEwan laid out Braid Hill at Edinburgh in the late 1800s in collaboration with Robert Ferguson.

John McGlynn

The first greenkeeping superintendent at Oakmont CC, John McGlynn worked under both

Henry and William Fownes. He later operated a design and build firm part time with Emil "Dutch" Loeffler, his successor at Oakmont.
Courses by John McGlynn: See Emil "Dutch" Loeffler.

J. B. McGovern (–1951)   ASGCA: Charter Member

J. B. McGovern spent most of his design career as an associate of Donald Ross with offices in Wynnewood, Pennsylvania. For a short period following World War II, he planned several courses on his own, including Overbrook CC near Philadelphia (c.X.G.Hassenplug,1951); Llanersch CC in Pennsylvania (1949) and revisions to Gulph Mills near Philadelphia and Irondoquoit near Rochester, New York.

Alexander G. McKay (1893–1964)

Born: Aberdeen, Scotland. Died: Nashville, Tennessee, at age 71.

Alex McKay learned golf at the Cruden Bay GC in Aberdeen and turned professional at a young age. After spending three years in Egypt, he moved to America following World War I. He worked at odd jobs before landing the position of supervisor of the Louisville (Kentucky) city parks in 1926. He remained there for ten years as professional and greenkeeper for the city's golf courses and in that capacity remodeled two existing courses and designed and built three new ones, including the popular Shawnee GC.

In the mid-1930s McKay designed the Meadowbrook CC in West Virginia and became its first pro-superintendent. Following World War II, he took a similar position at Holston Hills in Tennessee. In the late 1940s he began experimenting at Holston Hills with bentgrass greens, then a rarity in the South. His success resulted in commissions to convert other clubs from Bermuda to bent, and in the process he often recommended changes to the course layout.

In the early 1950s McKay resigned from Holston Hills to work full time as a course architect, contractor and turf consultant. He supervised the construction of several courses for other golf architects, notably William B. Langford, and also designed a number of courses himself.

Courses by Alexander G. McKay:
KENTUCKY: Audubon CC, Louisville; Greenville CC (9); Indian Springs CC, Barbourville (9,1963); L & N GC, Brooks; Owensboro Muni; Seneca Muni, Louisville (1928); Shawnee Muni, Louisville (1927).
MARYLAND: Chestnut Ridge CC, Lutherville (1956).
NEW YORK: Commack Hills G&CC (1955).
NORTH CAROLINA: Statesville CC (new site,1960).
OHIO: Wright-Patterson AFB GC, Dayton (r.9,a.9,1960).
TENNESSEE: CC of Bristol (1959); Green Meadow CC, Maryville (r.9,a.9,1958); Lakes View GC, Johnson City (9 par 3,1963); Nubbins Ridge CC, Knoxville; Pine Oaks Muni, Knoxville (1963).
VIRGINIA: Bristol CC (new site,1960); Glenrochie CC, Abington (9,1958); Lake Bonaventure CC, St. Paul (9,1957); Spotswood CC, Harrisburg (a.9,1965).
WEST VIRGINIA: Edgewood CC, Charleston; Meadowbrook CC, Charleston (1937).
Courses Remodeled by Alexander G. McKay:
KENTUCKY: Cherokee GC, Louisville (1927); Crescent Hill GC, Louisville (9,1926).
TENNESSEE: Chattanooga G&CC (1953); Cherokee CC, Knoxville (1950); Holston Hills CC, Knoxville (1946); Riverview CC, Chattanooga (1961).

Chester Mendenhall (1895–   )

Born: Montgomery County, Kansas.

Raised on a farm in Oklahoma, Chester Mendenhall was hired in 1921 to construct the Sims Park Municipal GC in Wichita, Kansas. He remained there as greenkeeper until 1929, when he took a similar position with the Wichita CC. In 1934 he moved to the Mission Hills CC in Kansas City, serving as superintendent until his retirement in 1965. He began designing and remodeling courses as a "second career" after retirement.

Mendenhall was a charter member of the National Association of Greenkeepers of America (1927) and served as president in 1948. He was also a member for several years of the USGA Green Section Committee.

Courses by Chester Mendenhall:
KANSAS: Osawatomie Muni (a.2nd 9,1972).
MISSOURI: California CC (9); Centralia CC; Claycrest CC, Liberty (1969); Linn CC; Shirkey GC, Richmond (1968); Tarkio CC.
Courses Remodeled by Chester Mendenhall:
KANSAS: Fort Hays CC, Hays (9); Lake Quivira CC (1968); Medicine Lodge Muni (9); Shawnee CC, Topeka; Topeka CC.

Fraser Middleton   BAGCA

Based in Scotland, golf architect Fraser Middleton designed a number of courses in the British Isles. Among those completed by 1980 were Hounslow Heath, Middlesex, and Davenport, Cheshire, both in England, together with Invergorden, Rossshire and Shetland (Dale GC), both in Scotland.

David T. Millar (1892–1946)

Born in Arbroath, Scotland, David Millar settled and worked in the Detroit area. Among his designs were Clinton Valley in Detroit, Milham Park Muni in Kalamazoo (1931) and a course at Kalamazoo State Teachers College, all in Michigan.

Lon Mills

Greenkeeper at the Knoxville (Tennessee) Municipal GC from its opening in 1931, Lon Mills practiced golf course architecture in the 1950s. Two courses of his design were Beaver Brook G&CC, Knoxville (1956) and Green Valley GC, Kingsport, both in Tennessee.

Samuel S. Mitchell (1909–   ) ASGCA

Born: Manchester, Massachusetts.

Samuel Mitchell was the second of four sons (Robert, Samuel, Henry and William) of Robert A. Mitchell, greenkeeper at Kernwood CC, Salem, Massachusetts. He and his brothers all became active in golf course design, construction or maintenance.

Samuel graduated from the Stockbridge School of Agriculture of Massachusetts Agricultural College in 1928. He worked in golf design, construction and maintenance for the firm of Langford and Moreau, and was later employed with the Metropolitan District Commission of Boston as greenkeeping superintendent at Ponkapoag GC in Canton, Massachusetts. While at Ponkapoag, he added a third nine to the design of Donald Ross.

In the 1950s Mitchell was involved in a design and build partnership with brothers William and Henry; and in 1960–61 he collaborated with Geoffrey Cornish in the development of Spring Valley CC at Sharon, Massachusetts, and the addition of nine holes to the Woonsocket (Rhode Island) CC. He entered private practice as a golf architect in 1962.

Mitchell also operated an extensive sod business and managed a course of his own design, the Easton (Massachusetts) GC. Two sons, Samuel Jr. and Philip, became golf course superintendents.

Courses by Samuel S. Mitchell:

MASSACHUSETTS: Brookmeadow GC, Canton (9,1966;9,1968); Chestnut Hill CC, Newton (9,1962); City of New Bedford Muni (9,1964); D.W. Field GC, Brockton (2,1972); Dighton Par 3 GC (9,1963); Easton CC (9,1961;9,1967); Great Neck GC, Wareham (1963); Hatherly CC, North Scituate (a.3,1968;r.2,1976); Leo J. Martin GC, Weston (9,1962); Natick CC (r.4,a.9,1960); Norwood CC (1975); Town of Braintree Muni (11,1967); Lost Brook Par 3, Norwood.

RHODE ISLAND: Melody Hill GC, Harmony (9,1965).

Courses Remodeled by Samuel S. Mitchell:

MASSACHUSETTS: City of Gardner Muni (2,1968).

RHODE ISLAND: Kirkbrae CC, Lincoln (3,1969).

William F. Mitchell (1912–1974) ASGCA

Born: Salem, Massachusetts. Died: West Palm Beach, Florida, at age 62.

William Mitchell was involved with golf courses from an early age. The son of Robert Mitchell, respected course superintendent who taught at the Essex County (Massachusetts) Agricultural School in the 1920s and later became superintendent at Kernwood CC in Salem, Massachusetts, Bill Mitchell obtained his first greenkeeper's job at the age of nineteen. A few years later, while working as greenkeeper at the Lake Sunapee GC in North Sutton, New Hampshire, he established a turf farm specializing in velvet bentgrass for greens that he operated successfully for decades. Through his turf business he gained first-hand experience in golf course construction and by the late 1930s was assisting architect Orrin Smith in the construction or reconstruction of several New England layouts.

After serving as a Navy pilot during World War II, Mitchell became superintendent at the Charles River CC near Boston. In the late 1940s he and two of his brothers, Samuel and Henry, formed a golf design and construction firm, Mitchell Brothers, which continued until the mid-fifties. Sam then left to do designing and consulting on his own; and Henry returned to a superintendent's position with a little design work on the side, notably Dennis Pines and the second nine of Cummaquid, both on Cape Cod. William himself was associated for several years during the fifties with golf architect Albert Zikorus. Another brother, Bob, was a long-time superintendent and manager at the Edison CC in New York.

By the 1960s William Mitchell was doing golf course architecture exclusively and had planned courses as far south as Florida and as far west as Michigan. He estimated that by the early 1970s he had done some 150 original designs and 200 remodeling jobs. He was an early and vocal advocate of separate courses designed specifically for women golfers, and shortly before his death he had been retained by the Ladies Professional Golfers Association to build such a course. He is also credited with having coined the title "executive course."

Courses by William F. Mitchell:

CONNECTICUT: Sleeping Giant GC, Hamden (1951); Tumble Brook CC, Bloomfield (1948).

FLORIDA: Atlantis CC; Brooksville G&CC (1972); Carrollwood G&TC, Tampa (1967); Deerfield CC (1964); East Bay CC, Largo (1962); El Pomar GC, West Palm Beach (Par 3,1971); Hollybrook G&CC, Hollywood (1968); Kassuba GC, West Palm Beach (18 par 3,1972); Lochmoor GC, North Ft. Myers (1972); Longboat Key Club, Sarasota (1961); Palm Aire CC, Pompano Beach (Palms course,1960); Palm Beach Lakes GC (1966); President GC, West Palm Beach (North course,1970;South course,1972); Rolling Hills CC, Altamonte Springs; Rolling Hills CC, Ft. Lauderdale (1961); Southern Manor CC, Boca Raton (1962); University of South Florida GC, Tampa (1967); Tavares Cove Exec. GC.

MAINE: Loring AFB GC, Limestone (1959).

MARYLAND: Eaglehead G&CC, New Market (1971).

MASSACHUSETTS: Colonial GC, Lynnfield (r.Old course,1948;a.9,1963); Framingham CC (a.9,1960); Green Hill Muni, Worcester (New course,1968); Martin Memorial GC, Weston (1952); Mt. Pleasant CC, Boylston (New site,1959); CC of New Seabury, South Mashpee (Blue course,1964;Green course,1965); North Hill CC, Duxbury (1967); Ponkapoag GC, Canton (r.,a.9,1955); Saddle Hill CC, Hopkinton (1962); Webb Brook GC, Burlington (1952).

MICHIGAN: Bedford Valley CC, Battle Creek (1965); Gull Lake View GC, Richland (East course,r.West course,1967).

NEW HAMPSHIRE: Amherst CC (1962); Goffstown CC (1962); Kearsarge Valley CC, North Sutton (r.9,a.9,1963); Plausawa Valley CC, Concord (1965).

NEW JERSEY: Fairview GC (1954).

NEW YORK: Bergen Point Muni, Babylon (1972); Colonie Muni (1969); Crab Meadow GC, Northport (1963); Emerald Green GC, Rock Hill (1970); Glen Cove Muni (1970); Hard Estate Park Muni, West Sayville (1970); Indian Island Park GC, Riverhead (1973); Kutsher's Hotel GC, Monticello (1962); Lido Springs GC, Lido Beach (Par 3,1963); Lowell Thomas Estate GC, Pawling (1951); McCann Memorial GC, Poughkeepsie (1973); Noyac G&CC, Sag Harbor (1964); Old Westbury G&CC (27,1962); Otterkill G&CC, Newburgh (1957); Park District GC, Fallsburgh (1959); Pine Hollow CC, East Norwich (1954); Putnam CC, Lake Mahopac; Stevensville Lake G&CC, Swan Lake (1966); Tarry Brae GC, South Fallsburg (1958); Timber

Point Park GC (1972); Waldemere Hotel GC, Livingston Manor (1959); Willows GC [formerly Wahalla CC], Rexford (1967); The Woodcrest Club, Syosset (1963).

OHIO: Dorlon Park GC, Columbiana (1972); Pebble Creek GC, Lexington (1974); Tanglewood GC, Chagrin Falls (1966), Walden G&TC, Aurora (1974).

PENNSYLVANIA: Cedarbrook CC, Blue Bell (1962); General Washington CC, Audubon (1962).

VERMONT: Crown Point CC, Springfield (9,1953;a.9,1959); Stowe CC (1962).

CANADA: Golf Du Parc Carleton, Quebec (9,1963); Golf Fort Preval, Quebec (9,1961); Mactaquac Provincial Park GC, New Brunswick (1970); Maple Downs G&CC, Toronto, Ontario (1954).

PORTUGAL: Club de Quintado de Lago, Faro, Algarve (27,1973).

Courses Remodeled by William F. Mitchell: [o]

CALIFORNIA: Canyon CC, Palm Springs (North & South courses,1965).

CONNECTICUT: Birchwood CC, Westport (1946); Minnechaug CC (1952); High Ridge GC, Norwalk (1946); Meadowbrook CC, Hamden (1947); Milford CC (1948); Old Lyme GC (1949); Rockledge CC, Hartford (1947).

MAINE: Riverside CC, Portland (1948).

MASSACHUSETTS: Bear Hill CC, Wakefield (1950); Charles River CC, Newton (1946); Duxbury Y&CC (1951); Franklin CC (1949); Furnace Brook GC, Quincy (1947); Holden GC (1957); Kernwood CC, Salem (1950); Leicester CC (1950); Lynnfield Center GC (1949); New Bedford Muni (1958); North Andover CC (1947); Red Hill CC, Reading (1951); Riverside CC, Weston (1948); Springfield CC (1948); Wayland CC (1952); Winthrop CC (1949); Wollaston CC, Quincy (1956).

NEW HAMPSHIRE: Franklin CC (1956); Nashua CC (1949).

NEW JERSEY: White Beeches CC, Haworth (1953).

NEW YORK: Dellwood CC, New City (1951); Glen Head CC, Glen Cove (1949); Grossinger's Hotel GC (1959); Hiawatha CC, Syracuse (1948); Huntington CC (1949); I.B.M. CC, Endicott (1948); Island Hill CC, Sayville (1967); Old Oaks CC, Purchase (1949); Poughkeepsie Muni (1953); Quaker Hill CC, Pawling (1959); Sadaquada GC, Utica (1969); Saratoga Spa GC (1959); Southampton CC (1965); Teugega CC, Rome (1948); Van Cortlandt Park GC, Bronx (1947).

NORTH CAROLINA: Southern Pines CC (1947).

VERMONT: Basin Harbor GC, Vergennes (1952); Brattleboro CC (1948); Equinox CC, Manchester (1967).

CANADA: Mt. Magog Park GC, Magog, Quebec (1960).

[o] Some of Mitchell's remodeling in the late 1940s and early 1950s was in conjunction with re-sodding greens from his velvet bent nursery.

Theodore Moone

A British golf writer of the 1930s, Theodore Moone's best-known publication was *Golf From A New Angle*. He designed or remodeled at least four courses in the British Isles, including the Carlisle GC and Eastwood GC near Glasgow. as well as revisions to Kilmarnock (Barassie) (CC) and the Dumfries and Galloway GC.

Hugh C. Moore, Sr. (1895-1972)

After helping to construct Sea Island GC and Jekyll Island GC to Walter Travis's plans, Hugh Moore became superintendent at Sea Island and later constructed a second nine designed by Colt and Alison. He resigned in 1933 to work as a baseball umpire in Southern semi-pro leagues but returned to golf in 1942, remodeling and operating a course in Georgia. He later designed Bowden Muni in Macon, Georgia, and remained as superintendent until 1953, when he was hired to renovate the Dunedin (Florida) CC into the national base of the PGA.

Courses by Hugh C. Moore, Sr.:

ALABAMA: Dothan CC.

GEORGIA: Blakely CC (9,1959); Bowden Muni, Macon (1949); Dawson CC; Sunset CC, Moultrie (1944); Turner AFB GC, Albany (9,1953); Warner Robins AFB GC, Macon (9,1951).

Courses Remodeled by Hugh C. Moore, Sr.:

GEORGIA: American Legion GC, Albany (1954); Glen Arven GC, Thomasville (4,1942); Pelham CC.

David Stanley Moote (1928–   )

David Moote received a B.S.A. degree from Ontario Agricultural College and a masters degree in Turf from Rutgers University. He worked as course superintendent at Rosedale GC, Toronto; Essex GC, Windsor, Ontario; and Scarboro GC, Toronto. He became active in course design in Ontario in 1963, in partnership (part-time) with his brother Robert. Moote served as president of the Golf Course Superintendents Association of America in 1964. See Robert F. Moote.

Robert Frederick Moote (1924–   ) ASGCA

Born: Dunnville, Ontario, Canada.

Robert Moote received a B.S.A. degree in Ornamental Horticulture from the Ontario Agricultural College in 1948 and then worked for golf architect Stanley Thompson in Canada, the United States and Jamaica. In 1951 he became assistant landscape supervisor with Central Mortgage and Housing, where he remained for five years.

Around 1956 Moote became construction supervisor at Oakdale G&CC near Toronto, staying on as course superintendent for some twenty years. During these years he did some part-time work with golf architect C. E. Robinson and served as a greens consultant to the Royal Canadian Golf Association. He was also associated in course design with his brother David for a time. In 1976 he entered private practice as a full-time architect under the firm name of R. F. Moote and Associates.

Courses by Robert Frederick Moote:

ONTARIO: Barrie GC (c.D.Moote); Blair Hampton GC, Minden (c.D.Moote); Brampton GC (co-architect); Galt GC (c.D.Moote); Hawthorne Valley GC; Hornby Tower GC, Kingsville GC

(c.D.Moote); Lively GC, Sudbury; Lynnwood GC, London; North Halton, Georgetown (c.D.Moote); Orillia GC; Streetsville Glen GC (c.D.Moote); Trehaven GC; Westview GC, Aurora (c.D.Moote).
JAMAICA: Ironshores GC, Montego Bay.
MARTINIQUE: La Pointe du Diamant.
Courses Remodeled by Robert Frederick Moote:
ALBERTA: Shawnee Slopes, Calgary.
ONTARIO: Huntington GC (c.C.E.Robinson); Owen Sound GC; Port Colborne GC; Westview GC, Aurora (1st 9).
JAMAICA: Paradise Park GC.

Theodore J. Moreau (1890–1942)
Died: Wilmette, Illinois, at age 51.
Civil engineer Theodore J. Moreau teamed with William B. Langford after World War I in a golf design and construction business based in Chicago. The firm of Langford & Moreau was among the busiest in the Midwest in the 1920s and 30s. While Moreau primarily handled the construction aspects of their projects, he also did a few original designs. See William B. Langford.

Sloan Morpeth
Noted Australian amateur golfer Sloan Morpeth won New Zealand's Open tournament in 1928 and its Amateur in 1920, '27, and '28. In 1967 he remodeled the Australian GC following a highway land taking. He also designed Surfer's Paradise GC in Queensland, Australia.

George Morris
George Morris assisted his brother, "Old Tom" Morris, in laying out several courses and then planned the first nine holes of Hoylake (Royal Liverpool) in England (1869) in collaboration with Robert Chambers, Jr. Morris remained as greenkeeper and professional at Hoylake, where he influenced the careers of several men who later emigrated to North America, including designers H. J. Tweedie of Chicago and William F. Davis of Royal Montreal and Newport CC.
Two of Morris's grandsons, Tom and George Morris, also emigrated to the United States. The younger George Morris became professional at Grand Beach GC in Michigan and was later professional at Colonial CC, Harrisburg, Pennsylvania, for more than fifty years.

Thomas "Old Tom" Morris (1821–1908)
Born: St. Andrews, Scotland. Died: St. Andrews, Scotland.
"Old Tom" Morris apprenticed under Allan Robertson at the Old Course at St. Andrews from 1839 to 1851. Following a bitter disagreement with Robertson concerning use of the gutta-percha ball, of which Robertson disapproved, Morris moved to Prestwick, where he held the position of greenkeeper and professional until 1865. He then returned to similar duties at St. Andrews, where he remained until his retirement in 1904. Morris won the British Open in 1861, '62, '64 and '67; and his son "Young Tom," who had won the Open four times by the age of twenty-two, ranks among the greatest golfers of all time. Morris's life was saddened by his son's death in 1875 at the age of 25.
Those who knew him described "Old Tom" as a man it was impossible to dislike. Throughout his productive life he refused to play golf on Sundays and kept the Old Course closed on that day, because he felt it also needed a rest. His philosophy in regard to putting surface maintenance embraced sand and more sand as top-dressing.
Morris ranked at the top of recognized links designers in the last half of the nineteenth century. He practiced the art in an age when it was virtually impossible to alter existing contours in laying out a new course. A native of the links with an eye for every shot in golf, he developed a skill for utilizing natural terrain and its features, which he passed on to an apprentice, Donald Ross (of Dornoch, Scotland and Pinehurst, North Carolina).
Artificial features found on Morris's layouts were probably not his but rather the poorly conceived alterations of others made years or decades later. "Old Tom" was the first to plan double loop routings to take maximum advantage of the wind.
Courses by "Old Tom" Morris:
ENGLAND: Wallasey GC, Cheshire (1891); West Herts (1897); Westward Ho! (Royal North Devon).
IRELAND: Lahinch (1893); Rosapenna GC (1893).
NORTHERN IRELAND: Royal County Down (1891).
SCOTLAND: Askernish, Western Isles; Barry Angus, Carnoustie (r.,a.several holes); Crail GC (1892); Dornoch (a.9); Dunbar GC, East Lothian; Elie GC; Glasgow GC (1904); King James VI GC, Perth (1896); Ladybank GC, Fife (1879); Luffness New GC, East Lothian; Muirfield (1891); Prestwick (finalized 12-hole layout); Royal Burgess of Edinburgh (1895); St. Andrews New Course; Stirling GC (1892); Tain GC, Ross-shire.
WALES: Pwllheli GC (Original 9,1900).
Courses Remodeled by "Old Tom" Morris:
SCOTLAND: Macrihanish; Nairn Highlands; St. Andrews (modifications to the Old Course).

John Stanton Fleming Morrison (1892–1961)
Born: Deal, England. Died: Farnham, England, at age 68. Interred: Woking.
J. S. F. Morrison attended Trinity College, Cambridge, where he won blues in cricket and soccer before World War I. After service in the Royal Flying Corps, he returned to Cambridge and won another blue in golf. He later won the 1929 Belgian Amateur. Morrison was especially fond of partners' play and won the Worplesdon Foursomes in 1928 with Joyce Wethered and the Halford-Hewitt Cup five times with Henry Longhurst, British golf writer and member of Parliament.
Morrison joined the golf design firm of Colt and Alison in the 1920s and by the early 1930s was made a partner and director of the firm of Colt, Alison and Morrison. He worked closely

with H. S. Colt on a number of courses on the Continent and in Britain. Following World War II, he was involved in several restoration projects, including Prince's GC in collaboration with Sir Guy Campbell. Morrison was active well into the 1950s, assisted by J. Hamilton Stutt.
Courses by John Stanton Fleming Morrison:
BRITAIN: Wentworth GC, Surrey (East and West courses,c.Colt,1924); Fulwell GC, Middlesex.
GERMANY: Falkenstein GC, Hamburg (c.Colt,1930); Frankfurter GC (1928,c.Colt;r.1952,c.Stutt); Hamburger Land und GC (c.Colt).
ITALY: GC Biella, Biellese; La Mandria GC, Turin (1956).
NETHERLANDS: Eindhoren GC, Valkensward (c.Colt,1930); Haagsche GC, Wassenaar (c.Colt,1939); Kennemer G&CC, Zandvoort (c.Colt,1928); Utrecht GC (c.Colt,1929).
SPAIN: Real Pedrena GC, Santander (c.Colt).
SWEDEN: Stockholm GC (new site,c.Colt,1932).
Courses Remodeled by J.S.F. Morrison:
BRITAIN: Liphook GC, Hampshire (r.,a.2,1946); Prince's GC; Sandwich, Kent (r.18,a.9,1951,c.Campbell); Seaford GC, Sussex; Sunningdale GC, Surrey (New course).
IRELAND: Royal Portrush GC (Dunluce and Valley courses).

Desmond Muirhead (1924–   )
Born: England.
Desmond Muirhead studied architecture and engineering at Cambridge and horticulture at the University of British Columbia and Oregon University. He worked for several years as a landscape planner in British Columbia before moving to the United States in the late 1950's to work on retirement villages. He planned one course during his years in British Columbia.
Muirhead's next interest in golf course design occured while he was working on the Sun City, Arizona, development. The son of a Scottish golfer, Muirhead claimed never to have been more than a high handicapper himself. But he recognized the need to make golf courses and housing developments compatible with one another. While he took no part in the routing of the course at Sun City, he was offered the opportunity to lay out his own design within a real estate project in California in 1962.
By that time Muirhead had made a whirlwind tour of the great courses of America and Britain and came away convinced that he could offer some new ideas in the field of golf design. Much of his early work involved the remodeling of existing West Coast courses; but as his designs gained national attention, the demand for his services increased. By the early 1970s Muirhead was busy on both coasts.
Two tournament golfers lent their names to various Muirhead projects. Initally Gene Sarazen was listed as his partner. Later Jack Nicklaus worked with him on several projects and in turn asked for his help with the routing and land planning of Nicklaus's first solo design, the Muirfield Village GC in Ohio.
Courses by Desmond Muirhead:
ARIZONA: McCormick Ranch GC, Scottsdale (Palm course, 1972; Pine course, 1973).
CALIFORNIA: Capistrano Saddle Club (1963; Desert Island CC, Rancho Mirage (1970); Disneyland Hotel GC, Anaheim (9 par 3, 1963,n.l.e.); Ironwood GC, Palm Desert (South course,1974); Mission Hills G&GC, Cathedral City (original 18, 1970; Quail Lake CC, Moreno (1968); Rossmoor Leisure World GC, Laguna Hills (1965); San Luis Bay Inn & CC, Avila Beach (original 9, 1968); Soboba Springs CC, San Jacinto (1967); The Springs Club, Rancho Mirage (1975).
CONNECTICUT: Heritage Woods CC, Farmington (1970); Oronoque Village GC, Stratford (1971).
FLORIDA: Baymeadows GC, Jacksonville (1969); Boca Raton West G&CC (Course #1, 1969; Course #2, 1970); Mayacoo Lakes CC, West Palm Beach (c.Nicklaus,1973); Silver Spring Shores G&CC, Ocala (1970).
MARYLAND: Rossmoor Leisure World GC, Silver Spring (1966).
MICHIGAN: Bay Valley GC, Bay City (1973).
NEW JERSEY: Rossmoor Leisure World GC, Cranbury (1967).
NEW MEXICO: Rio Rancho G&CC [formerly Panorama G&CC9], Albuquerque (1970).
NEW YORK: River Oaks CC, Grand Island (1972).
OHIO: Jack Nicklaus GC, Mason (Bruin and Grizzly courses, 1972); Muirfield Village GC, Dublin (c. Nicklaus, 1974).
TEXAS: Bent Tree GC, Dallas (1974); Woodlake CC, San Antonio (1972).
VERMONT: Haystack CC, Wilmington (1972).
CANADA: Quilchena G&CC, British Columbia (before leaving Canada).
JAPAN: New St. Andrews GC, Ontawara City (1974) c.Nicklaus.
SPAIN: La Moraleja GC, Madrid (1973) c. Nichlaus.
Courses Remodeled by Desmond Muirneau:
CALIFORNIA: Alameda Muni (North course, 1967); Brookside Muni, Pasadena (Course1 #1, 1966); Fort Irwin GC, Barstow; Presidio GC, San Francisco (1973); Santa Ana CC; South Hills CC, West Covina; Visalia CC.
MARYLAND: All view G.C, Columbia.
WASHINGTON: Overlake G&CC, Medina (1964).

Claude Muret (1936–   )
Born: Brussels, Belgium.
Claude Muret received a B.Sc. degree in mechanical engineering from the University of Manitoba and later formed the company of Taylor-Muret of Winnipeg. In 1970 he joined Lombardy North Ltd., Calgary, Alberta, one of the largest landscape architecture and environmental planning firms in western Canada.
Courses by Claude Muret:
ALBERTA: Silverspring G&CC, Calgary (c.R. Phelps, 1970).
MANITOBA: N.E. Park, Winnipeg (par 3, 1978).
SASKATCHEWAN: Murray Muni, Regina (1977).
Courses Remodeled by Claude Muret:
ALBERTA: Elks GC, Calgary (1976).

Albert Murray (1888–1974)
Born: England.

Albert Murray emigrated to Canada before World War I and became professional at Outremont GC, Beaconsfield GC and other clubs in the Montreal area. His brother was a revered professional at Royal Montreal from 1905 to 1930. Albert laid out a number of courses in eastern Canada and upstate New York during his career.

Courses by Albert Murray:
NEW YORK: Malone CC (9); Massena GC.
CANADA: CC of Montreal (original course); Edmunston G&CC, New Brunswick; Montreal Muni (2nd 18,n.l.e.).

Frank Murra Born: St. Louis, Missouri. Died: Chico, California.

In the late 1940s Frank Murray served as green committee chairman at the Congressional CC in Maryland. He became interested in golf course construction at this time while helping to build the Norbeck CC. He soon completed another course designed by golf architect Alfred Tull, the Westbriar CC, and then decided to build one for himself. Brooke Manor Farms CC, constructed to Tull's design, was completed in 1955. Murray was so fascinated with golf course design by this time that he formed a design and construction firm with Russell Roberts, who was in charge of maintenance at Brooke Manor Farms.

Murray soon sold his club in order to devote full time to his practice with Roberts. The two designed and built a number of courses along the eastern seaboard in the late 1950s. In 1959 the partnership was terminated and Murray moved to Florida, where he did several resort courses in the 1960s.

Courses by Frank Murray: (See Russell Roberts for courses planned jointly by Murray and Roberts:
FLORIDA: Crooked Creek G&CC, Miami (1968); Kendale CC, Miami (Executive course, 1967); North Dade CC, Miami (1961); Placid Lakes Inn & CC, Lake Placid (1966); Pompano Park GC, Pompano Beach (Executive course,1970); Sabal Palms CC, Tamarac (1968); Tierra Verde GC (1965); University Park CC, Boca Raton (1960).
WASHINGTON, D.C.: Andrews AFB GC (West course,1961).
PUERTO RICO: Berwind CC, Rio Grande (new site,1966).

Renee and Charles Muylaert

Based near Toronto, Renee Muylaert and his brother Charles laid out numerous courses in the 1960s and 70s, working almost entirely in the Canadian province of Ontario. Both Muylaerts had been well-known course superintendents and were graduates of the Winter School for Turfgrass Managers at the University of Massachusetts.

Renee began designing courses on a part-time basis in 1960 and entered the field full time in 1966. When Charles joined him in 1976, they set up the design and build firm of Green-Par Golf Construction Ltd. In addition to courses of their own design, the brothers made major or minor modifications to many established layouts. They also operated an extensive sod business.

Courses by Renee and Charles Muylaert:
ONTARIO: Aurora Highlands GC, Aurora (1980); Binbrook GC, Hamilton (1963); Brookside GC, Agincourt (27,1967); Buttonville GC (9,1980); Chinguacousy CC, Brampton (27,1960); Derrydale GC, Brampton (18 exec.,1968); Glen Cedars GC, Markham (1967); Glen Eagles GC, Bolton (1961); Gormley Green GC (18,1972;9,1974); Greenhills GC, Lambeth (27,-1977); Horseshoe Valley GC, Barrie (1972); Indian Wells GC, Burlington (1972); Nanticoke GC, Simcoe (1977); Nobleton Lakes GC (1974); Pheasant Run CC, Newmarket (1979); Royal Downs GC, Thornhill (18 exec.,1966); St. Catharines Muni (18 exec.,1973); Spring Lakes GC, Stouffville (18,1976;18,1980); Steed and Evans GC, Fonthill (9,1971); Strathroy CC (9,1975); Sunset Golf Centre, Fort Erie (18 par 3,1973); Thistledown GC, Owen Sound (9,1974); Trent GC, Bolsouer (9,1974); Unionville Fairways (18 par 3,1962); Vaughan Valley GC (18 exec., 1969); Victoria Park Golf Centre, Guelph (18,1967;18,1972).

Torakichi "Pete" Nakamura (1915–   )

Prominent Japanese golfer Torakichi Nakamura was individual winner of the 1957 Canada Cup Match held at Kasumigaseki GC. It was during this event that he acquired the nickname "Pete" through mutual agreement with his American competitors who found "Torakichi" difficult to pronounce.

Nakamura's victory at Kasumigaseki was thought to have initiated the golf boom in Japan. By 1968 he had planned thirteen courses on his own, including his first design, Kawagoe CC (1963).

Greg Nash (1949–   ) ASGCA
Born: Harper, Kansas.

Greg Nash attended the University of Arizona, earning the B.Sc. degree in landscape architecture in 1972. He worked for two years as a golf course designer and construction supervisor with the Del E. Webb Corporation and in December 1972 became associated with the firm of Jeff Hardin, Inc., eight months after its establishment.

Courses by Greg Nash: See Jeff Hardin.

William Henrichsen Neff (1905–   ) ASGCA
Born: Holladay, Utah.

Bill Neff attended the University of Utah and graduated from the American Landscape School in Des Moines, Iowa. He practiced landscape architecture in Utah and Arizona for over twenty years.

A member of the Salt Lake City CC, Neff was appointed to a committee in charge of remodeling the course in 1952. He hired Californian William P. Bell to design the changes and worked with the architect on the reconstruction. After Bell's death, Neff was hired by the architect's son, William F. Bell, to supervise construction of the Riverside CC in Provo, Utah.

Neff served as construction boss on three other Bell projects in Salt Lake City and then in 1956 decided to try his own hand at golf design. Over the next twenty years he created a number of Utah's top courses.

Courses by William Henrichsen Neff:
UTAH: Alpine CC, American Fork (1960); Bloomington CC, St. George (1972); Bonneville GC, Salt Lake City (9,1956,c.Bell); Bountiful GC (1975); Cascade Fairways GC, Orem (9,1968); Cottonwood Club, Salt Lake City (r.9,a.9 par 3,1963); Davis Park GC, Kaysville (9,1963;9,1968); Fore Lakes CC, Taylorsville (Executive 9,1974); Glenmore G&CC, South Jordan (1967); Hidden Valley CC, Draper (a.9); Majestic Oaks GC, Salt Lake City (4 par 3,1973); Mountain Dell GC, Salt Lake City (1960,c.Bell); Mountain View GC, West Jordan (1968); Oakridge CC, Farmington (1957); Park City GC (original 9,1962); Riverside CC, Provo (1960,c.Bell); Rose Park GC, Salt Lake City (9,1960,c.Bell); Stansbury Park CC, Tooele (1972); Sweetwater GC, Bear Lake (9,1974;9,1980); Wasatch State Park GC, Midway (1966;a.3rd 9,1972); Westland Hills GC, South Jordan (9).
WYOMING: Little America GC, Cheyenne (Executive 9,1974).
Courses Remodeled by William Henrichsen Neff.
UTAH: CC of Salt Lake City (9,1954); Willow Creek CC, Sandy.

William Howard Neff (1933–   ) ASGCA
Born: Limon, Colorado.

William Howard Neff received a B.F.A. degree in architecture from the University of Utah in 1958. He worked as a draftsman for the land planning firm of Harmon, O'Donnell and Henniger of Denver, the Salt Lake City Planning Commission and the Salt Lake County Planning Commission, and as a planning consultant and graphic designer for R. Clay Allred and Associates of Salt Lake City. In 1966 he embarked on a career as a golf course architect, entering the practice of William Henrichsen Neff (no relation) of Salt Lake City.

Courses by William Howard Neff:
See William Henrichsen Neff.

John Francis "Jack" Neville (1895–1978)
Born: St. Louis, Missouri.

Jack Neville moved to Oakland, California, as a young boy and learned golf from Macdonald Smith and Jim Barnes. He was an excellent competitive golfer, winning the California State Amateur Championship in 1912, 1913, 1919, 1922 and 1929, and defeating H. Chandler Egan for the Pacific Northwest Title in 1914. He was also on the 1923 Walker Cup team.

In 1915 Neville became a real estate salesman with the Pacific Improvement Company of Monterey, California. Shortly thereafter, company president S. F. B. Morse gave him the assignment of building a golf course on ocean frontage along Seventeen Mile Drive. The result was the Pebble Beach Golf Links, which opened in 1919. Neville did the preliminary routing of the course and then called in his friend Douglas Grant, another former California Amateur champion, to help with the bunkering. The Pebble Beach course remains today as originally laid out except for alteration of the bunkering, changes in several holes and some natural erosion of the shore line.

Neville designed several other courses in the late 1920s, but these were never built. He did assist George C. Thomas, Jr., with the design of the Bel Air CC in Los Angeles and Bob Baldock with the layout of the Shore course for the Monterey Peninsula GC in 1961. He also laid out a second nine on dunes for the Pacific Grove Municipal GC in 1959. But he remained a real estate salesman all his life and never practiced golf course architecture as a vocation. His influence at Pebble Beach, nevertheless, remained so strong that officials continued to consult him throughout his life before making even modest changes to the course.

William K. Newcomb, Jr. (1940–   )
Born: Logansport, Indiana.

William Newcomb attended the University of Michigan, receiving a Bachelor of Architecture degree in 1963 and a Master of Landscape Architecture in 1965. From 1965 to 1967 he was associated with golf architect "Pete" Dye. In 1968 he formed William Newcomb Associates, which included golf architect John Robinson (later based in Ontario) from 1972 to 1974. Newcomb also served as a lecturer at the University of Michigan's Department of Natural Resources and Michigan State University's Department of Agricultural Technology.

Courses by William K. Newcomb, Jr.:
INDIANA: Noblesville City GC.
KENTUCKY: Greenbrier CC, Lexington.
MICHIGAN: Boyne Highlands GC, Harbor Springs; Boyne Mountain GC, Boyne Falls; Brookwood CC, Rochester (9); Grand Traverse GC, Traverse City; Great Oaks GC, Rochester; Green Hills, Linwood; Hickory Falls GC, Jackson (a.9,1977); Indianfield GC, Michigan Technological University, Houghton; Prairie Creek GC, DeWitt (9,1978); Riverview City GC; Travis Pointe CC, Saline; West Branch GC (a.9); Willow GC, Huron-Clinton Metro-Park, Detroit; Willow Muni, New Boston (1978).
OHIO: Apple Valley GC, Mt. Vernon; Fon du Lac CC, Youngstown (a.9); Seven Hills GC, Hartville; Union CC, New Philadelphia; Wooster CC (a.9).
Courses Remodeled by William K. Newcomb, Jr.:
MICHIGAN: Barton Hills CC, Ann Arbor; Plum Hollow GC, Southfield; Spring Lake CC.
OHIO: Congress Lake CC, Hartville; Trumbull CC, Warren.

Jack William Nicklaus (1940–   )
Born: Columbus, Ohio.

Jack Nicklaus became one of the truly great golfers of all time and according to photojournalist David Cupp, "he owns the record books." He was also an author of several books on golf, including four with Ken Bowden, one with Herbert Warren Wind and two on his own.

Entering the field of golf course design, Nicklaus collaborated first with "Pete" Dye and later with Desmond Muirhead before starting his own practice. His firm, known as Golden Bear, included Jerry Pierman and Robert Cupp in design and Jay Morrish in construction. Nicklaus himself, however, designed the courses on which he was listed as architect of record and personally inspected them during and after construction.

Nicklaus's design philosophy was examined in an article by Dan Jenkins entitled "The Course That Jack Built" (Sports Illustrated, October 14, 1974, p. 34). A profile of Nicklaus and his design practice by George Peper appeared in Golf Magazine (March 1981).

Courses by Jack William Nicklaus:
ALABAMA: Shoal Creek GC, Birmingham (1976).
COLORADO: Castle Pines CC.
FLORIDA: Bear's Paw, Naples (1979); Cheeka Lodge, Islamorda; John's Island, Vero Beach (c.P.Dye,1970); Mayacoo Lakes GC, West Palm Beach (c.D.Muirhead,1972).
MICHIGAN: Fleming Hills CC; Wabeek GC, Bloomfield Hills (c.P.Dye,1971).
MISSISSIPPI: Annandale CC.
OHIO: (The) CC at Muirfield Village, Dublin (1979); Jack Nicklaus Golf Center, Kings Island, Cincinnati (2 courses,c.D.Muirhead,1973); Muirfield Village GC, Dublin (c.D.Muirhead,1973).
SOUTH CAROLINA: Harbour Town GC, Hilton Head (c.P.Dye); Kiawah Golf Links (a.18,1979).
TEXAS: Hills of Lakeway, Austin (a.18,1980); Lochinvar GC, Houston (1979).
UTAH: Park Meadow GC, Park City.
WISCONSIN: (The) Briar Patch, Playboy Club, Lake Geneva (c.P.Dye).
CANADA: Glen Abbey GC, Toronto (1974).
JAPAN: New St. Andrews GC, Ontawara City (c.D.Muirhead,1974).
SPAIN: LaMoraleja GC, Madrid (c.D.Muirhead,1973).
Courses Remodeled by Jack Williams Nicklaus:
FLORIDA: Lost Tree Club, North Palm Beach (1978).
NEW YORK: St. Andrews on the Hudson.
WEST VIRGINIA: Greenbrier Course, White Sulphur Springs (1977).
AUSTRALIA: Australian GC, Sydney (1978).

Tom Nicoll

Scottish-born professional Tom Nicoll designed and built a number of courses in California before and after spending several years in Asia. In 1917 he moved to Manila to build and operate a course there for the United States government. In Manila, he taught a group of Japanese golfers who persuaded him to become the professional at Komazawa Golf Course in Tokyo. As such, he was one of, if not the first teaching professional in Japan. Four courses of his design in California are San Jose CC (1912), where he once served as professional; Los Altos G&CC; Burlingame CC in San Francisco, and Menlo CC.

Tom Nicoll should not be confused with Tom Nicol who planned several courses in Alabama in the 1960's.

Richard Nugent (1931–) ASGCA: President, 1981
Born: Highland Park, Illinois.

Richard Nugent received the B.S.L.A. degree in 1958 from the University of Illinois and from 1958 until 1964 was employed with golf architect Robert Bruce Harris. In 1964 he and Kenneth Killian formed the Illinois firm of Killian and Nugent, Inc., Golf Course Architects, which actively experimented with such design techniques as computer planning of automatic irrigation and the use of waste water in turf maintenance. Killian and Nugent prepared the booklet "Planning and Building the Golf Course", published by the National Golf Foundation in 1980.

Courses by Richard Nugent: See Kenneth Killian.

John E. O'Connor, Jr.

Miami PGA professional John O'Connor designed and built a series of executive courses in the 1960s that he owned and operated himself. He also designed several regulation courses for others.

Courses by John E. O'Connor, Jr.:
FLORIDA: Colonial Palms CC, South Miami (Exec. course,1961); Key Colony Beach GC (9 par 3,1970); Land O'Golf GC, Miami (Par 3); Miami Lakes Inn & CC (a.18 par 3,1965); San Carlos Park G&CC (1973); West End GC, Gainesville (Exec. course,1969).

William "Willie" Ogg (1889–1960)
Born: Carnoustie, Scotland. Died: Tampa, Florida, at age 71.

Willie Ogg emigrated to the United States in 1914 and became professional at the Dedham (Massachusetts) Polo and Hunt Club, remaining there until 1921, when he took a similar position at the Worcester CC. He was an early graduate of the Massachusetts Agricultural College's Winter School for Greenkeepers and during his career designed several golf courses on the side.

Courses by William "Willie" Ogg:
FLORIDA: Ridge Manor CC (2nd 9,1957).
GEORGIA: Atlanta's City Course [now James L. Key Muni].
MASSACHUSETTS: Greenhill Muni, Worcester (1930); Wilbraham CC (c.A.Macdonald,1927).
Courses Remodeled by William "Willie" Ogg:
MASSACHUSETTS: Dedham Polo and Hunt Club.
NEW YORK: Albany CC.

George O'Neil (1883–1955)
Born: Philadelphia, Pennsylvania. Died: Miami, Florida, at age 72.

George O'Neil, one of the early American golf professionals, was employed with several Chicago-area clubs, including Midlothian, Beverly, Lake Shore and Edgewater. He was a fine teacher and helped develop the skills of young Charles "Chick" Evans while Evans was a caddy at Edgewater.

O'Neil practiced golf architecture as a sideline for several years and at one time or another worked with Chicago professional designers Jack Daray, Joseph Roseman and Jack Croke. He formed his own full-time practice with offices in Chicago and Cleveland in the 1920s, but this was lost in the Depression. Undaunted, O'Neil then became active in the promotion of professional football.

The last twenty years of O'Neil's life were spent battling serious illnesses. His medical expenses were covered by friend and former pupil Albert D. Lasker, the Chicago advertising magnate for whom O'Neill had built the Melody Farm Course.

Courses by George O'Neil:
FLORIDA: El Conquistador GC, Valparaiso (1917,n.l.e.).
ILLINOIS: Barrington Hills CC (1920); Cedar Crest GC, Antioch; Illinois GC, Glencoe (n.l.e.); Melody Farms (n.l.e.).
INDIANA: South Bend CC.
WEST VIRGINIA: The Greenbrier, White Sulphur Springs (Greenbrier course,1925).
WISCONSIN: Maxwelton Braes Resort & GC, Green Bay (c.Roseman).
Courses Remodeled by George O'Neil:
CALIFORNIA: Pasadena GC, (1920,n.l.e.).
ILLINOIS: Glenview GC, Golf.
VIRGINIA: CC of Virginia, Richmond (r.James River course,1927).

Edward Lawrence Packard (1912–) ASGCA: President, 1970
Born: Northampton, Massachusetts.

Lawrence Packard received a degree in landscape architecture from Massachusetts State College in 1935 and worked as a landscape architect with the National Park Service in Maine, the U. S. Corps of Engineers in Massachusetts (Westover Field) and the Chicago (Illinois) Park District.

In 1946 Packard joined the staff of golf architect Robert Bruce Harris, where he remained until 1954, when he formed the design firm of Packard and Wadsworth with Brenton Wadsworth. This association later divided into two separate organizations, the design firm of Packard Inc. and the construction firm of Wadsworth Company.

Packard exerted a powerful influence on design trends, professional policy and innovations in the field of course architecture. He hastened the trend toward gentler sculpturing and pioneered free forms in shaping of course features. Some believe he played the most important role of any post-World War II architect in establishing the profession's outlook on American society and environmental concerns. He was among the earliest advocates of the use of waste water for golf course irrigation, and his Innisbrook Resort & CC near Tarpon Springs, Florida, is considered one of the finest examples of golf condominium integration in existence.

Courses by Edward Lawrence Packard:
CALIFORNIA: Leisure Village GC, Camirillo.
FLORIDA: Countryside CC, Clearwater; Innisbrook Resort & CC (63); Winewood GC, Tallahassee.
ILLINOIS: Apple Valley CC, Bartlett; Belk Park GC, Wood River; Brookhill GC, Rantoul; Calumet CC, Homewood (2nd 9); Canton Park District GC (9); Carlinville GC (9); Champaign CC; Chanute ABB GC, Rantoul (2nd 9); Coal Creek CC, Atkinson (9); CC Estates GC, De Kalb; Crestwicke CC, Bloomington; Da-De-Co, Ottawa; Danville CC (9); Deer Creek GC, Park Forest; Deerfield GC, Riverwoods; Eagle Ridge GC, Galena (1977); Earl F. Elliot Park GC, Rockford; Elgin GC; Faries Park GC, Decatur; Granite City GC (9); Greenville CC (9); Hickory Point GC, Decatur; Indian Spring GC, Saybrook (9); Jacksonville CC (2nd 9); Jerseyville GC (9); Kellogg GC, Peoria (27); Lake Barrington Shores GC; Ledges CC, Roscoe; Lick Creek GC, Pekin; Lincolnshire Fields GC, Champaign; Mattoon CC (2nd 9); Mission Hills GC, Northbrook; Northbrook Hills CC; Oak Brook Muni; Palatine Hills GC; Pekin CC; Prestwick CC, Frankfort; Ravinia Green CC, Riverwoods; Rend Lake GC, Benton; Spring Lake CC, Quincy (2nd 9); Springbrook GC, Naperville; Sunset Hills CC, Edwardsville (2nd 9); Turnberry CC, Crystal Lake; Urban, Chicago Heights; Richton Park; Vermillion Hills CC, Danville; Wagon Wheel, Rockton; Wedgewood GC, Joliet; Zion Park District GC (9); Indian Boundary Exec. GC, Boling Brook (1980).
INDIANA: Burning Bush CC, Munster; Briar Ridge CC, 1981.
IOWA: A. H. Blank GC, Des Moines (9); Beaver Hills CC, Cedar Falls; Burlington GC; Echo Valley CC, Des Moines; Sunnyside CC, Waterloo.
KANSAS: Sunflower Hills GC, Kansas City.
KENTUCKY: Audubon Park GC, Henderson (9); Barkley Lake State Park GC, Cadaz; Iroquois GC, Louisville (2nd 9); Midland Trail GC, Louisville; Pennyrile State Park GC, Dawson Springs; Standard Club, Louisville (2nd 9).
MICHIGAN: Bay City GC; Hamshire GC, Dowagiac; Leslie Park GC, Ann Arbor; Pine Grove CC, Iron Mountain (2nd 9); Spring Meadows CC, Flint.
MINNESOTA: Columbia Park GC, Minneapolis; Theodore Wirth GC, Minneapolis (2nd 9).
MISSOURI: Jefferson City CC; Westmoreland G&CC, Sedalia (9); Whiteman AFB GC, Sedalia (9); Crescent CC, Crescent (9,1979).
NEBRASKA: Benson Park GC, Omaha; Platteview CC, Omaha.
NEW JERSEY: Leisure Village, Woodlake; Woodlake CC, Lakewood.
NEW YORK: Riverside GC, Syracuse; Wayne Recreation Association GC, Lyons.
NORTH DAKOTA: Maple River GC, West Fargo (9).
OHIO: Rawiga CC, Rittman (9); Rosemont CC, Akron (2nd 9); Silver Lake CC, Akron; Wright-Patterson AFB GC, Dayton (9).
SOUTH DAKOTA: Elmwood Park GC, Sioux Falls; Westward Ho! CC, Sioux.
TENNESSEE: McMinnville CC.
WISCONSIN: Antigo-Bass Lake CC (2nd 9); Baraboo CC (9); Big Foot CC; Black River Falls GC (9); Brown County GC, Green Bay; Bull's Eye CC, Wisconsin Rapids (9); Chaska GC, Appleton; Chenequa CC, Hartland (9); Iola Community GC (9); Mascoutin GC, Berlin; Naga-Waukee Park War Memorial GC, Waukesha; Oakwood Park GC, Milwaukee; Peninsula State Park GC, Fish Creek; Rib Mountain Lodge, Wausau; River Island GC, Oconto Falls (9); Stevens Point CC; Timber Ridge CC, Minocqua; Tumblebrook GC, Pewaukee; Watertown CC (2nd 9); Wausau CC; Westview CC, Marshfield (9);
KOREA: Bomun Lake, Kyongju.
VENEZUELA: El Morro, Puerto La Cruz.

Roger Bruce Packard (1947–   ) ASGCA
Born: Chicago, Illinois.
   Roger Packard graduated in 1970 from Colorado State University at Fort Collins. As an undergraduate, he worked summers in course construction for the Wadsworth Company of Plainfield, Illinois, and upon graduation joined his father's golf design firm, Packard Inc. After 1970 he took an active role in the planning of all Packard courses in the United States and abroad.
Courses by Roger Bruce Packard: See Edward Lawrence Packard.

Harold D. Paddock, Sr. (1888–1969) Born: San Diego, California. Died: Aurora, Ohio.
   Professional golfer Harold Paddock owned and operated Moreland Hills CC and Aurora CC in Cleveland, Ohio. He began designing courses in the 1920s and reactivated his practice in the 1950s, doing a number of courses in the Cleveland area. Paddock's son, Harold Jr., a fine amateur golfer, later served as professional at Moreland Hills.
Courses by Harold D. Paddock, Sr.:
   FLORIDA: Mount Dora GC (r.9,a.9,1959).
   MISSOURI: Westwood CC, St. Louis (1928).
   OHIO: Astorhurst CC, Bedford; Avon Oaks CC, Avon; Chuckle Creek GC, Bowling Green (1959); Griffiths Park GC, Akron; Hinckley Hills GC (1964); Mercer County Elks CC, Le Cina; Pine Hills GC, Cleveland (27,1958); Sugarbush CC, Garrettsville (1965); Valley View GC, Lancaster (1956); Velleaire GC, North Royalton; Willard GC (1959).

Arnold D. Palmer (1919–   )
Born: Latrobe, Pennsylvania.
   Arnold Palmer, son of the pro-superintendent at Latrobe CC, won most of the major championships and became the first golfer to win a million dollars on the pro tour. He was also credited with being a major force in the golf boom of the 1960s.
   Palmer formed a course design association with golf architect Francis Duane in 1969. In 1974 he became associated with architect Edwin Seay, and the two founded the Palmer Course Design Company in 1979. In addition, Palmer collaborated with X. G. Hassenplug on one course at Indian Lake Lodge in Pennsylvania and remodeled the Bay Hill Club in Florida on his own.
Courses by Arnold D. Palmer: See Francis J. Duane and Edwin B. Seay.

Gary A. Panks (1941–   )
Born: Flint, Michigan.
   Gary Panks was the son of a golf professional at the Sault Ste. Marie CC. In 1964 he received a B.S. degree in landscape architecture from Michigan State University, where he played on the golf team and served as its captain in 1963. By 1980 he had won sixteen amateur tournaments.
   Panks worked for a short time as assistant superintendent at Michigan State University GC and then held successive positions as a landscape architect or planning consultant with New York State Roadside Development, the Maricopa County (Arizona) Park Department, the Bureau of Indian Affairs, Department of the Interior and the City of Phoenix Parks Department. In 1971 he entered private practice as a golf course and landscape architect under the firm name of Gary Panks Associates.
Courses by Gary A. Panks:
   ARIZONA: Ahwatukee GC, Phoenix (Executive course); Casa Grande Muni (9); Fort Huachuca GC, Sierra Vista (a.9,c.Coggins); Winslow Muni (c.Snyder).
   CALIFORNIA: Fahrens Park GC, Merced (9).
Courses Remodeled by Gary A. Panks:
   ARIZONA: Arizona CC, Scottsdale; Encanto Park Muni, Phoenix (27); Orange Tree GC, Scottsdale.

The Park Family
   The Parks of Scotland were one of golf's early "First Families." Several of the five sons and numerous grandchildren of farmer James Park played influential roles in the history of course design. A Park family tree of those members actively involved in the world of golf is as follows:

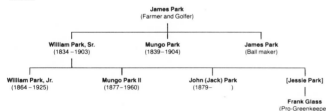

William "Willie" Park, Sr. and **Mungo Park:** Natives of Musselburgh, Scotland, Willie Park, Sr., won the first British Open at Prestwick in 1860 as well as three subsequent Opens; and Mungo Park was Open Champion in 1874. Willie Sr. was involved in laying out golf courses on his own, with his brother Mungo, and with his son, Willie Jr. Although it is difficult to distinguish between the work of Park Sr. and the earliest courses of his son, it is believed that Willie Sr. may have revised Bruntisfield Links in Scotland (on his own or in collaboration with Mungo) and may have planned the original nine at Killarney. Mungo laid out the original Alnmouth course in England, where he served as professional for several years.
William "Willie' Park, Jr. and **Mungo Park II:** See separate biographies.
John "Jack" Park: Jack Park supervised construction at the Maidstone (New York) CC around 1898 and then worked with brothers Willie (in Britain) and Mungo (in Argentina)

before returning to Maidstone as its professional in 1915. He continued to assist brother Willie following the latter's return to North America in 1916.
   Another member of the Park golf dynasty, Frank Glass, the son of Willie Jr.'s sister Jessie, served as pro-greenkeeper at the Mt. Bruno Club near Montreal from 1920 to 1951. A complete account of the Park family will be found in J. W. L. Adams's *Willie Park, Jr. and His Family* (unpublished by 1980).

Mungo Park II (1877–1960)
Born: Scotland.
   Mungo Park II served as professional at Dyker Meadow GC in New York and Galveston CC in Texas around 1898. Between 1901 and 1904 he was at Huntercombe GC in England, working as director of the Chiltern Estates, where his brother Willie was managing director.
   From 1904 to 1913 Mungo was employed as a professional golfer in Argentina, where he planned the San Andres GC at San Martin (home of the Buenos Aires CC) and other courses. Following service with the British Army during World War I, he returned to Argentina, laying out the Adolfo Siro GC for the Swifts of meat packing fame. Altogether, he claimed some fifty-nine courses of his own design in that country.
   Mungo went to the United States from Argentina in 1924 to escort his brother Willie Jr., then fatally ill, home to Scotland. In 1925 he returned to the United States to complete Willie's unfinished courses, probably to lay out several of his own, including one at Peekskill, New York, and to occupy a number of professional berths in the East and in Arizona. He returned to Scotland permanently in the 1930s and planned several changes at Musselburgh (Preston Grange). Mungo's youngest son, Dr. Jack Park, was a famous Scottish International rugby player.

William "Willie" Park, Jr. (1864–1925)
Born: Musselburgh, Scotland. Died: Edinburgh, Scotland, at age 61.
   The name of Willie Park, Jr., is one of the most respected in the history of golf. He was a multi-faceted personality, a talented and prolific golf architect, one of the greatest golfers of his day, an entrepreneur and businessman, a club maker, inventor and author. A big man physically, his influence has been profound.
   As a boy, Willie often played golf at Musselburgh with "Young Willie" Dunn, who was also destined to make his mark on the history of course architecture. From 1880 to 1894 Park Jr. served as assistant greenkeeper and professional under his uncle Mungo at Ryton in England. He then returned to Musselburgh, joining his father in the club and ballmaking firm of W. Park and Son. Continuing to refine his golf game, he won the British Open in 1887 and 1889, and was runner-up in 1898.
   Willie was a perfectionist. He believed that matches were settled by putting and would spend twelve hours without a break on a practice green. He brought the same intensity to his design work. He laid out links and courses with his father and uncle, and later on his own with construction assistance from brothers Mungo II and Jack. Two of Park's courses, Sunningdale GC and Huntercombe GC (opened in England in 1901) became landmarks in the history of course architecture. Huntercombe, of which Willie was a major stockholder and promoter, was among the first golf courses planned for integration with housing. The housing scheme was never executed, however, and the project turned out to be a financial problem for Willie for many years.
   Willie first traveled to the United States around 1895 and worked there until 1898, promoting golf in general but also laying out some courses. When he returned to North America in 1916 (where he remained, except for visits home and abroad, until 1924), he was inundated with requests to design and redesign courses. He undertook a prodigious number, claiming seventy courses in North America in the years following World War I. Although he maintained several offices in the United States and Canada, and was assisted by a loyal gang of construction bosses in addition to his two brothers, Willie himself visited each of his courses periodically during construction. He personally supervised the construction of Sunningdale and Huntercombe in England; Mt. Bruno and Summerlea near Montreal; the CCs of Woodway, Tumblebrook, New Haven and Shuttlemeadow in Connecticut; New Bedford CC in Massachusetts; Ashland GC in Ohio; Castine GC in Maine; State College GC in Pennsylvania; and Maidstone GC on Long Island, New York.
   In the course of his indefatigable career, Willie also found time to write two books, *The Game of Golf* (1896) and *The Art of Putting* (1920), part of which is autobiographical. He was finally stricken with fatal illness in 1924 and made his last journey home to Scotland, where he died in 1925. But his brilliant legacy survives: Sir Guy Campbell called him the "doyen" of course architects and credited him with setting the standards adhered to by the countless designers who followed. Willie Park, Jr., was surely one of the greatest golf architects of all time.
Courses by William "Willie" Park, Jr.:*
   ARKANSAS: Hot Springs G&CC.
   CONNECTICUT: Farmington CC; Madison CC; New Canaan CC; New Haven CC; Shuttlemeadow CC, New Britain (1916); Tumblebrook CC, Bloomington; Woodway CC, Darien.
   FLORIDA: Alton Beach CC, Miami.
   ILLINOIS: Olympia Fields CC (4th course,1922).
   INDIANA: Highland G&CC, Indianapolis.
   MAINE: Castine GC.
   MARYLAND: Baltimore CC; Rolland Road GC, Baltimore.
   MASSACHUSETTS: Fall River CC (Original 9); Hoosic-Whisick Club, Canton; New Bedford CC.
   MICHIGAN: Automobile CC, Detroit; Battle Creek CC; Flint CC; Grand Rapids GC; Meadowbrook CC, Detroit; Pine Lake GC, Pontiac (New site,1915); Red Run GC, Royal Oak, Detroit.
   MINNESOTA: Minneapolis GC, St. Louis Park (1917).
   NEW JERSEY: Atlantic City CC, Northfield; Glen Ridge GC; Ocean City CC.
   NEW YORK: Maidstone Club (c.J.Park; 2nd 9,1899; a.9,1923); Moon Brook CC, Jamestown; St. Albans CC, Long Island.
   NORTH CAROLINA: Asheville CC (now Grove Park Inn CC).
   OHIO: Ashland CC; Congress Lake CC, Hartville; Defiance CC; Sylvania CC, Toledo

(1917); Toledo CC.

PENNSYLVANIA: Berkshire CC, Reading; Chartiers CC, Pittsburgh; Green Valley CC, Roxborough; Indiana CC; Philmont CC, Philadelphia; Pittsburgh Field Club (r.1923); State College GC (Original 18); Youghiogheny CC, McKeesport.

RHODE ISLAND: Metacomet CC, East Providence; Pawtucket GC.

VERMONT: St. Johnsbury CC (9).

AUSTRIA: Vienna GC.

BELGIUM: Lombardzide; Royal Antwerp GC.

CANADA: Abitibi Power & Paper Co., Iroquois Falls, Ont.; Beaconsfield GC, Montreal, P.Q.; Bowness GC, Calgary, Alta.; Brightwood G&CC, Dartmouth, N.S.; Calgary G&CC, Alta. (1911; New course,1925); Calgary St. Andrews GC, Alta.; Islesmere GC, P.Q.; Kentville GC, N.S.; Laval Sur Le Lac Club, Montreal, P.Q.; Mt. Bruno GC, Montreal, P.Q.; Ottawa Hunt and Motor Club, Ont.; Royal Montreal GC, Dixie, P.Q. (r. South course, a.North course,1922;n.l.e.); Royal Quebec (Royal course, back 9 Present course,1925); Senneville CC, P.Q.; (Old) Summerlea G&CC, Lachine, P.Q. (27); Toronto Hunt Club, Ont.; Weston GC, Ont.; Whitlock GC, Hudson Heights, P.Q.; Winnipeg GC, Man.; Winnipeg Hunt Club, Man.

FRANCE: Costebelle Golf Links, Hyeres; Dieppe; Dinard; Evian-les-Baines; LaBoulie; Monte Carlo; Rouen.

BRITAIN & IRELAND: Acton; Aldeburgh; Alnmouth; Baberton; Barnton; Barry, Glamorganshire; Bathgate; Berkhamsted; Berwick-on-Tweed; Bexhill; Blundellsands; Bo'ness; Bridge-of-Weir; Brighton and Hove; Broadstone; Bruntisfield Links; Burhill; Burntisland; Cambridge University; Cannon's Park; Carnoustie; Chiselhurst; Coombe Hill; Crieff; Cuckfield; Dalkeith & Newbattle; Duddington; Edgware; Formby; Forres; Frinton-on-Sea; Gailes, Ayrshire; Glasgow Club; Glencorse; Goswick; Grantown-on-Spey; Gravesend; Gullane; Hartlepool; Headingley; Hendon; Hollinwell; Huntercombe; Innellan; Innerleithen; Jedburgh; Killarney; Kilspindie; Knebworth; Larne; Lauder, Londonderry; Melrose; Monifieth; Montrose (r); Murrayfield; Muswell Hill; Neasdon; Newbigging-by-Sea; New Luffness; Northampton; Nottingham; Notts; Parkstone; Port Stewart; Richmond, Sudbrook; Seaford; Selkirk; Sheerness; Shiskine; Shooters Hill; Silloth; South Herts; Southampton; Southerndown, Glamorganshire; St. Boswells; Stonham; Sundridge Park; Sunningdale; Temple, Maidenhead; Tooting Bec; Torwoodlee; Totteridge; Tramore; Turnhouse; Tynemouth; Waterford; Wembley; West Middlesex; Wimbledon; Worplesdon; Westhill, Surrey; Biggar, Scotland.

° Names in France and Great Britain (which also includes Irish courses) are sometimes those of towns and cities where courses are located and not the names of courses.

Stuart Paton
See John Low

George A. "Pat" Pattison, Jr.

"Pat" Pattison worked as pro/superintendent/manager at Buckhannon (West Virginia) CC in the early 1950s. Toward the end of the decade, he supervised construction of several Florida courses and went on to form his own design and construction firm in Fort Lauderdale.

Courses by George A. "Pat" Pattison, Jr.:

FLORIDA: Cooper Colony CC, Hollywood (Executive course,1959); Crystal Lake CC, Pompano Beach (1969); Hidden Valley GC, Boca Raton (Par 3 course,1957); Whispering Lakes GC, Pompano Beach (18 par 3,1963).

(Colonel) W. E. Pedley
See Charles Maud

Stanley F. Pelchar

Stanley Pelchar was active as a course designer in the 1920s, forming the Chicago firm of United States Golf Architects, Inc. with landscape architect Otto Clauss and engineer James Prendergast. Among their courses were Burnham Woods, Garden of Eden, Lake Anna and Woman's CC, all in Illinois, and Beloit CC and Oneida GC in Wisconsin. In the 1950s Pelchar served as club manager at the Biltmore CC, Barrington, Illinois.

John Jacob Frank Pennink (1913–)   BAGCA
Born: The Netherlands.

Frank Pennink attended Tonbridge School and Magdalen College of Oxford University. He was winner of the English Amateur (1937 and '38), the Royal St. Georges Challenge Cup (1938), the Boy's International (1930) and many other amateur tournaments. He was also a member of the Walker Cup team in 1938 and was on English international teams for several years as a player and later as a nonplaying captain. He authored three books, *Home of Sports—Golf, Golfer's Companion* and *Frank Pennink's Choice of Golf Course.*

In 1954 Pennink joined the established course design practice of Charles Kenneth Cotton. He eventually headed the firm that came to be known as Cotton (C.K.), Pennink, Lawrie and Partners, Ltd. By 1978 the firm included directors D. M. A. Steel, M. F. Bonallack and R. Clempson, and associates R. F. Besnard, Dr. J. de Sousa Mello, W. J. J. Ferguson (Northern Ireland) and C. F. Crosbie (Eire).

Courses by John Jacob Frank Pennink°   Among the best known of more than 300 courses worked on by Cotton (C.K.), Pennink, Lawrie & Partners, Ltd. are:

BRITISH ISLES: Abbey Hill, Milton Keynes (c.C.D.Lawrie); Alderney; Army GC, Aldershot (r); Ashbourne GC, Derby; Bandon GC, Ireland; Barnham Broom; Basildon; Beauport Park, Hastings; Bedale; Bedlington; Belhus Park, Essex; Billingham; Blackhills-Hoveringham; Blackwell Grange, Darlington; Bradley Park (Huddersfield); Brandon Wood, Coventry; Brickendon on Grange GC, Heath (c.C.K.Cotton); Bury St. Edmonds; Bushey Golf & Squash Club, Herts (9); Carlisle; Chippenham; Cradoc GC, Wales; Craigavon; Crookhill Park, Doncaster; Darlington; Dartford; Dunmurry; Eastleigh; Ellesmere; Eton; Fakenham; Farnham Park, Stoke Poges; Frilford Heath; Harrow School; Hastings GC, Sussex; Haverhill GC; Hawkhurst; H.M.S. Dryad; Hoveringham GC, Worcester; Immingham; Lamberhurst GC, Kent; Lee Park; Little Island (Cork); Livingston; Louth; Lowestoft; Lurgan; Mendip; Newtonstewart, Northern Ireland (r); North Downs; Oxton; Radcliffe on Trent, Nottingham (r); Rochdale; Romsey;

Ross-on-Wye; Royal Aberdeen (Ladies course); Royal Lytham & St. Annes (9); Royal St. Georges (r.1974); Rye (a.9); St. Pierre; Saunton (West course); Shifnal; Shrewesbury; Skips, Essex; Stocksfield; Stockwood Park, Luton; Stony Holme, Carlisle; Stornoway; Stowe School; Tewkesbury; Thurrock; Twickenham; Walton Hall, Cheshire; Warrington; Westhill, Aberdeen; Wigan; Winter Hill, Cookham; Woburn (Duke's course).

BANGLADESH: Dacca.
BELGIUM: Keerbergen.
CZECHOSLOVAKIA: Prague.
DENMARK: Kokkedal; St. Knud.
FRANCE: Amiens; La Bretesche; Le Mans; Nantes.
GERMANY: Dueren; Wik-Auf-Fohr.
HOLLAND: de Gelpenberg; Geysteren; Noordwijk; Rosendael.
INDONESIA: Sumatra.
ITALY: Is Molas (Sardinia); Olgiata.
LEBANON: Beirut.
LIBYA: Benghazi; Tripoli.
MALAYSIA: Sibu (Sarawak).
MOROCCO: Tangier.
PAKISTAN: Islamabad.
POLAND: Jablonna.
PORTUGAL: Aroeira; Palmares; CdeG Vilamoura; CdeG Don Pedro Vilamoura.
SINGAPORE: Jurong Town; Sentosa; Singapore Island (r.Bukit and Island courses a.new and Sime courses).
SWEDEN: Halmstad; Kungsbacka; Stannum.
SWITZERLAND: Breitenloo.
ZAMBIA: Lusaka.

° Names are sometimes those of towns and cities where courses by J. J. F. Pennink are located and not names of the courses.

Richard M. Phelps (1937–)   ASGCA: President, 1980
Born: Colorado Springs, Colorado.

Richard Phelps received B.S. and M.L.A. degrees from Iowa State University prior to training under golf architect Robert Bruce Harris. In the mid-1960s he entered private practice as a course designer and after a short association with landscape architect Donald Brauer in the firm of Phelps-Brauer, established the Colorado-based firm of Phelps-Benz and Associates with Bradford Benz. In 1980 this became Phelps, Benz and Poellot when J.M. Poellot joined the firm.

Courses by Richard M. Phelps:

COLORADO: Colorado Springs CC(a.9,1964); Copper Mountain Executive (9,1978); Englewood Muni (1976); Foothills GC, Lakewood (27,1971); Ft. Carson GC (1971); Grand Lake GC (a.9,1976); Greenway GC, Broomfield (9,1972); Heathergardens CC, Aurora (9,1973); Heatheridge CC, Aurora (1972); Indian Tree GC, Arvada (27,1971); Perry Park CC, Larkspur (1974); Peterson Field GC, Colorado Springs (9,1974); The Ranch GC, Westminster (1974); South Suburban GC, Littleton (27,1974); Springhill GC, Aurora (a.9,1976).

IOWA: Charles City CC (1964); Dysart GC & CC (9,1964); Glenhaven CC, Oelwein (9,1965); Jester Park GC, Des Moines (27,1968); Waverly GC (a.9,1966); Willow Creek GC, Des Moines (a.9,1964).

MINNESOTA: Braemar GC, Edina (27,1965); Minnreg GC, Orchard Gardens (27,1965).
MISSOURI: Windbrook CC, Parkville (r.7,a.9,1974); Liberty Hills CC (r.9.a9).
MONTANA: Riverside CC, Bozeman (a.9,1974).
NEBRASKA: Elks CC, Columbus (18 & 9,1965).
NEVADA: Wildcreek GC, Sparks (1979).
NEW MEXICO: Elephant Butte GC, Truth or Consequences (9,1974); Ladera Muni, Albuquerque (1979).
NORTH DAKOTA: Prairiewood GC, Fargo (9,1976).
SOUTH DAKOTA: Huron GC (r.7,a.9,1974); Southern Hills GC, Hot Springs (9,1977).
WYOMING: Riverton CC, Riverton (a.9,1980).
CANADA: Maple Ridge GC, Calgary, Alberta (9,1968); Silver Spring CC, Calgary, Alberta (1970).

Courses Remodeled by Richard M. Phelps:
MINNESOTA: Southview CC, West St. Paul (7,1966).

Gary Player (1935–)

Born and educated in South Africa, Gary Player became a professional golfer in 1953 and won scores of major tournaments, including the British Open, the U. S. Open, the PGA and the Masters. In the 1970s he joined forces with golf architect Ronald Kirby to form Kirby, Player and Associates, Inc., Golf Course Architects. Player had earlier planned several courses in South Africa and Rhodesia in collaboration with professional golfer Sidney F. Brews and Dr. Van Vincent. Among these were Elephant Hills at Victoria Falls, Rhodesia; Four Ways GC in Johannesburg, South Africa; and the remodeling of Crown Mines GC, also in Johannesburg.

Courses by Gary Player: For courses after 1972, see Ronald Kirby.

Ralph M. Plummer (1900–)   ASGCA: President, 1962
Born: Smithfield, Texas.

Ralph Plummer started out as professional at a small South Texas club in the early 1920s. In the late twenties he was hired as professional for the new Galveston Municipal course being laid out by Houston pro and part-time designer John Bredemus. Impressed with Plummer's interest in course design, Bredemus invited his assistance in laying out several area courses. In the early 1930s Plummer resigned his professional's position to work with Bredemus full time on courses in Texas where the Depression had relatively little effect on golf development.

When Bredemus moved to Mexico in the early 1930s, Plummer secured a position as professional at the Greenville (Texas) GC. During and after World War II, he designed and built several short courses at veteran's hospitals and then formed his own firm for constructing and restoring courses. By the 1950s he was once again designing.

In his most active years Plummer constructed all the courses he designed, but by the 1970s he was permitting other firms to build them. He was still active as late as 1979, when he designed and supervised construction of a course near Fort Worth, Texas. Plummer was known for the attractiveness of his layouts and for his remarkable ability to estimate cuts and fills and shape greens and bunkers by eye.

Courses by Ralph M. Plummer:
ARIZONA: Francisco Grande CC, Casa Grande (1964).
LOUISIANA: Lake Charles G&CC (1956).
NEW MEXICO: Artesia CC (9); Ruidoso CC (9).
OKLAHOMA: Altus CC.
TEXAS: Alice CC (1951); Atascocita CC, Humble (1956); Benbrook Muni, Ft. Worth (1962); Brownfield Muni (1954); Buckingham CC, Dallas (1960); Champions GC, Houston (Cypress Creek course,1959); Columbian Club, Carrollton (Original 9,1955); Dallas Athletic Club CC (18,1954;18,1962); Denton CC; Eastern Hills CC, Garland (1856); Elkins Lake GC, Huntsville (1971); Gainesville Muni (1955); Grande Prairie Muni (27,1965 & 67); Great Southwest GC, Arlington (1965); Greenville CC (a.2nd 9,1955); Hillcrest CC, Lubbock (1956); Hilltop Lakes GC, Normangee (Original 9,1963); Humble CC (1955); Indian Creek CC, Abilene (1966); Lake Arlington GC, Arlington (1963); Lake Country Estates GC, Fort Worth (9,1973); Lakeside CC, Houston (1952); Lakewood CC, Dallas (1947); Magnolia Ridge CC, Liberty (9,1951); McAllen Muni (1960); McKinney V.A. Hospital GC (1945); Meadowbrook Muni, Ft. Worth (1960); Midland CC (1954); Mission CC (1959); Palm View Muni, McAllen (1971); Pharoah's CC, Corpus Christi (1964); Port Arthur CC (1955); Preston Trail GC, Dallas (1965); Prestonwood CC, Dallas (1965); Ranchland Hills GC, Midland (a.2nd 9,1950); Ridgelea CC, Ft. Worth (Championship course,1966); Riverside CC, Lake Jackson (1951); Riverside Muni, Victoria (Original 9,1951); Rolling Hills CC, Arlington (1963); Sequin CC (a.2nd 9,1979); Shady Oaks CC, Ft. Worth (1959); Sharpstown CC, Houston (1957); (The) Shores CC, Lake Ray Hubbard (1979); Squaw Creek CC, Ft. Worth (1977); Temple CC (9); Tenison Muni, Dallas (East course,1960); Tennwood CC, Hockley (1961); Terrell CC (1979); Texas A&M University GC, College Station (1950); Waco Muni (1956); Willow Brook CC, Tyler (r.9,a.9,1953); Woodlawn Park Muni [now Pecan Valley Muni], Ft. Worth (27,1963).
JAMAICA: Tryall Golf & Beach Club, Montego Bay (1960).
Courses Remodeled by Ralph M. Plummer:
LOUISIANA: City Park GC, New Orleans (Course #1); Lafayette CC.
MINNESOTA: Minikahda Club, Minneapolis (1962).
TEXAS: Brook Hollow GC, Dallas (1956); Canyon Creek CC, San Antonio (1959); Dallas CC (1947); Glen Lakes CC, Dallas (1942); Golf Crest CC, Houston (1951); Hermann Park GC, Houston (9,1952); Houston GC (1957); Northwood Club, Dallas; Pine Forest CC, Houston (9,1956); Ridgelea CC, Ft. Worth (r.6,North course,1959); Ridgewood CC, Waco (1962); River Crest CC, Ft. Worth (1946); River Oaks CC, Houston (1957); Rockwood Muni, Ft. Worth (27,1964); Wichita Falls GC, Wichita (1964); Z Boaz GC, Ft. Worth (1962).
UTAH: (The) CC of Salt Lake City (1963).

J. Michael Poellot (1943–   ) ASGCA
Born: Pittsburgh, Pennsylvania.

J. Michael Poellot received a B.S. degree in landscape architecture from Iowa State University. His education also included undergraduate work in biological sciences at West Virginia Wesleyan College and graduate courses in turf management at Clemson University.

A third generation golfer, Poellot took up the game at the age of twelve. While living in Thailand in the early 1970s, he met Robert Trent Jones, Jr., who was working on the Navateene GC in Bangkok at the time. In 1972 Poellot was hired to head a Jones office in Asia and later continued to direct work in Southeast Asia from the Jones, Jr. California office.

By 1980, as Senior Architect/Planner of the Robert Trent Jones II Group, Poellot had worked on the design and construction supervision of twenty Jones courses in Arizona, California, New Mexico, Texas, Wisconsin, Hong Kong, Japan, Macao, Malaysia and the Philippines. In addition, he planned alterations on many established courses and conducted numerous studies relating to golf course and recreational planning. In 1980 he joined golf architects Richard Phelps and Brad Benz in the firm of Phelps, Benz, and Poellot.

Glen Proctor
See Roy L. Goss

Robert D. Pryde (1871-1951)
Born: Tayport, Scotland. Died: Connecticut, at age 79.

Robert Pryde grew up near St. Andrews, where he learned to play golf. He attended Harris Academy in Dundee and the Technical College of Glasgow. In 1892 he emigrated to the United States, becoming a cabinetmaker in New Haven, Connecticut, and designing several buildings as well.

In 1895 Pryde was persuaded to build his first golf course, and from then on his life was devoted to golf. He laid out a number of courses in Connecticut and possibly in other states, although they were not recorded. Pryde was also an early golf coach at Yale University and from 1922 to 1946 served as secretary-treasurer of the Connecticut State Golf Association.

Courses by Robert D. Pryde:
CONNECTICUT: Meriden CC; New Haven CC (Original course; for a short time this was the Yale University GC); New Haven Muni; Pine Orchards CC, Brantford; Race Brook CC; Wethersfield CC (original course).

Nicholas T. Psiahas (1930–   )
Born: Montclair, New Jersey.

Nicholas Psiahas began his career as an eleven-year-old caddie at the Upper Montclair CC in New Jersey. After working on the maintenance crew at that course, he joined the golf construction firm of William Baldwin, Inc. in 1955. Over the next eight years he served as construction superintendent for several Robert Trent Jones-designed courses built by Baldwin's company, including the new Upper Montclair CC, the Air Force Academy course in

Colorado and Half Moon-Rose Hall in Jamaica.

In 1963 Psiahas formed his own business, Golf Construction, Inc., and built courses for golf architects Frank Duane, David Gordon and Hal Purdy. In 1965 he began to design as well as construct courses.

Courses by Nicholas T. Psiahas:
NEW JERSEY: Berkeley Township GC; Darlington County GC, Darlington (1974); Jumping Brook CC, Neptune; Overpeck County GC, Teaneck; Rolling Greens GC, Newton (1970); Two Bridges CC, Lincoln Park (Exec. course); Wantage Golf Center (18 par 3); Wayne Golf Center (18 par 3,1972),
PENNSYLVANIA: Fernwood Resort & CC, Bushkill (1972).
Courses Remodeled by Nicholas T. Psiahas:
NEW JERSEY: North Jersey CC, Wayne.

Algie M. Pulley ASGCA

Algie Pulley worked with golf architect Ed Ault in the 1960s and then formed a contracting firm with "Buddy" Loving and E. H. Coffey, which built several courses, including the Manchester (Vermont) CC to the plans of Cornish and Robinson. In the early 1970s he formed Golf America, a firm that designed, built and operated golf courses.

Courses by Algie M. Pulley:
CALIFORNIA: Alhambra Muni (r.9,a.9,1977); Milpitas GC (1977); Dixon Landing CC (1979).
FLORIDA: Century XXI Club.
MARYLAND: Century XXI Club, Germantown (1974); The Duke of Marlborough GC, Upper Marlboro (1974); Germantown Exec GC (9); Hunt Valley CC (a.9).
VIRGINIA: Confederate Hills CC, Richmond (c.Loving,1972); Evergreen CC, Haymarket (1970); Jefferson Park GC, Fairfax Co. (9,1977); Lake Monticello CC, Charlottesville (c.Loving,1972); Montclair CC, Dumfries (1972).
WEST VIRGINIA: The Potomac Club, Keyser (9,1974).
Courses Remodeled by Algie M. Pulley:
CALIFORNIA: Arrowhead CC, San Bernardino (2,1977); San Bernardino GC (5,1976).
VIRGINIA: Army-Navy CC, Arlington (5,1970), Fairfax (2,1972); The CC of Fairfax (2,1969); Washington GC, Arlington (3,1969).

Hal Purdy (1905–   )
Born: Wabash, Indiana.

Hal Purdy graduated from high school in Wabash and went to work as a surveyor for the engineering firm of Stone and Webster. During the Depression, he was assistant manager and later manager at Lost Creek CC in Lima, Ohio, before working for two years as a draftsman. He then owned and operated the Sidney (Ohio) CC until 1945, when he became executive vice-president of a construction firm.

Purdy entered private practice as a golf course architect in 1956. He was joined by his son, Dr. Mal Purdy, in the 1960s and was also assisted for a few years by a second son, Chan.

Courses by Hal Purdy:
CONNECTICUT: Burning Tree CC, Greenwich (1962); Whitney Farms CC, Monroe (1979).
INDIANA: Elks CC, Elkhart (9,1964); McMillen Park GC, Ft. Wayne (1971); Norwood GC, Huntington (1970); Shoaff Park GC, Ft. Wayne (9,1966).
KENTUCKY: Carter Caves State Park (9,1963); General Butler State Park, Carrolton (9,1964); Harmony Landing CC, Goshen (9,1966); Jefferson High School (9,1964); Jenny Wiley State Park, Pikeville (9,1963); Kentucky Dam State Park, Paducah (1964).
NEW JERSEY: Atlantic City Electric Company, Somers Point (1964); Bamm Hollow CC, Middletown (27); Battleground CC, Freehold (1967); Bey-Lea GC, Toms River (1970); Clearview CC, Lincoln Park (1966); Fairmont CC, Chatnam (1961); Fiddler's Elbow CC, Bedminster (27,1966); Flanders Valley GC (27,1963); Forsgate CC, Jamesburg (a.West course,1974); Hickman Par 3, Wayne (9,1970); Knoll East GC, Boonton (1961); Mays Landing GC, Atlantic City (1964); Medford Lakes CC (9,1969); Millburn Par 3 (9,1970); Nevesink CC, Red Bank (1964); Ocean Acres GC, Manahawkin (9,1964); Old Tappan GC (9,1970); Ramsey G&CC (9,1965); Roxiticus CC, Mendham (1965); Rutgers University, New Brunswick (a.9,1963); Summit Par 3 (9,1968); Sunset Valley GC, Pequannock (1974); Tamarack GC, New Brunswick (27,1973); Warrenbrook CC, Plainfield (1966); Weequahic GC, Newark (9,1969).
NEW YORK: Catratonk GC, Candor (9,1966); Cazenovia GC (1969); Central Valley GC (9,1968); Chenango Valley GC, Binghampton (9,1967); Columbia G&CC, Hudson (9,1962); Deer Park GC, Utica (9,1966); Dinsmore GC, Staatsburg (1957); Greenview GC, Central Square (1967); Hillandale GC, Huntington (9,1961); Huguenot Manor GC, New Paltz (9,1971); Kanon Valley CC, Oneida (1969); Monroe County GC, Churchville (9,1968); Narrowsburg GC, Syracuse (9,1959); Newburgh GC (9,1965); Pompey Hills, Syracuse (1964); Rondout GC, Accord (9,1969); Roxbury Run GC, Denver (9,1974); Skaneatelas CC (9,1966); Stony Ford GC, Goshen (1962); Sunny Hill GC, Greenville (9,1967); Tioga GC, Nichols (1969); West Hill CC, Camillus (1967); Windham GC (9,1969).
Courses Remodeled by Hal Purdy:
CALIFORNIA: Thunderbird CC, Palm Springs (1973).
CONNECTICUT: Darien CC (1974).
INDIANA: French Lick CC (36,1965).
NEW JERSEY: Asbury Park GC (1970); Colonia CC (1969); Canoebrook CC, Summit (1971); Covered Bridge GC, Englishtown (1974); Florham Park CC (1974); Morris County GC, Morristown (1968); North Jersey CC, Wayne (1965); Raritan Arsenal, Edison (9,1968); Rivervale CC (1968); Rock Spring CC, West Orange (1965); Rockaway River CC, Denville (1974).
NEW YORK: IBM CC, Sands Point (9,1961); Inwood CC (1959); Mid Island CC, Oceanside (1963); Onondaga CC, Syracuse (1964); Wykagyl CC (1966).
OHIO: Losantiville GC (1961); Lost Creek CC, Lima (1961); Middletown GC (1962); Sidney G&CC (9,1945).

Mal Purdy (1932–   )
Born: Lima, Ohio.

Mal Purdy grew up on golf courses managed or operated by his father. He earned a doctorate in industrial psychology from Purdue University and worked in that field for fifteen

years. In the late 1960s he joined his father's course design firm, which became known as The Purdys.
Courses by Mal Purdy   See Hal Purdy. Courses for which Mal Purdy had major responsibility include:
CONNECTICUT: Aspetuck Valley CC, Weston (1966); Smith-Richardson GC, Fairfield (1970).
MARYLAND: Lighthouse Sound GC, Ocean City (1974).
NEW JERSEY: Braidburn CC, Florham Park (9,1972); Clear Brook GC, Cranbury (9,1974).
NEW YORK: Village Green GC, Syracuse (1974).
VIRGINIA: Luray Caverns CC (1974).
Courses Remodeled by Mal Purdy:
FLORIDA: Bellevue-Biltmore CC, Sarasota (9,1973).
NEW JERSEY: Essex Fells CC (1971).

Robert Dean Putnam
Robert Putnam worked as a commercial artist and then for golf architect Robert Baldock. In 1954 he established his own firm, based in California.
Courses by Robert Dean Putnam:
CALIFORNIA: Rancho Canada GC, Carmel (East and West courses,1970); Visalia Plaza GC (1973).
NEW MEXICO: Sandia Mountain Par 3 GC, Albuquerque (1962); Tijeras Arroyo GC, Kirkland AFB (1971).
WASHINGTON: Harrington G&CC (9,1957).
SPAIN: La Manga Campo de Golf, Costa Blanca (North and South courses,1972); Las Lomas El Bosque GC, Madrid (1973).
Courses Remodeled by Robert Dean Putnam:
CALIFORNIA: San Joaquin CC, Fresno (1972); Sunnyside CC, Fresno (1973).

Everett Pyle
Everett Pyle worked under Donald Ross in the 1930s, building Twigg Memorial GC in Providence, Rhode Island. From the 1940s through the 1960s he served as Superintendent of Parks in Hartford, Connecticut, planning extensive changes at Keney and Goodwin Park golf courses. He also designed or revised several Connecticut courses on the side, including Pine Hill GC at Windsor.

David A. Rainville (1936–   )
Born: Deadwood, South Dakota.
David Rainville received an A.A. degree in Engineering from Fullerton Junior College in California in 1957. Beginning at age twelve, he worked at golf course maintenance or construction during the summers.
In 1962, following military service, Rainville joined his father in the full-time practice of golf course design. Their California-based firm became known as David Rainville–Harry Rainville, Golf Course Architects, in the early 1970s.
Courses by David A. Rainville:
See Harry M. Rainville.

Harry M. Rainville (1905–   )
Born: St. Onge, South Dakota.
Harry Rainville's early years were spent in a variety of occupations, including ranching, mining, general construction and selling. In the early 1940s he moved his family to California, where he worked at Cal-Tech Rocket Assembly until 1944.
A friend of golf architect Lawrence Hughes, Rainville became construction superintendent on what is now the Stardust GC in San Diego in 1945. He went on to build five more courses for Hughes and was responsible for construction of, among others, the Desert Inn in Las Vegas and the Thunderbird in Palm Springs.
In 1952 Rainville entered private practice as a golf course designer. He was joined by his son David in 1962 and by additional partners in the late 1960s, including professional golfer Billy Casper (1969–71). In the 1970s the firm of David Rainville–Harry Rainville, Golf Course Architects began to build and operate, as well as design, golf facilities, and by 1979 owned an interest in five successful courses.
Courses by Harry M. Rainville and David A. Rainville:
CALIFORNIA: Alta Vista GC, Placentia; Bellflower GC (9 par 3) [Now Gene List Par 3 Muni]; Brea GC; Birch Hills GC, Brea; Candlewood CC, Whittier; Casa La Cumbre GC [Formerly Bonita Valley CC]; Santa Barbara (9 par 3); Cathedral Canyon CC, Palm Springs; Chula Vista GC; El Prado GC (Butterfield Stage and Chino Creek courses), Chino; El Rancho Verde CC, Rialto; Escondido CC; Fallbrook CC; Golf Rancho, Gardena (9 par 3); Imperial GC, Brea; Indian Wells CC, Palm Desert; Laguna Hills GC; Lake San Marcos; Mile Square GC, Fountain Valley; Needles GC; Panorama Village GC, Hemet (9 par 3); Pine Tree GC, Santa Ana (9 par 3); Rossmoor GC (Exec. course); Walnut Creek; San Juan Hills CC, San Juan Capistrano; Seven Hills GC, Hemet; University Village GC, Goleta (9); Warner Springs Resort; Western Hills CC, Chino; Whispering Palms GC, Rancho Santa Fe (27); Yorba Linda CC.
NEVADA: Boulder City GC (9).
Courses Remodeled by Harry M. Rainville and David A. Rainville:
CALIFORNIA: Chevy Chase CC, Glendale; Irvine Coast CC, Newport Beach; Los Serranos G&CC, Chino; Rancho Santa Fe CC; Red Hill CC, Upland; San Diego CC; Santa Ana CC; Thunderbird CC, Palm Springs; Torrey Pines GC, San Diego (North & South courses).

Seth J. Raynor (1878–1926)
Born: Suffolk County, New York. Died: Palm Beach, Florida, at age 47.
Seth J. Raynor trained as a surveyor and did not become interested in golf design until 1908, when he was hired by Charles Blair Macdonald to survey property that would become the

National Golf Links of America. Raynor so impressed Macdonald that he was hired to supervise construction of the National; and he went on to construct several more courses for Macdonald, including Piping Rock, Sleepy Hollow, Greenbrier, St. Louis CC and Lido.
In 1915 Raynor joined Macdonald as a partner and in the next ten years designed or remodeled nearly one hundred courses that appeared under his own name. C. B. Macdonald, by his own admission, concentrated on only a half dozen pet projects. In 1926 Seth Raynor died of pneumonia, leaving his assistants, Charles H. Banks and Ralph M. Barton, to complete his in-progress projects and to carry on the Macdonald tradition.
Courses by Seth J. Raynor:
CALIFORNIA: Monterey Peninsula CC, Pebble Beach (Dunes course,1926).
CONNECTICUT: CC of Fairfield (1921); Greenwich CC; Hotchkiss School GC, Lakeville; Yale University GC, New Haven (c.Macdonald,1926).
FLORIDA: Everglades Club, Palm Beach (Original 9,1919). Mountain Lakes C, Lake Wales.
GEORGIA: Bon Air Vanderbilt Hotel GC, Augusta (Lake course,n.l.e.).
HAWAII: Waialae CC, Honolulu (1925); Mid Pacific GC (original 9).
ILLINOIS: Shoreacres, Lake Bluff (1921).
MARYLAND: Gibson Island Club (c.Macdonald).
MINNESOTA: University of Minnesota GC, St. Paul (1925).
NEW JERSEY: Roselle CC.
NEW YORK: Blind Brook CC; The Creek Club, Locust Valley (c.Macdonald); Deepdale CC, Great Neck (c.Macdonald,n.l.e.); Fishers Island GC (1917); H. P. Whitney Estate GC, Manhasset (c.Macdonald); The Links GC, Roslyn (c.Macdonald,1919); Otto Kahn Estate GC, Cold Springs Harbour; Suffolk County CC, East Islip (n.l.e.); Thousand Islands Club, Alexandria Bay.
NORTH CAROLINA: Green Park-Norwood GC, Blowing Rock (n.l.e.).
PENNSYLVANIA: Fox Chapel GC, Pittsburgh (1925).
RHODE ISLAND: Tailer's Ocean Links (9,1920; n.l.e.).
SOUTH CAROLINA: Yeaman's Hall Club, Charleston (1925).
WISCONSIN: Blue Mound CC, Wauwautosa (1924).
Courses Remodeled by Seth J. Raynor:
ILLINOIS: Chicago GC, Wheaton (c.Macdonald,1923).
NEW YORK: Crawford CC.

Wilfrid Reid (1884–1973)
Born: Bulwell, Nottingham, England. Died: West Palm Beach, Florida, at age 89.
Wilfrid Reid studied club and ball making with Tommy Armour's father, Willie, in Edinburgh, Scotland. A scratch golfer at fifteen, he turned professional at seventeen and was a protégé of Harry Vardon, who helped him land a club professional job in Paris, France, in the early 1900s. Reid was a fine competitive golfer despite his diminutive size; and he beat his mentor, Vardon, on several occasions.
Reid competed in the United States during several seasons before moving there at the behest of the DuPont family after the outbreak of the first World War. He became a member of the PGA in 1917 and took out U. S. citizenship in 1921. He served as professional at several of America's top clubs, including the CC of Detroit, Michigan; Beverly CC in Illinois; the Broadmoor GC in Colorado; and Seminole GC in Florida. He defeated Gene Sarazen in the 1924 Augusta Open, won the 1926 Michigan PGA tournament and had twenty-six aces in his long playing career.
Reid began designing golf courses at an early age and had laid out courses in Europe and Britain before settling in the United States. It is estimated that he designed fifty-eight courses and remodeled some forty-three others in his career. While based in Michigan during the 1920s, he partnered with another club professional, William Connellan, and the firm of Reid and Connellan designed some twenty courses in that state alone. Wilfrid Reid retired to Florida in the early 1950s and consistently bettered his age in both social and competitive rounds.
Courses by Wilfrid Reid:
CALIFORNIA: Olympic Club [formerly Lakeside G&CC], San Francisco (Lake course) (1917).
DELAWARE: DuPont CC, Wilmington (n.l.e.); Green Hill Muni [formerly Wilmington CC], Wilmington; Newark CC (n.l.e.).
MICHIGAN: Bald Mountain GC, Detroit (c.Connellan); Black River CC, Port Huron (a.2nd 9,c.Connellan); Bob O'Link GC, Novi (c.Connellan); Brae Burn GC, Plymouth (c.Connellan); Harsens Island GC (c.Connellan); Indianwood G&CC, Lake Orion (c.Connellan,1928); Orchard Lake CC (c.Connellan); Plum Hollow G&CC, Southfield (c.Connellan); Sunnybrook CC, Grandville (c.Connellan).
OHIO: Ashtabula CC.
BELGIUM: Royal Belgique GC, Brussels (1904).
ENGLAND: Garrats Hall GC.
FRANCE: Cannes CC; GC D'Aix-Les-Bains; Golf du Racing Club "La Boulie"; Golf Ile De Berder; Pont St. Maxence GC.
Courses Remodeled by Wilfrid Reid:
MICHIGAN: Birmingham CC (c.Connellan); Gaylord CC (1949); Grosse Ile G&CC (r.bunkering); Tam O'Shanter CC, Orchard Lake (c.Connellan).
ENGLAND: Banstead Downs GC; Seacroft GC, Skegness (r.9).

Robert A. Renaud
Born: Canada.
Robert Renaud became pro-manager at the Pickens County CC in South Carolina in the early 1950s. After renovating the course which had been closed during World War II, he moved on to the Thomson CC in Georgia, where he performed the same task. He later served as head professional at a number of clubs and was twice voted South Carolina Golf Professional of the Year by his peers.
Renaud designed golf courses on a part-time basis during the 1950s and 60s, and in 1972 resigned from his position as head professional at Hillwood CC in Nashville to pursue a full-time career in golf architecture. In 1979 he retired to maintain and manage a course he had

built in Crossville, Tennessee.

Courses by Robert A. Renaud:
FLORIDA: The Admiralty CC, Rockledge (1974).
SOUTH CAROLINA: Fairfield CC, Winnsboro (1961); Springlake CC, York (a.2nd 9,1962).
TENNESSEE: Green River CC, Waynesboro (1972); Tansi Resort GC, Crossville (1973).
Courses Remodeled by Robert A. Renaud:
GEORGIA: Thomson CC (9,1954).
SOUTH CAROLINA: Pickens County CC, Pickens (1953).
TENNESSEE: Hillwood CC, Nashville (1970).

Garrett J. Renn (1913–1968)
Born: Mt. Holly, New Jersey. Died: Camden, New Jersey, at age 55.
Garrett Renn held the position of Superintendent of Philadelphia Municipal Golf Courses from 1950 until his death in 1968. A member of the PGA of America and the GCSAA, he designed several courses on a part-time basis. Among these were Bryn Llawen CC in Ivyland, Pennsylvania, and Little Mill CC in Marlton, New Jersey.

Joseph Michael "Mick" Riley (1905–1964)
Born: Burke, Idaho. Died: Salt Lake City, Utah, at age 59.
"Mick" Riley competed against George Von Elm as a youngster and turned professional while still in his teens. In the 1920s he helped to construct the Nibley Park GC in Salt Lake City and stayed on as its first professional. He served as pro at a series of Salt Lake City courses throughout his life and in 1951 was awarded a citation of merit by the National PGA for his efforts in promoting the game of golf. He has often been called the "Father of Golf in Utah."
Riley was responsible for the design and construction of several Utah golf courses and was especially active in the years just after World War II. After his death, the Salt Lake County Commission named their newest course, Riley's last design, in his honor.

Courses by Joseph Michael "Mick" Riley:
UTAH: Brigham City G&CC (9,1949); Copper GC (original 9); El Monte GC, Ogden (9,1950); Empire G&CC, Vernal (9); Forest Dale GC, Salt Lake City (9,1935); Fort Douglas V.A. Hospital GC (9 par 3,1957); Logan G&CC (1949); Meadowbrook Muni, Salt Lake City (1950); Mick Riley GC, Murray (1965); Mt. Lomond G&CC, Ogden (1949); Oquirrah Hills Muni; Rose Park GC, Salt Lake City (original 9); Timpanogas Muni, Provo (1950); Tooele GC (9,1949).
WYOMING: Purple Sage GC, Evanston (9,1952).
Courses Remodeled by Joseph Michael "Mick" Riley:
UTAH: Nibley Park GC, Salt Lake City (1949).

Bertrand Jay Riviere (1933–   )
Born: Houston, Texas.
Jay Riviere was an outstanding high school and college athlete and while playing tackle on the Rice University football team was an all-Southwest Conference selection in 1954, '55 and '56. He also lettered on the Rice golf team. After college he worked as an assistant professional under Claude Harmon at Winged Foot GC in New York.
Returning to Texas in 1962, Riviere became involved in golf course construction, assisting George Fazio with the creation of the Jackrabbit Course of the Champions Golf Club. After working on other Fazio projects, Riviere struck out on his own as a golf course architect in 1965. In 1970 he founded Golf Course Construction Co., Inc. based in Houston and in 1980 made professional golfer Dave Marr a partner in his design firm. Marr, a former PGA Champion, had also been an assistant to Claude Harmon in the late 1950s.

Courses by Bertrand Jay Riviere:
MISSOURI: Lakewood Oaks GC, Lees Summit (1980).
TEXAS: Bear Creek Golf World, Houston (Masters course ,1973); Bluebonnet CC, Navasota (1973); Clear Lake CC, Houston (1965); Frisch Auf Valley CC (9); Green Meadows CC, Katy; Hearthstone CC, Houston (1977); Inwood Forest GC, Houston (a.3rd 9); Killeen Muni; Lake Houston GC, Huffmann; McAllen CC (New site); Pasadena Ellington GC, Pasadena; Pinecrest GC, Trinity; Pine Forest CC, Houston (27); Point Aquarius GC, Conroe; Quail Valley CC, Missouri City; Rayburn CC, Jasper (Original 9,1968); River Plantation G&CC, Conroe (27,1968); Roman Hills GC, Splendora; Sun Meadow GC [formerly Chigger Creek CC], Houston; Temple CC (r.9,a.9).
PANAMA: Club de Golf Panama, Panama City (New site).
Courses Remodeled by Bertrand Jay Riviere:
LOUISIANA: Acadian Hills CC, Lafayette; Bayou Bend CC, Crowley; Lake Charles CC, Oakbourne CC, Lafayette; Pine Hills GC, Monroe.
MICHIGAN: Blythfield CC, Grand Rapids.
TEXAS: Baywood CC, Houston; CC of Austin; Riverbend CC, Sugarland; Sharpstown CC, Houston; Stephen F. Austin GC, San Felipe.

Harry Robb, Sr. (1894–1952)
Born: Montrose, Scotland. Died: Kansas City, Kansas, at age 58.
Harry Robb apprenticed with pro James Winton on the links at Montrose. Besides learning club making from Winton, he also developed a fine competitive game and won several local Artisan tournaments. In 1912 he emigrated to America with his boyhood friend Tom Clark, also a golf professional. After serving a short time as assistant pro at the Houston (Texas) CC, Robb moved to the Hutchinson (Kansas) GC, succeeding Clark as head professional. While in Hutchinson, he introduced the game to many small Kansas communities and laid out nine-hole courses in several of those towns.
In 1916 Robb moved to Kansas City, Kansas, again at Clark's behest. There he supervised construction of the Milburn G&CC to the plans of William Langford and stayed on as head professional. He remained at Milburn for the rest of his life, except for military service during World War I and a brief trip back to Scotland to marry his childhood sweetheart. He con-

tinued to design an occasional course while at Milburn and laid out several in the Kansas City-area during the 1920s. Upon his retirement from Milburn in the early 50s, his son succeeded him as professional.

Courses by Harry Robb Sr.:
KANSAS: Dodge City CC (9); Emporia CC (9); Iola CC (9;n.l.e.); Lake Barton GC, Great Bend; Lawrence CC; Newton CC (9); Ottawa CC (9); Tomahawk Hills GC, Lenexa [originally Shawnee CC]; White Lakes GC, Topeka (n.l.e.).

Russell Roberts (1922–   )
Born: Gaithersburg, Maryland.
Russell Roberts studied engineering while serving with the U. S. Navy during World War II. After the War he joined Frank Murray in the construction of several courses to the plans of golf architect Alfred Tull, and between 1955 and 1959 the partnership of Murray and Roberts was involved in designing and building courses of their own. When Murray moved to Florida in 1959, Roberts continued to practice on his own, adding course remodeling and drainage as well as flood control work for other types of projects to his design and building activities.
See Frank Murray.

Courses by Russell Roberts:
DELAWARE: Cavaliers CC, New Castle (c.Murray); Mapledale CC, Dover; Newark CC (a.9,c.Murray,1956); Old Landing GC, Rehobeth (9); Rehobeth Beach CC (c.Murray,1962).
MARYLAND: Bel Aire G&CC, Bowie (27,c.Murray,1959); Chantilly Manor CC, Rising Sun; Chestnut Ridge CC,Lutherville (9); Hagerstown Muni (1957); Holly Hill CC, Frederick; Maryland G&CC, Belair (9); Nassawango CC, Snow Hill; Needwood GC, Rockville; Newbridge CC, Largo; Ocean City CC, Berlin (9); Rocky Point GC, Essex; Swan Creek CC, Belair (9,c.Murray,1956); Valley Springs GC, Oxen Hill (9); Washingtonian CC, Gaithersburg (36).
PENNSYLVANIA: Fairview G&CC, Quentin (c.Murray,1959); Lebanon CC (c.Murray); Penn Oaks CC, West Chester.
VIRGINIA: Eastern Shore Y&CC, Onancock (9); Lakeview CC, New Market; Woodlawn CC, Mt. Vernon.
WASHINGTON, D.C.: Andrews AFB GC (East course,c.Murray,1951).
WEST VIRGINIA: Moorefield-Petersburg GC, Moorefield.

Allan Robertson (1815–1859)
Born: St. Andrews, Scotland. Died: St. Andrews, Scotland, at age 44.
Allan Robertson, a prominent St. Andrews ball maker and the greatest golfer of his day, is considered the first professional golfer in history. In 1858 he became the first person to break 80 at St. Andrews, an incredible feat for those days. He used a gutta-percha ball to do this, although, as a maker of feather balls, he had stubbornly opposed their introduction.
At the urging of Sir Hugh Playfair, who became Provost of St. Andrews in 1842 and set about improving both town and links, "Robertson in some unofficial and unremunerated way exercised a general supervision of the green." [4] He is also credited with the 1848 modifications to the Old Course that involved widening the fairways and creating huge double greens and the new seventeenth green; with laying out ten formal holes at Barry Angus (Carnoustie) in 1850; and, according to Robert Clark,[5] with laying out links in various districts of Scotland. He was, therefore, if unofficially, the first greenkeeper and course designer in golfing history, as well as the first professional.
4 Robert Clark, Golf, A Royal and Ancient Game, London. MacMillan and Co. (1899), p. 67.
5 Ibid., in an excerpt from Robertson's obituary, Dundee Gazette, September 1859, reprinted in an appendix.

David "Davie" Robertson
The elder brother of Allan and son of David Robertson, Davie Robertson was a ball maker and senior caddy at St. Andrews. In 1848 he emigrated to Australia, where he introduced golf and later helped to establish the Australian Golf Society. He is thought to have laid out the country's first links and courses in the process of introducing the game.

Roland Robertson
Roland Robertson served as professional at the Darlington (South Carolina) CC in the 1960s, designing several courses on the side. He then became professional/owner of the Sunkist GC in Biloxi, Mississippi, a layout of his own design.

Courses by Roland Robertson:
MISSISSIPPI: Sunkist CC, Biloxi (1970).
SOUTH CAROLINA: Darlington CC (a.2nd 9,1964); Oakdale GC (1968); Tifton GC, Darlington (1968).

Clinton E. Robinson (1907–   )   ASGCA: President, 1961, 1971
Born: St. Amadee, Province of Quebec, Canada.
"Robbie" Robinson received a B.S.A. degree in 1929 from the University of Toronto's Agricultural College at Guelph, Ontario. He became interested in golf course architecture during his undergraduate years, when he updated and renovated the private course of Sir Joseph Flavelle (Canadian magnate and prominent World War I statesman) at Fenelon Hall, Ontario. After graduation he embarked on an apprenticeship of several years duration with golf architect Stanley Thompson, who arranged a stint as course manager and superintendent at the Sunningdale CC, London, Ontario, for Robinson.
In 1936 Robinson returned to the Thompson firm and then served with the Royal Canadian Air Force during World War II. Following military service, he was employed in site selection and development of housing with the Canadian government's Central Mortgage and Housing.
Robinson entered private practice as a course architect in 1961 but had designed or redesigned several courses prior to that time. Soon recognized as a leading course designer, he was also an authority on turfgrass culture and for several years was director of the Royal

209

Canadian Golf Association Green Section. Robinson exerted considerable influence on the policies of his profession, and the top names in Canadian golf architecture after the death of Stanley Thompson were generally held to be those of Clinton Robinson and Howard Watson. In addition to his native Canada, Robinson worked in the United States and consulted on courses in Greece, Mexico, the Caribbean and South America.

Courses by Clinton E. Robinson:

ALBERTA: Windermere G&CC, Edmonton.
MANITOBA: John Blumberg Muni, Winnipeg (27,1950); Portage La Prairie GC (r.9,a.9); Stein Back Fly Inn GC.
NEW BRUNSWICK: CFG Gagetown GC, Oromocto (9); Gowan Brae GC, Bathurst; Miramichi G&CC, Bushville; Moncton G&CC (a.3rd 9); Restigouche G&CC, Campbellton (a.9); Sussex G&CC; Westfield G&CC (r.9,a.9).
NEWFOUNDLAND: Terra Nova National Park GC.
NOVA SCOTIA: Abercrombie CC, New Glasgow; Ken-Wo G&CC, New Minas (a.9); Lingan CC, Sydney (a.9); Northumberland G&CC, Pugwash; Oakfield CC, Grand Lake; Seaview GC, North Sydney (r.9,a.9); Truro G&CC (r.9,a.9).
ONTARIO: Bay of Quinte GC, Belleview (a.9); Bayview CC, Thornhill; Belleville G&CC, Marysville (a.9); Beverly G&CC, Copetown; Blue Mountain G&CC, Collingwood; Bowmanville CC (1st 9); Brampton GC; Briars G&CC, Jackson's Point (2nd 9); Bridgeport Fairways, Connestoga (Exec. course,1969); Borckville CC (2nd 9); Cedar Brae G&CC, Milliken; Conestogo G&TC; Coral Creek G&CC, Fisherville (9); Dalewood G&CC, Port Hope; Doon Valley GC, Kitchener; Dryden G&CC; East Park Executive GC, London; Elgin House GC, Port Carling (1969); Fort Frances GC (9); Hamilton G&CC, Ancaster (3rd 9); Hawthorne Valley G&CC, Mississauga; Hidden Valley GC (Executive course,1968); Lake St. George G&CC, Orillia (r.9,a.9); Lido Golf Centre, Oakville; London Hunt & CC (c.R.T.Jones); Maple City CC, Chatham (1st 9); Mount Hope G&CC; Muskoka Lakes G&CC (a.3rd 9); Oakdale G&CC, Downsview (3rd 9); Oakland Greens GC, Norwood (2nd 9); Oxford G&CC, Woodstock; Parkview GC, Milliken; Pine Lake GC (a.2nd 9); Richmond Hill G&CC; Richview G&CC, Oakville; Rideau View G&CC; Manotick (2nd 9); Saint Thomas G&CC (a.9); South Muskoka G&CC, Bracebridge; Strathcona G&CC, Huntsville (Exec. course,1978); Sunningdale CC, London (2nd 18); Trafalgar G&CC, Milton; Twenty Valley G&CC, Beamsville; Tyandaga Muni, Burlington; Upper Canada GC, Morrisburg (1966); Windermere G&CC.
PRINCE EDWARD ISLAND: Brudenell GC, Montague; Green Gables GC, Cavendish (r.18,a.9); Mill River GC, O'Leary; Stanhope G&CC.
QUEBEC: Baie Comeau CdG (1st 9).
SASKATCHEWAN: Holiday Park GC, Saskatoon; Kenopsee Lake Men's GC (r.9,a.9); Madge Lake GC, Kamsask (r.9,a.9).
UNITED STATES: Lemontree GC, Ford Lake, Michigan; Warren GC, Warren, Pennsylvania.
Courses Remodeled by Clinton E. Robinson:
ALBERTA: Calgary G&CC; Earl Grey GC, Calgary.
BRITISH COLUMBIA: Burnaby Mountain Men's GC; Vancouver GC, Coquitlam.
MANITOBA: Assiniboine GC, Winnipeg; Elmurst CC (3); Pine Ridge GC, Winnipeg; St. Charles CC, Winnipeg (2).
NEW BRUNSWICK: Fredericton GC (2); Riverside CC, St. John.
NOVA SCOTIA: Amherst G&CC (3rd 9).
ONTARIO: Barcoven G&CC (2); Beach Grove G&CC, St. Clair Beach; Brantford G&CC; CFB Borden G&CC (9); Cherry Hill GC, Ridgeway; Credit Valley G&CC, Mississauga; Dundas Valley GC; Glendale GC; Glen Lawrence G&CC; Golfland, Hamilton; Huntington G&CC, Nashville Lambton G&CC, Toronto; Oakville GC; Oshawa GC (3); Rosedale GC, Toronto; St. Catharines G&CC; St. George's GC, Islington; Sarnia G&CC; Thornhill CC; Westmount G&CC, Kitchener; Whirlpool GC, Niagara Falls.
PRINCE EDWARD ISLAND: Belvedere G & Winter C, Charlottetown.
QUEBEC: Beaconsfield GC, Pointe Claire; Elm Ridge CC, Ile Bizard (r.traps); Kanawaki GC, Caughnawaga; Royal Ottawa GC, Aylmer.
SASKATCHEWAN: Regina GC; Wascana G&CC, Regina; Waskesiu Lake GC.
COLOMBIA: Calis GC; Medellin GC; Mennezales GC.
UNITED STATES; Dearborn CC, Michigan; Monroe CC, Michigan.

Cabell B. Robinson (1941–   )   ASGCA
Born: Washington, D.C.
    Cabell Robinson received a B.A. degree in history from Princeton University in 1963 and then studied design for a year at Harvard, where he was a classmate of Rees L. Jones. In 1967 he obtained a B.L.A. degree from the University of California at Berkeley and in the autumn of that year went to work for the firm of Robert Trent Jones in New Jersey. In 1970 Robinson moved to Spain to organize a permanent Jones European office.
Courses by Cabell B. Robinson: See Robert Trent Jones.

John F. Robinson (1947–   )
Born: Toronto, Ontario, Canada.
    John Robinson, younger brother of golf architect William G. Robinson, attended the University of Michigan, receiving a bachelor's degree in landscape architecture in 1970. During his college years, he worked summers for golf architect William K. Newcomb and upon graduation became Newcomb's senior associate, assisting him in the design and construction of eight courses over a three-year period.
    In 1972–73, Robinson was employed as senior landscape architect with Marshall, Macklin, Monaghan Engineers and Planners of Toronto. He planned five courses while with the firm although none had been constructed by the end of the decade. Between 1973 and 1979, he laid out six courses of his own in Ontario, Kentucky and Antigua. Among them were the nine-hole Woodson Bend Resort in Kentucky (1975) and a nine-hole addition to Cedar Glen G&CC, Sudbury, Ontario (1979). Both were built.
    Robinson was associated for a short period with golf architect Dave Bennett and also collaborated on several projects with his own brother's firm. In addition, he planned a housing development in Algeria and taught course architecture for Professor Jack Eggens at the University of Guelph.

Theodore G. Robinson (1923–   )   ASGCA
Born: California;
    Theodore Robinson received an A.B. degree in naval science from the University of California in 1944 and an M.S. in urban planning and landscape architecture from the University of Southern California in 1948. Following graduation, he was employed with a general land planning and park design firm. In 1954 he established his own practice and was involved in land planning, subdivisions, park design and golf course routing.
    Robinson had been introduced to golf by his father, who was active and well known in amateur golf circles and had long been involved with the game. Nevertheless, the transition from land planner to golf architect took nearly ten years. By the late 1970s Robinson had worked extensively in the western United States, Mexico and the Pacific, and was engaged in planning two courses in Iran that were never built as a result of political unrest.
Courses by Theodore G. Robinson:

ARIZONA: El Dorado CC, Tucson (1970); Rio Salado Muni, Elwood (9,1979).
CALIFORNIA: Braemar CC (East and West courses); Camarillo Springs CC (1971); Casta Del Sol, Mission Viejo (1973); Cerritos GC (9,1976); Chaparral Executive CC, Palm Desert (1979); Crow Canyon CC, Danville (1976); De Anza Palm Springs Exec. GC; Desert Aire CC (27); Desert Horizons CC, Indian Wells (1979); Diamond Oaks CC, Roseville (1964); El Dorado GC, Long Beach (r.12,a.18,1964); Fullerton Muni (9,1965); Inglewood GC (1965); Ironwood CC, Palm Desert (North and South courses,1977); Laguna Canyon CC; Lomas Santa Fe, Solana Beach (1974); Marrakesh CC, Palm Desert (1970); Mission Bay GC, San Diego (1964); Mission Lakes CC, Desert Hot Springs (1966–7); Monterey CC, Rancho Mirage (27,1979); Mountain Meadows GC, Pomona (1975); Mountaingate CC, Hollywood Hills (1966–7); Navy GC, Los Alamitos Naval Air Station, Seal Beach (9,1974); North Ranch CC, Westlake (1975); Oak Tree, Techacapi (9,1973); Oakmont CC, Santa Rosa (18,-1964;18,1977); Old Ranch CC, Seal Beach (1968); Palm Desert Greens (1971); Portar Valley GC, Chatsworth (1968); Rancho Bernardo East, East San Diego (1967); Rancho Las Palmas, Rancho Mirage (27,1976); Rancho Murieta CC, Sacramento (South course,1978); Rancho San Vincente GC, Ramona (1972); Rolling Hills CC (1968); San Vicente CC; Seven Lakes CC, Palm Springs (1964); Silver Lakes GC, Victorville (27,1971); Stoneridge CC, Poway (1971); Sunrise CC, Rancho Mirage (1974); Sunset Hills CC, Thousand Oaks (1974); Vista Valley CC, Vista (9,1979); Westlake CC (18,1966;18,1974).
HAWAII: Kalua Kai GC (Sheraton Molokai), Molokai (1976).
NEVADA: Nellis AFB GC, Las Vegas (9,1970).
NEW MEXICO: Inn of the Mountain Gods, Mescalero Resort (1974).
OREGON: Chabonneau GC (Exec.9,1979); Charbonneau CC, Wilsonville (27,1973); Tokatee CC, Blue River (1967).
TEXAS: Bear Creek G&RC, Arlington (East and West courses,1980); Euless GC (36,1979).
WASHINGTON: Everett CC (r.6,a.18,1969); Highland GC, Tacoma (9,1968); Meridian Valley CC, Kent (1966–7); Mill Creek CC, Seattle (1974); Sahalee CC, Redmond (27,1969); Sudden Valley CC, Bellingham (1970).
WASHINGTON, D.C.: Tantallon CC (1961).
BERMUDA: Princess Southampton (1972).
JAPAN: Lakewood GC, Oiso Machi Kanagawa Ken (West course,1970;East course,1973).
MEXICO: Princess Acapulco (1971).
Courses Remodeled by Theodore G. Robinson:
CALIFORNIA: Alondra Park CC, Gardena (2,1976); Alondra Park Muni (18,1978); Candle Wood CC, La Miranda (6,1971); Hacienda CC, Whittier (2,1965); LaJolla CC (3,1968–73); Los Coyotes CC, Buena Park (6,1970); Navy GC-Admiral Baker Field, San Diego (6,1970); Palos Verdes GC (3,1975); Stardust CC, San Diego (6,1976); Tamarisk CC, Palm Springs (17,1972–3).
WASHINGTON: Royal Oak CC, Vancouver (2,1970); Seattle GC (18,1969); Yakima CC (5,1974).

William G. Robinson (1941–   )   ASGCA
Born: Ontario, Canada.
    William Robinson turned down an opportunity to play professional hockey, having decided early on for a career in golf design. He studied landscape architecture at Pennsylvania State University and graduated in 1964 with two summers' experience working for the firm of Robert Trent Jones. A scratch golfer, he was a member of the Penn State golf team.
    Following graduation, Robinson joined the practice of golf architect Geoffrey S. Cornish. In 1977 he formed and became president of Cornish and Robinson Golf Course Designers Ltd. of Calgary, Alberta, engaged in designing courses in oil-rich Alberta and surrounding provinces. Robinson pioneered methods for modifying established layouts through long-range planning; researched putting green design and bunker placement in relation to play, eye appeal and maintenance; coauthored with Cornish the booklet "Golf Course Design—An Introduction" distributed by the National Golf Foundation; and led a trend to planning courses to be nature walks.
Courses by William G. Robinson   From 1964 through 1979 he collaborated on all Cornish courses. He is architect of record for all Cornish and Robinson Ltd. courses, including:
ALBERTA: Inglewood Muni, Calgary (a.9,1978); Sturgeon Valley G&CC, St. Alberts (a.12, 1979); Spruce Grove GC, Edmonton; Carstairs G&CC (a.9).
BRITISH COLUMBIA: Fort Nelson GC (9,1979); Kelowna Pines G&CC (1978–79) [now Gallaghers Canyon GC]; Okanagon Park, Kelowna (9 par 3,1979).
Courses Remodeled by William G. Robinson:
ALBERTA: Calgary G&CC (1978); Canyon Meadows G&CC, Calgary (1978); Edmonton G&CC (1979); Red Deer G&CC (1977–80).
SASKATCHEWAN: Riverside G&CC, Saskatoon (1977–80).
BRITISH COLUMBIA: Vancouver GC.

William James Rockefeller (1864–1932)
Born: Binghampton, New York. Died: Toledo, Ohio, at age 67.
    W. J. Rockefeller grew up on his family's farm in New York, studied music for a time and worked as a hospital orderly before being hired as greenkeeper at the newly formed Inver-

ness Club in Toledo, Ohio, in 1903. He remained at Inverness for the rest of his life and in 1918–19 supervised construction, when the course was remodeled and extended to eighteen holes by Donald Ross. The experience led him to take on several other design or reconstruction projects in the Toledo area.

Rockefeller was also known as a fine turfsman and teacher of course maintenance. Two of his students became outstanding course superintendents, Joe Mayo of Pebble Beach and Al Schardt of Buffalo.

Rockefeller's final project was the preparation of the Inverness Club to host the 1931 USGA Open Championship, an exhaustive effort completed only a short time before his death in 1932.

Courses by William James Rockefeller:

OHIO: Catawba Island Club, Port Clinton; Defiance GC; Heather Downs CC, Toledo (1927); Lakemont GC, Reno; Mohawk GC, Tiffin; Napoleon GC (9).

Douglas Rolland (1860–1914)

Born: Scotland. Died: England, at age 54.

Trained as a stonemason, Douglas Rolland became one of the leading professional golfers of his day. Although he never won a major championship, he was runner-up in the British Opens of 1884 and 1894. For several years he lived in the United States.

Rolland practiced course design in Great Britain. Much of his work is thought to have comprised planning of modifications to existing courses.

Joseph A. Roseman, Sr. (1888–1944)

Born: Philadelphia, Pennsylvania. Died: Chicago, Illinois, at age 55.

Joseph Roseman began his golf career as a caddy at the Philadelphia CC. In 1907 he was hired as professional for the Des Moines (Iowa) CC and shortly after his arrival took on the additional duties of greenkeeper. Gifted as an inventor, he created a hitch for horses that could accommodate three gang mowers at once. He later adapted a Model T Ford to serve as a tractor unit to pull his gang mowers and then invented a hollow mower roller to preserve the turf as it mowed.

Following a brief stint as pro-greenkeeper in Racine, Wisconsin, Roseman moved to the Chicago area in 1916. In neighboring Evanston, Illinois, he founded the Roseman Tractor Mower Company, a concern in existence in 1980. A short time later he laid out his first golf course, the Westmoreland CC in Wilmette. He remained there as pro-superintendent until 1928, when he resigned to devote more time to his mower equipment company.

While course design was always a part-time endeavor, Roseman estimated that he had worked on more than fifty courses, many in collaboration with Jack Croke and George O'Neil. He also pioneered complete underground watering systems on several Chicago-area courses and built one of the first night-lighted par-3 courses in the country in 1933.

Courses by Joseph A. Roseman, Sr.:

FLORIDA: Fort Lauderdale CC (North course,1925).

ILLINOIS: Glenview Naval Air Station GC (Courses #1&2,1927); [formerly Pickwick GC]; Glenview Park GC [formerly Elmgate CC]; Jackson Park GC, Chicago; Park District GC, East St. Louis; Waveland GC, Chicago (9); Westmoreland CC, Wilmette (1917); West Wilmette Illuminated GC (Par 3,1933); Wilmette GC (1923); Wilmette Park GC, Glenview.

INDIANA: Tippecanoe CC, Monticello (1920).

MICHIGAN: Walnut Hills CC, Lansing.

WISCONSIN: Maxwelton Brae CC, Baileys Harbor (c.O'Neil); Petrifying Springs GC, Kenosha (1922); Racine CC.

Courses Remodeled by Joseph A. Roseman, Sr.:

ILLINOIS: Glenview GC, Golf (c.O'Neil); Green Acres CC [formerly Illinois GC]. Northbrook.

Donald James Ross (1872–1948) ASGCA: Charter Member, Honorary President, 1947–48

Born: Dornoch, Scotland. Died: Pinehurst, North Carolina, at age 76.

Donald Ross, son of stonemason Mundo Ross, began as an apprentice carpenter under Peter Murray of Dornoch. On the advice of John Sutherland, secretary of the Dornoch GC, he went to St. Andrews, where he learned club making at Forgan's Shop and studied golf with "Old" Tom Morris. In 1893 he returned to Dornoch GC, becoming greenkeeper and professional and gaining from his mentor, Sutherland, a lifelong interest in the propagation and maintenance of grass for golf and in the fundamental qualities of a good golf hole.

In 1898, at the urging of Harvard astronomy professor Robert Wilson, Ross emigrated to Boston, Massachusetts, where he became pro-greenkeeper at Oakley CC, a layout that he quickly formalized. At Oakley he met members of the wealthy Tufts family of Medford, one of whom had previously known him at Dornoch. The Tufts persuaded Ross to become winter golf professional at the resort they were developing at Pinehurst, North Carolina. For several years he continued to spend summers at Oakley CC and later Essex CC in Massachusetts, and winters at Pinehurst.

The planning and refining of courses at the Pinehurst golf complex brought Ross national fame. His services as a golf architect were soon in demand throughout North America; and in the years from around 1912 until his death in 1948, Ross was considered by many to be America's best-known and most active course designer. By 1925, 3,000 men were employed annually in the construction of Ross courses. Donald J. Ross Associates, Inc. had winter offices at Pinehurst; summer offices at Little Compton, Rhode Island; and branch offices at North Amherst, Massachusetts (headed by Walter B. Hatch) and Wynnewood, Pennsylvania (headed by J. B. McGovern). Despite his extensive practice, Ross continued as golf manager at Pinehurst until his death.

Ross's design style incorporated naturalness and a "links touch," deriving from his Dornoch background and training with John Sutherland. Although he sculptured his greens, he always tried to utilize existing contours with only minor modifications.

Donald Ross played a major role in forming the American Society of Golf Course Architects and is considered the Society's "patron saint." Its official jacket is the Ross plaid, and the 1980 Annual Banquet and presentation of the Ross Award was held in Dornoch.

Ross's family included a daughter, Mrs. Richard Pippitt, by his first wife, who died in 1922, and a stepson John, the child of his second wife, Mrs. Florence Blacklington, whom he married in 1926. Donald's brother, Alex Ross, a well-known professional golfer, worked for many years at Braeburn CC near Boston and at the Detroit CC in Michigan.

Donald Ross of Pinehurst and Royal Durnoch by Donald Grant provides insight into Ross's career, while *America's Greatest Golfing Resorts* by Dick Miller presents an excellent description of the courses at Pinehurst. Another account is found in the two-part series written by Mike Dann for Golf World in 1974. Brian M. Silva of the U.S.G.A. Green Section is considered an authority on Donald Ross and is the author of an unpublished paper (as of 1980) on this architect.

Courses by Donald James Ross: (Although sometimes credited with 600–700 courses, Ross probably did fewer. The following list is believed to include most of his courses.)

ALABAMA: CC of Birmingham (East & West courses,1927); CC of Mobile; Mountain Brook CC,Birmingham.

CALIFORNIA: Beresford CC [now Peninsula G&CC], San Mateo.

COLORADO: Broadmoor GC, Colorado Springs (Original 9, East & West courses,1918); Wellshire GC, Denver (1926).

CONNECTICUT: CC of Waterbury (1922); Hartford GC, West Hartford; Norwich Hotel GC [now Norwich Muni]; Shennecossett GC, Groton; Wampanoag CC, West Hartford (1926).

FLORIDA: Belleair CC (36); Belleview-Biltmore Hotel & Club, Clearwater (r.9,a.9 West course; a. East course,1915) [Formerly Belleair CC]; Bobby Jones GC, Sarasota (1927); Brentwood GC, Jacksonville (1923); Coral Gables (Miami) Biltmore CC (1924); Daytona Beach G&CC (South course,1924); Dunedin Isles CC (1925); Everglades CC, Palm Beach (2nd 9,1928); Florida CC, Jacksonville; Fort Myers G&CC (1918); Gulf Stream GC, Delray Beach (1923); Hyde Park CC, Jacksonville; Jacksonville Muni; Keystone G&CC (9,1927); Miami CC (n.l.e.); New Smyrna GC (1922); Palm Beach CC (1917); Panama CC; Pelican GC, Clearwater (1926); Ponce de Leon CC, St. Augustine (1916); San Jose CC, Jacksonville (1935); Seminole GC, North Palm Beach (1929); St. Augustine Links (36; one 18 now Ponce de Leon CC; other 18, n.l.e.); Sunset GC, St. Petersburg (1923); Timuquana CC, Jacksonville (1923).

GEORGIA: Athens CC (1926); Augusta CC (Hill course); Bacon Park GC, Savannah (1926); Brunswick GC (Original 9,1936); East Lake CC, Atlanta (r. #1,1915;a. #2,1923;n.l.e.); Forrest Hill GC, Augusta; Gainesville Muni (9;n.l.e.); Highland CC, LaGrange (9); Savannah Inn & CC (1927); Savannah Muni (36).

ILLINOIS: Beverly (Auburn Park) CC, Chicago (1907); Bob O'Link CC, Highland Park (1916); Calumet CC, Homewood (1901); Evanston CC, Skokie (1917); Northmoor CC, Highland Park (1918); Old Elm Club, Fort Sheridan (1913).

INDIANA: Broadmoor CC, Indianapolis (1928); Fairview GC, Ft. Wayne (Original 9); French Lick-Sheraton Hotel & Club (Hill course).

IOWA: Cedar Rapids CC.

KANSAS: Shawnee CC, Topeka (1921).

KENTUCKY: Idle Hour CC [formerly Ashland GC], (1916,n.l.e.).

MAINE: Augusta CC, Augusta (Original 9;1919); Lake Kezar Club, Lovell (9); Penobscot Valley CC, Bangor; Portland CC, Falmouth; York G&CC.

MARYLAND: Chevy Chase CC (1910); Hagerstown CC; Indian Spring Club, Silver Springs (n.l.e.); Prince George's G&CC [formerly Beaver Dam CC], Landover (1921).

MASSACHUSETTS: Andover GC; Belmont CC; Brae Burn CC, West Newton; Charles River CC, Newton Centre (1921); Cohasset GC, Quincy; Concord CC; Essex County CC, Manchester (1910); George Wright Muni, Boston (1931); Kernwood CC, Salem; Longmeadow CC, Springfield (1922); Mt. Tom CC, Holyoke; North Andover CC; Oak Hill CC, Fitchburg; Oakley CC, Watertown (1899); Orchards GC, South Hadley; Oyster Harbors Club, Osterville (1927); Pittsfield CC; Plymouth CC; Pocasset GC; Ponkapoag GC, Boston (1933); Salem CC, Peabody (1926); Sandy Burr CC, Wayland; Sankaty Head GC, Nantucket (1927); Tatnuck CC, Worcester; Toy Town Tavern GC, Winchendon; Vespers CC, Lowell (r.9,a.9); Wachusset CC, West Boylston; Wellesley CC (Original 9); Weston GC; Whaling City Muni, New Bedford (Original 9); Whitinsville GC; Winchester CC (1903;r.1928); Worcester CC (1914).

MICHIGAN: Barton Hills, Ann Arbor; Birmingham CC (1916); Dearborn CC; Detroit GC (North & South courses,1916); Franklin Hills CC; Franklin Woods, Detroit; Grosse Isle G&CC; Highland GC, Grand Rapids; Kent CC, Grand Rapids; Monroe CC; Muskegon CC; Oakland Hills CC, Birmingham (South course,1917; North course,1918); Rackham Park Muni, Huntington Woods (1925,n.l.e.); Redford Muni GC, Detroit (1910); Warren Valley CC, Wayne; Washtenaw CC, Ypsilanti (r.9,a.9,1922).

MINNESOTA: Northland CC, Duluth (1927); Woodhill CC, Wayzata (1916;r.1934).

MISSOURI: Hillcrest CC, Kansas City (1917).

NEW HAMPSHIRE: Balsam's Hotel & CC, Dixville Notch; Bretton Woods GC, Mt. Washington (27); Carter CC, Lebanon (1923); Lake Sunapee CC, New London; Lake Tarleton Club, Pike; Manchester CC (1923); Maplewood CC, Bethlehem; Mt. Crotched CC, Francestown (9,1929,n.l.e.); Mount Washington Hotel & CC, Bretton Woods (1915); Wentworth-By-The-Sea GC, Portsmouth (Original 9,1910).

NEW JERSEY: Crestmont CC, West Orange; Englewood CC; Homestead CC, Spring Lake; Knickerbocker CC, Tenafly (New course,1915); Montclair GC; Newark Athletic Club, Essex Fells; Plainfield CC (1920); Riverton CC; Seaview CC, Absecon (Bay course,1915).

NEW YORK: Bellevue CC, Syracuse (1915); Brooklea CC, Rochester (1924); Chappequa CC, Mt. Kisco (1929); Cold Spring CC; CC of Buffalo, Williamsville (1924); CC of Rochester (1914); Essex County Club, Hempstead; Fairview CC, Elmsford; Glenns Falls CC; Irondequoit CC, Rochester (9); Malone GC (Original 9); Mark Twain GC, Elmira (1940); Mayfield CC; Monroe GC, Pittsford (1924); Oak Hill CC, Rochester (West course,1925; East course,1926); Sagamore GC, Bolton Landing (1928); Siwanoy GC, Bronxville (1914;r.1927); Teugega CC, Rome; Thendara CC, Old Forge (Original 9); Tupper Lake GC; Whippoorwill CC, Armonk (1925).

NORTH CAROLINA: Alamance CC, Burlington (1948); Asheville Muni (1927); Beaver Lake GC, Asheville (1924); Benevenue CC, Rocky Mount (1931); Biltmore Forest, Asheville (1922); Carolina G&CC, Charlotte (1928); Charlotte CC (1912); CC of Salisbury (Original 9,1927); Eseelo Lodge, Linville; Forsythe CC , Winston-Salem; Hendersonville CC (1936); Highland CC, Fayetteville (1947); Highlands CC (1926); Hope Valley CC, Durham (1926);

Linville GC (1929); Mid Pines CC, Southern Pines (1921); Mimosa Hills CC, Morganton (1931); Monroe CC (9,1943); Myers Park CC, Charlotte; Pinehurst CC (#1,1899; #2,1903; #3,1907,2nd 9,1910; #4,Original 9,1919;r.1925,1935); Pine Needles Lodge & CC, Southern Pines (1927); Raleigh CC (1949); Richmond Pines CC, Rockingham (1926); Roaring Gap G&CC (1914); Sedgefield CC, Greensboro (36); Southern Pines CC (36); Wilmington Muni (1927).

OHIO: Acacia CC, Cleveland; Athens CC (original 9); Brookside CC, Canton (1922); Columbus CC (9,1907;9,1914); Congress Lake Club, Hartville; Elks CC, Columbus; Granville Inn GC; Hamilton CC; Hyde Park GC, Cincinnati; Inverness Club, Toledo (1919); Manakiki G&CC, Willoughby (1929); Miami Shores GC, Troy (1947); Miami Valley GC, Dayton; Mill Creek GC, Youngstown (North & South courses); Piqua CC (9); Portsmouth CC; Scioto CC, Columbus (1916); Shaker Heights CC; Springfield CC; Wyandot Muni, Worthington (1922); Youngstown CC.

PENNSYLVANIA: Aronimink GC, Newtown Square (1928); Buck Hill Inn & GC (Original 18,1915); Charles Schwab Estate GC, Loretto (9,1917); CC of York; Edgewood CC, Pittsburgh; Flourtown (Sunnybrook) CC, Plymouth Meeting; Gulph Mills GC, King of Prussia (1919); Kahkwa Club, Erie (1915); Lu Lu Temple CC, Philadelphia; Philadelphia Cricket Club; Pittsburgh Field Club (1915); Rolling Rock GC, Ligonier; St. David's GC, Philadelphia; Sunnybrook CC; Torresdale Frankford, Philadelphia.

RHODE ISLAND: Metacomet CC, East Providence (1921); Rhode Island CC, West Barrington; Sakonnet GC, Little Compton (1921); Twiggs (Providence Muni); Wannamoisett CC, Rumford; Warwick CC (Original 9,r. 2nd 9).

SOUTH CAROLINA: Camden CC (1934); CC of Charleston; Myrtle Beach (1927).

TENNESSEE: Belle Meade CC, Nashville; Chattanooga G&CC; Holston Hills CC, Knoxville (1933); Memphis CC; Richland.

TEXAS: Galveston Muni (New site,1948); Pinehurst CC, Orange; River Oaks CC, Houston (1924).

VERMONT: Burlington CC.

VIRGINIA: CC of Petersburg (9,1921); Hampton (Rhodes) GC; Jefferson-Lakeside CC, Richmond (1921); Washington G&CC, Arlington (1915).

WISCONSIN: Kenosha CC.

CANADA: Algonquin GC, St. Andrews by the Sea, New Brunswick (27); Brightwood G&CC, Dartmouth, Nova Scotia; Elmhurst Golf Links, Winnipeg, Manitoba; Essex G&CC, Sandwich, Ontario (1929); Roseland G&CC, Windsor, Ontario (27); St. Charles CC, Winnipeg, Manitoba (South 9).

CUBA: CC of Havana (1911); Havana Biltmore CC.

Courses Remodeled by Donald James Ross:

CONNECTICUT: Greenwich CC (1946).

FLORIDA: Breakers GC, Palm Beach (1926); Palma Ceia G&CC, Tampa (1923); Punta Gorda CC (1927).

GEORGIA: Bon Air-Vanderbilt Hotel GC, Augusta (Hill course).

ILLINOIS: Exmoor CC, Highland Park; Indian Hill Club, Winnetka (1914); Ravisloe CC, Homewood.

MASSACHUSETTS: Bass River Muni, Yarmouth; Hyannisport Club; New Bedford CC; Woodland GC, Auburndale (1927).

MICHIGAN: Bloomfield Hills CC, Birmingham (1936).

MINNESOTA: Interlachen CC, Edina (1919); Minikahda Club, Minneapolis (1917).

NEW JERSEY: Essex County CC, West Orange (East & West courses,1925); Ridgewood CC (1916,n.l.e.).

NEW YORK: Fox Hills GC, Staten Island; Hudson River GC, Yonkers (1916,n.l.e.); Wykagyl CC, New Rochelle (1920).

OHIO: Oakwood CC, Cleveland (r.18).

PENNSYLVANIA: Allegheny CC, Sewickley (r.,a.3,1923); Bedford Springs CC; Cedarbrook CC, Philadelphia (1921,n.l.e.); Whitemarsh Valley CC, Philadelphia.

RHODE ISLAND: Agawam Hunt Club, Providence; Misquemicut GC, Watch Hill; Pt. Judith CC; Newport CC.

VERMONT: Woodstock CC.

VIRGINIA: Hermitage CC, Richmond.

CANADA: Riverside G&CC, New Brunswick (1933–37); Rosedale CC, Toronto, Ontario.

SCOTLAND: Royal Dornoch GC (c.Sutherland).

Robert J. Ross

A Hartford-based civil engineer and prominent amateur golfer, Robert Ross designed several Connecticut courses in the 1920s and 30s, including the original Avon CC, Canton GC, Indian Hills CC at Newington, Middleton GC, revisions to Wethersfield CC and the original 18 at Stanley GC in New Britain.

Philip Mackenzie Ross (1890–1974) BAGCA: President, 1971
Born: Edinburgh, Scotland. Died: London, England, at age 83.

Philip Ross learned golf at Royal Musselburgh and won several amateur medals as a youth. He served with the British Army during World War I and upon discharge looked for a golf-related job. By chance he met golf architect Tom Simpson, who hired him as a construction boss in 1920. By the mid-twenties Ross was a full partner in the firm of Simpson and Ross.

By the 1930s Ross was working on his own and had developed a fine reputation as a designer in Great Britain and on the Continent. After the second World War he demonstrated his talents to a new generation by reconstructing or restoring many war-ravaged courses.

In 1972 Ross was elected the first president of the British Association of Golf Course Architects.

Courses by Philip Mackenzie Ross:
BELGIUM: Royal Antwerp GC, Kapellenbos (r.18,a.9,c.Simpson,1924); Royal Golf Club des Fagnes, Spa (c.Simpson).

CHANNEL ISLANDS: Royal Guernsey GC.

ENGLAND: Carlisle GC, Cumberland (1938); Castletown GC, Isle of Man; Hythe Imperial GC,Kent.

FRANCE: GC d'Amiens (9); GC d'Hardelot, Boulogne (c.Simpson); Mazamet, New GC,

Deauville (c.Simpson,1929).

NORTHERN IRELAND: Balmoral GC, Belfast.

PORTUGAL: Estoril GC (a.18,1938); Furnas GC; San Miguel GC, The Azores; Club de Golf de Vidago (9).

SCOTLAND: Cramond GC; Dumfries & County GC (1949); Southerness GC, Dumfrieshire (1949); Glen GC, East Lothian.

SPAIN: Club de Golf Las Palmas, Canary Islands (1957); Club de Campo de Malaga, Torremolinos (1928); Maspolomas GC, Canary Islands.

WALES: Pyle and Kenfig.

Courses Remodeled by Philip Mackenzie Ross:

CHANNEL ISLANDS: Royal Guernsey GC.

ENGLAND: Alnmouth GC.

FRANCE: Golf Club du Touquet (r.Forest and Sea courses,1958).

NORTHERN IRELAND: Bangor GC, County Down.

PORTUGAL: Oporto GC, Espinho (1958).

SCOTLAND: Longniddry Club, East Lothian; North Berwick Muni, East Lothian (r.Burgh course); Turnberry GC, Ayrshire (r.Ailsa course,1951).

V. C. "Dick" Rossen

Dick Rossen, golf course superintendent at the Rainbow Canyon Golf Resort in California, designed and built the course (then known as the Rancho California Golf Resort) in 1970. He also remodeled the Pala Mesa (California) GC.

In 1978 Rainbow Canyon GC received forty-nine inches of rain in ninety days but was able to remain open throughout due to its excellent drainage. The fact that it was the only area golf course not closed during the period was a tribute to Rossen's abilities as designer and superintendent.

Roger G. Rulewich (1936–   ) ASGCA
Born: New Brunswick, New Jersey.

Roger Rulewich received a B.E. degree in civil engineering from Yale University in 1958. Following graduation, he was employed with Clarke and Rapuano, consulting engineers and landscape architects. In 1961 he joined the firm of Robert Trent Jones, Inc., where he quickly took an active role in the design and construction inspection of Jones courses in the United States and abroad.

By the late 1970s Rulewich was recognized as a major force, both in the Jones organization and in the profession of golf architecture at large, and was numbered among the most active course architects. A member of the American Society of Golf Course Architects, he established the Society's exhibit on the history of course design at the Golf Hall of Fame in Pinehurst, North Carolina.

Courses by Roger G. Rulewich: See Robert Trent Jones.

Alex Russell

Australian amateur golfer Alex Russell won the 1924 Australian Open. In 1926 he assisted Alister Mackenzie in laying out the original (West) course at Royal Melbourne GC. Following Mackenzie's departure, Russell laid out an additional course (the East) at Royal Melbourne, as well as several others in Australia and New Zealand.

Courses by Alex Russell:
AUSTRALIA: Lake Karrinyupuc GC (1930); Royal Melbourne GC (West course,c.Mackenzie,1926; East course,1932); Yarra Yarra GC, Melbourne (1929).

NEW ZEALAND: Paraparaumu Beach GC (1949).

Edward Ryder

Edward Ryder was a partner with Val Carlson in the Connecticut firm of Carlson and Ryder, which designed and built courses in the 1960s. He planned several courses in Fairfield County and neighboring areas of Connecticut and New York, including Danbury Muni and the original nine of the Redding CC in Connecticut, and Salem CC and one nine at Back O' Beyond GC (formerly Morfar GC, Brewster) in New York. He also planned the original eighteen of Suntree GC in Florida.

Jaime Saenz

A member of the Mexican design firm of Saenz and Teran, Jaime Saenz planned La Ceiba on the Yucatan Peninsula in 1974.

Bernard Sayers (1857–1924)
Born: Leith, Scotland. Died: North Berwick, Scotland at age 67.

Famed Scottish professional golfer Bernard Sayers of Leith claimed to have laid out many courses in a chapter he wrote for Great Golfers in the Making. Among them were Broomieknowe, Midlothian, in Scotland, and Castlerock in Northern Ireland.

Mario Schjetnan

Mario Schjetnan, the son of a Norwegian settler in Mexico, became a club professional in that country. He designed at least two Mexican courses, Campestre de Leon (1960) and Club Loman de Cocoyoc (1978).

Hans Carl Schmeisser (1892–1980)
Born: Ulm, Germany. Died: West Palm Beach, Florida at age 88.

Superintendent of the Fort Lauderdale (Florida) CC in the early 1950's, and later superintendent of the Miami Beach Parks Department, Hans Schmeisser designed several courses in the late 1950's and early 60's. One son, John, was on the staff of Robert Trent Jones, while a second, Otto, was superintendent of the Everglades Club at Palm Beach. Hans Schmeisser was selected to receive one of the three G.C.S.A.A. Distinguished Service Awards in 1981.

Courses by Hans Schmeisser:
FLORIDA: Forest Hill GC, West Palm Beach (Executive course,1966); Glen Oaks GC, Clearwater (9 par 3,1960); Oak Ridge CC, Ft. Lauderdale (1962); Pines GC, Hollywood (Par 3,1961); Ridge Manor CC, Dade City (Original 9,1956); Sebring Shores GC (Par 3,1964).
Courses Remodeled by Hans Schmeisser:
FLORIDA: Shore Acres GC, St. Petersburg (1956).

Emmanuel J. Schwartz
See A. Russell Tryon.

Edwin B. Seay   (1938–   )   ASGCA, President 1976.
Born: Dade City, Florida.
Edwin Seay graduated from the University of Florida with a bachelor's degree in landscape architecture, and was then commissioned as an officer in the US Marine Corps. His professional career began in 1964 with an association with golf architect Ellis Maples, which resulted in the design and construction of 27 courses.
Seay entered private practice under the firm name of Edwin B. Seay Inc. in 1972, and later was joined by professional golfer Arnold Palmer. The corporation which included golf architect Robert Walker as an assistant, became known as the Palmer Course Design Company in 1979.

Courses by Edwin B. Seay: (Courses after 1974 with Robert Walker)
CALIFORNIA: Ironwood CC, Palm Desert (a.9 Par 3,c. Palmer,1975); Mission Hills CC, Rancho Mirage (a.New course, c.Palmer,1979).
COLORADO: Bear Creek GC, Golden (c.Palmer,1981); The Broadmoor GC, Colorado Springs (South course, c.Palmer,1976).
FLORIDA: Grenelefe G&RC, Haines City (a.East course,27,c.Palmer,1976); Palm Coast GC (a.18,c.Palmer,1980); Sawgrass GC, Ponte Vedra Beach (original 18,1974); Spessard Holland GC, Cocoa Beach (c.Palmer,1977); Suntree CC, Melbourne (a.18, c.Palmer,1981); Wildcat Run CC, Ft. Myers (c.Palmer,1981).
GEORGIA: The Landings at Skidaway Island (a.18, c.Palmer,1979).
HAWAII: Kapalua GC, Maui (Village course,c.Palmer,1980).
MARYLAND: Prince Georges G&CC, Mitchellville (new site,27,c.Palmer,1980).
UTAH: Jeremy Ranch GC, Salt Lake City (c.Palmer,1980).
CANADA: Whistler GC,Vancouver, B.C. (c.Palmer,1980).
JAPAN: Hiroshima Athletic CC (c.Palmer,1974); Iga Ueno CC, Nara, (c.Palmer,1974); Furano CC [formerly Kitanomine CC, c.Palmer,1975]; Manago CC, Tochigi (27,c.Palmer,1974); Niseko GC, Sapporo (c.Palmer,1981); Nishi Biwako GC, Osaka (c.Palmer,1974); Shimotsuke CC, Kanuma (c.Palmer,1974).
MEXICO: Nuevo Vallarta GC, Puerto Vallarta (27,c.Palmer,1980).
THAILAND: Bangpoo GC, Bangkok (c.Palmer,1981).
Courses remodeled by Edwin B. Seay:
ALABAMA: Anniston CC (1975).
COLORADO: Cherry Hills CC, Englewood (c.Palmer,1977); Denver CC (1975); Snowmass-at-Aspen (c.Palmer,1980).
FLORIDA: San Jose CC, Jacksonville (1977); Sawgrass GC, Ponte Vedra Beach (West course,1980).
PENNSYLVANIA: Allegheny CC, Pittsburgh (1976); Oakmont CC (c.Palmer,1978).

Donald R. Sechrest   (1933–   )
Born: St. Joseph, Missouri.
Don Sechrest received the B.S. degree in business in 1956 from Oklahoma State University where he had played on the golf team under Labron Harris, Sr. Turning professional upon graduation, Sechrest worked with his former coach at Oklahoma State in Stillwater for 10 years, and during that time tried his hand at the PGA Tour. In 1966 he laid out and supervised the building of a course for the Stillwater G&CC, and then served a short term as club pro. In 1968 Sechrest entered private practice as a golf course architect, based in Tulsa, Oklahoma.

Courses by Donald R. Sechrest:
IOWA: Ames G&CC.
KANSAS: Southwind CC, Garden City (1980).
MISSOURI: Loma Linda CC, Joplin (1978).
OKLAHOMA: Boiling Springs GC, Woodward; (The) Greens G&RC, Oklahoma City (1972); Heritage Hills GC, Claremont; Indian Springs CC, Broken Arrow (Gold course,1974); Meadowbrook CC, Tulsa (a.2nd 9); Miami G&CC (a.2nd 9); Potowatomi Tribal GC, Shawnee; Shangri-La CC, Afton (27,1971); Stillwater G&CC (1966).
TEXAS: Brownsville CC (1977); Monte Cristo CC, Edinburg (1974).
Courses Remodeled by Donald R. Sechrest:
MISSOURI: Greenbriar Hills CC, Kirkwood.
OKLAHOMA: Elk City G&CC; Fort Sill GC, Lawton: Muskogee CC (1970); Oklahoma City G&CC; Ponca City CC; Twin Hills G&CC, Oklahoma City.

Alberto Serra
Brazilian golf architect Alberto Serra redid the Sao Fernando GC in Sao Paulo in 1972 and planned the Asuncion GC in Paraguay.

Robert A. Simmons
Born: Camden, Indiana.
Robert Simmons became a caddy at the age of 9 at the Mississinewa CC. He later became

its caddymaster, assistant professional and finally, head pro. While at Mississinewa, he made scale model greens of famous golf holes as a hobby, and during the early 1950s laid out 3 courses in nearby Indiana communities.
In 1956 Simmons became a construction supervisor for golf architect Dick Wilson. He was responsible for constructing a number of outstanding Wilson designs including Moon Valley in Arizona, Bay Hill and Cypress Lakes in Florida, Coldstream in Ohio, Lyford Cay and Paradise Island in the Bahamas, and Royal Montreal in Canada. In 1961 Simmons entered private practice as a golf course architect.

Courses by Bob Simmons:
ALABAMA: Olympia Spa & CC, Dothan (1968).
FLORIDA: Atlantis CC (a.3rd 9,1973); Bay Hill Club, Orlando (a.Charger 9,1969); Orange Tree CC, Orlando (1972).
INDIANA: Arrowhead Park GC, Minster (1966); The Club of Prestwick, Danville (1975); The CC of Connersville (a.2nd 9,1962); County Lind and Sherman GC, Indianapolis; Green Acres CC, Kokomo (1967); Highland Lake GC, Richmond (1971); Hillview CC; Lafayette City GC (1974); Lafayette CC (Battleground course,1968); Lake Monroe GC, Bloomington (1973); Valle Vista CC, Greenwood.
KENTUCKY: Bent Creek CC, Louisville; Glenwood Hall CC, Perry Park.
OHIO: Salem CC (a.9,1967).
Courses Remodeled by Bob Simmons:
KENTUCKY: Idle Hour CC, Lexington.

Archibald Simpson
Born in Elie, Fife, Scotland, Archie Simpson and his five brothers learned golf at Carnoustie. He later designed Nairn GC (1887) and Murcar GC (27,1909), both in Scotland.

Thomas C. Simpson   (1877-1964)
Born: Winkley Hall Estate, Lancashire, England. Died: Basingstoke, Hampshire, England at age 87.
Tom Simpson, who came from a wealthy family, studied law at Trinity Hall, Cambridge, and was admitted to the bar in 1905. A scratch golfer, he was a member of the Oxford and Cambridge Golfing Society and played a great deal at Woking. There his interest in golf design developed as he observed the remodeling of the course by club members John Low and Stuart Paton, and on more than one occasion defended their advanced designs. Simpson began to develop particular ideas about course architecture himself, and by 1910 he had closed his legal practice and joined golf architect Herbert Fowler in the business.
After World War I, Simpson and Fowler were partners in a firm which for a short time included J.F. Abercrombie and A.C.M. Croome. Simpson handled most of the firm's work on the Continent, and his best designs can be found in France. In the 1920's Simpson hired Philip Mackenzie Ross on a whim to assist him in the construction of courses. By the late 20's Fowler and Simpson had split up, and Simpson made the talented and enterprising Ross a partner.
Always a colorful figure, Tom Simpson toured the English countryside in a chauffer-driven silver Rolls Royce and often appeared for site inspections in an embroidered cloak and beret. Although he experimented with golf holes, he believed the Old Course at St. Andrews to be the only enduring text on course design. He was well-known, however, for his excellent essays on the philosophy of golf architecture, and, in addition to numerous articles, wrote *The Architectural Side of Golf* with Herbert Newton Wethered (1929; 2nd edition, *Design for Golf*, 1952) and contributed to *The Game of Golf* (1931) and *Golf Courses: Design, Construction and Upkeep* (1933; 2nd edition, 1950). A consummate artist, Simpson illustrated his works with ink sketches and color washes, and wrote and illustrated *Modern Etchings and Their Collectors* in 1919. He also practiced silk embroidery.
Simpson prided himself on supervising the construction of his designs, and as a result was not as prolific as some of his contemporaries. He retired from active course design with the outbreak of World War II. After the War he continued to write about the subject but did no further work in the field, and his final years were spent in seclusion at his estate in Hampshire.

Courses by Tom Simpson:
BELGIUM: Keerbergen GC; Royal Antwerp GC, Kapellenbos, Antwerp (r.18,a.9,1924, c.P.M. Ross); Royal GC des Fagnes, Spa, Balmoral (c.P.M. Ross); Royal GC du Sart-Tilman, Liege.
ENGLAND; Berkshire GC, Ascot (Blue and Red courses,c.Fowler,1928); Bootle GC, Lancashire; Carlton GC, Nottinghamshire; Keighley GC, Utley Yorkshire; New Zealand GC, Byfleet,Surrey (new site,1931); Windlesham Moor GC.
FRANCE: Baron Edward de Rothchild Estate GC; Baron Henri de Rothchild Estate GC; Comte de Rougemont Estate GC; Duc de Gramont Estate GC; GC d'Hardelot, Boulogne (c.P.M. Ross); G de d'Hossegor; G de Chantilly (27); G de Chiberta, Biarritz (1925); G de Dieppe; G de Fontainebleau; G de International Club du Lys, Chantilly (27,1927); G de Morfontaine, Senlis (27,1927); G de Voisins; New Golf Club, Deauville (original 18, 1929,c.P.M.Ross).
IRELAND: Carlow GC.
SCOTLAND: Cruden Bay G&CC, Aberdeen (27,c.Fowler).
SPAIN: Real CC de San Sebastian; Royal Madrid GC. (Add 18).
Courses Remodeled by Tom Simpson:
BELGIUM: Royal GC de Belfique, Brussels.
ENGLAND: Ashridge GC, Berkhamsted, Hertfordshire; Hayling GC, Hampshire; Liphook GC; Royal Lytham & St. Annes GC; Sunningdale GC (New course), North Foreland, Kent (c.Fowler & Morrison).
IRELAND: Ballybunion GC, County Kerry (1936); County Louth GC, Baltray, (1938).
SCOTLAND: Muirfield GC, Cullane, East Lothian.
SPAIN: Real Club de la Puerto de Hierro, Madrid (1938).
SWITZERLAND: Zurich G&CC (1935).
WALES: Royal Porthcawl GC, Glamorgan.

Al Smith

Seattle-based golf course designer Al Smith had constructed courses for several Pacific Northwest architects in the 1920's and 1930's, including A.V. Macan. In the Fifties Smith designed several courses on his own in the state of Washington.

Courses by Al Smith;

WASHINGTON: Brae Burn CC, Bellevue; Brookdale CC, Tacoma; Cross Roads Par 3 GC, Seattle; Everett Muni (1971); Glendale CC, Bellevue; Glendale G&CC, Bothel; Lake Samanish State Park GC, Issaquah (1958); Maplewood CC; North Shore CC, Tacoma (1962); Redmond Golf Links; Tam O'Shanter CC, Bellevue; Twin Lakes CC, Tacoma; Wayne Public GC, Bothel (executive course).

Ernest E. Smith

(1901–   )

Born: Vestal, New York.

Ernest Smith began caddying at age 9 in Binghampton, New York. At age 20 he became an assistant professional at the Binghampton CC, and a professional at 25. His first design was the Geneganslet GC in Greene, New York, completed in 1926. He then helped the Endicott-Johnson Shoe Co. route and consruct a company course, the En-Joie CC, which opened in 1927.

In the early 1930's Smith designed and constructed the Ely Park GC in Binghampton, and remained as its pro/superintendent. Although he did no further golf design work for some 25 years, he proved himself an able teacher and avid promoter of the game. He served as a Vice President of the National PGA in 1941, and was on the executive board of the New York PGA for 28 years.

In the early 1950's Smith wintered in Florida where his interest in course design was renewed. He received commissions on a few Florida projects, and when he retired from Ely Park in 1963 Smith moved to that state to practice golf architecture full-time. He remained active through the late 1960's.

Courses by Ernest E. Smith:

FLORIDA: Hobe Sound CC; Riomar CC, Vero Beach (a.2nd 9,1964); Selva Marina CC, Atlantic Beach (1958); Seven Lakes CC, Fort Myers (Executive course,1971); Silver Lake G&CC, Leesburg (1962); South Seas Plantation GC, Captiva Island (9,1969).

NEW YORK: Ely Park GC, Binghampton (1933;a.par 3 course,1962); En-Joie CC, Endicott (1927); Geneganslet GC, Grene (1926); Kass Inn & CC, Margaretville (a.par 3 course,1964).

Courses Remodeled by Ernest E. Smith:

FLORIDA: Martin County G&CC, Stuart.

Orrin Edward Smith   (1883–1958)

Born: Southington, Connecticut. Died: New Britain, Connecticut at age 75.

Orrin Smith began his career as a construction superintendent for Willie Park, Jr. on the Shuttle Meadow CC in New Britain, Connecticut. He was later associated with Donald Ross on several projects, including the Longmeadow (Massachusetts) CC, both before and after beginning his own design practice.

Smith entered private practice as a course designer around 1925 and remained active through the mid-1950's, based in Hartford, Connecticut. He was influential in the early design career of James Harrison. He also trained golf architect William Mitchell, as well as Albert Zikorus, who took over Smith's practice on his retirement around 1955.

Courses by Orrin E. Smith:

ARKANSAS: Melbourne CC.

CONNECTICUT: Birchwood CC, Westport (9); Deercrest CC, Greenwich; East Hartford GC; Edgewood CC, Cromwell; Hyfield CC, Middlebury; Longshore Beach Club, Westport; Louis Stoner Private Course, West Hartford; Rock-Rimmon CC, Stamford (9); Stanley CC, New Britain (9); Suffield CC (9); Torrington CC; Tumblebrook, Bloomfield; Woodbridge CC.

MAINE: Waterville CC (original 9).

MASSACHUSETTS: Duamyre CC, Enfield (9,n.l.e.); Framingham CC (9); Packachug Hills CC, Worcester (9); Westover AFB GC, Chicopee (c.Zikorus).

MISSOURI: J.J. Lynn Private Course, Kansas City (9).

NEW YORK: Embassy Club, Armonk; Empire State, Spring Valley (27); Hilly Dale, Carmel; Plandome CC, Long Island; Riverdale CC, River Vale; Signal Hill CC, Armonk; Willowdale CC, Buffalo (9).

PENNSYLVANIA: Baldoc CC, Erwin; Pennhurst CC, Turtle Creek (n.l.e.).

Courses Remodeled by Orrin E. Smith:

CONNECTICUT: Farmington CC; Hartford CC: Rockledge, West Hartford; Salmon Brook CC, Granby (n.l.e.).

KANSAS: Wichita CC.

MASSACHUSETTS: Belmont CC.

MISSOURI: Joplin CC.

NEBRASKA: East Ridge CC, Lincoln (n.l.e.).

OHIO: Columbus CC; Zanesville CC.

William "Willie" Smith   (1872–1916)

Born: Carnoustie, Scotland. Died: Mexico City, Mexico at age 44.

Willie Smith, member of a famous Carnoustie golfing family, won the U.S. Open in 1899. Around that time he laid out Mexico's first golf course, the 9-hole San Pedro CC.

Smith eventually settled in Mexico, planning the first version of the CC of Mexico City and the Chapultepec CC. After he died in the Revolution of 1914–16, his brother Alex completed construction of Chapultepec in 1921.

Arthur Jack Snyder   (1917–   ) ASGCA

Born: Rosedale, Pennsylvania

Arthur Jack Snyder received a B.Sc. degree in landscape architecture from Pennsylvania State University in 1939. From 1939 to 1955 he owned two landscape architectural firms,

Arthur J. Snyder Co. and Snyder, Inc. During World War II he was involved in defense design and for a brief period afterwards in land surveying.

Snyder was one of six brothers, all of whom became course superintendents, who were trained by their father, Arthur Snyder. The senior Snyder had himself been trained by Loeffler and McGlynn at Oakmont. Arthur Jack served as superintendent at Oakmont in 1951-52, and during that time rebuilt the "awful" 8th green and adjusted positions (but not shapes) of several others. From 1956 to 1959 he was superintendent at White Mountain CC, Pinetop, Arizona.

Snyder entered private practice as a golf architect in 1958. Prior to that time he had been involved with course remodeling since 1930 and had designed one course at Jane Lew, West Virginia (n.l.e.) as early as 1940.

Courses by Arthur Jack Snyder:

ARIZONA: Apache CC [now Golden Hills], Mesa (1960); Apache Wells CC, Mesa (East 9,1963); Arizona City CC; Black Canyon GC, Phoenix (9,1961); (The) Boulders GC, Carefree (East 9,1973); Camelback GC, Scottsdale (a.18,1978); Canon del Oro CC, Sedona (9,1961); Casa Grande Muni (9,1977); Concho Valley CC (9,1970); Coronado GC, Scottsdale (9,1965); Desert Sands Exec. GC; CC of Green Valley (South 9,1963;North 9,1965); Hospitality Muni, Winslow (9,1979); Ironwood GC (9); Lake Montezuma G&CC, Rimrock (9,1960;9,1962); London Bridge GC, Lake Havasu (a.9,1979); Mountain Shadows CC, Scottsdale (1961); Poco Diablo GC, Sedona (9 Par 3,1966); Santa Cruz Park Muni; Show Low CC (9,1961); Silverbell Muni, Tucson (1979); Tempe Muni (1974); White Mountain CC, Pinetop (South 9,1959); Wigwam CC, Litchfield Park (r.9,a.9,1961 n.l.e.).

CALIFORNIA: Kern City GC (North 9,1961); Stockdale CC (Original 9).

HAWAII: Kaanapali Kai GC, Lahaina, Maui (exec,n.l.e.); Royal Kaanapali GC, Lahaina, Maui (South course,1976); Seamountain Ninole GC, Ka'u (1973); Volcano G&CC, Kilauea Volcano (r.9,a.9,1969); Wailea GC, Maui (Blue course,1971;Orange course,1977).

NEVADA: Carson City Muni (1975); Eagle Valley Muni, Carson City (1977); Ruby View Muni, Elko (9,1967;9,1969).

NEW MEXICO: Arroyo del Oso Muni, Albuquerque (1965); Civitan Park Muni, Farmington (9,1965); Scott Park Muni, Silver City (9,1962).

UTAH: Copper GC (a.9); Montecello GC (9).

VIRGINIA: Cedar Point Club, Norfolk (1963).

Courses Remodeled by Arthur Jack Snyder:

ARIZONA: Tucson CC (1972)I.

NEW MEXICO: Sunport Muni, Albuquerque (9,1978).

HAWAII: Makaha Inn G&CC (3, 1981).

Gary L. Sorenson

Gary Sorenson received the degree of Doctor of Environmental Design from Texas A & M University in 1976. The same year, he published (privately) *The Architecture of Golf*, a work dealing both with the history of course design and with the art itself. Some readers felt this remarkable treatise presented a perceptive view of the future of golf architecture.

Daniel G. "Des" Soutar

Trained at Carnoustie, Scottish professional Des Soutar emigrated to Sydney, Australia where he became a leading golfer and, in 1906, authored the book *The Australian Golfer*. In 1925 he planned Kingston Heath GC in Melbourne and Christchurch CC (new site) in New Zealand.

William J. Spear   ASGCA

William Spear trained under golf architect Robert Bruce Harris, entering private practice in 1960.

Courses by William J. Spear:

GEORGIA: Turtle Cove GC, Atlanta (9,1971).

ILLINOIS: Arrowhead CC, Chillicothe (9,1960); Crawford County CC, Robinson (9,1965); Danville Elks Club (1969); Effingham CC (9,1968); Hawthorn Ridge GC, Aledo (1977); Highland Springs CC, Rock Island (1968); Highland Woods GC, Hoffman Estates (1975); Lake Taylorville GC (1968); Lakewood G&CC, Havana (9,1966); Little Tam GC, Niles (9,1970); Marengo Ridge GC (9,1964); Midland CC, Kewanee (1970); Park Place GC, DeKalb (9,1965); Randall Oaks GC, Dundee (1965); Renwood CC, Grays Lake (9,1977); Rock River CC, Sterling (9,1966); St. Elmo GC (9,1969); Swan Hills GC, Avon (1971).

INDIANA: Elbel Park GC, South Bend (1964); Forest Park GC, Valparaiso (9,1971); Playland Park Golf Center, South Bend (9,1962).

IOWA: Palmer Hills GC, Bettendorf (1974).

MICHIGAN: Brookwood GC, Buchanan (9,1964); Grand Prairie GC, Kalamazoo (9,1962).

NORTH DAKOTA: Souris Valley GC, Minot (1967).

OHIO: Auglaize CC, Defiance (9,1963); Edgecreek GC, Van Wert (1960).

WISCONSIN: Hickory Grove CC, Fennimore (9,1966); Voyager Village GC, Danbury (1971).

Bert Stamps (1911–   )

Born: Visalia, California.

Bert Stamps began as a caddie at the old Rancho CC in Los Angeles. An excellent golfer, he turned professional at age eighteen but was soon reinstated as an amateur, winning seven local tournaments in succession by one point. He again turned pro in 1932 and went to work in a pro shop. He was admitted to the PGA of America in 1938.

Stamps was stationed with the U. S. Army in the Far East during World War II. While there he won the Japanese Open in Osaka. Following military service, he became head professional at the Cleveland (Tennessee) CC. Between 1945 and 1948, he competed sporadically on the PGA Tour and had his first course design experience, remodeling the Cleveland layout. He was soon hired to plan a new course in Baton Rouge, Louisiana; and he continued to practice golf design on a part-time basis in California, where he returned to serve as a club professional in the 1950s.

Stamps was chosen Northern California PGA Professional of the Year in 1974. The same

214

year he retired to become professional emeritus at the Rancho Murieta CC near Sacramento, a course of his own design and construction.

Courses by Bert Stamps:
CALIFORNIA: Airways GC, Fresno (1951); Belmont CC, Fresno (1956); Cameron Park CC, Shingle Springs (1965); Camino Heights GC, Delano GC (9); DeLaveaga CC, Santa Cruz; Elkhorn GC, Lodi (1962); Kings County CC, Hanford (a.2nd 9,1961); Lawrence Links CC; Oak Ridge GC, San Jose (1967); Paso-Robles G&CC (1960); Rancho Murieta GC, Sloughhouse (North course,1971); San Luis Obispo CC (1959); Woodbridge G&CC, Lodi (1974).
LOUISIANA: Baton Rouge CC (1950).
NEVADA: Sahara/Nevada CC, Las Vegas (1962); Tropicana CC, Las Vegas (1961).
Courses Remodeled by Bert Stamps:
CALIFORNIA: Rio Del Mar GC [formerly Aptos Seascape GC], Aptos (1957).
TENNESSEE: Cleveland CC (1947).

Donald M. A. Steel (1937–   )   BAGCA
Born: Hillingdon near London, England.
D. M. A. Steel attended Fettes College, Edinburgh, and graduated with a degree in agriculture from Cambridge University. In 1965 he joined the golf architecture firm of Cotton (C.K.), Pennink, Lawrie and Partners, Ltd. as a consultant trainee, becoming a partner in 1971.

Well known as a rugby and cricket player, Steel also became a scratch golfer and represented England in international matches. He served as golf correspondent for the *London Sunday Telegraph*, and edited *The Golfer's Bedside Book* (two editions), *The Golf Course Guide* (3 editions of a detailed list of British courses) and *The Encyclopedia of Golf* (with Peter Ryde and Herbert Warren Wind). He was also honorary secretary and treasurer of the British Association of Golf Course Architects. In 1980 he assembled Guiness's *Golf Facts and Feats*.

Courses by Donald M.A. Steel:
ENGLAND: Beacon Park, West Lancashire; Blackhills near Dudley; Boothferry; Bradley Park GC, Huddersfield; Bushey (9); Carlisle Race Course GC; Farnham Park at Stoke Poges (1st 9); Harrey Park at Bushey; Harrow School GC (9); Ingol at Preston; Woburn (Dutchess course, completed after death of Charles Lawrie).
SCOTLAND: Deeside GC, Aberdeen (a.9).
Courses Remodeled by D.M. Steel
SCOTLAND: Machrie GC.

Wayne E. Stiles (1884–1953   ASGCA: Charter Member
Born: Boston, Massachusetts. Died: Wellesley, Massachusetts, at age 68.
Wayne Stiles did not train formally for a career in landscape architecture but began working at age eighteen as an office boy for landscape designer Franklin Brett. After being made a draftsman and finally a junior partner, Stiles opened his own landscape design and town planning office in Boston in 1915. He branched into golf design in the early 1920s.

Stiles formed a partnership with John R. Van Kleek in 1924. The firm of Stiles and Van Kleek had offices in Boston, Massachusetts; New York; and St. Petersburg, Florida, and concentrated mainly on golf courses, accompanying subdivisions and town planning. Over the years associates of the firm included: professional golfer Walter Hagen, who was a consultant in course design, particularly at Pasadena CC near St. Petersburg; Thomas D. Church and Butler Sturdivant, nationally known landscape architects; and W. Bruce Matthews, later a prominent course designer.

The firm dissolved before the Depression, as the real estate boom faded in Florida; but Stiles remained in practice almost exclusively as a golf course architect. During the Depression, he supervised CCC projects for the National Park Service. After World War II he was active again.

Stiles served as president of the Boston Society of Landscape Architects for several years and was a member of the American Society of Landscape Architects.

Courses by Wayne E. Stiles (Courses from 1924–1930 with J.R. Van Kleek):
ALABAMA: Municipal Club, Birmingham.
CONNECTICUT: Paul Block Private Course, Greenwich (9).
FLORIDA: Highland Park GC; Lake Wales (1925); Holly Hill G&CC, Davenport; Jovita CC, San Antonio; Palmetto CC; Pasadena CC, St. Petersburg (c.Hagen); Tarpon Springs Muni.
GEORGIA: Glen Arven CC, Thomasville (1929); Skywater CC, Albany (c.Kirkwood).
MAINE: Augusta CC, Augusta (a.9,1926); Boothbay Harbor CC (9); Brunswick GC (Original 9); Prouts Neck GC (r.9,a.9); Riverside Portland Muni (Original 18); Wawenock GC, Damariscotta (9).
MASSACHUSETTS: Albemarle CC, West Newton; Commonwealth CC, Newton; Duxbury GC (9); Franconia Muni, Springfield (1930); Haverhill CC; Marlboro CC (9); Marshfield CC (9,1922;9,1931); Memorial Muni, Springfield (n.l.e.); Needham CC (9); Oak Hill CC, Fitchburg (9); Oak Ridge Muni, Brockton (9); Pine Brook Valley CC, Weston; Putterham Meadows Muni, Brookline; South Shore CC, Hingham; Stony Brae GC, Quincy; Taconic GC, Williamstown (1927); Thorny Lea GC, Brockton (1925); Unicorn CC, Stoneham; Wahconah CC, Dalton (9); Weld GC; Wyndhurst Club, Lenox; Cranwell School GC, Lenox.
MISSOURI: Norwood Hills CC [formerly North Hills CC], St. Louis (36,1922).
NEW HAMPSHIRE: Cocheco CC, Dover (Original 9); Dover CC (9); Hooper GC, Walpole (9); Kearsage CC, North Conway (9); Laconia CC (9); Mojalaki CC, Franklin; Nashua CC; Wentworth Hall GC, Jackson.
NEW JERSEY: Brigantine Beach GC; Wildwood CC.
NEW YORK: Woodstock CC; I.B.M. CC, Endicott.
NORTH CAROLINA: Hamilton Lakes CC; Lake Lure CC, Chimney Rock.
SOUTH CAROLINA: Hartford Estate GC, Charleston.
VERMONT: Barre CC (9); Brattleboro CC (r.9,a.9); Rutland CC (r.9,a.9); Woodstock CC (1924).
Courses Remodeled by Wayne E. Stiles:
MAINE: Northhaven GC (9).
MASSACHUSETTS: CC of Pittsfield (1932); Franklin CC; Monoosnock CC, Leominster (9); Sharon CC (9); Wellesley CC (9); Wollaston GC; Woods Hole CC.
NEW HAMPSHIRE: Crawford Notch CC.

Earl Stone (1926–   )
Born: Alachua, Florida.
Earl Stone graduated from Auburn University in 1949 after service with the U. S. Navy during World War II. He worked in the electrical appliance business and as a heating and air conditioning contractor until the mid-1950s, when he began installing irrigation systems on golf courses. This led to jobs rebuilding greens and in 1958 to a commission to design and build an entire course. An admirer of golf architect Dick Wilson's work, Stone designed numerous courses in the Southeast over the next twenty years.

Courses by Earl Stone:
ALABAMA: Bessemer Muni (1972); Camden State Park GC (1970); CC of Mobile (a.3rd 9,1966); Deer Run GC; Gulf Shores GC (1965); Gulf State Park GC, Gulf Shores (1972); Holly Hills CC, Bay Minette (9,1966); Joe Wheeler State Park GC, Rogersville (1974); Lake Forest CC, Daphne (r.9,a.9,1978); Little Mountain State Park GC, Guntersville (1972); McFarland Park GC, Florence (1973); Moulton Muni (9,1980); Oak Mountain State Park GC, Pelham (1972); Skyline CC, Mobile (a.3rd 9,1974); Southmoor CC [formerly Cypress Creek CC], Mobile (1971).
ARKANSAS: Rivercliff GC, Bull Shoals (9,1977).
FLORIDA: Indian Bayou G&CC, Destin (1978).
MISSISSIPPI: Briarwood CC, Meridian (1967); Broadwater Beach Hotel GC, Biloxi (r.Sea course,1962;a.Par 3 Fun course and Sun course,1968); Diamondhead Y&CC, Bay St. Louis (a.3rd 9,1977); Gulfport Naval Air Station GC (9,1978); Hickory Hills CC, Gautier (1965); Pine Burr CC, Wiggens (9,1977); Rainbow Bay GC (formerly Edgewater GC), Biloxi (r.12,a.6,1976); Riverside Muni, Jackson (9,1974,n.l.e.); Waynesboro (9,1960).
BAHRAIN: Bahrain Equestrian & Racing Club, Manama (1980).

David Strath (1840–1879)
Born: St. Andrews, Scotland. Died: En route to Australia, at age 39.
David Strath served as greenkeeper at North Berwick from 1876 to 1878. He formalized the course and extended it to eighteen holes, and his revisions to the Perfection (#14) and the Redan (#15) made these holes famous worldwide. The Redan's concept has been adapted repeatedly on courses throughout the world.

Concerning this classic hole, golf architect David Gill wrote: "... the wind and the contours of apron and green determine the stroke to the pin and club to be used. With the wind directly in one's face, the play for a scratch golfer would be directly over the bunker to the pin. With a following wind the play would be a slight draw to the opening of the green on the right with the player relying on the contours of apron and green to guide the ball to the pin. With a wind from the left quarter the golfer can simply play the pin with a slight draw. But with a wind from the right the contours must be relied upon to carry the ball to the cup. It is an intriguing hole that plays differently with each season and wind shift." [7]
[7] Letter, David Gill to Geoffrey S. Cornish, January 10, 1980 (unpublished).

Herbert Bertram Strong (1879–1944)
Born: Ramsgate, Kent, England. Died: Fort Pierce, Florida, at age 65.
Herbert Strong began his golf career as professional and club maker at St. Georges GC, Sandwich, Kent, England. In 1905 he emigrated to New York, becoming professional at the Apawamis Club in Rye. Six years later he moved to the Inwood GC in Far Rockaway and while there, remodeled the course. This led to other design jobs; and within a few years, Strong was devoting virtually full time to golf course architecture.

Throughout his career, Strong did his own surveying and usually remained at the sites to supervise construction. He was assisted on some of his later jobs by younger brother Leonard, who later became a prominent course superintendent. Leonard claimed that Strong had invented the first golf pull cart in the 1920s, but someone else had obtained a patent on such a device before he applied.

Like many architects of that era, Herbert Strong was a victim of the Depression. He lost a fortune when the golf course market collapsed, although he remained in the golf business until the end. In his day he had been a fine player and was considered among the longest drivers, having nearly a dozen holes-in-one to his credit, including one of 320 yards. He was a charter member of the PGA and served as its first treasurer from 1917 to 1919.

Courses by Herbert Bertram Strong:
FLORIDA: Clearwater CC (1920); Fort Pierce CC; Lakewood CC, St. Petersburg; Ponte; Vedra Club (original 18,1932); Vero Beach CC.
MARYLAND: Aviation Y&CC, Leonardstown; South Sherwood Forest GC, Annapolis; Woodholme CC, Pikesville.
NEW JERSEY: Linwood CC; Mountain Ridge CC, West Caldwell.
NEW YORK: Beacon CC (r.9,a.9,1929); Engineers CC, Roslyn (new site,1918); Huntington Bay Club; Metropolis CC, White Plains; Sayville CC.
OHIO: Canterbury CC, Shaker Heights (1922); Lake Forest CC, Hudson.
PENNSYLVANIA: Saucon Valley CC, Bethlehem (Saucon course, 1922).
VERMONT: Lake Shore CC, Burlington (9).
VIRGINIA: Army/Navy GC, Arlington (original 18).
WEST VIRGINIA: Guyen G&CC, Huntington.
CANADA: Club Laval Sur Le Lac, Villa de Laval, Quebec; Kent Links, Montgomery Falls; Lakeview CC, Toronto, Ontario; Manoir Richelieu GC, Murray Bay, Quebec (1927); St. Andrew CC, Saint-Andre Est, Quebec.
CUBA: Veradera Beach CC, Havana (n.l.e.)
Courses Remodeled by Herbert Bertram Strong:
NEW JERSEY: Knickerbocker CC, Tenafly.
NEW YORK: Deepdale CC, Great Neck (n.l.e.); Inwood CC, Far Rockaway (1911); Nassau CC, Glen Cove.
PENNSYLVANIA: Harrisburg CC.

215

J. Hamilton Stutt (1924–   ) BAGCA: Founding Member; Chairman, 1975; President, 1980
Born: Scotland.

J. Hamilton Stutt attended Glasgow Academy and received a B.Sc. degree in mathematics and botany from St. Andrews University, where he was a member of the golf and tennis teams. As a boy, he accompanied his father, John R. Stutt, and business associate James Braid, to many construction sites. Following service with the Royal Air Force during World War II, he entered his father's firm, John R. Stutt, Golf and Sports Ground Construction. At the same time, he began studying civil engineering and surveying at Strathclyde University.

Over the next fifteen years Stutt constructed many golf courses, several of them planned by golf architects Philip Mackenzie Ross and J. S. M. Morrison. Ross and Morrison instructed and encouraged Stutt in course design, and by 1949 he had begun doing some work on his own. In the course of the next decade, he gradually gave up the family construction business to devote full time to golf course architecture.

Stutt's courses were characterized by bold, sweeping features with emphasis on appearance and natural beauty. He spent considerable time on the initial layout plan in order to make as much use as possible of natural features in the design. Throughout his design career, he limited the number of commissions accepted so that he could deal personally with all aspects of design and supervision from beginning to end. He never worked with partners or regular assistants.

Stutt was the author of "Restoration of Derelict Lands for Golf," published by the Golf Development Council (3, The Quadrant, Richmond, Surrey, England) and sponsored by the British Sports Council. He was a member of the Royal and Ancient; captain of Parkstone Golf Club, Dorset; and an honorary member of several other clubs. In addition to his native tongue he spoke fluent French, German, Spanish and Norwegian, and by 1979 had designed courses in the British Isles, France, Spain, Scandinavia and the Middle East.

Courses by J. Hamilton Stutt:
EIRE: Wexford (9).
ENGLAND: Ashley Wood, Blandford; Aycliffe New Town, Durham (27); Blyth, Northumberland (Colliery restoration); Bramshott Hill, Hythe; Carlyon Bay, Cornwall; Cowes, Isle of Wight (New 9); Ferndown, Dorset (a.9); Launceston, Cornwall (a.9); Marlborough, Wilts (a.9); Meon Valley G&CC, near Wickham, Hampshire; Middlesbrough, Yorkshire; Ramsey, Huntingdonshire; St. Mellion G&CC, Plymouth; Solent Meads, Bournemouth; Ventnor, Isle of Wight (9); Vivary Park, Taunton.
FRANCE: Corsica (Par 3); International Club Du Lys, Paris; Normandie (9); Piencourt, Normandie.
LEBANON: Delhamyeh CC, Beirut.
SCOTLAND: Cumbernauld New Town; Fort William; Gleddoch House CC, Firth of Clyde; Glenrothes; Irvine, Ayrshire; Kirkcaldy, Fifeshire; Murrayshall G&CC, Perth; Prestwick St. Cuthbert, Ayrshire; Ardees GC, Ayrshire; Inverurie GC.
SPAIN: Colorado on Costa Del Sol; Costa Brava GC, San Feliu; Coto de Donana, Seville.
Courses Remodeled by J. Hamilton Stutt:
EIRE: Dundalk; Rosslare.
ENGLAND: Ashridge, Herts; Brockenhurst, Hampshire; Came Down, Dorchester; Lee-on-the-Solent, Hampshire; Morpeth, Northumberland; Mullion, Cornwall; Parkstone, Dorset; Royal Eastbourne; Ryde GC, Isle of Wight; St. Georges Hill, Surrey; Shanklin & Sandown, Isle of Wight; S. Herts GC, London; Whitby, Yorkshire.
SCOTLAND: Colville Park GC, Motherwell, Lanarkshire; Monifieth, Carnoustie; plus various Scottish Tourist Board courses.
WALES: Pyle & Kenfig, Porthcawl.

John R. Stutt (1897–   )
Born: Paisley, Scotland.

In 1923 John Stutt founded the landscape and sports ground construction firm of John R. Stutt Ltd. Soon branching into golf, Stutt had built some eighty-two courses by 1939, many to the plans of James Braid with whom he had become associated in 1923.

The Braid–Stutt association lasted until Braid's death in 1950. In the beginning Braid did all the course planning, but he encouraged Stutt to take on some of the design work as well as construction. Eventually, Stutt became architect and builder of numerous courses of his own, in addition to constructing those of Braid and other architects, including John Morrison and Theodore Moon.

Courses by John R. Stutt: (Included are courses where Stutt participated to a greater or lesser degree in the design or redesign.)
BRITISH ISLES: Arcott Hall; Bangor, Ulster; Belle Isle; Boat of Garten, Inverness; Buchanan Castle; Countess Wear GC, Island of Lewis; Eastwood; Finchley; Hainault Forest; Hamilton Park; Hilton Park; Howth, Dublin; Kedleston; Kingswood; Mullingar; Musselburgh Boat of Garten; North Cliffe; Orsett; Oswestry; Parkstone; Prestwick GC (a.4); Ramsey, Isle of Man; Scarborough; Stornoway, Island of Lewis; Tamworth GC at Birmingham; Tiverton; Torquay, Devon; Truro, Cornwall; Welshpool.
Courses Remodeled by John R. Stutt:
BRITISH ISLES: Carnoustie (for 1937 Open); Rosemount.
SCOTLAND: Blairgowrie GC (Rosemount Course).

John Sutherland

John Sutherland served as secretary of Dornoch GC in Scotland for fifty years from the 1880s into the late 1920s. He also wrote a weekly article on golf for the *London Daily News* from 1902 into the 1920s. A lifelong student of course architecture and greenkeeping, he exerted an enormous influence on Doanld Ross during his years as greenkeeper and professional at Dornoch. The two made a point of walking the course every evening to see where improvements could be made. According to Donald Grant, who knew them both, Sutherland and Ross were constantly experimenting with grass and often discussed "what constitutes a good golf course." [1]

Sutherland also did some designing on his own. He laid out a private course for his friend Andrew Carnegie, the American steel magnate, at Carnegie's Scottish estate, Skibo Castle.

He also revised Tom Morris's nine at Dornoch, added a second nine and planned several other links in the northern counties of Scotland, including one version of Tain GC in Rossshire. J. H. Taylor collaborated with Sutherland in planning changes to several holes at Dornoch.
[1] Donald Grant, *Donald Ross of Pinehurst and Royal Dornoch*, Golspie, Scotland: The Sutherland Press.(1973) p. 15.

Philip Tattersfield

A landscape architect based in Vancouver, British Columbia, Philip Tattersfield designed or redesigned several courses in the 1970s in collaboration with famed Canadian professional golfer Stanley Leonard. By the early 1980s his firm, Tattersfield Associates, had several additional courses in collaboration with Leonard under construction or in the planning stages.
Courses by Philip Tattersfield: See Stanley Leonard.

John Henry Taylor (1871–1963)
Born: Devonshire, England. Died: Devonshire, England, at age 92.

John Henry Taylor, one of British golf's "Great Triumvirate," originally trained as a gardener at the boyhood home of Horace Hutchinson. He served as assistant greenkeeper at Westward Ho! and later as professional and greenkeeper at Burnham in Somerset, Winchester, Wimbledon, and for many years at Royal Mid Surrey. He won the British Open five times, as well as many other major championships.

Taylor used his enormous influence to promote public golf courses in England. He had laid out several courses before World War I and continued to plan new ones as part of a design and build partnership formed with Frederick G. Hawtree. Founded in 1924, the firm of Hawtree and Taylor was active until World War II.

Taylor had little formal education, having left school by age eleven; but he was an avid reader and insisted on writing his memoirs, *Golf, My Life's Work*, without the assistance of a ghost writer.

Courses by John Henry Taylor: (For courses after 1924, see Frederick G. Hawtree.)
ENGLAND: Chadwell Springs, Herts (9); Clevedon, Avon (1909); Eastbourne Downs, Sussex; Hainault Forest GC, Essex (1920); Heaton Park, Manchester; Norfolk GC; Queens Park GC, Bournemouth (1905); Seaford GC, Sussex (1906); Sidmouth, Devon; West Wiltshire (1898); Willingdon GC, Sussex.
Courses Remodeled by John Henry Taylor:
ENGLAND: Aldeburgh GC; Morton Hall (1906); Notts GC (a.bunkers); Royal Mid Surrey (1918).
SCOTLAND: Royal Dornoch (1907).
WALES; Ashburnham GC (1914).

Felix Teran
See Jaime Saenz

Alec Ternyei, born Elek Viktor Ternyey (1909–   )
Born: Briarcliff, New York.

The son of Hungarian immigrants, Elek Ternyey became a caddie at age nine and within a year was working for the club professional, cleaning up after club-making sessions. By observing the club maker and by salvaging old parts, Ternyey soon became adept at club making and repaired many a club for fellow caddies. Leaving high school at the age of sixteen, Ternyey turned professional and worked as an apprentice to Englewood (N.J.) CC professional Cyril Walker. He became a member of the PGA of America at eighteen and in the manner of star golfer Gene Sarazen, modified his name to "Alec Ternyei." The "Alec," he once explained, had a Scottish ring; and the "Ternyei" was a concession to those who constantly misspelled his last name.

After stints at Knickerbocker CC and Maidstone CC, Ternyei got his first head professional job in 1931 at the Rivervale CC in New Jersey. Over the next twenty-five years he worked as professional at several New Jersey clubs, playing in local and regional PGA events and earning a fine reputation as an expert club maker. He also served in the Air Force during World War II.

In the late 1950s Ternyei designed and built his first golf course. He resigned his professional duties in the 1960s to devote his full energies to golf architecture and prided himself on the fact that he personally constructed the dozen courses he designed in the New Jersey area during that period. In 1970 Ternyei retired to a teaching professional position in Florida.
Courses by Alec Ternyei:
FLORIDA: Crystal Lago CC, Pompano Beach.
NEW JERSEY: Beacon Hill CC, Atlantic Highlands (1962); Beaver Brook GC, Clinton (1965); Glenhurst CC, Watchung (1966); Green Pond GC (9,1964); High Mountain CC, Franklin Lakes (1968); The Pines GC, Emerson (1963); Princeton Hills Golf Academy, Princeton (1970).
Courses Remodeled by Elek Viktor Ternyey:
NEW JERSEY: Englewood CC (1968).
PENNSYLVANIA: Winding Brook CC (formerly Atzinachson CC), Milton (a.2,1957).

David C. Thomas (1934–   )
well-known Britisher golfer David Thomas collaborated with Peter Alliss in course design after planning the Chapel-en-le-Frith GC in England on his own.

George Clifford Thomas, Jr. (1873–1932)
Born: Philadelphia, Pennsylvania. Died: Beverly Hills, California, at age 58.

George C. Thomas, Jr., scion of a prominent Philadelphia family, was educated at Episcopal

Academy and at the University of Pennsylvania. He worked with his father in the banking firm of Drexel & Co. until 1907, but his early avocation was gardening. He was a nationally recognized authoriy on the care and breeding of roses and wrote several books about them.

Thomas was a marginal golfer but was interested in the landscaping aspects of golf course design. His first course, a nine-hole layout at Marion, Massachusetts (not Kittansett), was designed in the early 1900s. Thomas went on to design other courses in the East and to study the various techniques of prominent architects. He worked as a committeeman with Donald Ross at Flourtown and Sunnybrook in Pennsylvania, and with Tillinghast on a second course for the Philadelphia Cricket Club. He also observed the progress of his friend Hugh Wilson at Merion and of George Crump at Pine Valley. In 1908 Thomas completed the Mount Airy CC (now the Whitemarsh Valley CC) built on his family's estate at Chestnut Hill, Pennsylvania. The family home served for years as the clubhouse.

During World War I, Thomas served in Europe with the U. S. Army Air Corps as captain of a unit rumored to have been totally outfitted at his expense. In 1919 he moved to California, ostensibly to carry on his rose breeding. He devoted much of his time, however, to course architecture and over the next ten years designed and built some twenty-five courses, many with the assistance of William P. Bell. Throughout his career, it is believed that Thomas never accepted a fee for his services as course designer.

Thomas's classic work, *Golf Architecture in America: Its Strategy and Construction,* was published in 1927; but soon after its appearance the author began to lose interest in the subject. The last years of Thomas's life were spent in working on a book about Pacific game fish.

Courses by George Clifford Thomas, Jr.:

CALIFORNIA: Baldwin Hills GC, Culver City (1926,n.l.e.); Bel Air CC, Los Angeles (1927); El Caballero GC, Tarzana (1924,n.l.e.); Fox Hills CC, Culver City (1926,n.l.e.); Griffith Park GC, Los Angeles (Harding course,1926); Los Angeles CC (North course,1921); Ojai Valley Inn & CC (1925); Red Hill CC, Cucamonga (9,1921); Riviera CC, Pacific Palisades (1927); Saticoy Pubiic Links [formerly Ventura County CC] (9,1921).

MASSACHUSETTS: Marion GC (9).

NEW JERSEY: Spring Lake G&CC (1910).

PENNSYLVANIA: Whitemarsh Valley CC [formerly Mount Airy CC], Chestnut Hill (1908).

Courses Remodeled by George Clifford Thomas, Jr.:

CALIFORNIA: Griffith Park GC, Los Angeles (Wilson course,1923); La Cumbre G&CC, Santa Barbara (1920); Los Angeles CC (South course,1921).

John Alexander Thompson (1920–)

Born: Winnipeg, Canada.

"Jack" Thompson (no relation to the legendary Canadian golf architect Stanley Thompson) graduated from the American School of Landscape Design in Chicago in 1938. After World War I he formed a garden supply and landscape contracting firm in Canada.

While a contractor, Thompson formed an association with Alexander Mann, a golf course designer and turfgrass consultant from Aberdeen, Scotland. Thompson worked closely with Mann on the renovation and redesign of numerous courses from 1946 until Mann's death in 1952, and credited the Scot with providing his formal education in golf course architecture. After 1952 Thompson returned full time to his landscape contracting business until 1966, when he branched into golf course and landscape architecture.

Courses by John Alexander Thompson:

ALBERTA: Black Bull G&CC, Mam-E-O Beach (9).

MANITOBA: Carmen G&CC; Hecla GC (1975); Minnedosa G&CC (9); Selkirk GC (a.2nd 9).

SASKATCHEWAN: Craig GC, Regina (9); Tor Hill GC, Regina.

Courses Remodeled by John Alexander Thompson:

MANITOBA: Southwood G&CC, Winnipeg; Windsor GC, Winnipeg.

Stanley Thompson (1894–1952) ASGCA: Charter Member; President, 1949

Born: Scotland. Died: Toronto, Canada, at age 58.

Stanley Thompson emigrated with his family to Toronto, Ontario, before the first World War. He was one of five brothers, Nicol, William, Mathew, Stanley and Frank, all of whom became internationally known professional or amateur golfers. Stanley attended Ontario Agricultural College, Guelph, but left in 1915 to serve with the Canadian Expeditionary Force in France.

In 1922 Thompson entered practice as a course architect with modest projects in Toronto, followed shortly by the design of his first eighteen-hole course, Southwood GC in Winnipeg. Other courses in Winnipeg and Toronto preceded two of his greatest triumphs, Banff Springs and Jasper Park Golf courses, both in the Canadian Rockies. Banff, built for the Canadian Pacific Railway and officially opened by the Prince of Wales, and Jasper, built for the Canadian National Railway and opened by Field Marshall Haig, met with worldwide acclaim. Dramatic mountain layouts, "playgrounds for British nobility and American wealth," they exhibited a degree of strategic design unprecedented in North America. Thompson's fame spread as a result of the general enjoyment found in playing his strategic courses. Even Winston Churchill, by no means a golf devotee, is said to have enjoyed games played at Banff on his visits to Canada between the Wars.

Thompson himself, nicknamed "the Toronto Terror," was one of the more colorful figures in golf design history, ranking with "Young Willie" Dunn, Tom Simpson and "Tillie the Terror" Tillinghast. Many close to him felt him to be a genius. He made and spent fortunes. But he was also conscientious in the training of a number of assistants who later made names for themselves in course design, including Robert Trent Jones (who became a partner in the firm of Thompson–Jones & Co. Ltd.), Howard Watson, C. E. Robinson, Norman Woods, Kenneth Welton, Robert Moote and Geoffrey S. Cornish. Joe Lacerda gave a vivid account of the flamboyant Thompson and his career in an article that appeared in *The Saturday Evening Post,* June 8, 1948.

Four of Thompson's courses, Banff, Jasper, Capilano and Cape Breton Highlands, rank among the world's greatest. Shortly after his death in 1952, the *Ottawa Citizen* eulogized him with these words: "Stanley Thompson has left a mark on the Canadian landscape from coast to coast. No man could ask for a more handsome set of memorials." Those who knew Thompson well sensed depth beneath his flamboyance. In 1980 he was inducted posthumously into the Canadian Golf Hall of Fame.

Courses by Stanley Thompson:

ALBERTA: Banff Springs; Jasper Park GC (1925); Mayfair G&CC, Edmonton; Waterton National Park GC.

ATLANTIC PROVINCES: Ann of Green Gables, P.E.I.; Old Ashburn G&CC, Halifax (rt.); Cape Breton Highlands National Park GC, Keltic Lodge (1935); Fundy National Park GC; Pines GC, Digby.

BRITISH COLUMBIA: Capilano G&CC, West Vancouver.

MANITOBA: Clear Lake GC; Glendale G&CC, Winnipeg; Niakwa G&CC, Winnipeg; Pine Ridge G&CC, Winnipeg; Southwood G&CC, Winnipeg.

ONTARIO: Allandale GC (9); Aurora GC (9); Beach Grove G&CC, Walkerville; Big Boy G&CC, Lake Simcoe (9); Bigwin Inn GC, Lake of Bays; Briars G&CC, Jackson Point (9); Burlington G&CC, Hamilton; Cataraqui G&CC, Kingston; Cedarbrook G&CC, Toronto; Chedoke GC, Hamilton (r.18,a.18); Civic GC, Kitchener (9); Credit Valley GC, Toronto (9); Dundas Valley G&CC; Essex GC, St. Thomas; Fort William G&CC; Geraldton GC (9); Glen Marr GC, Toronto; Highland GC, London; Humber Valley GC, Toronto; Islington GC, Toronto; Kawartha GC, Peterboro; Kenora GC, Lake of the Woods (9); Ladies GC, Toronto; Marathon GC (9); Mardon Lodge GC, Barrie (9); Minaki Lodge Hotel GC (9); Muskoka Beach GC, Gravenhurst; Muskoka Lakes G&CC, Port Carling; North Bay GC (9); Northwood G&CC, Toronto; Oakdale GC, Toronto; Orchard Beach G&CC, Lake Simcoe (9); Owen Sound GC (9); Peninsula Park GC, Portage (9); Rio Vista GC, Bridgeburg (9); St. Andrews GC, Toronto (27,n.l.e.); St. Catharines G&CC; St. Georges [formerly Royal York GC], Toronto; Sir Harry Oakes Private Course, Niagra Falls (9); Sunningdale GC, London; Whirlpool, Niagara Falls Park Course.

QUEBEC: Arvida GC (9); Beaconsfield GC; International Club, Richford; K.I.-8-ab CC, Three Rivers (9); Le Chateau Montebello [formerly Seigniory Club], Lucerne in Quebec, Montebello; Marlborough GC, Montreal (27 n.l.e.); Model City Commercial Course, Montreal; Noranda Mines GC (9); Lachute GC.

SASKATCHEWAN: Waskesiuu GC.

FLORIDA: Floridale GC, Milford; Hyde Park GC, Jacksonville; Nealhurst GC, Jacksonville.

MINNESOTA: North Oaks CC, St. Paul (1951).

NEW YORK: Midvale CC, Penfield (c.Jones,1930); Onondogo CC, Syracuse.

OHIO: Chagrin Valley CC, Chagrin Falls, Beachmont CC, Cleveland.

BRAZIL: Itanhanga GC; Teresopolis GC (1932).

COLOMBIA: Medellin GC; San Andres GC, Bogota (1946).

JAMAICA: Constant Springs GC (1930).

Courses Remodeled by Stanley Thompson:

ATLANTIC PROVINCES: Moncton GC; Sydney GC (9); Truto GC (9).

ONTARIO: Brampton GC (9); Brantford G&CC; Brockville CC (9); Lake Shore G&CC, Toronto; Lambton G&CC, Toronto; Mississaugua G&CC, Toronto; Norway Point GC (9); Oshawa G&CC; Peterborough G&CC; Sault St. Marie CC; Thornhill GC, Toronto; York Downs G&CC [former site]; Scarboro G&CC, Toronto.

FLORIDA: Hyde Park GC, Jacksonville.

MINNESOTA: Somerset GC, St. Paul.

QUEBEC: Beaconsfield GC (1940).

BRAZIL: Gavea G&CC, Rio de Janeiro; Sao Paulo GC (1935).

Peter Thomson, C.B.E. (1929–)

Born: Melbourne, Australia.

Five times winner of the British Open and winner of seventy-five other major tournaments, Peter Thomson became senior partner of Thomson, Wolveridge, Fream and Associates, Golf Course Architects of Australia, California and London. He was also a contributor to the *Melbourne Herald* and *Melbourne Age,* and coauthor of *The World Atlas of Golf.*

Thomson served as president (1976) of the Australian PGA, as special advisor for the Asia golf circuit and as a member of the India Golf Union Committee. He planned major changes at the Bombay Presidency Club in Chembur, India (originally designed by C. R. Clayton), making this one of India's finest golf courses, and designed the Gulmarg GC, India. He also redesigned the Old course at the Royal Calcutta Club, India and Middlemore GC in New Zealand. With his associates, he planned Jagorawi National GC in Indonesia, Fujioka CC, Japan with T. Yamada, and numerous other courses.

Albert Warren Tillinghast (1874–1942)

Born: North Philadelphia, Pennsylvania. Died: Toledo, Ohio.

A. W. "Tillie" Tillinghast began playing golf in the 1890s, making an extended visit to St. Andrews in Scotland in that decade. There the wealthy young American formed a warm friendship with the canny Scot, "Old Tom" Morris, then in his late seventies. Back home, Tillinghast played in the U. S. Amateur several times between 1905 and 1912, acquitting himself well in matches lost to such golfing luminaries as Walter Travis, Chandler Egan and "Chick" Evans.

In 1906, with the blessing of Charles Worthington of pump and later course equipment fame, Tillinghast began laying out a golf course on Worthington family property near Stroudsburg, Pennsylvania. The result eventually became Shawnee-on-Delaware. Within a short time, Tillinghast was actively designing courses. An author and artist as well, he wrote and illustrated *Cobble Valley Golf Yarns and Other Sketches* and *The Mutt and Other Golf Yarns,* and was a frequent contributor to *Golf Illustrated,* of which he became editor in 1933. He introduced the word "birdie" to the golfing lexicon

During the Depression, Tillinghast worked full time for the PGA, studying members' courses and recommending changes. He is said to have removed several thousand bunkers in those years. By the end of the Depression he had lost both his fortune and his interest in golf course architecture, and he retired to California to open an antique store.

In his day "Tillie the Terror" was one of the most colorful figures in course design history. An outstanding account of his life and work can be found in Frank Hannigan's article "Golf's Forgotten Genius" (*The Golf Journal,* May 1974). It is perhaps a fitting testimonial to the man's talent that in 1974 four USGA Championships were played on courses of his design:

Winged Foot, San Francisco GC, The Brooklawn CC and Ridgewood CC.

Courses by Albert Warren Tillinghast:

CALIFORNIA: San Francisco GC (1915).

FLORIDA: Atlantic Beach CC (n.l.e.); Davis Shores CC, St. Augustine (n.l.e.); St. Petersburg CC.

MARYLAND: Baltimore CC at Five Farms.

MASSACHUSETTS: Berkshire Hills CC, Pittsfield.

MINNESOTA: Golden Valley GC, Minneapolis; Rochester G&CC (r.9,a.9,1925).

NEW JERSEY: Alpine CC [formerly Aldercress CC] (1931); Baltusrol, Springfield (Lower and Upper courses,1922); Essex County CC, West Orange; Mountain Ridge CC (new site,1916); Myosotis CC, Eatontown (n.l.e.); Norwood CC, Long Branch (n.l.e.); Ridgewood CC (new site,27,1929); Shackamaxon G&CC, Westfield (1917); Somerset Hills CC, Bernardsville (1917); Wilton Grove CC (1916).

NEW YORK: Bethpage State Park GC [formerly Lenox Hills CC], Farmingdale (Red course,1935;Blue course,1935;Black course,1936;r.Green course,1935); Binghampton CC, Endwell (1918); Bluff Point CC, Lake Champlain; CC of Ithaca (n.l.e.); Elmwood CC, White Plains; Fenway GC [formerly Fenimore CC], White Plains (1924); Fresh Meadow CC, Flushing (n.l.e); Harmon CC (1918); Knollwood CC, White Plains (new site); Marble Island GC, Essex Junction; Hempstead CC, Port Washington (a.9,1916); Oswego CC (9); Port Jervis CC (9); St. Albans CC (1916, n.l.e.); Southward Ho! CC, Bayshore; Winged Foot, Mamaroneck (East and West courses,1923).

NORTH CAROLINA: Myers Park CC, Charlotte (original 9,1921).

OHIO: Lakewood CC, Westlake (1925).

OKLAHOMA: The Oaks CC, Tulsa (1924); Tulsa (new site,1920).

PENNSYLVANIA: Cedarbrook CC, Philadelphia (n.l.e.); Irem Temple CC, Wilkes Barre; New Castle CC; Philadelphia Cricket Club, Flourtown; Shawnee CC; Sunnehanna CC, Johnstown; Wyoming Valley CC, Wilkes Barre (1923).

RHODE ISLAND: Newport CC.

SOUTH CAROLINA: Rock Hill CC (9).

TENNESSEE: Johnson City CC; Kingsport CC.

TEXAS: Brackinridge Park GC, San Antonio (1915); Brook Hollow GC, Dallas (1921); Cedar Crest GC, Dallas; Oak Hill CC [formerly Alamo CC], San Antonio (1921).

VERMONT: Marble Island GC, Essex Junction (9).

VIRGINIA: Hermitage CC, Richmond (1916).

CANADA: Anglo-American Club, Lec., L'Achign; Elm Ridge CC, Montreal (n.l.e.).

Courses Remodeled by Albert Warren Tillinghast:

CONNECTICUT: Brooklawn CC (1928).

ILLINOIS: Westmoreland CC, Wilmette.

KANSAS: Indian Hills CC, Prairie Village; Kansas City CC, Shawnee Mission.

MISSOURI: Swope Park GC, Kansas City (Course #1,1934).

NEW JERSEY: Seaview CC (Bay course); Spring Lake G&CC; Suburban GC, Union; Upper Montclair CC, Clifton (n.l.e.).

NEW YORK: Bonnie Briar CC, Larchmont; Elmira CC; Grossingers (1933); Jackson Heights CC, Jamaica (n.l.e.); Meadowbrook Club, Westbury (n.l.e.); Mount Kisco CC; Quaker Ridge CC (1926); Rockaway Hunting Club, Cedarhurst; Scarsdale GC, Hartsdale, (r.,a.9); Sleepy Hollow CC, Scarborough-on-Hudson (9); Wykagyl (1931); Wolferts Roost CC, Albany.

OHIO: Inverness CC, Toledo (1930).

OKLAHOMA: Oklahoma City G&CC.

PENNSYLVANIA: Fox Hill CC, Exeter; Nemacolin CC, Beallsville; Old York Road CC, Jenkintown (n.l.e.); Pittsburgh Field Club; St. Davids GC, Wayne; Valley CC, Conyngham; Wanago CC, Reno; Williamsport CC.

VIRGINIA: Roanoke CC.

CANADA: Scarboro CC, Toronto (1926).

H. C. C. Tippets

Amateur golfer H. C. C. Tippets was runner-up one year in the New York Metropolitan Amateur. He planned three courses for Fisher Resorts in the 1920s.

Courses by H. C. C. Tippets:

FLORIDA: Bayshore GC, Miami Beach (1925); Hollywood Beach Hotel CC; La Gorce CC, Miami (1927).

NEW YORK: Montauk Downs (1927).

Howard C. Toomey

An engineer specializing in railroad construction, Howard Toomey formed the partnership of Toomey and Flynn with William Flynn shortly after World War I and was responsible for much of the firm's construction.

See William Flynn.

Walter J. Travis (1862–1927)

Born: Australia. Died: Denver, Colorado, at age 65.

Educated at public schools and at Trinity College in Australia, Walter Travis emigrated to the United States at age twenty-three. Although he did not take up golf until he was thirty-five, he was soon the winner of the U. S. Amateur (1900, 1901 and 1903); and of the British Amateur (1904) and was runner-up at the 1902 U. S. Open. In addition, he was founder and editor of *American Golfer* magazine, and author of *The Art of Putting* and *Practical Golf*. He was known in golf circles as the "Grand Old Man."

Travis, unlike his contemporary C. B. Macdonald, often criticized British golf and in turn was not always treated kindly by the British press. He was originally appointed to Macdonald's select committee for the National Golf Links but was later dropped from it.

Walter Travis created many distinguished courses, some in collaboration with John Duncan Dunn, and a number on his own. He was particularly fond of the state of Vermont and is buried at Manchester near one of his and Dunn's greatest creations, Ekwanok CC. The routing at Ekwanok remains today almost identical to its opening in 1900, a tribute to the genius of its planners.

Courses by Walter J. Travis:

CONNECTICUT: Round Hill Club, Greenwich.

GEORGIA: Sea Island GC (Plantation 9,1927).

KENTUCKY: Louisville CC (r.9,a.9).

MAINE: Cape Arundel GC, Kennebunkport.

PENNSYLVANIA: CC of Scranton (1927).

NEW JERSEY: Hollywood GC, Deal; White Beaches G&CC, Hawroth.

NEW YORK: Garden City CC (1919); Old Country Club, Flushing (n.l.e.); Westchester CC, Rye (36,1922); Yahnundasis CC, Utica.

VERMONT: Ekwanok CC, Manchester (1900,c.Dunn); Equinox Golf Links, Manchester.

CANADA: Welland CC (formerly Lookout Point CC), Ontario; Cherry Hill GC, Ontario.

Courses Remodeled by Walter J. Travis:

GEORGIA: Jekyll Island GC (Oceanside course,1926).

NEW JERSEY: North Jersey CC (1915).

NEW YORK: Garden City GC (several times); Park CC, Williamsville.

A. Russell Tryon

Prominent landscape architect A. Russell Tryon headed the firm of Tryon and Schwartz & Associates, Inc. of East Aurora, New York. After 1950 he and partner E. J. Schwartz, designed a number of courses and consulted on several others, often in collaboration with a third associate, William E. Harries.

Courses by A. Russell Tryon: See William E. Harries.

William Henry Tucker, Sr. (1871–1954)

Born: Redhill, Surrey, England. Died; Albuquerque, New Mexico, at age 83.

William Tucker learned the art of sod rolling from his father, an employee of the Wimbledon Commons. He served as professional at two English clubs as a teenager, and then worked on course construction crews for Tom and "Young" Willie Dunn in England, France and Switzerland.

In 1895 Tucker emigrated to the United States, joining his brother Samuel, professional at the St. Andrews GC in New York. They formed the equipment firm of Tucker Brothers, and their handmade "Defiance" brand clubs were sold for years. When St. Andrews moved to a new site, Tucker was hired to construct it to the design of Harry Tallmadge and to serve as greenkeeper. Within a year of the course's opening, he had rearranged some holes and built several new ones.

Tucker laid out several other courses in the New York area while at St. Andrews and later at the Ardsley CC. He also worked in the early 1900s as pro-greenkeeper at the Chevy Chase Club near Washington, D.C., where he collaborated with Dr. Walter S. Harban, the wealthy and eccentric dentist to presidents who dabbled in course design and maintenance. In the 1920s Tucker and his son, William H. Tucker, Jr., established a full-time golf architecture firm with offices in New York, Los Angeles and Portland, Oregon. After World War II, he retired to Albuquerque, New Mexico, where he designed, built and maintained the University of New Mexico course. It is estimated that he designed or remodeled over 120 courses in his career.

Tucker was also a nationally known turfgrass expert and in his New York days had been called upon to install and nurture the original turf at such sports facilities as Yankee Stadium and the West Side Tennis Club (Forest Hills).

Courses by William Henry Tucker:

MARYLAND: Argyle CC (formerly Columbia CC), Chevy Chase (c.Harban); Bannockburn G&CC, Glen Echo (c.Harban;n.l.e.).

NEBRASKA: CC of Lincoln (1923); Hillcrest CC [formerly Shrine GC], Lincoln; Pioneers Park GC, Lincoln (27,1932; only 9 remain).

NEW JERSEY: Preakness Hills CC (1927). *NEW MEXICO:* Portales CC (1948); University of New Mexico GC, Albuquerque (original course, now North course,1951; a.9 par 3,1954).

NEW YORK: Ardsley CC, Ardsley-on-Hudson; Maidstone Club, East Hampton (original 9,1896).

PENNSYLVANIA: Bala CC [formerly Philadelphia CC], Philadelphia (a.2nd 9).

VERMONT: Woodstock CC (1906).

Courses Remodeled by William Henry Tucker:

NEW YORK: St. Andrews GC, Hastings-on-Hudson.

William Henry Tucker, Jr. (1895–1962)

Born: New York. Died: Los Angeles, California, at age 67.

William H. Tucker, Jr., was the son of pioneer golf course architect and builder William H. Tucker. He joined his father's business after service in World War I and except for a stint in World War II, worked most of his life on the design, construction and maintenance of courses for his father.

Tucker Jr. did not work under his own name until after his father's death in 1954, although some of the courses that bore the name of the father were actually the work of the son. Tucker Jr. practiced on his own for slightly less than a decade, designing courses in the Southwest from his base in Los Angeles.

Courses by William Henry Tucker, Jr.:

ARIZONA: Glendale Muni (n.l.e.).

CALIFORNIA: Anderson Tucker Oaks GC, Anderson (9,1964); Elkins Ranch GC, Fillmore (1962); Fletcher Hills CC, Santee (1960); Ontario National GC (original course; a.18 par 3).

The Tufts Family

Biographies of four members of the Tufts family are included because of the impact they and their famous resort, Pinehurst, had on the development of golf and golf architecture in the United States.

James Walker Tufts (1835–1902)

Born: Charlestown, Massachusetts. Died: Pinehurst, North Carolina, at age 67.

James Tufts, a cousin of the Charles Tufts who donated land for the campus of Tufts University in Medford, Massachusetts, became an apprentice druggist at the age of sixteen. By age twenty-one the enterprising young man owned three stores and was on his way to becoming a tycoon in the soda fountain business. One of the first to forsee the coming popularity of soda fountains, Tufts installed them in his stores, developed extracts and dispensers that he used himself and marketed elsewhere and created a line of silver-plated accessories sold nationwide, based on his own more efficient method of silver plating. In 1891 Tufts consolidated his booming business with several others to become the American Soda Fountain Company.

But Tufts remained as head of his organization for only four years. Turning the operation over to his son, he moved south for his health, settling in central North Carolina. There he bought 5,000 acres of barren sand hills for $7,500.00; and though many claimed this proved Tarheel woodsmen to be better businessmen than Yankee merchants, Tufts was so enamored of the place that he dreamed of developing it into a resort. He hired eminent landscape architect Frederick Law Olmstead to lay out a formal village, built several hotels and negotiated for a railroad spur. The resort was named Pinehurst.

Pinehurst proved a popular winter retreat; and in 1898 Tufts and a friend, Dr. D. LeRoy Culver, laid out a primitive nine-hole course for guests. A year later they added nine more. This was the beginning of what would become the largest single golf resort in the world.

In 1900 Tufts met a young Scottish professional golfer in Massachusetts and hired him to become winter pro at Pinehurst and to develop its courses. The young golfer, Donald J. Ross, began an association with Pinehurst in the winter of 1901 that would last the rest of his life.

James W. Tufts died in 1902 while his proudest accomplishment, Pinehurst, was still evolving.

Leonard Tufts (1870–1945)

Born: Medford Massachusetts. Died: Pinehurst, North Carolina, at age 75. Son of James Walker Tufts.

Leonard Tufts, who attended MIT, worked for his father in the soda fountain business after leaving college. Though not yet twenty-six at the time of his father's retirement, Leonard was placed on the executive staff of the giant American Soda Fountain Company. But he was more interested in the new Pinehurst resort his father was building in North Carolina.

Tufts assisted his father and Dr. Culver in laying out Pinehurst's first course in 1898–99. Although this was his only active golf design experience, he was instrumental in the early 1900s in convincing Donald Ross to rebuild the course and eventually add several others to the resort, in accordance with James Tufts's dream.

Leonard Tufts became director of Pinehurst after his father's death. In 1906 he terminated all executive involvement with American Soda Fountain, devoting full time to the resort. He became nationally known for his cattle-breeding experiments, begun originally in an effort to supply fresh milk and butter to the Pinehurst guests.

Tufts resigned his control of Pinehurst in 1930 due to ill health; but he continued to reside there, assisting his eldest son, Richard, in running the resort. He died of pneumonia in 1930, leaving three sons and a daughter.

Richard Sise Tufts (1896–1980)

Born: Medford, Massachusetts. Son of Leonard Tufts and Gertrude War Tufts, nee Sise.

Richard Tufts learned his golf at Pinehurst from Donald Ross, starting at the age of eight and becoming the most proficient golfer of the Tufts clan. After graduation from Harvard in 1917, he served with the U. S. Navy in World War I and then returned to Pinehurst to work with his father. He took over in 1930 after his father's retirement and continued as director of Pinehurst, Inc. into the 1960s.

A lifelong friend of Donald Ross and devotee of his work, Tufts dabbled in course design after the great architect's death. He laid out a new Pinehurst No. 4 course in the early 1950s since the original No. 4, a Ross design, had been abandoned during World War II as an austerity measure. He revised several holes of the No. 2 course for the 1962 USGA Amateur, and he also assisted golf architect Ellis Maples with the routing of Pinehurst No. 5 in the 1960s.

Richard Tufts was involved in every facet of golf administration and was often consulted in setting up courses for championship play. At one time or another he served on every committee of the USGA and was its president in 1956–57. He was awarded the Richardson Award in 1950 by the Golf Writers Association of America for outstanding contributions to the game, and the Bob Jones Award in 1966 by the USGA for distinguished sportsmanship in golf. He also wrote many articles on golf, some pertaining to golf architecture, and was author of *The Principles Behind the Rules of Golf* (1960) and *The Scottish Invasion: A Brief Review of American Golf in Relation to Pinehurst* (1962).

In 1971 Tufts's two brothers, who owned a majority of the stock in Pinehurst, Inc., voted to sell the grand old resort. Undaunted, Richard Tufts helped his son Peter start a new golf resort a short distance away. And in the late 1970s he was pleased to see the Pinehurst management restore the courses, particularly the masterful No. 2.

Peter Vail Tufts

Son of Richard S. Tufts and Alice Tufts, nee Vail. Godson of Donald Ross.

Peter Tufts worked his way up in the management of Pinehurst. Beginning as manager of laundry and garage facilities, he worked on course maintenance crews, served as club manager and was finally appointed golf operations manager at Pinehurst in the 1960s. When the resort was sold in 1971, he resigned his position, and he and his father searched for a new location in which to carry on their family traditions. They established the Seven Lakes GC in nearby West End, North Carolina, a residential housing complex.

Peter Tufts designed and supervised construction of the Seven Lakes course, his first experience in golf architecture. When the course opened in 1976, he was quick to down play any comparison with Donald Ross works. Nevertheless, Tufts, who grew up playing Ross's courses in the company of the great designer, professed his admiration for Ross's designs and announced his hope of someday reestablishing Ross's philosophy of course design.

In 1977 Tufts opened his own course design firm and soon landed a few promising contracts, including partial renovation of the famous Pinehurst No. 2 course. There he set about restoring some of the original Ross mounds, removing the Bermuda roughs and redefining the fairway contours. For a man who had hoped to someday practice the art as Donald Ross had, it was the fulfillment of a dream.

Alfred H. Tull (1897–   ) ASGCA

Born: England.

Alfred Tull moved with his family to Canada in 1907 and to the United States in 1914. He began his career as a construction superintendent for Walter Travis in 1921 and for A. W. Tillinghast in 1922. In 1923 he took a similar position with Devereux Emmet.

Tull's association with Emmet lasted for twelve years, culminating in the design partnership of Emmet, Emmet and Tull (1930–35). He entered private practice as a course architect in 1935 following Emmet's death.

Clients and others he worked with were struck by Tull's remarkable ability to lay out individual holes and establish a circuit by walking the land and staking the holes without resort to a topographical plan. Later he would place his circuit on a topo to convey his ideas to others.

Courses by Alfred H. Tull: (Most courses before 1935 were done in collaboration with Emmet and also appear on his list).

ARKANSAS: Rosswood CC, Pine Bluff (1961).

CONNECTICUT: CC of Darien (1958); CC of New Canaan (2nd 9,1947); Hob Nob Hill, Salisbury (1934,n.l.e.); Oak Hill GC, Norwalk (1967); Pilgrim's Harbor CC, Wallingford (9,1970); Pine Tree CC, Brooksville (9,1953); Rolling Hills CC, Wilton (1965); Silver Mine, Norwalk.

DELAWARE: Brandywine CC, Wilmington (1951); DuPont CC, Wilmington (Nemours course,1938;DuPont course,1950); Hercules CC, Wilmington (1st 9,1937;2nd 9,1941;3rd 9,1966); Seaford CC (9,1941).

MARYLAND: Norbeck CC, Rockville (1952); Woodmont CC, Bethesda (2nd 9,1948,n.l.e.); Woodmont CC, Rockville (18,1951;a.9,1955).

MASSACHUSETTS: Clauson's Inn, North Falmouth (9,1929); Jug End Inn, Egremont (9,1961); Rhode Island Club.

NEW JERSEY: Ashbrook, Union County Park Commission (1951); Canoe Brook CC, Summit (North 9,1949); Cooper River CC, Camden (1929,n.l.e.); Greenacres CC, Trenton (1932); Mendham G&TC (1967); Passaic County (Park Commission) Course (9,1955); Rockleigh, Bergen County Park Commission (1958).

NEW YORK: Bethpage State Park (White course,1958); Broadmoor CC, New Rochelle (1929,n.l.e.); Concord Hotel, Kiamesha (International and Challenger courses, 1951); Crescent-Hamilton CC, Huntington (36,1931;18,n.l.e.); Hampshire CC, Larchmont (1927); Harbor Hills CC, Port Jefferson (1955); Harrison Williams Private Course, Bayville (3,1932); Indian Hills CC, Pine Bush (9 par 3,1965); Lake Ann CC, Monroe (9,1963); Mayflower, N.Y.C. Park Commission (1930); Morningside Hotel, Hurleyville (1961); Mrs. Graham F. Vanderbilt, Manhasset (9,1929,n.l.e.); Muttontown CC, East Norwich (1959); Nevele Hotel, Ellenville (1963); Pine Ridge CC, Newcastle (1954); Poxebogue GC, Bridgehampton (9,1962); Rockwood Hall CC, Tarrytown (1929,n.l.e.); Schuyler Meadows Club, Loudenville (1928); Seawane Harbor Club, Hewlett (1927); Sunken Meadow Park, L.I. State Park Commission (1968); Tenanah Lake House, Roscoe (1960); Vernon Hills CC, Mt. Vernon (1928).

NORTH CAROLINA: Hog Back Mountain Club, Tryon (9,1931;n.l.e.).

PENNSYLVANIA: Radley Run CC, West Chester (1965); Valley Forge V.A. (1943).

RHODE ISLAND: Ledgemont CC, Providence (1948).

SOUTH CAROLINA: Georgetown CC (9,1956).

VIRGINIA: Brook Manor CC, Brooke (1955); Westwood CC [formerly West Briar CC], Vienna (1954).

BERMUDA: Belmont Manor CC (2nd 9,1929); Southampton Princess (18 par 3,1964).

CANADA: Blomidon Club, Corner Brook, Newfoundland (1967).

DOMINICAN REPUBLIC: Bella Vista Course (1957).

PUERTO RICO: Berwind CC, San Juan (2nd 9,1959;n.l.e.); Ponce GC (9,1953).

VIRGIN ISLANDS: Estate Carlton, St. Croix (9,1960).

Courses Remodeled by Alfred H. Tull:

ALABAMA: CC of Mobile (1967).

CONNECTICUT: Meriden Parks Course (1968); Silver Mine CC, Norwalk; Silver Springs CC, Ridgefield (1968).

DELAWARE: Green Hill, Wilmington Park Dept. (1962); Henry F. duPont, Wilmington (9,1929).

MARYLAND: Green Hill Y&CC, Salisbury (1951).

MASSACHUSETTS: Belmont CC (1969); Mt. Pleasant CC, Leicester (1951).

NEW JERSEY: Fairmont CC, Chatham (1968); Galloping Hills, Union County Park Commission (1953); White Beeches CC, Haworth (1950).

NEW YORK: Apawamis Club, Rye (1962); Bonnie Briar CC, Larchmont (1928); Elmwood CC, Elmsford (1954); Fairview CC, Elmsford (1964); Glen Head CC, Glen Cove (1968); Maidstone CC, East Hampton (1965); Middle Bay CC, Oceanside (1955); Pelham CC (1954); Red Hook GC (1967); Rockland County CC, Sparkill (1965); Waccabuc CC (1967); Westchester CC, Rye (1969); Wheatley Hills CC, Williston (1929).

Herbert James Tweedie (–1921)

Born: Hoylake, Cheshire, England. Died: Chicago, Illinois.

H. J. Tweedie came to the United States with his brother L. P. in 1887. Both golfers from the Royal Liverpool Club, they settled in Chicago and managed the A. G. Spalding & Bros., Inc. sporting goods store.

The Tweedies became friends of C. B. Macdonald and were members of his original Chicago Golf Club. When the Chicago GC moved to Wheaton, Illinois, Tweedie and others organized the Belmont GC at the old site and built a new course there. Over the next ten years, Tweedie built a number of Chicago-area clubs. He also continued to manage the Spalding Chicago concern until his death, when his son Douglas assumed the position.

Courses by Herbert James Tweedie:

ILLINOIS: Belmont GC (1898); Bryn Mawr Club, Chicago; Exmoor CC, Highland Park; Flossmoor CC [formerly Homewood CC] (1898); Glen View GC (1904); La Grange CC (9,1899,n.l.e.); Midlothian CC (1898); Onwentsia Club (c.Whigham & Foulis, a.9,1898); Park Ridge CC (1906); Ridge CC, Chicago (1902); Washington Park CC, Chicago (n.l.e.); Westward Ho! CC, Oak Park, Rockford CC (1899).

Lawrence E. Van Etten (1865–1951)

Born: Kingston, New York. Died: New Rochelle, New York, at age 85.

Lawrence Van Etten attended Princeton University, receiving an engineering degree in 1886 and later obtaining a law degree as well. For most of his life he worked as a civil engineer, planning and developing residential subdivisions in metropolitan New York.

Van Etten was also a prominent player in the early days of American golf and won many local titles. His golfing abilities and engineering training provided excellent course design background, and he planned many in the New York area. Though most have long since been abandoned, the Wykagyll CC in New Rochelle, where Van Etten maintained a lifelong membership, still exists in modified form.

Courses by Lawrence E. Van Etten:

NEW JERSEY: Deal GC, Deal Beach (1898).

NEW YORK: Knollwood CC, Elmsford (1898,n.l.e.); Pelham CC (9,1908); Pelham Bay Park GC, Bronx (original 9,1899); Wykagyl CC, New Rochelle (1905).

Harry Vardon (1870–1937)

Hailing from the Isle of Jersey, Harry Vardon became one of Britain's ''Great Triumvirate'' of professional golfers. He won six British Opens and one U. S. Open. Despite demand for his services as a course architect, his planning was limited by poor health.

Courses by Harry Vardon:

ENGLAND: Brockton Hall, Stafford; Ganton (1899); Letchworth, Herts; Little Aston (1909); Moore Place GC; Oxney (1909); Saffron Walden; South Herts; West Herts (1910); Woodhall Spa (1905).

IRELAND: Bundoran.

SCOTLAND: Kingussie.

WALES: Knighton GC; Llandindrod Wells.

Courses Remodeled by Harry Vardon:

NORTHERN IRELAND: Royal County Down, Ulster (1908).

John R. Van Kleek (–1957)

Died: Tryon, North Carolina.

After graduating with a degree in landscape architecture from Cornell University, John Van Kleek formed a partnership with Wayne E. Stiles of Boston, Massachusetts. Van Kleek managed the firm's St. Petersburg, Florida, office. This was one of the nation's busiest by the mid-1920s although not all the courses planned were actually built. Before the Depression, the Stiles and Van Kleek partnership was dissolved, but each continued a modest practice on his own until after World War II.

Courses by John R. Van Kleek See Wayne E. Stiles. Among courses designed solely by Van Kleek are:

NEW MEXICO: Albuquerque CC (1929).

NEW YORK: La Tourette, Staten Island (1935); White Face Inn GC, Lake Placid.

COLOMBIA: CC of Bogota (West course,new site,1947; East course,1950).

VENEZUELA: Cara Belleda G&YC, Macuto (9).

George Von Elm (1901–1961)

George Von Elm was well known as an amateur golfer between the first and second World Wars and had an impressive record in both the British and U. S. Opens. He designed several courses in the western United States.

Courses by George Von Elm:

IDAHO: Airport GC (1957).

UTAH: Mt. Ogden Muni.

Courses Remodeled by George Von Elm:

CALIFORNIA: Hacienda CC.

IDAHO: Sun Valley CC.

Robert Bernhardt Von Hagge (1930–   )

Born: West Texas.

Robert Hagge, the adopted son of Indiana superintendent Bernhardt F. ''Ben'' Hagge literally grew up on a golf course. Ben Hagge had constructed courses in the 1920s for such architects as William Diddel, Donald Ross and George O'Neil, and had tried a few designs himself.

After two years at Annapolis Hagge transferred to Purdue University, where he graduated with a degree in agricultural engineering in 1951. He then spent a few years on the PGA tour, worked as a club professional in the Catskill Mountains of New York, and tried his hand at acting in Hollywood. In 1957 he joined the golf architectural firm of Dick Wilson, Inc. in Florida. Training under Wilson, he quickly proved adept at course design and building and changed his surname to Von Hagge.

Von Hagge established his own practice in Delray Beach, Florida, in 1963. Some of his early works, particularly Boca Rio GC in Florida and the spectacular El Conquistador in Puerto Rico, attracted widespread attention. In the mid-1960s he was hired to redesign The Lakes GC in Australia at the recommendation of professional golfer Bruce Devlin. Von Hagge and Devlin became friends and colleagues, forming a course design partnership in Australia in 1968. The following year, the firm of Von Hagge and Devlin was established in the United States.

Courses by Robert Bernhardt Von Hagge: (All courses since 1968 in collaboration with Bruce Devlin)

ARIZONA: La Mancha CC, Phoenix (1975).

CALIFORNIA: Marre Ranch GC, Avila Beach; Tierra Del Sol GC, California City (1978).

COLORADO: Eagle Vail CC, Vail (1975). Zapata Falls GC, Alamosa (9,1977).

FLORIDA: Bayshore Muni, Miami Beach (1969); Boca Del Mar G&TC, Boca Raton (North course,1972); Boca Lago CC, Boca Raton (East and West courses,1975); Boca Rio GC, Boca Raton (1967); Boca West CC, Boca Raton (Course #3,1974); Briar Bay CC, Miami (9

par 3,1975); Colony West GC, Tamarac (1970;a.Exec. course,1974); CC of Sarasota (1976); Cypress Creek CC, Boynton Beach (1964); Doral CC, Miami (Green and White courses,1967;Gold course,1969;r.Blue course,1971); East Lake Woodlands CC, Oldmar (a.18,1980); Eastwood Muni, Ft. Myers (1978); Emerald Hills CC, Hollywood (1969); The Fountains G&RC, Lake Worth (27,1971); Hillcrest G&CC, Hollywood (1966); Holiday Springs CC, Margate (1975); Hunters Run GC, Boynton Beach (a.18,1979); Indian Spring CC, Boynton Beach; Key Biscayne GC (1972); Marco Shores CC (1974); Ocean Reef Club, North Key Largo (Barracuda and Harbour courses,1976;r.Dolphin course,1969); Palm-Aire CC, Pompano Beach (Palms and Sabals courses,1969); Poinciana G&RC, Kissimmee (1973); Pompano Beach CC (Pines course,1967;r.Palms course,1967); Sandalfoot Cove G&CC, Margate (27,1970); Sheoah GC, Winter Springs (1973) [now Big Cypress GC]; Sherbrooke G&CC; Wekiva GC, Forest City (1973); Wellington GC, West Palm Beach (1979); The Woodlands CC, Tamarac (East and West courses,1969); Woodmont CC, Tamarac (Cypress and Pines courses,1976).

KENTUCKY: Boone Aire GC, Florence (1968).

MISSOURI: Hidden Lake GC, Osage Beach (9,1969); Tan-Tar-A Resort GC, Osage Beach (1980).

NEW MEXICO: Tanoan GC, Albuquerque (27,1978).

NORTH CAROLINA: Brandywine Bay GC; Mill Creek CC.

OHIO: Carolina Trace GC, Harrison (9,1969); Quail Hollow Inn & CC, Painesville (1975).

TENNESSEE: Crockett Springs National G&CC, Brentwood (1972).

TEXAS: Crown Colony CC; Ravenneaux CC (1980); Vista Hills CC, El Paso (1975); Walden on Lake Conroe GC (1976); The Woodlands CC (East course,1978).

WISCONSIN: Brookfield Hills GC (1971).

AUSTRALIA: Campbelltown GC, Sydney (1976); Cannon Hill CC, Brisbane (1976); Magnolia Hills CC, Suncoast (1975); Ocean Shores GC, Brunswick.

BAHAMAS: Cape Eleuthera GC (1971).

PUERTO RICO: El Conquistador Hotel & Club, Fujardo (1967).

Courses Remodeled by Robert Bernhardt Von Hagge:

ARIZONA: Tucson National GC (1979).

OHIO: Camargo Club, Cincinnati.

AUSTRALIA: The Lakes GC, Sydney (1970).

Bernhard von Limburger (1901–   )

Born: Leipzig, Germany. Died: Stuttgart.

Bernhard von Limburger learned golf in Scotland at age thirteen and later won the German Amateur in 1921, '22 and '25. He represented Germany thirty-five times in international competition. He earned a degree in law but never practiced, choosing instead to publish a German golf magazine that he edited until the mid-1930s. During this period, he laid out a few courses that were, by his own admission, terrible designs.

In the 1930s Limburger formed a partnership with Berlin golf professional Karl Hoffman, already an accomplished designer. Hoffmann and Limburger created several courses in Germany before World War II and operated a number of them. But their business was terminated by the War, and Limburger returned to his native Leipzig to work as a club manager. In 1943 he fled to south Germany and never returned to Leipzig, which became part of the Communist zone after the War.

Hoffman and Limburger tried to resume their practice at the close of the War, but Hoffmann died shortly thereafter. Limburger was successful in landing several commissions to build courses for American military bases in the newly created West Germany in the late 1940s, and by the 1950s he was designing full time. In the 1960s and 70s he was busy designing and constructing courses in many parts of Europe.

Always a strong advocate of strategic design and a strong opponent of water hazards and over-bunkering (especially with what he termed ''zigsaw-puzzle pieces''), Limburger developed a distinctly European style of golf architecture. All German Open tournaments after World War II through 1978 were played on courses he had designed or revised. Limburger was also the author of three books: *The Big 1 x 1 of the Golfer*, *Beloved Golfing* and *Golf at the Fireplace*.

Courses by Bernhard von Limburger;

AUSTRIA: Badgastein GC (9); Bellach GC; Schloss Fuschl G&CC (9 par 3); Schloss Pichlarn GC (9); Steiermarischer GC, Frohnleiten.

GERMANY (EAST): (All c. Hoffmann) Chemnitzer GC, Slauv-Floeha; Gaschwitz GC, Leipzig; Neustadt GC (9); Wittenberg GC (9).

GERMANY (WEST): Augsburg GC, Burgwalden (9); Bad Driburge GC (9); Bad Durrenburg GC; Bad Harzburg GC (9); Bad Herrenalb GC (9); Bad Saaron GC (9); Bad Salzuflen GC; Bad Waldsee GC (9); Bayreuth GC (9); Braunfels GC (9); Breslau GC (9); Donaueschingen GC; Dortmunder GC; Essener GC, Haus Oefte (9,c.Hoffmann); Feldafing GC (c.Hoffmann); Freiburg GC (9); Furth GC (U.S. Army Base); Garmisch-Partnekirchen GC (c.Hoffmann); Golf und Land club Cologne, Refrath (c.Hoffmann); GuLC Ostwestfalen-Lippe, Bad Salzuflen (9); Hamburg GC, Ahrensburg; Hamburg-Walddorfer GC, Hoisbuettel; Hannover GC, Garbsen (c.Hoffmann); Heidelburg GC (U.S. Army Base); Intercontinental GC, Dusseldorf (9); Kassel-Wilhelmshohe GC (9); Konstanzer GC (c.Hoffmann); Kornwestheim GC, Stuttgardt (U.S. Army Base) Krefelder GC, Krefeld-Lind (1940,c.Hoffmann); Land und Golfclub Dusseldorf, Hubbelrath (East and West courses,1963); Lindau GC, Bad Schachen (1954); Lohersand GC, Rendsburg (9); Mannheim GC (9,c.Hoffmann); Marienburger GC, Cologne; Monsheim GC, Stuttgardt; Morsum-Sylt GC, Sylt (9); Munchener GC, Munich; Neheim-Huston GC (9); Oberfranken GC, Bayreuth (9); Oldenburgischer GC (9); Reichswald GC, Nuremburg; Schloss Anholt GC (9); Schloss Myllendonk GC, Monchengladbach (9); Schloss Rheden GC (9); Siegen-Olpe GC, Seigen (9); Spangdahlem GC (U.S. Army Base,9); Timmendorferstrand GC (9); Ulm-GC, Ulm (9); Weidenbruck-Gutersloh GC, Gutersloh (9); Zur Vahr GC, Bremen (Garlstedter course,1966).

IRELAND: Clandeboye GC, Conlig, County Down (36).

SPAIN: Atalaya Park Hotel G&CC, Marbella (1976).

SWITZERLAND: Basel G&CC; Blumisberg G&CC, Bern (1959); Neuchatel GC, Pierre a Bots (9); Zurich-Hittnau G&CC.

Courses Remodeled by Bernhard von Limburger:

CZECHOSLOVAKIA: Marienbad GC.
GERMANY: Falkenstein GC, Hamburg; Frankfurt; Kiel; Kronberg; Wuppertal.

Brenton Wadsworth

A graduate landscape architect, Brenton Wadsworth joined golf architect E. Lawrence Packard in a golf and landscape architecture partnership in 1954. Packard and Wadsworth was dissolved in 1957, when Wadsworth left to form his own firm specializing in golf course construction.

Charles Dudley Wagstaff (1894–1977)

Born: Tipton, Indiana. Died: Boca Raton, Florida, at age 82.

C. D. Wagstaff attended the University of Illinois, where he was captain of the varsity gymnastic team, and graduated in 1918 with a B.S. degree in landscape architecture.

After serving in the U. S. Navy for two years, the diminutive Wagstaff (5'3", 110 pounds) moved to Glenview, Illinois, where he formed a landscape and golf course architecture business in 1923. Over the next 46 years he worked on many prominent landscaping projects, including the Chicago World's Fair of 1933, the Great Lakes Exposition in Cleveland in 1936, and the La Gorce Island housing project in Florida.

But Wagstaff devoted much of his attention to golf course design and construction, creating such well-known Illinois layouts as Tam O'Shanter CC, Kildeer CC (now Twin Orchards CC) and, after World War II, thirty-six holes for the University of Illinois.

In his later years Wagstaff was asissted by Donald R. Anderson and by his own son, Charles D. Wagstaff, Jr. C. D. Wagstaff disbanded his firm in 1969 and retired to Florida, where he died in 1977.

Courses by Charles Dudley Wagstaff:
ILLINOIS: Bonnie Dundee GC, Dundee; Brookridge CC, Park Ridge; Brookwood CC, Addison; Elsbert Farm GC, Chicago (3 hole course,1964); Great Lakes NTC GC, North Chicago (original 9); Hickory Hills CC, Oak Lawn (a.Executive course,1963);Indian Boundary CC,Chicago; Mission Hills CC, Northbrook (a. Par 3 course); Mauh-Na-Tee-See CC, Rockford; Olympic G&CC, Arlington Heights (1927); Park Hills GC, Freeport (East course, 1953; West course, 1964); Park Lane GC, DesPlaines; Sandy Hollow Muni, Rockford; Tam O'Shanter CC, Niles (1925,n.l.e.); Twin Orchards CC [formerly Kildeer CC], Long Grove (Red and White courses, 1928); Twin Ponds GC, Crystal Lake (9 par 3, 1964); University of Illinois GC, Champaign (Orange course, 1950; Blue course, 1964); Winnetka Park GC (Original course; a.18 par 3, 1961).
IOWA: Emeis Park GC, Davenport (1961); Sheaffer Memorial Park GC, Fort Madison (1962); Starhaven GC, Keokuk (3 hole course, 1969).
MICHIGAN: Leland CC (1965); Sugar Loaf Mountain GC, Cedar (1966).
MISSOURI: Greenbrier Hills CC [formerly Osage Hills CC], Kirkwood (Original 9,1937;a.9,1958).
NORTH CAROLINA: Sippihaw CC [formerly Fuquay-Varina CC], Fuquay-Varina (Original 9,1961).
Courses Remodeled by Charles Dudley Wagstaff:
ILLINOIS: Barrington Hills CC; Oregon CC; Rockford CC (1949); Sunset Ridge CC, Winnetka (1926).

Robert C. Walker (1948–) ASGCA

Born: Sherman, Texas.

Robert Walker received a B.S. degree in engineering and architecture from East Texas State University in 1971, and later undertook post-graduate studies in soil science and parks and recreation at Texas A & M University. He was employed in 1972–73 with the Club Corporation of America, where he worked with golf architects Ralph Plummer and Joe Finger. In 1974 he joined the firm of Edwin B. Seay, Inc., which was associated with Arnold Palmer. In 1979 the Palmer Course Design Company was formed, with Seay and Walker actively associated. Walker collaborated on all Seay courses after 1974, including those done under the Seay name and those under the Seay and Palmer name.

Courses by Robert C. Walker: See Edwin B. Seay.

Art Wall (1923)

Art Wall was leading money winner on the PGA tour in 1959, the year in which he won the Masters Tournament. He was associated in course design with the architectural firm of Bellante and Clauss of Scranton, Pennsylvania. Three of his designs while with that firm were Seascape at Kittyhawk, North Carolina (1969); Pocono Farm CC in Pennsylvania (1971); and a nine-hole addition at the Scranton CC (1979), also in Pennsylvania.

David L. Wallace

David Wallace's first golf design experience was his collaboration with Mark Mahannah on the addition of a second course at the Port St. Lucie Resort in Florida, where he was employed as superintendent of grounds. In the 1970s, based in Tampa, he created a score of courses.

Courses by David L. Wallace:
FLORIDA: Burnt Store GC, Punta Gorda Isles (9,1970;9,1976); Cove Cay G&TC, Clearwater (1972); Deltona G&CC (1964); Grenelefe G&CC, Winter Haven (West course,1971); High Point CC, Naples (Par 3,1972); Lake Region Y&CC, Winter Haven (1964); Lely Community GC, Naples (1969); Lely CC, Naples (1975); Lucerne GC, Winter Haven (Par 3,1967); Marco Island CC (1966); Rocky Point GC, Tampa (a.3rd 9); Royal Poinciana GC, Naples (North course,1969;South course,1970); Sandpiper CC [formerly St. Lucie CC], Port St. Lucie (Saints course,1963); Southridge GC, Delano (1968); Spring Hill G&CC (1969); Willow Brook GC, Winter Haven (1968).
Courses Remodeled by David L. Wallace:
FLORIDA: Gasparilla Inn & CC, Boca Grande.

Laurie B. Waters

A native of St. Andrews, Laurie Waters apprenticed under "Old" Tom Morris. In 1901 he emigrated to South Africa, where he introduced grass greens and became known as the "Father of South African Golf."

Courses by Laurie B. Waters:
ZIMBABWE (RHODESIA): Royal Salisbury (1922); Ruma CC (c.George Waterman).
SOUTH AFRICA: Durban CC (1920); Royal Johannesburg (West course,1910).

Howard Watson (1907–) ASGCA: President, 1958

Born: Dresden, Ontario, Canada.

Howard Watson attended the University of Toronto, majoring in bacteriology at the School of Agriculture in Guelph. He met golf architect Stanley Thompson through a classmate, Edwin I. Wood, who later became an influential Canadian landscape architect. Thompson started Watson and another classmate, C. E. "Robbie" Robinson, on their respective careers on the same day in June 1929 at the Royal York GC, then under construction in Toronto. Both went on to become well-known designers.

In 1930 Watson was sent to work with Robert Trent Jones in Rochester, New York, in the newly formed Thompson, Jones & Company. As the Depression progressed, he became involved in a variety of occupations in addition to his work at Thompson, Jones. Among these were a position as greenkeeper at the Port Arthur (Ontario) GC, self-employment as a turf consultant in Toronto, the design of his first solo course at Seaforth, Ontario, and the redesign of the golf course at Noranda Mines (Quebec), where he also became a diamond driller, mucker boss and blasting foreman. During the war years from 1940 to 1945, he served overseas with the Royal Canadian Engineers.

In 1945 Watson rejoined Stanley Thompson, remaining until 1949, when he established Canadian Golf Landscaping Ltd. of Lachute, Quebec, a firm engaged in course design. He was joined in this firm by his son John in 1969.

Watson felt that his thoughts on course architecture were adequately summed up in David A. Forgan's definition of golf: "It is a science, the study of a lifetime in which you may exhaust yourself but never your subject."

Courses by Howard Watson:
MANITOBA: Pinawa GC (9,1964).
NEW BRUNSWICK: Pokemouche GC, Caraquet (1974).
ONTARIO: Aguasabon GC, Terrace Bay (1955); Bay of Quinte GC, Bellville (1964); Brian Thicke Estate, Orangeville (1974); Brockville GC (36,1966); Cherry Downs GC, Claremont (27,1962); Chrysler Memorial Park, Morrisburg (9,1958); Crang Estate, Toronto (1953); Deep River GC (9,1952); Don Valley Muni, Toronto (18,1955;r.27,1973); Downsview G&CC, Toronto (27,1955); F.A. McConnel, Caledon (3,1954); Flemingdon Park GC, Toronto (9,1959); Idylwylde G&CC, Sudbury (r.9,a.9,1961); Kanata GC, Ottawa (9,1966); Manderly GC, North Gower (1962); Manitouwadge GC (1971); Metro Toronto Board of Trade (36,-1963); Mississauga GC, Port Credit (r.3,a.9,1973); North Bay G&CC (r.9,a.9,1963); Pine Valley GC, Woodbridge (1960); Pineview GC, Ottawa (36,1968); R.H. Storrer Estate, Woodbridge (1966); Rideau View CC, Manotick (1957); Scarlett Woods GC, Toronto (1972); Seaforth GC (9,1953); Spruce Needles GC, Timmins (1959); Sumner Heights GC, Cornwall (9,1968); Tam O'Shanter Muni, Toronto (1974); Upper Canada CC, Oakville (1964); Woodbine Downs GC, Toronto (1960).
QUEBEC: Asbestos G&CC (1966); Bonaventure GC, Fauvel (9,1973); Bonniebrook GC, St. Colomban (1966); Carling Lake GC, Pine Hill (1961); Cedarbrook GC, Ste. Sophie (1959); Champlain GC, Ville, Brossard (1963); Le Chantecler, Ste. Adel (1964); Chicoutimi GC (1955); CdG Adstock, Thetford Mines (1970); CdG Baie Comeau (r.9,a.9,1973); CdG Berthier, Berthierville (1959); CdG Bromont, Shefford (1963); CdG Cap Rouge (1959); CdG Chambly (1960); CdG Charny (r.9,a.9,1971); CdG Chicoutimi (1965); CdG de Joliette (1951); CdG du Bic, Rimouski (1962); CdG Granby-St. Paul (r.18,a.18,1974); CdG Grand Pabos, Chandler (r.9,a.9,1972); CdG Lac Beauport (1961); CdG Lapraire, Montreal (27,-1963); CdG le Portage, L'Assomtion (1963); CdG les Dunes, Sorel (r.18,a.18,1952); CdG Longchamps, Sherbrooke (1969); CdG St. Laurent, Ile D'Orleans (1971); CdG St. Michel, St. Michel De Vaudreuil (36,1960); CdG Ste. Anne, Beaupre (36,1972); CdG Ste. Marie, Mont Ste. Marie (1974); CdG Triangle D'Or, St. Remi (1968); CdG Vallee de Parc, Grandmere (1972); CdG Victoriaville (r.9,a.9,1960); Le Club Seigneurie de Grand Pre Inc., Louisville (1962); Club Vielles Forges, Three Rivers (1973); Concordia GC, Ste. Therese (1962); Cowansville GC (1963); Dorval GC (1974); Douglas H. Keen Estate, Austin (9,1974); Harve des Isles GC, Montreal (1966); Hillsdale G&CC, Ste. Therese (18,1953;18,1958); Hudson G & Curling C, Hudson Heights (1969); Ile Bourdon GC, Montreal (1969); Islesmere G&CC, Ste. Dorothee (9,1965); Knowlton GC, Brome (r.9,a.9,1970); La Tuque G& Curling C (r.9,a.9,1969); Lac Thomas GC, St. Didace (9,1962); Lachute GC (r.9,a.18,1948); Lachute G&CC (1956); Lennoxville GC (1964); Leonard Wheatley, Hillhead (3,1962); Lorette GC, Quebec (r.9,a.9,1962); Mountain Ranches GC, Rigaud (1967); Nun's Island GC, Montreal (1967); Pinegrove G&CC, Montreal (27,1958); Riviere Du Loup GC (r.9,a.9,1974); Royal Quebec GC, Boischatel (9,1958;9,1964); St. Georges GC, St. Georges de Beauce (1959); St. Luc GC (1971); Ste. Marie de Beauce GC (9,1967); Ste. Marguerite, Sept Isles (9,1954); Salzborg Property, Morin Heights (1954); Le Seigneurie de Vaudreuil (1969); Shawinigan G&CC (1962); Thetford Mines G & Curling C (r.9,a.9,1971); Wentworth GC, Ille Perrot (1964); Whitlock G&CC, Hudson (9,1961;r.18,1970).
COLOMBIA: Club Campestre de Cucuta (1958); CC de Manizales (1953); CC El Rodeo, Medellin (1953); CC Militar, Melgar (1954).
JAMAICA: Caynamas G&CC, Spanish Town (1955).
UNITED STATES: A.D. Dana Estate, Stowe, Vermont (9,1966); Aroostook Valley GC, Fort Fairfield (r.9,a.9,1958); Obrien Estate, Plattsburgh, New York (27,1962); Pembroke Lakes GC, Hollywood, Florida (18,1973;27,1974).
Courses Remodeled by Howard Watson:
ONTARIO: Forest Hills GC, Toronto (27,1956); Larrimac GC, Ottawa (9,1973); Rosedale GC, Toronto (1951); Thornhill GC, Toronto (1954); Toronto GC, Port Credit (9,1962;5.1968).
QUEBEC: Beaconsfield GC, Montreal (6,1970); Candiac GC (1974); CdG Alpin, Ste. Brigitte de Laval (1972); CdG Port, Port Alfred (9,1963); Fort Prevel GC (9,1974); Grandmere GC (3,1967); Green Valley GC, Ste. Monique (1965); Kanawaki GC, Montreal (9,1963); Ki-8-EB

221

GC, Three Rivers (2,1974); Laval-sur-le-Lac GC (9,1966); Levis GC (1956); Marlborough GC, Montreal (1964); Mont Tremblant GC (9,1974); New Glasgow (1974); Noranda Mines GC (9,1935); Royal Ottawa GC, Hull (27,1966); Val Morin GC (1971).
   JAMAICA: Upton G&CC, Ocho Rios (9,1961).

John Watson (1933–   ) ASGCA
Born: Toronto, Ontario, Canada.
   John Watson served as a pilot in the Royal Canadian Air Force, resigning his commission in 1967 to accept a flight test position with North American Rockwell. In 1969 he joined the practice of his father, golf architect Howard Watson, training under and working with him on about twenty projects. He entered private practice under the firm name of John Watson Golf Design Limited in 1975.
Courses by John Watson: (Courses prior to 1976 are in collaboration with Howard Watson)
   NEW BRUNSWICK: CdG Pokemouche, Caraguet (9,1977).
   ONTARIO: Amberwood Village GC, Stittsville (9,1977).
   QUEBEC: Bonaventure GC, Fauvel, Gaspe (9,1975); CdG Charny (9,1973); CdG Montcalm, St-Liguori (1976); CdG St-Luc (9,1976); CdG St-Patrick (r.9,a.9,1974); CdG Terrebonne (r.3,a.9,1976); CdG Vielles Forges, Trois-Rivieres (1974); Granby-St-Paul GC, Granby (36,1974); Mont Ste-Anne GC, Ste-Anne de Beaupre (1975); Mont Ste-Marie GC, Lac Ste-Marie (9,1975;9,1977); Mount Adstock GC (9,1975); Royal Quebec GC, Montmorency (a.2,1974); Sorel-Tracy GC (r.6,a.9,1976); Thetford Mines GC (r.9,a.9,1975); Val Niegette GC, Rimouski (9,1979).
Courses Remodeled by John Watson:
   QUEBEC: Baie Comeau GC (1,1975); Candiac GC (2,1976); CdG Alpin, Ste-Brigite (3,1973); Hillsdale GC, Ste-Therese (1,1974); Kanawaki GC, Caugnawauga (3,1976); Ki-8-EB GC, Trois-Rivieres (2,1975); Larrimac GC (3,1974).

Richard Watson (1932–   )
Born: Fairbury, Nebraska.
   Richard Watson attended Fairbury Jr. College and Doane College, and received a B.S. degree in zoology from Nebraska University. He then served for four years with the U. S. Navy, learning to play golf while stationed in Pensacola, Florida. Upon his return to Nebraska, he was employed as district sales manager with a major pharmaceutical company, and he continued to play golf, competing successfully in many local and regional tournaments, and winning the 1962 Lincoln (Nebraska) City Publinks title.
   In 1963 Watson resigned to build and operate a par-3 course in Lincoln. He retained Denver golf architect Henry Hughes to assist him with the project. Hughes stayed on in Nebraska to build several small town courses, and Watson collaborated on both design and construction phases. The two formed a partnership in the mid-1960s, planning several courses in the Midwest.
   In 1970 Hughes retired to Colorado, and Watson continued to practice on his own in Nebraska. He had designed or remodeled some forty courses by the end of the 1970s.
Courses by Richard Watson:
   IOWA: Creston GC (9); Iowa National GC, Panora (1972); Lake Panorama GC (9 par 3,1973).
   KANSAS: Belleville CC (9,c.Hughes); Chapman CC (9); Scott County CC, Scott City (9,c.Hughes); Indian Hills Muni, Chapman (9,1977).
   KENTUCKY: Doe Valley G&CC, Brandenberg (1973).
   NEBRASKA: Ashland CC (9,1968,c.Hughes); Bloomfield-Wausa CC (9,c.Hughes); Colonial GC, Lincoln (9 par 3,1964;c.Hughes;n.l.e.); Friend CC (9,1967,c.Hughes); Mid-County CC, Arapahoe (9,c.Hughes); Pine Lake GC, Lincoln (9 par 3,1973); Tara Hills GC, Papillion (1978); Wayne CC (original 9,c.Hughes).
   SOUTH DAKOTA: Mitchell CC (original 9); Lakeview Muni.
   TEXAS: Sinton Muni (1968,c.Hughes).
   VIRGINIA: Massanuetten Mountain Greens GC, Harrisburg (a.2nd 9); The Summit GC at Lake Holiday, Winchester (1972).
   WEST VIRGINIA: Claymont Chase CC.
   WYOMING: Midway CC, Greybull (9,c.Hughes).

William "Willie" Watson
   Willie Watson emigrated to the United States from Scotland in 1898 to help Robert Foulis lay out and build the original nine holes at Minikahda CC in Minneapolis. He remained at Minikahda as pro-greenkeeper during the summer months, and as early as 1901 was also serving as golf instructor at the Hotel Green GC in Pasadena, California, during the winter.
   Prior to World War I, most of Watson's design work was done in Minnesota, Michigan and Illinois. Following the War he was based in Los Angeles until 1931. He then became professional at the Charlevoix (Michigan) CC, when golf course construction was severely curtailed by the Depression.
Courses by William "Willie" Watson:
   CALIFORNIA: Fort Washington CC; Harding Park GC, San Francisco (1925); Hillcrest CC, Los Angeles (1920); Hotel Green GC, Pasadena (9,1901;n.l.e.); Lake Arrowhead CC (Original 9); Olympic Club, San Francisco (Ocean course,1924,c.S. Whiting); Orinda CC (1924); Sunset Canyon Par 3 GC, Burbank (9,1921;n.l.e.); [Watson may also have designed Sonoma National (1928) and Berkeley GC [now Miravista] and remodeled Olympic Club's Lakeside course (1924).
   ILLINOIS: Garden of Eden GC, Momence (9); Momenoe CC; Olympia Fields CC (Course #2,1919;n.l.e.).
   MICHIGAN: Belvedere GC, Charlevoix (1917); Charlevoix Muni (9).
   MINNESOTA: Interlachen CC, Edina (Original course,1910); Minikahda CC, Minneapolis (Original 9,1899 c.R.Foulis).

William R. Watts (1932–   )
Born: Miami, Florida.
   William Watts attended the University of Miami, where he was a member of the golf team. A

lifelong amateur golfer, he won more than thirty local and regional titles in southern Florida. In the late 1950s Watts designed and built the Sunrise CC, which he owned and managed. Over the next twenty years he designed a dozen other courses in the Gold Coast area of Florida. In the late 1970s he joined with golf architect William Dietsch to form a course design firm known as Ecolo-Golf.
Courses by William R. Watts:
   FLORIDA: Arrowhead CC, Fort Lauderdale (1968); Broken Woods G&RC, Coral Springs (Exec. course,1966); Deer Creek G&CC, Deerfield Beach; Foxcroft CC [formerly Fairway CC], Miramar (1968); Hollywood Lakes CC (East course,1965;West course,1967); Lago Mar CC, Fort Lauderdale (1970); Miami Lakes Inn & CC (1963;a.18); Sun'n Lake CC, Lake Placid (Exec. course,1969); Sun'n Lake of Sebring; Sunrise CC, Fort Lauderdale (1960).
   GEORGIA: Sky Valley CC, Dillard.

Ernest W. Way (–1943)
Born: Westward Ho!, Devonshire, England. Died: Miami, Florida.
   Ernest Way was the son of an English cabinetmaker and the brother of golfers Ed, Jack and "Bert" Way. He and Jack emigrated to the United States around 1905 to join their elder brother Bert, already a successful golfer in America at the time. After brief jobs at golf clubs in Pittsburgh and Richmond, Virginia, Ernest moved to the Detroit GC, where Bert had just built a new course. He remained as head professional at Detroit until 1919 and during his tenure, supervised construction of the club's two Donald Ross courses. Jack became the professional of the Canterbury Club near Cleveland, Ohio, where he remodeled the course and added three holes in the early 1920s.
   A charter member of the Michigan PGA and a member of both the PGA of America and the National Greenkeepers Association, Ernest resigned from the Detroit GC to design and build courses in Michigan in the 1920s. He returned to his position as course superintendent at Detroit in the 1930s; but ill health forced him to retire in 1937, and he moved to Florida, where he resided until his death.
Courses by Ernest W. Way:
   FLORIDA: Hotel Indiatlantic GC, Melbourne (n.l.e.).
   MICHIGAN: Belle Isle Muni, Detroit (9,1922;n.l.e.); Birch Hill GC, Detroit (n.l.e.); Edgewood CC, Union Lakes; Grosse Ile G&CC (1919); Pine Lake CC, Orchard Lake (1923); Pontiac CC.

William H. "Bert" Way (1873–1963)
Born: Westward Ho!, Devonshire, England. Died: Miami, Florida, at age 90.
   "Bert" Way and his brothers grew up alongside the North Devon (now Royal) GC. All were proficient golfers who moved to America to further their careers. The first of his family to emigrate to the United States, Bert took a roundabout route. He had worked as an apprentice to Tom and "Young Willie" Dunn in England and Biarritz, France; and when Willie traveled to America to design and build Shinnecock Hills, Bert Way soon followed.
   In 1896 Bert found one of the few available club professional jobs in the U. S., at the Meadow Brook Club in New York, where he worked for $100.00 a month. His duties left him plenty of time to work on his game, and he soon became a successful tournament golfer. In 1899 he was joint runner-up in the U. S. Open, though a distant eleven shots behind the winner, Willie Smith.
   By that time, Bert had moved to Detroit, Michigan, where he was hired to lay out several courses. He was also active in the Cleveland, Ohio, area. In 1909 he designed the Mayfield (Ohio) CC and stayed on as its professional until 1952. In this capacity he introduced John D. Rockefeller to golf. Bert continued to design and remodel courses while at Mayfield, and his best-known creation is the Firestone CC in Akron, which was considerably toughened by Robert Trent Jones in the 1950s.
   A member of the national PGA and the NAGA, Bert was especially active in Senior golf activities. He served as PGA Senior president in 1946–47, won several Senior events and was at one time the oldest living PGA professional. He died in Miami in August of 1963, just two weeks short of his ninety-first birthday.
Courses by William H. "Bert" Way:
   KENTUCKY: Sundowner GC, Ashland (9,1953).
   MICHIGAN: CC of Detroit, Lake St. Clair (1898,n.l.e.); Detroit CC (1905,n.l.e.).
   OHIO: Euclid Heights CC (1900,n.l.e.); Firestone CC, Akron (original 18, now "South course",1929); Firestone Public GC, Akron (1929,n.l.e.); Mayfield CC, South Euclid (1911).

Tom Wells
   Professional golfer Tom Wells established a golf school in New York in 1898. In the 1920s he advertised as a golf architect and planned several New York courses, including Bayside Links, Belleclaire Golf Links and Elmsford CC.

Kenneth Welton
   Kenneth Welton trained under golf architect Stanley Thompson in the 1920s, leaving to take a job with the Green Section of the USGA. In the course of his work there he wrote numerous articles on course design, construction and maintenance. Following retirement in 1963, he formed the golf design firm of Welton and Collett in California but died a short time afterward.

Henry James Whigham (1869–1954)
Born: Prestwick, Scotland. Died: Southampton, New York, at age 85.
   H. J. Whigham, descended from one of Prestwick's oldest golfing families, was the son of one of C. B. Macdonald's golfing friends when Macdonald was an undergraduate at St. Andrews University. An Oxford graduate, Whigham traveled to the United States in 1895 to lecture on English literature and political economy at the university level. Shortly after his arrival, he became drama critic for the *Chicago Tribune*, a post from which he took time off in 1896 and '97 to win the U. S. Amateur Championship.

From 1896 to 1907 Whigham served as war correspondent for several British and American newspapers, covering the Battle of San Juan (where he was captured), the Boer War, the Boxer Rebellion of 1899, the Macedonian Rebellion and the Russo–Japanese War. He returned to the United States in 1908, becoming editor of *Metropolitan* magazine and of *Town and Country* in 1909. He was author of *How to Play Golf* and of books on a variety of other subjects, from the *Persian Problem* (1903) to one on the New Deal (1936).

In his first years in the United States, Whigham had laid out the original Onwentsia CC in Chicago in collaboration with H. J. Tweedie and James and Robert Foulis. After his marriage in 1909 to C. B. Macdonald's daughter Frances, he assisted his father-in-law in planning the National Golf Links of America. Whigham took a friendly interest in Macdonald's design work and in the work of other early golf architects on the East Coast. He also remodeled the Morris County CC in New Jersey, rerouting several holes and adding others.

Jack White (1873–1949)
Born: Dirleton, Scotland.

Jack White, professional golfer at Sunningdale in England for many years, won the British Open in 1904. He assisted Willie Park, Jr., with the design and construction of several courses and is thought to have consulted on modifications to numerous established layouts in the London area. On his own he designed the Clacton-On-Sea GC in Essex, England.

Robert White (1874–1959) ASGCA: Charter Member
Born: St Andrews Scotland, died Myrtle Beach, South Carolina at age 85.

In 1894 Robert White emigrated from St. Andrews, Scotland, to the United States to study agronomy. For a short period around 1895 he served as pro-greenkeeper at Myopia Hunt Club in Massachusetts and in 1902 moved to Ravisloe CC in Illinois. Later he was professional at Wykagyl CC in Westchester County, New York. During his career, White laid out a number of courses at which he remained as pro-superintendent for several years, as well as planning or revising others.

White became the first president of the PGA, a founding member of the ASGCA, a pioneer in scientific turfgrass management and a leading golf businessman. His career is outlined in *The PGA* by Herb Graffis.

Courses by Robert White
KENTUCKY: Louisville CC, (Original 9).
MASSACHUSETTS: North Salem Links, Salem (9,1885, nle).
NEW JERSEY: Green Brook CC, Caldwell.
NORTH CAROLINA: Pine Lakes GC.
OHIO: Cincinnati CC (r.9, add 9)
PENNSYLVANIA: Longue Vue Club, Verona; Skytop Club, Skytop; Watergap CC [formerly Wolf Hollow CC], Delaware Watergap.
SOUTH CAROLINA: Ocean Forest CC [now Pine Lakes International GC]; Myrtle Beach.
Courses Remodeled by Robert White:
ILLINOIS: Ravisloe CC.
NEW YORK: Richmond County CC, Staten Island; Wykagyl CC.

Sam Whiting (1880–1956)
Sam Whiting was professional at the Lakeside G&CC from 1920 to 1924, when the course was sold to the Olympic Club of San Francisco. Whiting was then hired as superintendent of the "Lakeside Course" of Olympic and in that capacity supervised construction in 1924 of a second eighteen, the "Ocean Course" designed by Willie Watson. He also supervised construction of Watson's design of nearby Harding Park Muni.

Whiting is credited with remodeling Olympic's Lakeside Course in 1924, although it is likely that architect Watson planned the changes. Whiting was certainly responsible for the massive tree-planting program that eventually made Lakeside one of the tightest courses in the country. He is also credited with "building" Sonoma National GC in California (1928), but records are unclear as to whether he built it to his own design or to Watson's. In either case, Whiting's work is a good example of the overlapping roles of architect, superintendent and professional so prevalent in the history of course design.

Sam Whiting continued as superintendent at Olympic until his poor health forced his retirement in 1954. It was a disappointment to him that he was unable to handle the course for the U. S. Open tournament scheduled there in the following year.

Ronald Edward Whitten (1950–   )
Born: Omaha, Nebraska.

Ronald Whitten received a B.S. degree in 1972 from the University of Nebraska, and a J.D. degree in 1977 from the Washburn University School of Law. A practicing trial attorney, he served as an assistant district attorney in Topeka, Kansas.

Whitten's interest in golf course design was born in 1967, when he visited the Chicago GC and Beverly CC courses in Illinois. He began compiling information about courses and course architects in 1969, eventually establishing one of the world's most complete data banks on the subject. In 1974 Whitten was a contributor to Frank Hannigan's article on golf architect A. W. Tillinghast that appeared in the *USGA Journal*.

Thomas Winton (1871–1944)
Born: Montrose, Scotland. Died: Tuckahoe, New York, at age 73.

Thomas Winton, descended from a famous Scottish golfing family, was the son of James Winton, longtime pro and club maker at Montrose. Tom's brothers all became professionals and club makers, and Tom studied under his father as well but moved to London at the turn of the century. There he became involved in golf course construction, working for several architects and building such courses as Coombe Hill and South Herts.

At the outbreak of World War I, Winton joined Willie Park Jr.'s crew and moved to the United States, but course construction soon stopped there as well as in Britain. Winton took a

position as superintendent for the Westchester (New York) County Park Commission, where he remained for many years. He was in charge of maintaining the county's golf courses and other parks, and of constructing new facilities as well. In this capacity he designed several public courses in the New York suburbs.

Winton soon found additional design jobs and in the 1920s was active along the eastern seaboard, laying out courses and supervising their construction. When design business fell off in the Depression, he continued in his park commission position and also served as a maintenance consultant for several New York clubs.

Courses by Thomas Winton:
CONNECTICUT: Mill River CC, Bridgeport.
MASSACHUSETTS: Woods Hole GC.
NEW JERSEY: Cranmoor CC, Toms River; Hopewell Valley GC, Hopewell Junction.
NEW YORK: Amityville CC; Colgate University GC, Hamilton (n.l.e.); Corning CC; Hollow Brook CC, Peekskill; Kingsridge CC, Portchester (1929); Lawrence Farms CC, Mt. Kisco; Maplemoor GC, White Plains (1927); Mohansic Park GC, Yorktown Heights (1925); Pelham Bay Park GC (Split Rock course,1934); Saxon Woods GC, Mamaroneck; Sprain Brook GC, Yonkers (27,1928); Westport GC (1928).
VIRGINIA: Lynn Haven CC, Norfolk.
Courses Remodeled by Thomas Winton:
NEW YORK: Apawamis Club, Rye (r.greens); Siwanoy CC, Mt. Vernon; Sleepy Hollow CC, Scarborough-On-Hudson; Westchester CC, Rye (r.greens,36 holes).

Benjamin J. Wihry (1913–   ) ASGCA
Born: Haverhill, Massachusetts.

Ben Wihry received a B.S. (1935) and B.L.A. (1941) degree from what is now the University of Massachusetts. He was employed as a recreational planner for the U. S. Forest Service from 1935 to 1940, and from 1941 to 1946 served with the U. S. Army Corps of Engineers.

In 1946 Wihry entered private practice in planning, engineering and landscape architecture. His firm, which became Miller, Wihry, Lee, Inc. of Louisville, Kentucky, branched into golf course architecture around 1964, after Wihry had worked with and studied under his friend and former classmate, E. Lawrence Packard.

Courses by Benjamin J. Wihry:
INDIANA: Elks Lodge GC, Jeffersonville (9,1969).
KENTUCKY: Barren River State Park, Glasgow (9,1970;9,1979); Bobby Nichols, Jefferson County (9,1964); Chenoweth Run, Jefferson County (9,1967); Danville CC (9,1974); Eagle's Nest CC, Somerset (1977); Eastern Kentucky University, Richmond (1972); Elizabethtown CC (9,1968); Hunting Creek CC, Prospect (1965); Iroquois, Louisville (r.3,a.9,1964); Lexington CC (r.4,a.5,1975); Long Run, Jefferson County (9,1965;9,1980); Rough River State Park, Falls of Rough (9,1972); Seneca Muni, Louisville (r.8,a,18,1972); Shelbyville CC (2,1974).
TENNESSEE: Nashboro National CC, Nashville (1974); Paris Landing State Park (1970), Pickwick Landing State Park (1973).
Courses Remodeled by Benjamin J. Wihry:
KENTUCKY: Louisville CC (r.1,a.1,1974); Sun Valley GC, Louisville (9,1972).
TENNESSEE: Swan Lake CC, Clarksville (1977).

Willard G. Wilkinson (1889–1979) ASGCA
Born: Wimbledon, England. Died: Arizona.

After service with the Royal Flying Corps during World War I, Willard Wilkinson moved to the United States, where he attended Rutgers University and then went to work as assistant to golf architect A. W. Tillinghast. Eventually, he became vice-president of A. W. Tillinghast Golf Construction Company Inc., and during these years supervised construction at Winged Foot, Fresh Meadows and other renowned layouts.

In 1921 Wilkinson entered private practice, aided by his former employer, who arranged for him to complete three Tillinghast courses and receive the fees still due on them. He went on to design eighty-seven courses and remodel sixteen, in the continental United States, Hawaii (where he resided for many years), the Caribbean, the Philippines, Guam, Japan and Tahiti. He was assisted by his son, Col. Robert N. Wilkinson (USAF, ret.), during several of the years when his practice was based in Honolulu. Wilkinson moved to Arizona shortly after his retirement in 1969.

Courses by Willard G. Wilkinson:
HAWAII: Fort Shafter GC, Honolulu; Hilo Muni; Kauai Surf G&CC, Kauai (1969); Mid Pacific (a.9); GC Honolulu; Pali Muni; Pacific Palisades Par 3.
NEW JERSEY: Galloping Hills GC; Jumping Brook GC, Neptune; Echo Lake (r.3,1928).
JAPAN: Hayana International GC (1967).
PHILIPPINES: Binicitan GC, Manila; Subic Bay GC (1966).
TAHITI: Atimoona G&CC (1965).

Joseph B. Williams
Joseph Williams served as superintendent at the Santa Clara (California) CC in the 1960s and then designed Shorecliffs CC in San Clemente and became its superintendent. He later planned several more courses in the Southwest.

Courses by Joseph B. Williams:
CALIFORNIA: Golden Hills GC, Tehachapi (1966); Navy GC, Cypress; Nixon Estate GC, San Clemente (1970); Shorecliffs CC (Estrella GC); San Clemente (1964); Tahoe Donner GC, Truckee (1975).
UTAH: Davis County GC, Layton (1974); Roosevelt Muni (1973); Tri-City GC, American Fork.

John Harold Williams, Sr. (1920–   )
Born: Alabama.

John H. Williams attended the University of Alabama and served in the military for four and one half years during World War II. He became a professional golfer in 1945, joining the PGA of America and becoming a charter member of the Alabama PGA.

Williams owned and operated the Meadowbrook Golf Club in Tuscaloosa, Alabama, until 1962. He played frequently on the Pro Tour during that time and won the Alabama Open once, the Mississippi Open twice and the Alabama PGA Championship on several occasions. Williams began designing golf courses on a part-time basis in the late 1950s.

Courses by John Harold Williams, Sr.:

ALABAMA: Anniston CC (r.); Canoe Creek CC, Gadsen; The Country Club, Reform; Grayson Valley CC, Birmingham; Indian Hills CC, Tuscaloosa (c.T.Nicol,1960); Indian Oaks CC, Anniston (1968); Pine Harbor Champions G&CC, Pell City; Terrapin Hills GC, Ft. Payne; University of Alabama GC, Tuscaloosa (original 9,c.T.Nicol,1959).

Tom Williamson (1880–1950)

Born: England. Died: England.

Tom Williamson's career as pro-greenkeeper and club maker at the Notts Golf Club spanned more than half a century, from 1896 until his death in 1950. He laid out numerous courses on the side and in 1919 claimed to have worked on all but one of the courses within a fifty-mile radius of Nottingham. Over the years he designed or remodeled some sixty courses and was assisted by his brother Hugh with the construction of several. Tom Williamson was an early advocate of plasticine models of new greens.

Courses by Tom Williamson:

ENGLAND: Ashover, Derbys; Beeston Fields, Nottm.; Belton Park, Grantham, Lincs.; Bulwell Hall, Notts.; Burton-on-Trent, Staffs.; Cavendish, Buxton, Derbys.; Edgbaston, B'ham.; Garforth, near Leeds; Hillsborough, Sheffield; Ladbrook Park, Warks; Leek, Staffs.; Longcliffe, Leics.; Louth, Lincs. (before 1906;New course,after1919); Mapperley, Nottm.; Matlock, Derbys.; Melton Mowbray, Leics.; Mullion, Cornwall; Nuneaton, Warks; Ratcliffe-on-Trent, Notts.; Retford, Notts.; Rothley Park, Leics.; Rushcliffe, Notts.; Rushden, Northants.; Scraptoft, Leics.; Serlby Park, Retford (before 1906; New course,after 1907); Sleaford, Lincs.; Southwell, Notts.; Stanton-on-the-Wold, Derbys.; Tibworth, Leics.; Trentham, Staffs.; Wellingborough, N'hants.; Wollaton Park, Nottm.; Worksop, Notts.

SWITZERLAND: Zurich (1929).

Courses Remodeled by Tom Williamson:

ENGLAND: Birstall, Leics. (after 1914); Bulwell Forest, Nottm (aft.1914); Buxton High Peaks, Derbys.(aft.1914); Chatsworth, Derbys.(before 1914); Chesterfield, Derbys. (bef.1914); Chilwell Manor, Notts.(aft.1914); Edgbaston GC, Erewash Valley GC, Derby (bef.1914); Grimsby, Lincs.(aft.1914); Hollinwell, Notts.(bef.1914); Lees Hall, Sheffield (bef.1914); Ockbrook (bef.1914); Radcliffe-on-Trent, Notts.(aft.1914); Renishaw, Yorks. (aft.1914); Sherwood Forest, Notts.(aft.1914); Sickleholme (bef.1914); Sutton-on-Sea, Lincs.(bef. and aft.1914); West Runton, Norfolk (aft.1914).

Hugh Irvine Wilson (1879–1925)

Born: Philadelphia, Pennsylvania. Died: Bryn Mawr, Pennsylvania, at age 45.

Hugh Wilson graduated in 1902 from Princeton University, where he had been captain of the golf team. Following college, he joined a Philadelphia insurance brokerage firm and eventually became its president.

A lifelong amateur golfer, Wilson was a member of Aronimink GC and the Merion Cricket Club. In 1910 he was chosen to make a survey of great British courses in preparation for a new Merion course. Wilson spent seven months in England and Scotland, returning with armloads of sketches and notes, and then proceeded, with the assistance of Richard S. Francis, to lay out a new course at Ardmore, Pennsylvania. With the exception of later changes to four holes and the rebunkering of most, Merion East remains as Wilson designed it in 1912.

Hugh Wilson also planned the West course at Merion (1914) and the Cobb's Creek Municipal GC in Philadelphia (1917). With the assistance of his brother, Alan, he finished the remaining four holes at Pine Valley after George Crump's death in 1919; and he consulted with William S. Flynn on the design of the Kittansett Club in Marion, Massachusetts, a design not executed in its entirety.

Louis Sibbett "Dick" Wilson (1904–1965)

Born: Philadelphia, Pennsylvania. Died: Boynton Beach, Florida, at age 61.

"Dick" Wilson was a fine athlete as a youth and attended the University of Vermont on a football scholarship, although he did not graduate. He had served as water boy for a construction crew at Merion West in 1914, and later worked on a Toomey and Flynn crew during the revision of Merion in the mid-1920s.

Wilson remained with Toomey and Flynn, becoming a construction superintendent and later a design associate. He is credited with making major contributions to Flynn's redesign of Shinnecock Hills GC, New York, which reopened in 1931. In the early thirties Wilson moved to Florida to construct the Indian Creek Club, Miami Beach, to Flynn's plans. But with Toomey's death and the decline of Flynn's business due to the Depression, Wilson took a job as course superintendent at Delray Beach CC. He remained there until World War II, accepting a few local design or reconstruction jobs on the side. He spent the war years constructing and camouflaging airfields.

In 1945 Wilson formed his own golf design company in association with a Miami earthmoving firm, the Troup Brothers. His early post-war works, especially the West Palm Beach CC and the NCR CC in Dayton, Ohio, established him as one of the most sought-after architects of the 1950s and 60s. Wilson did relatively few courses in the later years of his life, however. Quality, not quantity, was his concern, and he tried to give personal attention to each work bearing his name. He also had a staff of loyal and talented assistants who handled much of the actual design and construction work on some projects, including Joseph L. Lee (Wilson's partner after 1959), Frank Batto, Robert Von Hagge, Ward Northrup and Robert Simmons.

Courses by Louis Sibbett "Dick" Wilson:

ARIZONA: Moon Valley CC, Phoenix (1958).

CALIFORNIA: Annenberg Estate GC, Rancho Mirage; La Costa CC, Carlsbad (1964).

DELAWARE: Bidermann GC, Wilmington; Wilmington CC, Greenville (North course,1962).

FLORIDA: Bay Hill Club, Orlando (1961); Cape Coral CC (1963); Cypress Lakes CC, Ft. Myers (1960); Doral CC, Miami (Blue & Red courses,1962); Golden Gate CC, Naples (1965); Harder Hall Hotel GC, Sebring (1958); Hole-in-the-Wall GC, Naples (1959); J.D.M. CC [formerly PGA National GC], Palm Beach Gardens (East & West courses,1964; now parts of South & North courses at J.D.M.); Lone Palm GC, Lakeland (1965); Melreese GC [formerly LeJenue Road CC], Miami (1962); Palm Aire CC of Sarasota [formerly DeSoto Lakes I G&CC] (1958); Palm Beach Par 3 GC (9,1961); Palmetto CC, South Miami (1960); Pine Tree CC, Delray Beach (1962); Royal Oak G&CC, Titusville (1964); Tamarac CC, Ft. Lauderdale (1961); Tequesta CC, Jupiter, (1958); West Palm Beach CC (1947); Westview CC, Miami (original 9, 1949).

GEORGIA: Callaway Gardens GC, Pine Mountain (Lakeview course: 9,1952;a.9,1963; Mountainview course,1963); Canongate GC, Palmetto (1965); Jekyll Island GC (Oleander course,1961); Mystery Valley GC, Lithonia (1966); Sea Island GC (Retreat 9,1959).

ILLINOIS: Cog Hill GC, Lemont (r.Courses/1&2,1963;a.Courses/3&4 ("Dubsdread"), 1964).

LOUISIANA: Oakbourne CC, Lafayette (1958).

MISSISSIPPI: The CC of Jackson (27,1963).

NEVADA: Winterwood GC, Las Vegas (1964).

NEW JERSEY: Bedens Brook Club, Skillman.

NEW YORK: Cavalry Club, Manlius (1966); Deepdale CC, Manhasset (1956;r.1962); Meadow Brook Club, Jericho (1955); North Redoubt Club, Garrison-on-Hudson (1963) (now Garrison CC).

OHIO: Coldstream CC, Cincinnati (1960); NCR CC, Dayton (North & South courses,1954).

PENNSYLVANIA: Laurel Valley CC, Ligonier (1960); Penn Hills Club, Bradford (r.9,a.9); Radnor Valley CC, Villanova (1953).

TENNESSEE: American GC, Chattanooga (18 par 3,1963); Brainerd G&CC, Chattanooga.

TEXAS: Jersey Village CC, Houston (1957); Long Meadows CC.

VIRGINIA: Glen Oak CC, Danville (9,1951); Hidden Valley CC, Salem (1952); Kinderton CC, Clarksville (1947).

WEST VIRGINIA: Fincastle CC, Bluefield (1963); The Greenbrier, White Sulphur Springs (Lakeside course,1962).

AUSTRALIA: Metropolitan GC, Victoria (r.11,a.8,1961).

BAHAMAS: King's Inn G&CC, Freeport (Emerald course,1965); Lucayan CC, Freeport (1964); Lyford Cay Club, New Providence (1960); Paradise Island GC [formerly Arawak GC], Nassau (1962); Treasure Cay GC, Abaco (1966); Tower GC, Bahamas Princess Hotel, Grand Bahamas Is.

CANADA: Royal Montreal GC, Ile Bizard (Blue, Green (9) & Red courses,1959).

CUBA: Villa Real GC, Havana (1957).

VENEZUELA: Lagunita CC, Caracas (1958).

Courses Remodeled by Louis Sibbett "Dick" Wilson:

CALIFORNIA: Bel Air CC, Los Angeles (1961).

FLORIDA: Dunedin CC (1960); Gulfstream GC; Indian Creek Club, Miami Beach; Lakewood GC, St. Petersburg (r.greens,1957); Riviera CC, Coral Gables (1962).

NEW JERSEY: Hollywood GC, Deal (1956).

NEW YORK: Scarsdale GC, Hartsdale (1956); Winged Foot GC, Mamaroneck (r.3,West course,1958).

OHIO: Columbus CC (1962); Inverness Club, Toledo (1956); Moraine CC, Dayton (1955); Scioto Cc, Columbus (1963).

PENNSYLVANIA: Aronimink GC, Newtown Square (1962).

TEXAS: Colonial CC, Ft. Worth (1956).

AUSTRALIA: Royal Melbourne GC (East & West courses,1959).

MEXICO: Club Campestre, Mexico City

James Winans

As an in-house golf architect for Sun City in Phoenix, Arizona, James Winans collaborated on many of the corporation's courses.

Theodore J. Wirth (1927–   )

Born: New Orleans, Louisiana.

Ted Wirth attended St. Thomas College, Kansas University and Iowa State University, where he received a B.S. degree in landscape architecture in 1950. After working as a park planner with the National Park Service for ten years, he entered private practice as a landscape architect in Montana in the early 1960s. Wirth served as president of the National Council of Park and Recreation Consultants and as vice-president of the American Society of Landscape Architects. Branching into golf course design in the late 1960s, he had planned several courses in the Montana area by the end of the 1970s.

Courses by Theodore J. Wirth:

MONTANA: Billings Muni (par 3,c.D. Bennett); Laurel G&RC (1968); Point North GC, Billings; Riverside GC, Bozeman; Valley View GC, Bozeman.

WYOMING: Powell Muni (9,1971).

Eugene F. "Skip" Wogan (1890–1957)

Born: Roxbury, Massachusetts. Died: Manchester, Massachusetts, at age 67.

"Skip" Wogan attended public schools in Watertown, Massachusetts, and after graduation from high school went to work as assistant professional under Donald Ross at the Essex County Club in Manchester. Ross retained the position of head professional at Essex through 1912 despite his involvement at Pinehurst and his growing design practice.

Upon Ross's retirement in 1913, Wogan succeeded him at Essex, remaining there as head professional and grounds manager until his death. He also carried on a design practice on the side, planning a number of courses in Massachusetts and other eastern states. Wogan's son Philip became a course architect; and two other sons, Louis and Richard, became contractors specializing in golf construction.

Courses by Eugene F. "Skip" Wogan:
MAINE: Mingo Springs, Rangeley Lakes (9); Webhannett GC, Kennebunkport; Willowdale GC, Portland.
MASSACHUSETTS: Arlmont CC, Arlington (9); Bellevue CC, Melrose (9); Blue Hills CC, Canton; Bristol County CC, Taunton (9); Cape Ann GC, Essex (9); Labor-in-Vain, Ipswich (9); Merrimack GC, Methuen (9); Needham GC (9); Sankaty Head GC, Nantucket; Walpole CC (9).
NEW JERSEY: Picatinny Arsenal G&TC, Dover.
Courses Remodeled by Eugene F. "Skip" Wogan:
MASSACHUSETTS: Bear Hill GC, Stoneham; Essex CC, Manchester; Tedesco CC, Marblehead; United Shoe CC, Beverly.

Philip A. Wogan (1918–   ) ASGCA
Born: Beverly, Massachusetts.
Philip Wogan attended North Carolina State College, Pennsylvania State College, Lehigh University and Boston University, where he received a bachelor's degree in biology and a master's degree in education. From 1947 to 1956 he taught biology on the high school level and during the same years, assisted his father, Eugene "Skip" Wogan, in golf course design on a part-time basis.
In 1956 Wogan retired from teaching to devote full time to golf architecture; and in 1958, after his father's death, he continued in practice on his own. Employing his joint background in biology and course design, he became a leading authority on the relationship of golf courses to the environment and prepared the ASGCA's widely distributed paper on the subject.
Courses by Philip A. Wogan:
MAINE: Bucksport G&CC (9,1969); Martindale CC, Auburn (2nd 9,1963); Tidewater CC, Trenton (1968); Val Halla CC, Cumberland (9,1965).
MASSACHUSETTS: Blue Hill CC, Canton (3rd 9,1955); CC of Billerica (9,1971); Franklin CC (a.10,1974); Halifax CC (1969); New Meadows GC, Topsfield (9,1963); Pembroke CC (1973); Rockland CC (18 par 3,1965); Rowley CC (9,1970).
NEW HAMPSHIRE: Charmingfare Links, Candia (1964); Cochecho CC, Dover (2nd 9,1965); Hoodkroft CC, Derry (9,1971); North Conway CC (2nd 9,1974); Rochester CC, Gonic (2nd 9,1964).
RHODE ISLAND: Spring Haven CC, Hope Valley (18 par 3,1966).
Courses Remodeled by Philip A. Wogan:
MASSACHUSETTS: Juniper Hills GC, Northboro (4,1972); Putterham Meadows, Brookline (2,1962); Rockport GC (2,1962).

Michael Stephen Wolveridge (1937–   )
Born: Essex, England.
After playing for a time on the professional tour in the United States, Michael Wolveridge worked with John Harris in the 1950s in New Zealand and other countries. In 1976 he formed a partnership with Peter Thomson, John Harris and Ronald Fream. The firm of Thomson, Wolveridge, Fream and Associates gained an international reputation for course design and construction. By 1980 the firm of Thomson and Wolveridge was the most active of any "Down Under" and in the Far East (some say the world).

Charles Campbell Worthington (1854–1944)
C. C. Worthington was famed as a pump manufacturer and later as a developer of mowing and other types of golf course maintenance equipment. He laid out several rudimentary courses on estates in the eastern United States. These included; a six-hole course on his own estate at Irvington-on-Hudson, New York, laid out before the turn of the century; Manwallimink GC at Shawnee on Delaware near Stroudsburg, Pennsylvania, built in 1898 on another of his own properties and believed to be the largest private estate east of the Mississippi; and the Calendo GC, a nine-hole layout in Calendo, Pennsylvania.
Worthington started A. W. Tillinghast on his road to fame as a course architect, when he hired him to design a quality course at Shawnee on Delaware in 1907. This was Tillinghast's first project. Worthington was also the grandfather of several men whose careers in the development and production of maintenance equipment were significant in the business world of golf. They included Edmund (Ross), Chester and Charles Sawtelle, and Edward Worthington, Jr., the son of a long-time president of the Worthington Mower Company.

Norman Woods
Norman Woods attended the Ontario Agricultural College at Guelph in the early 1930s and later became associated with golf architect Stanley Thompson. In the early 1950s he began his own practice in western Canada with offices in British Columbia.
Courses by Norman Woods:
ALBERTA: Broadmoor CC; Glendale CC; Indian Hills GC, Calgary; Willow Park CC, Calgary; Henderson Lake GC, Lethbridge; Stoney Plain GC.
BRITISH COLUMBIA: Harrison GC, Harrison Hotel (9,1961); Hirsch Creek CC, Kitimat; Kokanee Springs CC, Crawford Bay (1968); Mission GC; Penticton GC (a.9); Tsawwassen CC.
MANITOBA: Birds Hill CC; Falcon Beach Lake CC, Grand Beach GC; Rossmere G&CC, Winnipeg; St. Charles CC, Winnipeg (West 9,1954).
MONTANA: Hilands GC, Billings; Marias Valley G&CC, Shelby (1971); Signal Point CC, Fort Benton.
PENNSYLVANIA: Lords Valley CC, Hawley.
WASHINGTON: Capitol City GC, Olympia; Nile CC, Edmonds; Lake Wilderness CC (a.9).

George Wright (1847–   )
The founder of Wright and Ditson Sporting Goods of Boston, Massachusetts, George Wright laid out several informal courses in the 1890s in parks and vacant lots in the Boston area. Among these were a course at Franklin Park, the old Allston GC (n.l.e.) and an early version

of Wollaston GC. They were laid out in an attempt to popularize the recently introduced game of golf and thus increase the sales of playing equipment imported from Great Britain. An account of Wright's career can be found in *The Golf History of New England* by Jack Mahoney who notes that Wright has been called the "Father of New England Golf."

Ralph Wymer
Chicago-based engineer Ralph Wymer formed the design and build firm of Pioneer Golf and Landscape Company with James Foulis in 1927.
See James Foulis.

Tameshi Yamada
Course designer Tameshi Yamada is known to have planned Fujioka GC in his native Japan in 1971 with advice from Peter Thompson.

Arthur M. Young (1917–   )
Born: Kalamazoo, Michigan.
Arthur Young attended Northwestern University and was employed as a CPA with Swift & Co. in Chicago. He served in the U. S. Army during World War II and the Korean Conflict, and then resigned his accounting position to build his first golf course in Shelbyville, Michigan, in the early 1950s. After operating that course for several years and being admitted to the PGA of America, he designed and built other small town courses in Michigan.
Young moved to Florida in the late 1960s and designed and built several executive courses, which he owned and operated. In the 1970s he retired to operate the Crane Creek GC, which he helped Charles Ankrom to design.
Courses by Arthur M. Young:
FLORIDA: Crane Creek GC, Stuart (c.Ankrom,1977); Holiday CC, Ft. Pierce (Exec. course,1972); Holiday CC, Lake Park (Exec. course,1969); Holiday CC, Stuart (Exec. course,1971); North River Shores CC, Stuart (1972).
MICHIGAN: Duck Lake CC, Albion (a.9); Shelbyville GC (9,1955;9,1960); Whiffletree Hill GC, Concord (1970).

Albert Zikorus (1921–   ) ASGCA
Born: Needham, Massachusetts.
After caddying at Needham GC and Wellesley CC, Albert Zikorus attended the winter school for turfgrass managers at the University of Massachusetts and then served overseas with the U. S. Army Air Force. After the War he became superintendent at Old Newbury CC and later Wellesley CC, both in Massachusetts, and still later at Woodbridge CC in Connecticut.
Zikorus was associated in course design with golf architect William F. Mitchell for a short time and then with Orrin Smith, until Smith's retirement in the mid-1950s. Zikorus took over the practice and continued to plan courses on his own. Several of these were built by his brothers Walter and Edward, who operated a course construction company.
Courses by Albert Zikorus:
CONNECTICUT: Banner Lodge, Moodus (a.9,1965); Crestbrook CC (a.9,1980); Deercrest CC, Greenwich (1956); East Hartford GC (9,c.Smith); Glastonbury Hills CC (1965); Great Hills CC, Seymour (9,1960); Harry G. Brownson CC, Huntington (9,1960;9,1963); Heritage Village, Southbury (1966); Highland Greens GC, Prospect (9 par 3,1965); Hillandale CC, Trumbull (1960); Hyfield CC, Middlebury (9,1954;r.1964); Prospect CC (1961); Riverview CC, Milford (1961); Rockledge CC, West Hartford (9,1954); Rockrimmon CC, Stamford (9,c.Smith); Stanley GC, New Britain (9 c.Smith); Stony Brook CC, Litchfield (9,1964); Tashua Knoll, Town of Trumbull Muni (1972); Timberlin, Town of Berlin Muni (1969); Tunxis Plantations CC, Farmington (27,1961); Woodhaven CC, Bethany (1968).
MASSACHUSETTS: Billerica Par 3 Course (9,c.Mitchell,1952); Elmcrest CC, East Longmeadow (1964); Framingham CC (4,1953;1,1954;c.Mitchell); Hampden CC (1971); Red Hill CC, North Reading (9,c.Mitchell,1952); Twin Hills CC, Longmeadow (1964); Walpole CC (1973); Westover AFB, Chicopee (c.Smith).
NEW JERSEY: Lakeshore CC, Oradell (1965).
NEW YORK: Bel Aire CC, Armonk (1963); Cedar Brook CC, Brookville (1960); Lakeover CC, Bedford Village (1967); Plattsburgh AFB (1960); Somers CC (r.9,a.9,1961).
SOUTH CAROLINA: Green River CC, Chesterfield (9,1964;9,1966).
PUERTO RICO: Punta Borinquen CC (formerly Ramey AFB GC) (1960).
Courses Remodeled by Albert Zikorus:
CONNECTICUT: Alling Memorial, City of New Haven Muni (18,1972;18,1974); Greenwoods CC, Torrington (1,1961); High Ridge CC, Stamford (2,c.Mitchell,1951); Minnechaug GC, Glastonbury (9,c.Mitchell,1951); New Haven CC (1,1957); Pine Orchard CC, Branford (4,1961); Racebrook CC, Orange (2,1957); Wallingford CC (6,1958–61); Washington CC (9,1954–64); Wepaug CC, Orange (13,1961); Woodway CC, Stamford (1,1961).
MASSACHUSETTS: Colonial CC, Lynfield (5,c.Mitchell,1954); Cohassee CC, Southbridge (9,1971); Winthrop GC (1953); Wykcoff Park GC, Holyoke (1966).
NEW HAMPSHIRE: Portsmouth AFB (1960).
NEW YORK: Orange County CC, Middletown (3,1961); Village of Lake Success GC, Long Island (1957–58,c.Smith).
VIRGINIA: Langley AFB (1963–65).

Benjamin W. Zink
A charter member of the Golf Course Superintendents of America, Benjamin Zink served as superintendent of Acadia CC (1927) and later of Kirkland CC, both in Ohio. His design firm, Ben W. Zink and Son, planned a number of courses in Ohio and Florida.
Courses by Benjamin W. Zink:
FLORIDA: Palm Rivers CC, Naples (1960).
OHIO: Erie Shores GC (1958); Lander Haven CC (a.9,1965); Pebble Brook CC, Cleveland; Shawnee Hills GC, near Cleveland (9,1957); Tomahawk CC (1963).

PART THREE

Golf Courses in the United States
Selected years—1900 through 1979
(National Golf Foundation Figures)

Year	Golf Courses	Year	Golf Courses
1900	982	1958	5,745
1916	742	1959	5,991
1923	1,903	1960	6,385
1929	5,648	1961	6,623
1930	5,856	1962	7,070
1931	5,691	1963	7,477
1934	5,727	1964	7,893
1937	5,196	1965	8,323
1939	5,303	1966	8,672
1941	5,209	1967	9,336
1946	4,817	1968	9,615
1947	4,870	1969	9,926
1948	4,901	1970	10,188
1949	4,926	1971	10,494
1950	4,931	1972	10,665
1951	4,970	1973	10,896
1952	5,026	1974	11,134
1953	5,056	1975	11,370
1954	5,076	1976	11,562
1955	5,218	1977	11,745
1956	5,358	1978	11,885
1957	5,553	1979	11,966

Courses

A Master List of Golf Courses Cross-referenced to Designers

When two or more architects were involved in a partnership or joint effort, it is often impossible to ascertain those courses they planned alone or jointly and, in the case of collaborations, which architect took the more active role. For father-son combinations, this is particularly difficult.

Abbreviations used are the same as those in Section II, ''Profiles'' (see page 162). If the designer's name appears in parentheses on this master list, he is not profiled.

When the name of a course has changed, an effort has been made to list it under both its former and present title. Also an effort has been made to list work on an individual course by different architects chronologically.

Aalborg CC
Denmark
J. D. Harris

Abbeydale GC
England
W. H. Fowler

Abbey Hill at Milton Keynes GC
England
J. J. F. Pennink, C. D. Lawrie

Abbey Springs CC
Wisconsin
K. Killian, R. Nugent

Abenaqui Club (r.)
New Hampshire
M. L. Francis

Abenaqui Club (r)
New Hampshire
G. S. Cornish, W. G Robinson

Abercrombie CC (a.9)
Nova Scotia, Canada
C. E. Robinson

Aberdeen GC, Royal (Ladies course)
Scotland
J. J. F. Pennink

Aberdeen Proving Ground GC
Maryland
E. B. Ault

Aberdour GC (a. 3, 1981)
Scotland
F. Middleton

Aberdovey GC (r.)
Wales
J. Braid

Aberdovey GC (r.)
Wales
H. S. Colt

Aberdovey GC (r.)
Wales
W. H. Fowler

Abergele and Pensarn GC
Wales
F. W. Hawtree

Abiko CC
Japan
Akaboshi Brothers

Abilene CC (r.)
Kansas
(Dewitt ''Maury'' Bell)

Abilene CC (r.)
Texas
M. H. Ferguson

Abitibi Power and Paper Co. GC
Ontario, Canada
W. Park, Jr.

Abridge GC
England
H. Cotton

Acacia CC (n.1.e.)
Illinois
W. Langford, T. J. Moreau

Acacia CC (r.; n.1.e.)
Illinois
R. B. Harris

Acacia CC
Ohio
D. J. Ross

Acadian Hills CC
Lousiana
(Luca Barbato)

Acadian Hills CC (r.)
Louisiana
B. J. Riviere

Acapulco CC
Mexico
J. Bredemus

Acapulco CC (a.9)
Mexico
P. Clifford

Acapulco Princess GC
Mexico
T. G. Robinson

Acozak, Club de Golf
Mexico
L. M. Hughes

A. C. Read GC (r. Mainside, a. Seaside courses)
Florida
W. W. Amick

Acton GC
England
W. Park, Jr.

Adams County GC
Colorado
H. B. Hughes

Adams Muni
Oklahoma
F. Farley

Adam Spring G&CC (9)
California
J. Fleming

A. D. Dana Estate at Stowe (9)
Vermont
H. Watson

Addington Court GC (Old course)
England
F. G. Hawtree

Addington Court GC (New course)
England
F. W. Hawtree

Addington GC (Old and New courses)
England
J. F. Abercromby

Addington Palace GC
England
F. G. Hawtree

Addison Pinnacle CC
New York
G. S. Cornish, W. G. Robinson

Adelaide GC, Royal (r.)
Australia
A. Mackenzie

Admiral Baker Memorial GC (U. S. Navy Base, San Diego)
California
J. L Daray

Admiralty CC
Florida
R. A. Renaud

Adolfo Siro GC
Argentina
M. Park II

Adstock, Club de Golf
Province of Québec, Canada
H. Watson

Adventure Inn Par 3 GC
South Carolina
G. W. Cobb

Aeroclub de Azragoza, Royal (9)
Spain
F. W. Hawtree

Agate Beach GC (9)
Oregon
F. Federspiel

Agawam Hunt Club (r.)
Rhode Island
D. J. Ross

Agawan Hunt Club (r.)
Rhode Island
G. S. Cornish

Agua Caliente GC [now Tijuana CC]
Mexico
W. P. Bell

Aguasabon GC
Ontario, Canada
H. Watson

A. H. Blank GC
Iowa
E. L. Packard

Ahwatukee Exec. GC
Arizona
G. A. Panks

Airco GC
Florida
C. H. Adams

Airdrie GC
Scotland
J. Braid

Airport GC
Idaho
G. Von Elm

Airport GC [now Port Columbus GC]
Ohio
J. Kidwell

Airport GC (n.1.e.)
Oklahoma
A. J. Jackson

Airways GC
California
B. Stamps

A. J. Gustin, Jr. Memorial GC (University of Missouri)
Missouri
F. Farley

Akarana GC (r.)
New Zealand
P.W. Thomson, M. Wolveridge

Alabama International CC (Point AcAquarius Hotel; 36; now Alpine Bay)
Alabama
R. T. Jones, R. L. Jones

Alabang G&CC
Philippines
R. T. Jones, Jr.

Alamance CC
North Carolina
D. J. Ross

Alamance CC (r.)
North Carolina
W. C. Byrd

Alameda Muni (North course)
California
W. P. Bell

Alameda Muni (South course)
California
W. F. Bell

Alameda Muni (r. North course)
California
D. Muirhead

Alamo CC [now Oakhill CC]
Texas
A. W. Tillinghast

Alassio GC
Italy
J. D. Harris

Ala Wai GC (r.)
Hawaii
R. E. Baldock

Albany CC (a. 2nd 9)
Minnesota
W. H. Kidd, Sr.

Albany CC (r. Former site)
New York
W. Ogg

Albany CC (New site)
New York
R. T. Jones

Albarella CC
Italy
J.D. Harris

Albermarle CC
Massachusetts
W. E. Stiles, J. R. Van Kleek

Albrug CC
Vermont
(Walter Barcomb)

Albuquerque CC
New Mexico
J. R. Van Kleek

Albuquerque CC (r.)
New Mexico
W. D. Cantrell

Albuquerque CC (r.)
New Mexico
L. Howard

Alcoma CC
Pennsylvania
E. F. Loeffler, J. McGlynn

Aldeburgh GC
England
W. Park, Jr.

Aldeburgh CC (r.)
England
J. H. Taylor

Aldcress CC [now Alpine CC] (r.)
New Jersey
W. F. Gordon

Alden Pines GC
Florida
W. Maddox

Alderbrook Inn G&CC
Washington
R.L.Goss, (Glen Proctor)

Aldecress CC [now Alpine CC]
New Jersey
A. W. Tillinghast

Alderney (Channel Islands) GC
England
J. J. F. Pennink

Alderwood CC (n.1.e.)
Oregon
A. V. Macan

Algona CC (9)
Iowa
''Young'' W. Dunn

Algonquin CC
Missouri
R. Foulis

Algonquin GC (r.)
Missouri
K. Killian, R. Nugent

Algonquin Hotel GC (St. Andrews By The Sea)
New Brunswick, Canada
D. J. Ross

Alhambra G&TC
Florida
W. W. Amick

Alice Springs CC
Northern Territory, Australia
P.W. Thomson, M. Wolveridge

Alhambra Muni (r.9, a.9)
California
A. M. Pulley

Alice CC
Texas
R. Plummer

Alladin Hotel Par 3 GC
Nevada
R. E. Baldock

All America Par 3 GC
Florida
R. T. Jones

Allandale GC (9)
Ontario, Canada
S. Thompson

Allegheny CC
Pennsylvania
T. Bendelow

Allegheny CC (r.,a.3)
Pennsylvania
W. H. Fowler

Allegheny CC (r.)
Pennsylvania
D. J. Ross

Allegheny CC (r.)
Pennsylvania
E. B. Seay

Allendale CC
Massachusetts
G. S. Cornish

Alling Memorial GC. New Haven Muni (r.)
Connecticut
A. Zikorus

All Seasons GC (now Four Seasons GC)
Missouri
R. T. Jones

Allston GC (n.l.e.)
Massachusetts
G. Wright

All-View GC
Maryland
E. B. Ault

All-View GC (r.)
Maryland
D. Muirhead

All Weather Golf Practice
England
F. G. Hawtree

Almaden GC
California
J. Fleming

Almaden GC (r.)
California
R. M. Graves

Almansor GC
California
W. F. Bell

Almerimar, Club de Golf
Spain
R. Kirby, G. Player

Alnmouth GC (Original course)
England
M. Park I

Alnmouth GC
England
W. Park, Jr.

Alnmouth GC (r.)
England
P. M. Ross

Alondro Park GC (Course #1)
California
W. P. Bell, W. H. Johnson

Alondro Park GC (r.2, Course #1)
California
T. G. Robinson

Alondro Park GC (a. 18 par 3)
California
C. B. Hollingsworth

Alondro Ranch CC
California
W. H. Johnson

Alpin at Ste. Brigite, Club de Golf (r.)
Province of Québec, Canada
H. and J. Watson

Alpin, Club de Golf (r.)
Province of Québec, Canada
H. Watson

Alpine CC [formerly Aldercress]
New Jersey
A. W. Tillinghast

Alpine CC (r.)
New Jersey
W. F. Gordon

Alpine CC
Rhode Island
G. S. Cornish

Alpine CC
Utah
W. H. Neff

Alpine CC
Michigan
M. DeVries

Alpine Bay CC (36)
Alabama
R. T. Jones, R. L. Jones

Alpine Valley GC (9)
Georgia
R. Kirby, A. Davis, G. Player

Altadena GC
California
W. P. Bell

Alta Sierra CC
California
R. E. Baldock

Alta Vista CC
California
H. M. and D. A. Rainville

Altimoona G&CC
Tahiti
W. G. Wilkinson

Alton Beach GC
Florida
W. Park, Jr.

Alto Village GC (Original 9)
New Mexico
R. Kirby, A. Davis, G. Player

Alto Village GC (a.9)
New Mexico
P. Dye

Altus CC (9)
New Mexico
R. Plummer

Alum Creek Park GC
Ohio
J. Kidwell, M. Hurdzan

Alva CC (9)
Oklahoma
F. Farley

Alvamar Hill (Jayhawk and Quail Creek 9's)
Kansas
R. C. Dunning

Alvamar Hills (Sunflower 9, Hidden Valley 9, and Orchard Exec. 9)
Kansas
(Melvin Wesley Anderson)

Alwoodley GC
England
H. S. Colt, A. Mackenzie

Amarillo AFB GC (9)
Texas
J. Finger

Amarillo CC (r.)
Texas
W. D. Cantrell

Ambassador Beach GC [formerly Nassau CC]
Bahamas
D. Emmet

Ambassador Hotel GC (n.1.e.)
California
W. H. Fowler

Amberwood Village GC
Ontario, Canada
J. Watson

Ambridge CC
Pennsylvania
E. F. Loeffler, J. McGlynn

Amelia Island Plantation (27)
Florida
P. Dye

American Golfers Club Exec. Course
Florida
R. T. Jones

American Legion GC (r.)
Georgia
H. C. Moore, Sr.

American Legion GC
Iowa
C. H. Adams

American Legion GC (r.)
Kansas
F. Hummel

American Par 3 GC
Tennessee
L. S. "Dick" Wilson

Amery GC (r.9,a.9)
Wisconsin
D. Herfort

Ames G&CC
Iowa
D.R. Sechrest

Amherst G&CC (r.) Nova Scotia, Canada
C. E. Robinson

Amherst GC
Massachusetts
W. B. Hatch

Amherst GC
New Hampshire
W. F. Mitchell

Amiens (r.)
France
J.J.F. Pennink

Amiens, GC d'
France
P.M. Ross

Amityville CC
New York
T. Winton

Ammonoosuc Inn CC
New Hampshire
R. M. Barton

Ampfield Par 3 GC
England
H. Cotton

Am Reichswald GC
West Germany
B. Von Limburger

Amsterdam Muni
New York
R. T. Jones

Anaheim Hills GC
California
(Richard Bigler)

Ancil Hoffman Muni
California
W. F. Bell

Andalucia La Nueve GC (36 plus Par 3)
Spain
R. T. Jones

Anderson AFB GC
Guam
J. L. Lee

Anderson Tucker Oaks CC
California
W. H. Tucker, Jr.

Andorra Springs Exec. GC
Pennsylvania
(Horace W. Smith)

Andover GC
Massachusetts
D. J. Ross

Andrews AFB (East course)
Washington, D.C.
F. Murray, R. Roberts

Andrews AFB (West course)
Washington, D.C.
F. Murray

Andrews Muni
Texas
W. D. Cantrell

Andros Island Par 3 GC
Bahamas
G. W. Cobb

Angel Fire GC
New Mexico
R. Garl

Anglo-American Club
Province of Québec, Canada
A. W. Tillinghast

Anholt, Schloss GC
West Germany
B. Von Limburger

Ankara GC
Turkey
(Ambassador George Wadsworth)

Annandale CC (r.)
California
N. Macbeth

Ankeny CC
Iowa
L. Johnson

Ankeny G&CC
Iowa
L. Johnson

Annandale CC (r.2)
California
W. P. Bell

Annandale CC (r.)
California
R. T. Jones, Sr. and Jr.

Annandale GC
Mississippi
J. Nicklaus

Annapolis Roads GC (9)
Maryland
C. Banks

Annenberg Estate GC
California
L. S. "Dick" Wilson

Anne of Green Gables GC
Prince Edward Island, Canada
S. Thompson

Anne of Green Gables GC (r. 18, a.9)
Prince Edward Island, Canada
C.E. Robinson

Anniston CC (r.)
Alabama
J. H. Williams, Sr.

Anniston CC (r.)
Alabama
E. B. Seay

Ansley CC
Georgia
W. C. Byrd

Antelope Hills GC
Arizona
L. M. Hughes

Antelope Valley GC
California
W. F. Bell

Antigo Bass Lake CC
Wisconsin
E. L. Packard

Antimaona CC, Golf D'
Tahiti
R. E. Baldock

Antioch Muni (a.9)
California
R. E. Baldock

Antrim Dells GC
Michigan
W. B. and G. H. Matthews

Antwerp GC
Belgium
S. Dunn

Antwerp, GC, Royal
Belgium
W. Park, Jr.

Antwerp GC, Royal (r. 18,a.9)
Belgium
T. C. Simpson, P. M. Ross

Apache CC [now Golden Hills CC]
Arizona
A. J. Snyder

Apache Wells GC
Arizona
M. Coggins

Apache Wells GC (East 9)
Arizona
A. J. Snyder

Apache Wells GC (a. West 9)
Arizona
M. Coggins

Apawamis Club (r.)
New York
T. Winton

Apawamis Club (r.)
New York
G. and T. Fazio

Apollo Beach CC
Florida
R. T. Jones, Sr. and Jr.

Apple Creek G&CC [formerly Bismarck CC]
North Dakota
R. B. Harris

Apple Orchard CC (r.)
Illinois
D. Gill

Apple Valley CC
Illinois
E. L. Packard

Apple Valley GC
Ohio
W. K. Newcomb

Apple Valley Inn & CC
California
W. P. Bell, W.F. Bell

Applewood GC [formerly Rolling Hills CC]
Colorado
J. P. Maxwell
Applewood Muni
Nebraska
L. Howard
Appomattox CC
Virginia
F. Findlay C.R.F. Loving Sr.
April Sound CC
Texas
(Carlton Gipson)
Aptos Seascape GC [now Rio del Mar GC] (r.)
California
B. Stamps
Arawak GC [now Paradise Island GC]
Bahamas
L. S. "Dick" Wilson
Arcadian Shores GC
South Carolina
R. T. Jones, R.L. Jones
Arcola CC (r.)
New Jersey
R. T. Jones
Arcot Hall GC
England
J. Braid, J. R. Stutt
Ardee GC (r.)
Ireland
E. Hackett
Ardeer GC
Scotland
J. H. Stutt
Ardsley on Hudson CC
New York
"Young" W. Dunn
Argyle CC [formerly Columbia CC]
Maryland
W. H. Tucker, Sr., W. S. Harban
Argyle CC (r.)
Maryland
E. B. Ault
Arispie Lake CC (9)
Illinois
J. R. Darrah
Arizona Biltmore GC (Adobe course)
Arizona
W. P. Bell
Arizona Biltmore GC (Links course)
Arizona
(Bill Johnston)
Arizona City CC
Arizona
A. J. Snyder
Arizona CC (r.)
Arizona
J. Finger
Arizona CC (r.)
Arizona
G. A. Panks
Arkansas City CC (Original 9)
Kansas
P. D. Maxwell
Arkansas City CC (a.9)
Kansas
(Dick Metz)
Arklow GC
Ireland
F. G. Hawtree, J. H. Taylor
Arklow GC (r.)
Ireland
E. Hackett
Arlington CC
Illinois
D. Gill

Arlington CC [formerly Pedley Farms GC, now Victoria GC]
California
C. E. Maud
Arlington Lakes Muni
Illinois
D. Gill
Arlington Park GC
Illinois
D. Gill
Arlmont CC
Maine
E. F. Wogan
Armco Park CC
Ohio
A. Hills
Armco Park GC
Ohio
A. Hills
Armour Fields GC
Kansas
E. L. Bell
Army GC
England
(Captain Bagot, R.E.)
Army GC (r.)
England C. K. Cotton, J. J. F. Pennink
Army-Navy GC (Fairfax course)
Virginia
H. B. Strong
Army-Navy GC (Arlington course)
Virginia
(Major Richard D. Newman)
Army-Navy GC (r. Fairfax course)
Virginia
G. W. Cobb
Army-Navy GC (r.)
Virginia
E. B. Ault
Army-Navy GC (r,)
Virginia
A.M. Pulley, R.F. Loving
Aroeira GC
Portugal
J. J. F. Pennink
Aronimink CC (original course, n.l.e.)
Pennsylvania
A. Findlay
Aronimink CC
Pennsylvania
D. J. Ross
Aronimink CC (r.)
Pennsylvania
L. S. "Dick" Wilson
Aroostook Valley GC (r.9,a.9)
Maine
H. Watson
Arrowbrook CC
Indiana
J. R. Darrah
Arrowhead CC
California
W. P. Bell
Arrowhead CC (r. 2)
California
A.M. Pulley
Arrowhead CC
Florida
W. R. Watts
Arrowhead CC
Illinois
W. J. Spear
Arrowhead GC [Formerly Roxborough Park CC]
Colorado
R. T. Jones, Jr.

Arrowhead GC (9)
Georgia
A. L. Davis
Arrowhead GC
Illinois
D. Gill
Arrowhead Park GC
Indiana
R. A. Simmons
Arrowhead State Park GC (9)
Oklahoma
D. Bennett
Arrowhead State Park GC (a.9)
Oklahoma
F. Farley
Arrowwood CC [now Countryside CC]
Virginia
E. Maples
Arroyo del Oso Muni
New Mexico
A. J. Snyder
Arroyo Seco Par 3 GC
California
W. H. Johnson
Arsenal Club (Rock Island) (r.)
Illinois
D. Gill
Artesia CC
New Mexico
R. Plummer
Arthur Pack GC
Arizona
D. Bennett
Arthur Raymond Memorial GC
Ohio
R. T. Jones
Arvida GC
Province of Québec, Canada
S. Thompson
Asbestos G&CC
Province of Québec, Canada
H. Watson
Asbury Park GC (r.)
New Jersey
H. Purdy
Ascarte Park Muni (27)
Texas
G. A. Hoffman
Ashbourne GC
England
J. J. F. Pennink
Ashbrook, Union County P.C.
New Jersey
A. H. Tull
Ashburn Course (Old) of Halifax G&CC (route plan)
Nova Scotia, Canada
S. Thompson
Ashburnham GC (r. 1914)
Wales
J. H. Taylor
Ashburnham GC (r. 1923)
Wales
F. G. Hawtree, J. H. Taylor
Ashburnham GC (r.)
Wales
C. K. Cotton
Ashburton GC (r.)
New Zealand
P.W. Thomson, M. Wolveridge
Asheville CC [now Grove Park Inn CC]
North Carolina
W. Park, Jr.
Asheville CC [formerly Beaver Lake CC]
North Carolina
D. J. Ross

Asheville Muni
North Carolina
D. J. Ross
Ashland CC [now Idle Hour CC]
Kentucky
D. J. Ross
Ashland CC (9)
Nebraska
H. B. Hughes, R. Watson
Ashland CC
Ohio
W. Park, Jr.
Ashley Park CC
England
T. Dunn
Ashley Wood
England
J. H. Stutt
Ashover GC
England
T. Williamson
Ashridge GC
England
G. Campbell, S. Hotchkin, C. Hutchison
Ashridge GC (r.)
England
T. C. Simpson
Ashridge GC (r.)
England
J. H. Stutt
Ashtabula CC
Ohio
W. Reid, W. Connellan
Ashton-In-Makerfield GC (9)
England
F. W. Hawtree
Askernish GC
Scotland
T. Morris
Aspen Meadows GC
Alberta, Canada
R.T. Jones, Jr.
Aspen Muni
Colorado
F. Hummel
Aspetuck, GC at [now Connecticut GC]
Connecticut
G. S. Cornish, W. G. Robinson
Aspetuck Valley CC
Connecticut
M. and H. Purdy
Aspley Guise and Woburn Sands GC
England
(Charles Wilmott), S. Herd
Assiniboine GC (r.)
Manitoba, Canada
C. E. Robinson
Astorhurst CC
Ohio
H. D. Paddock, Sr.
Astoria G&CC
Oregon
(George Junor)
Asuncion GC
Paraguay
A. Serra
Atalaya Park Hotel G&CC
Spain
B. Von Limburger
Atascadero
California
J. D. Dunn
Atascocita CC
Texas
R. Plummer
Athens CC
Georgia
D. J. Ross

Athens CC (original 9)
Ohio
D. J. Ross
Athens CC (a. 9, 1979)
Georgia
G.W. Cobb
Atkinson Stuart GC
Nebraska
H. B. Hughes, R. Watson
Atlanta Athletic Club [now East Lake CC]
Georgia
T. Bendelow
Atlanta Athletic Club (Riverside 18 and Original 9 of Highlands)
Georgia
R. T. Jones
Atlanta Athletic Club (a.9, Highlands)
Georgia
J. Finger
Atlanta Athletic Club (r. Highlands)
Georgia
G. and T. Fazio
Atlanta City Course [now James L. Key Muni]
Georgia
W. Ogg
Atlanta CC
Georgia
W. Byrd, J. Finger
Atlantic Beach CC (n.l.e.)
Florida
A. W. Tillinghast
Atlantic City CC (a.13, n.l.e.)
New Jersey
W. Park, Jr.
Atlantic City CC (New site, 27)
New Jersey
W. S. Flynn
Atlantic City Electric Company GC
New Jersey
H. Purdy
Atlantis CC
Florida
W. F. Mitchell
Atlantis CC (a.9)
Florida
R. A. Simmons
Atlantis GC
New Jersey
G. Fazio
Atlas, Club
Mexico
J. Finger
Atoka Muni (9)
Oklahoma
F. Farley
Atwood GC
Illinois
C. E. Maddox
Atzinachson CC (now Wynding Brook CC) a.9
Pennsylvania
E. V. Ternyey
Auckland GC
New Zealand
(F. G. Hood)
Auckland GC (r.)
New Zealand
P.W. Thomson, M. Wolveridge
Audubon CC
Kentucky
A. G. McKay
Audubon GC
New York
W. E. Harries
Audubon Park GC
Kentucky
E. L. Packard

231

Auglaize CC
Ohio
W. J. Spear

Augsburg GC
West Germany
B. Von Limburger

Augusta CC
Georgia
D. J. Ross

Augusta CC (Original 9)
Maine
D. J. Ross

Augusta CC (a.9)
Maine
W. E. Stiles, J. R. Van Kleek

Augusta CC
Virginia
F. A. Findlay

Augusta National GC
Georgia
A. Mackenzie, R. T. "Bobby" Jones

Augusta National GC (r.)
Georgia
P. D. Maxwell

Augusta National CC (r.3)
Georgia
R. T. Jones

Augusta National GC (r.)
Georgia
G. and T. Fazio

Augusta National GC (r.)
Georgia
G. Cobb

Augusta National GC (a. Par 3 course)
Georgia
G. Cobb, R. T. "Bobby" Jones

Aurora CC
Ohio
G. G. Alves

Aurora GC
Ontario, Canada
S. Thompson

Aurora Highlands GC
Ontario, Canada
R. and C. Muylaert

Aurora Hills GC
Colorado
H. B. Hughes

Ausable Club
New York
S. Dunn

Austin, CC of
Texas
J. P. and P. D. Maxwell

Austin, CC of (r.)
Texas
B. J. Riviere

Australian GC (27)
Australia
A. Mackenzie

Australian GC (r.27)
Australia
S. Morpeth

Australian GC (r.)
Australia
J. Nicklaus

Automobile Club, Royal (n.l.e.)
England
W. H. Fowler

Automobile CC (n.l.e.)
Michigan
W. Park, Jr.

Automovil GC, Real
Spain
J. Arana

Ava G&CC
Missouri
F. Farley

Avalon [now Catalina GC]
California
J. D. Dunn

Avalon Lakes GC
Ohio
P. Dye, W. Newcomb

Avandara, Club de Golf
Mexico
P. Clifford

Aventura CC [now Turnberry Isle] (36)
Florida
R. T. Jones, R. L. Jones

Aviation Y&CC
Maryland
H. B. Strong

Aviation Y&CC (New site)
Maryland
E. B. Ault

Aviation Y&CC (r.)
Maryland
G. W. Cobb

Avila G&CC
Florida
R. Garl

Avon CC (Original 18)
Connecticut
R. J. Ross

Avon CC (r.18,a.9)
Connecticut
G. S. Cornish, W. G. Robinson

Avon Oaks CC
Ohio
H. D. Paddock, Sr.

Avon Oaks CC (r.6)
Ohio
G. S. Cornish, W. G. Robinson

Avondale-on-Hayden GC
Idaho
(Melvin A. Hueston)

Aycliffe New Town GC (27)
England
J. H. Stutt

Ayr Belleisle
Scotland
J. Braid

Ayr Seafield
Scotland
J. Braid

Azalea City GC
Alabama
R. B. Harris

Azalea Sands GC
South Carolina
E. Hamm

Azuza Greens GC
California
R. E. Baldock

Baberton GC
England
W. Park, Jr.

Babe Zaharias GC
Florida
R. Garl

Babraham GC
England
T. Dunn

Back Acres GC (r.9,a.9)
Mississippi
J. R. Darrah

Back O' Beyond GC [formerly Morfar]
New York
E. Ryder

Bacon Park GC
Georgia
D. J. Ross

Bacon Park GC (r.)
Georgia
J. P. Gibson, J. Finger

Bad Driburge GC
West Germany
B. Von Limburger

Bad Durrenburg GC
West Germany
B. Von Limburger

Bad Gastein GC
Austria
B. Von Limburger

Bad Harzburg GC
West Germany
B. Von Limburger

Bad Herrenalb GC
West Germany
B. Von Limburger

Bad Pyrmont
Germany
D. Harradine

Bad Ragaz GC
Switzerland
F. W. Hawtree

Bad Ragaz GC (r.)
Switzerland
D. Harradine

Bad Saaron GC
West Germany
B. Von Limburger

Bad Salzuflen GC
West Germany
B. Von Limburger

Bad Scuol, GC
Switzerland
(Gordon Spencer)

Bad Waldsee GC
West Germany
B. Von Limburger

Bad Woerishofen
Germany
D. Harradine

Baederwood CC [formerly Huntingdon Valley] (r.)
Pennsylvania
H. S. Colt

Bahama Reef G&CC
Bahamas
(Arthur Rude)

Bahamas CC
Bahamas
D. Emmet

Bahamas Princess (Emerald course)
Bahamas
L. S. "Dick" Wilson

Bahamas Princess (Ruby course)
Bahamas
J. Lee

Bahia De Banderas
Mexico
P. Clifford

Bahrain Equestrian & Racing Club
Bahrain
E. Stone

Baie Comeau, Club de Golf
Province of Québec, Canada
C. E. Robinson

Baie Comeau, Club de Golf (r.9,a.9)
Province of Québec, Canada
H. and J. Watson

Baiting Hollow CC
New York
R. T. Jones

Bajamar, Club de Golf
Mexico
P. Clifford

Bakersfield CC
California
W. P. Bell

Bala CC [formerly Philadelphia CC]
Pennsylvania
"Young" W. Dunn

Bala CC (a. 2nd 9)
Pennsylvania
W. H. Tucker, Sr.

Bala CC (r.)
Pennsylvania
W. S. Flynn

Balandra Beach GC
Trinidad
P.W. Thomson, M. Wolveridge, R. Fream

Balboa Park GC
California
W. P. Bell

Balbriggan GC (r.)
Ireland
E. Hackett

Bald Head Island GC
North Carolina
G. W. Cobb

Bald Mountain GC
Michigan
W. Reid, W. Connellan

Baldoc CC
Pennsylvania
O. E. Smith

Baldwin Hills GC (n.l.e.)
California
G. C. Thomas, Jr., W. P. Bell

Balham GC
Great Britain
T. Dunn

Bali Handara CC
Bali
P.W. Thomson, M. Wolveridge, R. W. Fream

Bali Handara CC
Indonesia
J. D. Harris, P. W. Thomson, M. Wolveridge, R. W. Fream

Ballaghadereen GC
Ireland
(D. Skerritt)

Ballina GC (r.)
Ireland
E. Hackett

Ballinasloe GC (r.)
Ireland
E. Hackett

Ballinrobe GC (r.)
Ireland
E. Hackett

Ballston Spa & CC (r.9,a.9)
New York
A. Craig

Ballybofey GC
Ireland
E. Hackett

Ballybunion GC (Original 9)
Ireland
(P. Murphy)

Ballybunion GC (a.9)
Ireland
(M. Smyth, Carter Seeds)

Ballybunion GC (a.18)
Ireland
E. Hackett

Ballybunion GC (r.)
Ireland
T.C. Simpson

Ballybunion GC (r.)
Ireland
E. Hackett

Ballybunion GC (a. 18)
Ireland
R.T. Jones

Ballyclare GC
Northern Ireland
P. Alliss

Ballyclare GC (r.)
Northern Ireland
T. J. A. McAuley

Balmoral GC
Northern Ireland
P. M. Ross

Balmore
Scotland
J. Braid

Balnagask
Scotland
F. W. Hawtree

Balsams Hotel & CC
New Hampshire
D. J. Ross

Baltimore CC (Roland Park CRS) (n.1.e.)
Maryland
"Young" W. Dunn

Baltimore CC (Roland Park) (n.1.e.)
Maryland
W. Park, Jr.

Baltimore CC (Five Farms)
Maryland
A. W. Tillinghast

Baltimore CC (Five Farms, West Course)
Maryland
E. B. Ault

Baltinglas GC (r.)
Ireland
E. Hackett

Baltray GC (Country Louth; r.)
Ireland
T. C. Simpson

Baltusrol CC (Lower and Upper courses)
New Jersey
A. W. Tillinghast

Baltusrol CC (r. Lower course)
New Jersey
R. T. Jones

Bamm Hollow CC
New Jersey
H. Purdy

Bandon
Ireland
J. J. F. Pennink

Banff Springs GC
Alberta, Canada
S. Thompson

Bangalore GC
India
P.W. Thomson, M. Wolveridge

Bangor GC
Northern Ireland
J. Braid, J. R. Stutt

Bangor GC (r.)
Northern Ireland
P. M. Ross

Bangor Muni
Maine
G. S. Cornish

Bangpoo CC
Thailand
E. B. Seay, A. Palmer

Banks Exec. GC
Ohio
J. Kidwell, M. Hurdzan

Banner Lodge Hotel GC (a.9)
Connecticut
A. Zikorus

Banning CC (9)
California
W. J. Johnson

Banning Muni
California
W. F. Bell

Bannockburn G&CC (n.l.e.)
Maryland
W. Harban, W. H. Tucker, Sr.

Banstead Downs GC (r.)
England
W. Reid

Bantry GC
Ireland
E. Hackett

Banyan GC
Florida
J. L. Lee

Baraboo CC (9)
Wisconsin
E. L. Packard

Barassie GC (Kilmarnock)
Scotland
T. Moone

Barbados G&CC
Barbados
J.D. Harris

Barbara Worth CC [now Imperial G&CC] (r.)
California
L. M. Hughes

Barcoven G&CC (r.)
Ontario, Canada
C. E. Robinson

Bardmoor CC (East and South courses)
Florida
W. Diddel

Barefoot Bay G&CC
Florida
J. L. Lee

Bar-K CC
Texas
L. Howard

Barnham Broom GC
England
J. J. F. Pennink

Barnhurst GC
England
J. Braid

Barnton GC
England
W. Park, Jr.

Barquisimeto CC
Venezuela
J. L. Lee

Barranquila CC
Colombia
Frank Applebye

Barre CC (Original 9)
Vermont
W. E. Stiles, J. R. Van Kleek

Barre CC (a.9)
Vermont
M. Hurdzan

Barren River State Park GC
Kentucky
B. J. Wihry

Barrie CC
Ontario, Canada
R. and D. Moote

Barrien Hills CC
Michigan
K. Killian, R. Nugent

Barrington Hills CC
Illinois
G. O'Neill, (Jack Croke)

Barrington Hills CC (r.)
Illinois
E.L. Packard

Barrington Hills CC (r.)
Illinois
C. D. Wagstaff

Barry Angus (Carnoustie; Original 10)
Scotland
A. Robertson

Barry Angus (Carnoustie; a.8)
Scotland
T. Morris

Barry GC (Glamorgan)
Wales
W. Park, Jr.

Bartlett CC (r.)
New York
R. T. Jones

Bartlett Hills G&CC
Illinois
F. MacDonald, C. E. Maddox

Barton CC (9)
Vermont
(Andrew Freeland)
W. Diddel

Barton Hills CC (r.)
Michigan
D. J. Ross

Barton Hills CC (r.)
Michigan
W. Diddel

Barton Hills CC (r.)
Michigan
W. K. Newcomb

Barton On Sea
England
H. S. Colt

Baru, Club de Golf
Colombia
P. Clifford

Bash Recreation Exec. GC (9)
Ohio
J. Kidwell

Basildon GC
England
J. J. F. Pinnink

Basil G&CC
Switzerland
B. Von Limburger

Basingstoke GC
England
J. Braid

Basin Harbor Club (Original 9)
Vermont
A. Campbell

Basin Harbor Club (r.)
Vermont
W. Mitchell

Bass River GC (r.)
Massachusetts
D. J. Ross

Bass Rocks GC
Massachusetts
H. C. Leeds

Bastad GC
Sweden
F. G. Hawtree, J. H. Taylor

Batchwood Hall Muni (St. Albans Corp.)
England
F. G. Hawtree, J. H. Taylor

Bath GC
England
T. Dunn

Bathgate CC
Scotland
W. Park, Jr.

Baton Rouge CC
Louisiana
B. Stamps

Baton Rouge CC (r.)
Louisiana
J. Finger

Baton Rouge CC (r.)
Louisiana
J. L. Lee

Battle Creek CC
Michigan
W. Park, Jr.

Battle Creek CC (new course)
Michigan
M. J. McCarthy, Sr.

Battleground CC
New Jersey
H. Purdy

Bay City CC (r.9,a.9; n.l.e.)
Michigan
R. B. Harris

Bay City CC (New site)
Michigan
E. L. Packard

Bay Hill Club
Florida
L. S. "Dick" Wilson

Bay Hill Club (r.)
Florida
A. Palmer

Bay Hill Club (Charger 9)
Florida
R. A. Simmons

Bay Hills
Maryland
E. B. Ault

Bay Isles
Florida
W. C. Byrd

Bay-Lea GC
New Jersey
H. Purdy

Baymeadows CC
Florida
D. Muirhead

Baymeadow Exec. GC
California
J. Fleming

Bay of Quinte GC
Ontario, Canada
H. Watson

Bay of Quinte GC (a.9)
Ontario, Canada
C. E. Robinson

Bayou Barriere GC (27)
Louisiana
(Jimmy Self)

Bayou Bend CC
Louisiana
B . J. Riviere

Bayou DeSiard CC
Louisiana
P. D. Maxwell

Bayou DeSiard CC (r.)
Louisiana
J. N. Cochran

Bayou Muni
Texas
J. Finger

Bay Park GC
New York
D. W. Gordon

Bay Pointe GC
Michigan
(Ernest Fuller)

Bay Point G&CC (27)
Florida
W. C. Byrd

Bayreuth GC
West Germany
B. Von Limburger

Bayshore GC (n.l.e.)
Florida
H. C. C. Tippets

Bayshore Muni (New course)
Florida
G. Von Hagge, B. Devlin

Bayside CC
California
W. P. Bell

Bayside Links (n.l.e.)
New York
T. Wells

Bayside Links (r.; n.l.e.)
New York
A. Mackenzie

Bayside Muni
California
H. C. Egan

Bay Tree GC (54, route plan)
South Carolina
R. F. Breeden

Bay Tree Golf Plantation (Gold, Green and Silver courses)
South Carolina
G. and T. Fazio

Bay Valley GC
Michigan
D. Muirhead, J. Nicklaus

Bayview G&CC
Ontario, Canada
C. E. Robinson

Bay West Lodge & CC
Florida
C. H. Adams

Bay Wood CC
Texas
J. Finger

Bay Wood CC (r.)
Texas
B. J. Riviere

Baywood G&CC
California
R. E. Baldock

Beach Club Hotel (Naples Beach GC, r.)
Florida
M. Mahannah

Beach Grove G&CC
Ontario, Canada
S. Thompson

Beach Grove G&CC (r.)
Ontario, Canada
C. E. Robinson

Beachmont CC
Ohio
S. Thompson

Beachwood GC
South Carolina
E. Hamm

Beacon CC (r.9,a.9)
New York
H. B. Strong

Beacon Hill GC
New Jersey
E. V. Ternyey

Beacon Park CC
England
D. M. A. Steel

Beaconsfield GC
Province of Québec, Canada
W. Park, Jr.

Beaconsfield GC (r.)
Province of Québec, Canada
S. Thompson

Beaconsfield GC (r.)
Province of Québec, Canada
C. E. Robinson

Beaconsfield GC (r.)
Province of Québec, Canada
H. Watson

Beacon Woods CC
Florida
W. W. Amick

Bear Creek
Colorado
E. B. Seay, A. Palmer

Bear Creek G&RC (Dallas, Fort Worth; East and West courses)
Texas
T. G. Robinson

Bear Creek GC
South Carolina
R. L. Jones

Bear Creek Golf World (Houston; Exec. and Presidents courses)
Texas
(Bruce Littell)

Bear Creek Golf World (Houston: Masters)
Texas
B. J. Riviere

Bear Hill CC (r.)
Massachusetts
E. F. Wogan

Bear Hill CC (r.)
Massachusetts
W. F. Mitchell

Bear Lake West
Idaho
(Keith Downs)

Bear's Paw
Florida
J. Nicklaus

Bear Valley GC
California
R. E. Baldock

Beau Chene CC
Louisiana
J. L. Lee

Beau Clerc CC (Original 9)
Florida
R. T. Jones

Beau Clerc CC (a.9)
Florida
G. W. Cobb

Beau Desert GC
England
W. H. Fowler

Beaumont CC
Pennsylvania
J. G. Harrison

Beauport Park
British Isles
J. J. F. Pennink

Beaver Brook G&CC
Tennessee
L. Mills

Beaver Brook GC
New Jersey
E. V. Ternyey

Beaver Creek CC
Maryland
R. P. Hines

Beaver Creek GC
Colorado
R. T. Jones, Jr.

Beaver Dam CC [now Prince Georges G&CC]
Maryland
D. J. Ross

Beaver Hills CC
Iowa
E. L. Packard

Beaver Hills CC
Virginia
F. Garbin

Beaver Island GC
New York
W. E. Harries

Beaver Lake GC [now Asheville CC]
North Carolina
D. J. Ross

Beaver Lakes CC
Pennsylvania
F. Garbin

Beaver Meadow CC
New York
R. D. Bailey
Beaver Meadows Muni (a.9)
New Hampshire
G. S. Cornish, W. G. Robinson
Beavers Bend State Park GC
Oklahoma
F. Farley
Beaver Valley CC (Original 9)
Pennsylvania
E. F. Loeffler, J. McGlynn
Beaver Valley CC (r.9,a.9)
Pennsylvania
J. G. Harrison
Bebington GC (a.9)
England
F. W. Hawtree
Beckenham GC
England
T. Dunn
Beckett Ridge G&CC
Ohio
J. Kidwell
Bedale GC
England
J. J. F. Pennink
Bedens Brook Club
New Jersey
L. S. "Dick" Wilson
Bedford Springs CC
Pennsylvania
(Arthur Goss)
Bedford Springs CC (r.)
Pennsylvania
D.J. Ross
Bedford Springs CC (r.)
Pennsylvania
J. G. Harrison
Bedford Valley CC
Michigan
W. F. Mitchell
Bedlington GC
England
J. J. F. Pennink
Bedstone Court GC
England
T. Dunn
Bedwell Park GC
England
F. W. Hawtree
Bedwell Park GC
England
M. Hawtree
Beech Mountain
North Carolina
W. C. Byrd
Beechwood GC
Indiana
W. Diddel
Beeston Fields GC
England
T. Williamson
Beirut GC
Lebanon
J. J. F. Pennink
Beirut GC (Delhamyeh GC)
Lebanon
J. H. Stutt
Bel-Air CC
California
G. C. Thomas, Jr., W. P. Bell
Bel-Air CC (r.)
California
W. H. Johnson

Bel-Air CC (r.)
California
L. S. "Dick" Wilson
Bel-Air CC (r.)
California
R. T. Jones, Sr., and Jr.
Bel Air CC
Pennsylvania
W. F. and D. W. Gordon
Bel Aire CC
New York
A. Zikorus
Belair G&CC
Maryland
F. Murray, R. Roberts
Bel Compo GC
Connecticut
(Joseph Brunoli)
Belfast GC, Royal
Nothern Ireland
H. S. Colt
Belfrey GC (Brabazon and Derby courses)
England
P. Alliss, D. Thomas
Belgique GC, Royal (1904)
Belgium
W. Reid
Belgique GC, Royal (r.)
Belgium
T. C. Simpson
Belham River Valley GC
Montserrat, West Indies
E. B. Ault
Belhus Park
England
J. J. F. Pennink
Belk Park GC
Illinois
E. L. Packard
Bellach GC
Austria
B. Von Limburger
Bellavista, Club de Golf de
Mexico
P. Clifford
Bellavista, Club de Golf de (r.)
Mexico
M. L. Francis
Bella Vista CC (Kingswood and Berksdale courses)
Arkansas
E. B. Ault
Bella Vista CC (Bella Vista course)
Arkansas
J. Finger
Bella Vista CC
Tennessee
(John Frazier)
Bella Vista GC
Dominican Republic
A. H. Tull
Belleair CC
Arizona
R. Lawrence, J. Hardin, G. Nash
Belleair CC (9; n.l.e.)
Florida
J. D. Dunn
Belleair CC [now Belleview Biltmore West] (r.9,a.9; also, a.18) [now Belleview Biltmore East]
Florida
D. J. Ross
Belleclaire Golf Links (n.l.e.)
New York
T. Wells

Bellefonte CC (r.)
Kentucky
J. G. Harrison
Belle Haven CC
Virginia
L. Macomber
Belle Haven CC (R)
Virginia
E. B. Ault
Belle Haven CC (r.)
Virginia
G. W. Cobb
Belle Isle GC
Scotland
J. Braid, J. R. Stutt
Belle Isle Muni (n.l.e.)
Michigan
E. W. Way
Belle Meade CC
Tennessee
D. J. Ross
Belle Meade CC (r.)
Tennessee
R. T. Jones
Bellerive CC (n.l.e.)
Missouri
R. Foulis
Bellerive CC (New site)
Missouri
R. T. Jones
Belles Spring CC
Pennsylvania
E. B. Ault
Belle Terre CC
Louisiana
P. Dye
Belleville CC (9)
Kansas
H. Hughes, R. Watson
Belleville G&CC (a.9)
Ontario, Canada
C. E. Robinson
Belleview Biltmore Hotel & Club (r.9,a.9, West course; a.18, East course)
Florida
D. J. Ross
Belleview Biltmore Hotel & Club (r. East and West courses)
Florida
M. and H. Purdy
Bellevue CC
Massachusetts
E. F. Wogan
Bellevue CC
New York
D. J. Ross
Bellevue CC (r.14,a.4)
New York
F. Duane
Bellevue Muni
Washington
D. Kent
Bellflower Par 3 GC [now Gene List Muni]
California
H. M. and D. A. Rainville
Bellhaven CC
Virginia
L. Macomber
Bellingham GC
England
J. J. F. Pennink
Bel-Meadow G&CC
West Virginia
R. T. Jones
Belmont CC
California
B. Stamps

Belmont CC (r.)
California
R. E. Baldock
Belmont CC
Massachusetts
D. J. Ross
Belmont CC (r.)
Massachusetts
O. E. Smith
Belmont CC (r.)
Massachusetts
A. H. Tull
Belmont CC
Ohio
R. B. Harris
Belmont CC (r.)
Ohio
A. Hills
Belmont GC
Illinois
H. J. Tweedie
Belmont Hotel GC
Bermuda
D. Emmet, A. H. Tull
Beloit CC
Wisconsin
S. F. Pelchar
Belton Muni (formerly Richards Gebaur AFB GC)
Missouri
R.E. Baldock
Belton Park GC
England
T. Williamson
Belvedere CC
Arkansas
H. C. Hackbarth
Belvedere GC
Michigan
W. Watson
Belvedere GC (r.)
Prince Edward Island, Canada
C. E. Robinson
Belvoir Park
Northern Ireland
H.S. Colt
Benbrook Muni
Texas
R. Plummer
Bend CC (9)
Oregon
H. C. Egan
Bend CC (a.9)
Oregon
R. E. Baldock
Bend Muni
Oregon
(Gene S. Mason)
Ben Geren GC
Arkansas
M. H. Ferguson
Benghazi GC
Libya
J. J. F. Pennink
Bennett Valley GC
California
T. B. Harmon
Benona Shores GC
Michigan
K. W. Bowen
Benson Park GC
Nebraska
E. L. Packard
Bent Creek CC
Kentucky
R. A. Simmons
Bent Oak GC
Missouri
R.A. Simmons

Benton County GC
Indiana
W. Diddel
Bent Pine GC
Florida
J. L. Lee
Bent Tree CC
Georgia
J. L. Lee
Bent Tree CC
Texas
D. Muirhead
Bent Tree G&RC
Florida
W. B. Lewis
Benevenue GC
North Carolina
D. J. Ross
Bercuit, Golf de
Belgium
R. T. Jones
Beresford CC [now Peninsula GC]
California
D. J. Ross
Bergen County GC
New Jersey
A. H. Tull
Bergen Point Muni
New York
W. F. Mitchell
Berkeley CC [now Mira Vista CC]
California
W. R. Hunter
Berkeley CC
South Carolina
G. W. Cobb
Berkeley Hills GC
Georgia
A. Davis, R. Kirby
Berkeley Township GC
New Jersey
N. T. Psiahas
Berkhamsted GC
England
W. Park, Jr.
Berkhamsted GC
England (C. J. Gilbert)
Berkhamsted GC (r.,a.6)
England
J. Braid
Berkley Lake State Park GC
Kentucky
E. L. Packard
Berkly Hills GC
Georgia
R. Kirby, G. Player
Berkshire CC
Pennsylvania
W. Park, Jr.
Berkshire GC (Red & Blue courses)
England
W. H. Fowler, H. S. Colt, T. C. Simpson
Berkshire Hills CC
Massachusetts
A. W. Tillinghast
Berkshire Hills CC (r.4)
Massachusetts
G. S. Cornish, W. G. Robinson
Berlin G&CC
Germany
C. S. Butchart
Bermuda Dunes G&CC
California
W. F. Bell
Bermuda Run G&CC
North Carolina
E. Maples

Berry Hills CC
West Virginia
W. F. Gordon
Berthier, Club de Golf
Province of Québec, Canada
H. Watson
Berwick-On-Tweed GC
England
W. Park, Jr.
Berwick-On-Tweed GC (r.)
England
J. Braid
Berwick-Upon-Tweed GC (a.9)
England
F. W. Hawtree
Berwind CC (a.9; n.l.e.)
Puerto Rico
A. H. Tull
Berwind CC (New site)
Puerto Rico
F. Murray
Bessemer Muni
Alabama
E. Stone
Bethel Island GC
California
R. E. Baldock
Bethesda GC (r.)
Maryland
E. B. Ault
Bethlehem Muni
Pennsylvania
W. F. and D. W. Gordon
Bethlehem Steel Club [now Sparrows Point CC](27)
Maryland
W. F. and D. W. Gordon
Bethlehem Steel Club
New York
W. F. and D. W. Gordon
Bethlehem Steel Club
Pennsylvania
W. F. and D. W. Gordon
Bethpage GC (Red, Blue, Black and r. Green courses)
New York
A. W. Tillinghast
Bethpage GC (White course)
New York
A. H. Tull
Beverly CC
Illinois
D. J. Ross
Beverly G&CC
Ontario, Canada
C. E. Robinson
Beverly G&TC (r.)
Massachusetts
E. F. Wogan
Beverly Shores GC
Indiana
C. E. Maddox, F. MacDonald
Bexhill GC
England
W. Park, Jr.
Biarritz, Golf de
France
T. Dunn, "Young" W. Dunn
Biarritz, Golf de (r.)
France
H. S. Colt
Bic, Club de Golf du
Province of Québec
H. Watson
Bide-A-Wee CC
Virginia
F. A. Findlay

Bidermann GC
Delaware
L. S. "Dick" Wilson
Bielefeld GC
Germany
D. Harradine
Biella GC
Italy
J. S. F. Morrison
Big Bay G&CC
Ontario, Canada
S. Thompson
Big Canoe GC
Georgia
J. L. Lee
Big Canyon GC
California
R. M. Graves
Big Canyon CC
California
R.W. Fream, P.W. Thomson, M. Wolveridge
Big Cypress GC
Florida
R. Von Hagge
B. Devlin
Big Foot CC
Wisconsin
T. Bendelow
Big Foot CC (r.)
Wisconsin
E. L. and R. Packard
Big Oaks CC
Illinois
E. B. Dearie, Jr.
Big Pine GC
Indiana
R. D. Beard
Big Rapids CC
Michigan
J. L. Daray
Big Sky Meadow Village GC
Montana
F. Duane, A. Palmer
Big Spring CC
Kentucky
(George Davies)
Big Spring CC (r.)
Kentucky
W. Diddel
Big Springs CC (New site)
Texas
W. D. Cantrell
Big Spring GC (r.)
Kentucky
E.L. Packard
Big Tee Par 3 GC (9)
California
W. H. Johnson
Bigwin Inn GC
Ontario, Canada
S. Thompson
Bigwood GC
Idaho
R. M. Graves
Billerica, CC of
Massachusetts
P. A. Wogan
Billerica Par 3 GC
Massachusetts
A. Zikorus
Billings Muni (Point North GC)
Montana
T. J. Wirth, D. Bennett
Bill Roberts Muni
Montana
R. M. Graves

Biltmore Forest GC
North Carolina
D. J. Ross
Binbrook GC
Ontario, Canada
R. and C. Muylaert
Binghamton CC
New York
A. W. Tillinghast
Binghamton CC (r.)
New York
W. F. and D. W. Gordon
Bing Mahoney Muni
California
(Michael J. McDonagh)
Binicitan GC
Philippines
W. G. Wilkinson
Birch Hill GC
Michigan
E. W. Way
Birch Hills GC
California
H. W. and D. A. Rainville
Birchwood CC
Connecticut
O. E. Smith
Birchwood CC (r.)
Connecticut
W. F. Mitchell
Birchwood Farm G&CC
Michigan
W. B. and G. H. Matthews
Birchwood GC (r.9,a.9)
Ohio
F. Garbin
Birchwood GC
England
T. J. A. McAuley
Bird Bay Exec. GC
Florida
R. Garl
Birds Hill CC
Manitoba, Canada
N. Woods
Birdwood GC
Virginia
L. B. Ervin
Biri GC (r.)
Ireland
E. Hackett
Birkdale GC, Royal (Original course)
England
G. Lowe
Birkdale GC, Royal (r.)
England
F. G. Hawtree, J. H. Taylor
Birkdale GC, Royal (r.)
England
F. W. Hawtree
Birmingham Corporation (Marston Green & Pype Hayes' Muni)
England
F. G. Hawtree
Birmingham CC (r.)
Alabama
G. W. Cobb
Birmingham CC
Michigan
D. J. Ross
Birmingham CC (r.)
Michigan
W. Reid, W. Connellan
Birmingham CC (r.)
Michigan
R. T. Jones

Birmingham CC (r.3)
Michigan
W. B. and G. H. Matthews
Birmingham, CC of (East and West courses)
Alabama
D. J. Ross
Birmingham, CC of (r. East course)
Alabama
G. W. Cobb
Birmingham, CC of (r. West course)
Alabama
R. T. Jones
Birnam Wood GC
California
R. T. Jones, Sr. and Jr.
Birnamwood GC (9)
Minnesota
D. Herfort
Birstall GC (r.)
England
T. Williamson
Bismarck CC [now Apple Creek G&CC]
North Dakota
R. B. Harris
Bitterend GC (1978)
Missouri
E.L., R.B. Packard
Bitterroot River CC
Montana
W. F. Bell
Bixby Village GC (9)
California
R. W. Fream D.W. Thomson, M. Wolveridge
Blackberry Farm GC
California
R. M. Graves
Black Bull G&CC
Alberta, Canada
J. A. Thompson
Black Butte Ranch GC (Big Meadows)
Oregon
R. M. Graves
Black Butte Ranch (Glaze Meadows)
Oregon
(Gene S. Mason)
Black Canyon CC
California
W. F. Bell
Black Canyon GC
Arizona
A. J. Snyder
Black Hall Club
Connecticut
R. T. Jones
Black Hawk GC
Ohio
J. Kidwell
Blackheath GC, Royal (r.)
England
"Old" W. Dunn
Blackheath GC, Royal (New course, Eltham)
England
J. Braid
Blackhills-Hoveringham GC
England
J. J. F. Pennink
Blackhills Near Dudley GC
England
D. M. A. Steel
Blackhorse Par 3 GC
Illinois
C. E. Maddox

Blackledge CC
Connecticut
G. S. Cornish, W. G. Robinson
Blacklick Woods GC (r.5; a. Exec. 18)
Ohio
J. Kidwell
Blacklion (r.)
Ireland
E. Hackett
Blackmoor
England
H. S. Colt
Blackmountain CC (r.9,a.9)
North Carolina
(Ross Taylor)
Blac.. Mountain G&CC
Nevada
R. E. Baldock
Black Pool—Stanley Park
England
A. Mackenzie
Black River CC (Original 9)
Michigan
W. Reid, W. Connellan
Black River CC (r.9,a.9)
Michigan
W. Diddel
Black River Falls GC (9)
Wisconsin
E. L. Packard
Blackhawk CC
California
R. Von Hagge and B. Devlin
Blacksburg CC (Valley course)
Virginia
F. Garbin
Blackwell GC
England
W. H. Fowler
Blackwell GC (r.)
England C. K. Cotton
Blackwell Grange GC
England
J. J. F. Pennink
Blackwood CC
Pennsylvania
D. W. and W. F. Gordon
Blainroe GC
Ireland
F. W. Hawtree
Blair Academy GC (9)
New Jersey
(D. Irving Sewall)
Blairgowrie GC (r.a. 8)
Scotland
J. Braid
Blairgowrie GC (Rosemount Course)
Scotland
A Mackenzie
Blairgowrie GC (Lansdowne course)
Scotland
P. Alliss, D. Thomas
Blair Hampton GC
Ontario, Canada
R. and D. Moote
Blairmore and Strone
Scotland
J. Braid
Blairsville CC
Pennsylvania
J. G. Harrison
Blakely CC
Georgia
H. C. Moore, Sr.
Blandford GC (r.)
England
J. H. Stutt

Blanding Boulevard GC
Florida
F. Bolton
Bled GC
Yugoslavia
D. Harradine
Blind Brook CC (Route Plan)
New York
S. Raynor
Blind Brook CC
New York
G. Low
Blomidon Club
Newfoundland, Canada
A. H. Tull
Bloomfield Hills CC
Michigan
W. Diddel
Bloomfield Hills CC (r.)
Michigan
D. J. Ross
Bloomfield Hills CC (r.)
Michigan
R. T. Jones
Bloomfield-Wausa CC (9)
Nebraska
H. Hughes, R. Watson
Bloomington CC
Minnesota
P. Coates
Bloomington CC
Utah
W. H. Neff
Bloomington Hill CC
Utah (David Bingeman)
Bloomsburg CC (r.)
Pennsylvania
J. G. Harrison
Blossom Trails GC
Michigan
W. B. Matthews
Bloxswitch GC
England
(J. Sixsmith)
Blue Ash Muni (a.9)
Ohio
J. Kidwell, M Hurdzan
Blueberry Hill GC
Pennsylvania
J. G. Harrison, F. Garbin
Bluebonnet CC
Texas
B. J. Riviere
Bluegrass CC
Tennessee
R. B. Harris
Blue Hill CC
Massachusetts
E. F. Wogan
Blue Hill CC (a.9)
Massachusetts
P. A. Wogan
Blue Hill GC (r.4)
Massachusetts
M. L. Francis
Blue Hill GC (r.)
New York
E. B. Ault
Blue Hill GC (r.)
New York
F. Duane
Blue Hills CC (n.l.e.)
Missouri
F. Farley
Blue Hills CC (n.l.e.) (r.)
Missouri
R. C. Dunning

Blue Knob Resort
Pennsylvania
F. Garbin
Blue Lake Estates GC
Texas
J. Finger
Blue Lakes Springs GC
California
R. E. Baldock
Blue Mound CC
Wisconsin
S.J. Raynor
Blue Mound CC (r.)
Wisconsin
D. Gill
Blue Mountain CC
Pennsylvania
D. W. Gordon
Blue Mountain G&CC (Original 9)
Ontario, Canada
C. E. Robinson
Blue Ridge CC (r.)
Pennsylvania
J. G. Harrison, F. Garbin
Blue Rock Par 3 GC
Massachusetts
G. S. Cornish
Blue Rock Springs GC
California
J. Fleming
Blue Skies CC
California
W. F. Bell
Blue Water Bay CC
Florida
G. and T. Fazio
Bluff Point CC
New York
A. W. Tillinghast
Blumisberg G&CC
Switzerland
B. Von Limburger
Blundellsands GC
England
W. Park, Jr.
Blythefield CC (r.5)
Michigan
W. B. and G. H. Matthews
Blythe Field CC (r.)
Michigan
B. J. Riviere
Blythe Muni
California
W. F. Bell
Blytheville CC (r.9,a.9)
Arkansas
J. Finger
Blyth GC (Borough of Blyth Valley)
England
J. H. Stutt
Board of Trade GC (Toronto)
Ontario, Canada
H. Watson
Board of Trade GC (Toronto; r.9,a.9)
Ontario, Canada
A. Hills
Boars Head Inn Par 3 GC (9)
Virginia
R. F. Loving
Boat-Of-Garten GC
Scotland
J. Braid, J. R. Stutt
Bobby Jones GC ("British" and "American" courses)
Florida
D. J. Ross

Bobby Jones Muni (r.36)
Florida
R. A. Anderson
Bobby Jones Muni (a. 9 Exec.)
Florida
L. Marshall
Bobby Nichols GC
Kentucky
B. J. Wihry
Bob Goalby/Yorktown Par 3 GC
Illinois
P. Dye
Bob O Link CC
Illinois
D. J. Ross
Bob O Link CC (r.)
Illinois
H. S. Colt, C. H. Alison, A. Mackenzie
Bob O Link CC (r.)
Illinois
K. Killian, R. Nugent
Bob O Link CC
Michigan
W. Reid, W. Connellan
Boca Del Mar G&TC (North course)
Florida
R. Von Hagge, B. Devlin
Boca Del Mar G&TC (South course)
Florida
J. L. Lee
Boca Grande CC
Florida
M. Mahannah
Boca Greens GC
Florida
J. L. Lee
Boca Lago CC (East and West courses)
Florida
R. Von Hagge, B. Devlin
Boca Raton Hotel & CC (South course)
Florida
W. S. Flynn
Boca Raton Hotel & CC (North course)
Florida
W. S. Flynn
Boca Raton Hotel & CC (r.)
Florida
R. T. Jones
Boca Raton Muni (9 par 3)
C. Ankrom
Boca (Raton) West G&CC (Courses #1 and #2)
Florida
D. Muirhead
Boca (Raton) West G&CC (Course #3)
Florida
R. Von Hagge, B. Devlin
Boca Rio GC
Florida
R. Von Hagge
Boca Teeca CC (27)
Florida
M. Mahannah
Boca Woods GC
Florida
J.L. Lee
Bodega Harbour GC (9)
California
R. T. Jones, Sr. and Jr.
Bodenstown GC
Ireland
E. Hackett
Bogey CC
Missouri
R. Foulis

Bognor Regis
England
J. Braid
Bogota, CC of (n.l.e.)
Colombia
C. H. Banks
Bogota, CC of (New site, 36)
Colombia
J. R. Van Kleek
Boiling Springs GC
Oklahoma
D. R. Sechrest
Boldmere GC
England
(Carl Bretherston)
Bolling AFB GC
Virginia
E. B. Ault
Bolton Field GC
Ohio
J. Kidwell
Bombay Presidency Club
India
(C. R. Clayton)
Bombay Presidency Club (r.)
India
P. Thomson, M. Wolveridge
Bomun Lake GC
Korea
E. L. and R. B. Packard
Bon Air CC
Pennsylvania
W. F. Gordon
Bon Air Vanderbilt Hotel GC (Lake course)
Georgia
S. J. Raynor
Bon Air-Vanderbilt Hotel GC (r. Hill Course)
Georgia
D. J. Ross
Bonaventure CC (East course)
Florida
J. L. Lee
Bonaventure CC (West course)
Florida
M. and C. Mahannah
Bonaventure GC
Province of Québec, Canada
H. and J. Watson
Bondues, Golf de (a. 3rd 9)
France
R. T. Jones
Bondues, Golf de
France
F. W. Hawtree
Bo'ness GC
Scotland
W. Park, Jr
Bonita CC
California
W. F. Bell
Bonneville GC
Utah
W. H. Neff
Bonneville Muni
Utah
W. P. and W. F. Bell
Bonnie Brae CC
South Carolina
R. Breeden
Bonnie Briar CC (r.)
New York
D. Emmet
Bonnie Briar CC (r.)
New York
A. W. Tillinghast

Bonnie Briar CC (r.)
New York
A. H. Tull
Bonnie Brook
Illinois
J. Foulis
Bonniebrook GC
Province of
Québec, Canada
H. Watson
Bonnie Dundee GC
Illinois
C. D. Wagstaff
Bonnie View CC (r.)
Maryland
E. B. Ault
Bonnie View GC (r.)
Michigan
W. B. and G. H. Matthews
Bookcliff CC
Colorado
H. B. Hughes
Boone Aire CC
Kentucky
R. Von Hagge
Boone CC
North Carolina
E. Maples
Boonsboro CC (orig)
Virginia
W. Park Jr.
Boonsboro CC
Virginia
F. A. Findlay
Boothbay Harbour CC
Maine
W. E. Stiles, J. R. Van Kleek
Boothferry GC
England
D. M. A. Steel
Bootle GC
England
T. C. Simpson
Borrego Springs CC (9)
California
L. M. Hughes
Borris GC
Ireland
(Col. J. H. Curry)
Borris GC (r.)
Ireland
E. Hackett
Borth and Ynslas GC
Wales
H. S. Colt
Boscobel G&CC
South Carolina
F. Bolton
Bosques del Lago GC (East and West courses)
Mexico
J. Finger
Bosques de San Isidro GC
Mexico
L. H. Hughes
Botany Woods Par 3 GC
South Carolina
G. W. Cobb
Boughton Ridge G.C (9, 1980)
Illinois
E.L., R.B. Packard
Boulder City GC
Nevada
H. M. and D. A. Rainville
Boulder CC [now Flat Irons CC]
Colorado
R. B. Harris

Boulder CC (New site, 27)
Colorado
J. P. Maxwell
Boulder Creek Exec. GC
California
J. Fleming
Boulders GC
Arizona
R. F. Lawrence
Boulders GC (a.9)
Arizona
A. J. Snyder
Bountiful GC
Utah
W. H. Neff
Bowden Muni
Georgia
H. C. Moore, Sr.
Bowling Green CC
Kentucky
W. B. Langford
Bowling Green GC
New Jersey
G. S. Cornish, W. G. Robinson
Bowling Green University GC (a.9)
Ohio
X. G. Hassenplug
Bowling Green University GC (r.)
Ohio
A. W. Hills
Bowmanville CC (First 9)
Ontario, Canada
C. E. Robinson
Bowness GC
Alberta, Canada
W. Park, Jr.
Bowring Park GC
England
F. W. Hawtree
Boyce Hill GC (r.)
England
F. G. Hawtree
Boyne Highlands GC (Original 18, now 9 of Moor and 9 of Heather courses)
Michigan
R. T. Jones
Boyne Highlands GC (a.9, Moor course and a.9, Heather course)
Michigan
W. K. Newcomb
Boyne Mountain GC (Alpine and Exec. courses)
Michigan
W. K. Newcomb
Brackenridge Park GC
Texas
A. W. Tillinghast
Bradford GC
Pennsylvania
J. G. Harrison, F. Garbin
Bradford GC
England
W. H. Fowler
Bradley Park GC
England
D. M. A. Steel
Bradley Park (Huddersfield) GC
England
J. J. F. Pennink
Brae Burn CC
Massachusetts
D. J. Ross
Brae Burn CC (r.2)
Massachusetts
G. S. Cornish, W. G. Robinson

Brae Burn CC
New York
F. Duane
Brae Burn CC [formerly Colonial CC]
Texas
J. Bredemus
Brae Burn CC (r.)
Texas
R. Plummer
Brae Burn CC (r.)
Texas
M. H. Ferguson
Brae Burn CC (r.)
Texas
J. Finger
Brae Burn CC
Washington
A. Smith
Braeburn GC
Michigan
W. Reid, W. Connellan
Braemar CC (East and West courses)
California
T. G. Robinson
Braemar GC (27)
Minnesota
R. N. Phelps
Braidburn CC (Original 9)
New Jersey
(Duer Irving Sewall)
Braidburn CC (a.9)
New Jersey
M. and H. Purdy
Braid Hill GC
Scotland
P. McEwen, R. Ferguson
Braidwood Rec. Centre GC
Illinois
H. D. Fieldhouse
Brainerd G&CC
Tennessee
L. S. "Dick" Wilson
Braintree GC
England
F. W. Hawtree
Braintree Muni (a.11)
Massachusetts
S. Mitchell
Bramley GC
England
(Charles Mayo)
Bramley GC (r.)
England
J. Braid
Brampton GC (9)
Ontario, Canada
S. Thompson
Brampton GC (r.)
Ontario, Canada
C. E. Robinson, R. Moote
Bramshaw Manor GC
England
(W. Wiltshire)
Bramshott Hill GC
England
J. H. Stutt
Brancepeth Castle
England
H. S. Colt
Brandermill CC
Virginia
R. Kirby, G. Player
Brandon GC (r.)
Ireland
E. Hackett

Brandon Wood GC
England
J. J. F. Pennink
Brandywine Bay GC
North Carolina
R. Von Hagge, B. Devlin
Brandywine CC
Delaware
A. H. Tull
Brandywine CC
Michigan
P. Dye
Brandywine CC
Ohio
(Earl Yesberger)
Brantford G&CC (r.)
Ontario, Canada
S. Thompson
Brantford G&CC (r.)
Ontario, Canada
C. E. Robinson
Brasilia GC
Brazil
R. T. Jones
Brattleboro CC
Vermont
W. E. Stiles
Brattleboro CC (r.)
Vermont
W. Mitchell
Braunfels GC
West Germany
B. Von Limburger
Brea GC
California
H. M. and D. A. Rainville
Breakers Beach CC
Illinois
L. Macomber
(The) Breakers GC (r. Ocean course)
Florida
D. J. Ross
(The) Breakers GC [formerly Royal Poinciana](r.9,a.9, Ocean course)
Florida
W. B. Langford, T. J. Moreau
(The) Breakers GC [formerly Royal Poinciana] Ocean course)
Florida
J. L. Lee
Breakers West GC
Florida
W. C. Byrd
Brechin GC
Scotland
J. Braid
Breezy Bend CC (r.)
Manitoba, Canada
G. S. Cornish, W. G. Robinson
Breitenloo GC
Switzerland
D. Harradine
Breitenloo GC
Switzerland
J. J. F. Pennink
Brentwood CC (r.)
California
M. Behr
Brentwood CC
Texas
B. Martindale
Brentwood GC
Florida
D. J. Ross
Breslau GC
West Germany
B. Von Limburger

Breton Bay GC
Maryland
J. P. Gibson
Bretton Woods GC
Maryland
E. B. Ault
Bretton Woods GC (Mt. Washington Hotel)
New Hampshire
D. J. Ross
Bretwood GC
New Hampshire
G. S. Cornish, W. G. Robinson
Brewster Green CC (a.2)
Massachusetts
G. S. Cornish, W. G. Robinson
Brian Thicke Estate
Ontario, Canada
H. Watson
Briar Bay Exec. GC (9)
Florida
R. Von Hagge, B. Devlin
Briarcliff CC
Washington
F. Federspiel
Briarcliff Manor GC
New York
D. Emmet
Briar Creek CC
Georgia
W. W. Amick
Briarcrest CC
Texas
M. H. Ferguson
Briardale Muni
Ohio
R. LaConte, E. McAnlis
Briar Ridge CC
Indiana,
E.L., R.B. Packard
Briars G&CC (9)
Ontario, Canada
S. Thompson
Briars G&CC (a.9)
Ontario, Canada
C. E. Robinson
Briarwood CC [formerly Briergate CC]
Illinois
H. S. Colt, C. H. Alison
Briarwood CC (r.)
Illinois
R. B. Harris
Briarwood CC
Mississippi
E. Stone
Briarwood CC
Ohio
R. LaConte, E. McAnlis
Brickendon Grange GC
England
C. K. Cotton, J. J. F. Pennink
Bridge-Of-Weir GC
Scotland
W. Park, Jr.
Bridgeport CC
West Virginia
J. G. Harrison
Bridgeport Fairways Exec. GC
Ontario, Canada
C. E. Robinson
Bridgman CC
Michigan
(George B. Ferry)
Bridport and West Dorset
England
J. Braid

Briergate CC [now Briarwood CC]
Illinois
H. S. Colt, C. H. Alison
Brigantine Beach GC
New Jersey
W. E. Stiles, J. R. Van Kleek
Brigham City G&CC
Utah
J. M. Riley
Bright Leaf GC
Kentucky
C. R. Blankenship
Brighton and Hove GC
England
W. Park, Jr.
Brighton and Hove GC
England
J. Braid
Brighton Corporation (Hollingbury Park and Dyke GC)
England
F. G. Hawtree
Brighton CC
New York
W. E. Harries
Brighton Dale Muni
Wisconsin
E. B. Ault
Brighton GC
England
T. Dunn
Brightwood G&CC
Nova Scotia, Canada
W. Park, Jr.
Brightwood G&CC
Nova Scotia, Canada
D. J. Ross
Brightwood Hills GC (9)
Minnesota
L. I. Johnson
Bristol CC
Virginia
A. G. McKay
Bristol, CC of
Tennessee
A. G. McKay
Bristol County CC (9)
Massachusetts
E. F. Wogan
Bristol Harbour Village GC
New York
R. T. Jones, R. L. Jones
Bristol Wood Par 3 GC
New York
G. Fazio
Broadmoor CC
Indiana
D. J. Ross
Broadmoor CC
Indiana
R. A. Anderson
Broadmoor CC (n.l.e.)
New York
D. Emmet, A. H. Tull
Broadmoor CC
Alberta, Canada
N. Woods
Broadmoore CC [now Franke CC]
Oklahoma
F. Farley
(The) Broadmoor GC (Original course, now 9 of East and 9 of West courses)
Colorado
D. J. Ross

(The) Broadmoor GC (r. 9, a. 9 East and
   West courses)
Colorado
R. T. Jones
The) Broadmoor GC (South course)
Colorado
E. B. Seay, A. Palmer
Broadmoor GC
Michigan
M. DeVries
Broadmoor GC
Washington
A. V. Macan
Broadstone GC
England
T. Dunn
Broadstone GC (r.)
England
H. S. Colt
Broadstone GC (r.)
England
W. H. Fowler
Broadview GC (9)
Ohio
J. Kidwell
Broadwater Beach Hotel GC (Original 9,
   Sea course)
Mississippi
(Bert Jones)
Broadwater Beach Hotel GC (r. Sea
   course, a. Sun and Par 3 courses)
Mississippi
E. Stone
Brockton Hall
England
H. Vardon
Brockton Hall GC (r.)
England
R. Beale
Brockville CC (r.)
Ontario, Canada
S. Thompson
Brockville CC (a.18)
Ontario, Canada
H. Watson
Brockville CC (a.9)
Ontario, Canada
C. E. Robinson
Brockway GC (9)
California
J. D. Dunn
Broekpolder GC
(of the Rotterdan CC)
The Netherlands
J.J.F. Pennink
Brokenhurst GC
England
H. S. Colt
Brokenhurst GC (r.)
England
J. H. Stutt
Broken Sound CC
Florida
J. L. Lee
Broken Woods Exec. GC
Florida
W. R. Watts
Broken Woods G&TC (r. Exec. course)
Florida
E. B. Ault
Bromley GC
England
T. Dunn
Bromont, Club de Golf
Province of Québec, Canada
H. Watson

Brookdale CC
Washington
A. Smith
Brooke GC
England
T. Dunn
Brooke Hills Park
West Virginia
X. G. Hassenplug
Brookfield CC
New York
W. E. Harries
Brookfield Hills CC (Exec.)
Wisconsin
R. Von Hagge, B. Devlin
Brookfield West G&CC
Georgia
G. W. Cobb
Brook Green CC (9)
North Carolina
W. C. Byrd
Brookhaven CC (Championship, Masters
   and Presidents courses)
Texas
J. P. Maxwell
Brookhill GC
Illinois
E. L. Packard
Brookhill GC (9)
Indiana
G. Kern
Brook Hollow CC
Michigan
W. B. Matthews
Brook Hollow GC
Texas
A. W. Tillinghast
Brook Hollow GC (r.)
Texas
R. Plummer
Brooklawn CC (r.)
Connecticut
A. W. Tillinghast
Brooklea CC
New York
D. J. Ross
Brooklea CC (r.)
New York
W. E. Harries
Brooklyn
New York
T. Bendelow
Brook Manor CC
Virginia
A. H. Tull
Brookmeadow CC
Massachusetts
S. Mitchell
Brookridge CC
Illinois
C. D. Wagstaff
Brookridge G&CC (27)
Kansas
C. H. Adams
Brookshire GC
Indiana
W. Diddel
Brookside CC
Pennsylvania
J. G. Harrison
Brookside CC (r.9,a.9)
Pennsylvania
W. F. Gordon
Brookside CC, Canton
Ohio
D. J. Ross
Brookside CC, Columbus (r.2)
Ohio
J. Kidwell, M. Hurdzan

Brookside GC
Iowa
L. I. Johnson
Brookside GC at Reno [now Reno Brook-
   side GC]
Nevada
R. E. Baldock
Brookside GC
Oklahoma
F. Farley
Brookside GC (27)
Ontario, Canada
R. and C. Muylaert
Brookside Muni (Courses #1 and #2)
California
W. P. Bell
Brookside Muni (r. Course #1)
California
D. Muirhead
Brookside Muni (Original 9)
Ohio
X. G. Hassenplug
Brookside Muni (a.9)
Ohio
J. Kidwell, M. Hurdzan
Brooksville G&CC
Florida
W. F. Mitchell
Brook Valley GC
North Carolina
E. Maples
Brookview CC (27)
Minnesota
C. E. Maddox
Brookview CC (a. 9 par 3)
Minnesota
(Emil F. Perret)
Brookwood CC
Illinois
C. D. Wagstaff
Brookwood CC (9)
Michigan
W. K. Newcomb
Brookwood GC (a.9)
Michigan
W. J. Spear.
Broome Manor GC
England
F. W. Hawtree
Broome Park GC
England
D. Steel
Broomfield CC (9)
Colorado
L. Howard
Broomieknowe
Scotland
B. Sayers
Broomieknowe (a.9)
Scotland
J. Braid
Broward CC
Florida
M. Mahannah
Brora
Scotland
J. Braid
Brown County GC
Wisconsin
E. L. Packard
Brown Deer Muni
Wisconsin
G. Hansen
Brownfield Muni
Texas
R. Plummer

Brown's Lake GC (r.)
Wisconsin
D. Gill
Brown's Mill GC
Georgia
G. W. Cobb
Browns Run CC
Ohio
D. W. Gordon
Brownsville CC
Texas
D. R. Sechrest
Bruce Memorial GC
Connecticut
R. T. Jones
Brundenell GC
Prince Edward Island, Canada
C. E. Robinson
Brunswick GC (Original 9)
Georgia
D. J. Ross
Brunswick GC (Original 9)
Maine
W. E. Stiles, J. R. Van Kleek
Brunswick GC (a.9)
Maine
G. S. Cornish, W. G. Robinson
Bruntisfield Links (r.)
Scotland
W. Park, Sr.
Bruntisfield Links (Davidson Main.)
Scotland
W. Park, Jr.
Bruntisfield Links (r.)
Scotland
J. Braid
Bruntisfield Links (r.)
Scotland
F. W. Hawtree
Bryan CC
Ohio
H. D. Paddock Sr.
Bryan Muni (r.)
Texas
M. H. Ferguson
Bryan Park Muni
North Carolina
G. W. Cobb, J. B. LaFoy
Bryanston GC
South Africa
C. H. Alison
Bryce Mountain GC
Virginia
E. B. Ault
Brynhill GC
Wales
C. K. Cotton
Bryn Mawr GC
Illinois
H.J. Tweedle
Bryn Mawr GC (r.)
Illinois
G. J. Renn
Bryn Llawen GC
Pennsylvania
G. J. Renn
Bryn Mawr GC
Illinois
W. B. Langford, T. J. Moreau
Brynwood CC (r.1,a.2)
Michigan
W. B. and G. H. Matthews
Brynwood CC (r.)
Wisconsin
D. Gill
Brynwood CC (r.)
Wisconsin
K. Killian, R. Nugent
Buchanan Castle GC
Scotland
J. Braid, J. R. Stutt
Buckeye Hills GC
Ohio
X. G. Hassenplug

Buck Hill Inn & CC (Original 18)
Pennsylvania
D. J. Ross
Buck Hill Inn GC (r.)
Pennsylvania
W. F. Gordon
Buckhurst Park GC
England
F. G. Hawtree
Buckingham CC
Texas
R. Plummer
Bucknell University GC (a.9)
Pennsylvania
E. B. Ault
Bucks County GC
Pennsylvania
W. F. and D. W. Gordon
Bucksport G&CC
Maine
P. A. Wogan
Buddock Vean
England
J. Braid
Buena Vista CC
New Jersey
W. F. and D. W. Gordon
Buenos Aires CC (San Andres GC)
Argentina
M. Park II
Buffalo, CC of
New York
D. J. Ross
Buffalo, CC of (r.)
New York
R. T. Jones
Buffalo, CC of (r.2)
New York
G. S. Cornish, W. G. Robinson
Buffalo Dunes Muni
Kansas
F. Hummel
Buffalo Grove CC
Illinois
K. Killian, R. Nugent
Buffalo Hill GC (r.18,a.9)
Montana
R. M. Graves
Buffalo Muni (9)
Wyoming
F. Hummel
Bugambilian. Club de Golf
Mexico
P. Clifford
Bukit Jambul GC
Malaysia
R. T. Jones, Jr.
Bull Bay GC
Wales
W. H. Fowler
Bull Creek CC
Georgia
J. L. Lee
Bulls Eye CC
Wisconsin
E. L. Packard
Bulwell Forest GC
England
T. Dunn
Bulwell Forest GC (r.)
England
T. Williamson
Bulwell Hall GC
England
T. Williamson
Bundoran
Ireland
H. Vardon

Bunker Hill CC
Maryland
(Charles B. Schaelstock)
Bunker Hills Muni (27)
Minnesota
D. Gill
Bunn Park GC
Illinois
R. B. Harris
Bunn Park GC (r.)
Illinois
E.L. Packard
Butterfield CC (r.)
Illinois
E.L. Packard
Burgess of Edinburgh, Royal
Scotland
T. Morris
Burgess of Edinburgh, Royal
Scotland
J. Braid
Burhill GC
England
H. S. Colt
Burke Lake Par 3 GC
Virginia
L. Howard
Burleigh GC
Australia
(James D. Scott)
Burlingame CC
California
T. Nicoll
Burlington CC
Vermont
D. J. Ross
Burlington G&CC
Ontario, Canada
S. Thompson
Burlington GC
Iowa
E. L. Packard
Burlington GC
Kentucky
C. R. Blankenship
Burlington Industries Par 3 GC
North Carolina
E. Hamm
Burnaby Mountain Men's GC (r.)
British Columbia, Canada
C. E. Robinson
Burnham & Berrow GC (a.9)
England
F. W. Hawtree
Burnham Woods GC
Illinois
S. F. Pelchar
Burning Bush CC
Indiana
E. L. and R. B. Packard
Burning Ridge CC
North Carolina
E. Hamm
Burning Tree Club
Maryland
H. S. Colt, C. H. Alison, A. Mackenzie
Burning Tree Club (r.)
Maryland
W. S. Flynn
Burning Tree Club (r.)
Maryland
R. T. Jones
Burning Tree Club (r.)
Maryland
E. B. Ault
Burningtree CC
Alabama
G. W. Cobb

Burning Tree CC
Connecticut
H. Purdy
Burns Park Muni (27)
Arkansas
J. Finger
Burnt Store GC
Florida
D. L. Wallace
Burton-On-Trent GC
England
T. Williamson
Burton-On-Trent GC
England
(Henry Beck)
Bury St. Edmunds GC
England
(Edward "Ted" Ray)
Bury St. Edmunds GC (r.)
England
J. J. F. Pennink
Buscot GC
England
T. Dunn
Bushey G & Squash Club (9)
England
J. J. F. Pennink
Bushfield CC
Virginia
E. B. Ault, A. Jamison
Bushfoot GC
Northern Ireland
J. D. Harris
Butler CC
Pennsylvania
T. Bendelow
Butler CC (r.9)
Pennsylvania
E. F. Loeffler, J. McGlynn
Butler CC (r.9,a.9)
Pennsylvania
L. Macomber
Butler CC (r.)
Pennsylvania
E. B. Ault
Butler National GC
Illinois
G. and T. Fazio
Butte Creek G&CC
California
R. E. Baldock
Butterfield CC
Illinois
W. B. Langford, T. J. Moreau
Cabool Mountain Grove CC by F. Farley is in
   Missouri, not Mississippi
Buttermilk Falls GC
Ohio
J. Kidwell, M. Hurdzan
Buttes Blanches, Royal GC Les (r.)
Belgium
F. W. Hawtree
Buttonville GC (9)
Ontario, Canada
R. and C. Muylaert
Buxton High Peak GC
England
A. Mackenzie
Buxton High Peak GC (r.)
England
T. Williamson
Byrncliff
New York
W. E. Harries
Byrn Manor
Illinois
H. J. Tweedie

Byrnwych CC (27)
Ohio
A. Hills
Byron Meadows CC
New York
W. E. Harries
Cabarrus CC
North Carolina
G. W. Cobb
Cabool-Mountain Grove CC
Missouri
F. Farley
Cacapon Springs GC
West Virginia
R. T. Jones
Cactus Heights GC
South Dakota
(Clifford A. Anderson)
Caesarea G&CC
Israel
(Charles Mandelstam)
Cahir Park GC
Ireland
E. Hackett
Cairndhu Larne GC (r.)
Ireland
E. Hackett
Cairo CC
Georgia
R. A. Anderson
Calabasas Park CC
California
R. T. Jones, Sr. and Jr.
Calais GC (r.)
Colombia
C. E. Robinson
Calatagan G&CC
Philippines
R. T. Jones, Jr.
Calcutta, Royal (r. Old course)
India
P. Thomson
Caldwell GC
Scotland
G. Fernie
Calendo GC
Pennsylvania
C. D. Worthington
Calero Hills CC
California
J. Fleming
Calgary G&CC
Alberta, Canada
W. Park, Jr.
Calgary G&CC (r.)
Alberta, Canada
W. G. Robinson
Calgary Muni
Alberta, Canada
T. Bendelow
Calgary St. Andrews GC
Alberta, Canada
W. Park, Jr.
Calhoun Club (9)
South Carolina
E. Maples
California CC (n.l.e.)
California
M. Behr
California CC (New site)
California
W. F. Bell
California CC
Missouri
C. Mendenhall

California GC (r.)
California
R. T. Jones, Jr.
California GC (a.5)
Ohio
J. Kidwell, M. Hurdzan
California GC of San Francisco
California
A. V. Macan
California GC of San Francisco (r.)
California
A. Mackenzie
California GC of San Francisco (r.,a.5)
California
R.T. Jones, Sr. and Jr.
Callan GC
Ireland
(P. Mahon)
Callan GC (r.)
Ireland
E. Hackett
Callawassie Island
South Carolina
W. C. Byrd
Callaway Gardens GC (Lakeview and
   Mountain View courses)
Georgia
L. S. "Dick" Wilson
Callaway Gardens GC (Gardens View
   and Exec. Sky View courses)
Georgia
J. L. Lee
Caloosa G&CC
Florida
R. Garl
Calumet CC
Illinois
D. J. Ross
Calumet CC (a.9)
Illinois
E. L. Packard
Calusa CC
Florida
M. Mahannah
Calvada Valley G&CC
Nevada
W. F. Bell
Camarlo GC
Nevada
R. E. Baldock
Camargo Club
Ohio
S.J. Raynor
Camargo Club (r.)
Ohio
R. Von Hagge
Camarillo Springs CC
California
T. G. Robinson
Camberley Heath
England
H. S. Colt
Camden CC
South Carolina
D. J. Ross
Camden State Park GC
Alabama
E. Stone
Came Down GC (r.)
England
J. H. Stutt
Camelback GC (Padre course)
Arizona
R. F. Lawrence
Camelback GC (Indian Bend course)
Arizona
J. Snyder

Camelot CC
Texas
L. Howard
Camelot CC
Wisconsin
H. D. Fieldhouse
Camelot GC (27)
Arizona
M. Coggins
Camels GC
Colorado
J. P. Maxwell
Cameron Park CC
California
B. Stamps
Camino Heights GC
California
B. Stamps
Campbelltown GC
Australia
R. Von Hagge, B. Devlin
Camp Crowder GC
Missouri
E. L. Bell
Camp David GC (1 hole course)
Maryland
R. T. Jones
Campestre, Club
Mexico
P. Clifford
Campestre de Cucuta, Club
Colombia
H. Watson
Campestre de Hermosillo Club
Mexico
L. M. Hughes
Campestre de Lagunero
Mexico
P. Clifford
Campestre de Leon GC
Mexico
M. Schjetnan
Camp Hood GC
Texas
P. D. and J. P. Maxwell
Campobello Prov. Park GC
New Brunswick, Canada
G. S. Cornish, W. G. Robinson
Campo, Club de
Spain
J. Arana
Campo, Club de
Spain
J. D. Harris
Campo de Golf Cajuiles GC (Teeth of the
   Dog and Links courses)
Dominican Republic
P. Dye
Campo de Golf Parcelas
Spain
J. D. Harris
Campo de Golf Somosaguas
Spain
J. D. Harris
Campo de Golf Tres Vidas
Mexico
R. T. Jones, Sr. and Jr.
Campo de Malaga, Club de
Spain
P. M. Ross
Campo de Golf Maspalomas (Canary Is-
   lands; South course)
Spain
P. M. Ross

Campo de Golf Maspalomas (Canary Islands; North course)
Spain
R. Kirby, G. Player
Canaan Valley State Park GC
West Virginia
G. S. Cornish, W. G. Robinson
Canadian-American GC
Pennsylvania
P. Erath
Canberra GC, Royal
Australia
J. D. Harris
Cancun Pok-Ta-Pok Resort Course
Mexico
R. T. Jones, Sr. and Jr.
Candiac GC
Province of Québec, Canada
H. Watson
Candiac GC (r.)
Province of Québec, Canada
J. Watson
Candlestone GC
Michigan
W. B. and G. H. Matthews
Candlewood CC [formerly Clock CC]
California
H. M. Rainville
Candlewood CC (r.)
California
T. G. Robinson
Cando GC (9)
North Dakota
L. I. Johnson
Candywood GC
Ohio
H. D. Fieldhouse
Canlubang GC (2 courses)
Philippines
R. T. Jones, Jr.
Cannes CC
France
H. S. Colt
Cannes GC
France
W. Reid
Cannon Hill GC
Australia
R. Von Hagge, B. Devlin
Canoe Brook CC (South course)
New Jersey
C. H. Alison
Canoe Brook CC (North course)
New Jersey
A. H. Tull
Canoe Brook CC (r.)
New Jersey
W. F. Gordon
Canoe Brook CC (r.2)
New Jersey
H. Purdy
Canoe Brook CC (r.)
New Jersey
R. T. Jones
Canoe Creek CC
Alabama
J. H. Williams, Sr.
Canon del Oro CC at Sedona
Arizona
A. J. Snyder
Canongate CC
Florida
J. L. Lee
Canongate GC
Georgia
L. S. "Dick" Wilson

Canongate-On-Lanier GC
Georgia
J. L. Lee
Canon's Brook
England
H. Cotton
Canterbury CC
Ohio
H. B. Strong
Canterbury CC (r.)
Ohio
(Jack Way)
Canterbury CC (r.)
Ohio
G. S. Cornish, W. G. Robinson
Canterbury Green GC
Indiana
R. D. Beard
Canton GC
Connecticut
R. J.Ross
Canton Park District GC
Illinois
E. L. Packard
Canyon CC (North and South courses)
California
W. F. Bell
Canyon CC (r.)
California
W. F. Mitchell
Canyon Creek CC
Texas
J. P. Maxwell
Canyon Creek CC (r.)
Texas
R. Plummer
Canyon Lakes G&CC
Washington
R. Fream, P. Thomson, M. Wolveridge
Canyon Meadows G&CC (r.)
Alberta, Canada
W. G. Robinson
Canyon R&GC
California
W. F. Bell
Cape Ann GC
Massachusetts
E. F. Wogan
Cape Arundel GC
Maine
W. J. Travis
Cape Breton Highlands National Park GC (Keltic Lodge)
Nova Scotia, Canada
S. Thompson
Cape Coral CC
Florida
L. S. "Dick" Wilson
Cape Coral Exec. GC
Florida
(Sid Clarke)
Cape Eleuthera GC
Bahamas
R. Von Hagge, B. Devlin
Cape Fear CC [now Green Valley CC](r.)
North Carolina
E. Hamm
Cape Giradeau CC (Original 9)
Missouri
A. Linkogel
Cape Giradeau CC (a.9)
Missouri
D. Gill
Capehart GC at Offutt AFB
Nebraska
R. T. Jones

Cape Haze G&CC
Florida
R. A. Anderson
Capilano G&CC
British Columbia, Canada
S. Thompson
Capistrano Saddle Club
California
D. Muirhead
Capital City Club
Florida
(John Budd)
Capital City Club (r.)
Florida
R. A. Anderson
Capital City CC (r.)
Georgia
G. W. Cobb
Capitol City GC
Washington
N. Woods
Capitol Hills CC
Philippines
(Francisco D. Santana)
Capri Isle GC
Florida
R. A. Anderson
Capri Isles GC, Sarasota
Florida
L. Marshall
Cap Rouge, Club de Golf
Province of Québec, Canada
H. Watson
Carabelleda G&YC
Venezuela
J. R. Van Kleek
Caracas, Club de Golf
Venezuela
D. Bennett
Cardiff GC
Alberta, Canada
W.G. Robinson
(The) Cardinal GC
North Carolina
P. Dye
Cardross GC
Scotland
W. Fernie
Card Sound GC
Florida
Von Hagle and B. Devlin
Carefree Ranch GC
Arizona
P. and R. Dye
Cariari International CC
Costa Rica
G. and T. Fazio
Carling Lake GC
Province of Québec, Canada
H. Watson
Carlinville GC
Illinois
E. L. Packard
Carlisle GC
England
T. Moone
Carlisle GC (r.)
England
P. M. Ross
Carlisle GC (r.)
England
J. J. F. Pennink
Carlisle Race Course GC
England
D. M. A. Steel

Carlow GC
Ireland
T. C. Simpson
Carlow GC (r.)
Ireland
E. Hackett
Carlson Farms CC (Greensboro CC, Carlson Farms course)
North Carolina
E. Maples
Carlton GC
England
T. C. Simpson
Carlton Oaks CC
California
(William Mast)
Carlyon Bay
England
J. H. Stutt
Carmargo Club (r.)
Ohio
R. Von Hagge
Carmel CC (North course)
North Carolina
G. W. Cobb
Carmel CC (South course)
North Carolina
E. Maples
Carmel Valley G&CC
California
R. M. Graves
Carmel Valley Ranch GC
California
P. Dye
Carmen G&CC
Manitoba, Canada
J. A. Thompson
Carmoden GC
Scotland
C. D. Lawrie
Carnalea
Northern Ireland
J. Braid
Carnoustie (Barry Angus) CC (Original 10 holes)
Scotland
A. Robertson
Carnoustie (Barry Angus) CC (a.8)
Scotland
T. Morris
Carnoustie GC (r.)
Scotland
W. Park, Jr.
Carnoustie CC (r.)
Scotland
J. Braid, J. R. Stutt
Carolina G&CC
North Carolina
D. J. Ross
Carolina Sands
North Carolina
W. C. Byrd
Carolina Shores CC
North Carolina
T. Jackson
Carolina Trace G&CC (27)
North Carolina
R. T. Jones
Carolina Trace GC
Ohio
R. Von Hagge
Caroline CC
Maryland
E. B. Ault
Carper Valley GC
Virginia
F. Findlay

Carradam CC
Pennsylvania
J. G. Harrison
Carrick-On-Shannon GC (r.)
Ireland
E. Hackett
Carrick-On-Suir GC (r.)
Ireland
E. Hackett
Carrol Lake CC
Tennessee
R. A. Anderson
Carrol County GC (9)
Arkansas
H. C. Hackbarth
Carroll Park Muni
Maryland
C. Hook
Carrollton CC (r.)
Missouri
M. H. Ferguson
Carrollwood G&TC (27)
Florida
W. F. Mitchell
Carrollwood G&TC (a.18)
Florida
E. B. Ault
Carson City Muni [now Eagle Valley Muni]
Nevada
A. J. Snyder
Carson City Muni (a.9)
Nevada
R. E. Baldock
Carstairs G & Community Club (a. 9)
Alberta, Canada
W.G. Robinson
Carswell AFB GC
Texas
(Charles B. Akey)
Carter Caves State Park GC
Kentucky
H. Purdy
Carter CC
New Hampshire
D. J. Ross
Cartersville CC
Georgia
A. Davis, R. Kirby, G. Player
Cartersville Muni
Georgia
R. Kirby, G. Player
Cary CC
Indiana
R. A. Anderson
Casa De Campo Hotel (Campo De Golf)
Dominican Republic
P. Dye
Casa del Mar CC [now Longwood]
Indiana
H. Collis
Casa Grande Muni [now Santa Cruz Park](9)
Arizona
A. J. Snyder
Casa Grande Muni (9)
Arizona
G. A. Panks
Casa La Cumbre Par 3 GC
California
H. M. and D. A. Rainville
Casaview CC
Texas
L. Howard
Cascade Fairways GC
Utah
W. H. Neff
Cascade Hills CC
Michigan
J. L. Daray
(Charles B. Akey)

240

Cascade Hills CC (r.)
Michigan
D. Gill

Cascade Hills CC (r.)
Michigan
W. B. and G. H. Matthews

Cascade Hills CC (r.)
Michigan
E.L. Packard

Cascades Course (The Homestead)
Virginia
W. S. Flynn

Cascades Course (The Homestead) (r.)
Virginia
R. T. Jones

Case Leasing GC
Ohio
R. D. Beard

(The) Casino Club
El Salvador
F. W. Hawtree

Caslano GC (r.)
Switzerland
E. B. Ault

Casper CC (Original course)
Wyoming
(James Mason)

Casper CC (a.9)
Wyoming
R. M. Graves

Casper CC (r.9,a.9)
Wyoming
R. E. Baldock

Casper Muni (r.)
Wyoming
R. M. Graves

Casta Del Sol GC (Exec.)
California
T. G. Robinson

Castine GC
Maine
W. Park, Jr.

Castle AFB GC (9)
California
R. E. Baldock

Castlebar GC (r.)
Ireland
E. Hackett

Castle Eden and Peterlee
England
C.K. Cotton

Castle GC
Ireland
H. S. Colt

Castle Harbor GC
Bermuda
C. H. Banks

Castle Inn Par 3 GC (n.l.e.)
Bermuda
D. Emmet

Castle Pines CC
Colorado
J. Nicklaus

Castlerea GC (r.9)
Ireland
E. Hackett

Castle Rock
Northern Ireland
B. Sayers

Castle Rock GC
Virginia
F. Garbin

Castleroy GC
Ireland
(Maj. R. Deekin)

Castletown GC, Isle of Man
England
A. Mackenzie

Castletown GC, Isle of Man (r.)
England
P. M. Ross

Castletroy GC (r.)
Ireland
E. Hackett

Castle View Muni
California
R. E. Baldock

Castle View T&CC
Georgia
C. H. Adams

Castlewood CC (Hill and Valley courses)
California
W. P. Bell

Catalina GC
California
J. D. Dunn

Cataraqui G&CC
Ontario, Canada
S. Thompson

Catawba CC (27)
North Carolina
W. C. Byrd

Catawba Island Club
Ohio
W. J. Rockefeller

Caterham GC
England
F. G. Hawtree

Cathedral Canyon CC
California
H. M. and D. A. Rainville

Catatonk GC
New York
H. Purdy

Cavaliers CC
Delaware
F. Murray, R. Roberts

Cavalry Club
New York
L. S. "Dick" Wilson, J. L. Lee

Cavan GC
Ireland
E. Hackett

Cavendish GC
England
A. Mackenzie

Cavendish GC (r.)
England
T. Williamson

Cawder GC (Cawder and Keir courses)
Scotland
J. Braid

Caymanas G&CC
Jamaica
H. Watson

Cazenovia CC (Original 9)
New York
S. Dunn

Cazenovia CC (a.9)
New York
H. Purdy

Ceann Seibeal, Golf Cursa
Ireland
E. Hackett

Cedar Brae G&CC
Ontario, Canada
C. E. Robinson

Cedar Brook CC
North Carolina
E. Maples

Cedar Brook CC
New York
A. Zikorus

Cedarbrook CC (n.l.e.)
Pennsylvania
A. W. Tillinghast

Cedarbrook CC, Belle Vernon
Pennsylvania
J. G. Harrison

Cedarbrook CC (New site), Blue Bell
Pennsylvania
W. F. Mitchell

Cedarbrook GC
Ontario, Canada
S. Thompson

Cedarbrook GC
Province of Québec, Canada
H. Watson

Cedar Creek GC
Indiana
R. D. Beard

Cedar Creek GC
Michigan
R. D. Beard

Cedar Crest CC
Kansas
(Dewitt "Maury" Bell)

Cedar Crest GC
Illinois
G. O'Neill

Cedar Crest GC
Texas
A. W. Tillinghast

Cedar Glenn G&CC (a.9)
Ontario, Canada
J. F. Robinson

Cedar Hills Exec. GC
Nebraska
H. W. Glissmann

Cedarholm Muni (9)
Minnesota
P. Coates

Cedar Knob GC
Connecticut
G. S. Cornish

Cedar Knoll GC (9)
Kentucky
J. G. Harrison

Cedar Lake GC
Indiana
R. A. Anderson

Cedar Point Club
Virginia
A. J. Snyder

Cedar Rapids CC
Iowa
D. J. Ross

Cedar Ridge CC
Oklahoma
J. Finger

Cedar Rock CC
North Carolina
E. Maples

Cedar Valley GC (27)
Oklahoma
F. Farley

Cedar Wood CC
North Carolina
E. Maples

(The) Centennial CC
Florida
R. Garl

Centennial Estates CC
Tennessee
A. L. Davis

Centennial Farms GC
Michigan
W. Bowen

Centennial Par 3 GC (9)
Colorado
J. Fleming

Center Square GC
Pennsylvania
E. B. Ault

Central City CC
Kentucky
(Harold England)

Central City CC
Nebraska
H. W. Glissmann

Centralia CC
Missouri
C. Mendenhall

Central Valley GC
New York
H. Purdy

Centre Hills CC (Original 9)
Pennsylvania
J. G. Harrison

Centre Hills CC (a.9)
Pennsylvania
R. T. Jones

Centro Deportive GC (9)
Mexico
P. Clifford

Century CC [now Orange Tree CC]
Arizona
L.M. Hughes, (Johnny Bulla)

Century CC
New York
H. S. Colt, C. H. Alison

Century CC (r.)
New York
R. T. Jones

Century GC
Florida
J. L. Lee

Century Hills CC
Connecticut
G. S. Cornish, W. G. Robinson

Century XXI Club
Florida
A. M. Pulley

Century XXI Club
Maryland
A. M. Pulley

Century Village GC
Florida
J. L. Lee

Cerro Alto, Club de Golf
Mexico
P. Clifford

Cerromar Beach GC (North and South courses)
Puerto Rico
R. T. Jones

Cervinia GC
Italy
D. Harradine

C.F.B. Borden GC (r.)
Ontario, Canada
C. E. Robinson

Chabonneau Exec. GC (r.)
Oregon
T. G. Robinson

Chadron GC (9)
Nebraska
F. Hummel

Chadwell Springs
England
J. H. Taylor

Chagrin Valley CC
Ohio
S. Thompson

Chahinkapa Park GC
North Dakota
R. B. Harris

Chalampe GC
France
D. Harradine

Chalk Mountain Muni
California
R. M. Graves

Chamberlain CC (New site)
South Dakota
R. B. Harris

Chambersburg CC (r.)
Pennsylvania
W. F. Gordon

Chambersburg GC
Pennsylvania
E. B. Ault

Chambly, Club de Golf
Province of
Québec, Canada
H. Watson

Chamonix GC
France
R. T. Jones

Champion Lakes CC
Pennsylvania
P. Erath

Champions GC (Cypress Creek course)
Texas
R. Plummer

Champions GC (Jackrabbit course)
Texas
G. Fazio

Champlain GC
Province of Québec, Canada
H. Watson

(Le) Chantecler GC
Province of Québec, Canada
H. Watson

Chantilly de Lys (International GC)
France
T. C. Simpson

Chantilly, Golf de (27)
France
T. C. Simpson

Chantilly Manor CC
Maryland
R. Roberts

Chantilly National G&CC
Virginia
E. B. Ault

Chanute AFB GC (a.9)
Illinois
E. L. Packard

Chapala, CC of
Mexico
(Harry C. Offut, Jr.)

Chaparral CC
Texas
L. Howard

Chaparral Exec. GC
California
T. G. Robinson

Chapel-En-Le Frith
England
D. Thomas

Chapel Hill CC
North Carolina
F. A. Findlay

Chapel Hill CC (r.)
North Carolina
E. Hamm

Chapel Hill CC (r.)
North Carolina
G. W. Cobb

Chapman CC
Kansas
R. Watson
Chappell GC (9)
Nebraska
F. Hummel
Chappequa CC
New York
D. J. Ross
Chapultepec CC
Mexico
W. Smith (completed by A. Smith)
Chapultepec GC (r.)
Mexico
P. Clifford
Charbonneau CC (27)
Oregon
T. G. Robinson
Charles City CC
Iowa
R. N. Phelps
Charles River CC
Massachusetts
D. J. Ross
Charles River CC (r.)
Massachusetts
W. F. Mitchell
Charles Schwab Estate GC
Pennsylvania
D. J. Ross
Charleston AFB GC (9)
South Carolina
G. W. Cobb
Charleston, CC of
South Carolina
D. J. Ross
Charleston, CC of
West Virginia
G. W. Cobb
Charleville GC (r.)
Ireland
E. Hackett
Charlevoix Muni
Michigan
W. Watson
Charlie Chaplin Estate GC
California
A. Mackenzie
Charlotte CC
North Carolina
D. J. Ross
Charlotte CC (r.)
North Carolina
R. T. Jones
Charmingfare Links
New Hampshire
P. A. Wogan
Charnita GC
Pennsylvania
E. B. Ault
Charnwood Forest
England
J. Braid
Charny, Club de Golf (r.9,a.9)
Province of Québec
H. and J. Watson
Charter World G&RC (Exec.)
Florida
J. L. Lee
Chartiers CC
Pennsylvania
W. Park, Jr.
Chartiers CC (r.)
Pennsylvania
E. F. Loeffler, J. McGlynn

Chartiers CC (r.)
Pennsylvania
X. G. Hassenplug
Chartwell G&CC
Maryland
E. B. Ault
Chase Hammond GC
Michigan
M. DeVries
Chaska GC
Wisconsin
E. L. Packard
Chatfield GC
Colorado
F. Hummel
Chatham CC
Virginia
E. Hamm
Chatmoss CC
Virginia
E. Maples
Chatsworth GC (r.)
England
T. Williamson
Chattahoochee CC
Alabama
W. W. Amick
Chatthoochee GC (New site)
Georgia
R. T. Jones
Chattanooga G&CC (r.)
Tennessee
A. G. McKay
Chattanooga G&CC
Tennessee
D. J. Ross
Chattanooga G&CC (r.)
Tennessee
A. L. Davis
Chattaqua CC
New York
S. Dunn
Chatuge Shores CC
North Carolina
(John V. Townsend)
Chaumont En Vexin
France
D. Harradine
Cheat Lake GC
West Virginia
J. G. Harrison
Chedoke GC (r.18,a.18)
Ontario, Canada
S. Thompson
Cheeca Lodge
Florida
J. Nicklaus, (Bob Cupp)
Chemnitze GC
East Germany
B. Von Limburger, K. Hoffmann
Chenango Valley GC (a.9)
New York
H. Purdy
Chenequa CC (a.9)
Wisconsin
E. L. Packard
Chenoweth Run GC
Kentucky
B. J. Wihry
Cherokee GC
Alabama
(Neil R. Bruce)
Cherokee GC (r.)
Kentucky
A. G. McKay

Cherokee GC (r.)
Tennessee
A. G. McKay
Cherokee National G&CC
South Carolina
J. P. Gibson
Cherokee Park CC
Wisconsin
D. Gill
Cherokee Town & CC
Georgia
D. Gill
Cherokee Town & CC (a.9)
Georgia
W. C. Byrd
Cherokee Village GC (North and South courses)
Arkansas
E. B. Ault
Cherry Chase GC
California
R. M. Graves
Cherry Downs GC (27)
Ontario, Canada
H. Watson
Cherry Hill GC
Massachusetts
(David Maxon)
Cherry Hill GC
Ontario, Canada
W. Travis
Cherry Hill GC (r.)
Ontario, Canada
C. E. Robinson
Cherry Hills CC
Colorado
W. S. Flynn
Cherry Hills CC (r., a. Par 3)
Colorado
J. P. Maxwell
Cherry Hills CC (r.)
Colorado
E. B. Seay, A. Palmer
Cherry Hills CC (Original 18)
Illinois
H. Collis, J. Daray
Cherry Hills CC (a.18; n.l.e.)
Illinois
(J. Meister)
Cherry Hills CC (a. Exec. 9)
Illinois
D. Gill
Cherry Lane GC (9)
Idaho
R. E. Baldock
Cherry Lodge GC
England
(John Day)
Cherry Point GC
North Carolina
G. W. Cobb
Cherry Valley CC
New York
D. Emmet
Cherry Valley CC (r.12)
New York
F. Duane
Cherry Valley CC (r.)
New York
R. T. Jones
Cheshunt Park GC
England
F. W. Hawtree
Chester CC
Illinois
W. W. Amick
Chesterfield GC (r.)
England
T. Williamson

Chester GC
South Carolina
R. Breeden
Chester River Y&CC (r.)
Maryland
E. B. Ault
Chester Valley CC
Pennsylvania
G. and T. Fazio
Chestnut Hill CC
Maryland
A. G. McKay
Chestnut Hill CC
Massachusetts
W. E. Stiles, J. R. Van Kleek
Chestnut Hill CC (r.)
Massachusetts
S. Mitchell
Chestnut Ridge CC
Maryland
R. Roberts
Chestnut Ridge CC
Pennsylvania
J. G. Harrison, F. Garbin
Chestuee G&CC
Tennessee
W. W. Amick
Cheviot Hills GC
North Carolina
E. Hamm
Chevy Chase CC (r.)
California
H. M. and D. A. Rainville
Chevy Chase CC (n.l.e.)
Kansas
J. Dalgleish
Chevy Chase CC (Original 18)
Maryland
D. J. Ross
Chevy Chase CC (r.)
Maryland
H. S. Colt, C. H. Alison, A. Mackenzie
Chevy Chase CC (r.)
Maryland
R. T. Jones
Cheyenne CC
Wyoming
(Herbert Lockwood)
Chiba CC
Japan
K. Fujita
Chiberta, Golf de
France
T. C. Simpson
Chicago GC, Belmont [now Downer's Grove GC]
Illinois
C. B. Macdonald
Chicago GC, Wheaton
Illinois
C. B. Macdonald
Chicago GC, Wheaton (r.)
Illinois
C. B. Macdonald, S. J. Raynor
Chickaming GC
Michigan
H. Collis
Chickasaw GC
South Carolina
R. Breeden
Chicopee CC Muni
Massachusetts
G. S. Cornish
Chicorae CC (r.)
North Carolina
E. Hamm
Chicoria CC (r.)
Virginia
E. Hamm

Chicoutimi GC
Province of Québec, Canada
H. Watson
Chigger Creek CC [Formerly Sun Meadow CC]
Texas
B. J. Riviere
Chigusa CC
Japan
P.W. Thomson, M. Wolveridge
Chigwell GC
England
F. G. Hawtree
Chihuahua CC
Mexico
P. Clifford
Chiluca GC
Mexico
L. M. Hughes
Chilwell Manor GC (r.)
England
T. Williamson
Chimney Rock GC
California
R. E. Baldock
Chingford GC
England
"Young" W. Dunn
Chinguacousy CC (27)
Ontario, Canada
R. and C. Muylaert
Chippanee GC
Connecticut
(Herbert Lagerblade)
Chippenham GC
England
J. J. F. Pennink
Chippewa CC (2)
Ohio
J. G. Harrison, F. Garbin
Chipping Sodbury GC
England
F. W. Hawtree
Chiselhurst GC
England
T. Dunn
Chiselhurst GC (r.)
England
W. Park, Jr.
Chockoyette CC
North Carolina
E. Maples
Chorley GC
England
(J. A. Steer)
Christchurch CC (n.l.e.)
New Zealand
(Denis O'Rourke, L. B. Wood)
Christchurch CC (New site)
New Zealand
D. G. Soutar
Christown GC
Arizona
M. Coggins
Christmas Lake G&CC
Indiana
E. B. Ault
Chromonix CC (9)
Minnesota
D. Herfort
Chrysler Memorial Park GC
Ontario, Canada
H. Watson
Chula Vista GC [formerly Bonita Valley CC]
California
H. M. and D. A. Rainville

Chulmleigh GC
England
(J. W. Goodman, W. G. Mortimer)
Church Stretton GC
England
J. Braid
Churchill Valley CC (r.)
Pennsylvania
J. G. Harrison
Churston GC (r.)
England
H. S. Colt
Churubusco CC
Mexico
J. Bredmus
Churubusco CC (r.)
Mexico
M. L. Francis
Cielo Vista Muni
Texas
M. H. Ferguson
Cimarron GC
Minnesota
D. Herfort
Cimarron Hills CC
Colorado
J. P. Maxwell
Cincinatti CC (r.9,a.9)
Ohio
R. White
Cincinnati Muni
Ohio
J. Kidwell, M. Hurdzan
Cinque Ports, Royal (Deal)
England
T. Dunn
Cinque Ports, Royal (Deal; r.)
England
G. Campbell
Circle J GC
California
W. P. Bell
Circle R Ranch GC
California
J. Daray
Circle R. Ranch GC (r.)
California
(Jack Daray, Jr.)
Circleston CC
Georgia
(Sid Clarke)
City of Derry GC
Ireland
E. Hackett
City of New Bedford Muni [now Whaling City GC] (Original 9)
Massachusetts
D. J. Ross
City of New Bedford Muni [now Whaling City GC] (a.9)
Massachusetts
S. Mitchell
City Park GC (r. 18a.9)
Colorado
J. N. Cochran
City Park GC (r.)
Louisiana
R. Plummer
Civic GC
Ontario, Canada
S. Thompson
Civitan Park Muni
New Mexico
A. J. Snyder

Clacton On Sea
England
J. White
Clandeboye GC (Old course)
Northern Ireland
B. Von Limburger, T. J. A. McAuley, (W. R. Robinson)
Clandeboye GC (New course)
Northern Ireland
P. Alliss, D.J. Thomas
Claremont CC (r.)
California
A. Mackenzie
Claremorris GC (r.)
Ireland
E. Hackett
Clarksburg CC (r.9,a.9)
West Virginia
E. B. Ault
Clarksville CC
Tennessee
G. W. Cobb
Clauson's Inn GC (Original 9)
Massachusetts
D. Emmet
Clauson's Inn GC (a.9)
Massachusetts
A. H. Tull
Clay Center CC
Kansas
F. Farley
Clay County GC
Texas
(Bruce Littell)
Claycrest CC
Missouri
C. Mendenhall
Claymont Chase CC
West Virginia
H. Watson
Clear Brook GC
New Jersey
M. and H. Purdy
Clear Lake CC, Houston
Texas
B. J. Riviere
Clear Creek GC, Camp Hood
Texas
L. Howard
Clear Lake CC (Routed)
Texas
M. Coggins
Clear Lake GC
Manitoba, Canada
S. Thompson
Clearview CC
New Jersey
H. Purdy
Clearwater Bay G&CC
Hong Kong
R. T. Jones, Jr.
Clearwater CC
Florida
H. B. Strong
Clearwater CC (r.)
Florida
J. L. Lee
Clearwater Golf Park (Exec.)
Florida
R. Garl
Cleburne Muni
Texas
L. Howard
Cleghorn Plantation G&CC
North Carolina
G. W. Cobb

Clemson University GC
South Carolina
G. W. Cobb, J. B. LaFoy
Clevedon
England
J. H. Taylor
Cleveland CC (r.)
Tennessee
E. Hamm
Cleveland G&CC
Tennessee
B. Stamps
Cleveland G&CC (r.)
Tennessee
E. Hamm
Cleveland Heights G&CC
Florida
W. S. Flynn
Clewiston CC
Florida
R. A. Anderson
Cliffside CC
Connecticut
G. S. Cornish
Clifton Highlands GC
Wisconsin
H. D. Fieldhouse
Clifton Park Muni (r.)
Maryland
C. Hook
Clifton Springs CC
New York
A. Craig
Clinton CC
Connecticut
G. S. Cornish, W. G. Robinson
Clinton CC
Pennsylvania
E. B. Ault
Clinton Jaycees GC
Illinois
R. B. Harris
Clinton Valley
Michigan
D. T. Millar
Clitheroe
England
J. Braid
Clock CC [now Candlewood CC]
California
H. M. Rainville
Cloisters
Georgia
See Sea Island
Clongowes Wood College GC
Ireland
E. Hackett
Clonmel GC
Ireland
E. Hackett
Clontarf GC (r.)
Ireland
E. Hackett
Cloverleaf GC
Pennsylvania
(Wynn Tredway)
Club Atlas
Mexico
J. Finger
Club at Pelican Bay
Florida
A. Hills
Club Campestra, Mexico City
Mexico
L. S. "Dick" Wilson
Club Campestre
Chihuahua, Mexico
P. Clifford

Club Campestre de Bucaramanga
Chile
M. Mahannah, J. Saenz
Club Campestre, Sonoro
Mexico
P. Clifford
Club Campestre, Torreon
Mexico
P. Clifford
Club Campestre de Cucuta
Colombia
H. Watson
Club Campestra de Hermosillo
Mexico
L. M. Hughes
Club Compestie La Colina
Colombia
J. Hardin, G. Nash
Club de Campo
Spain
J. Arana
Club de Campo (Real Sociedad Hipica Espinola)
Spain
J. D. Harris
Club de Campo de Malaga
Spain
P. M. Ross
Club de Campo El Bosque
Spain
R. T. Jones
Club de Golf Acozak
Mexico
L. M. Hughes
CdG Adstock
Province of Québec, Canada
H. Watson
CdG Alpin (r.)
Province of Québec, Canada
H. Watson
CdG Alpin (r.)
Province of Québec, Canada
H. and J. Watson
CdG Avandaro
Mexico
P. Clifford
CdG Baie Comeau (r.9,a.9)
Province of Québec, Canada
H. Watson
CdG Baja Mar
Mexico
P. Clifford
CdG Baru
Colombia
P. Clifford
CdG Bellavista
Mexico
P. Clifford
Club de Golf Berthier
Province of Québec, Canada
H. Watson
CdG Bromont
Province of Québec, Canada
H. Watson
CdG Bugambilian
Mexico
P. Clifford
CdG Cap Rouge
Provine of Québec, Canada
H. Watson
CdG Caracas
Venezuela
D. Bennett
CdG Cerdana
Spain
J. Arana

CdG Cerro Alto
Mexico
P. Clifford
CdG Chambly
Province of Québec, Canada
H. Watson
CdG Charny (r.9,a.9)
Province of Québec, Canada
H. and J. Watson
CdG Chicoutimi
Province of Québec, Canada
H. Watson
CdG Costalita
Spain
J. Gancedo
CdG de Bellavista
Mexico
P. Clifford
CdG de Bellavista (r.)
Mexico
M. L. Francis
CdG Don Pedro Vilamoura
Portugal
J. J. F. Pennink
CdG de Vidago
Portugal
P. M. Ross
CdG Dos Mares
Mexico
P. Clifford
CdG du Bic
Province of Québec, Canada
H. Watson
CdG Erandeni
Mexico
P. Clifford
CdG Escorpion (36)
Spain
R. Kirby, G. Player
CdG Granby-St. Paul (r.18,a.18)
Province of Québec, Canada
H. Watson
Club de Golf Grand Pabor (r.9,a.9)
Province of Québec, Canada
H. Watson
CdG Hacienda
Mexico
P. Clifford
CdG Hermosila
Mexico
J. Bredemus
CdG Joliette
Province of Québec, Canada
H. Watson
CdG La Canada (36)
Mexico
P. Clifford
CdG Lac Beaufort
Province of Québec, Canada
H. Watson
CdG Laguna (36)
Mexico
P. Clifford
CdG Laprairie
Province of Québec, Canada
H. Watson
CdG Las Palmas, Grand Canary Islands
Spain
P. M. Ross
CdG La Villa Rica (9)
Mexico
P. Clifford
CdG le Portage
Province of Québec, Canada
H. Watson

CdG les Dunes (r.18,a.18)
Province of Québec, Canada
H. Watson
Cdg Llavaneras (9)
Spain
J. P. Gannon
CdG Llavaneras (r.)
Spain
F. W. Hawtree
CdG Longchamps
Province of Québec, Canada
H. Watson
CdG Mexico (27)
Mexico
P. Clifford, L. M. Hughes
CdG Montcalm
Province of Québec, Canada
J. Watson
CdG Montecastillo
Mexico
P. Clifford
CdG Monte Costello
Mexico
C. H. Adams
Club de Golf Panama (New site)
Panama
B. J. Riviere
CdG Pierre-Marques
Mexico
P. Clifford
CdG Piramides (36)
Mexico
P. Clifford
CdG Pokemouche
New Brunswick, Canada
J. Watson
CdG Poniente
Spain
J. Gancedo
CdG Port Alfred (r.)
Province of Québec, Canada
H. Watson
CdG Ranchitos
Mexico
P. Clifford
CdG Rio Seco (9)
Mexico
P. Clifford
CdG Ste. Anne Beaupre
Province of Québec, Canada
H. Watson
CdG Ste. Marie
Province of Québec, Canada
H. Watson
Cdg St. Laurent
Province of Québec, Canada
H. Watson
CdG St. Luc
Province of Québec, Canada
J. Watson
CdG St. Michel
Province of Québec, Canada
H. Watson
CdG St. Patrick
Province of Québec, Canada
H. and J. Watson
CdG San Carlos, Toluca
Mexico
P. Clifford
CdG San Gaspar
Mexico
P. Clifford
CdG San Luis
Mexico
P. Clifford
CdG Santa Anita
Mexico
L. M. Hughes

CdG Santo Domingo
Chile
(A. Macdonald)
CdG Santo Ponsa (r.)
Spain
J. Gancedo
Club de Golf Sotogrande (Old, New and
        Par 3 courses)
Spain
R. T. Jones
CdG Tabashines
Mexico
P. Clifford
CdG Terramar (a.9)
Spain
F. W. Hawtree
CdG Terrebone
Province of Québec, Canada
J. Watson
CdG Torrequebrado
Spain
J. Gancedo
CdG Triangle D'or
Province of Québec, Canada
H. Watson
CdG Vallee de Parc
Province of Québec, Canada
H. Watson
CdG Vallescondido
Mexico
P. Clifford
CdG Vallromanos
Spain
F. W. Hawtree
CdG Victoriaville (r.9,a.9)
Province of Québec, Canada
H. Watson
CdG Vielles Forges
Province of Québec, Canada
H. and J. Watson
CdG Vilamoura
Portugal
J. J. F. Pennink
Club de Quintado de Lago (27)
Portugal
W. F. Mitchell
Club Lagos de Caujarel
Colombia
J. L. Lee
Club Laval Sur Le Lac
Province of Québec, Canada
H. B. Strong
Club Lomas de Cocoyoc
Mexico
M. Schjetnan
Club Mazatlan Sur
Mexico
R. T. Jones, Jr.
Club of Prestwick
Indiana
R. A. Simmons
Club Santiago
Mexico
L. M. Hughes
Clyne GC
Wales
H. S. Colt
Coal Creek CC
Illinois
E. L. Packard
Cobbly Nob GC
Tennessee
A. Davis, R. Kirby, G. Player
Cobbs Creek Muni
Pennsylvania
H. I. Wilson
Cobbs Glen
South Carolina
G. W. Cobb, J. B. LaFoy

Cobtree GC
England
M. Hawtree
Cochecho CC (original 9)
New Hampshire
W. E. Stiles
Cochecho CC (a. 9)
New Hampshire
P. A. Wogan
Cochiti Lake GC
New Mexico
R. T. Jones, Jr.
Cockermouth GC (r.)
England
J. Braid
Cocoa Beach Rec. Course
Florida
M. Mahannah
Coconino CC [now Continental CC]
Arizona
R. E. Baldock
Cocoyoc CC
Mexico
P. Clifford, J. Finger
Coffeyville CC
Kansas
E. L. Bell
Coffeyville CC (r.)
Kansas
R. C. Dunning
Coffin Muni [formerly Highland G&CC]
Indiana
W. Park Jr.
Cog Hill GC (Courses #1 and #2)
Illinois
(Bert F. Coghill)
Cog Hill GC (r. Courses #1 and #2; a.
      Courses #3 and #4)
Illinois
L. S. "Dick" Wilson
Cog Hill GC (r. Course #4)
Illinois
J. L. Lee
Cohassee CC (r.)
Massachusetts
A. Zikorus
Cohasset GC
Massachusetts
D. J. Ross
Coherie CC
North Carolina
E. Maples
Colchester GC
England
J. Braid
Cold Norton GC
England
F. W. Hawtree
Cold Spring CC
New York
D. J. Ross
Cold Spring CC (r.)
New York
R. T. Jones
Cold Spring G C (White Mountain CC)
New Hampshire
G. S. Cornish, W. G. Robinson
Coldstream CC
Ohio
L. S. "Dick" Wilson
Coldwater CC
Michigan
R. D. Beard
Cole Park GC (r.)
Kentucky
E.L. Packard
Collier Park GC, Western Australia, P.W.
       Thomson, M. Wolveridge
Colonia CC, New Jersey, R. White

Colgate university GC (n.l.e.)
New York
T. Winton
Colgate University GC (New site) also
      known as Seven Oaks GC
New York
R. T. Jones
College GC at Delhi
New York
A. Craig
College of the Sequoias (4 hole course)
California
R. E. Baldock
Collindale GC
Colorado
F. Hummel
Coloana Island GC
Macao
R. T. Jones, Jr.
Colonia CC (r.)
New Jersey
H. Purdy
Colonial CC (r.5)
Massachusetts
W. Mitchell, A. Zikorus
Colonial CC (a.9)
Massachusetts
W. F. Mitchell
Colonial CC
North Carolina
E. Hamm
Colonial CC (n.l.e.)
Tennessee
W. B. Langford
Colonial CC (North and South courses)
Tennessee
J. Finger
Colonial   CC   [now   Braeburn   CC]
      (Bellaire)
Texas
J. Bredemus
Colonial CC (Ft. Worth)
Texas
J. Bredemus
Colonial CC (Ft. Worth; a. holes #3,4 &
      5)
Texas
P. D. Maxwell
Colonial CC (Ft. Worth; r.)
Texas
L. S. "Dick" Wilson
Colonial CC of Harrisburg (New site)
Pennsylvania
W. F. and D. W. Gordon
Colonial GC
Pennsylvania
F. Garbin
Colonial Palms Exec. GC
Florida
J. E. O'Connor, Jr.
Colonial Park CC
New Mexico
W. D. Cantrell
Colonial Par 3 GC
Nebraska
H. Hughes, R. Watson
Colonie CC
New York
G. S. Cornish
Colonie Muni (Original 18)
New York
W. F. Mitchell
Colonie Muni (a.9)
New York
R. T. Jones

Colony CC
New York
C. H. Alison, H. S. Colt
Colony West GC (East, West and Exec.
      courses)
Florida
R. Von Hagge, B. Devlin
Colorado, CC of
Colorado
P. and R. Dye
Colorado on Costa del Sol
Spain
J. H. Stutt
Colorado Springs CC (original 9)
Colorado
(John Monteith)
Colorado Springs CC (a.9)
Colorado
R.M. Phelps
Columbia CC (now Argyle CC)
Maryland
W. S. Tucker, Sr., W. S. Harban
Columbia CC (New site)
Maryland
H.H. Barker
Columbia CC (r., a. holes)
Maryland
W. J. Travis
Columbia CC (r.)
Maryland
W. S. Flynn
Columbia CC (r.)
Maryland
G. and T. Fazio
Columbia CC (r.)
Missouri
E. L. Bell
Columbia CC (27)
South Carolina
E. Maples
Colombia Edgewater CC (r.)
Oregon
R. M. Graves
Columbia Edgewater CC (r.)
Oregon
W. F. Bell
Columbia G&CC (a.9)
New York
H. Purdy
Columbia GC
Illinois
A. Linkogel
Columbia Hills CC
Ohio
H. D. Paddock Sr.
Columbia Lakes CC
Texas
(Jack B. Miller)
Columbia Muni
Missouri
E. L. Bell
Columbian Club (Original 9)
Texas
R. Plummer
Columbian Club (a.9)
Texas
L. Howard
Columbian Club (r.)
Texas
J. Finger
Columbia Park GC
Minnesota
E. L. Packard
Columbine CC
Colorado
H. B. Hughes

Columbine CC (r.)
Colorado
J. P. Maxwell
Columbus CC
Mississippi
(John Frazier)
Columbus CC
Ohio
D. J. Ross
Columbus CC (r.)
Ohio
O. E. Smith
Columbus CC (r.)
Ohio
R. B. Harris
Columbus CC (r.)
Ohio
L. S. "Dick" Wilson
Colville Park GC (r.)
Scotland
J. Braid, J. H. Stutt
Colwood G&CC, Royal
British Columbia, Canada
A. V. Macan
Combat Center GC (9)
California
D. Kent
Commack Hills G&CC
New York
A. G. McKay
Commonwealth CC [now Chestnut Hill]
Massachusetts
W. c. Stiles, J. R. Van Kleek
Commonwealth CC [now Chestnut Hill](r.)
Massachusetts
S. Mitchell
Compestie La Colina, Club
Colombia
J. Hardin, G. Nash
Compton GC
California
W. H. Johnson
Comstock CC
California
R. E. Baldock
Concho Valley CC
Arizona
A. J. Snyder
Concord CC
Massachusetts
D. J. Ross
Concord CC (original 9)
New Hampsire
R. M. Barton
Concord Green Par 3 GC
Illinois
K. Killian, R. Nugent
Concord Hotel GC (International course and Challenger 9)
New York
A. H. Tull
Concord Hotel GC (Championship course)
New York
J. Finger
Concordia GC
Province of Québec, Canada
H. Watson
Concord Muni [now Diablo Creek Muni]
California
R. E. Baldock
Concord Muni [now Diablo Creek Muni](r.)
California
R. M. Graves

Concordville CC (a.4)
Pennsylvania
G. S. Cornish, W. G. Robinson
Conestoga CC
Pennsylvania
W. F. Gordon
Conestoga G&TC
Ontario, Canada
C. E. Robinson
Conewango Valley CC (r.)
Pennsylvania
E. B. Ault
Confederate Hills CC
Virginia
R. F. Loving, A. M. Pulley
Congressional CC (Original 18)
Maryland
D. Emmet
Congressional CC (r.9,a.9)
Maryland
R. T. Jones
Congressional CC (a.9)
Maryland
G and T. Fazio
Congress Lakes Club
Ohio
W. Park, Jr.
Congress Lakes Club (new course)
Ohio
D. J. Ross
Congress Lakes CC (r.)
Ohio
W. K. Newcomb
Conneaut Shores CC
Ohio
(J. Thomas Francis)
(THE) Connecticut GC [formerly, The GC at Aspetuck]
Connecticut
G. S. Cornish, W. G. Robinson
Connemara Golf Links
Ireland
E. Hackett
Connersville, CC of
Indiana
R. A. Simmons
Connestee Falls CC
North Carolina
G. W. Cobb
(El) Conquistador (n.l.e.)
Florida
G. O'Neill
(El) Conquistador CC
Florida
M. Mahannah
Conshohocken GC
Pennsylvania
W. S. Flynn
Conshohocken GC (r.)
Pennsylvania
J. G. Harrison
Constant Springs GC
Jamaica
S. Thompson
Continental CC [formerly Coconino CC]
Arizona
R. E. Baldock
Continental CC
Florida
R. Garl
Continental GC Flagstaff (a. 18)
Arizona
J. Hardin, G. Nash
Continental GC (Scottsdale)
Arizona
J. Hardin, G. Nash

Conyngham Valley CC (r.)
Pennsylvania
A. W. Tillinghast
Cool Creek CC
Pennsylvania
(Chester Ruby)
Coolidge Par 3 GC
California
W. H. Johnson
Coolattin GC (r.)
Ireland
E. Hackett
Coombe Hill GC (Route Plan)
England
W. Park, Jr.
Coombe Hill GC
England
J. F. Abercromby
Coonamesset CC (Original 9)
Massachusetts
D. Emmet
Coonskin Park Par 3 GC
West Virginia
X. G. Hassenplug
Cooper Colony Exec. GC
Florida
G. A. Pattison, Jr.
Cooper River CC (n.l.e.)
New Jersey
D. Emmet, A. H. Tull
Coosa CC (r.)
Georgia
G. W. Cobb
Coos CC
Oregon
H. C. Egan
Copeland Hills CC
Ohio
R. A. Anderson
Copenhagen GC
Denmark
J. D. Harris
Copper GC (original 9)
Utah
J. M. Riley
Copper GC (a.9)
Utah
A. J. Snyder
Copper Mountain Muni
Colorado
R. N. Phelps, B. Benz
Copthorne GC
England
J. Braid
Coral Creek G&CC
Ontario, Canada
C. E. Robinson
Coral Gables Biltmore CC [formerly Miami Biltmore]
Florida
D. J. Ross
Coral Gables Biltmore CC (r.)
Florida
W. B. Langford
Coral Gables Biltmore CC (r.)
Florida
M. Mahannah
Coral Harbour GC
Bahamas
G. Fazio
Coral Ridge CC
Florida
R. T. Jones
Coral Springs G&TC
Florida
E. B. Ault

Corbalis GC
Ireland
F. W. Hawtree
Corballis GC (r.)
Ireland
E. Hackett
Corfu GC
Greece
D. Harradine
Corhampton GC (a.9)
England
C. D. Lawrie
Cork GC
Ireland
J. J. F. Pennink
Cornell University GC
New York
R. T. Jones
Corning CC
New York
T. Winton
Cornwells CC
Pennsylvania
W. F. and D. W. Gordon
Coronado Beach GC
Panama
G. and T. Fazio
Coronado G&CC
Texas
L. M. Hughes
Coronado G&CC (r.)
Texas
M. H. Ferguson
Coronado GC (a. 9)
Arizona
M. Coggins
Coronado GC (9)
Arizona
A. J. Snyder
Coronada GC
Arkansas
E. B. Ault
Coronado Muni
California
J. Daray
Coronado Muni (r.)
California
W. F. Bell
Corona National GC [formerly Pepper Tree CC]
California
L. M. Hughes
Corpus Christi CC (New site)
Texas
R. T. Jones
Corpus Christi Golf Center (27)
Texas
L Howard
Corral de Tierra CC
California
R. E. Baldock
Corry Muni
Pennsylvania
E. B. Ault
Corsica Par 3 GC
France
J. H. Stutt
Cortez GC
Arkansas
E. B. Ault
Cortez Muni
Colorado
J. P. Maxwell
Costa Brava GC
Spain
J. H. Stutt
Costa del Sol G&CC
Florida
(Bobb Cupp)

Costalita GC
Spain
J. Gancedo
Costa Mesa CC (Los Lagos and Mesa Linda courses)
California
W. F. Bell
Costebello Golf Links
France
W. Park, Jr.
Coto de Caza GC
California
R.T. Jones, Jr.
Coto De Donano GC
Spain
J. H. Stutt
Cottesloe GC (r.)
Australia
P.W. Thomson, M. Wolveridge
Cottesmore GC
England
(M. Rogerson)
Cotton Bay Club
Bahamas
R. T. Jones
Cottonwood Club
Utah
W. H. Neff
Cottonwood CC (Ivanhoe and Monte Vista courses)
California
(O. W. Moorman, A. C. Sears)
Cottonwood CC
Montana
L. I. Johnson
Cotswold Hill GC
England
(M. D. Little)
Coubert GC
France
T. Dunn
Council Bluffs CC (r.; n.l.e.)
Iowa
H.W. Glissmann
Council Grove CC (r.)
Kansas
L. I. Johnson
Countess Wear GC (Island of Lewis)
Scotland
J. R. Stutt
(The) Country Club
Alabama
J. H. Williams, Sr.
(The) Country Club
Massachusetts
W. Campbell
(The) Country Club (a. Primrose 9)
Massachusetts
W. S. Flynn
(The) Country Club (r.5)
Massachusetts
G. S. Cornish, W. G. Robinson
(The) Country Club
Ohio
W. S. Flynn
(The) Country Club (27)
South Africa
F. W. Hawtree
CC at Muirfield Village GC, Club course)
Ohio
J. Nicklaus
CC Cuzcatlan
El Salvador
F. W. Hawtree

CC of Decatur (r.)
Illinois
E.L. Packard
CC de Manizales
Colombia
H. Watson
CC El Rodeo
Colombia
H. Watson
CC Estates GC
Illinois
E. L. Packard
CC Jurica
Mexico
L. M. Hughes
CC Lake
Virginia
R. F. Loving
CC Militar
Colombia
H. Watson
CC Morelia
Mexico
P. Clifford
CC Obregon
Mexico
P. Clifford
CC of Asheville [formerly Beaver Lake CC]
North Carolina
D. J. Ross
CC of Austin (New site)
Texas
J. P. and P. D. Maxwell
CC of Austin (r.)
Texas
B. J. Riviere
CC of Billerica
Massachusetts
P. A. Wogan
CC of Birmingham (East and West courses)
Alabama
D. J. Ross
CC of Birmingham (r. East course)
Alabama
G. W. Cobb
CC of Birmingham (r. West course)
Alabama
R. T. Jones
CC of Bogota (n.l.e.)
Colombia
C. H. Banks
CC of Bogota (New site, 36)
Colombia
J. R. Van Kleek
CC of Bristol
Tennessee
A. G. McKay
CC of Buffalo
New York
D. J. Ross
CC of Buffalo (r.)
New York
R. T. Jones
CC of Buffalo (r.2)
New York
G. S. Cornish, W. G. Robinson
CC of Chapala
Mexico
(Harry C. Offut, Jr.)
CC of Charleston
South Carolina
D. J. Ross
CC of Charleston
West Virginia
G. W. Cobb
CC of Colorado
Colorado
P. and R. Dye

CC of Connersville
Indiana
R. A. Simmons
CC of Cuzcatlan (9)
El Salvador
F. W. Hawtree
CC of Darien
Connecticut
A. H. Tull
CC of Darien (r.)
Connecticut
H. Purdy
CC of Detroit (n.l.e.)
Michigan
W. H. Way
CC of Detroit (r.)
Michigan
H. S. Colt, C. H. Alison
CC of Detroit (New site)
Michigan
H. S. Colt
CC of Detroit (r.)
Michigan
R. T. Jones
CC of Detroit (r.)
Michigan
A. Hills
W. B. and G. H. Matthews
CC of Detroit (Short course)
Michigan
R. T. Jones
CC of Fairfax
Virginia
See Fairfax CC
CC of Fairfield
Connecticut
S. J. Raynor
CC of Fairfield (r.)
Connecticut
G. S. Cornish
CC of Florida
Florida
R. B. Harris
CC of Fort Collins
Colorado
H. B. Hughes
CC of Green Valley
Arizona
R. F. Lawrence
CC of Green Valley (a.9)
Arizona
A. J. Snyder
CC of Harrisburg
Pennsylvania
W. S. Flynn
CC of Havana
Cuba
D. J. Ross
CC of Hudson
Ohio
H. D. Paddock Sr.
CC of Indianapolis
Indiana
W. Diddel
CC of Indianapolis (r.)
Indiana
P. Dye
CC of Ithaca (Original course n.l.e.)
New York
A. W. Tillinghast
CC of Ithaca (Original course r., n.l.e.)
New York
R. T. Jones
CC of Ithaca (New site)
New York
G. S. Cornish

CC of Jackson (27)
Mississippi
L. S. "Dick" Wilson
CC of Johnston County
North Carolina
E. Maples
CC of Lansing
Michigan
W. B. Langford, T. J. Moreau
CC of Lansing (r.)
Michigan
E.L. Packard
CC of Lincoln
Nebraska
W. H. Tucker, Sr.
CC of Lincoln (r.2)
Nebraska
P. Dye
CC of Little Rock
Arkansas
H. C. Hackbarth
Cc of Little Rock (r.)
Arkansas
E. B. Ault
CC of Mexico City
Mexico
W. Smith
CC of Mexico City (r.)
Mexico
J. Bredemus
CC of Miami (East and West courses)
Florida
R. T. Jones
CC of Miami (South course)
Florida
W. H. Dietsch, Jr.
CC of Missouri
Missouri
M. H. Ferguson
CC of Mobile
Alabama
D. J. Ross
CC of Mobile (r.)
Alabama
A. H. Tull
CC of Mobile (a.9)
Alabama
E. Stone
CC of Montreal
Province of Québec, Canada
A. Murray
CC of Montreal (r.)
Province of Québec, Canada
P. and R. Dye
CC of Morristown
Tennessee
W. B. Langford
CC of Naples [formerly Big Cypress CC]
Florida
W. Diddel
CC of New Canaan (Original course)
Connecticut
W. Dunn
CC of New Canaan
Connecticut
W. Park, Jr.
CC of New Canaan (a.9)
Connecticut
A. H. Tull
CC of New Canaan (r.)
Connecticut
R. T. Jones
CC of New Seabury (Blue and Green courses)
Massachusetts
W. F. Mitchell
CC of North Carolina (Original 9, Cardinal course)
North Carolina
W. C. Byrd

CC of North Carolina (Dogwood course)
North Carolina
E. Maples, W. C. Byrd
CC of North Carolina (r., a.9)
North Carolina
R. T. Jones
CC of North Carolina (r.)
North Carolina
R. L. Jones
CC of North Port Charlotte
Florida
C. F. Ankrom
CC of Orlando (r.)
Florida
R. T. Jones
CC of Paducah
Kentucky
R. T. Jones
CC of Peoria
Illinois
(F. M. Birks)
CC of Petersburg (n.l.e.)
Virginia
D. J. Ross
CC of Petersburg (New site)
Virginia
E. B. Ault
CC of Pittsfield
Massachusetts
D. J. Ross
CC of Pittsfield (r.)
Massachusetts
W. E. Stiles, J. R. Van Kleek
CC of Rochester
New York
D. J. Ross
CC of Rochester (a.3)
New York
R. T. Jones
CC of Salisbury (Original 9)
North Carolina
D. J. Ross
CC of Salt Lake City (r.)
Utah
R. Plummer
CC of Salt Lake City
Utah
H. Lamb
CC of Salt Lake City (r.)
Utah
W. P. Bell
CC of Salt Lake City (r.9)
Utah
W. H. Neff
CC of Sarasota
Florida
R. Von Hagge, B. Devlin
CC of Scranton
Pennsylvania
W. J. Travis
CC of Scranton (a.9)
Pennsylvania
A. Wall
CC of South Carolina
South Carolina
E. Maples
CC of Staunton
Virginia
E. B. Ault
CC of Virginia (Westhampton course)
Virginia
H. N. Barker
CC of Virginia (r. James River course)
Virginia
G. O'Neill

CC of Virginia (r. Westhampton and James River courses)
Virginia
F. A. Findlay
CC of Virginia (James River course)
Virginia
W. S. Flynn
CC of Virginia (a.9, James River course)
Virginia
E. B. Ault
CC of Waterbury
Connecticut
D. J. Ross
CC of York
Pennsylvania
D. J. Ross
CC Queretaro
Mexico
P. Clifford
CC Torreon
Mexico
P. Clifford
CC Villages of America
Ohio
E. B. Ault
Countryside CC
Florida
E. L. and R. B. Packard
Countryside CC
Virginia
E. Maples
Country View Par 3 GC
Minnesota
D. Herfort
County Creek GC
Michigan
K. W. Bowen
County Down, Royal (Original course)
Northern Ireland
T. Morris
County Down, Royal (r.)
Northern Ireland
S. Dunn
County Down, Royal (r.)
Northern Ireland
H. Vardon
County Line and Sherman GC [now Carl E. Smock GC]
Indiana
R. A. Simmons
County Longford
Ireland
E. Hackett
County Louth GC (Baltray; r.)
Ireland
T. C. Simpson
County Sligo GC
Ireland
H. S. Colt, C. H. Alison
Courthouse CC
Virginia
R. P. Hines
Courtland Hills GC
Michigan
M. DeVries
Courtown GC
Ireland
J. D. Harris, C. K. Cotton
Courtown GC (r.)
Ireland
E. Hackett
Cove Cay G&TC
Florida
D. L. Wallace

Cove Creek CC
Maryland
L.B. Ervin

Coventry GC
England
H. Cotton

Covered Bridge GC (r.)
New Jersey
H. Purdy

Cowal GC
Scotland
J. Braid

Cowansville GC
Province of Québec, Canada
H. Watson

Cowdray Park GC
England
J. F. Abercromby, H. Fowler

Cowes, Isle of Wight GC
England
J. H. Stutt

Crab Meadow GC
New York
W. F. Mitchell

Crackerneck CC
Missouri
C. E. Maddox

Cradoc GC
Wales
J. J. F. Pennink

Crag Burn Club
New York
R. T. Jones

Cragie Brae CC
New York
J. G. Harrison

Craigavon
British Isles
J. J. F. Pennink

Craig GC
Saskatchewan, Canada
J. A. Thompson

Craig Hill GC [now Deerfield GC]
New York
A. Craig

Craigie Hill GC
Scotland
(J. Anderson)

Craig Wood CC (Original 9)
New York
S. Dunn

Crail GC
Scotland
T. Morris

Cramond GC
Scotland
P. M. Ross

Cranberry Valley GC (Harwich Muni)
Massachusetts
G. S. Cornish, W. G. Robinson

Cranbrook GC
England
J. D. Harris

Crane Creek CC
Iowa
R. E. Baldock

Crane Creek GC [now Martin Downt GC]
Florida
C. F. Ankrom, A. M. Young

Crane Creek Road GC
Florida
C. F. Ankrom

Crang Estate
Ontario, Canada
H. Watson

Cranmoor CC
New Jersey
T. Winton

Crans Sur Sierre GC (Original 9)
Switzerland
(Sir Arnold Lunn)

Cranston CC
Rhode Island
G. S. Cornish, W. G. Robinson

Cranwell GC, Royal Air Force
England
S. V. Hotchkin

Cranwell School GC
Massachusetts
W. Stiles, J. Van Kleek, W. Tucker, Sr.

Crater CC
Virginia
F. A. Findlay

Crawford CC (r.)
New York
S. J. Raynor

Crawford County GC (r. 9, a. 9)
Illinois
W. J. Spear

Crawford Notch CC (r.)
New Hampshire
W. E. Stiles, J. R. Van Kleek

Crawfordsville Muni
Indiana
W. Diddel

Cray Valley
England
(John Day)

Credit Island GC
Iowa
W. B. Langford, T. J. Moreau

Credit Valley GC
Ontario, Canada
S. Thompson

Credit Valley G&CC (r.9,a.9)
Ontario, Canada
C. E. Robinson

Creek Club
New York
C. B. Macdonald, S. J. Raynor

Creek Club (r.)
New York
W. S. Flynn

Crescent CC
Missouri
E. L. Packard

Crescent-Hamilton CC at Huntington [now Huntington Crescent]
New York
D. Emmet, A. H. Tull

Crescent Hill CC (r.)
Kentucky
A. G. McKay

Cress Creek CC
Illinois
D. Gill

Crestbrook CC (Original 9)
Connecticut
G. S. Cornish

Crestbrook CC (a.9)
Connecticut
A. Zikorus

Crestmont CC
New Jersey
D. J. Ross

Crestmont CC (r.3)
New Jersey
F. Duane

Crestmont CC (r.)
New Jersey
R. T. Jones

Creston GC
Iowa
R. Watson

Crestview CC
Florida
W. W. Amick

Crestview CC
Indiana
R. D. Beard

Crestview CC (New site; North and South courses)
Kansas
R. T. Jones, Sr. and Jr.

Crestview CC
Massachusetts
G. S. Cornish

Crestview GC (New site)
Indiana
R. D. Beard

Crestwicke CC
Illinois
E. L. and R. B. Packard

Crestwood CC (r.9,a.9)
Kansas
F. Farley

Crestwood CC
Massachusetts
G. S. Cornish

Crieff GC
Scotland
W. Park, Jr.

Crieff GC (r.)
Scotland
J. Braid

Cripple Creek CC
Colorado
(Dewitt "Maury" Bell)

Croasdale CC
North Carolina
G. W. Cobb

Crockery Hills GC
Michigan
W. B. and G. H. Matthews

Crockett Springs National G&CC
Tennessee
R. Von Hagge, B. Devlin

Crofton CC
Maryland
E. B. Ault

Crohamhurst GC
England
J. Braid, F. G. Hawtree

Cromer, Royal
England
J. Braid

Crooked Creek G&CC [now International]
Florida
F. Murray

Crooked Creek CC (1979)
Indiana
E.L., R.B. Packard

Crooked Stick GC
Indiana
P. Dye

Crookhill Park
British Isles
J. J. F. Pennink

Croos Creek GC (27)
Pennsylvania
F. Garbin

Cross Creek CC
Georgia
A. L. Davis

Cross Creek CC
North Carolina
J. L. Lee

Crooked River Ranch GC
Oregon
(Gene S. Mason)

Cross Roads Par 3 GC
Washington
A. Smith

Crow Canyon CC
California
T. G. Robinson

Crown City Ranch GC
California
W. F. and W. P. Bell

Crown Colony G&CC
Texas
R. Von Hagge, B. Devlin

Crown Mines GC (r.)
South Africa
G. Player, (S. Brews), V. Vincent)

Crown Point CC
Vermont
W. F. Mitchell

Crow Valley CC
Iowa
J.N. Cochran

Crow Wood
Scotland
J. Braid

Cruden Bay G&CC
Scotland
W. H. Fowler, T. C. Simpson

Crumpin Fox Club
Massachusetts
R. T. Jones

Crystalaire CC
California
W. F. Bell

Crystal Downs GC (Original 9)
Michigan
(Eugene Goebel)

Crystal Downs GC (r.9,a.9)
Michigan
A. Mackenzie, P. D. Maxwell

Crystal Lago CC
Florida
A. Ternyei

Crystal Lake CC
Florida
G. A. Pattison, Jr.

Crystal Lake GC
Michigan
W. B. and G. H. Matthews

Crystal Lakes GC
Florida
C. F. Ankrom

Crystal River GC (r.)
Florida
M. Mahannah

Crystal Springs GC
Massachusetts
G. S. Cornish

Cuckfield
Great Britain
W. Park, Jr.

Cuddington GC
England
H. S. Colt

Culpepper CC (9)
Virginia
F. A. Findlay

Culver Military Academy GC
Indiana
W. B. Langford, T. J. Moreau

Cumaquid GC (a.9)
Massachusetts
(Henry Mitchell)

Cumberland CC (r.)
Maryland
X. G. Hassenplug

Cumberland CC
Pennsylvania
J. G. Harrison, F. Garbin

Cumberland Lake CC
Alabama
W. W. Amick

Cumbernauld New Town GC
Scotland
J. H. Stutt

Current River CC (9)
Missouri
F. Farley

Currie Muni
Wisconsin
G. Hansen

Custer Hills GC (Original 9)
Kansas
R. T. Jones

Cutten Fields GC
Ontario, Canada
C. Evans

Cuyuna CC (r.9,a.9)
Minnesota
D. Herfort

Cuzcatlan, CC of (9)
El Salvador
F. W. Hawtree

Cypress Bay GC
South Carolina
R. F. Breeden

Cypress Creek CC (Boynton Beach)
Florida
R. Von Hagge

Cypress Creek CC (Orlando)
Florida
L. Clifton

Cypress Creek CC at Mobile [now Southmoor CC]
Alabama
E. Stone

Cypress Hills GC (9 exec. plus 9 regulation)
California
J. Fleming

Cypress Lake CC
Florida
L. S. "Dick" Wilson

Cypress Lakes GC (Travis AFB)
California
J. Finger

Cypress Lakes GC
North Carolina
(L. B. Floyd)

Cypress Links Course
Florida
(Ward Northrup)

Cypress Point Club
California
A. Mackenzie, W. R. Hunter

Cypress Wood G&CC
Florida
R. Garl

Dacca GC
Bangladesh
J. J. F. Pennink

Da-De-Co
Illinois
E. L. Packard

Dahlgreen GC
Minnesota
(Emile F. Perret)

D'Aix-Les-Bains GC
France
W. Reid

Dalewood Golf & Curling Club
Ontario, Canada
C. E. Robinson

Dalkeith & Newbattle GC
Scotland
W. Park, Jr.
Dallas Athletic Club (East and West courses)
Texas
R. Plummer
Dallas CC (r.)
Texas
R. Plummer
Dalmahoy GC (East and West courses)
Scotland
J. Braid
Dalton CC (r.)
Georgia
R. Kirby, G. Player
Danbury Muni [now Richter Memorial GC]
Connecticut
E. Ryder
Dania CC (9)
Florida
R. F. Lawrence
Danville CC
Illinois
E. L. Packard
Danville CC
Kentucky
B. J. Wihry
Danville CC (r.)
North Carolina
E. Hamm
Danville CC (r.)
Virginia
E. Hamm
Danville Elks Club
Illinois
W. J. Spear
Danville V. A. Hospital GC (9)
Illinois
C. E. Maddox
Darenth Valley GC
England
(R. Tempest)
Dar Es Salam (Royal Golf Rabat; 45)
Morocco
R. T. Jones
Darien CC
Connecticut
A. H. Tull
Darien CC (r.)
Connecticut
H. Purdy
Darlington CC (a. 2nd 9)
South Carolina
R. Robertson
Darlington County GC
New Jersey
N. T. Psiahas
Darlington GC
England
A. Mackenzie
Darlington GC (r.)
England
J. J. F. Pennink
Dartford GC
England
J. J. F. Pennink
Darwin GC
Northern Territory, Australia
P.W. Thomson, M. Wolveridge
D'Atimaona CC
Tahiti
R.E. Baldock
Davenport CC
Iowa
C. H. Alison
Davenport CC (r.)
Iowa
E. G. Lockie

Davenport GC
England
F. Middleton
Davis County GC
Utah
J. B. Williams
Davis-Monthan AFB Par GC
Arizona
R. E. Baldock
Davis Park GC
Utah
W. H. Neff
Davis Shores CC (n.l.e.)
Florida
A. W. Tillinghast
Davos GC
Switzerland
D. Harradine
Dawn Hill CC
Arkansas
(Virgil Brookshire)
Dawson CC
Georgia
H. C. Moore, Sr.
Dayton CC (Original 9)
Ohio
(Willie V. Hoare)
Daytona Beach G&CC (South course)
Florida
D. J. Ross
Dayton CC (r.2)
Ohio
G. S. Cornish, W. G. Robinson
Deaconsbank
Scotland
J. Braid
Deal GC
New Jersey
L. E. Van Etten
Deal GC [now Royal Cinque Ports] (Original 9)
England
T. Dunn
Deangate Ridge GC
England
F. W. Hawtree
De Anza Desert CC
California
L. M. Hughes
De Anza Palm Springs Exec. GC
California
T. G. Robinson
Dearborn CC
Michigan
D. J. Ross
Dearborn CC (r.)
Michigan
C. E. Robinson
De Bell GC
California
W. F. Bell, W. H. Johnson
De Cardova Bend GC
Texas
L. Howard
Decatur CC (r.)
Alabama
D. Gill
Decatur GC (9)
Illinois
R. B. Harris
Dedham Polo and Hunt Club (r.)
Massachusetts
W. Ogg
Dedham Polo and Hunt Club (r.)
Massachusetts
G. S. Cornish, W. G. Robinson
Deep Cliff GC
California
C. Glasson

Deepdale CC (n.l.e.)
New York
C. B. Macdonald, S. J. Raynor
Deepdale CC (r.; n.l.e.)
New York
H. B. Strong
Deepdale CC (New course)
New York
L. S. "Dick" Wilson
Deep River GC
Ontario, Canada
H. Watson
Deep Springs CC
North Carolina
E. Maples
Deep Springs CC (a.9)
North Carolina
D. and E. Maples
Deer Creek G&CC
Florida
W. R. Watts
Deer Creek GC
Illinois
E. L. and R. B. Packard
Deer Creek State Park Muni
Ohio
J. Kidwell, M. Hurdzan
Deercrest CC
Connecticut
O. E. Smith, A. Zikorus
Deerfield CC
Florida
W. F. Mitchell
Deerfield CC
Mississippi
J. Finger
Deerfield GC
Illinois
E. L. Packard
Deerfield GC [formerly Craig Hill]
New York
A. Craig
Deerpath GC (r.), Illinois,
E.L. Packard
Deer Park at Richmond
England
T. Dunn
Deer Park GC
New York
H. Purdy
Deerpath GC (r.)
Illinois
K. Killian, R. Nugent
Deer Run GC (9)
Florida
R. Garl
Deer Run Muni
Alabama
E. Stone
Deer Track CC (I and II)
South Carolina
J. P. Gibson, (R. Toski)
Deer Track CC
South Carolina
J.P. Gibson
Deerwood CC
Florida
G. W. Cobb
Deerwood CC (r.)
Florida
W. C. Byrd
Deeside GC (a.9)
Scotland
D. M. A. Steel
Defence GC
South Africa
R. G. Grimsdell
Defiance GC
Ohio
W. Park, Jr.

Defiance GC (a. 9)
Ohio
W. J. Rockefeller
de Gelpenberg GC
Holland
J. J. F. Pennink
Del-Aire CC (27)
Florida
J. L. Lee
Delamere Forest GC
England
W. H. Fowler
Delamere Forest GC (r.)
England
F. W. Hawtree
Delano GC
California
B. Stamps
Delano Muni (9)
California
R. E. Baldock
Delapree Golf Complex
England
(John Jacobs)
De Laveaga CC
California
B. Stamps
Delcastle Farms GC
Delaware
E. B. Ault
Delhamyeh CC
Lebanon
J. H. Stutt
Delhi GC (r., a. 9)
India
P.W. Thomson, M. Wolveridge
Delhi Muni
New York
W. F. Gordon
Delkenheim near Wiesbaden
B. Von Limburger
1981
Del Lago GC
Mexico
P. Clifford
Dellwood CC (r.)
New York
R. T. Jones
Dellwood CC (r.)
New York
W. Mitchell
Dellwood National GC
Minnesota
D. Herfort
Delmar GC (Original 9)
California
C. Maud
Del Monte CC (Original 9)
California
C. Maud
Del Monte CC (r.9,a.9)
California
W. H. Fowler
Del Paso GC
California
(John L. Black)
Del Paso GC (r.)
California
W. H.Fowler
Del Paso GC (r.)
California
W. F. Bell
Delray Beach CC (a. 9)
Florida
R. F. Lawrence
Delray Beach CC (r.)
Florida
R. B. Harris

Delray Dunes CC
Florida
P. Dye
Delray Dunes CC (a.18)
Florida
W. H. Dietsch, Jr.
Del Rio G&CC
California
W. P. Bell
Deltona G&CC
Florida
D. L. Wallace
Denbigh GC
Wales
(J. Stockton)
Denham GC
England
H. S. Colt
Denham GC (r.)
England
J. Braid
Dennis Pines Muni
Massachusetts
(Henry Mitchell)
Denton CC
Texas
R. Plummer
Denton GC
England
(B. Allen)
Denver CC (n.l.e.)
Colorado
J. Foulis
Denver CC (New site)
Colorado
W. Diddel
Denver CC (r.)
Colorado
W. S. Flynn
Denver CC (r.)
Colorado
J. P. Maxwell
Denver CC (r.3)
Colorado
J. N. Cochran
Denver CC (r.)
Colorado
E. B. Seay
Dereham GC
England
(E. C. Gray)
Derrick Club
Alberta, Canada
W. Brinkworth
Derrydale Exec. GC
Ontario, Canada
R. and C. Muylaert
Desaru Resort GC
Malaysia
R.T. Jones, Jr.
Desert Air CC
California
(Jimmy Hines)
Desert Aire CC (27)
California
T. G. Robinson
Desert Cove CC [now Vintage CC]
California
G. and T. Fazio
Desert Forest GC
Arizona
R. F. Lawrence
Desert Hills CC
Arizona
D. Bennett
Desert Horizon CC
California
T. G. Robinson

Desert Inn & CC
Nevada
L. M. Hughes
Desert Inn & CC (r.)
Nevada
D. Collett
Desert Island GC
California
D. Muirhead
Desert Island GC (r.)
California
S. Leonard
Desert Sands Exec. GC
Arizona
A. J. Snyder
Design Master
Arizona
J. Hardin, G. Nash
Des Moines G&CC (North and South courses)
Iowa
P. Dye
Desoto GC (Hot Springs Village CC)
Arkansas
E. B. Ault
De Soto Lakes GC [now Palm Aire of Sarasota]
Florida
L. S. "Dick" Wilson
De Soto Lakes G&CC (r.)
Florida
R. A. Anderson
Detroit, CC of (n.l.e.)
Michigan
W. H. Way
Detroit, CC of (new site)
Michigan
H. S. Colt, C. H. Alison
Detroit, CC of (r.)
Michigan
R. T. Jones
Detroit, CC of (r.)
Michigan
W. B. and G. H. Matthews
Detroit, CC of (Short course)
Michigan
R. T. Jones
Detroit GC (n.l.e.)
Michigan
W. H. Way
Detroit GC (North and South courses)
Michigan
D. J. Ross
Detroit GC (North and South courses) (r.)
Michigan
R. T. Jones
Detroit Lakes GC (a. 9)
Minnesota
D. Herfort
Detroit GC (r.)
Michigan
A. Hills
Detwiler GC
Ohio
A. Hills
Development Corporation of America Spring Tree Exec. GC
Florida
W. H. Dietsch, Jr.
Devil's Elbow (36)
South Carolina
G. and T. Fazio
Devils GC
California
W. F. Bell
Devil's Head Lodge GC
Wisconsin
(Art Johnson)

Devil's Knob (Wintergreen)
Virginia
D. and E. Maples
Devon CC
Pennsylvania
(Lemuel Altemus)
Devonshire Par 3 GC (27)
California
W. H. Johnson
Dewsbury District
England
P. Alliss, D.C. Thomas
Diablo Creek Muni [formerly Concord Muni]
California
R. E. Baldock
Diablo Creek Muni (r.5)
California
R. M. Graves
Diablo G&CC (r.)
California
R. M. Graves
Diablo Hills GC (r.9,a.9)
California
R. M. Graves
Diamond Bar Muni
California
W. F. Bell
Diamondhead Yacht & CC (Original 18)
Mississippi
(Bill Atkins)
Diamondhead Yacht & CC (a.9)
Mississippi
E. Stone
Diamond Hills G&CC
Florida
C. H. Adams
Diamond Oaks CC
California
T. G. Robinson
Diamond Oaks G& CC
Texas
(Charles B. Akey)
Diamond Ridge CC
Maryland
E. B. Ault
Diboll Muni
Texas
L. Howard
Dieppe, Golf de
France
W. Park, Jr.
Dieppe, Golf de
France
T. C. Simpson
Digby Pines Hotel GC
Nova Scotia, Canada
S. Thompson
Dighton Par 3 GC
Massachusetts
S. Mitchell
Dinard, Golf de
France
T. and J. D. Dunn
Dinard, Golf de
France
W. Park, Jr.
Dinsmore GC
New York
H. Purdy
Diplomat CC
Florida
R. F. Lawrence
Diplomat CC (Presidential course)
Florida
M. Mahannah

Discovery Bay GC
California
R. M. Graves
Disneyland Hotel Par 3 GC (n.l.e.)
California
D. Muirhead, T. G. Robinson
(Walt) Disney World (Palm, Magnolia and Lake Buena Vista courses)
Florida
J. L. Lee
(Walt) Disney World Exec. Juniors GC
Florida
R. Garl
Dixon Landing GC
California
A. M. Pulley
Dobbins AFB GC
Georgia
C. H. Adams
Dobson Ranch GC
Arizona
J. Hardin, G. Nash, R. F. Lawrence
Dodge City CC
Kansas
H. Robb, Sr.
Dodge Park GC (r.)
Iowa
D. Gill
Dodgertown GC (9)
Florida
(Walter F. O'Malley, Ira Hoyt)
Doe Valley G&CC
Kentucky
R. Watson
Dogwood Hills GC
Missouri
H. C. Hackbarth
Dogwood Lakes CC
Florida
(James Root)
Dolphin Head GC
South Carolina
R. Kirby, G. Player, A. Davis
Domont, Golf de
France
F. W. Hawtree
Dom Pedro, CdG
Portugal
J. J. F. Pennink
Donabate GC (r.)
Ireland
E. Hackett
Donala CC
Colorado
F. Hummel
Donalsonville CC
Georgia
W. W. Amick
Donavechigen GC
West Germany
B. Von Limburger
Doncaster GC (r.)
England
F. W. Hawtree
Donegal Murwagh GC
Ireland
E. Hackett
Donney Brook Par 3 GC
California
W. H. Johnson
Don Valley Muni (36)
Ontario, Canada
H. Watson
Dooks GC (r.)
Ireland
E. Hackett

Doon Valley GC
Ontario, Canada
C. E. Robinson
Doorn GC
Holland
J. D. Dunn
Dorado CC
Arizona
T.G. Robinson
Dorado Beach G&TC (East and West courses)
Puerto Rico
R. T. Jones
Dorado Del Mar CC
Puerto Rico
J. G. Harrison, F. Garbin
Dorado Del Mar CC (r.)
Puerto Rico
E. B. Ault
Doral CC (a. Silver course)
R. Von Hagge and B. Devlin
Doral CC (Blue and Red courses)
Florida
L. S. "Dick" Wilson
Doral CC (Par 3, White, Silver and Gold courses)
Florida
R. Von Hagge
Dorking GC
England
J. Braid
Dorlon Park GC
Ohio
W. Mitchell, R. LaConte, E. McAnlis
Dornick Hills G&CC
Oklahoma
P. D. Maxwell
Dornoch GC [now Royal Dornoch]
Scotland
T. Morris
Dornoch GC (r.9,a.9)
Scotland
J. Sutherland
Dornoch GC (r.)
Scotland
J. Sutherland, J. H. Taylor
Dornoch GC (a.4)
Scotland
G. Duncan
Dortmunder GC
West Germany
B. Von Limburger
Dorval GC
Province of Québec, Canada
H. Watson
Dorval Muni
Province of Québec, Canada
G. Cooke
Dos Mares, Club de Golf
Mexico
P. Clifford
Dos Rios GC (9)
Colorado
J. N. Cochran
Dothan CC
Alabama
H. C. Moore, Sr.
Doublegate Plantation CC
Georgia
G. W. Cobb
Dougalston GC
Scotland
J. D. Harris
Douglas CC
Arizona
A. H. Jolly

Douglas GC (r.)
Ireland
E. Hackett
Douglas H. Keen Estate
Province of Québec, Canada
H. Watson
Douglas Muni, Isle of Man
England
A. Mackenzie
Douglaston CC
Scotland
J. D. Harris
Douglaston Park GC [formerly North Hills GC](r.5)
New York
F. Duane
Dover AFB GC
Delaware
E. B. Ault, A. Jamison
Dover CC (r.)
Delaware
E. B. Ault
Dover CC (Original 9)
New Hampshire
W. E. Stiles, J. R. Van Kleek
Downer's Grove GC [formerly Chicago GC] (9)
Illinois
C. B. Macdonald
Downer's Grove GC (r.)
Illinois
D. Gill
Downey V. A. Hospital GC
Illinois
C. E. Maddox
Downfield GC
England
C. K. Cotton
Downing Muni
Pennsylvania
J. C. Harrison, F. Garbin
Downingtown Inn GC
Pennsylvania
G. Fazio
Downshire
England
F. W. Hawtree
Downsview G&CC (27)
Ontario, Canada
H. Watson
Drayton Park GC
England
J. Braid
Dretzka Muni
Wisconsin
(Evert Kincaid)
Druid Hills CC
Georgia
H. N. Barker
Druid Hills GC (r.)
Georgia
R. Kirby, G. Player
Drumline GC
New York
L. Macomber
Dry Creek GC
California
J. Fleming
Dryden G&CC
Ontario, Canada
C. E. Robinson
Dryden Park Muni
California
W. F. Bell
Duamyre CC (n.1.e.)
Massachusetts
O. E. Smith

Dublin CC (r.9,a.9)
Georgia
G. W. Cobb
Dublin GC, Royal (r.)
Ireland
H. S. Colt
Dublin CC, Royal (r.)
Ireland
G. Campbell
Dublin Muni
Ireland
E. Hackett
Dublin Sports Club
Ireland
E. Hackett
Dubois CC (r.)
Pennsylvania
X. G. Hassenplug
Dub's Dread GC (r.)
Florida
L. Clifton
Dub's Dread GC
Kansas
R. C. Dunning
Dubuque G&CC (r. 9, 1979)
Iowa
E.L., R.B. Packard
Duck Creek GC (r.)
Iowa
D. Gill
Duck Creek Park GC
Iowa
W. D. Langford, T. J. Moreau
Duck Creek Park GC (r.)
Iowa
R. B. Harris
Duck Lake CC (a. 2nd 9)
Michigan
A. M. Young
Duck Woods GC
North Carolina
E. Maples
Duddingston GC
Scotland
W. Park, Jr.
Dueren
Germany
J. J. F. Pennink
Duff House GC
Scotland
A. Mackenzie
Duke Estate GC (9)
New Jersey
R. T. Jones
Duke of Marlborough GC [now Marlboro CC]
Maryland
A. M. Pulley
Duke University GC
North Carolina
R. T. Jones
Dullatur
Scotland
J. Braid
Dunmurry GC (New site, 1981)
Northern Ireland
T. McAuley
Dunfries and County GC
Scotland
P. M. Ross
Dumfries and Galloway GC (r.)
Scotland
T. Moone
Dunbar GC
Scotland
T. Morris
Dundalk GC (r.)
Ireland
J.H. Stutt

Dundas Valley G&CC
Ontario, Canada
S. Thompson
Dundas Valley G&CC (r.)
Ontario, Canada
C. E. Robinson
Dundee CC
Illinois
H. Collis, (Jack Croke)
Dundee Park GC (n.l.e.)
Nebraska
(Harry Lawrie)
Dunedin CC
Florida
D. J. Ross
Dunedin CC (r.)
Florida
L. S. "Dick" Wilson
Dunedin CC (r.)
Florida
A. W. Hills
Dunes Golf & Beach Club
South Carolina
R. T. Jones
Dunes Hotel GC (Emerald course)
Nevada
W. F. Bell
Dunfey's Resort Course (Hyannis Par 3)
Massachusetts
G. S. Cornish, W. G. Robinson
Dungarven GC (r.)
Ireland
E. Hackett
Dunham Muni
Ohio
A. Hills
Dunlaoghaire GC (r.)
Ireland
E. Hackett
Dunmurry GC
Northern Ireland
J. J. F. Pennink
Dun Roamin GC
Massachusetts
M. L. Francis
Dun Rovin CC
Michigan
W. B. Matthews
Dunstable Downs GC
England
J. Braid
Dunwoody CC
Georgia
W. C. Byrd, A. L. Davis
Du Pont CC (Original course, n.l.e.)
Delaware
W. Reid
Du Pont CC (Du Pont and Nemours courses)
Delaware
A. H. Tull
Du Pont CC (r. Du Pont and Nemours courses; a. Montchanin and Louviers courses)
Delaware
W. F. and D. W. Gordon
Du Pont CC (r. Du Pont, Louviers, Montchanin and Nemours courses)
Delaware
G. S. Cornish, W. G. Robinson
Du Pont Estate GC (9)
Delaware
D. Emmet
Du Pont Estate GC (r.)
Delaware
D. Emmet

Du Pont GC (r.9,a.9)
Virginia
E. Hamm
Durand-Eastman Muni
New York
R. T. Jones
Durango Muni (9)
Colorado
F. Hummel
Durant CC
Oklahoma
L. Howard
Durban CC
South Africa
L.B. Waters (George Waterman)
Durban CC (r.)
South Africa
S. V. Hotchkin
Durban CC (r.)
South Africa
R. G. Grimsdell
Dusseldorf (Hubbelrath) Land und GC
Germany
F. W. Hawtree
Du Touguet GC (45)
France
H. S. Colt
Duwayne Motel Par 3 GC
Illinois
C. E. Maddox
Duxbury Park Muni
England
F. W. Hawtree
Duxbury Yacht Club (Original 9)
Massachusetts
W. E. Stiles, J. R. Van Kleek
Duxbury Yacht Club (r.)
Massachusetts
W. F. Mitchell
Duxbury Yacht Club (a.9)
Massachusetts
G. S. Cornish, W. G. Robinson
D'Uxelles GC
France
J. D. Harris
Dwan Muni
Minnesota
D. Gill
D. W. Fields GC
Massachusetts
W. E. Stiles, J. R. Van Kleek
D. W. Fields GC (a.2)
Massachusetts
S. Mitchell
Dwight D. Eisenhower GC
Maryland
E. B. Ault
Dyess AFB GC (9)
Texas
L. Howard
Dyke GC (Brighton Corporation; r.)
England
F. G. Hawtree
Dyker Beach GC [formerly Marine and Field Club]
New York
T. Bendelow
Dyker Meadow GC (n.l.e.)
New York
T. Bendelow
Dysart G&CC
Iowa
R.M. Phelps

Eagle Bluff CC
Wisconsin
H. D. Fieldhouse
Eagle Creek Muni (27)
Indiana
P. Dye
Eaglehead G&CC
Maryland
W. F. Mitchell
Eagle Hills GC
Idaho
(C. Edward Trout)
Eagle Hills GC (a.9)
Idaho
R. E. Baldock
Eagle Lodge GC (r.)
Pennsylvania
R. L. Jones
Eagle National G&CC
Florida
R. Garl
Eagle Ridge GC
Illinois
E. L. and R. B. Packard
Eaglescliffe and District GC
England
J. Braid
Eaglescliffe and District GC (r.)
England
H. Cotton
Eaglesmere CC (r.)
Pennsylvania
W. S. Flynn
Eagles Nest CC
Kentucky
B. J. Wihry
Eagles Nest GC
South Carolina
E. Hamm
Eagles Nest GC of Towson CC
Maryland
G. S. Cornish, W. G. Robinson
Eagle Vail GC
Colorado
R. Von Hagge, B. Devlin
Eagle Valley Muni
Nevada
A. J. Snyder
Earl F. Elliot Park GC
Illinois
E. L. Packard
Earl Grey GC (r.)
Alberta, Canada
C. E. Robinson
Earlsville Island GC
Illinois
(E. Joseph Meister)
Earlywine Park Muni
Oklahoma
F. Farley
Easingwold
England
F. W. Hawtree
East Aurora CC (r.)
New York
W. P. Harries
East Aurora CC (r. 9, a. 9)
New York
A.R. Tryon
East Bay CC
Florida
W. F. Mitchell
East Berkshire GC
England
(Peter Paxton)
Eastbourne Downs
England
J. H. Taylor

Eastbourne GC [now Royal Eastbourne]
England
H. G. Hutchinson, (C. Mayhewe)
Eastbourne GC, Royal (r.)
England
J. H. Stutt
East Cork GC (r.)
Ireland
E. Hackett
Eastern Hills CC
Texas
R. Plummer
Eastern Kentucky University GC
Kentucky
B. J. Wihry
Eastern Shore Yacht & CC
Virginia
R. Roberts
Eastern Shore Yacht & CC (r.)
Virginia
E. B. Ault
Eastham Lodge
England
F. W. Hawtree
Easthampstead Park Muni
England
F. W. Hawtree
East Hartford GC (Original 9)
Connecticut
O. E. Smith
East Hartford GC (a.9)
Connecticut
O. E. Smith, A. Zikorus
East Kilbride GC
Scotland
F. W. Hawtree
East Kilbride Muni
Scotland
F. W. Hawtree, M. Hawtree
East Lake CC (Original course)
Georgia
T. Bendelow
East Lake CC (r. Course #1; a. Course #2, n.l.e.)
Georgia
D. J. Ross
East Lake CC (r. Course #2)(n.l.e.)
Georgia
C. H. Adams
East Lake CC (r. Course #1)
Georgia
G. W. Cobb
Eastlakes CC
Florida
G. and T. Fazio
East Lake Woodlands CC
Florida
T. Jackson
East Lake Woodlands CC (a. 18)
Florida
R. Von Hagge, B. Devlin
Eastleigh
British Isles
J. J. F. Pennink
East Liverpool CC
Ohio
G. S. Alves
East London CC (r.)
South Africa
S. V. Hotchkin
Eastman CC
New Hampshire
G. S. Cornish, W. G. Robinson
Eastmoreland GC
Oregon
H. C. Egan
Easton CC
Massachusetts
S. Mitchell

East Park Exec. GC
Ontario, Canada
C. E. Robinson
East Pointe CC
Florida
G. and T. Fazio
East Potomac Park GC (r.)
Washington, D. C.
W. S. Flynn
East Ranch GC
Texas
L. Howard
East Ridge CC
Louisiana
J. P. Maxwell
East Ridge CC at Lincoln (r.)(n.l.e.)
Nebraska
O. E. Smith
Eastward Ho! CC
Massachusetts
W. H. Fowler
Eastwood Fairways GC
Louisiana
(Thomas Moore)
Eastwood GC
Scotland
T. Moore
Eastwood GC
Scotland
J. R. Stutt
Eastwood Muni
Florida
R. Von Hagge, B. Devlin
Eaton Canyon GC (6)
California
W. F. Bell
Eaton Hall GC
England
F. W. Hawtree
Echo Farms C&CC
North Carolina
E. Hamm
Echo Lake CC
New Jersey
D.J. Ross, C.G. Low
Echo Lake CC, (r. 6)
New Jersey
R. White
Echo Lake CC (r. 3)
New Jersey
W. Wilkinson
Echo Lakes CC (r. 3)
New Jersey
G.S. Cornish, W.G. Robinson
Echo Valley CC
Iowa
E. L. Packard
(The) Eden Course, St. Andrews
Scotland
H. S. Colt, A. Mackenzie
Eden Isles CC
Louisiana
E. B. Ault
Edenvale GC
Minnesota
D. Herfort
Edgbaston GC
England
H. S. Colt
Edgbaston GC (r.)
England
T. Williamson
Edgebrook GC
Illinois
K. Killian, R. Nugent
Edgebrook GC
South Dakota
(Donald K. Rippel)

Edgecreek CC
Ohio
W. J. Spear
Edgewater CC (9; n.l.e.)
Illinois
T. Bendelow
Edgewater CC [now Rainbow Bay CC]
Mississippi
H. Collis, J. Daray
Edgewater CC [now Rainbow Bay CC] (r.)
Mississippi
E. Stone
Edgewater Muni
Washington
A. V. Macan
Edgewood CC
Connecticut
O. E. Smith
Edgewood CC
Illinois
C. E. Maddox
Edgewood CC
Massachusetts
G. S. Cornish
Edgewood CC
Michigan
E. W. Way
Edgewood CC
Pennsylvania
D. J. Ross
Edgewood CC (r.)
Pennsylvania
E. F. Loeffler, J. McGlynn
Edgewood CC (r.)
Pennsylvania
J. G. Harrison
Edgewood CC
West Virginia
A. G. McKay
Edgewood Muni (r.)
North Dakota
R. B. Harris
Edgewood Tahoe CC
Nevada
G. Fazio
Edgewood Valley CC
Illinois
W. Diddel
Edgware
Great Britain
W. Park, Jr.
Edinburg CC (9)
Texas
J. Bredemus
Edison CC
New York
D. Emmet
Edmonstown GC (r.)
Ireland
E. Hackett
Edmonton G&CC
Alberta, Canada
W. Brinkworth
Edmonton G&CC (r.)
Alberta, Canada
W. G. Robinson
Edmunston G&CC
New Brunswick, Canada
A. Murray
Edwin R. Carr GC
Virginia
E. B. Ault
Edzell GC
Scotland
J. Braid
Effingham CC
Illinois
W. J. Spear
Effingham GC
England
H. S. Colt

Eglin AFB GC [formerly Chicago GC]
Florida
W. B. Langford, T. J. Moreau
Eglin AFB GC (r.)
Florida
W. W. Amick
Eindhoven GC
Holland
H. S. Colt, J. S. F. Morrison
Eisenhower College Exec. GC
New York
G. W. Cobb
Eisenhower GC, Dwight D.
Maryland
E. B. Ault
Eisenhower GC, USAF Academy (Blue course)
Colorado
R. T. Jones
Eisenhower GC, USAF Academy (Silver course)
Colorado
F. Hummel
Eisenhower Park GC [formerly Salisbury Golf Links](Red course) Nassau County
New York
D. Emmet
Eisenhower Park GC (Blue and White courses) Nassau County
New York
R. T. Jones
Ekwanok CC
Vermont
J. D. Dunn, W. J. Travis
Ekwanok CC (r.8)
Vermont
G. S. Cornish
Elbel Park GC
Indiana
W. J. Spear
El Bosque GC
Spain
R. T. Jones
Elbow River CC
Alberta, Canada
R.T. Jones, Jr.
El Caballero GC (n.l.e.)
California
G. C. Thomas, Jr. W. P. Bell
El Caballero GC (New site)
California
W. H. Johnson
El Caballero GC (r.)
California
R. T. Jones
El Camino G&CC
California
W. H. Johnson
El Camino G&CC
California
W. F. Bell
El Campestre Chiluca
Mexico
L. M. Hughes
El Campestre Jurica
Mexico
L. M. Hughes
El Campo GC [now Newark GC]
California
J. Fleming
El Cariso GC
California
R. M. Graves
El Cerrito (r.)
California
R. M. Graves

El Cid G&CC (Original 9)
Mexico
(Manore Orthoco)
El Cid G&CC (a.9)
Mexico
L. M. Hughes
Elcona CC
Indiana
W. Diddel
Elcona CC (r.)
Indiana
W. B. and G. H. Matthews
El Conquistador CC (Bradenton)
Florida
M. Mahannah
El Conquistador CC (Valparaiso; n.l.e.)
Florida
G. O'Neill
El Conquistador Hotel and Club
Puerto Rico
R. Von Hagge
Eldorado CC
California
L. M. Hughes
El Dorado CC (r. 12, a. 18)
California
T. G. Robinson
El Dorado CC (Original 9)
Indiana
P. Dye
El Dorado CC (a.9)
Indiana
G. Kern
El Dorado CC
Kansas
E. L. Bell
El Dorado CC
Texas
G. Fazio
El Dorado CC
Texas
G.R. Baird
El Dorado GC
Michigan
W. B. and G. H. Matthews
El Dorado Hills Exec. GC
California
R. T. Jones
El Dorado Park GC
California
W. P. Bell
Elephant Butte GC
New Mexico
R.M. Phelps, B. Benz
Elephant Hills
Rhodesia
G. Player, (S. Brews, V. Vincent)
Elfordleigh Hotel GC
England
F.G. Hawtree, J.H. Taylor
Elgin GC
Illinois
E. L. Packard
Elgin House GC
Ontario, Canada
C. E. Robinson
Elgin Wing Park GC
Illinois
T. Bendelow
Elie Golf House Club
Scotland
T. Morris
Elie Golf House Club (r.)
Scotland
J. Braid
Elizabeth City GC
North Carolina
J. P. Gibson
Elizabeth Manor CC
Virginia
L.S. "Dick" Wilson

Elizabethtown CC
Kentucky
B. J. Wihry
El Kantaoui GC
Tunisia
J.D. Harris, P.W. Thomson, M. Wolveridge, R. Fream
Elk City G&CC
Oklahoma
R. C. Dunning
Elk City G&CC (r.)
Oklahoma
D. R. Sechrest
Elk County CC (r.)
Pennsylvania
X. G. Hassenplug
Elk Creek GC
Ohio
A. Hills
Elkhart GC (r.)
Kansas
L. I. Johnson
Elkhorn GC at Sun Valley
Idaho
R. T. Jones, Sr. and Jr.
Elkhorn GC
California
B. Stamps
Elkhorn Valley GC
Oregon
(Don Cutler)
Elkins CC (Now Cedar Brook CC)
North Carolina
E. Maples
Elkins Lake GC
Texas
R. Plummer
Elkins Ranch GC
California
W. H. Tucker, Jr.
Elk Island National Park GC
Alberta, Canada
W. P. Brinkworth
Elkridge CC (r.)
Maryland
R. T. Jones
Elkridge CC (r.)
Maryland
E. B. Ault
Elk River CC
Minnesota
W. H. Kidd, Sr.
Elks CC (Elkhart) (a. 9)
Indiana
H. Purdy
Elks CC (Seymour)
Indiana
(Harold England)
Elks CC [now Lakeshore CC](a.9)
Iowa
D. Gill
Elks CC
Michigan
C. E. Maddox
Elks CC
Oklahoma
F. Farley
Elks CC at Columbus (27)
Nebraska
R.M. Phelps
Elks CC at Columbus
Ohio
D. J. Ross
Elks GC (r.)
Alberta, Canada
C. Muret
Elks Lodge CC (9)
Indiana
B. J. Wihry

Elks Lodge #2186 GC
Indiana
P. Dye

Ellendale CC
Louisiana
J. Finger

Ellesmere GC
England
J. J. F. Pennink

Ellington Ridge CC
Connecticut
G. S. Cornish

Ellinwood CC (a.9)
Massachusetts
G. S. Cornish, W. G. Robinson

Ellwood Greens CC
Illinois
C. E. Maddox

El Macero CC
California
R. E. Baldock

Elma Meadows GC
New York
W. E. Harries

Elmcrest CC
Massachusetts
A. Zikorus

Elmendorf AFB GC
Alaska
R. T. Jones, Sr. and Jr.

Elm Fork Muni (now L.B. Houston Muni)
Texas
L. Howard

Elmgate CC [now Glenview Park GC]
Illinois
J. A. Roseman, Sr.

Elmhurst CC (r.)
Illinois
K. Killian, R. Nugent

Elmhurst CC
Manitoba, Canada
D. J. Ross

Elmhurst CC (r.3)
Manitoba, Canada
C. E. Robinson

Elmhurst CC (r.2)
Manitoba, Canada
G. S. Cornish, W. G. Robinson

Elmira CC (Original 9)
New York
"Young" W. Dunn

Elmira CC (a.9)
New York
A. W. Tillinghast

Elmira CC (a.7)
New York
F. Garbin

El Monte GC
Utah
J. M. Riley

El Morro GC
Venezuela
E. L. and R. B. Packard

Elm Park (r.)
Ireland
E. Hackett

Elm Ridge CC (Former course)
Province of Québec, Canada
A. W. Tillinghast

Elm Ridge CC (New site; Courses #1 and #2)
Province of Québec, Canada
W. F. and D. W. Gordon

Elm Ridge CC (r.)
Province of Qèbec, Canada
C. E. Robinson

Elmsford CC
New York
T. Wells

Elmwood CC
New York
A. W. Tillinghast

Elmwood CC (r.)
New York
A. H. Tull

Elmwood CC (r.1)
New York
F. Duane

Elmwood Park GC
South Dakota
E. L. Packard

Elmwood Park GC (a.9)
South Dakota
C. E. Maddox

Elmwood Park GC (r.9)
South Dakota
D. Herfort

Elmwood Park Muni
Nebraska
T. Bendelow

El Niguel CC
California
D. Kent

El Palmar GC
Mexico
P. and R. Dye

El Paraiso GC
Spain
R. Kirby, G. Player, A. Davis

El Pomas Par 3 GC [now Tavares Cove CC]
Florida
W. F. Mitchell

El Prado GC (Butterfield Stage and Chino Creek courses)
California
H. M. and D. A. Rainville

El Prat, Real Club de Golf
Spain
J. Arana

El Rancho Verde CC
California
H. M. and D. A. Rainville

El Reno CC
Oklahoma
F. Farley

El Rincon Club
Colombia
R. T. Jones

El Rio CC
Arizona
W. F. Bell

El Rivino CC
California
(Joe Calwell)

El Rodeo, CC
Colombia
H. Watson

El Saler
Spain
J. Arana

Elsbert Farm GC (3)
Illinois
C. D. Wagstaff

Eltham Warren GC
England
T. Dunn

Ely City GC
England
H. Cotton

Ely Muni [now White Pine Muni]
Nevada
R. E. Baldock

Ely Park GC and Par 3 GC
New York
E. E. Smith

Elyria CC
Ohio
W. S. Flynn

Elyria CC (r.)
Ohio
J. Kidwell, M. Hurdzan

Embassy Club at Armonk
New York
O. E. Smith

Emeis Park GC
Iowa
C. D. Wagstaff

Emerald Green GC
New York
W. F. Mitchell

Emerald Hills GC
California
C. Glasson

Emerald Hills CC
Florida
R. Von Hagge, B. Devlin

Emerald Hills GC
Iowa
L. I. Johnson

Emerald Valley GC
Oregon
R. E. Baldock

Emmetsburg CC (9)
Iowa
H. W. and H. C. Glissmann

Emorywood Club (r.)
North Carolina
E. Maples

Empire G&CC
Utah
J. M. Riley

Empire State GC at Spring Valley
New York
O. E. Smith

Emporia CC
Kansas
H. Robb, Sr.

Emporia Muni
Kansas
F. Hummel

Emporium CC
Pennsylvania
F. Garbin

Encanto Muni (27)
Arizona
W. P. Bell

Encanto Park Muni (r.)
Arizona
G. A. Panks

Enderlin GC
North Dakota
D. Herfort

Endwell Greens GC
New York
G. S. Cornish, W. G. Robinson

Enfield GC
England
T. Dunn

Enfield GC (r.)
England
J. Braid

Engineers Club
New York
H. B. Strong

Engineers Club (r.)
New York
D. Emmet

Engineers Club (r.)
New York
W. F. and D. W. Gordon

Engineers Club (r.)
New York
F. Duane

Englewood CC (now Rolling Hills CC)
New Jersey
D. J. Ross

Englewood GC
Florida
R. A. Anderson

Englewood CC (r. 9)
New Jersey
E. V. Ternyey

Englewood Muni
Colorado
R.M. Phelps, B. Benz

English Hills GC
Michigan
M. DeVries

En Joie CC
New York
E. E. Smith

En Joie CC (r.)
New York
W. Mitchell

Enmore Park GC
England
F. W. Hawtree

Enniscorthy GC (r.)
Ireland
E. Hackett

Enniscrone GC
Ireland
E. Hackett

Ennis GC (r.)
Ireland
E. Hackett

Enniskillen GC (r.)
Ireland
E. Hackett

Ennis Muni (9)
Montana
F. Hummel

Enzesfeld GC
Austria
J. D. Harris

Equinox GC
Vermont
W. J. Travis

Equinox GC (r.)
Vermont
W. Mitchell

Erandeni, Club de Golf
Mexico
P. Clifford

Erding GC
Germany
D. Harradine

Erewash Valley GC (r.)
England
T. Williamson

Eridge Park
Great Britain
T. Dunn

Erie MacCaune CC
Pennsylvania
J. G. Harrison

Erie Shores GC
Ohio
B. W. Zink

Errol Estates Inn & CC (27)
Florida
J. L. Lee

Escondido CC
California
H. M. and D. A. Rainville

Escorpion, Club de Golf (36)
Spain
R. Kirby, G. Player

Eseeola Lodge CC(n.l.e.)
North Carolina
A. Findlay

Eseeola Lodge CC [now Linville CC](a. 2nd 18)
North Carolina
D. J. Ross

Esquire CC
West Virginia
X. G. Hassenplug

Essener GC
West Germany
B. Von Limburger, K. Hoffmann

Essex County Club
New York
D. J. Ross

Essex County CC
Massachusetts
H. C. Leeds

Essex County CC (Existing course)
Massachusetts
D. J. Ross

Essex County CC (r.)
Massachusetts
E. F. Wogan

Essex County CC (East course)
New Jersey
T. Bendelow

Essex County CC (r.; a.4)
New Jersey
D. S. Hunter

Essex County CC (West course
New Jersey
C. H. Banks

Essex County CC (r. East and West courses)
New Jersey
D. J. Ross

Essex County CC (r.)
New Jersey
A. W. Tillinghast

Essex County CC (r. 36)
New Jersey
R. T. Jones

Essex County CC (r.9)
New Jersey
F. Duane

Essex Fells CC
New Jersey
D. J. Ross

Essex Fells CC (r.)
New Jersey
M. and H. Purdy

Essex G&CC
Ontario, Canada
D. J. Ross

Essex G&CC (r.)
Ontario, Canada
A. Hills

Essex G&CC (r.2)
Ontario, Canada
W. B. and G. H. Matthews

Essex GC at St. Thomas
Ontario, Canada
S. Thompson

Estate Carlton Hotel GC
Virgin Islands
A. H. Tull

Estero Woods GC
Florida
A. Hills

Estes Park GC
Colorado
H. B. Hughes

252

Estoril GC (Original 9)
Portugal
(Jean Gassiat)
Estoril GC (r.9,a.9)
Portugal
P. M. Ross
Estoril Sol GC
Portugal
J.D. Harris, M. Wolveridge, R. Frean
Estrella CC (Shorecliffs)
California
J. B. Williams
Estrella Mountain GC
Arizona
R. F. Lawrence
Ethelwood CC
Virginia
W. F. and D. W. Gordon
Eton GC
England
J. J. F. Pennink
Etowah Valley CC
North Carolina
E. B. Ault
Euclid Heights CC
Ohio
W. H. Way
Euclid Hills CC [now Silver Lake GC, North course]
Illinois
L. Macomber
Eugene CC
Oregon
H. C. Egan
Eugene CC (r.)
Oregon
R. T. Jones, Sr. and Jr.
Eugene Grace Estate GC
Oklahoma
P. D. Maxwell
Euless GC
Texas
T. G. Robinson
Eureka GC (r.9)
Kansas
L. I. Johnson
Eureka Muni
California
R. E. Baldock
Eustis CC (n.l.e.)
Florida
C. S. Butchart
Evan Heights GC (r.)
Georgia
A. L. Davis
Evanston CC
Illinois
D. J. Ross
Evanston CC (r.)
Illinois
K. Killian, R. Nugent
Evanston GC (n.l.e.)
Missouri
J. Dalgleish
Evansville CC (r.)
Indiana
W. Diddel •
Evansville Muni [now Fendrich GC]
Indiana
T. Bendelow
Everett CC (27)
Washington
T. G. Robinson
Everett Muni
Washington
A. Smith

Everglades Club
Florida
S. J. Raynor
Everglades Club (a.9)
Florida
D. J. Ross
Everglades Club (r.)
Florida
W. B. Langford, T. J. Moreau
Everglades Club (r.)
Florida
M. Mahannah
Everglades Club (r.)
Florida
G. and T. Fazio
Evergreen CC
Virginia
A.M. Pulley, R.F. Loving
Evergreen GC
Michigan
R. D. Beard
Evergreen GC
Wisconsin
K. Killian, R. Nugent
Evergreen Valley GC
Maine
R. T. Jones
Evian-les-Baines GC
France
W. Park, Jr.
Excelsior Springs CC (r.)
Missouri
E. L. Bell
Excelsior Springs CC (a. Par 3)
Missouri
R. C. Dunning
Excelsior Springs Par 3 GC (n.l.e.)
Missouri
P. D. Maxwell
Exeter CC (r.)
New Hampshire
M. L. Francis
Exeter CC
Rhode Island
G. S. Cornish
Exeter Muni
California
R. E. Baldock
Exmoor CC
Illinois
H. J. Tweedie
Exmoor CC (r.)
Illinois
D. J. Ross
Exmoor CC (r.)
Illinois
K. Killian, R. Nugent

Fagnes GC, Royal
Belgium
T. C. Simpson, P. M. Ross
Fahrens Park GC
California
G. A. Panks
Fairborn CC
Ohio
W. Diddel
Fairchild Wheeler GC (36)
Connecticut
R. White
Fairfax CC (Original 9)
Virginia
R. T. Jones
Fairfax CC (a.9)
Virginia
W. F. Gordon
Fairfax, CC of (r.2)
Virginia
A.M. Pulley, R.F. Loving

Fairfield Bay GC
Arkansas
L. Howard
Fairfield Bay GC (r.)
Arkansas
E. B. Ault
Fairfield CC
Connecticut
S. J. Raynor
Fairfield CC (a. Hole #10)
Connecticut
G. S. Cornish
Fairfield CC
South Carolina
R. A. Renaud
Fairfield Harbour G&CC
North Carolina
E. Hamm
Fairfield Mountain GC (The Mountains CC)
North Carolina
W. B. Lewis
Fairfield Muni [now South Pine Creek Par 3 GC](9)
Connecticut
G. S. Cornish, W. G. Robinson
Fairgreen GC
Florida
W. W. Amick
Fairington G&TC
Georgia
R. T. Jones, R. L. Jones
Fairlawn CC
Maine
C. H. Adams
Fairlawn CC (r.)
Ohio
A. Hills
Fairmont CC (r.)
New Jersey
A. H. Tull
Fairmont Hot Springs CC
British Columbia, Canada
(C. L. Wilder)
Fairmount CC
New Jersey
H. Purdy
Fairmount GC
North Carolina
J. P. Gibson
Fair Oaks CC
Texas
R. Kirby, G. Player
Fairview CC (New site)
Connecticut
R. T. Jones
Fairview CC (n.l.e.)
New York
D. J. Ross
Fairview CC (r.) (n.l.e.)
New York
A. H. Tull
Fairview G&CC
Pennsylvania
F. Murray, R. Roberts
Fairview GC (Original 9)
Indiana
D. J. Ross
Fairview GC (a.9)
Indiana
(Everett A. Monroe)
Fairview GC
New Jersey
W. F. Mitchell

Fairway CC
Pennsylvania
W. F. and D. W. Gordon
Fairway CC at Miramar [now Foxcroft CC]
Florida
W. R. Watts
Fairway Glen GC
California
R. E. Baldock
Fairway GC
Florida
W. W. Amick
Fairway Oaks G&CC
Texas
R. Garl
Fairway Park GC
Western Australia
P.W. Thomson, M. Wolveridge
Fairways CC [now Lake Valley CC]
Colorado
J. P. Maxwell
Fairway-to-the-Stars GC
Nevada
(Louis Prima)
Fairwood Park
Wales
F. W. Hawtree
Fakenham
Great Britain
C. D. Lawrie, J. J. F. Pennink
Falcon Beach Lake GC
Manitoba, Canada
N. Woods
Falcon Head Lodge CC [formerly Turner Lodge CC]
Oklahoma
(Waco Turner) R.C. Dunning
Falkenstein GC
Germany
H. S. Colt, J. S. F. Morrison, C. H. Alison
Falkenstein GC (r.)
West Germany
B. Von Limburger
Fallbrook CC
California
H. M. and D. A. Rainville
Fall Creek Falls State Park GC
Tennessee
J. L. Lee
Falling Creek GC
North Carolina
E. Hamm
Fall River CC (Original 9)
Massachusetts
W. Park, Jr.
Fall River CC (a.9)
Massachusetts
G. S. Cornish, W. G. Robinson
Fall River Valley G&CC
California
C. Glasson
Falls Road Muni
Maryland
E. B. Ault
Fallsview Hotel GC (9)
New York
R. T. Jones
Falsterbo GC
Sweden
(Gunnar A. Bauer)
F. A. McConnel (3 hole course)
Ontario, Canada
H. Watson
Fan Court GC
Great Britain
T. Dunn

Far Corner Farm GC
Massachusetts
G. S. Cornish, W. G. Robinson
Fargo CC (r.)
North Dakota
D. Herfort
Faribault G&CC
Minnesota
W. H. Kidd, Sr.
Faries Park GC
Illinois
E. L. Packard
Farmington CC
Connecticut
W. Park, Jr.
Farmington CC (r.)
Connecticut
O. E. Smith
Farmington CC (r.1)
Connecticut
G. S. Cornish
Farmington CC (r.)
Michigan
W. B. and G. H. Matthews
Farmington CC (9)
New Mexico
W. D. Cantrell
Farmington CC
Tennessee
J. P. Maxwell
Farmington CC
Virginia
F. A. Findlay
Farmington CC (a. 3rd 9)
Virginia
R. F. Loving
Farmington Woods CC
Connecticut
D. Muirhead
Farm Neck GC [formerly The Links on the Vineyard](Original 9)
Massachusetts
G. S. Cornish, W. G. Robinson
Farm Neck GC (a.9)
Massachusetts
(Patrick Mulligan)
Farms CC
Connecticut
G. S. Cornish
Farms Motel Par 3 GC
Vermont
G. S. Cornish, W. G. Robinson
Farnborough GC
England
J.D. Harris, P.W. Thomson, M. Wolveridge
Farnham Park GC
England
J. J. F. Pennink, D. M. A. Steel
Farnham Park GC (a.9)
England
M. Hawtree
Fawn Club
New York
S. Dunn
Feather Sound CC
Florida
J. L. Lee
Feldafing GC
West Germany
B. Von Limburger, K. Hoffmann
Felixstowe Ferry GC (r.)
England
W. Fernie
Felixstowe Ferry GC (n.l.e.)
England
A. Mackenzie
Felixstowe Ferry GC (new course)
England
G. Campbell, H. Cotton

Felixstowe Ferry GC (r.)
England
H. Cotton
Fellows GC
Michigan
W. B. and G. H. Matthews
Fendrich GC [formerly Evansville Muni]
Indiana
T. Bendelow
Fendrich GC (r.)
Indiana
E. B. Ault
Fenimore CC [now Fenway CC]
New York
A. W. Tillinghast
Fenway CC [formerly Fenimore CC]
New York
A. W. Tillinghast
Fermoy GC
Ireland
J. D. Harris
Fermoy GC (r.)
Ireland
E. Hackett
Fernandina Beach CC (Original 18)
Florida
(Ed Matteson)
Fernandina Beach CC (a.9)
Florida
J. L. Lee
Ferncliffe CC
New Hampshire
S. Dunn
Ferncroft CC [formerly Topsfield CC]
Massachusetts
R. T. Jones, R. L. Jones
Ferndown GC
England
(Harold Hilton)
Ferndown GC (a.9)
England
J. H. Stutt
Fernwood CC
Mississippi
G. Curtis
Fernwood Resort & CC
Pennsylvania
N. T. Psiahas
Ferreter's Cove
Ireland
E. Hackett
Fianna Hills CC
Arkansas
(Jim Holmes)
Fiddler's Elbow CC
New Jersey
H. Purdy
Fiddlesticks CC
Florida
R. Garl
Field Club of Omaha
Nebraska
(Harry Lawrie)
Fiji Hotel GC
Fiji Island
P.W. Thomson, M. Wolveridge
Fig Garden GC
California
(Nick Lombardo)
Filton GC (r.)
England
F. G. Hawtree
Fincastle CC
West Virginia
L. S. "Dick" Wilson
Finchley GC
England
J. Braid, J. R. Stutt
Finley GC, University of N.C.
North Carolina
G. W. Cobb

Finger Lakes GC
New York
D. W. Gordon
Finham Park (r.)
England
F. W. Hawtree
Fircrest GC
Washington
A. V. Macan
Firefly Exec. GC
Massachusetts
D. Hoenig
Firestone CC (South course)
Ohio
W. H. Way
Firestone CC (r. South course, a. North course)
Ohio
R. T. Jones
Firestone Public GC (n.l.e.)
Ohio
W. H. Way
Fishers Island GC
New York
S. J. Raynor
Fish Lake CC
Mississippi
L. Howard
Five-by-80 GC (9)
Iowa
H. W. Glissmann
Five Farms (Baltimore CC, Five Farms course)
Maryland
A. W. Tillinghast
Five Farms (Baltimore CC, a. West course)
Maryland
E. B. Ault
Flagstaff Hill G&CC
Australia
(D.N. Hillan)
Flanders Valley GC (27)
New Jersey
H. Purdy
Flat Creek GC
Georgia
J. L. Lee
Flatirons CC [formerly Boulder CC]
Colorado
R. B. Harris
Fleetwood GC
England
(J. A. Steer)
Fleming Creek CC
Michigan
J. Nicklaus
Flemington Park GC
Ontario, Canada
H. Watson
Fletcher Hills GC
California
W. H. Tucker, Jr.
Flinders GC
Australia
A. Mackenzie
Flint CC
Michigan
W. Park, Jr.
Flint Elks GC
Michigan
W. B. and G. H. Matthews
Florence GC
Italy
S. Dunn
Florham Park CC (r.)
New Jersey
H. Purdy

Florida CC (n.l.e.)
Florida
D. J. Ross
Florida, CC of
Florida
R. B. Harris
Floridale GC (n.l.e.)
Florida
S. Thompson
Florida State University GC (Seminole GC)
Florida
R. A. Anderson
Florida State University GC (r.3,a.9)
Florida
W. W. Amick
Floridian CC [now Mission Inn & CC]
Florida
(Captain Charles Clarke)
Flossmoor CC
Illinois
H. J. Tweedie
Flossmoor CC (r.)
Illinois
H. Collis
Flourtown CC (Sunnybrook)
Pennsylvania
D. J. Ross
Floyd CC (9)
Virginia
E. Hamm
Flushing GC (n.l.e.)
New York
T. Bendelow
Folmont Resort GC
Pennsylvania
F. Garbin
Fon Du Lac CC (a.9)
Ohio
W. K. Newcomb
Fountainbleau GC (36)
Florida
M. Mahannah
Fontainebleau, Golf de
France
T. C. Simpson
Fontainebleau, Golf de (r.)
France
F. W. Hawtree
Foothills G&CC
California
W. P. Bell
Foothills GC
Colorado
R.M. Phelps
Forbes AFB GC (9)
Kansas
R. E. Baldock
Fore Lakes Exec. GC
Utah
W. H. Neff
Foremost Insurance Company GC
Michigan
M. DeVries
Forest Akers GC, State University
Michigan
W. B. Matthews
(The) Forest CC
Florida
W. Maddox
Forest Dale GC
Utah
J. M. Riley
Forest Heights CC
Georgia
G. W. Cobb

Forest Hill Exec. GC at West Palm Beach
Florida
H. Schmeisser
Forest Hill GC
Georgia
D. J. Ross
Forest Hills CC
Florida
(J. Franklin Meehan)
Forest Hills CC
Illinois
C. E. Maddox
Forest Hills GC
Oregon
W. F. and W. P. Bell
Forest Hills GC (r.)
Ontario, Canada
H. Watson
Forest Lake CC
Florida
R. A. Anderson
Forest Lake CC
Michigan
W. Diddel
Forest Lake CC
Virginia
E. B. Ault, A. Jamison
Forest Lakes Club
South Carolina
M.J. McCarthy, Sr.
Forest Little
Ireland
F. W. Hawtree
Forest Meadows Exec. GC
California
R. T. Jones, Sr. and Jr.
Forest Nottingham
England
T. Dunn
Forest Oaks CC
North Carolina
E. Maples
Forest Park CC (r.9,a.9)
Virginia
E. Hamm
Forest Park GC
Indiana
W. J. Spear
Forest Park GC
New York
T. Bendelow
Forest Park Muni (r.)
Maryland
C. Hook
Forest Park Muni (27)
Missouri
R. Foulis
Forfar GC
Scotland
J. Braid
Formby GC
England
W. Park, Jr.
Formby GC (r.)
England
H. S. Colt
Forres
Scotland
W. Park, Jr.
Forres
Scotland
J. Braid
Forsgate CC (East course)
New Jersey
C. H. Banks

Forsgate CC (West course)
New Jersey
H. Purdy
Forsyth CC
North Carolina
D. J. Ross
Forsyth CC (r.)
North Carolina
W. C. Byrd
Fort Belvoir GC
Virginia
E.B. Ault
Fort Belvoir GC (r.)
Virginia
R. T. Jones
Fort Benning GC (a. 9, Pineside course and Lakeside course)
Georgia
(Lester Lawrence)
Fort Benning GC (a.9, Lakeside course)
Georgia
R. T. Jones
Fort Carson GC
Colorado
R.M. Phelps
Fort Cobb Lake State Park GC
Oklahoma
F. Farley
Fort Collins, CC of
Colorado
H. B. Hughes
Fort Devens GC
Massachusetts
(Melvin B. Lucas, Jr.)
Fort Eustis GC
Maryland
G. W. Cobb
Fort Frances GC
Ontario, Canada
C. E. Robinson
Fort George Island GC (Original 9)
Florida
W. W. Amick
Fort Harrison GC
Indiana
W. Diddel
Fort Hays CC (r.)
Kansas
C. Mendenhall
Fort Huachuca GC
Arizona
M. Coggins, G. A. Panks
Fort Irwin GC (r.)
California
D. Muirhead
Fort Jackson GC
South Carolina
G. W. Cobb
Fort Lauderdale CC (North course)
Florida
J. A. Roseman, Sr.
Fort Lauderdale CC (South course)
Florida
R. F. Lawrence
Fort Leavenworth GC (r.;a.9)
Kansas
(Art Hall)
Fort Leonard Wood GC
Missouri
F. Farley
Fort Lewis GC
Washington
(William Teufel)

Fort McClellan GC (a.9)
Alabama
G. W. Cobb
Fort McPherson CC (r.)
Georgia
G. W. Cobb
Fort Meade GC (Park course)
Maryland
G. W. Cobb
Fort Meade GC (Meade course)
Maryland
(Major Robert McClure)
Fort Mitchell CC (r.)
Kentucky
A. Hills
Fort Myers CC
Florida
D. J. Ross
Fort Myers Exec. GC
Florida
W. B. Lewis
Fort Nelson GC [now Poplar Hills G&CC]
British Columbia, Canada
W. G. Robinson
Fort Ord GC (Bayonnet course)
California
(Major Robert McClure, Lawson Little)
Fort Pierce CC [now Indian Hills CC]
Florida
H. B. Strong
Fort Preval GC
Province of Québec, Canada
W. F. Mitchell
Fort Preval GC (r.)
Province of Québec, Canada
H. Watson
Fort Riley GC [now Custer Hill GC]
Kansas
R. T. Jones
Fort Riley Officer's GC
Kansas
(Major Richard D. Newman)
Fort Royal
Northern Ireland
T. J. A. McAuley
Fort Shafter GC
Hawaii
W. G. Wilkinson
Fort Sill GC (r.)
Oklahoma
D. R. Sechrest
Fortune Hills GC
Bahamas
J. L. Lee
Fort Walton Beach Muni
Florida
W. W. Amick
Fort Washington CC
California
W. Watson
Fort Washington CC (r.)
California
R. E. Baldock
Fort Wayne CC (r.)
Indiana
W. Diddel
Fort Wayne CC (r.)
Indiana
R. L. Jones
Fort Wayne CC (r.)
Indiana
W. B. and G. H. Matthews
Fort William G&CC
Ontario, Canada
S. Thompson

Fort William GC
Scotland
J. H. Stutt
Forty Niners CC
Arizona
W. F. Bell
Fostoria GC (r.8,a.10)
Ohio
J. Kidwell
Fountain Head CC (r.)
Maryland
E. B. Ault
Fountainhead State Park GC
Oklahoma
F. Farley
Fountain of the Sun Exec. GC
Arizona
R. F. Lawrence
Fountains G&RC (27)
Florida
R. Von Hagge, B. Devlin
Fountain Valley GC
Virgin Islands
R. T. Jones
Four Hills CC
New Mexico
R. E. Baldock
(The) 400 Club
Florida
R. Garl
Four Lakes CC
Colorado
F. Hummel
Four Seasons CC of Georgia
Georgia
R. A. Anderson
Four Seasons CC of Tennessee
Tennessee
R. A. Anderson
Four Seasons G&CC
Missouri
R. T. Jones
Four Seasons Resort & Exec. GC
Pennsylvania
F. Garbin
Four Ways GC
South Africa
G. Player (S. Brewer, V. Vincent)
Fox Acres CC (9)
Colorado
J. N. Cochran
Foxborough CC
Massachusetts
G. S. Cornish, W. G. Robinson
Foxburg CC
Pennsylvania
J. G. Harrison
Fox Chapel GC
Pennsylvania
S. J. Raynor
Fox Chapel GC (r.)
Pennsylvania
J. G. Harrison
Fox Chapel GC (r.)
Pennsylvania
P. Erath
Fox Cliff CC
Indiana
W. Diddel
Fox Creek CC
Missouri
H. G. Herpel
Foxcroft CC at Miramar
Florida
W. R. Watts
Fox Den CC
Tennessee
W. C. Byrd

Foxfire CC
Florida
A. Hills
Foxfire G&CC (27)
North Carolina
E. Hamm
Foxfire G&TC
Florida
L. L. Marshall
Foxhill CC
Colorado
F. Hummel
Foxhill CC (r.)
Pennsylvania
A. W. Tillinghast
Fox Hills CC (n.l.e.)
California
G. C. Thomas, Jr., W. P. Bell
Fox Hills GC
New York
T. Bendelow
Fox Hills GC (r.)
New York
D. J. Ross
Fox Hills GC (Chertsey and Longcross courses)
England
F. W. Hawtree
Fox Lake CC
Illinois
W. B. Langford, T. J. Moreau
Fox Lake CC (r.)
Illinois
K. Killian, R. Nugent
Fox Lake CC (a.9)
Wisconsin
H. D. Fieldhouse
Fox Meadows CC
Tennessee
C. H. Adams
Foxrock GC (r.)
Ireland
E. Hackett
Fox Run GC (9)
Vermont
F. Duane
Fox Valley CC
Illinois
(Joe Meister)
Framingham CC (Original course)
Massachusetts
O. E. Smith
Framingham CC (r.5)
Massachusetts
A. Zikorus
Framingham CC (a.9)
Massachusetts
W. F. Mitchell
Framingham CC (a.3)
Massachusetts
G. S. Cornish, W. G. Robinson
Framingham CC (r.)
Massachusetts
M. L. Francis
Francisco Grande CC
Arizona
R. Plummer
Francis Lake GC
Georgia
W. C. Byrd
Franconia Muni at Springfield
Massachusetts
W. E. Stiles, J. R. Van Kleek
Franconia Muni (r.7)
Massachusetts
G. S. Cornish, W. G. Robinson

Francourt Farms GC
New York
A. Craig
Franke CC
Oklahoma
F. Farley
Frankfort GC
Indiana
C. E. Maddox
Frankfurt (r.)
Germany
B. Von Limburger
Frankfurter GC
Germany
H. S. Colt, J. S. F. Morrison
Frankfurter GC (r.)
Germany
J. S. F. Morrison, J. H. Stutt
Franklin Canyon GC
California
R. M. Graves
Franklin CC (r.)
Massachusetts
W. E. Stiles, J. R. Van Kleek
Franklin CC (r.;a.2)
Massachusetts
W. F. Mitchell
Franklin CC (a.10)
Massachusetts
P. A. Wogan
Franklin CC (r.)
New Hampshire
W. F. Mitchell
Franklin County CC
Illinois
W. B. Langford, T. J. Moreau
Franklin Hills CC
Michigan
D. J. Ross
Franklin Park Muni (Original course; n.l.e.)
Massachusetts
G. Wright
Franklin Park Muni (9)
Massachusetts
W. Campbell
Franklin Pierce Muni
Michigan
(Fred A. Ellis)
Franklin Woods
Michigan
D. J. Ross
Fransisco Grande CC
Arizona
R. Plummer
Frear Park GC (a.9)
New York
R. T. Jones
Frederick GC (r.)
Oklahoma
A. J. Jackson
Fredericton GC (r.1)
New Brunswick, Canada
C. E. Robinson
Fredericton GC (r.2)
New Brunswick, Canada
G. S. Cornish, W. G. Robinson
Freeport CC
Illinois
H. Collis
Freiburg GC
West Germany
B. Von Limburger
Fremont GC
Nebraska
D. Gill

Fremont Hills CC
Missouri
J. P. Maxwell
French Lick CC (Sheraton Hotel & Club; Hill course)
Indiana
D. J. Ross
French Lick CC (r. Valley course)
Indiana
G. S. Alves
French Lick CC (r. Hill and Valley courses)
Indiana
H. Purdy
Frenchman's Creek GC (North and South courses)
Florida
G. Dickinson
Frerick GC (r.)
Oklahoma
A. J. Jackson
Fresh Meadows CC (n.l.e.)
New York
A. W. Tillinghast
Fresh Meadow GC (r.)
Illinois
W. B. Langford
Fresh Pond Muni
Massachusetts
W. Johnson
Fresh Pond Muni (r.)
Massachusetts
G. S. Cornish, W. G. Robinson
Freshwater GC (r.)
England
F. G. Hawtree
Fresnillo GC
Mexico
(McLain-Rose Engineers)
Friend CC
Nebraska
H. B. Hughes, R. Watson
Friendly Hills CC
California
(Jimmy Hines)
Frilford Heath GC (New course)
England
C. K. Cotton, J. J. F. Pennink
Frinton-On-Sea GC
England
T. Dunn
Frinton-On-Sea GC (r.)
England
W. Park, Jr.
Fripp Island CC
South Carolina
G. W. Cobb, J. B. LaFoy
Frisch Auf Valley CC
Texas
B. J. Riviere
Frome
Great Britain
T. Dunn
Frosty Valley CC
Pennsylvania
D. W. Gordon
Fuji GC
Japan
C. H. Alison
Fuji Lakeside GC
Japan
(Makato Harada)
Fujikoshi CC
Japan
R. T. Jones, Jr.
Fujioka GC
Japan
P. Thomson, M. Wolveridge, T. Yamada

Fulford GC
England
A. Mackenzie
Fulford Heath
England
J. Braid
Fullerton G&CC (27)
California
W. F. Bell
Fullerton Muni (a. 9)
California
T. G. Robinson
Fulton Estate GC
Connecticut
D. Emmet, A. H. Tull
Fulwell GC
England
J. S. F. Morrison
Fundy National Park GC
Nova Scotia, Canada
S. Thompson
Fuquay Varina CC (Original 9)
North Carolina
C. D. Wagstaff
Furano GC [formerly Kitanomine CC]
Japan
E. B. Seay, A. Palmer
Furnace Brook CC (r.)
Massachusetts
W. F. Mitchell
Furnace Creek GC (Original 9)
California
W. P. Bell
Furnace Creek GC (r.9,a.9)
California
W. F. Bell
Furnas GC
Portugal
P. M. Ross
Furth GC (U. S. Army Base)
West Germany
B. Von Limburger
Furzedown GC
England
T. Dunn
Fuschl, Schloss Par 3 GC
Austria
B. Von Limburger
Futurama GC
Florida
R. A. Anderson

Gables GC (9)
Florida
J. D. Dunn
Gadsden CC
Florida
J. L. Lee
Gagetown GC (Original 9)
New Brunswick, Canada
C. E. Robinson
Gailes GC [now Western Gailes]
Scotland
W. Park, Jr.
Gaines County GC
Texas
W. D. Cantrell
Gainesville CC
Florida
G. W. Cobb
Gainesville Muni (9)
Georgia
D. J. Ross
Gainesville Muni
Texas
R. Plummer

Galen Hall CC (r.)
Pennsylvania
W. F. and D W. Gordon
Galion CC (a.9)
Ohio
J. Kidwell
Gallagher's Canyon CC
British Columbia, Canada
W. G. Robinson
Galloping Hills GC
New Jersey
L. Wilkinson
Galloping Hills GC (r.)
New Jersey
R. T. Jones
Galloping Hills GC (r.)
New Jersey
A. H. Tull
Galls GC (r.)
Minnesota
D. Herfort
Gallup Muni
New Mexico
L. Howard
Galt GC
Ontario, Canada
R. and D. Moote
Galveston CC
Texas
J. Bredemus
Galveston CC (r.)
Texas
J. Finger
Galveston Muni (n.l.e.)
Texas
J. Bredemus
Galveston Muni (New site)
Texas
D. J. Ross
Ganton GC
England
T. Dunn
Ganton GC
England
H. Vardon
Ganton GC (r.)
England
J. Braid
Ganton GC (r.4)
England
H. S. Colt
Ganton GC (r.)
England
W. H. Fowler
Ganton GC (r.)
England
C. K. Hutchison
Ganton GC (r.)
England.d
C. K. Cotton
Garden City CC (r.)
Kansas
E. L. Bell
Garden City CC (Southwinds course)
Kansas
D. Sechrest
Garden City CC
New York
W. J. Travis
Garden City CC (r.6)
New York
F. Duane
Garden City CC (r.)
New York
R. T. Jones
(The) Garden City GC
New York
D. Emmet

(The) Garden City GC (r.)
New York
W. J. Travis
Garden of Eden GC
Illinois
S. F. Pelchar
Garden of Eden GC
Illinois
W. Watson
Gardner Muni (a.2)
Massachusetts
S. Mitchell
Garforth near Leeds
England
T. Williamson
Garlenda CC
Italy
J. D. Harris
Garmisch-Partnekirchen GC
West Germany
B. Von Limburger, K. Hoffmann
Garrats Hall GC
England
W. Reid
Garrison GC (formerly North Redoubt GC)
New York
L. S. "Dick" Wilson
Garrison's Lake GC
Delaware
E. B. Ault
Gary CC
Indiana
W. B. Langford, T. J. Moreau
Gary Player GC (27)
Japan
R. Kirby, G. Player
Gary Player GC (Sun City)
South Africa
R. Kirby, G. Player
Gaschwitz GC
East Germany
B. Von Limburger, K. Hoffmann
Gasparilla Inn & CC (r.)
Florida
D. L. Wallace
Gasparillo Pines
Florida
L. L. Marshall
Gaston CC
North Carolina
E. Maples
Gastonia National GC
North Carolina
J. P. Gibson
Gates Four G&CC
North Carolina
W. C. Byrd
Gatlinburg G&CC
Tennessee
W. B. Langford
Gatlinburg G&CC (r.)
Tennessee
D. and E. Maples
Gator Greek GC
Florida
J. L. Lee
Gator Hole GC
South Carolina
R. L. Jones
Gavea G&CC (r.)
Brazil
S. Thompson
Gay Hill CC
Virginia
E. Hamm
Gaylord CC (r.)
Michigan
W. Reid

Gem Lake Public GC (9)
Minnesota
P. Coates
Geneganslet GC
New York
E. E. Smith
Gene List Muni. Par 3 GC
California
H. M. and D. A. Rainville
General Blanchard GC
Arizona
R. E. Baldock
General Butler State Park GC
Kentucky
H. Purdy
General Electric A. A. GC
Massachusetts
R. Armacost
General Washington CC
Pennsylvania
W. F. Mitchell
Geneva G&CC
Iowa
D. Gill
Geneva on the Lake GC
Ohio
J. G. Harrison
Geneve, GC de
Switzerland
R. T. Jones
Genting Highlands GC
Malaysia
P.W. Thomson, M. Wolveridge
George AFB GC (West Winds 9)
California
R. E. Baldock
Georgetown CC (9)
South Carolina
A. H. Tull
Georgetown Par 3 GC (9)
Michigan
(C. Maddox, Jr.)
George Wright Muni
Massachusetts
D. J. Ross
Geraldton GC
Ontario, Canada
S. Thompson
Germantown Exec. GC (9)
Maryland
A. M. Pulley
Geysteren GC
Holland
J. J. F. Pennink
Giant Oak GC
Michigan
A. Hills
Gibson Island Club
Maryland
C. B. Macdonald, S. J. Raynor
Gibson Woods Muni
Illinois
H. D. Fieldhouse
Gillespie GC
Florida
J. H. Gillespie
Gillette CC
Wyoming
F. Hummel
Gilman GC
California
W. H. Johnson
Glacier View GC
Montana
R. E. Baldock
Glacier View GC (r.)
Montana
R. W. Fream

Glade Springs CC (Original course)
West Virginia
G. W. Cobb
Glade Springs CC (a.18)
West Virginia
G. W. Cobb, J. B. LaFoy
Gladstone Community GC
Michigan
A. H. Jolly
Glamorganshire GC
Wales
W. Park, Jr.
Glasgow AFB GC
Montana
R. E. Baldock
Glasgow GC
Scotland
T. Morris
Glasgow GC
Scotland
W. Park, Jr.
Glastonbury Hills CC
Connecticut
A. Zikorus
Glastonbury Hills CC (r.4)
Connecticut
G. S. Cornish, W. G. Robinson
Gleddoch House CC
Scotland
J. H. Stutt
Glen Abbey GC
Ontario, Canada
J. Nicklaus
Glen Arven CC
Georgia
W. E. Stiles
Glen Arven CC (r.)
Georgia
H. C. Moore, Sr.
Glenbernie GC
Scotland
J. Braid
Glenbrook CC (r.)
Nevada
R. M. Graves
Glen Cannon CC
North Carolina
W. B. Lewis
Glen Cedars GC
Ontario, Canada
R. and C. Muylaert
Glencoe GC (r.)
Illinois
K. Killian, R. Nugent
Glencorse GC
Scotland
W. Park, Jr.
Glen County GC
California
B. Harmon
Glen Cove Muni
New York
W. F. Mitchell
Glencruitten
Scotland
J. Braid
Glendale CC
Alberta, Canada
N. Woods
Glendale CC
Bellevue
Washington
A. Smith
Glendale G&CC
Manitoba, Canada
S. Thompson

Glendale G&CC (r.)
Ontario, Canada
C. E. Robinson
Glendale G&CC
Bothel
Washington
A. Smith
Glendale GC
Arizona
M. Coggins
Glendale Muni (n.l.e.)
Arizona
W. H. Tucker, Jr.
Glendale Muni
Utah
W. F. Bell
Glendora CC (Original 9)
California
(E. Warren Beach)
Glendora CC (r.9)
California
W. H. Johnson
Glendora CC (r.9,a.9)
California
R. T. Jones,Sr. and Jr.
Gleneagles GC (Red and White courses)
Illinois
F. MacDonald, C. E. Maddox
Glen Eagles GC
Ontario, Canada
R. Muylaert
Gleneagles Hotel (Kings and Queens courses)
Scotland
J. Braid
Gleneagles Hotel (Princes course)
Scotland
J. Alexander (with Marchbanks and Telford)
Gleneagles Hotel (r. Queens course)
Scotland
J. Alexander
Gleneagles Hotel (Glendevon course)
Scotland
T. J. A. McAuley
Glen Echo CC
Missouri
J. Foulis
Glen Echo CC (r.)
Missouri
R. Foulis
Glengarry CC (r.9,a.9)
Ohio
R. B. Harris
Glen GC
Scotland
P. M. Ross
Glenhardie CC
Pennsylvania
D. W. Gordon
Glenhaven CC
Iowa
R.M. Phelps
Glen Haven G&CC
California
J. Fleming
Glen Head CC [formerly Women's National CC]
New York
D. Emmet
Glen Head CC (r.)
New York
W. F. Mitchell
Glen Head CC (r.)
New York
A. H. Tull
Glenhurst CC
New Jersey
E. V. Ternyey

Glen Lakes CC (r.)
Texas
R. Plummer
Glen Lakes Exec. GC (9)
Arizona
M. Coggins
Glen Lawrence G&CC (r.)
Ontario, Canada
C. E. Robinson, (W. C. Harvey)
Glen Marr GC
Ontario, Canada
S. Thompson
Glenmore G&CC
Utah
W. H. Neff
Glenn G&CC (9)
California
T. B. Harmon
Glenn Dale CC (r.)
Maryland
(Ray and Roy Shields)
Glen Oak Club (r.1, Original course)
New York
F. Duane
Glen Oak Club (New course)
New York
J. Finger
Glen Oak CC (r.)
Illinois
W. B. Langford
Glen Oak CC (r.)
Illinois
D. Gill
Glen Oak CC
Pennsylvania
J. G. Harrison
Glen Oak CC
Virginia
L. S. "Dick" Wilson
Glen Oaks Par 3 GC
Florida
H. Schmeisser
Glenridge CC
New Jersey
W. Park, Jr.
Glenridge CC (r.)
New Jersey
R. T. Jones
Glenrochie CC
Virginia
A. G. McKay
Glenrothes New Town GC
Scotland
J. H. Stutt
Glens Falls CC
New York
D. J. Ross
Glen View GC
Illinois
H. J. Tweedie
Glen View GC (r.)
Illinois
G. O'Neil, J. A. Roseman
Glen View GC (r.)
Illinois
W. S. Flynn
Glenview Muni (Original and 2nd 18's)
Ohio
A. Hills
Glenview Naval Air Station GC (Courses #1 and #2)
Illinois
J. A. Roseman, Sr.
Glenview Park GC
Illinois
J. A. Roseman, Sr.

Glenwood CC
New York
D. Emmet
Glenwood CC
Virginia
F. A. Findlay
Glenwood Hall CC
Kentucky
R. A. Simmons
Glenwoodie CC
Illinois
H. Collis, J. Daray
Glenwoodie CC (r.)
Illinois
J. L. Lee
Glenwood Muni (9)
Ohio
X. G. Hassenplug
Glenwood Springs GC
Colorado
H. B. Hughes
Glyfada GC
Greece
D. Harradine
Glyfada GC (r.)
Greece
R. T. Jones
Glynhir GC
Wales
F. W. Hawtree
Godwin Glen GC (27)
Michigan
W. B. and G. H. Matthews
Goeppingen GC
Germany
D. Harradine
Goettingen GC
Germany
D. Harradine
Goffstown CC
New Hampshire
W. F. Mitchell
Gog Magog GC (a. 3rd 9)
England
F. W. Hawtree
Gold Canyon GC
Arizona
G. Hardin, J. Nash
Gold Coast CC
Queensland, Australia
P.W. Thomson, M. Wolveridge
Golden Eagle GC (Tides Inn)
Virginia
G. W. Cobb, J. B. LaFoy
Golden Gate CC
Florida
L. S. "Dick" Wilson
Golden Gate Fields Par 3 GC
California
J. Fleming
Golden Gate Par 3 GC (San Francisco)
California
J. Fleming
Golden GC
Colorado
J. P. Maxwell
Golden Hills CC
Arizona
A. J. Snyder
Golden Hills GC
California
J. B. William
Golden Horseshoe GC and Spotswood Exec. GC (Williamsburg Inn)
Virginia
R. T. Jones

Golden Sands GC
Wisconsin
H. D. Fieldhouse
Golden Tee GC
Ohio
R. A. Anderson
Golden Triangle GC
Maryland
R. T. Jones
Golden Valley GC
Minnesota
A. W. Tillinghast
Gold Hills CC
California
R. E. Baldock
(The) Golf Club
Ohio
P. Dye
(The) Golf Club at Aspetuck [now The Connecticut GC]
Connecticut
G. S. Cornish, W. G. Robinson
Golf Club at the Pyramids
Egypt
R. T. Jones, Jr.
Golf Club Bad Scuol
Switzerland
(Gordon Spencer)
Golf Club d'Amiens
France
P. M. Ross
Golf Club de Geneve
Switzerland
R. T. Jones
Golf Club de Uruguay
Uruguay
A. Mackenzie
Golf Club d'Hardelot
France
T. C. Simpson, P. M. Ross
Golf Club d'Hossegor
France
T. C. Simpson
Golf Club du Touquet (r. Sea and Forest courses)
France
P. M. Ross
Golf Club of Indiana
Indiana
C. E. Maddox
Golf Club Son Vida (Majorca)
Spain
F. W. Hawtree
Golf Club Wien
Austria
(M. C. Noskowski)
Golf Course Padova
Italy
J. D. Harris
Golfcrest CC
Texas
R. Plummer
Golfcrest CC (new site)
Texas
J. Finger
Golf Cursa Ceann Seibeal
Ireland
E. Hackett
Golf D'Atimaona CC
Tahiti
R. E. Baldock
Golf de Bercuit
Belgium
R. T. Jones
Golf de Biarritz
France
T. Dunn, "Young" W. Dunn

Golf de Biarritz (r.)
France
H. S. Colt
Golf de Bondues (a. 3d 9)
FrancE
R. T. Jones
Golf de Bondues
France
F. W. Hawtree
Golf de Chantilly (27)
France
T. C. Simpson
Golf de Chiberta
France
T. C. Simpson
Golf de Cornauaille (9) (formerly Golf de Quimper)
France
F. W. Hawtree
Golf de Dieppe
France
T. C. Simpson
Golf de Domont
France
F. W. Hawtree
Golf de Fontainebleau
France
T. C. Simpson
Golf de Fontainebleau (r.)
France
F. W. Hawtree
Golf de International Club du Lys (27)
France
T. C. Simpson
Golf de La Baule (r.)
France
P. Allis
Golf de L'Esperance (Golf de la Martinique)
Martinique
R. T. Jones
Golf de Lyon (27)
France
F. W. Hawtree
Golf de Metz
France
F. W. Hawtree
Golf de Morfontaine (27)
France
T. C. Simpson
Golf de Pals
Spain
F. W. Hawtree
Golf de Prieure (East and West courses)
France
F. W. Hawtree
Golf de Quimper [now Golf de Cornauaille](9)
France
F. W. Hawtree
Golf de Rochefort
France
F. W. Hawtree
Golf de St. Nom La Breteche (Red and Blue courses)
France
F. W. Hawtree
Golf de Saint Samson (9)
France
F. W. Hawtree
Golf de Seraincourt
France
F. W. Hawtree
Golf de Toulouse (a.9)
France
F. W. Hawtree

257

Golf de Valcros
France
F. W. Hawtree

Golf de Vaudreuil
France
F. W. Hawtree

Golf de Voisins
France
T. C. Simpson

Golf du Park Carleton
Province of Québec, Canada
W. F. Mitchell

Golf du Racing Club "La Boulie"
France
S. Dunn

Golf du Racing Club "La Boulie"
France
W. Reid

Golf du Racing Club "La Boulie"
France
W. Park, Jr.

Golf Hammock CC
Florida
R. Garl

Golf Hill G&CC
New York
F. Duane

Golf Internationale de St. Francoise
Guadeloupe
R. T. Jones

Golfland (Hamilton)
Ontario, Canada
C. E. Robinson

Golfland Par 3 GC
Georgia
C. H. Adams

Golfmohr GC at East Moline
Illinois
E. G. Lockie

Golf Rancho Par 3 GC
California
H. M. and D. A. Rainville

Golf Rio Real
Spain
J. Arana

Golf '72 (90) (Karuizawa GC)
Japan
R. T. Jones, Sr. and Jr.

Golf Und Land Club
West Germany
B. Von Limburger, K. Hoffmann

Golf Und Landclub Ostwestfallen-Lippe
West Germany
B. Von Limburger

Golf Village Exec. GC
Wisconsin
H. D. Fieldhouse

Goodland GC (r.)
Kansas
H D. Fieldhouse

Goodwin Park GC (r.)
Connecticut
E. Pyle

Goodyear G&CC (Wigwam Inn; Gold and Blue courses)
Arizona
R. T. Jones

Goodyear G&CC (West course)
Arizona
R. F. Lawrence, J. Hardin, G. Nash

Goose Creek CC
Virginia
W. F. Gordon

Goose Pond Colony GC
Alabama
G. W. Cobb

Gordon Lakes GC
Georgia
R. T. Jones, R. L. Jones

Gordon Trent GC
Virginia
A. Jamison

Gormley Green GC (27)
Ontario, Canada
R. and C. Muylaert

Gort GC (r.)
Ireland
E. Hackett

Goshen Plantation CC
Georgia
E. Maples

Goswick GC
Great Britain
W. Park, Jr.

Gourock GC
Scotland
H. Cotton

Gowan Brae GC
New Brunswick, Canada
C. E. Robinson

Gowanda CC
New York
A.R. Tryon

Graham F. Vanderbilt (Mrs.) Course at Manhasset
New York
A. H. Tull

Gramont (Duc de) Estate GC
France
T. C. Simpson

Granada Farms CC
North Carolina
T. Jackson

Granbury CC
Texas
L. Howard

Granada G&CC
Granada, West Indies
(Ewart Hughes)

Granby-St. Paul, Club de Golf (r.18,a.18)Province of Québec, Canada
H. and J. Watson

Grand Bahama Hotel & CC (27)
Bahamas
M. Mahannah

Grand Beach GC
Manitoba, Canada
N. Woods

Grand Blanc GC
Michigan
W. B. and G. H. Matthews

Grande Prairie GC
Michigan
W. J. Spear

Grandfather G&CC
North Carolina
E. Maples

Grand Forks CC (New site)
North Dakota
R. B. Harris

Grand Forks CC [now Riverbend CC](r.)
North Dakota
R. B. Harris

Grand Haven GC
Michigan
W. B. and G. H. Matthews

Grand Hotel (Lakewood course)
Alabama
P. D. Maxwell

Grand Hotel (a. Magnolia 9)
Alabama
J. L. Lee

Grand Island Muni
Nebraska
F. Hummel

Grand Lake GC
Colorado
R. N. Phelps, B. Benz

Grand Marais GC [formerly Park District GC]
Illinois
J.A. Roseman

Grandmere GC (r.)
Province of Québec, Canada
H. Watson

Grand Oak CC
Michigan
A. Hills

Grand Pabor, Club de Golf (r.9,a.9)
Province of Québec, Canada
H. Watson

Grand Prairie Muni (27)
Texas
R. Plummer

Grand Rapids CC (Original course)
Michigan
W. Park, Jr.

Grand Rapids CC
Michigan
J. L. Daray

Grand Teton Lodge GC (r.)
Wyoming
R. T. Jones, Jr.

Grand Traverse GC
Michigan
W. K. Newcomb

Grand View CC
Wisconsin
E. G. Lockie

Grandview GC
Pennsylvania
J. G. Harrison

Grandview Muni
Missouri
P. D. Maxwell

Grand Vue Park Par 3 GC
West Virginia
X. G. Hassenplug

Grange Conventry (r. 6)
England
T. McAuley

Grangemouth Muni
Scotland
F. W. Hawtree

Grange-Over-Sands GC
England
A. Mackenzie

Granite City CC
Illinois
E. L. Packard

Grantown-On-Spey
Scotland
W. Park, Jr.

Grant Park Muni
Wisconsin
G. Hansen

Grant's Pass GC (r.4,a.14)
Oregon
R. E. Baldock

Grantwood CC
Ohio
H. D. Paddock Sr.

Granville GC
Ohio
D. J. Ross

Grapevine Muni
Texas
J. Finger

Grasmere Par 3 at Falmouth
Massachusetts
G. S. Cornish, W. G. Robinson

Grassy Brook GC
New York
G. S. Cornish, W. G. Robinson

Gravesend GC
England
W. Park, Jr.

Graysburg Hills GC
Tennessee
R. L. Jones

Grayson Valley CC
Alabama
J. H. Williams, Sr.

Great Bend Petroleum Club (9)
Kansas
F. Hummel

Great Bend Pet. Club (a.2nd 9)
Kansas
R. Watson

Great Cove GC
Pennsylvania
E. B. Ault

Great Harbor Cay GC
Bahamas
J. L. Lee

Great Hay GC
England
J. D. Harris

Great Hills CC
Connecticut
A. Zikorus

Great Hills CC
Texas
D. January, B. Martindale

Great Lakes N.T.C. GC
Illinois
C. D. Wagstaff

Great Lakes GC (a.9)
Illinois
K. Killian, R. Nugent

Great Neck Par 3 GC
Massachusetts
S. Mitchell

Great Oaks CC
Michigan
W. K. Newcomb

Great Smokies GC (Hilton Inn & CC)
North Carolina
W. B. Lewis, Jr.

Great Southwest GC
Texas
R. Plummer (Bryon Nelson)

Greeley CC
Colorado
J. P. Maxwell

Green Acres CC
Illinois
G. O'neil

Green Acres CC (r.)
Illinois
J. A. Roseman, Sr.

Green Acres CC
Indiana
R. A. Simmons

Green Acres CC
New Jersey
D. Emmet, A. H. Tull

Green Acres CC (r.)
New Jersey
W. F. and D. W. Gordon

Green Acres GC
Georgia
A. L. Davis

Greenbriar CC
Kentucky
W. K. Newcomb

Greenbriar Hills CC [formerly Osage Hills]
Missouri
C. D. Wagstaff

Greenbriar Hills CC (r.)
Missouri
D. R. Sechrest

Greenbrier GC (27)
Virginia
G. W. Cobb

(The) Greenbrier (Old White)
West Virginia
C. B. Macdonald, S. J. Raynor

(The) Greenbrier (Greenbrier course)
West Virginia
G. O'Neill

(The) Greenbrier (Lakeside course)
West Virginia
L. S. "Dick" Wilson

(The) Greenbrier (r. Greenbrier course)
West Virginia
J. Nicklaus

Green Brook CC
New Jersey
R. White

Green Brook CC (r.)
New Jersey
R. T. Jones

Green County GC
Pennsylvania
E. F. Loeffler, J. McGlynn

Greendale Muni
Virginia
L. Howard

Greene Hills CC (9)
Missouri
F. Farley

Greenfield CC
Indiana
G. Kern

Greenfield CC
Massachusetts
R. M. Barton

Greenfield Muni
Wisconsin
G. Hansen

Greenfield Ramada Camp Inn CC
Indiana
G. Kern

Green Gables GC, Anne of
Prince Edward Island, Canada
S. Thompson

Green Gables GC, Anne of (r.18,a.9)
Prince Edward Island, Canada
C. E. Robinson

Green Harbor CC
Massachusetts
M. L. Francis

Green Haven GC (r.)
Minnesota
D. Gill

Green Hill Muni
Delaware
W. Reid

Green Hill Muni (r.)
Delaware
A. H. Tull

Green Hill Muni (r.)
Delaware
E. B. Ault

Greenhill Muni (Original course)
Massachusetts
W. Ogg

Greenhill Muni (New course)
Massachusetts
W. F. Mitchell

Green Hills CC
California
A. Mackenzie

Green Hills CC
New York
A. Craig

Green Hills CC
West Virginia
E. B. Ault

258

Greenhills CC (27)
Ontario, Canada
R. and C. Muylaert
Green Hills CC (r.)
California
R. M. Graves
Green Hills G&CC
Indiana
W. Diddel
Green Hills GC
Michigan
W. K. Newcomb
Greenhill Yacht & CC (r.)
Maryland
A. H. Tull
Green Island CC
Georgia
G. W. Cobb
Green Island CC (r.)
Georgia
J. L. Lee
Green Knoll CC
New Jersey
W. F. and D. W. Gordon
Green Lakes State Park GC
New York
R. T. Jones
Green Meadow CC (a. 9)
Montana
R. M. Graves
Green Meadow CC (9)
Montana
(William Teufel)
Green Meadow CC
New York
M.J. McCarthy, Sr.
Green Meadow CC (Original 9)
Tennessee
W. B. Langford
Green Meadow CC (r.9,a.9)
Tennessee
A. G. McKay
Green Meadow CC (r.)
Tennessee
W. C. Byrd
Green Meadows CC
Georgia
W. W. Amick
Green Meadows CC
Texas
B.J. Riviere
Green Meadows Golf & Sports Club
Texas
R. T. Jones, Jr.
Green Meadows GC (36)
New Hampshire
(Phil Friel)
Greenock GC (27)
Scotland
J. Braid
Greenore GC (r.)
Ireland
E. Hackett
Green Park-Norwood GC
North Carolina
S. J. Raynor
Green Pond GC
New Jersey
E. V. Ternyey
Green Ridge CC
Michigan
W.B. Matthews
Green Ridge CC
Michigan
W. B. Matthews
Green River CC (Riverside course)
California
L. M. Hughes
Green Ridge CC (r.)
Michigan
Tom Bendelow

Green River CC
South Carolina
A. Zikorus
Green River CC
Tennessee
R. A. Renaud
Greensboro CC (r. Irvine Park course)
North Carolina
G. W. Cobb
(The) Greens G&RC
Oklahoma
D. Sechrest
Greensboro CC (Carlson Farms Course)
North Carolina
E. Maples
Greenshire GC (9)
Illinois
K. Killian, R. Nugent
Green Spring Valley Hunt Club (r.9,a.9)
Maryland
R. T. Jones
Greentree CC
Indiana
W. Diddel
Greentree G&TC
California
W. F. Bell
Green Valley CC (r.)
Alabama
G. W. Cobb
Green Valley, CC of
Arizona
A. J. Snyder
Green Valley CC
North Carolina
G. W. Cobb
Green Valley CC [formerly Cape Fear
CC](r.)
North Carolina
E. Hamm
Green Valley CC (a.9)
North Carolina
D. and E. Maples
Green Valley CC (Original course)
Pennsylvania
W. Park, Jr.
Green Valley CC [formerly Marble Hall
CC]
Pennsylvania
W. S. Flynn
Green Valley, CC of (Original 9)
Arizona
A.J. Snyder
Green Valley CC
South Carolina
G. W. Cobb
Green Valley, CC of (a.9)
Arizona
L. Howard
Green Valley, CC of (a.9)
Arizona
R. F. Lawrence
Green Valley G&CC (r.)
California
R. M. Graves
Green Valley GC
Tennessee
L. Mills
Green Valley GC (r.)
Province of Québec, Canada
H. Watson
Green Valley Muni
Iowa
D. Gill
Greenview GC
New York
H. Purdy

Greenville CC
Illinois
E. L. Packard
Greenville CC
Kentucky
A. G. McKay
Greenville CC
Mississippi
J. L. Daray
Greenville CC (r.9,a.9)
Pennsylvania
F. Garbin
Greenville CC (Chanticleer course)
South Carolina
R. T. Jones
Greenville CC (r. Riverside course)
South Carolina
G. W. Cobb
Greenville CC (r. Riverside course)
South Carolina
R. Breeden
Greenville CC (a.9)
Texas
R. Plummer
Greenway GC
Colorado
R. N. Phelps
Greenwich CC
Connecticut
S. J. Raynor
Greenwich CC (r.)
Connecticut
D. J. Ross
Greenwich CC (r.)
Connecticut
R. T. Jones
Greenwood CC
South Carolina
G. W. Cobb
Greenwoods CC
Connecticut
A. Zikorus
Grenelefe G&CC [formerly Arrowhead
Lakes CC] (West course)
Florida
D. L. Wallace
Grenelefe G&RC (East course)
Florida
E.B. Seay, A. Palmer
Greylock Glen GC
Massachusetts
G. S. Cornish, W. G. Robinson
Greynold Park
Florida
M. Mahannah
Greystones GC (r.)
Ireland
E. Hackett
Griffin CC
Georgia
W. C. Byrd
Griffin Gate GC
Kentucky
R. L. Jones
Griffith Park GC (Wilson course)
California
T. Bendelow
Griffith Park GC (r. Wilson course, a.
Harding course)
California
G. C. Thomas, Jr.
Griffith Park GC (r. Harding and Wilson
courses; a. Roosevelt 9, Coolidge Par
3 and Los Feliz Par 3 courses)
California
W. H. Johnson
Griffiths Park GC
Ohio
H. D. Paddock, Sr.

Grimsby GC
England
S. V. Hotchkin
Grimsby GC (r.)
England
T. Williamson
Grosse Ile G&CC
Michigan
E. W. Way
Grosse Ile G&CC (r. bunkering)
Michigan
W. Reid
Grosse Isle G&CC (r.)
Michigan
D. J. Ross
Grossingers GC
New York
(Andrew Carl Salerno)
Grossingers GC (r.)
New York
A. W. Tillinghast
Grossingers GC (r.)
New York
W. F. Mitchell
Grossingers GC (r.)
New York
J. Finger
Grouse Moor GC
North Carolina
G. W. Cobb, J. B. LaFoy
Grove City GC
Pennsylvania
T. Bendelow
Grove Park GC
Mississippi
E. D. Guy
Grove Park Inn CC [formerly Asheville
CC]
North Carolina
W. Park, Jr.
Groveport GC
Ohio
J. Kidwell, M. Hurdzan
Grover Keaton Muni
Texas
D. Bennett
Guadalajara CC
Mexico
J. Bredemus
Guadalajara CC (r.)
Mexico
L. M. Hughes
Guadalmina GC (36)
Spain
J. Arana
Guensburg GC
Germany
D. Harradine
Guernsey CC, Royal
Channel Islands
P. M. Ross
Gulf Hills Inn & GC
Mississippi
J. Daray
Gulfport Naval Air Station GC
Mississippi
E. Stone
Gulf Shores GC
Alabama
E. Stone
Gulf State Park GC
Alabama
E. Stone
Gulfstream GC
Florida
D. J. Ross

Gulfstream GC (r.)
Florida
L. S. "Dick" Wilson
Gulfstream GC (r.)
Florida
J. L. Lee
Gulfstream Par 3 GC
Florida
M. Mahannah
Gullane GC
Scotland
W. Park, Jr.
Gull Lakeview GC (West course)
Michigan
(Charles D. Scott)
Gull Lakeview GC (r. West course, a.
East course)
Michigan
(Charles D. Scott)
Gulmarg GC (New course)
India
P. Thomson, M. Wolveridge
Gulph Mills CC
Pennsylvania
D. J. Ross
Gulph Mills CC (r.)
Pennsylvania
P. D. Maxwell
Gulph Mills CC (r.)
Pennsylvania
J. B. McGovern
Gulph Mills CC (r.)
Pennsylvania
R. T. Jones
Gulph Mills CC (r.)
Pennsylvania
W. F. and D. W. Gordon
Guyan G&CC
West Virginia
H. B. Strong
Guyan G&CC (r.3)
West Virginia
X. G. Hassenplug
Guymon CC
Oklahoma
R. C. Dunning

Haagsche CC (Original 9; n.l.e.)
Netherlands
J. D. Dunn
Haagsche CC (n.l.e.)
Netherlands
J. F. Abercromby
Haagsche CC (New site)
Netherlands
H. S. Colt, C. H. Alison, J. S. F. Morrison
Haagsche CC (r. New site)
Netherlands
G. Campbell
Hacienda, Club de Golf
Mexico
P. Clifford
Hacienda CC
California
M. Behr
Hacienda CC (r.)
California
G. Von Elm
Hacienda CC (r.)
California
R. T. Jones, Sr. and Jr.
Hacienda CC (r.)
California
T. G. Robinson

Hacienda Hotel Par 3 GC
California
R. E. Baldock
Hacienda Hotel Par 3 GC (n.l.e.)
Nevada
R. E. Baldock
Hackensack CC
New Jersey
C. H. Banks
Hadley Wood GC
England
A. Mackenzie
Hagerstown CC
Maryland
D. J. Ross
Hagerstown Muni
Maryland
R. Roberts
Haggin Oaks Muni (North course)
California
A. Mackenzie
Haggin Oaks Muni (South course)
California
(Michael J. McDonagh)
Haggs Castle
Scotland
P. Alliss, D.J. Thomas
Hainault Forest
England
F. G. Hawtree, J. H. Taylor
Hainault Forest (a. 18)
England
J. R. Stutt
Halfe Sink GC
Virginia
J. L. Lee
Half Moon Bay GC
California
F. Duane, A. Palmer
Half Moon-Rose Hall GC
Jamaica
R. T. Jones
Halifax CC
Massachusetts
P. A. Wogan
Halifax G&CC (New Ashburn)
Nova Scotia, Canada
G. S. Cornish, W. G. Robinson
Halifax G&CC (Old Ashburn, route plan)
Nova Scotia, Canada
S. Thompson
Halloud Muni (a.9)
Virginia
R. F. Breeden
Hallowes
England
G. Duncan, A. Mitchell
Halls Head Resort GC
Western Australia
P.W. Thomson, M. Wolveridge
Halmstad GC (Original course
Sweden
(Rafael Sandblom)
Halmstad GC
Sweden
J. J. Pennink
Hamburg-Ahrensburg GC (r.)
West Germany
R. T. Jones
Hamburger Land und GC
West Germany
H. S. Colt, J. S. F. Morrison
Hamburg-Falkenstein GC (r.)
West Germany
B. Von Limburger
Hamburg GC
West Germany
B. Von Limburger

Hamilton CC
Ohio
D. J. Ross
Hamilton G&CC
Ontario, Canada
H. S. Colt
Hamilton G&CC (r.)
Ontario, Canada
W. Diddel
Hamilton G&CC (a.9)
Ontario, Canada
C. E. Robinson
Hamilton Lakes CC
North Carolina
W. E. Stiles, J. R. Van Kleek
Hamilton Muni [now Twin Run GC]
Ohio
W. Diddel
Hamilton Park
Scotland
J. Braid, J. R. Stutt
(The) Hamlet of Delray Beach GC
Florida
J. L. Lee
Hammamatsu CC
Japan
P.W. Thomson, M. Wolveridge
Hampden CC
Massachusetts
A. Zikorus
Hampshire CC
New York
D. Emmet, A. H. Tull
Hampshire CC (r.)
New York
E. B. Ault
Hampshire CC (r.)
New York
F. Duane
Hampshire GC
Michigan
E. L. Packard
Hampton GC
New York
F. Duane
Hampton (Rhodes) GC
Virginia
D. J. Ross
Hampton GC (r.)
Virginia
E. B. Ault
Hancock Muni (9) (n.l.e.)
New York
R. T. Jones
H and H Guest Ranch GC
Texas
J. Finger
Handsworth GC (r.)
England
H. S. Colt
Hangman Valley Muni
Washington
R. E. Baldock
Hankley Common GC (r.9,a.9)
England
J. Braid
Hannover GC
West Germany
B. Von Limburger, K. Hoffmann
Hanover CC (Dartmouth College; a.9)
New Hampshire
R. M. Barton
Hanover CC (r.)
New Hampshire
G. S. Cornish, W. G. Robinson
Happy Acres CC
New York
J. G. Harrison

Happy Hollow Club
Nebraska
W. B. Langford, T. J. Moreau
Happy Hollow Club (r.)
Nebraska
D. Gill
Happy Hollow Club (r.)
Nebraska
(Jim Holmes)
Happy Hunting CC (9)
Kansas
R. C. Dunning
Harbor City Muni
Florida
R. A. Anderson
Harbor City Muni (r.)
Florida
W. W. Amick
Harbor Hills CC
New York
A. H. Tull
Harborne GC (r.)
England
H. S. Colt
Harbor Park GC (9)
California
W. H. Johnson
Harbor Point GC (r.; a.3)
Michigan
D. Gill
Harbour Town Golf Links
South Carolina
P. Dye, J. Nicklaus
Harbour Trees GC
Indiana
P. Dye
Hardelot, GC d'
France
T. C. Simpson, P. M. Ross
Harder Hall Hotel GC
Florida
L. S. "Dick" Wilson
Hard Estate Park Muni
New York
W. F. Mitchell
Harding Park Muni
California
W. Watson
Harding Park Muni (r.; a.9)
California
J. Fleming
Hardscrabble CC
Arkansas
H. C. Hackbarth
Hardscrabble CC (r.)
Arkansas
M. H. Ferguson
Hardscrabble CC (r.)
Arkansas
(Jim Holmes)
Harewood GC
New Zealand
J.D. Harris, P.W. Thomson, M. Wolveridge
Harker Heights Muni
Texas
L. Howard
Harlem Hills CC
Illinois
H. Collis
Harlingen CC
Texas
L. Howard
Harlingen Muni
Texas
(Dennis Arp)
Har-Lou GC
Michigan
W. Bowen

Harlow GC
Michigan
K. W. Bowen
Harmon CC
New York
A. W. Tillinghast
Harmony Landing CC
Kentucky
H. Purdy
Harold GC
Great Britain
T. Dunn
Harold Lloyd Estate GC
California
A. Mackenzie
Harpenden GC
England
F. G. Hawtree, J. H. Taylor
Harrey Park at Bushey
England
D. M. A. Steel
Harrington G&CC
Washington
R. D. Putnam
Harrisburg CC
Pennsylvania
W. S. Flynn
Harrisburg CC (r.)
Pennsylvania
H. B. Strong
Harrisburg Sportsman CC
Pennsylvania
J. G. Harrison
Harrison GC
British Columbia, Canada
N. Woods
Harrison Heights GC
Nebraska
H. W. Glissmann, (H. C. Glissmann)
Harrison Hills CC
Indiana
W. B. Langford, T. J. Moreau
Harrison Lake CC
Indiana
R.A. Simmons
Harrison Williams Course (3)
New York
D. Emmet, A. H. Tull
Harrogate GC
England
G. Duncan, A. Herd
Harrogate GC (r.)
England
A. Mackenzie
Harrow School GC
England
J. J. F. Pennink, D. M. A. Steel
Harry B. Brownson GC
Connecticut
A. Zikorus
(Sir) Harry Oakes Private GC Ontario,
Canada
S. Thompson
Harsens Island GC
Michigan
W. Reid, W. Connellan
Hartford CC
Connecticut
D. J. Ross
Hartford CC
Connecticut
O. E. Smith
Hartford CC (r.)
Connecticut
D. W. Gordon
Hartford CC (r.)
Connecticut
R. T. Jones

Hartford CC (r.2)
Connecticut
G. S. Cornish, W. G. Robinson
Hartford CC (r.9,a.9)
Wisconsin
K. Killian, R. Nugent
Hartford Estate GC
South Carolina
W. E. Stiles
Hartlepool GC
England
W. Park, Jr.
Hartsbourne Manor GC
England
F. G. Hawtree
Hartwell State Park GC
South Carolina
G.W. Cobb
Hartwellville CC (n.l.e.)
Vermont
W. S. Flynn
Harve des Isles GC
Province of Québec, Canada
H. Watson
Harve Elks Club (r.)
Montana
W. Diddel
Hastings CC (Original 9)
Michigan
J. L. Daray
Hastings CC
Minnesota
P. Coates
Hastings GC (r.)
England
T. Dunn
Hastings GC
England
J. J. F. Pennink
Hastings GC (r.)
New Zealand
P.W. Thomson, M. Wolveridge
Hatchford Brook Muni
England
F. W. Hawtree
Hatherly CC (r.2,a.3)
Massachusetts
S. Mitchell
Hattiesburg CC
Mississippi
J. P. Maxwell
Haulover Beach Hotel Par 3 GC
Florida
M. Mahannah
Havana Biltmore CC
Cuba
D. J. Ross
Havana Biltmore GC (r.)
Cuba
M. Mahannah
Havana CC
Florida
W. W. Amick
Havana, CC of
Cuba
D. J. Ross
Havenhurst GC
Indiana
R. D. Beard
Haverhill CC
Massachusetts
W. E. Stiles, J. R. Van Kleek
Haverhill GC
England
J. J. F. Pennink
Hawaii Kai CC
Hawaii
W. F. Bell

260

Hawaii Kai Exec. GC
Hawaii
R. T. Jones
Hawkhurst G&CC
England
J. J. F. Pennink
Hawk Valley CC
Pennsylvania
W. F. and D. W. Gordon
Hawthorne CC
Maryland
E. B. Ault
Hawthorne Hills CC
Indiana
W. Diddel
Hawthorne Valley G&CC
Ontario, Canada
C. E. Robinson, R. Moote
Hawthorn Ridge GC
Illinois
W. J. Spear
Hayana International GC
Japan
W. G. Wilkinson
Hayling GC (r.)
England
T. C. Simpson
Haystack CC (n.1.e.)
Vermont
D. Muirhead
Hayston
Scotland
J. Braid
Hazelden CC
Indiana
T. Bendelow
Hazeltine National CC
Minnesota
R. T. Jones
Headingley GC
England
W. Park, Jr.
Headingley GC
England
A. Mackenzie
Hearthstone CC
Texas
B. J. Riviere
Heart River Muni
North Dakota
D. Gill
Heather Downs CC
Ohio
W. J. Rockefeller
Heather Farms GC
California
R. E. Baldock
Heathergardens CC (9)
Colorado
R.M. Phelps
Heather Hills CC
Indiana
P. Dye
Heather Hills GC
Florida
R. A. Anderson
Heather Ridge CC
Colorado
R. N. Phelps
Heath GC (r.)
Ireland
E. Hackett
Heaton Park
England
J. H. Taylor

Hecla GC
Manitoba, Canada
J. A. Thompson
Heidelberg GC
Germany
D. Harradine
Heidelburg GC (U. S. Army Base)
West Germany
B. Von Limburger
Height Park CC
Oregon
(Ernest Schneiter)
Hempstead CC (Original 9)
New York
P. W. Lees
Hempstead CC (a.9)
New York
A. W. Tillinghast
Hempstead Park GC
England
T. Dunn
Henbury (r.)
England
F. G. Hawtree
Henderson CC (r.9,a.9)
North Carolina
E. Hamm
Henderson G&CC
Kentucky
W. B. Langford
Henderson G&CC
Nevada
R. E. Baldock
Henderson Lake GC
Alberta, Canada
N. Woods
Hendersonville CC
North Carolina
D. J. Ross
Hendon GC
England
W. Park, Jr.
Hendon GC
England
H. S. Colt
Henley GC
England
J. Braid
Henry F. Dupont Course (r.)
Delaware
A. H. Tull
Henson Creek Exec. GC
Maryland
E. B. Ault
Hercules Powder Club (r. Original course)
Delaware
W. S. Flynn
Hercules CC (27)
Delaware
A. H. Tull
Heretaunga GC
New Zealand
A. Mackenzie
Heritage Hills GC
Oklahoma
D. R. Sechrest
Heritage Hills Par 3 GC
Massachusetts
G. S. Cornish, W. G. Robinson
Heritage of Westchester (27)
New York
G. S. Cornish, W. G. Robinson
Heritage Ridge GC
Florida
C. Ankrom

Heritage Village at Southbury (Original 18)
Connecticut
A. Zikorus
Heritage Village at Southbury (a.9)
Connecticut
T. Manning
Heritage Woods CC [now Farmington Woods CC]
Connecticut
D. Muirhead
Hermann Park Muni
Texas
J. Bredemus
Hermann Park Muni (r.)
Texas
R. Plummer
Hermitage (r.)
Ireland
E. Hackett
Hermitage CC
Virginia
A. W. Tillinghast
Hermitage CC (r.)
Virginia
D. J. Ross
Hermitage CC (r.)
Virginia
D. W. Gordon
Hermitage CC (r.)
Virginia
E. B. Ault
Hermitage Woods GC
Tennessee
(James King)
Hermosilla, Club de Golf
Mexico
J. Bredemus
Herndon Centennial Muni
Virginia
E. B. Ault
Hershey CC (West course)
Pennsylvania
M. J. McCarthy, Sr.
Hershey Hotel GC (9)
Pennsylvania
M. J. McCarthy, Sr.
Hershey CC (East course)
Pennsylvania
G. Fazio
Hershey Poconos
Pennsylvania
G. S. Cornish, W. G. Robinson
Hershey's Mill CC
Pennsylvania
D. W. Gordon
Hesperia G&CC
California
W. F. Bell
Hessle GC
England
P. Alliss, D.C. Thomas
Hesston Muni
Kansas
F. Hummel
Hexham GC (r.)
England
C. K. Cotton, J. J. F. Pennink
Heysham GC
England
A. Herd
Heysham GC (r.)
England
F. G. Hawtree

Hiawatha CC (r.)
New York
W. F. Mitchell
Hiawatha GC (9)
Ohio
J. Kidwell
Hickleton GC
England
(Huggett, Coles, Dyer)
Hickman AFB GC
Hawaii
R. E. Baldock
Hickman Par 3 at Wayne
New Jersey
H. Purdy
Hickory Falls GC (a.9)
Michigan
W. K. Newcomb
Hickory Flat GC
Ohio
J. Kidwell
Hickory Grove CC
Wisconsin
W. J. Spear
Hickory Hill CC
Mississippi
E. Stone
Hickory Hill GC
Massachusetts
M. L. Francis
Hickory Hills CC
Illinois
J. Foulis
Hickory Hills CC (a. Par 3 course)
Illinois
W. B. Langford
Hickory Hills CC (a. Exec. course)
Illinois
C. D. Wagstaff
Hickory Hills CC (a.9)
Michigan
M. DeVries
Hickory Hills CC (r.)
Missouri
R. C. Dunning
Hickory Hills CC (r.)
Missouri
E. B. Ault
Hickory Hills CC
Ohio
J. Kidwell, M. Hurdzan
Hickory Knob State Park GC
South Carolina
T. Jackson
Hickory Point GC
Illinois
E. L. Packard
Hickory Ridge CC
Massachusetts
G. S. Cornish, W. G. Robinson
Hidden Hills CC
Florida
D. W. Gordon
Hidden Hills CC
Georgia
J. L. Lee
Hidden Lake GC (9)
Missouri
R. Von Hagge
Hidden Lakes CC [formerly Riverview CC]
Kansas
F. Farley

Hidden Valley Club
Michigan
W. Diddel
Hidden Valley CC
Nevada
W. F. Bell
Hidden Valley CC
Ohio
J. G. Harrison, F. Garbin
Hidden Valley CC (Reading)
Pennsylvania
J.G. Harrison
Hidden Valley CC (Pittsburgh)
Pennsylvania
E. B. Ault
Hidden Valley CC (Pittsburgh; r.)
Pennsylvania
J. L. Lee
Hidden Valley CC (n.l.e.)
Utah
W. P. Bell
Hidden Valley CC (New site, 27)
Utah
W. F. Bell
Hidden Valley CC (a.9)
Utah
W. H. Neff
Hidden Valley Exec. GC
Ontario, Canada
C. E. Robinson
Hidden Valley GC (9)
Indiana
J. Kidwell, M. Hurdzan
Hidden Valley GC (Pottstown)
Pennsylvania
J. G. Harrison, F. Garbin
Hidden Valley Lake GC
California
W. F. Bell
Hidden Valley Par 3 GC at Boca Raton
Florida
G. A. Pattison, Jr.
Hideaway-in-the-Pines GC
Texas
L. Howard
Higashi Ibaragi GC
Japan
A. Hills
Higashi Matsuyama GC
Japan
K. Fujita
Higby Hills CC
New York
G. S. Cornish, W. G. Robinson
High Elms GC
England
F. W. Hawtree
Highgate GC (r.)
England
C. S. Butchart
High Hampton GC
North Carolina
G. W. Cobb
Highland CC (9)
Georgia
D. J. Ross
Highland CC (9)
Georgia
J. Finger
Highland CC
Kentucky
W. Diddel
Highland CC
Michigan
J. L. Daray

Highland CC
Michigan
D. J. Ross

Highland CC
Nebraska
W. B. Langford, T. J. Moreau

Highland CC (r.)
Nebraska
D. Gill

Highland CC
North Carolina
D. J. Ross

Highland CC (r.)
North Carolina
W. C. Byrd

Highland CC
Pennsylvania
E. F. Loeffler, J. McGlynn

Highland CC (r.)
Pennsylvania
J. G. Harrison

Highland CC (r.)
Pennsylvania
E. B. Ault

Highland CC (r.)
Pennsylvania
F. Garbin

Highland G&CC [now Coffin Muni]
Indiana
W. Park, Jr.

Highland G&CC (New site)
Indiana
W. Diddel

Highland GC
Washington
T. G. Robinson

Highland GC
Ontario, Canada
S. Thompson

Highland Greens Par 3 GC
Connecticut
A. Zikorus

Highland Hills CC
Colorado
H. B. Hughes

Highland Hills GC
Michigan
W. B. and G. H. Matthews

Highland Hills Muni (a. 2nd 9)
Colorado
F. Hummel

Highland Lake GC
Indiana
R. A. Simmons

Highland Lakes GC (18 par 3)
Florida
L. Clifton

Highland Lakes GC
Texas
L. Howard

Highland Meadows CC
Ohio
G. S. Alves

Highland Meadows GC (r.)
Ohio
A. Hills

Highland Park CC (a.9)
New York
G. S. Cornish, W. G. Robinson

Highland Park GC
Florida
W. E. Stiles, J. R. Van Kleek

Highland Park GC (a.9)
Iowa
D. Gill

Highland Park GC (36)
Ohio
G. S. Alves

Highlands GC (Cape Breton Highlands, Keltic Lodge)
Nova Scotia, Canada
S. Thompson

Highland Spring CC
Illinois
W. J. Spear

Highland Springs CC
West Virginia
J. G. Harrison

Highland Woods GC
Illinois
W. J. Spear

High Meadows GC (r.)
North Carolina
G. W. Cobb

High Mountain CC
New Jersey
E. V. Ternyey

High Point Par 3 GC at Naples
Florida
D. L. Wallace

High Post
England
F. G. Hawtree

High Ridge GC (r.)
Connecticut
W. F. Mitchell, A. Zikorus

High Ridge GC
Florida
J. L. Lee

Highshore Hills CC
North Carolina
T. Jackson

High Vista GC
North Carolina
T. Jackson

Highwood GC
England
F. G. Hawtree, J. H. Taylor

Hilands GC
Montana
N. Woods

Hillandale GC at Huntington
New York
H. Purdy

Hill and Dale CC (r.)
North Carolina
G. W. Cobb

Hill Barn GC (Worthing Corporation)
England
F. G. Hawtree

Hillcrest CC
California
W. Watson

Hillcrest CC (a. Par 3 course)
California
W. P. Bell

Hilcrest CC (r.)
California
R. M. Graves

Hillcrest CC (r.9)
Colorado
H. B. Hughes

Hillcrest CC
Florida
R. Von Hagge

Hillcrest CC
Idaho
A. V. Macan

Hillcrest CC (r.)
Idaho
R. M. Graves

Hillcrest CC
Illinois
R. B. Harris

Hillcrest CC (r. 3, 1981)
Indiana
J. Kidwell,
M. Hurdzan

Hillcrest CC (r. 3, 1981)
Indiana
J. Kidwell, M. Hurdzan

Hillcrest CC
Missouri
D. J. Ross

Hillcrest CC (r.)
Missouri
M. H. Ferguson

Hillcrest CC
Nebraska
W. H. Tucker, Sr.

Hillcrest CC (Bartlesville; r.9)
Oklahoma
F. Farley

Hillcrest CC (Original 9)
Pennsylvania
E. F. Loeffler, J. McGlynn

Hillcrest CC (a.9)
Pennsylvania
J. G. Harrison

Hillcrest CC
Texas
R. Plummer

Hillcrest East Exec. GC
Florida
M. Mahannah

Hillcrest G&CC (Oklahoma City)
Oklahoma
F. Farley

Hillcrest G&CC (a. 2nd 9)
South Dakota
H. D. Fieldhouse

Hillcrest Muni (9)
Kansas
E. L. Bell

Hillcrest Par 3 GC (Washington)
Illinois
A. Linkogel

Hilldale GC
Illinois
R. T. Jones

Hillendale CC (New site)
Maryland
W. F. Gordon

Hillendale CC (r.)
Maryland
E. B. Ault

Hillmoor CC
Wisconsin
J. Foulis

Hillsborough GC
England
T. Williamson

Hillsdale G&CC
Province of Québec, Canada
H. Watson

Hillsdale CC (r.)
Province of Québec, Canada
H. and J. Watson

Hillside GC (r.9,a.9)
England
F. W. Hawtree

Hills of Lakeway (Lakeway Inn)
Texas
J. Nicklaus

Hilltop Farms GC [now Shady Hills GC]
Indiana
W. Diddel

Hilltop Lakes GC (Original 9)
Texas
R. Plummer

Hilltop Lakes GC (a.9)
Texas
L. Howard

Hilltop Muni
England
F. W. Hawtree

Hill Valley
England
P. Alliss, D. Thomas

Hillview CC
Indiana
R. A. Simmons

Hillwood CC (Original 9)
Tennessee
(Bubber Johnson)

Hillwood CC (r.)
Tennessee
R. A. Renaud

Hilly Dale at Carmel
New York
O. E. Smith

Hilo Muni
Hawaii
W. G. Wilkinson

Hilton G&RC [formerly Panama City Beach CC]
Florida
W. W. Amick

Hilton Head Plantation (Shipyard GC)
South Carolina
G. W. Cobb

Hilton Head Plantation (Dolphin Head GC)
South Carolina
R. Kirby, G. Player, A. Davis

Hilton Head Plantation (Bear Creek and Oyster Reef GC's)
South Carolina
R. L. Jones

Hilton Head Plantation (Long Cove Club)
South Carolina
P. Dye

Hilton Park GC (Allender course)
Scotland
J. Braid, J. R. Stutt.

Hilton Park GC (Hilton course)
Scotland
F. G. Hawtree

Hinckley Hills GC
Ohio
H. D. Paddock, Sr.

Hindman Park GC
Arkansas
L. Howard

Hinksen Marsh
England
T. Dunn

Hinsdale CC
Illinois
J. Foulis

Hirona CC
Japan
C. H. Alison

Hiroshima Athletic CC
Japan
E. B. Seay, A. Palmer

Hirsch Creek CC
British Columbia, Canada
N. Woods

Hiwan GC
Colorado
J. P. Maxwell

H. M. S. Dryad GC
Great Britain
J. J. F. Pennink

Hobart CC (9)
Oklahoma
R. C. Dunning

Hobbit's Glen GC
Maryland
E. B. Ault

Hobble Creek GC
Utah
W. F. Bell

Hobbs CC (r.9,a.9)
New Mexico
W. D. Cantrell

Hobe Sound CC
Florida
E. E. Smith

Hob Nob Hill GC (n.l.e.)
Connecticut
D. Emmet, A. H. Tull

Hodge Park Muni
Missouri
(Larry Runyon, Mike Malyn)

Hodogaya CC
Japan
Akaboshi Brothers

Hogan Park (a.9)
Texas
R. Kirby, G. Player

Hog Back Mountain Club (n.l.e.)
North Carolina
D. Emmet, A. H. Tull

Hog Neck GC (27)
Maryland
L. B. Ervin

Holden GC (r.)
Massachusetts
W. F. Mitchell

Hole-in-the-Wall GC
Florida
L. S. "Dick" Wilson

Holiday Exec. CC at Ft. Pierce
Florida
A. M. Young

Holiday Exec. CC at Lake Park
Florida
A. M. Young

Holiday Exec. CC at Stuart
Florida
A. M. Young

Holiday Hills CC
Missouri
R. C. Dunning

Holiday Inn CC
Illinois
A. Davis, R. Kirby

Holiday Inn - Holiday Lakes CC (36)
Florida
W. R. Watts

Holiday Island GC
Arkansas
(John Allen)

Holiday Springs CC
Florida
R. Von Hagge, B. Devlin

Holland Lake GC
Michigan
W. Bowen

Hollingbury Park (Brighton Corp.)
England
F. G. Hawtree

Hollinwell
England
W. Park, Jr.

Hollinwell (r.)
England
T. Williamson

Hollow Acres GC
Indiana
R. A. Anderson

Hollow Brook CC
New York
T. Winton
Hollybrook G&CC
Florida
W. F. Mitchell
Holly Forest GC
North Carolina
R. Garl
Holly Greens GC (27)
Michigan
R. B. Harris
Holly Hill CC
Maryland
R. Roberts
Holly Hill G&CC
Florida
W. E. Stiles, J. R. Van Kleek
Holly Hills CC
Alabama
E. Stone
Holly Hills CC
Tennessee
M. H. Ferguson
Hollylake Ranch GC
Texas
L. Howard
Holly Ridge Par 3 GC
Massachusetts
G. S. Cornish, W. G. Robinson
Holly Tree CC
South Carolina
G. W. Cobb, J. B. LaFoy
Hollywood Beach Hotel GC
Florida
H. C. C. Tippetts
Hollywood Beach Hotel GC (r.)
Florida
M. Mahannah
Hollywood GC
New Jersey
W. J. Travis
Hollywood GC (r.)
New Jersey
L. S. "Dick" Wilson
Hollywood Lakes GC (East and West courses)
Florida
W. R. Watts
Hollywood Par 3 GC
Florida
W. W. Amick
Holmes Park Muni
Nebraska
F. Farley
Holston Hills CC
Tennessee
D. J. Ross
Holston Hills CC (r.)
Tennessee
A. G. McKay
Holston Hills CC (a.9)
Virginia
E. B. Ault
Holyhead
Wales
J. Braid
Holywell Park GC
Wales
F. G. Hawtree
Homelawn Mineral Springs GC (a.9)
Indiana
W. Diddel
Home Park GC
England
J. Braid

(The) Homestead (Virginia Hot Springs G&TC; Cascades course)
Virginia
W. S. Flynn
(The) Homestead (r. Cascades course)
Virginia
R. T. Jones
(The) Homestead (Lower Cascades course)
Virginia
R. T. Jones
Homestead AFB GC
Florida
M. Mahannah
Homestead CC (n.l.e.)
Kansas
J. Dalgleish
Homestead CC
New Jersey
D. J. Ross
Homestead GC
Ohio
W. W. Amick
Homestead Mine GC [now Tomahawk Lake CC](9)
South Dakota
L. M. Hughes
Homewood CC [now Flossmoor GC]
Illinois
H. J. Tweedie
Hominy Hill GC
New Jersey
R. T. Jones
Homosassa CC
Florida
H. Collis
Honey Hill CC
Florida
M. Mahannah
Honey Hill CC
New York
G. S. Cornish, W. G. Robinson
Honey Run GC
Pennsylvania
E. B. Ault
Honeywell Muni (a.9)
Indiana
A. Hills
Hong Kong, Royal (Old course)
Hong Kong
(Capt. H. N. Dumbleton, R.E.)
Hong Kong, Royal (New course)
Hong Kong
(L. S. Greenhill)
Hong Kong, Royal (Eden course)
Hong Kong
J. D. Harris, M. Wolveridge
Honolulu International CC
Hawaii
F. Duane, A Palmer
Hoodkroft CC at Derry
New Hampshire
P. A. Wogan
Hook and Slice Par 3 GC
Oklahoma
F. Farley
Hooper GC
New Hampshire
W. E. Stiles, J. R. Van Kleek
Hoosie Whisick GC [now Milton Hoosic GC]
Massachusetts
W. Park, Jr.
(The) Hoosier Links
Indiana
C. E. Maddox

Hope Valley CC
North Carolina
D. J. Ross
Hope Valley CC (r.)
North Carolina
P. D. Maxwell
Hopewell CC
Virginia
F. A. Findlay
Hopewell Valley GC
New Jersey
T. Winton
Hopewood GC
England
H. S. Colt
Hopkinsville G&CC
Kentucky
J. R. Darrah
Hop Meadow CC
Connecticut
G. S. Cornish
Horizon CC (9)
New Mexico
R. F. Lawrence
Hornby Tower GC
Ontario, Canada
R. Moote
Horseshoe Bay CC (Original 18)
Texas
R. T. Jones
Horseshoe Bay CC (a.18)
Texas
R. T. Jones, Jr.
Horseshoe Bend CC
Georgia
J. L. Lee
Horseshoe Valley GC
Ontario, Canada
R. and C. Muylaert
Horse Thief G&CC
California
R. E. Baldock
Hospitality Muni
Arizona
A. J. Snyder
Hossegor, CC d'
France
T. C. Simpson
Host Farms Exec. 9
Pennsylvania
G. S. Cornish, W. G. Robinson
Hotchkiss School GC (9)
Connecticut
S. J. Raynor
Hotchkiss School GC (r.)
Connecticut
C. H. Banks
Hotel Champlain GC
New York
G. Low
Hotel Frascati Par 3 GC (n.l.e.)
Bermuda
D. Emmet
Hotel Green CC (n.l.e.)
California
W. Watson
Hotel Hershey GC
Pennsylvania
M. J. McCarthy, Sr.
Hotel Indiatlantic GC (n.l.e.)
Florida
E. W. Way
Hotel Intercontinental Rose Hall
Jamaica
(H. Smedley)

Hot Springs G&CC (Original course, n.l.e.)
Arkansas
W. Park, Jr.
Hot Springs G&CC (r. #1, a. #3)
Arkansas
W. Diddel
Hot Springs G&CC (#2)
Arkansas
(Bert Meade)
Hot Springs Village GC (DeSoto and Cortez courses)
Arkansas
E. B. Ault
Houghton Road GC
Arizona
R. T. Jones, Jr.
Hound's Ear CC
North Carolina
G. W. Cobb
Houndslake CC
South Carolina
J. L. Lee
Hounslow Heath
England
F. Middleton
Houston CC (r.) [now Houston GC]
Texas
R. Plummer
Houston CC (New site)
Texas
R. T. Jones
Houston CC (r.)
Texas
B.J. Riviere
Houston Lake CC
Georgia
(O. C. Jones)
Houston Levee GC
Tennessee
G. Curtis
Houth Castle GC
Ireland
F. W. Hawtree
Hoveringham GC (Yorkshire)
England
(E. and M. Baker, Ltd.)
Hoveringham GC (Worcester)
England
J. J. F. Pennink
Howell Park GC
New Jersey
F. Duane
Howell Station CC
Georgia
W. C. Byrd
Howth GC
Ireland
J. Braid, J. R. Stutt
Hoylake (Royal Liverpool; Original 9)
England
(R. Chambers, G. Morris)
Hoylake (Royal Liverpool) (r. 9, a. 9)
England
J. Braid
Hoylake (Royal Liverpool; r.)
England
H. S. Colt
Hoylake (r.)
England
J. F. Pennink
H. P. Whitney Estate GC
New York
C. B. Macdonald, S. J. Raynor

Hubbard Heights GC
Connecticut
M. J. McCarthy, Sr.
Hubbard Trail CC
Illinois
R. B. Harris
Huddersfield GC
England
W. H. Fowler
Hudson CC (Original 9)
Wisconsin
(Leo J. Feser)
Hudson CC (r.9,a.9)
Wisconsin
D. Herfort
Hudson, CC of
Ohio
H. D. Paddock Sr.
Hudson Golf & Curling Club
Province of Québec, Canada
H. Watson
Hudson River CC (r.; n.l.e.)
New York
D. J. Ross
Hueston Woods State Park GC
Ohio
J. Kidwell
Huguenot Manor GC
New York
H. Purdy
Hull GC
England
F. G. Hawtree
Hulman Links
Indiana
D. Gill
Humberstone Muni
England
F. W. and M. Hawtree
Humber Valley GC
Ontario, Canada
S. Thompson
Humble CC
Texas
R. Plummer
Humewood CC
South Africa
S. V. Hotchkin
Hunsley Hills CC (27)
Texas
H. B. Hughes
Hunstanton GC
England
G. Fernie
Hunstanton GC (r.)
England
J. Braid
Huntercombe GC
England
W. Park, Jr.
Hunters Run GC (North, South and East courses)
Florida
R. Von Hagge, B. Devlin
Hunting Creek CC
Kentucky
B. J. Wihry
Huntingdale GC
Australia
C. H. Alison
Huntingdon Valley CC [later Braederwood GC] (r.; n.l.e.)
Pennsylvania
H. S. Colt
Huntingdon Valley CC (New site)
Pennsylvania
W. S. Flynn

Hunting Hills CC
Virginia
R. F. Loving

Hunting Hills CC
Virginia
F. Findlay, C.R.F. Loving Sr.

Huntington Bay Club
New York
H. B. Strong

Huntington CC
New York
D. Emmet

Huntington CC (r.1)
New York
W. F. Mitchell

Huntington Crescent GC (Original 18)
New York
D. Emmet, A. H. Tull

Huntington Crescent (a.18; n.l.e.)
New York
D. Emmet, A. H. Tull

Huntington Elks CC
West Virginia
X. G. Hassenplug

Huntington G&CC (r.)
Ontario, Canada
C. E. Robinson, R. Moote

Huntington GC (9)
New York
T. Bendelow

Huntington Hills GC
South Carolina
R. F. Breeden

Huntington Park GC
Louisiana
(Thomas Moore)

Huntington Sea Cliff GC
California
J. P. Maxwell

Hunt Valley CC
Maryland
E. B. Ault

Hunt Valley CC (a. 3rd 9)
Maryland
A. M. Pulley

Hurlburt Field GC
Florida
D. Bennett

Hurlingham
Great Britain
T. Dunn

Huron GC (r.9,a.9)
South Dakota
R. N. Phelps, B. Benz

Hurricane Creek CC
Texas
L. Howard

Hurstbourne CC
Kentucky
C. H. Adams

Hutt GC (r.)
New Zealand
J. D. Harris

HV-JAC Exec. GC
Ohio
J. Kidwell

Hyannis Par 3 (Dunfey's Motel Course)
Massachusetts
G. S. Cornish, W. G. Robinson

Hyannisport Club (r.)
Massachusetts
D. J. Ross

Hyatt Pattaya CC
Thailand
(Ichisuke Izumi)

Hyde Manor GC
Vermont
(Horace Rollins, George Sargent)

Hyde Park CC
Florida
D. J. Ross

Hyde Park CC (r.)
Florida
S. Thompson

Hyde Park CC
Ohio
D. J. Ross

Hyde Park Muni (r. North and Red courses; a. White course)
New York
W. F. and D. W. Gordon

Hyfield CC
Connecticut
O. E. Smith

Hyfield CC (r.9,a.9)
Connecticut
A. Zikorus

Hyland Greens CC
Minnesota
P. Coates

Hyland Hills CC
Colorado
H. B. Hughes

Hyland Hills GC
North Carolina
T. Jackson

Hyperion Field C
Iowa
(Warren Dickinson)

Hythe Imperial GC
England
P. M. Ross

I.B.M. CC at Endicott
New York
W. Stiles

I.B.M. CC at Endicott (r.)
New York
W. F. Mitchell

I.B.M. CC (Port Washington; r.)
New York
R. T. Jones

I.B.M. CC (Poughkeepsie; r.9,a.9)
New York
R. T. Jones

I.B.M. CC (Sands Point; r.)
New York
H. Purdy

I.B.M. CC (Sands Point; r.)
New York
R. T. Jones, F. Duane

I.B.M. Par 3 GC at San Jose
California
J. Fleming

Ibusuki CC (r.)
Japan
P.W. Thomson, M. Wolveridge

Ida Grove G&CC
Iowa
H. W. Glissmann

Idaho Falls CC
Idaho
W. F. Bell

Idle Hour CC (r.)
Georgia
W. C. Byrd

Idle Hour CC [formerly Ashland CC]
Kentucky
D. J. Ross

Idle Hour CC (r.)
Kentucky
R. A. Simmons

Idlewild CC (r.)
Illinois
W. B. Langford, T. J. Moreau

Idylwylde G&CC (r.9,a.9)
Ontario, Canada
H. Watson

Ifield GC
England
F. G. Hawtree

Iga Ueno CC
Japan
E. B. Seay, A. Palmer

I. Kent Fulton Estate GC
Connecticut
D. Emmet

Ile Bourdon GC
Province of Québec, Canada
H. Watson

Illahee Hills CC
Oregon
W. F. Bell

Illini CC (r.)
Illinois
R. B. Harris

Illinois GC
Illinois
G. O'Neill

Illinois GC (r.)
Illinois
R. B. Harris

Illinois GC [now Wilmette GC]
Illinois
J. A. Roseman, Sr.

Illinois State University GC
Illinois
R. B. Harris

Immingham
British Isles
J. J. F. Pennink

Imperialake G&CC (36)
Florida
R. Garl

Imperial CC
Florida
A. Hills

Imperial G&CC [formerly Barbara Worth CC](r.)
California
L. M. Hughes

Imperial GC
California
H. M. and D. A. Rainville

Imperial Sports Club
Iran
F. W. Hawtree

Incline Village GC & Exec. GC
Nevada
R. T. Jones, Sr. and Jr.

Independence CC (r.)
Kansas
E. L. Bell

Independence Green GC
Michigan
W. B. and G. H. Matthews

Indiana CC (Original course)
Pennsylvania
W. Park, Jr.

Indiana CC
Pennsylvania
J. G. Harrison

Indiana CC (r.)
Pennsylvania
E. B. Ault

Indiana, GC of
Indiana
C. E. Maddox

Indianapolis, CC of
Indiana
W. Diddel

Indianapolis, CC of (r.)
Indiana
P. Dye

Indian Bayou G&CC
Florida
E. Stone

Indian Boundary CC
Illinois
C. D. Wagstaff

Indian Boundary Exec. GC
Illinois
E. L. Packard

Indian Canyon GC
Washington
H. C. Egan

Indian Creek CC
Florida
W. S. Flynn

Indian Creek CC (r.)
Florida
L. S. "Dick" Wilson

Indian Creek CC
Texas
R. Plummer

Indian Creek GC [now Kansas City CC]
Kansas
W. B. Langford, T. J. Moreau

Indianfield CC
Michigan
W. K. Newcomb

Indian Head GC (9)
Maryland
E. B. Ault

Indian Hill Club (r.)
Illinois
D. J. Ross

Indian Hill GC (r.)
California
W. P. Bell

Indian Hills CC
Alabama
(T. Nicol), J.H. Williams, Sr.

Indian Hills CC
Connecticut
R. J. Ross

Indian Hills CC
Georgia
J. L. Lee

Indian Hills CC
Kansas
W. B. Langford, T. J. Moreau

Indian Hills CC (r.)
Kansas
A. W. Tillinghast

Indian Hills CC (r.)
Kansas
R. C. Dunning

Indian Hills CC (r.)
Kansas
F. Farley

Indian Hills CC (r.)
Michigan
W. B. and G. H. Matthews

Indian Hills CC
Minnesota
D. Herfort

Indian Hills CC [now Rolling Hills CC]
Oklahoma
P. D. Maxwell

Indian Hills GC
Nebraska
H. W. Glissmann, (H. C. Glissmann)

Indian Hills G&CC [Formerly Fort Pierce CC]
Florida
H. Strong

Indian Hills GC
Alberta, Canada
N. Woods

Indian Hills Par 3 at Pine Bush
New York
A. H. Tull

Indian Island Park GC
New York
W. F. Mitchell

Indian Lake Lodge GC
Pennsylvania
X. G. Hassenplug, A. Palmer

Indian Lakes CC (Sioux Trail and Indian Trail courses)
Illinois
R. B. Harris

Indian Lakes GC (r.9,a.9)
Florida
G. W. Cobb

Indian Meadows CC
Massachusetts
G. S. Cornish

Indian Oaks CC, Phenix City   Phoenix City
Alabama
W. C. Byrd

Indian Oaks CC, Anniston
Alabama
(T. Nicol) H. Williams, Sr.

Indian Pines G&TC
California
C. Glasson

Indian Ridge CC
Massachusetts
G. S. Cornish

Indian River Plantation Exec. GC
Florida
C. F. Ankrom

Indian River Trails CC
Florida
R. Garl

Indian Rocks Exec. GC
Florida
(Walter Pursley)

Indian Run GC
Michigan
W. B. and G. H. Matthews

Indian Spring CC
Florida
R. Von Hagge, B. Devlin

Indian Spring CC (36) (now Silver Springs CC)
Maryland
D. J. Ross

Indian Spring CC (New site; Chief and Valley courses)
Maryland
W. F. and D. W. Gordon

Indian Spring CC
Washington, D.C.
F. Findlay

Indian Spring GC
Illinois
E. L. Packard

Indian Springs CC
Kentucky
A. G. McKay

Indian Springs CC (Original 18)
Oklahoma
G. Fazio

Indian Springs CC (a.18, Gold course)
Oklahoma
D. Sechrest

Indian Springs GC
New Jersey
W. F. and D. W. Gordon

Indian Tree GC (27)
Colorado
R.M. Phelps

Indian Valley CC
North Carolina
E. Maples

Indian Valley CC
Pennsylvania
W. F. and D. W. Gordon
Indian Wells
Ontario, Canada
R. Muylaert
Indian Wells CC
California
H. M. and D. A. Rainville
Indianwood G&CC
Michigan
W. Reid, W. Connellan
Indian Woods CC
Illinois
H. Collis
Indies Inn Par 3 GC
Florida
(C. H. Anderson)
Indigo G&TC (Inn at Indigo; 27)
Florida
L. Clifton
Indio Par 3 Muni
California
L. M. Hughes
Industry Hills GC (Eisenhower and Zaharias courses)
California
W. F. Bell
Ingersoll Muni
Illinois
T. Bendelow
Ingestre
England
F. W. Hawtree
Ingleside Augusta CC
Virginia
F. A. Findlay
Ingleside GC
California
R. Johnstone
Inglewood GC
California
T. G. Robinson
Inglewood Muni (a.9)
Alberta, Canada
W. G. Robinson
Ingol at Preston
England
J. J. F. Pennink, D. M. A. Steel
Inn at Cobbly Nob GC
Tennessee
A. Davis, R. Kirby, G. Player
Inn at Indigo G&TC (27)
Florida
L. Clifton
Inn at Sandisten
Florida
T. Jackson
Innellan GC
Scotland
W. Park, Jr.
Innerleithen GC
Scotland
W. Park, Jr.
Innis Arden GC (r.)
Connecticut
F. Duane
Innis Arden GC (r.)
Connecticut
R. T. Jones
Innisbrook Resort & CC (Island, Sandpiper and Copperhead courses)
Florida
E. L. and R. B. Packard
Innlet Beach GC (now Sawgrass, Oakridge C)
Florida
W. W. Amick

Inn of the Mountain Gods GC
New Mexico
T. G. Robinson
Intercity GC
California
R. E. Baldock
Intercontinental GC
West Germany
B. Von Limburger
Interlachen CC
Minnesota
W. Watson
Interlachen CC (r.)
Minnesota
D. J. Ross
Interlachen CC (r.)
Minnesota
R. T. Jones
Interlaken CC (r.9,a.9)
Minnesota
D. Herfort
International Club
Province of Québec, Canada
S. Thompson
International Club du Lys, Golf de (27)
France
T. C. Simpson
International Club du Lys, Golf de
France
J. H. Stutt
International CC
Massachusetts
G. S. Cornish
International CC (r.)
Massachusetts
R. T. Jones
International G&CC [formerly Crooked Creek G&CC]
Florida
F. Murray
International Park Club [now Jekyll-Hyde GC]
Florida
W. K. Bowen
International Town & CC (r.)
Virginia
E. B. Ault
Inverallochy GC
Scotland
(James Gibb)
Invercargill GC
New Zealand
(A. M. Howden)
Invergordon GC
Scotland
F. M. Middleton
Inverness Club (Original 9)
Ohio
(Bernard Nichols)
Inverness Club (r.9,a.9)
Ohio
D. J. Ross
Inverness Club (r.)
Ohio
A. W. Tillinghast
Inverness Club (r.)
Ohio
L. S. "Dick" Wilson
Inverness Club (r.)
Ohio
A. Hills
Inverness Club (R.; a.4)
Ohio
G. and T. Fazio
Inverness CC
Alabama
G. W. Cobb
Inverness GC (r.)
Illinois
E.L. Packard

Inverness GC
Colorado
J. P. Maxwell
Inverness GC
Scotland
P.W. Thomson, M. Wolveridge
Inverrary G&CC (East, West and Exec. South courses)
Florida
R. T. Jones, R. L. Jones
Inverurie
Scotland
J. H. Stutt
Inwood CC (r.)
New York
H. B. Strong
Inwood CC (r.)
New York
H. Purdy
Inwood CC (r.)
New York
F. Duane
Inwood Forest CC
Texas
D. Collett
Inwood Forest CC (a. 3rd 9)
Texas
B. J. Riviere
Iola Community GC
Wisconsin
E. L. Packard
Iola CC
Kansas
H. Robb, Sr.
Iowa State University GC (Veenker Memorial GC)
Iowa
P. D. Maxwell
Ipswich GC
England
J. Braid
Ipswich GC (r. original course)
England
F. G. and F. W. Hawtree
Ipswich GC (a. Exec. 9)
England
F. W. Hawtree
Iraan GC (r.)
Texas
L. Howard
Irem Temple CC
Pennsylvania
A. W. Tillinghast
Irondequoit CC (Original 9)
New York
D. J. Ross
Irondequoit CC
New York
W.F. Gordon, J.B. McGovern
Irongate CC [now Gates Four G&CC]
North Carolina
W. C. Byrd
Iron Masters CC
Pennsylvania
E. B. Ault
Iron River CC
Michigan
W. B. Langford, T. J. Moreau
Ironshore GC
Jamaica
R. Moote
Ironwood CC
Ohio
H.D. Paddock

Ironwood GC (9)
Arizona
A. J. Snyder
Ironwood GC (South course)
California
D. Muirhead
Ironwood GC (r. South course; a. North course)
California
T. G. Robinson
Ironwood GC
Tennessee
(L. Wesley Flatt)
Ironwood Par 3 at Palm Desert
California
E. B. Seay, A. Palmer
Iroquios GC (a.9)
Kentucky
E. L. Packard
Iroquois GC (a. 9)
Kentucky
B. J. Wihry
Iroquois GC
Kentucky
R. B. Harris
I. Roveri GC
Italy
R. T. Jones
Irvine Coast CC
California
W. P. Bell
Irvine Coast CC (r.)
California
W. F. Bell
Irvine Coast CC (r.)
California
H. M. and D. A. Rainville
Irvine Ravenspark GC
Scotland
(J. Walker)
Irving CC (9)
Texas
J. P. Maxwell
Irvington-on-Hudson (Private course)
New York
C. D. Worthington
Irwin CC (r.)
Pennsylvania
J. G. Harrison
Irwindale Muni
California
R. E. Baldock
Isla Del Sol G&RC
Florida
M. Mahannah
Islamabad GC
Pakistan
J. J. F. Pennink
Island Club of St. Simon's
Georgia
J. L. Lee
Island Dunes GC (Exec. 9)
Florida
J.L. Lee
Island GC at Malahide (r.)
Ireland
E. Hackett
Island Golf Links (9; n.l.e.)
New York
D. Emmet
Island Green CC (27)
South Carolina
(William Mooney)
Island Hill GC (r.)
New York
W. F. Mitchell
Island Valley GC
New York
A. Craig

Island View GC (9; a. Par 3)
Minnesota
W. H. Kidd, Sr.
Islay GC [now Machrie GC]
Scotland
W. Campbell
Islay GC (r.)
Scotland
D. M. Steel
Isle Dauphine CC
Alabama
C. E. Maddox
Isle de Berdes GC
France
W. Reid
Islemere G&CC (a. 9)
Province of Québec, Canada
W. Park, Jr.
Islemere G&CC
Province of Québec, Canada
H. Watson
Isle of Palms GC (Now Wild Dunes GC)
South Carolina
G. and T. Fazio
Isles of Scilly GC (9)
England
H. G. Hutchinson
Islington GC
Ontario, Canada
S. Thompson
Is Molas (Sardinia)
Italy
Pierro Mancinelli
Itanhanga GC
Brazil
S. Thompson
Itanhanga GC (r.)
Brazil
R. T. Jones
Itasca CC (r.)
Illinois
R. B. Harris
Ithaca, CC of (Former course n.l.e.)
New York
A. W. Tillinghast
Ithaca, CC of (Former course r.)
New York
R. T. Jones
Ithaca, CC of (New site)
New York
G. S. Cornish
Ito International GC
Japan
K. Fujita
Ives Groves GC
Wisconsin
D. Gill
Ives Hill CC (Original course)
New York
M. J. McCarthy, Sr.
Ives Hill CC (r. Original course)
New York
P. W. Lees
Ives Hill CC (a.9)
New York
G. S. Cornish, W. G. Robinson
Ivinghoe GC
England
(R. Garrad)
Ivy Hill CC
Virginia
J. P. Gibson
Iwaski Resort GC
Queensland, Australia
P.W. Thomson, M. Wolveridge
Ixtapa-Zihuatanejo Resort GC [now Palma Real GC]
Mexico
R. T. Jones, Jr.

Iyanough Hills GC
Massachusetts
G. S. Cornish, W. G. Robinson

Jablonna GC
Poland
J. J. F. Pennink
Jacaranda CC (36)
Florida
M. Mahannah
Jaracanda West CC
Florida
M. Mahannah
Jack Nicklaus Golf Center (Bruin and Grizzly courses)
Ohio
D. Muirhead, J. Nicklaus
Jackpot GC (9)
Nevada
R.M. Graves
Jackson CC (a.9)
Illinois
D. Gill
Jackson, CC of (27)
Mississippi
L. S. "Dick" Wilson
Jackson Heights CC (r.) (n.l.e.)
New York
A. W. Tillinghast
Jackson Hole G&TC
Wyoming
R. E. Baldock
Jackson Hole G&TC (r.)
Wyoming
R. T. Jones
Jackson Park GC
Illinois
J. A. Roseman
Jacksonville CC (a.9)
Illinois
E. L. Packard
Jacksonville CC
North Carolina
G. W. Cobb
Jacksonville Beach Muni
Florida
D. J. Ross
Jagorawi National GC
Indonesia
P. Thomson, M. Wolveridge, R. Fream
James Baird State Park GC
New York
R. T. Jones
James H. Ager, Jr. Par 3 GC [now Lincoln Junior GC]
Nebraska
F. Farley
James L. Key Muni
Georgia
W. Ogg
James River CC
Virginia
F. A. Findlay
James River CC (r.)
Virginia
R. F. Loving
Jamestown CC (9)
Missouri
F. Farley
Jamestown CC
North Dakota
R. B. Harris
Jasper Park GC
Alberta, Canada
S. Thompson

Jawbone Creek GC
Montana
F. Hummel
J. C. Long Estate
South Carolina
G. W. Cobb
J.D.M. CC (East and West courses; West course is now 9 of North and 9 of South courses)
Florida
L. S. "Dick" Wilson
J. D. M. CC (a. 2nd 9 of North and 2nd 9 of South courses)
Florida
J. L. Lee
J. D. Wright Recreation [now T. R. W. CC](27)
Ohio
P. and R. Dye
Jedburgh GC
Scotland
W. Park, Jr.
Jefferson City CC (Original 9)
Missouri
R. Foulis
Jefferson City CC (n. 9, a. 9)
Missouri
E. L. Packard
Jefferson CC (9)
Florida
W. W. Amick
Jefferson County GC [now Ives Hill GC]
New York
M. J. McCarthy, Sr.
Jefferson County GC (r.)
New York
P. W. Lees
Jefferson High School GC
Kentucky
H. Purdy
Jefferson-Lakeside CC
Virginia
D. J. Ross
Jefferson Park GC
Virginia
A.M. Pulley
Jefferson Park Muni
Washington
T. Bendelow
Jekyll, Hyde GC
Florida
W. K. Bowen
Jekyll Island GC (Oceanside 9)
Georgia
"Young" W. Dunn
Jekyll Island GC (r. Oceanside course)
Georgia
W. J. Travis
Jekyll Island GC (Oleander course)
Georgia
L. S. "Dick" Wilson
Jekyll Island GC (Pine Lakes and Indian Mounds courses)
Georgia
J. L. Lee
Jenny Wiley State Park
Kentucky
H. Purdy
(The) Jeremy Ranch GC
Utah
E. B. Seay, A. Palmer
Jersey Village GC [now Long Meadows CC]
Texas
L. S. "Dick" Wilson

Jerseyville CC
Illinois
E. L. Packard
Jester Park GC (27)
Iowa
R. N. Phelps
J. F. K. Memorial GC
California
J. Fleming, R. Baldock, B. Harmon
J. J. Lynn Private Course
Missouri
O. E. Smith
Jockey Club of San Isidro (Red and Blue courses)
Argentina
A. Mackenzie
Joe Wheeler State Park GC
Alabama
E. Stone
Johannesburg, Royal (West course)
South Africa
L. B. Waters
Johannesburg, Royal (East course)
South Africa
R. G. Grimsdell
John Blumberg GC (27)
Manitoba, Canada
C. E. Robinson
John D. Rockefeller Estate GC [now Pocantico Hills GC]
New York
W. S. Flynn
John F. Kennedy Muni
Colorado
H. B. Hughes
John Knox Village Exec. GC (9)
Missouri
(Larry Runyon, Mike Malyn)
John O'Gaunt GC (a.18)
England
F. W. Hawtree
Johns Island Club (South course)
Florida
P. Dye, J. Nicklaus
Johns Island Club (North course)
Florida
P. Dye
Johnson City CC
Tennessee
A. W. Tillinghast
Johnson Park GC
Texas
G. A. Hoffman
Johnston County, CC of
North Carolina
E. Maples
Jonathon Par 30 GC (Exec.)
Minnesota
R. T. Jones
Jonathon's Landing GC
Florida
G. and T. Fazio
Joliet CC (r.)
Illinois
K. Killian, R. Nugent
Joliette, Club de Golf
Province of Québec, Canada
H. Watson
Jolly Acres GC
South Dakota
(Clifford A. Anderson)
Joondalup GC (27)
Western Australia
P.W. Thomson, M. Wolveridge
Joplin CC (r.)
Missouri
O. E. Smith

Jordan Point CC (9)
Virginia
R. F. Breeden
Jos-EE-Lyn CC
Georgia
A. L. Davis
Jovita CC
Florida
W. E. Stiles, J. R. Van Kleek
Juaniata CC
Pennsylvania
E. B. Ault
Juarez CC
Mexico
G. A. Hoffman
Jubilee Course, St. Andrews
Scotland
W. Auchterlonie
Jug End Inn GC
Massachusetts
A. H. Tull
Jumping Brook CC
New Jersey
L. Wilkinson
Jumping Brook CC
New Jersey
N. T. Psiahas
(The) Junko CC
Venezuela
C. H. Banks
Junior Players Club (at Walt Disney World) Exec. GC
Florida
R. Garl
Juniper Hill GC (Original 9)
Massachusetts
(Homer Darling)
Juniper Hill GC (a.9)
Massachusetts
G. S. Cornish
Juniper Hill GC (r.4)
Massachusetts
P. A. Wogan
Juniper Hills GC
Kentucky
C. R. Blankenship
Jupiter Hills Club
Florida
G. and T. Fazio
Jupiter Hills Club (Village course)
Florida
G. and T. Fazio
Jupiter Island Club
Florida
W. Diddel
Jupiter Island Club (r.)
Florida
G. And T. Fazio
Jurica, CC
Mexico
L. M. Hughes
Jurong Town GC
Singapore
J. J. F. Pennink
Jurupa Hills CC
California
W. F. Bell

Kaanapali CC, Royal
Hawaii
R. T. Jones
Kaanapali CC, Royal (South course)
Hawaii
A. J. Snyder
Kaanapali Kai GC
Hawaii
A. J. Snyder

Kahkwa CC
Pennsylvania
D. J. Ross
Kajak Point Muni
Washington
R. W. Fream
Kalamazoo Elks CC (a.2)
Michigan
W. B. and G. H. Matthews
Kalamazoo State Teacher's College GC
Michigan
D. T. Miller
Kalua Koi GC (Sheraton Molokai)
Hawaii
T. G. Robinson
Kananaskis GC (36)
Alberta, Canada
R. T. Jones
Kanata GC
Ontario, Canada
H. Watson
Kanawaki GC (r.)
Province of Québec, Canada
C. E. Robinson
Kanawaki GC (r.)
Province of Québec, Canada
H. and J. Watson
Kanehoe Marine GC
Hawaii
W. P. Bell
Kanirag GC
Philippines
R. Kirby, G. Player
Kankakee GC (r.8,a.10)
Illinois
J. R. Darrah
Kanon Valley GC
New York
H. Purdy
Kansas City CC
Kansas
W. B. Langford, T. J. Moreau
Kansas City CC (r.)
Kansas
A. W. Tillinghast
Kansas City CC (r.)
Kansas
R. C. Dunning
Kansas City CC (r.)
Kansas
F. Farley
Kapalua GC (Village course)
Hawaii
E. B. Seay, A. Palmer
Kapalua GC (Bay course)
Hawaii
F. Duane, A. Palmer
Karori GC
New Zealand
P.W. Thomson, M. Wolveridge
Karlovy Vary GC
Czechoslovakia
(M. C. Noskowski)
Karuizawa GC (Golf 72; Courses #1, #2, #3, #4, #5)
Japan
R. T. Jones, Sr. and Jr.
Kassel-Wilhelmshohe GC
West Germany
B. Von Limburger
Kass Inn & CC (Par 3)
New York
E. E. Smith
Kassuba Par 3 GC
Florida
W. F. Mitchell
Kasugai CC (East and West courses)
Japan
S. Inouye

Kasumigaseki GC (East and West courses)
Japan
K. Fujita
Kasumigaseki GC (r.)
Japan
C. H. Alison
Katke-Cousins GC (Ferris State College)
Michigan
R. D. Beard
Katke GC (Oakland University)
Michigan
R. D. Beard
Kauai Surf G&CC (Original 9)
Hawaii
W. G. Wilkinson
Kauai Surf G&CC (a.9)
Hawaii
(Ray Cain)
Kaufman GC
Michigan
W. B. and G. H. Matthews
Kawagoe CC
Japan
T. Nakamura
Kawana GC (Fuji course)
Japan
C. H. Alison
Kawana GC (Oshima course)
Japan
(M. Otani)
Kawana GC (r. Fuji and Oshima courses)
Japan
K. Fujita
Kawartha GC
Ontario, Canada
S. Thompson
Kaw Lake GC
Oklahoma
R. T. Jones, Jr.
Kayak Point GC
Washington
R. Fream
Kearney CC (r.)
Nebraska
H. W. Glissmann
Kearney CC (r.9,a.9)
Nebraska
L. I. Johnson
Kearsarge CC (Original 9)
New Hampshire
W. E. Stiles, J. R. Van Kleek
Kearsarge CC (r.9,a.9)
New Hampshire
W. F. Mitchell
Keauhou Kona CC
Hawaii
W. F. Bell
Kebayoran GC (r.)
Indonesia
P.W. Thomson, M. Wolveridge, R. Fream
Kebo Valley Club (Original 9)
Maine
(A. Liscombe), H. Leeds
Kebo Valley Club (a. 2nd 9)
Maine
(A. Liscombe)
Kebo Valley Club (r. Original 9)
Maine
H. C. Leeds
Kedleston Park GC
England
J. R. Stutt, J. S. F. Morrison
Keebergen CC
Belgium
T. C. Simpson
Keehi Muni
Hawaii
W. F. Bell

Keene CC (r.)
New Hampshire
M. L. Francis
Keerbergen GC
T.C. Simpson
J. J. F. Pennink
Keesler AFB GC (9)
Mississippi
J. Finger
Kieghley GC
England
T. C. Simpson
Keith Hills CC, Campbell College
North Carolina
D. and E. Maples
Keller Muni
Minnesota
P. Coates
Keller Muni (r.)
Minnesota
D. Herfort
Kelley Ridge Golf Links
California
(Homer Flint)
Kellogg CC (27)
Illinois
E. L. Packard
Kelowma Pines G&CC [now Gallagher's Canyon CC]
British Columbia, Canada
W. G. Robinson
Kelsey City GC (n.l.e.)
Florida
W. B. Langford, T. J. Moreau
Kelso Elks GC
Oregon
R. M. Graves
Keltic Lodge (Cape Breton Highlands GC)
Nova Scotia, Canada
S. Thompson
Kemper Lakes GC
Illinois
K. Killian, R. Nugent
Kempsville Meadows G&CC
Virginia
E. Maples
Kendale Exec. CC
Florida
F. Murray
Kendale Lakes G&CC
Florida
C. Mahannah
Kendrick Muni (Sheridan)
Wyoming
F. Hummel
Keney Park Muni
Connecticut
D. Emmet
Keney Park Muni (r.)
Connecticut
E. Pyle
Keney Park Muni (r.3)
Connecticut
G. S. Cornish, W. G. Robinson
Ken Lock Exec. GC (9)
Illinois
D. Gill
Kenmore Estates GC
North Carolina
J. L. Lee
Kennemer G&CC
Netherlands
H. S. Colt, J. S. F. Morrison
Kenora GC (Lake of the Woods)
Ontario, Canada
S. Thompson

Kenosee Lakes Men's GC (a.9)
Saskatchewan, Canada
C. E. Robinson
Kenosha CC
Wisconsin
D. J. Ross
Kensington GC (r.)
South Africa
R. Kirby, G. Player
Kent CC (Original 9)
Michigan
J. Foulis
Kent CC (a. 9)
Michigan
D. J. Ross
Kent Links at Montgomery Falls
Province of Québec, Canada
H. B. Strong
Kenton County GC (a.9)
Kentucky
J. Kidwell
Kentucky Dam State Park GC (Pines course)
Kentucky
H. Purdy
Kentville GC
Nova Scotia, Canada
W. Park, Jr.
Ken-Wo G&CC (a.9)
Nova Scotia, Canada
C. E. Robinson
Kenwood CC (r.)
Maryland
E. B. Ault
Kenwood CC (Kendale and Kenview courses)
Ohio
W. Diddel
Kenwood CC (r. Kendale and Kenview courses)
Ohio
J. Kidwell, M. Hurdzan
Keowee Key CC
South Carolina
G. W. Cobb, J. B. LaFoy
Keokuk CC (r.)
Iowa
W. B. Langford
Kern City GC (North 9)
California
A. J. Snyder
Kern County GC
California
W. F. Bell
Kern River CC
California
W. P. Bell
Kernwood CC
Massachusetts
D. J. Ross
Kernwood CC (r.)
Massachusetts
W. F. Mitchell
Kerrville Hills CC
Texas
D. Collett
Keswick Club of Virginia
Virginia
F. A. Findlay
Key Biscayne GC
Florida
R. Von Hagge, B. Devlin
Key Biscayne Hotel Par 3 GC
Florida
M. Mahannah

Key Colony Beach Par 3 GC
Florida
J. E. O'Connor, Jr.
Key Colony Par 3 GC
Florida
M. Mahannah
Key Royale Par 3 GC (9)
Florida
(Walter Pursley)
Keystone G&CC
Florida
D. J. Ross
Keystone G&CC (r.)
Florida
R. A. Anderson
Keystone Ranch GC
Colorado
R. T. Jones, Jr.
Key West GC
Florida
W. B. Langford, T. J. Moreau
Kiahuna Golf Village GC
Hawaii
R. T. Jones, Jr.
Kiawah Island Golf Links (Original 18)
South Carolina
R. Kirby, G. Player
Kiawah Island Golf Links (a. Turtle Point Course)
South Carolina
J. Nicklaus
Kicking Bird GC
Oklahoma
F. Farley
Ki-8-Eb CC at Three Rivers
Province of Québec, Canada
S. Thompson
Ki-8-Eb CC at Three Rivers (r.)
Province of Québec, Canada
H. and J. Watson
Kiel GC (r.)
Germany
B. Von Limburger
Kildeer CC [now Twin Orchards CC]
Illinois
C. D. Wagstaff
Kilkeel GC
Northern Ireland
(Lord Justice Barrington)
Killarney GC (Original 9)
Ireland
W. Park, Sr.
Killarney GC (a. 9)
Ireland
W. Park, Jr.
Killarney Golf & Fishing Club (Mahoney's Point course)
Ireland
G. Campbell
Killarney Golf & Fishing Club (Killeen course)
Ireland
F. W. Hawtree
Killearn G&CC
Florida
W. W. Amick
Killeen Muni
Texas
B. J. Riviere
Killington GC (9)
Vermont
G.S. Cornish
Killymoon
Northern Ireland
F. W. Hawtree
Kilmarnock (Barassie)
Scotland
(John Allan)

Kilmarnock (Barassie; r.)
Scotland
T. Moone
Kilspindie GC
Scotland
W. Park, Jr.
Kimberton GC
Pennsylvania
G. Fazio
Kinderton CC
Virginia
L. S. "Dick" Wilson
King Emmanuel's Private Course
Italy
S. Dunn
King James VI GC at Perth
Scotland
T. Morris
King Leopold's Private Course
Belgium
S. Dunn
Kingman CC (Original 9)
Arizona
M. Coggins
King Point West G&CC
Florida
R.T. Jones, Sr.
Kings Bay Yacht & CC
Florida
M. Mahannah
Kings County CC (a.9)
California
B. Stamps
Kingsdown GC
England
T. Dunn
Kingsgate GC
England
W. H. Fowler
Kings Grant GC
South Carolina
R. F. Breeden
Kings Inn G&CC
Florida
M. Mahannah
Kings Inn G&CC [now Bahamas Princess Hotel &CC] (Emerald course)
Bahamas
L. S. "Dick" Wilson
Kings Inn G&CC [now Bahamas Princess Hotel & CC] (Ruby course)
Bahamas
J. L. Lee
Kingsknowe
Scotland
J. Braid
King's Lynn GC
England
P. Alliss, D. Thomas
Kings Mill GC (9)
Ohio
J. Kidwell
Kingsmill GC
Virginia
P. Dye
Kings Mountain CC
North Carolina
J. P. Gibson
Kings Norton GC (27)
England
F. W. Hawtree
Kings Point West Exec. G&CC (Sun City)
Florida
R. T. Jones

Kings Point Par 3 G&CC, (Delray Beach)
Florida
R. T. Jones
Kingsport CC
Tennessee
M. J. McCarthy, Sr.
Kingsport CC (r.)
Tennessee
A. W. Tillinghast
Kingsridge CC
New York
T. Winton
Kings River G&CC
California
R. E. Baldock
Kingsthorpe
England
C. H. Alison
Kingston CC
North Carolina
E. Maples
Kingston Heath GC
Australia
D. G. Soutar
Kingston Heath GC (a. bunkers)
Australia
A. Mackenzie
Kingston Heath GC (r.)
Australia
P.W. Thomson, W. Wolveridge
(North) Kingstown Muni [formerly
    Quonset Naval Air Station GC]
Rhode Island
W. Johnson
Kingsville GC
Ontario, Canada
R. and D. Moote
Kingsway CC
Florida
R. Garl
Kingswood GC
England
J. Braid, J. R. Stutt
Kington
England
C. K. Hutchison
Kingussie
Scotland
H. Vardon
Kingwood CC (Island course)
Texas
J. Finger
Kingwood CC (Lake course)
Texas
(Bruce Littell)
Kino Springs CC
Arizona
R. F. Lawrence
Kirkbrae CC
Rhode Island
G. S. Cornish
Kirkbrae CC (r.3)
Rhode Island
S. Mitchell
Kirkcaldy GC
Scotland
J. H. Stutt
Kirkistown Castle
Northern Ireland
J. Braid
Kirkland AFB GC (Tizeras Arroya GC)
New Mexico
R. D. Putnam
Kirkland CC
Ohio
C. H. Alison
Kishwaukee CC
Illinois
D. Gill

Kissamee GC
Florida
J. H. Gillespie
Kissing Camels GC
Colorado
J. P. Maxwell
Kitanomine CC [now Furano CC]
Japan
E. B. Seay, A. Palmer
Kittanning GC
Pennsylvania
E. F. Loeffler, J. McGlynn
Kittansett Club
Massachusetts
F. Hood, W. S. Flynn
Kittyhawk Muni (Eagle, Kitty and Hawk
    courses)
Ohio
R. B. Harris
Kleberg County GC
Texas
(Dennis Arp)
Knebworth GC
England
W. Park, Jr.
Knickerbocker CC (Original course)
New Jersey
M. J. McCarthy, Sr.
Knickerbocker CC (new site)
New Jersey
D. J. Ross
Knickerbocker CC (r.)
New Jersey
H. B. Strong
Knickerbocker CC (r.6)
New Jersey
G. S. Cornish, W. G. Robinson
Knighton GC
Wales
H. Vardon
Knightstown GC
Indiana
G. Kern
Knock Sur Mer GC
Belgium
S. Dunn
Knock Sur Mer (36)
Belgium
H. S. Colt
Knole Park GC
England
J. F. Abercromby, W. H. Fowler
Knoll GC (Original course)
New Jersey
C. H. Banks
Knoll East GC
New Jersey
H. Purdy
Knolls Par 3 GC
Nebraska
F. Farley
Knollwood Club
Illinois
H. S. Colt, C. H. Alison
Knollwood Club (r.)
Illinois
F I Packard
Knollwood CC
California
W. F. Bell, W. H. Johnson
Knollwood CC (r.)
Michigan
W. B. and G. H. Matthews
Knollwood CC (Original course)
New York
L. E. Van Etten
Knollwood CC (new site)
New York
A. W. Tillinghast

Knollwood CC (r.; a.7)
New York
C. H. Banks
Knollwood CC (n.l.e.)
Texas
P. D. and J. P. Maxwell
Knowle GC
England
F. G. Hawtree
Knowlton GC (r.9,a.9)
Province of Québec, Canada
H. Watson
Koganei GC
Japan
W. Hagen
Kokanee Springs CC
British Columbia, Canada
N. Woods
Kokkedal GC
Denmark
J. J. F. Pennink
Konstanzer GC
West Germany
B. Von Limburger, K. Hoffmann
Kooyonga GC (r.)
Australia
P.W. Thomson, M. Wolveridge
Korakuen CC
Japan
P.W. Thomson, M. Wolveridge
Kornwestheim GC (U. S. Army Base)
West Germany
B. Von Limburger
Kountze Place GC (n.l.e.)
Nebraska
(Harry Lawrie)
Krefelder GC
West Germany
B. Von Limburger, K. Hoffmann
Kronberg GC (r.)
Germany
B. Von Limburger
Kronberg GC (r.)
Germany
B. Von Limburger
Kuehn Park GC (9)
South Dakota
D. Herfort
Kuilima GC
Hawaii
G. and T. Fazio, J. Hardin, G. Nash
Kuilima GC (r.)
Hawaii
R. T. Jones, Jr.
Kungsbacka GC
Sweden
J. J. F. Pinnink
Kutsher's Hotel GC
New York
W. F. Mitchell
Kwiniaska GC
Vermont
(Paul J. O'Leary, Brad Caldwell)
Kyushu Shima CC
Japan
S. Inouye
La Baule, Golf de (r.)
France
P. Alliss, D. Thomas
La Boulie, GC of the Racing Club
France
S. Dunn
La Boulie, GC of the Racing Club
France
W. Park, Jr.
La Boulie, GC of the Racing Club
France
W. Reid
Labour-In-Vain at Ipswich
Massachusetts
E. F. Wogan
La Breteche, Golf de St. Nom
France
F. W. Hawtree

La Breteche, Golf de St. Nom (a. 18)
France
J. J. F. Pennink
Labuan GC
East Malaysia
R. M. Graves
La Canada, Club de Golf
Mexico
P. Clifford
La Canada-Flintridge GC
California
L. M. Hughes
Lac Beauport, Club de Golf
Province of Québec, Canada
H. Watson
La Ceiba GC
Mexico
J. Saenz, F. Teran
Lachute GC
Province of Québec, Canada
S. Thompson
Lachute GC (r.9,a.18)
Province of Québec, Canada
H. Watson
Lackland AFB GC (r.)
Texas
J. Finger
Laconia CC
New Hampshire
R. M. Barton
Laconia CC (a.9)
New Hampshire
W. E. Stiles, J. R. Van Kleek
La Contenta CC
California
(Richard Bigler)
La Costa CC
California
L. S. "Dick" Wilson
La Costa CC (a.9)
California
J. L. Lee
LaCrosse CC (r.)
Wisconsin
E.L. Packard
Lac Thomas GC
Province of Québec, Canada
H. Watson
La Cumbre G&CC (Original 9)
California
(Peter Cooper Bryce)
La Cumbre G&CC (r.9,a.9)
California
G. C. Thomas, Jr., W. P. Bell
La Cumbre G&CC (r.)
California
W. F. Bell
Ladbrook Park
England
T. Williamson
La Dera Muni
New Mexico
R.M. Phelps
Ladies GC
Ontario, Canada
S. Thompson
Ladies Island GC
South Carolina
R. F. Breeden
Ladybank GC
Scotland
T. Morris
Lafayette City GC
Indiana
R. A. Simmons
Lafayette CC (Battleground course)
Indiana
R. A. Simmons

Lafayette CC (r.)
Louisiana
R. Plummer
Lafayette CC
New York
S. Dunn
La Fortune Park Muni (27)
Oklahoma
F. Farley
La Galea GC (Real Sociedad De Golf
    Neguri)
Spain
J. Arana
Lago Mar CC
Florida
W. R. Watts
La Gorce CC
Florida
H. C. C. Tippetts
La Gorce CC (r.)
Florida
R. T. Jones
Lagos de Caujarel, Club
Columbia
J. L. Lee
Lago Vista CC
Texas
L. Howard
LaGrange CC (n.1.e.)
Illinois
H. J. Tweedie
LaGrange CC (new site)
Illinois
T. Bendelow
LaGrange CC (r.)
Illinois
E. B. Dearie, Jr.
La Grange CC (r.)
Illinois
E.L., R.B. Packard
Laguna Canyon GC
California
T. G. Robinson
Laguna, Club de Golf
Mexico
P. Clifford
Laguna CC
California
W. P. Bell
Laguna Hills GC
California
H. M. and D. A. Rainville
Laguna Niguel GC
California
R. T. Jones, Jr.
Laguna Seca Golf Ranch
California
R. T. Jones, Sr. and Jr.
Lagunita CC
Venezuela
L. S. "Dick" Wilson
La Heliere GC
France
F. W. Hawtree
Lahinch GC
Ireland
T. Morris
Lahinch GC (r.)
Ireland
A. Mackenzie
Lahinch GC (a. 3rd 9)
Ireland
J. D. Harris
La Huertas GC
Mexico
P. Clifford
La Jolla CC
California
W. P. Bell

La Jolla CC (r.)
California
T. G. Robinson
La Jeune Road CC [now Melreese GC]
Florida
L. S. "Dick" Wilson
Lake Anna GC
Illinois
S. F. Pelchar
Lake Ann CC
New York
A. H. Tull
Lake Arbor GC
Colorado
C. Glasson
Lake Arlington GC
Texas
R. Plummer
Lake Arrowhead CC (Original 9)
California
W. Watson
Lake Arrowhead CC (r.9,a.9)
California
W. F. Bell
Lake Barrington Shores CC
Illinois
E. L. and R. B. Packard
Lake Barton GC
Kansas
H. Robb, Sr.
Lake Bonaventure CC
Virginia
A. G. McKay
Lake Buena Vista Club
Florida
J. L. Lee
Lake Chabot GC
California
(William Locke)
Lake Chabot Vallejo Exec. GC
California
J. Fleming
Lake Charles G&CC
Louisiana
R. Plummer
Lake Charles G&CC (r.)
Louisiana
B. J. Riviere
Lake City CC
Florida
W. C. Byrd
Lake Country Estates GC (9)
Texas
R. Plummer
Lake Country Estates GC (a.9)
Texas
D. January, B. Martindale
Lake Creek CC
Iowa
H. D. Fieldhouse
Lake Don Pedro G&CC
California
W. F. Bell
Lake Elsinore CC (n.1.e.)
California
J. D. Dunn
Lake Estes Exec. GC (9)
Colorado
H. B. Hughes
Lake Fairfax GC
Virginia
E. B. Ault
Lake Fairways Exec. GC
Florida
R. Garl

Lake Forest CC (r.9,a.9)
Alabama
E. Stone
Lake Forest CC
Illinois
H. S. Colt
Lake Forest CC
Ohio
H. Strong
Lake Forest CC (r.)
Ohio
J. G. Harrison
Lake Geneva CC (Original 9)
Wisconsin
R. Foulis
Lake Havasu, London Bridge
Arizona
L. M. Hughes
Lake Havasu, London Bridge (a.9)
Arizona
A. J. Snyder
Lake Hefner Muni (North course)
Oklahoma
P. D. Maxwell
Lake Hefner Muni (South course)
Oklahoma
F. Farley
Lake Hefner Muni (r. North course)
Oklahoma
F. Farley
Lake Hickory CC (27)
North Carolina
W. C. Byrd
Lake Hills CC
Montana
(George Schneiter)
Lake Hills G&CC (27)
Indiana
F. Macdonald, C. E. Maddox
Lake Houston GC
Texas
B. J. Riviere
Lake Isabella GC
Michigan
W. B. and G. H. Matthews
Lake James CC
Indiana
R. D. Beard
Lake Karrinyup CC
Australia
A. Mackenzie, A. Russell
Lake Karrinyup CC (r.)
Western Australia
P.W. Thomson, M. Wolveridge
Lake Kezar Club
Maine
D. J. Ross
Lakelawn Exec. CC
Pennsylvania
F. Garbin
Lake Lorraine CC
Florida
W. W. Amick
Lake Lure CC
North Carolina
W. E. Stiles, J. R. Van Kleek
Lake Merced G&CC
California
W. H. Fowler
Lake Merced G&CC (r.)
California
A. Mackenzie
Lake Merced G&CC (r.)
California
R. M. Graves
Lake Mohawk GC
New Jersey
(Duer Irving Sewall)
Lake Monroe GC
Indiana
R. A. Simmons

Lakemont CC
Ohio
W. J. Rockefeller
Lake Montezuma G&CC
Arizona
A. J. Snyder
Lake Monticello GC
Virginia
R.F. Loving, A.M. Pulley
Lake Norconian
California
J. D. Dunn
Lake of the North GC
Michigan
W. B. and G. H. Matthews
Lake of the Woods GC
Illinois
R. B. Harris
Lake O' The Hills Par 3 GC
Michigan
W. B. and G. H. Matthews
Lakeover CC
New York
A. Zikorus
Lake Padden GC
Washington
R. Goss (Glen Proctor)
Lake Paoay GC
Philippines
R. Kirby, G. Player
Lake Placid Club
Florida
S. Dunn
Lake Placid CC (Upper course)
New York
A. Findlay
Lake Placid CC (Lower course)
New York
S. Dunn
Lake Placid CC (r.)
New York
A. Mackenzie
Lake Pointe CC (a.6; n.1.e.)
Michigan
W. B. and G. H. Matthews
Lakepointe State Park GC
Alabama
(Thomas B. Nicol)
Lakeport GC
New Hampshire
R. M. Barton
Lake Quivira CC
Kansas
W. B. Langford, T. J. Moreau
Lake Quivira CC (r.)
Kansas
F. Farley
Lake Quivira CC (r.)
Kansas
C. Mendenhall
Lake Region Yacht & CC
Florida
D. L. Wallace
Lake Ridge CC
Nevada
R. T. Jones, Sr. and Jr.
Lake St. George CC [now Mariner Sands]
Florida
F. Duane
Lake St. George G&CC (r.9,a.9)
Ontario, Canada
C. E. Robinson
Lake Samanish State Park GC
Washington
A. Smith

Lake San Marcos
California
H. M. and D. A. Rainville
(The) Lakes GC (r.)
Australia
R. Von Hagge, B. Devlin
Lake Shastina GC
California
R. T. Jones, Sr. and Jr.
Lake Shawnee GC
Kansas
(L. Wesley Flatt)
Lake Shore G&CC (Taylorville)
Illinois
R. Garl
Lake Shore CC (r.)
Illinois
K. Killian, R. Nugent
Lake Shore CC (a. 2nd 9)
Iowa
D. Gill
Lakeshore CC
Kentucky
C. R. Blankenship
Lakeshore CC
New Jersey
A. Zikorus
Lakeshore CC at Burlington
Vermont
H. B. Strong
Lakeside CC (r.)
Texas
J. Finger
Lakeside GC
Ohio
E. B. Ault
Lakeside GC of Hollywood
California
M. H. Behr
Lakeside GC of Hollywood (r.)
California
R. M. Graves
Lake Success GC (r. 9, a. 9)
New York
O. E. Smith, A. Zikorus
Lake Sunapee CC
New Hampshire
D. J. Ross
Lake Surf CC
North Carolina
D. and E. Maples
Lakes View Par 3 GC
Tennessee
A. G. McKay
Lake Tarleton CC (Original 9; n.1.e.)
New Hampshire
D. J. Ross
Lake Tarleton CC (a.13; n.1.e.)
New Hampshire
M. L. Francis
Lake Taylorville GC
Illinois
W. J. Spear
Lake Texoma State Park GC
Oklahoma
F. Farley
Lake Valley CC [formerly Fairways GC]
Colorado
J.P. Maxwell
Lake Valley G&CC
Missouri
F. Farley
Lake Venice GC
Florida
M. Mahannah
Lakeview CC
Virginia
F. Findlay, C.R.F. Loving Sr.
Lakeview CC
Illinois
C.E. Maddox

Lakeview CC (9; n.1.e.)
Oklahoma
L. Brownlee
Lake View CC
Pennsylvania
J. G. Harrison
Lakeview CC (27)
Virginia
R. Roberts
Lake View CC
West Virginia
J. G. Harrison
Lakeview CC
Ontario, Canada
H. B. Strong
Lakeview Exec. GC
Florida
W. H. Dietsch, Jr.
Lakeview Exec. GC
Virginia
R. F. Loving
Lakeview GC
Nebraska
H. W. Glissmann
Lakeview Muni
South Dakota
R. Watson
Lakeview West Boggs Muni
Indiana
E. B. Ault
Lake Waco CC (18 and Par 3)
Texas
W. D. Cantrell
Lakeway Inn & GC (Yaupon and Live Oaks courses)
Texas
L. Howard
Lake Wilderness CC (Original 9)
Washington
(R. Coleman)
Lake Wilderness CC (a.9)
Washington
N. Woods
Lake Wildwood CC
California
W. F. Bell
Lakewood CC (r.)
Alabama
R. T. Jones
Lakewood CC
Florida
H. B. Strong
Lakewood CC (r.)
Florida
L. S. Wilson
Lakewood CC (New site)
Lousiana
R. B. Harris
Lakewood CC
Maryland
E. B. Ault
Lakewood CC
New Jersey
"Young" W. Dunn
Lakewood CC
Ohio
A. W. Tillinghast
Lakewood CC (r.)
Ohio
J. Kidwell, M. Hurdzan
Lakewood CC
Texas
R. Plummer
Lakewood CC (r.)
Texas
L. Howard

269

Lakewood G&CC
Illinois
W. J. Spear

Lakewood GC (Grand Hotel) (r.)
Alabama
R. T. Jones

Lakewood GC (Grand Hotel); (Dogwood and Azalea 9's)
Alabama
P. D. Maxwell

Lakewood GC (Grand Hotel); (a. Magnolia 9)
Alabama
J. L. Lee

Lakewood GC
California
W. P. Bell

Lakewood GC (r.)
Colorado
J. P. Maxwell

Lakewood GC (East and West courses)
Japan
T. G. Robinson

Lakewood GC at St. Petersburg (r.)
Florida
L. S. "Dick" Wilson

Lakewood Oaks GC
Missouri
B. J. Riviere

Lakewood Par 3 GC
Florida
A. Hills

Lakewood Shores G&CC
Michigan
W. B. and G. H. Matthews

Lakewood Village GC
Texas
L. Howard

Lake Wright GC
Virginia
A. Jamison

Lakey Hill GC
England
(G. T. Holloway, Brian Bramford)

Lakota Hills CC
Ohio
J. Kidwell

La Mancha CC
Arizona
R. Von Hagge, B. Devlin

La Mandria GC (Original 9)
Italy
J. S. F. Morrison

La Mandria GC (a.9)
Italy
J. D. Harris

La Mango Campo de Golf (North and South courses)
Spain
R. D. Putnam

Lamberhurst GC
England
J. J. F. Pennink

Lambton G&CC (r.)
Ontario, Canada
S. Thompson

Lambton G&CC (r.)
Ontario, Canada
C. E. Robinson

La Mirada GC
California
W. F. Bell

Lamont Hill GC
Kansas
(Melvin Wesley Anderson)

La Moraleja GC
Spain
D. Muirhead, J. Nicklaus

Lamoye GC (Channel Islands)
England
(George Boomer)

Lamoye GC (Channel Islands; r.)
England
H. Cotton

Lancaster CC
Pennsylvania
W. S. Flynn

Lancaster CC (r.18,a.6)
Pennsylvania
W. F. and D. W. Gordon

Lancaster CC (r.)
South Carolina
R. F. Breeden

Lancaster GC
New Hampshire
R. M. Barton

Landa Park GC
Texas
L. Howard

Lander Haven CC (a.9)
Ohio
B. W. Zink

Land Harbors GC
North Carolina
T. Jackson

(The) Landings at Skidaway Island (Marshwood 18)
California
F. Duane, A. Palmer

(The) Landings at Skidaway Island
Georgia
W. C. Byrd

(The) Landings at Skidaway Island (a. 18)
Georgia
E. B. Seay, A. Palmer

L & N CC
Kentucky
A. G. McKay

Land of Lakes G&CC
Florida
L. Clifton

Land O' Golf Par 3 GC
Florida
J. E. O'Connor, Jr.

Landsdown GC (n.1.e.)
England
T. Dunn

Land und Golf Club (East and West courses)
West Germany
B. Von Limburger

Langhorn CC
Pennsylvania
G. Fazio

Landley AFB GC (9)
Virginia
E. B. Ault

Langley AFB GC (r.)
Virginia
A. Zikorus

Langston GC (a.9)
Washington, D.C.
W. F. and D. W. Gordon

Lansing, CC of
Michigan
W. B. Langford, T. J. Moreau

Lansing Sportsman's Club (a. 9, 1976)
Illinois
K. Killian, R. Nugent

Lantau Island GC
Hong Kong
R.T. Jones, Jr.

Lan-Yair GC
South Carolina
R. F. Breeden

La Palma CC (n.1.e.)
Arizona
H. Collis

La Pointe du Diamant
Martinique
R. Moote

Laprairie, Club de Golf
Province of Québec, Canada
H. Watson

La Quinta CC
California
L. M. Hughes

La Quinta Cove GC
California
P. Dye

Larch Tree CC
Ohio
J. Kidwell

Laredo AFB GC
Texas
L. Howard

Larne GC
Northern Ireland
W. Park, Jr.

Larrimac GC (r.)
Ontario, Canada
H. and J. Watson

Larrimore CC (9)
North Dakota
C. E. Maddox

Las Colinas CC
Texas
J. Finger

Las Colinas CC (a. 2nd 18)
Texas
R.T. Jones, Jr.

Las Hadas GC
Mexico
P. and R. Dye

Las Huertas CC
Mexico
P. Clifford

Las Lomas El Bosque GC (27)
Spain
R. D. Putnam

Las Palmas, Club de Golf
Spain
P. M. Ross

Las Posas CC
California
L. M. Hughes

Las Positas Muni
California
R. M. Graves

Las Vegas CC
Nevada
E. B. Ault

Las Vegas CC (r.)
Nevada
R. Garl

Las Vegas Muni (Original 9)
Nevada
W. P. Bell

Las Vegas Muni (a.9)
Nevada
W. F. Bell

La Tourette Muni
New York
J. R. Van Kleek

La Tourette Muni (r.)
New York
F. Duane

Latrobe CC (Original 9)
Pennsylvania
E. F. Loeffler, J. McGlynn

Latrobe CC (a.9)
Pennsylvania
J. G. Harrison

La Tuque Golf & Curling Club (r.9,a.9)
Province of Québec, Canada
H. Watson

Lauder
British Isles
W. Park, Jr.

Laughlin AFB GC (9)
Texas
J. Finger

Launceston GC (a.9)
England
J. H. Stutt

Laurel CC
Mississippi
S. Dunn

Laurel G&RC
Montana
T. J. Wirth

Laurel GC
Virginia
F. A. Findlay

Laurel Pines CC
Maryland
G. W. Cobb

Laurel Valley CC
Pennsylvania
L. S. "Dick" Wilson

Laurel View CC (r.)
Pennsylvania
P. Erath

Laurel View Muni (Hamden Muni)
Connecticut
G. S. Cornish, W. G. Robinson

Laval-Sur-Le-Lac, Club
Province of Québec, Canada
W. Park, Jr.

Laval-Sur-Le-Lac, Club
Province of Québec, Canada
H. B. Strong

Laval-Sur-Le-Lac, Club (r.)
Province of Québec, Canada
H. Watson

La Villa Rica, Club de Golf
Mexico
P. Clifford

Lawrenceburg GC (r.; a.9)
Tennessee
A. L. Davis

Lawrence CC (Original 9)
Kansas
H. Robb, Sr.

Lawrence CC (r.9,a.9)
Kansas
P. D. Maxwell

Lawrence Farms CC
New York
T. Winton

Lawrence Links GC (9)
California
B. Stamps

Lawrence Harbour CC
New Jersey
"Young" W. Dunn

Lawrence Park Village (r.)
New York
J. Finger

Lawrenceville CC
Virginia
F. A. Findlay

Lawrenceville School GC (r.)
New Jersey
W. F. and D. W. Gordon

Lawsonia Links
Wisconsin
W. B. Langford, T. J. Moreau

Lawton CC
Oklahoma
P. D. Maxwell

Lawton CC (a.9)
Oklahoma
F. Farley

Lazy H GC
California
R. E. Baldock

L.B. Houston Muni [formerly Elm Fork Muni]
Texas
L. Howard

Leamington and County GC
England
J. Braid

Leamington and County GC
England
H. S. Colt

Leaning Tree GC
Ohio
R. LaConte, E. McAnlis

Leatham Smith Lodge GC
Wisconsin
W. B. Langford, T. J. Moreau

Leatherstocking GC (Otesega Hotel)
New York
D. Emmet

Leawood South CC
Kansas
R. C. Dunning

Lebanon CC
Pennsylvania
F. Murray, R. Roberts

Le Chatecler
Province of Québec, Canada
H. Watson

Le Chateau CC [formerly Hershey Poconos]
Pennsylvania
G. S. Cornish, W. G. Robinson

Le Chateau Montebello GC [formerly The Seigniory Club]
Province of Québec, Canada
S. Thompson

Leckford GC
England
H. S. Colt, J. S. F. Morrison

Le Club Seigneurie de Grand Pre
Province of Québec, Canada
H. Watson

Ledgemont CC
Massachusetts
A. H. Tull

Ledger CC
Illinois
E. L. Packard

Leeds Castle GC
England
S. V. Hotchkin, C. K. Hutchison, G. Campbell

Leek GC
England
T. Williamson

Lee-on-Solent GC
England
J. D. Dunn

Lee-on-Solent GC (r.)
England
J. H. Stutt

Lee Park GC (a.9)
South Dakota
(Clifford A. Anderson)

Lee Park GC (r.18)
South Dakota
(Gary L. Nelson)

Lee Park GC
England
J. J. F. Pinnink

Leesburg CC
Virginia
E. B. Ault
Lees Hall
England
A. Herd
Lees Hall (r.)
England
T. Williamson
Leeward GC
Hawaii
R. E. Baldock
Lee Win GC
Ohio
J. Kidwell
Legion Memorial GC
Washington
H. C. Egan
Lehigh Acres CC
Florida
R. A. Anderson
Lehigh CC
Pennsylvania
W. S. Flynn
Lehigh CC (r.)
Pennsylvania
W. F. and D. W. Gordon
Leicester Hill GC (r. Original 9)
Massachusetts
A. H. Tull, W. F. Mitchell
Leisure Village
New Jersey
E. L. Packard
Leisure Village GC
California
E. L. Packard
Leisure World (Exec. 9)
Arizona
(Johnny Bulla)
Leisure World (a. 2nd 18)
Arizona
J. Hardin, G. Nash
Leland CC
Michigan
C. D. Wagstaff
Leland CC
Michigan
R. L. Jones
Leland Meadows Par 3 GC
California
R. E. Baldock
Lely Community GC
Florida
D. L. Wallace
Lely CC
Florida
D. L. Wallace
Le Mans GC
France
J. J. F. Pinnink
Lemontree GC
Michigan
C. E. Robinson
Lemoore Muni
California
R. E. Baldock
Lenape Heights GC (9)
Pennsylvania
F. Garbin
Lennoxville GC
Province of Québec, Canada
H. Watson
Lenox Hills CC [now Green course at Bethpage State Park](r.)
New York
A. W. Tillinghast

Lenzerheide GC (Original 9)
Switzerland
J. P. Gannon
Lenzerheide GC
Switzerland
D. Harradine
Lenzerheide GC
Switzerland
F. W. Hawtree
Leo J. Martin GC (a.9)
Massachusetts
S. Mitchell
Leonard Wheatley GC (3 holes)
Province of Québec, Canada
H. Watson
Le Portage, Club de Golf
Province of Québec, Canada
H. Watson
Leroy King Private Course (a.3)
Kansas
F. Farley
Les Buttes Blanche (r.)
Belgium
F. W. Hawtree
Les Dunes, Club de Golf (r. 18,a.18)
Province of Québec, Canada
H. Watson
Le Seigneurie de Vaudreuil
Province of Québec, Canada
H. Watson
Leslie Park CC
Michigan
E. L. Packard
L'Esperance, Golf de
Martinique
R. T. Jones
Les Vieux Chenes Muni
Louisiana
M. H. Ferguson
Letchworth
England
H. Vardon
Letsatsing GC
South Africa
R. Kirby, G. Player
Letterkenny GC
Ireland
E. Hackett
Levis GC (r.)
Province of Québec, Canada
H. Watson
Lew Galbraith Muni
California
R. E. Baldock
Lewiston GC
Indiana
R. E. Baldock
Lewiston CC
Pennsylvania
E. B. Ault
Lew Wentz Memorial Park GC (a.9)
Oklahoma
F. Farley
Lexington CC (r.4,a.4)
Kentucky
B. J. Wihry
Lexington GC
Virginia
E. Maples
Liberty Lake GC
Washington
(Melvin A. Hueston)
Libertyville CC
Illinois
L. Macomber
Lick Creek GC
Illinois
E. L. and R. B. Packard

Licking Springs G&TC
Ohio
J. Kidwell
Lido Golf Centre
Ontario, Canada
C. E. Robinson
Lido GC (n.1.e.)
New York
C. B. Macdonald
Lido GC (new course)
New York
R. T. Jones
Lido Springs Par 3 GC
New York
W. F. Mitchell
Lighthouse Sound GC
Maryland
M. and H. Purdy
Ligonier CC (r.9)
Pennsylvania
X. G. Hassenplug
Lilleshall Hall
England
H. S. Colt
Limburg GC
Belgium
F. W. Hawtree
Limerick GC
Ireland
J. Braid
Limon GC (9)
Colorado
H. B. Hughes
Lincoln, CC of
Nebraska
W. H. Tucker, Sr.
Lincoln, CC of
Nebraska
P. Dye
Lincoln Greens Muni
Illinois
R. B. Harris
Lincoln Hills GC
Michigan
W. B. and G. H. Matthews
Lincoln Junior Par 3 GC [formerly J. H. Ager Par 3 GC]
Nebraska
F. Farley
Lincoln Park GC (r.)
California
J. Fleming
Lincoln Park Muni (9)
Illinois
E. B. Dearie, Jr.
Lincoln Park Muni (East and West courses)
Oklahoma
A. J. Jackson
Lincoln Park Muni (r. greens)
Oklahoma
P. D. Maxwell
Lincoln Park Muni (r. East and West courses)
Oklahoma
F. Farley
Lincolnshire CC (r. East and West courses)
Illinois
K. Killian, R. Nugent
Lincolnshire Fields GC
Illinois
E. L. Packard
Lincolnshire Marriot Hotel & GC
Illinois
G. and T. Fazio

Lindale Greens GC
California
R. E. Baldock
Lindau GC
West Germany
B. Von Limburger
Linden GC
Alabama
(Neil R. Bruce)
Lindrick GC
England
T. Dunn
Lindrick GC (r.1)
England
F. W. Hawtree
Lindsay Muni
California
R. E. Baldock
Link Hills CC
Tennessee
R. T. Jones
Linkopines GC
Sweden
(G. Bauer)
Links
England
S. V. Hotchkin
(The) Links at Nichols Muni
Illinois
D. Gill
(The) Links at Porto Carras
Greece
G. S. Cornish, W. G. Robinson
(The) Links GC
New York
C. B. Macdonald, S. J. Raynor
(The) Links on the Vineyard [now Farm Neck GC](Original 9)
Massachusetts
G. S. Cornish, W. G. Robinson
Linn CC
Missouri
C. Mendenhall
Linrick GC
South Carolina
R. F. Breeden
Linville GC
North Carolina
D. J. Ross
Linville GC (r)
North Carolina
R. T. Jones
Linville Ridge CC 1980)
North Carolina
G.W. Cobb, J.B. LaFoy
Linwood CC
New Jersey
H. B. Strong
Linz GC
Austria
D. Harradine
Liphook GC
England
A. C. M. Croome
Liphook GC (r.)
England
J. S. F. Morrison
Liphook GC (r.)
England
T. C. Simpson
Lisbon Bissell GC (r.9)
North Dakota
D. Herfort
Lisbon Sports Club (Original 9)
Portugal
F. G. Hawtree
Lisbon Sports Club (a.9)
Portugal
F. W. Hawtree

Lisburn GC
Northern Ireland
F. W. Hawtree
Lismore GC (r.)
Ireland
E. Hackett
Litchfield GC
South Carolina
W. C. Byrd
Little America Exec. GC
Wyoming
W. H. Neff
Little Aston GC (r.)
England
H. S. Colt
Little Aston GC
England
H. Vardon
(The) Little Club Par 3
Florida
J. L. Lee
Little Crow GC
Minnesota
D. Herfort
Little Cypress GC
Florida
R. A. Anderson
Littlehampton GC (r.)
England
F. G. Hawtree, J. H. Taylor
Little Hay GC
England
F. W. and M. Hawtree
Little Island GC
Ireland
J. J. F. Pennink
Little Knoll GC
California
C. Glasson
Little Lakes GC
England
(Michael Cooksey)
Little Mill CC (Original 9)
New Jersey
G. J. Renn
Little Mill CC (a.9)
New Jersey
D. W. Gordon
Little Mountain GC (r.)
Georgia
A. L. Davis
Little Mountain State Park GC
Alabama
E. Stone
Little Rock CC
Arkansas
H. C. Hackbarth
Little Rock CC (r.3)
Arkansas
J. Finger
Little Rock CC (r.)
Arkansas
E. B. Ault
Littlestone GC
England
(N. Laidlaw Purves)
Littlestone GC (r.)
England
T. Dunn
Littlestone GC (r.)
England
J. Braid
Little Tam GC
Illinois
W. J. Spear

271

Little Turtle Club
Ohio
P. and R. Dye
Lively GC
Ontario, Canada
R. Moote
Liveoaks CC
Mississippi
G. Curtis
Liverpool GC, Royal (Hoylake; Original
  course)
England
(R. Chambers), G. Morris
Liverpool GC, Royal (Hoylake; r.)
England
H. S. Colt
Liverpool GC, Royal (Hoylake; r.)
England
J. J. F. Pennink
Liverpool Muni
England
(J. Large)
Livingston G&CC
Scotland
J. J. F. Pennink, C. Lawrie
Livingston Park GC
Mississippi
E. D. Guy
Llandeilo GC (Glynhir; 9)
Wales
F. W. Hawtree
Llandrindod Wells
Wales
H. Vardon
Llanerch CC
Pennsylvania
J. B. McGovern
Lochinvar GC
Texas
J. Nicklaus
Lochland GC
Nebraska
D. Gill
Lochmoor Club (r.)
Michigan
H. S. Colt, C. H. Alison
Lockhaven CC
Illinois
R. B. Harris
Locking Stumps GC
England
T. J. A. McAuley
Lockmoor GC
Florida
W. F. Mitchell
Locust Hill CC
New York
S. Dunn
Locust Hill CC (r.)
New York
R. T. Jones
Locust Valley CC
Pennsylvania
W. F. and D. W. Gordon
Lodge of the Four Seasons Exec. GC
Missouri
H. Herpel
Logan G&CC
Utah
J. M. Riley
Logansport CC
Indiana
R.A. Simmons
Log Cabin Club
Missouri
R. Foulis
Logo De Vita GC
Pennsylvania
F. Garbin

Lohersand GC
West Germany
B. Von Limburger
Loma Linda CC
Missouri
D. R. Sechrest
Loman de Cocoyoc, Club
Mexico
M. Schjetnan
Lomas Santa Fe CC
California
T. G. Robinson
Lomas Santa Fe CC (a. Exec. course)
California
W. F. Bell
Lombardzide GC
Belgium
W. Park, Jr.
London Bridge GC [formerly Lake
  Havasu City GC]
Arizona
L. M. Hughes
London Bridge GC (a.9)
Arizona
A. J. Snyder
Londonderry
Northern Ireland
W. Park, Jr.
London GC
Kentucky
J. R. Darrah
London Hunt & CC
Ontario, Canada
R. T. Jones, C. E. Robinson
London Scottish (Wimbledon)
England
"Old" W. Dunn, T. Dunn
Lone Oak CC
Kentucky
C. R. Blankenship
Lone Palm GC
Florida
L. S. "Dick" Wilson
Lone Pine Exec. GC
Florida
R. LaConte, E. McAnlis
Lone Pine GC
Pennsylvania
X. G. Hassenplug
Long Beach Hotel GC (n.1.e.)
New York
J. D. Dunn
Long Beach Muni (n.1.e.)
California
W. P. Bell
Longboat Key Club
Florida
W. F. Mitchell
Longboat Key CC (a. 18)
Florida
W. Byrd
Longbranch CC [formerly Old Orchard
  CC]
New Jersey
(Marty O'Loughlin)
Longchamps, Club de Golf
Province of Québec, Canada
H. Watson
Longcliffe GC
England
T. Williamson
Long Cove GC
South Carolina
P. Dye
Longmeadow CC
Massachusetts
D. J. Ross

Longmeadow CC (r.2)
Massachusetts
G. S. Cornish, W. G. Robinson
Long Meadows CC
Texas
L. S. "Dick" Wilson
Longniddry GC
Scotland
H. S. Colt, C. H. Alison
Longniddry GC (r.)
Scotland
P. M. Ross
Long Run GC
Kentucky
B. J. Wihry
Longshore Beach Club [now Longshore
  Club Park]
Connecticut
O. E. Smith
Longue Vue CC
Pennsylvania
R. White
Longview Muni
Washington
R. W. Fream
Longwood CC [formerly Casa del Mar
  CC]
Indiana
H. Collis
Lookout Point CC [now Welland CC]
Ontario, Canada
W. J. Travis
Lord Mountbatten Estate GC
England
W. H. Fowler
Lord's Properties Course (a.18)
South Carolina
G. and T. Fazio
Lords Valley CC
Pennsylvania
N. Woods
Lorette GC (r.9,a.9)
Province of Québec, Canada
H. Watson
Loring AFB GC
Maine
W. F. Mitchell
Los Alamitos GC
California
W. F. Bell
Los Altos G&CC
California
T. Nicoll
Los Altos G&CC (r.)
California
R. M. Graves
Los Altos Muni
New Mexico
R. E. Baldock
Los Angeles CC (South course)
California
W. H. Fowler
Los Angeles CC (r. South course, a.
  North course)
California
G. C. Thomas, Jr.
Losantville GC (r.)
Ohio
H. Purdy
Los Banos CC (9)
California
R. E. Baldock
Los Caballeros GC
Arizona
J. Hardin, G. Nash

Los Coyotes CC
California
W. F. Bell
Los Coyotes CC (r.)
California
T. C. Robinson
Los Flamingos
Mexico
P. Clifford
Los Gatos Exec GC
California
C. Glasson
Los Lagos GC
Spain
R. T. Jones
Los Leones GC
Chile
(A. Macdonald)
Los Monteros
Spain
J. Arana
Los Rios CC
Texas
D. January, B. Martindale
Los Robles Greens GC
California
R. E. Baldock
Los Serranos G&CC (North course)
California
J. D. Dunn
Los Serranos G&CC (South course)
California
(William Eaton)
Los Serranos G&CC (r. North course)
California
H. M. Rainville
Los Tabachines, Club de Golf
Mexico
P. Clifford
Lost Creek CC at Lima (r.)
Ohio
H. Purdy
Lost Creek GC
Texas
D. Bennett
Lost Lakes Woods GC (a.9)
Michigan
K. Killian, R. Nugent
Lost Tree Club
Florida
M. Mahannah
Lost Tree Club (r.)
Florida
J. Nicklaus
Los Verdes G&CC
California
W. F. Bell
Loudoun G&CC (9)
Virginia
E. B. Ault
Loughrea GC (r.)
Ireland
E. Hackett
Louis Stoner Private Course
Connecticut
O. E. Smith
Louisville CC (original 9)
Kentucky
R. White
Louisville CC (r.9,a.9)
Kentucky
W. J. Travis
Louisville CC (r.1,a.1)
Kentucky
B. J. Wihry

Louisville Muni
Colorado
F. Hummel
Louth GC
England
T. Williamson
Louth GC
England
J. J. F. Pennink
Loveland Muni
Colorado
H. B. Hughes
Loveland Muni (a.9)
Colorado
F. Hummel
Lovington Muni
New Mexico
W. D. Cantrell
Lowell Thomas Estate GC
New York
W. F. Mitchell
Lower Cascades GC (The Homestead)
Virginia
R. T. Jones
Lowestoft GC
England
J. J. F. Pennink
Lowry AFB GC
Colorado
R. E. Baldock
Lubbock CC (r.9,a.9)
Texas
W. D. Cantrell
Lucan GC (r.)
Ireland
E. Hackett
Lucayan CC
Bahamas
L. S. "Dick" Wilson
Lucerne GC
Florida
D. L. Wallace
Lucky Hills GC (9)
Pennsylvania
X.G. Hassenplug
Ludington Hills GC
Michigan
W. B. and G. H. Matthews
Luffenham Heath GC
England
J. Braid
Luffness New GC
Scotland
T. Morris
Lugano (r.)
Switzerland
D. Harradine
Luisita GC
Philippines
R. T. Jones
Lullingstone Park GC
England
F. W. Hawtree
Lu Lu Temple
Pennsylvania
D. J. Ross
Luray Caverns CC
Virginia
M. and H. Purdy
Luray GC (n.1.e.)
Virginia
F. A. Findlay
Lurgan GC
Northern Ireland
J. J. F. Pennink
Lusaka GC
Zambia
J. J. F. Pennink

272

Lutterworth GC
England
F. W. Hawtree
Lyford Cay Club
Bahamas
L. S. "Dick" Wilson
Lyford Cay Club (a.18)
Bahamas
J. Lee
Lyman Meadow GC
Connecticut
R. T. Jones
Lyndhurst GC
Ohio
G. S. Alves
Lynnfield Centre GC (r.)
Massachusetts
W. F. Mitchell
Lynn Haven CC
Virginia
T. Winton
Lynnwood GC
Ontario, Canada
R. Moote
Lyon, Golf de (27)
France
F. W. Hawtree
Lyons Den G&CC
Ohio
(Bill Lyons)
Lytham & St. Annes GC, Royal
England
G. Lowe
Lytham & St. Annes GC, Royal (r.)
England
W. H. Fowler
Lytham & St. Annes GC, Royal (r.)
England
H. S. Colt
Lytham & St. Annes GC, Royal (r.)
England
T. C. Simpson
Lytham & St. Annes GC, Royal (r.)
England
C. K. Cotton, J. J. F. Pennink
Lytham Short Course, Royal
England
C. D. Lawrie
Macarene GC
Colombia
M. Mahannah, J. Saenz
Maccauvlei CC
South Africa
S. V. Hotchkin
Macclenny G&CC [now Pineview G&CC]
Florida
W. W. Amick
Macdonald Park Muni [formerly Wichita CC]
Kansas
J. Dalgleish
Macdonald Park Muni (r.)
Kansas
P. D. Maxwell
Macdonald Park Muni (r.)
Kansas
W. Diddel
Macdonald Park Muni (r.)
Kansas
R. C. Dunning
Mace Meadows GC (9)
California
J. Fleming
Macgregor Downs
North Carolina
W. C. Byrd
Machrie GC (Islay GC)
Scotland
W. Campbell

Machrie GC (r.)
Scotland
D. M. Steel
Mackenzie's GC
New Hampshire
R. M. Barton
Macrihanish GC (Original course)
Scotland
C. Hunter
Macrihanish GC (r.)
Scotland
T. Morris
Mactaquac Provincial Park GC
New Brunswick, Canada
W. F. Mitchell
Madeline Island Golf Links
Wisconsin
R. T. Jones, Sr. and Jr.
Madera CC
California
R. E. Baldock
Madge Lake GC (r.9,a.9)
Saskatchewan, Canada
C. E. Robinson
Madison CC
Connecticut
W. Park, Jr.
Madison CC
Ohio
G. S. Alves
Madison Park Muni
Illinois
T. Bendelow
Madison Valley Muni
Montana
F. Hummel
Madrid GC, Royal
Spain
H. S. Colt
Madrid GC, Royal
Spain
T. C. Simpson
Madrid GC, Royal
Spain
J. D. Harris
Maggie Valley CC
North Carolina
(William Prevost)
Magnolia CC (9)
Arkansas
H. C. Hackbarth
Magnolia GC
Massachusetts
R. M. Barton
Magnolia GC (9)
Texas
R. Plummer
Magnolia Hills CC
Australia
R. Von Hagge, B. Devlin
Magnolia Valley CC (27)
Florida
(Walter Pursley)
Mahogany Run GC
St. Thomas, Virgin Islands
G. and T. Fazio
Mahoney Park Muni
Nebraska
F. Farley
Mahoning Valley CC (n.1.e.)
Pennsylvania
M. J. McCarthy, Sr.
Mahoning Valley CC (New site)
Pennsylvania
W. F. and D. W. Gordon

Mahon Muni
Ireland
E. Hackett
Maidenhead GC
England
T. Dunn
Maidenhead GC
England
W. Park, Jr.
Maidstone Club (Original 9)
New York
W. H. Tucker, Sr.
Maidstone Club (r.9,a.9)
New York
W. Park, Jr., J. Park
Maidstone Club (r.)
New York
(C. Wheaton Vaughan)
Maidstone CC (r.)
New York
A. H. Tull
Majestic Oaks CC (27)
Minnesota
C. E. Maddox
Majestic Oaks Par 3 (4 holes)
Utah
W. H. Neff
Makaha Inn & CC (East and West courses)
Hawaii
W. F. Bell
Makena GC
Hawaii
R. T. Jones, Jr.
Makstoke Park Castle Bromwich GC
England
F. G. Hawtree
Malahide GC
Ireland
(N. Hone)
Malibu CC
California
W. F. Bell
Malkins Bank
England
F. W. Hawtree
Mallard Head CC
North Carolina
J. P. Gibson
Malone GC (Original 9)
New York
D. J. Ross
Malone GC (a.9)
New York
A. Murray
Malton and Norton GC (a.9)
England
F. W. Hawtree
Malvern GC (a.9)
England
F. W. Hawtree
Manada Gap CC
Pennsylvania
D. W. Gordon
Manago CC (27)
Japan
E. B. Seay, A. Palmer
Manakiki G&CC
Ohio
D. J. Ross
Manatee County GC
Florida
L. Marshall
Manchester CC
New Hampshire
D. J. Ross
Manchester CC
Vermont
G. S. Cornish, W. G. Robinson

Manchester GC
England
A. Mackenzie
Manderly GC
Ontario, Canada
H. Watson
Mandurah Resort GC
Australia
R. T. Jones Jr.
M. and W. GC
Texas
L. Howard
Mangrove Bay Muni
Florida
W. W. Amick
Manhasset CC
New York
D. Emmet, A. H. Tull
Manhattan CC
Kansas
E. L. Bell
Manila G&CC
Philippines
(James Black)
Manila G&CC (r.)
Philippines
R. E. Baldock
Manistee GC
Michigan
W. B. Matthews
Manitouwadge GC
Ontario, Canada
H. Watson
Manizales, CC de
Colombia
H. Watson
Mankato GC (a.9)
Minnesota
W. B. Langford
Manleys GC
Michigan
R. D. Beard
Mannheim GC
West Germany
B. Von Limburger, K. Hoffmann
Manoir Richelieu
Province of Québec, Canada
H. B. Strong
Manor CC
Maryland
H. Collis
Manor CC (r.)
Maryland
P. P. Hines
Manor CC (r.)
Pennsylvania
W. S. Flynn
Manor House Hotel GC
England
J. F. Abercromby, W. H. Fowler
Manor House Hotel GC (r.)
England
J. Alexander
Manor Park CC
Washington, D.C.
H. Collis
Manteca Park GC (9)
California
J. Fleming
Manti Muni
Utah
(Keith Downs)
Manufacturer's G&CC
Pennsylvania
W. S. Flynn
Manufacturer's G&CC (r.)
Pennsylvania
W. F. Gordon

Manwallimick GC (Shawnee on Delaware)
Pennsylvania
C. D. Worthington
Maple Bluff CC
Wisconsin
(George B. Ferry)
Maple Bluff CC (r.)
Wisconsin
K. Killian, R. Nugent
Maple City CC
Ontario, Canada
C. E. Robinson
Maple Crest CC
Wisconsin
L. Macomber
Maplecrest GC
Illinois
R. B. Harris
Maple Crest Par 3 GC (9)
Illinois
W. B. Langford
Mapledale CC
Delaware
R. Roberts
Maple Downs G&CC
Ontario, Canada
W. F. Mitchell
Maple Hill GC
Michigan
R. D. Beard
Maplehurst CC (9)
Maryland
J. G. Harrison
Maple Leaf CC (Exec.)
Florida
(Ward Northrup)
Maplemoor GC
New York
T. Winton
Maple Ridge GC
Alberta, Canada
R. N. Phelps
Maple River GC
North Dakota
E. L. Packard
Mapleview GC
Washington
(Francis L. James)
Maplewood CC
Washington
A. Smith
Maplewood GC
New Hampshire
A. Findlay
Maplewood GC
New Hampshire
D. J. Ross
Maplewood Village Par 3 GC
Nebraska
F. Farley
Mapperley GC
England
T. Williamson
Maracaibo GC
Venezuela
(James B. Wilson)
Maracay
Venezuela
(Carl H. Anderson)
Maramarua GC
New Zealand
J. D. Harris, P. W. Thomson, M. Wolveridge
Marathon GC
Ontario, Canada
S. Thompson
Marble Hall CC [now Green Valley CC]
Pennsylvania
W. S. Flynn

Marble Island G&YC (9)
Vermont
A. W. Tillinghast
Marble Island G&YC (r.9)
Vermont
F. Duane
Marceline CC (9)
Missouri
F. Farley
Marco Island CC
Florida
D. L. Wallace
Marco Island CC (r.)
Florida
P. Dye
Marco Shores CC
Florida
R. Von Hagge, B. Devlin
Mar del Plata GC (r.)
Argentina
A. Mackenzie
Mardon Lodge GC at Barrie
Ontario, Canada
S. Thompson
Marengo Ridge GC
Illinois
W. J. Spear
Mariah Hills GC
Kansas
F. Hummel
Marias Valley G&CC
Montana
N. Woods
Marienbad GC (r.)
Czechoslovakia
B. Von Limburger
Marienburger GC
West Germany
B. Von Limburger
Marietta CC (r.)
Ohio
E. B. Ault
Marina Exec. GC
California
W. F. Bell
Marina G&CC
Florida
R. Garl
Marine and Field GC [now Dyker Beach GC]
New York
T. Bendelow
Marine Corps Par 3 at Nebo
California
L. M. Hughes
Marine Drive GC
British Columbia, Canada
A. V. Macan
Marine Memorial GC (Camp Pendleton)
California
W. P. Bell
Marine Memorial GC (Santa Anna)
California
W. P. Bell
Marine Park GC (27)
New York
R. T. Jones
Mariner Sands CC [formerly Lake St. George CC]
Florida
F. Duane
Marin GC
California
L. M. Hughes

Marion CC (r.)
Ohio
J. Kidwell, M. Hurdzan
Marion GC (9)
Massachusetts
G. C. Thomas, Jr.
Marion Institute GC (9)
Alabama
(Col. James O. Wade, Dr. James T. Murfee III)
Marion Oaks CC
Florida
(John Denton)
Mariposa Pines GC
California
R. E. Baldock
Mark Twain GC
New York
D. J. Ross
Marland Estate GC (9; n.l.e.)
Oklahoma
A. J. Jackson
Marlboro CC
Maryland
A. M. Pulley
Marlborough CC (Original 9)
Massachusetts
W. E. Stiles, J. R. Van Kleek
Marlborough CC (a.9)
Massachusetts
G. S. Cornish, W. G. Robinson
Marlborough GC (a.9)
England
J. H. Stutt
Marlborough GC (27) (n.l.e.)
Province of Québec, Canada
S. Thompson
Marlborough GC (r.) (n.l.e.)
Province of Québec, Canada
H. Watson
Marquette G&CC (a.9)
Michigan
D. Gill
Marquette Park GC (9)
Illinois
T. Bendelow
Marrakesh CC
California
T. G. Robinson
Marre Ranch CC
California
R. Von Hagge, B. Devlin
Marriot's Lincolnshire GC
Illinois
G. and T. Fazio
Marsden Park
England
C. K. Cotton, F. W. Hawtree
Marshall Park
West Virginia
X. G. Hassenplug
Marshfield CC
Massachusetts
W. E. Stiles, J. R. Van Kleek
Marsh Harbor Golf Links
South Carolina
D. Maples
Marsh Island GC [now Pine Island GC]
Mississippi
P. Dye
Marston Green GC
England
(Carl Bretherton)
Marston Green Muni (Birmingham Corp.)
England
F. G. Hawtree

Martin County G&CC (r.9,a.9)
Florida
W. B. Langford
Martin County G&CC (r.)
Florida
E. E. Smith
Martin County G&CC (r.)
Florida
R. Garl
Martindale CC (a.9)
Maine
P. A. Wogan
Martingham G&TC
Maryland
P. And R. Dye
Martin G&CC (r.8,a.9)
Florida
W. B. Langford
Martinique, Golf de la
Martinique
R. T. Jones
Martin Memorial GC
Massachusetts
S. Mitchell
Martinsville G&CC
Indiana
W. Diddel
Marvin Rupp GC
Ohio
R. D. Beard
Mary Calder GC (a.9)
Georgia
G. W. Cobb
Maryland Estate GC
Oklahoma
A. J. Jackson
Maryland G&CC
Maryland
F. Murray, R. Roberts
Maryland University GC
Maryland
E. B. Ault
Maryvale GC
Arizona
W. F. Bell
Mascoutin GC
Wisconsin
E. L. and R. B. Packard
Maspalomas GC (Grand Canary Islands) (South course)
Spain
P. M. Ross
Maspalomas GC (Grand Canary Islands) Spain (North course)
Spain
R. Kirby, G. Player
Massacre Canyon Inn & CC [formerly Gilman CC](River 9)
California
W. H. Johnson
Massanutten GC
Virginia
F. Duane
Massanutten GC (a.9)
Virginia
R. Watson
Massena GC
New York
A. Murray
Massereene GC (a.9)
Northern Ireland
F. W. Hawtree
Massereene GC (r.)
Northern Ireland
E. Hackett
Mather AFB GC
California
J. Fleming
Matlock GC
England
T. Williamson

Mattoon CC (a.9)
Illinois
E. L. and R. B. Packard
Mauh-Na-Tee-See GC
Illinois
C.D. Wagstaff
Maui CC (9)
Hawaii
(Alex Bell, William McEwan)
Mauna Lani Resort GC, Hawaii, (Homer Flint)
Maui Resort GC
Hawaii
R. T. Jones, Jr.
Maumelle G&CC
Arkansas
E. B. Ault
Mauna Kea Beach Hotel GC
Hawaii
R. T. Jones
Max Sharpe Park GC
Texas
(Shelly Mayfield)
Maxwell Muni (a.18)
Texas
D. Bennett
Maxwelton Braes Resort & GC
Wisconsin
G. O'Neil, J. A. Roseman
Maxwelton GC
Indiana
W. B. Langford
Mayacoo Lakes GC
Florida
D. Muirhead, J. Nicklaus
Mayfair CC
Florida
C. S. Butchart
Mayfair CC
Ohio
E. B. Ault
Mayfair G&CC
Alberta, Canada
S. Thompson
Mayfield CC
New York
D. J. Ross
Mayfield CC
Ohio
W. H. Way, H. N. Barker
Mayfield CC
Pennsylvania
X. G. Hassenplug
Mayflower GC
New York
D. Emmet, A. H. Tull
Mays Landing GC
New Jersey
H. Purdy
Mayview G&CC
Pennsylvania
X. G. Hassenplug
Mazamet GC (New course)
France
T. C. Simpson, P. M. Ross
Mazatlan Resort GC
Mexico
R. T. Jones, Sr. and Jr.
Mazatlan Sur, Club
Mexico
R. T. Jones, Jr.
McAlester CC (n.l.e.)
Oklahoma
A. J. Jackson
McAlester CC (New site)
Oklahoma
F. Farley
McAlester CC (r.)
Oklahoma
R. C. Dunning

McAllen CC (New site)
Texas
B. J. Riviere
McAllen Muni
Texas
R. Plummer
McCall GC
Idaho
R. M. Graves
McCann Memorial GC at Poughkeepsie
New York
W. F. Mitchell
McChord AFB GC (Whispering Firs); (9)
Washington
R. E. Baldock
McCleary GC
British Columbia, Canada
E. Brown
McConnell AFB GC (9)
Kansas
F. Farley
McCormick Ranch GC (Palm and Pine courses)
Arizona
D. Muirhead
McFarland Park GC
Alabama
E. Stone
McGregor GC
New York
D. Emmet
McGuire AFB GC
New York
E. B. Ault
McGuires GC
Michigan
W. B. Matthews
McIntire Park GC (9)
Virginia
F. A. Findlay
McKellar Park GC
Tennessee
(Charles W. Graves)
McKinney Veteran's Hospital GC
Texas
R. Plummer
McLaren Park Muni (9)
California
J. Fleming
McMillen Park GC
Indiana
H. Purdy
McMinville CC
Tennessee
R. A. Anderson
McMinville CC
Tennessee
E. L. Packard
Meadia Heights CC (r.)
Pennsylvania
(Chester Ruby)
Meadow Brook Club (n.l.e.)
New York
D. Emmet
Meadow Brook Club (r.; n.l.e.)
New York
A. W. Tillinghast
Meadow Brook Club (New site)
New York
L. S. "Dick" Wilson
Meadowbrook CC (r.)
Kansas
R. C. Dunning
Meadowbrook CC (r.)
Massachusetts
G. S. Cornish

Meadowbrook CC (Original course)
Michigan
W. Park, Jr.
Meadowbrook CC (r. 6, a. 12)
Michigan
H. Collis, J. Daray
Meadowbrook CC (r.)
Michigan
A. Hills
Meadowbrook CC (r.)
Michigan
W. B. and G. H. Matthews
Meadow Brook CC [formerly Midland Valley](n.l.e.)
Missouri
R. Foulis
Meadowbrook CC (New site)
Missouri
R. B. Harris
Meadowbrook CC (a.9)
Ohio
W. Diddel
Meadowbrook CC
Oklahoma
J. P. Maxwell
Meadowbrook CC (a.9)
Oklahoma
D. R. Sechrest
Meadowbrook CC
Virginia
F. A. Findlay
Meadowbrook CC (r.)
Virginia
E. B. Ault
Meadowbrook CC
West Virginia
A. G. McKay
Meadowbrook GC (r.)
Connecticut
W. F. Mitchell
Meadowbrook GC
South Dakota
D. Gill
Meadowbrook Muni (r.)
Texas
R. Plummer
Meadowbrook Muni (r.27)
Texas
W. D. Cantrell
Meadowbrook Muni
Utah
J. M. Riley
Meadowbrook Park 3 GC
Nebraska
F. Farley
Meadowbrook T&CC (r.)
Wisconsin
D. Gill
(The) Meadow Club
California
A. Mackenzie, C. Hunter
(The) Meadow Club (r.)
California
R. M. Graves
Meadow Greens CC
North Carolina
E. Maples
Meadow Hills CC
Arizona
R. F. Lawrence
Meadow Hills CC
Colorado
H. B. Hughes
Meadow Lake Acres CC
Missouri
E. B. Ault

Meadowlakes G&CC (9)
Texas
L. Howard
Meadowlands CC (r.)
Pennsylvania
W. F. Gordon
Meadowlands GC
Ohio
G. S. Alves
Meadowlink Farms GC
Pennsylvania
F. Garbin
Meadows CC
Florida
F. Duane
Meadow Springs G&CC (Original 9)
Washington
(Jack Reimer)
Meadow Springs G&CC (a.9)
Washington
R. M. Graves
Meadowvale GC
California
W. F. Bell
Meadowview GC (r.)
Tennessee
R. L. Jones
Medal Course (r.)
Scotland
T. Morris
Medellin GC
Colombia
S. Thompson
Medellin GC (r.)
Colombia
C. E. Robinson
Medford CC
Oregon
H. C. Egan
Medford Lakes CC
New Jersey
H. Purdy
Medford Village GC [formerly Sunny Jim GC]
New Jersey
W. F. Gordon
Medicine Lodge Muni (r.)
Kansas
C. Mendenhall
Medinah CC (Courses #1, #2 and #3)
Illinois
T. Bendelow
Medinah CC (r.; a.5, Course #3)
Illinois
H. Collis
Medinah CC (r. course #3)
Illinois
K. Killian, R. Nugent
Medina Public GC
Minnesota
(Leo J. Feser)
Meeker GC (9)
Colorado
H. B. Hughes
Meihan Kokusai CC
Japan
P.W. Thomson, M. Wolveridge
Melbourne CC
Arkansas
O. E. Smith
Melbourne G&CC (r.)
Florida
W. W. Amick
Melbourne GC, Royal (West course)
Australia
A. Mackenzie

Melbourne GC, Royal (East course)
Australia
A. Russell
Melbourne GC, Royal (r. East and West courses)
Australia
L. S. "Dick" Wilson
Melody Farms CC (n.l.e.)
Illinois
G. O'Neill, (Jack Croke)
Melody Hill GC
Rhode Island
S. Mitchell
Melreese GC [formerly Le Jeune Road CC]
Florida
L. S. "Dick" Wilson
Melreese GC (r.4)
Florida
R. T. Jones
Melrose CC
Pennsylvania
P. D. Maxwell
Melrose GC
Scotland
W. Park, Jr.
Melton Mowbray GC
England
T. Williamson
Melton Mowbray GC
England
(W. Barfoot)
Memorial Muni at Springfield (n.l.e.)
Massachusetts
W. E. Stiles, J. R. Van Kleek
Memorial Park GC
Texas
J. Bredemus
Memphis CC (Original 9; n.l.e.)
Tennessee
J. Foulis
Memphis CC
Tennessee
D. J. Ross
Menard GC
Illinois
C. E. Maddox
Mendham G&TC
New Jersey
A. H. Tull
Mendip
England
J. J. F. Pennink
Mendota Heights Par 3 GC
Minnesota
P. Coates
Mendota Heights Par 3 GC (r.)
Minnesota
(Emile F. Perret)
Menlo CC
California
T. Nicoll
Menlo CC (r.)
California
R. T. Jones, Sr. and Jr.
Mennagio E Cadenabbia GC
Italy
J. D. Harris
Mennezaies GC (r.)
Colombia
C. E. Robinson
Meon Valley G&CC
England
J. H. Stutt

Mercedes GC
Texas
J. Bredemus
Merced G&CC
California
R. E. Baldock
Mercer County Elks CC
Ohio
H. D. Paddock, Sr.
Mere G&CC
England
J. Braid, G. Duncan
Meriden Muni
Connecticut
R. D. Pryde
Meriden Muni (r.)
Connecticut
A. H. Tull
Meridian GC
Oklahoma
F. Farley
Meridian Hills GC
Indiana
W. Diddel
Meridian Hills GC (r.)
Indiana
G. and T. Fazio
Meridian Valley CC
Washington
T. G. Robinson
Merion GC (East and West courses)
Pennsylvania
H. I. Wilson
Merion GC (r. East course)
Pennsylvania
W. S. Flynn
Merion GC (r.)
Pennsylvania
P. D. Maxwell
Meriwether National GC
Oregon
F. Federspiel
Merrick Park GC
New York
F. Duane
Merrill GC (r.;a.9)
Wisconsin
D. Herfort
Merrimack GC (9)
Massachusetts
E. F. Wogan
Mesa CC
Arizona
W. P. Bell
Mesa del Sol GC
Arizona
E.B. Seay, A. Palmer
Mesa Verde CC
California
W. F. Bell
Mesquite Muni
Texas
L. Howard
Metacomet CC (original course)
Rhode Island
W. Park, Jr.
Metacomet CC (new course)
Rhode Island
D. J. Ross
Metacomet CC (r.2)
Rhode Island
G. S. Cornish
Metairie CC
Louisiana
J. L. Daray
Metropolis Club
New York
H. B. Strong

Metropolitan GC
Australia
(J.B. Mackenzie)
Metropolitan GC (r.)
Australia
L. S. "Dick" Wilson
Metropolitan GC (r.) (a. 8)
Australia
P.W. Thomson, M. Wolveridge
L.S. "Dick" Wilson
Metz, Golf de
France
F. W. Hawtree
Mexicali G&CC
Mexico
L. M. Hughes
Mexico City, CC of
Mexico
W. Smith
Mexico City, CC of (r.)
Mexico
J. Bredemus
Mexico, Club de Golf
Mexico
L. M. Hughes, P. Clifford
Meyrick Park
England
T. Dunn
Miami Beach CC
Florida
W. B. Langford, T. J. Moreau
Miami Beach Polo Club (r.; n.l.e.)
Florida
W. S. Flynn
Miami Biltmore CC
Florida
D. J. Ross
Miami Biltmore CC (now Coral Gables Biltmore CC)
Florida
W. B. Langford
Miami, CC of (East, West courses)
Florida
R. T. Jones
Miami, CC of (South course)
Florida
W. H. Dietsch, Jr.
Miami G&CC (a.9)
Oklahoma
D. R. Sechrest
Miami CC (n.l.e.)
Florida
D. J. Ross
Miami Golf Links (9; n.l.e.)
Florida
A. Findlay
Miami Lakes Inn & CC (18)
Florida
W. R. Watts
Miami Lakes Inn & CC (a.18 Par 3)
Florida
J. E. O'Connor, Jr.
Miami Shores CC
Florida
R. F. Lawrence
Miami Shores GC
Ohio
D. J. Ross
Miami Shores GC (r.)
Ohio
J. Kidwell, M. Hurdzan
Miami Springs CC
Florida
(Thomas W. Palmer)
Miami Valley CC
Ohio
D. J. Ross
Miami View CC
Ohio
W. Diddel

Michaywe Hills GC
Michigan
(Robert W. Bills, Donald L. Child)
Michigan State University (Forest Akers GC)
Michigan
W. B. Matthews
Michigan Tech University GC
Michigan
W. K. Newcomb
Mick Riley GC
Utah
J. M. Riley
Mid Carolina CC
South Carolina
R. F. Breeden
Mid City GC (n.l.e.)
Illinois
W. B. Langford, T. J. Moreau
Mid County CC (9)
Nebraska
H. Hughes, R. Watson
Middle Bass Island GC
Ohio
G. S. Alves
Middle Bay CC (r.)
New York
A. H. Tull
Middleburg Recreation Area GC
Pennsylvania
E. B. Ault
Middlemore GC (r.)
New Zealand
P. Thomson
Middle Plantation CC
Virginia
D. and E. Maples
Middlesborough GC
England
J. Braid
Middlesborough GC
England
J. H. Stutt
Middletown GC (now Edgewood CC)
Connecticut
R. J. Ross
Middleton Par 3 GC
Massachusetts
G. S. Cornish, W. G. Robinson
Middletown GC (r.)
Ohio
H. Purdy
Mid Florida GC
Florida
J. L. Lee
Mid Island CC (r.)
New York
H. Purdy
Midland CC
Illinois
R. B. Harris
Midland CC
Michigan
W. B. Matthews
Midland CC
Texas
R. Plummer
Midland CC (r.)
Texas
R. Kirby, G. Player
Midland G&CC (a.9)
Ontario, Canada
(J. Ross Parrott)
Midland Hills CC
Minnesota
R. M. Barton, S. J. Raynor
Midland Farms GC
North Carolina
T. Jackson
Midland Hills CC (r.)
Minnesota
P. Coates

Midlands GC
Victoria, Australia
P.W. Thomson, M. Wolveridge
Midland Trail GC
Kentucky
E. L. Packard
Midland Valley CC
Missouri
R. Foulis
Midland Valley CC
South Carolina
E. Maples
Midlane CC
Illinois
R. B. Harris
Midlane CC
Illinois
W. J. Spear
Midlothian CC
Illinois
H. J. Tweedie
Mid-Ocean GC
Bermuda
C. B. Macdonald
Mid-Ocean GC (r.;
Bermuda
R. T. Jones
Mid Pacific GC (original 9)
Hawaii
S. Raynor
Mid Pacific GC (a. 9)
Hawaii
W. G. Wilkinson
Mid Pacific GC (r.)
Hawaii
R. E. Baldock
Mid Pines CC
North Carolina
D. J. Ross
Mid Rivers Y&CC
Florida
(Charles P. Martin)
Mid-Surrey GC [now Royal]
England
T. Dunn
Mid-Surrey GC, Royal (r.)
England
J. H. Taylor
Mid-Surrey GC, Royal (r.)
England
R. Beale
Mid-Surrey GC, Royal (r. Ladies course)
England
J. H. Taylor
Midvale G&CC
New York
R. T. Jones, S. Thompson
Midway GC (9)
Wyoming
H. B. Hughes, R. Watson
Midwest City Muni Par 3 GC
Oklahoma
F. Farley
Midwest CC (r.9,a.9, East course; r. West course)
Illinois
R. B. Harris
Midwick CC (n.l.e.)
California
N. Macbeth
Milan CC (9)
Tennessee
G. Curtis
Milbrook GC (r.3)
Connecticut
F. Duane

Milburn G&CC
Kansas
W. B. Langford
Milburn G&CC (r.)
Kansas
F. Farley
Miles Grant Exec. GC
Florida
M. and C. Mahannah
Miles Grant Exec. GC (r.)
Florida
E. B. Ault
Mile Square GC
California
H. M. and D. A. Rainville
Milford CC (r.)
Connecticut
W. F. Mitchell
Milham Park Muni
Michigan
D. T. Millar
Mililani GC
Hawaii
R. E. Baldock
Militar, CC
Colombia
H. Watson
Millbrook GC (original 9)
Connecticut
G. S. Cornish
Millburn Par 3 GC
New Jersey
H. Purdy
Mill Creek CC
North Carolina
R. Von Hagge, B. Devlin
Mill Creek CC
Texas
R.T. Jones, Jr.
Mill Creek CC
Washington
T. G. Robinson
Mill Creek GC (North and South courses)
Ohio
D. J. Ross
Mill Creek GC
Tennessee
L. Howard
Milledgeville CC
Georgia
G. W. Cobb
Milligan Park GC
Indiana
G. Kern
Mill Quarter Plantation
Virginia
E. B. Ault
Millrace CC (36)
Michigan
A. Hills
Mill Race GC
Pennsylvania
G. S. Cornish, W. G. Robinson
Mill River CC
Connecticut
T. Winton
Mill River CC
New York
(Gerald C. Roby)
Mill River CC (r.4)
New York
F. Duane
Mill River GC
Prince Edward Island, Canada
C. E. Robinson
Mill Road Farm GC (n.l.e.)
Illinois
W. S. Flynn

Milltown (r.)
Ireland
E. Hackett
Milne Memorial GC (9;
Iowa
(Donald K. Rippel)
Milpitas GC
California
A. M. Pulley
Milton Hoosic GC [formerly Hoosic Whisic)
Massachusetts
W. Park, Jr.
Milwaukee CC
Wisconsin
H. S. Colt, C. H. Alison
Milwaukee CC (r.)
Wisconsin
R. T. Jones
Mimosa Hills GC
North Carolina
D. J. Ross
Minaki Lodge Hotel GC
Ontario, Canada
S. Thompson
Minchinhampton GC
England
F. W. Hawtree
Mingo Springs GC
Maine
E. F. Wogan
Minikahda Club (Original 9)
Minnesota
R. Foulis, W. Watson
Minikahda Club (r.9,a.9)
Minnesota
(Robert Taylor, C. T. Jaffray)
Minikahda Club (r.)
Minnesota
D. J. Ross
Minikahda Club (r.)
Minnesota
R. Plummer
Minneapolis GC
Minnesota
W. Park, Jr.
Minneapolis GC (r.)
Minnesota
(Emile F. Perret)
Minnechaug GC (rte.plan)
Connecticut
(Graham Clark)
Minnechaug GC (Greens, original 9)
Connecticut
W. F. Mitchell, A. Zikorus
Minnechaug GC (Greens, new 9)
Connecticut
G. S. Cornish
Minnedosa GC
Manitoba, Canada
J. A. Thompson
Minnehaha CC (r.)
South Dakota
E.L. Packard
Minnehaha CC (r. 6, 1976)
South Dakota
K. Killian, R. Nugent
Minnesota Valley CC (r.)
Minnesota
E. B. Seay, A. Palmer
Minnetonka CC (r.)
Minnesota
D. Herfort
Minnreg CC (27)
Minnesota
R. N. Phelps
Minor Park GC
Missouri
(L. Wesly Flatt)
Mint Valley Muni
California
R. W. Fream

Miracle Hill GC
Nebraska
F. Farley
Miramachi G&CC (a.9)
New Brunswick, Canada
C. E. Robinson
Miramar GC (r.)
New Zealand
P.W. Thomson, M. Wolveridge
Mira Vista G&CC [formerly Berkeley CC]
California
W. R. Hunter
Mira Vista G&CC (r.)
California
R. M. Graves
Mirror Lakes CC
Florida
M. Mahannah
Mirror Lake GC
Idaho
(Ed Hunnicutt)
Misquemicut GC (r.)
Rhode Island
D. J. Ross
Mission Bay CC
California
T. G. Robinsin
Mission CC
Texas
R. Plummer
Mission GC
British Columbia, Canada
N. Woods
Mission Hills CC (Old course)
California
D. Muirhead
Mission Hills CC (New course)
California
E. B. Seay, A. Palmer
Mission Hills CC (n.l.e.)
Illinois
L. Macomber
Mission Hills CC (a. Par 3 course)
Illinois
C. D. Wagstaff
Mission Hills CC (new course)
Illinois
E. L. and R. B. Packard
Mission Hills CC (r.)
Kansas
P. D. Maxwell
Mission Hills CC (r.)
Kansas
W. Diddel
Mission Hills CC (r.)
Kansas
R. C. Dunning
Mission Hills CC (r.)
Kansas
F. Farley
Mission Inn & CC [formerly Floridian CC]
Florida
(Captain Charles Clarke)
Mission Inn & CC (r.; a.3)
Florida
(Thomas Line)
Mission Lakes CC
California
T. G. Robinson
Mission Valley CC [now Stardust CC]
California
L. M. Hughes
Mission Viejo GC
California
R. T. Jones
Mississauga G&CC (r.)
Ontario, Canada
S. Thompson

Mississauga G&CC (r.3,a.9)
Ontario, Canada
H. Watson
Mississippi Valley College GC
Mississippi
L. Howard
Missoula CC (r.9,a.9)
Montana
(Francis L. James)
Missouri, CC of
Missouri
M. H. Ferguson
Mitchell Creek GC
Michigan
G. and W.B. Matthews
Mitchell CC (Original 9)
South Dakota
R. Watson
Mittelrheinscher GC
Bad Ems, West Germany
(Karl Hoffmann)
Moanalua GC
Hawaii
(Donald Macintyre)
Mitchelstown GC (r.)
Ireland
E. Hackett
Mobile, CC of
Alabama
D.J. Ross
Mobile, CC of (r.)
Alabama
A. H. Tull
Mobile, CC of (a.9)
Alabama
E. Stone
Mobray CC (r.)
South Africa
S. V. Hotchkin
Moccasin Creek CC [formerly Prairiewood CC]
South Dakota
C. E. Maddox
Model City Commercial Course
Province of Québec, Canada
S. Thompson
Moffat GC
Scotland
B. Sayers
Moffett Field GC
California
R. M. Graves
Mohansic Park GC
New York
T. Winton
Mohawk CC
Ohio
W. J. Rockefeller
Mohawk CC (r.18,a.9)
Ohio
F. Garbin
Mohawk GC
New York
D. Emmet
Mohawk Hills GC
Indiana
G. Kern
Mohawk Park Muni (Course #1)
Oklahoma
W. Diddel
Mohawk Park Muni (r. Course #1)
Oklahoma
P. D. Maxwell
Mohawk Park Muni (r. Course #1; a. Course #2)
Oklahoma
F. Farley
Mohican Hills GC (9)
Ohio
J. Kidwell, M. Hurdzan

Mojaliki CC
New Hampshire
W. E. Stiles, J. R. Van Kleek
Moka GC [formerly St. Andrews GC]
Trinidad
H. S. Colt
Moncton G&CC (r.)
New Brunswick, Canada
S. Thompson
Momence CC
Illinois
W. Watson
Moncton G&CC (a.9)
New Brunswick, Canada
C. E. Robinson
Monifieth
Scotland
W. Park, Jr.
Monifieth (r.)
Scotland
J. H. Stutt
Monkstown (r.)
Ireland
E. Hackett
Monkton Hall GC
Scotland
J. Braid
Monmouth CC
New Jersey
S. Dunn
Monmouthshire GC
Wales
J. Braid
Monongahela Valley CC
Pennsylvania
E. F. Loeffler, J. McGlynn
Monoosnock CC (r.)
Massachusetts
W. E. Stiles, J. R. Van Kleek
Monroe CC (Original 9)
Georgia
C. H. Adams
Monroe CC (a.9)
Georgia
W. W. Amick
Monroe CC
Michigan
D. J. Ross
Monroe CC (r.)
Michigan
C. E. Robinson
Monroe CC
New York
D. J. Ross
Monroe CC (r.2)
New York
G. S. Cornish, W. G. Robinson
Monroe CC
North Carolina
D. J. Ross
Monroe County GC
New York
H. Purdy
Monroe Creek GC
Pennsylvania
E. B. Ault
Monroe G&CC
Georgia
C. H. Adams
Monsanto Employees GC
Florida
W. W. Amick
Monsheim GC
West Germany
B. Von Limburger
Mont Adstock GC
Province of Québec, Canada
J. Watson

Montague GC (a.3)
Vermont
G. S. Cornish, W. G. Robinson
Montammy CC
New Jersey
F. Duane
Montammy CC (r.)
New Jersey
J. Finger
Montauk Downs CC (n.l.e.)
New York
H. C. C. Tippets
Montauk G&RC
New York
R. T. Jones
Montaus CC
Pennsylvania
J. G. Harrison
Montcalm, Club de Golf
Province of Québec, Canada
J. Watson
Montclair CC (r.9,a.9)
Tennessee
A. L. Davis
Montclair CC (a. Exec. 9)
Tennessee
J. L. Lee
Montclair GC (27)
New Jersey
D. J. Ross
Montclair GC (a.9)
New Jersey
C. H. Banks
Montclair GC (r. East course)
New Jersey
R. T. Jones
Montclair GC (r.)
New Jersey
R. L. Jones
Montclair GC
Virginia
A.M. Pulley
Mont D'Arbois GC
France
H. Cotton
Montebello GC
California
M. Behr
Montebello GC (r.)
California
W. F. Bell
Monte Carlo GC
France
W. Park, Jr.
Monte Carlo GC (r.)
France
F. G. Hawtree
Montecastillo, Club de Golf
Mexico
P. Clifford
Montecello GC (9)
Utah
A. J. Snyder
Montecito CC
California
M. Behr
Monte Costello, Club de Golf
Mexico
C. H. Adams
Monte Cristo CC
Texas
D. R. Sechrest
Monte Gordo CC
Portugal
H. Cotton
Monterey CC (Rancho Mirage; 27)
California
T. G. Robinson

Monterey Hill Par 3 GC
California
W. P. Bell
Monterey Mobile CC (Exec. 9)
California
R. Watson
Monterey Peninsula CC (Dunes course)
California
S. J. Raynor, C. H. Banks
Monterey Peninsula CC (r. Dunes course)
California
W. R. Hunter, A. Mackenzie
Monterey Peninsula CC (Shore course)
California
R. E. Baldock
Monterey Peninsula CC (r.Shore course)
California
R. B. Harris
Monterrey CC
Mexico
J. Bredemus
Monte Ste-Anne GC
Province of Québec, Canada
H. and J. Watson
Montgomery Village
Maryland
E. B. Ault
Monticello CC
Indiana
P. Dye
Montour Heights CC (Original 9)
Pennsylvania
E. F. Loeffler, J. McGlynn
Montour Heights CC (r.9,a.9)
Pennsylvania
J. G. Harrison, F. Garbin
Montreal, CC of
Province of Québec, Canada
A. Murray
Montreal, CC of (r.)
Province of Québec, Canada
P. and R. Dye
Montreal GC, Royal (Dixie; n.l.e.)
Province of Québec, Canada
"Young" W. Dunn
Montreal GC, Royal (Dixie; 36; n.l.e.)
Province of Québec, Canada
W. Park, Jr.
Montreal GC, Royal (r. South course; n.l.e.)
Province of Québec, Canada
H. S. Colt
Montreal GC, Royal (Isle Bizard; Blue, Red and Green courses)
Province of Québec, Canada
L. S. "Dick" Wilson
Montreal Muni (2nd 18)
Province of Québec, Canada
A. Murray
Montreux GC
Switzerland
D. Harradine
Montrose GC (9)
Colorado
H. B. Hughes
Montrose GC (r.)
Scotland
W. Park, Jr.
Mont St. Marie GC
Province of Québec, Canada
J. Watson
Mont Tremblant GC (r.)
Province of Québec, Canada
H. Watson
Moody AFB GC (9)
Georgia
J. Finger

Moonbrook CC (Original course)
New York
W. Park, Jr.
Moonbrook CC (r. 12, a. 6)
New York
W. F. and D. W. Gordon
Moonbrook CC (a.9)
New York
W. E. Harries
Moonbrook CC (r.)
New York
R. T. Jones
Moonlake GC
Illinois
K. Killian, R. Nugent
Moon Valley CC
Arizona
L. S. "Dick" Wilson
Moor Allerton GC (Former site)(n.l.e.)
England
A. Mackenzie
Moor Allerton GC (New site; 27)
England
R. T. Jones
Moore Estates GC
New York
C. B. Macdonald
Moorefield-Petersburg GC
West Virginia
R. Roberts
Moore Place GC
England
H. Vardon
Mooresville GC
North Carolina
J. P. Gibson
(The) Moorings GC
Florida
P. Dye
Moor Park GC (High)
England
H. S. Colt
Moor Park GC (West)
England
A. Mackenzie, H. S. Colt
Moor Park GC (r.)
England
F. G. Hawtree
(The) Moors of Portage
Michigan
A. Hills
Moortown GC
England
A. Mackenzie
Morago CC
California
R. M. Graves
Moraine CC
Ohio
A. Campbell
Moraine CC (r.)
Ohio
L. S. "Dick" Wilson
Morelia, CC
Mexico
P. Clifford
Moretonhampstead GC (r.)
England
T. J. A. McAuley
Morfar GC [now Back O' Beyond GC]
New York
E. Ryder
Morfontaine, Golf de (27)
France
T. C. Simpson

277

Morningside Hotel GC
New York
A. H. Tull
Morpeth GC (r.)
England
J. H. Stutt
Morris CC (n.l.e.)
Illinois
W. B. Langford, T. J. Moreau
Morris CC (New site)
Illinois
J. R. Darrah
Morris County GC (r.)
New Jersey
H. J. Whigham
Morris County GC (r.)
New Jersey
H. Purdy
Morristown, CC of
Tennessee
W. B. Langford
Morris Williams Muni
Texas
L. Howard
Morsum-Sylt GC
West Germany
B. Von Limburger
Mortimer Singer Estate GC
England
W. H. Fowler
Morton Hall GC (r.)
Scotland
J. H. Taylor
Morton Hall GC (r.)
Scotland
F. W. Hawtree
Moselem Springs CC
Pennsylvania
G. Fazio
Moses Lake GC
Washington
(Melvin A. Hueston)
Moss Creek Plantation (Devil's Elbow
  courses, North and South)
South Carolina
G. and T. Fazio
Moulton Muni
Alabama
E. Stone
Mountain Brook CC
Alabama
D. J. Ross
Mountain Brook CC (r.)
Alabama
G. W. Cobb
Mountain Dell CC
Utah
W. F. Bell
Mountain Gate CC
California
T. G. Robinson
Mountain Glen GC
North Carolina
G. W. Cobb
Mountain Home AFB GC
Idaho
R. E. Baldock
Mountain Lakes C
Florida
S. J. Raynor
Mountain Lakes Resort GC
Tennessee
L. Howard
Mountain Meadows CC (n.l.e.)
California
W. P. Bell
Mountain Meadows CC (New site)
California
T. G. Robinson

Mountain Ranches GC
Province of Québec, Canada
H. Watson
Mountain Ranch GC
Arkansas
E. B. Ault
Mountain Ridge CC (Original course;
  n.l.e.)
New Jersey
D. S. Hunter
Mountain Ridge CC (r. Original course)
New Jersey
H. B. Strong
Mountain Ridge CC (New site)
New Jersey
A. W. Tillinghast
Mountains GC
North Carolina
W. B. Lewis
Mountain Shadows GC
Arizona
A. J. Snyder
Mountain Shadows Muni (Original 18)
California
R. E. Baldock
Mountain Shadows Muni (a.18)
California
G. Baird
Mountain Springs Exec. GC
North Carolina
E. and D. Maples
Mountain Valley CC (Par 3 course)
North Carolina
G. W. Cobb
Mountain View GC
New Hampshire
R. M. Barton
Mountain View GC
Pennsylvania
E. B. Ault
Mountain View GC
Utah
W. H. Neff
Mountain View GC
Washington
(R. Coleman)
Mount Airy CC [now Whitemarsh Valley
  CC]
Pennsylvania
G. C. Thomas, Jr.
Mount Bruno
Province of Québec, Canada
W. Park, Jr.
Mount Cobb Muni
Pennsylvania
J. G. Harrison, F. Garbin
Mount Crotched CC (n.l.e.)
New Hampshire
D. J. Ross
Mount Dora CC
Florida
H. D. Paddock, Sr.
Mount Hope G&CC
Ontario, Canada
C. E. Robinson
Mount Irvine Bay Hotel GC
Tobago
J. D. Harris
Mount Kineo CC
Maine
(Arthur Townley)
Mount Kisco CC (r.)
New York
A. W. Tillinghast
Mount Lebanon CC
Pennsylvania
J. G. Harrison

Mount Lomond G&CC
Utah
J. M. Riley
Mount Magog Park GC (r.)
Province of Québec, Canada
W. F. Mitchell
Mount Mitchell GC
North Carolina
F. W. Hawtree
Mount Odin Muni (r.)
Pennsylvania
X. G. Hassenplug
Mount Ogden Muni
Utah
G. Von Elm
Mount Pleasant CC [now Leicester Hill]
  (r.)
Massachusetts
A. H. Tull, W. F. Mitchell
Mount Pleasant CC (New site)
Massachusetts
W. F. Mitchell
Mount Pleasant CC
New Hampshire
A. Findlay
Mount Pleasant CC
South Carolina
G. W. Cobb
Mount Pleasant Muni
Maryland
C. Hook
Mountrath GC (r.)
Ireland
E. Hackett
Mount St. Helena GC (9)
California
J. Fleming
Mount Snow GC
Vermont
G. S. Cornish, W. G. Robinson
Mount Tom CC [now Wyckoff Park]
Massachusetts
D. J. Ross
Mount Vernon CC (r.)
Ohio
J. Kidwell, M. Hurdzan
Mount Vernon GC (a.9)
Illinois
G. Kern
Mount Washington Hotel & GC (Bretton
  Woods)
New Hampshire
D. J. Ross
Mount Whitney CC (9)
California
R. E. Baldock
Mountwood Park
West Virginia
G. W. Cobb, J. B. LaFoy
Mowbray CC (r.)
South Africa
S. V. Hotchkin
Mowsbury Park Muni
England
F. W. Hawtree
Muirfield GC
Scotland
T. Morris
Muirfield GC (r.)
Scotland
H. S. Colt
Muirfield GC (r.)
Scotland
T. C. Simpson
Muirfield Links (n.l.e.)
New York
J. D. Dunn

Muirfield Village, CC at
Ohio
J. Nicklaus
Muirfield Village GC
Ohio
D. Muirhead, J. Nicklaus
Mullet Bay GC
St. Martin
J. L. Lee
Mullingar GC
Ireland
J. Braid, J. R. Stutt
Mullion GC
England
T. Williamson
Mullion GC (r.)
England
J. H. Stutt
Mulrany (r.)
Ireland
E. Hackett
Mummy Mountain GC
Arizona
P. and R. Dye
Munchener GC
West Germany
B. Von Limburger
Municipal Club
Alabama
W. E. Stiles, J. R. Van Kleek
Murcar GC (27)
Scotland
A. Simpson
Murcar GC (r.)
Scotland
J. Braid
Murrayfield GC ·
West Germany
W. Park, Jr.
Murray Muni
Saskatchewan, Canada
C. Muret
Murrayshall GC
Scotland
J. H. Stutt
Murrieta (Hot Springs) GC
California
R. T. Jones, Sr. and Jr.
Musashino CC
Japan
(Ichisuke Izumi)
Muskegon CC (r.)
Michigan
W. B. and G. H. Matthews
Muskerry GC
Ireland
A. Mackenzie
Muskogee CC (Original 9; n.l.e.)
Oklahoma
L. Brownlee
Muskogee CC
Oklahoma
P. D. Maxwell
Muskogee CC (r.)
Oklahoma
D. R. Sechrest
Muskoka Beach GC
Ontario, Canada
S. Thompson
Muskoka Lakes G&CC
Ontario, Canada
S. Thompson
Muskoka Lakes G&CC (a. 3rd 9)
Ontario, Canada
C. E. Robinson
Musselburgh, Royal (Preston Grange)
Scotland
J. Braid

Musselburgh, Royal (Preston Grange; r.)
Scotland
M. Park II
Muswell Hill GC
England
W. Park, Jr.
Muttontown CC
New York
A. H. Tull
Muttontown CC (r.)
New York
R. T. Jones, F. Duane
Muttontown G&CC (r.)
New York
J. Finger
Myakka Pines GC (27)
Florida
L. Marshall
Myerlee CC
Florida
A. Hills
Myers Park CC (Original 9)
North Carolina
(Earl S. Draper)
Myers Park CC (r.)
North Carolina
D. J. Ross
Myers Park CC (a.9)
North Carolina
A. W. Tillinghast
Myers Park CC (r.)
North Carolina
E. Maples
Myers Park CC (r.)
North Carolina
R. L. Jones
Myllendonk, Schloss GC
West Germany
B. Von Limburger
Myopia Hunt Club (Original course n.l.e.)
Massachusetts
(R. M. Appleton)
Myopia Hunt Club
Massachusetts
H. C. Leeds
Myopia Hunt Club (r.4)
Massachusetts
G. S. Cornish
Myosotis CC
New Jersey
A. W. Tillinghast
Myrtle Beach National GC (East, West
  and South courses)
South Carolina
F. Duane, A. Palmer
Myrtle Beach Par 3 GC
South Carolina
E. B. Ault
Myrtlewood GC (Palmetto course)
South Carolina
E. B. Ault
Myrtlewood GC (Pines course)
South Carolina
G. W. Cobb
Mystery Valley CC
Georgia
L. S. "Dick" Wilson

Nagawaukee Park War Memorial GC
Wisconsin
E. L. Packard
Nairn GC (Original course
Scotland
A. Simpson

278

Nairn GC (r.)
Scotland
T. Morris
Nairn GC (r.)
Scotland
J. Braid
Nambu Fuji GC
Japan
J.D. Harris, P. Thomas, M. Wolveridge
Nanaimo CC
British Columbia, Canada
A. V. Macan
Nantes GC
France
J. J. F. Pennink
Nanticoke GC
Ontario, Canada
R. and C. Muylaert
Napa Muni [now J. F. K. Memorial]
California
R. Baldock, J. Fleming, T. Harmon
Naperville CC (r.)
Illinois
D. Gill
Naples Beach Hotel GC (r.)
Florida
M. Mahannah
Naples Beach Hotel GC (r.)
Florida
R. Garl
Naples, CC of
Florida
W. Diddel
Napoleon GC
Ohio
W. J. Rockefeller
Nappanee Muni (a.9)
Indiana
G. Kern
Narashino CC (Kings and Queens courses)
Japan
K. Fujita
Narrowsburg GC
New York
H. Purdy
Naruo CC
Japan
Akaboshi Brothers
Nashawtuc CC
Massachusetts
G. S. Cornish
Nashboro National CC
Tennessee
B. J. Wihry
Nashville G & Athletic C [formerly Crocket Springs]
Tennessee
R. Von Hagge, B. Devlin
Nashua CC
New Hampshire
W. E. Stiles, J. R. Van Kleek
Nashua CC (r.)
New Hampshire
W. F. Mitchell
Nassau CC
New York
D. Emmet
Nassau CC (r.)
New York
H. B. Strong
Nassau CC (r.)
New York
F. Duane
Nassau County Park GC (36) (now Eisenhower Park)
New York
R. T. Jones

Nassau GC [now Ambassador Beach GC]
Bahamas
D. Emmet
Nassau Shores CC
New York
M. J. McCarthy, Sr.
Nassawango CC
Maryland
R. Roberts
Nasu GC
Japan
K. Fujita
Natchez Trace CC
Mississippi
(John Frazier)
Natick CC (a.9)
Massachusetts
S. Mitchell
National Cash Register (North and South courses)
Ohio
L. S. "Dick" Wilson
National GC
Ontario, Canada
G. and T. Fazio
(The) National Golf Links of America
New York
C. B. Macdonald
(The) National Golf Links of America (r.)
New York
R. T. Jones
National Navy Medical GC (r.9)
Maryland
E. B. Ault
Mauh-Na-Ta-See CC
Illinois
C. D. Wagstaff
Nautical Inn Exec. GC [formerly Stone Bridge GC]
Arizona
R. F. Lawrence
Navajo Canyon CC
California
W. P. Bell
Navajo Fields CC (n.l.e.)
Illinois
H. Collis
Naval Academy GC (r.)
Maryland
W. S. Flynn
Naval Postgraduate School GC
California
R. M. Graves
Navatanee GC
Thailand
R. T. Jones, Sr. and Jr.
Navy GC
California
J. B. Williams
Navy GC, Admiral Baker Field (r.)
California
T. G. Robinson
Navy GC, Los Alametos Air Station
California
T. G. Robinsin
Navy-Marine GC
Hawaii
W. P. Bell
Neal Choate GC
Michigan
R. D. Beard
Nealhurst GC (n.1.e.)
Florida
S. Thompson

Neasdon
Great Britain
W. Park, Jr.
Needham GC (Original course)
Massachusetts
(John Graham)
Needham GC
Massachusetts
W. E. Stiles, J. R. Van Kleek
Needham GC
Massachusetts
E. F. Wogan
Needles GC
California
H. M. and D. A. Rainville
Needwood GC
Maryland
R. Roberts
Nefyn GC (r.)
Wales
F. W. Hawtree
Neheim-Huston GC
West Germany
B. Von Limburger
Neipsic Par 3 at Glastonbury
Connecticut
G. S. Cornish, W. G. Robinson
Nelles AFB GC [now Sunrise GC]
Nevada
T. G. Robinson
Nelson GC (a.9)
England
F. W. Hawtree
Nelson GC (r.)
New Zealand
J.D. Harris, P.W. Thomson, M. Wolveridge
Nemacolin CC
Pennsylvania
E. F. Loeffler, J. McGlynn
Nemacolin CC (r.)
Pennsylvania
A. W. Tillinghast
Nemaha G&CC (n.l.e.)
Oklahoma
F. Farley
Nenagh GC
Ireland
E. Hackett
Neuchatel GC
Switzerland
B. Von Limburger
Neumann Park GC (a.9)
Ohio
J. Kidwell, M. Hurdzan
Neustadt GC
East Germany
B. Von Limburger, K. Hoffmann
Nevele Hotel GC
New York
A. H. Tull
Nevesink CC
New Jersey
H. Purdy
Newark Athletic Club
New Jersey
A. Findlay
Newark Athletic Club (at Essex Fells)
New Jersey
D. J. Ross
Newark CC
Delaware
W. Reid
Newark CC (a.9)
Delaware
F. Murray, R. Roberts
Newark GC [formerly El Campo GC]
California
J. Fleming

New Ashburn GC of Halifax G&CC
Nova Scotia, Canada
G. S. Cornish, W. G. Robinson
New Bedford CC
Massachusetts
W. Park, Jr.
New Bedford Muni [now Wahling City GC](Original course)
Massachusetts
D. J. Ross
New Bedford Muni (now Whaling City GC](r.)
Massachusetts
W. F. Mitchell
New Bedford Muni [now Whaling City GC](a.9)
Massachusetts
S. Mitchell
New Bern G&CC
North Carolina
E. Maples
Newberry CC
South Carolina
R. F. Breeden
Newbiggin-By-Sea
England
W. Park, Jr.
Newbold Common GC
England
(Frederick Gibberd
Newbridge CC
Maryland
R. Roberts
Newburgh GC (r.)
New York
H. Purdy
New Canaan, CC of (Original course)
Connecticut
"Young" W. Dunn
New Canaan, CC of
Connecticut
W. Park, Jr.
New Canaan, CC of (a.9)
Connecticut
A. H. Tull
New Canaan, CC of (r.)
Connecticut
R. T. Jones
Newcastle (City of) GC
England
A. Mackenzie
Newcastle CC
Pennsylvania
A. W. Tillinghast
Newcastle GC
Australia
(Eric L. Apperly)
Newcastle Under Lyme
England
F. W. Hawtree
Newcastlewest (r.)
Ireland
E. Hackett
New CC
Kentucky
C. R. Blankenship
(The) New Course, St. Andrews
Scotland
T. Morris
New Forest GC
England
(Peter Swann)
New Glasgow GC (r.)
Province of Québec, Canada
H. Watson

New GC (Original 18)
France
T. C. Simpson
New GC (a.9)
France
H. Cotton
New Haven CC (Original course)
Connecticut
R. D. Pryde
New Haven CC
Connecticut
W. Park, Jr.
New Haven CC (r.1)
Connecticut
A. Zikorus
New Haven Muni
Connecticut
R. D. Pryde
New Haven Muni (Alling Memorial GC; r.)
Connecticut
A. Zikorus
Newlands
Ireland
J. Braid
Newlands (r.)
Ireland
E. Hackett
New London CC (r.5)
Connecticut
G. S. Cornish, W. G. Robinson
New Luffness
Scotland
W. Park, Jr.
Newmarket GC [now Royal Worlington]
England
T. Dunn
New Meadows GC
Massachusetts
P. A. Wogan
New Mexico Military Institute GC
New Mexico
F. Farley
New Mexico State University GC
New Mexico
F. Farley
Newport CC (a.9)
Arkansas
E. B. Ault
Newport CC
New Hampshire
R. M. Barton
Newport CC (Original 9)
Rhode Island
W. F. Davis
Newport CC (r.)
Rhode Island
D. J. Ross
Newport CC
Rhode Island
A. W. Tillinghast
Newport CC (Original 9)
Vermont
R. M. Barton
Newport CC (a.9)
Vermont
M. Hurdzan
Newporter Inn Par 3 GC
California
W. F. Bell
Newport News Muni
Virginia
E. B. Ault
New Prague GC (a.9)
Minnesota
D. Herfort

279

New Quarter Park GC
Virginia
G. W. Cobb, J. B. LaFoy
Newquay
England
H. S. Colt
New St. Andrews GC
Japan
D. Muirhead, J. Nicklaus
New San Carlos G&CC (27)
Florida
A. Hills
New Seabury, CC of (Blue and Green courses)
Massachusetts
W. F. Mitchell
New South Wales GC
Australia
A. Mackenzie
Newton Abbot GC
England
J. Braid
Newton CC (9)
Iowa
H. Collis
Newton CC (9)
Kansas
H. Robb, Sr.
Newton CC (a.9)
New Jersey
W. F. and D. W. Gordon
Newtonmore
Scotland
A. Mackenzie, J. Braid
Newtonstewart (r.)
Northern Ireland
J. J. F. Pennink
New Ulm CC (a.9)
Minnesota
D. Herfort
New World of Resorts GC
Texas
L. Howard
New York Hospital GC (r.)
New York
R.T. Jones
New Zealand GC (Original course)
England
S. Mure Ferguson
New Zealand GC (New course)
England
T. C. Simpson
Niagara Falls CC (r.)
New York
R. T. Jones
Niagara Falls Muni
New York
W. E. Harries
Niagara Falls Park Commission Whirlpool GC
Ontario, Canada
S. Thompson
Niakwa G&CC
Manitoba, Canada
S. Thompson
Nibley Park Muni (9)
Utah
H. Lamb
Nibley Park Muni (r.)
Utah
J. M. Riley
Nicholes GC
South Carolina
E. Hamm
Nichols Park GC
Illinois
D. Gill
Niigata Forest (36)
Japan
R. Kirby, G. Player

Nile CC
Washington
N. Woods
Nimes
France
D. Harradine
Ninole Seamountain GC
Hawaii
A. J. Snyder
Niobrara GC (9)
Wyoming
F. Hummel
Niseko CC
Japan
E. B. Seay, A. Palmer
Nishi Biwako CC
Japan
E. B. Seay, A. Palmer
Nishi Nihon CC
Japan
R. Kirby, G. Player
Nixon Estate GC (3 holes)
California
J. B. Williams
Noblesville City GC
Indiana
W. K. Newcomb
Nobleton Lakes GC
Ontario, Canada
R. and C. Muylaert
Nob North GC
Georgia
R. Kirby, G. Player
Nocona Hills GC
Texas
L. Howard
Nogales CC
Arizona
A. H. Jolly
Nolan River CC
Texas
L. Howard
Noordwijk
Holland
J. J. F. Pennink
Noranda Mines GC
Province of Québec, Canada
S. Thompson
Noranda Mines GC (r.)
Province of Québec, Canada
H. Watson
Norbeck CC
Maryland
A. H. Tull
Norbeck CC (r.)
Maryland
E. B. Ault
Norbury GC
Great Britain
T. Dunn
Norfolk CC (r.13,a.5)
Nebraska
F. Farley
Norfolk CC (r.)
Virginia
W. S. Flynn
Norfolk GC
England
J. H. Taylor
Norman CC [formerly Twin Lakes CC](9)
Oklahoma
F. Farley
Normandie GC
Missouri
R. Foulis

Normandy CC
Illinois
H. Collis
Normandy Shores GC [formerly Normandy Island GC](r.)
Florida
W. S. Flynn
Normandy Shores GC (r.)
Florida
M. Mahannah
Normanside CC
New York
W. E. Harries
Northampton County GC
Pennsylvania
D. W. Gordon
Northampton GC
England
W. Park, Jr.
Northamptonshire County GC
England
H. S. Colt
Northamptonshire County GC (r.)
England
J. Braid
Northampton Valley GC
Pennsylvania
E. B. Ault
North Andover CC
Massachusetts
D. J. Ross
North Andover GC (r.)
Massachusetts
W. F. Mitchell
North and South Parks, Allegheny County (r.)
Pennsylvania
X. G. Hassenplug
North Bay G&CC
Ontario, Canada
S. Thompson
North Bay G&CC (r.9,a.9)
Ontario, Canada
H. Watson
North Berwick GC (r.)
Scotland
D. Strath
North Berwick GC (r. West Links)
Scotland
G. Campbell
North Berwick Muni (r. Burgh course)
Scotland
P. M. Ross
Northbrook Hills CC
Illinois
E. L. and R. B. Packard
North Carolina, CC of
North Carolina
E. Maples, W. C. Byrd
North Carolina, CC of (a.9)
North Carolina
W. C. Byrd
North Carolina, CC of (r., a. 9)
North Carolina
R. T. Jones
North Carolina, CC of (r.)
North Carolina
R. L. Jones
Northcliffe GC
England
J. R. Stutt
North Colvin GC (9)
New York
A.R. Tryon
North Conway GC
New Hampshire
R. M. Barton

North Conway GC (a.9)
New Hampshire
P. A. Wogan
North Dade CC (now Vizcaya CC)
Florida
F. Murray
North Dale G&CC
Florida
R. Garl
North Devon GC, Royal (Westward Ho!; Original course)
England
T. Morris
North Devon GC, Royal (Westward Ho!; r.)
England
W. H. Fowler
North Downs GC
England
J. J. F. Pennink
North East Park Par 3 GC
Manitoba, Canada
C. Muret
North Eastway Muni (now William S. Sahm GC)
Indiana
P. Dye
Northfield GC (r.9,a.9)
Minnesota
D. Herfort
North Foreland
England
T. Simpson, H. Fowler, J. S. F. Morrison
North Fork CC
Pennsylvania
J. G. Harrison
Northgreen Village CC
North Carolina
J. P. Gibson
North Halton GC
Ontario, Canada
R. and D. Moote
North Hants GC
England
J. Braid
Northhaven GC (r.)
Maine
W. E. Stiles, J. R. Van Kleek
North Hempstead GC
New York
A. W. Tillinghast
North Hempstead GC (r.)
New York
R. T. Jones
North Hill CC
Massachusetts
W. F. Mitchell
North Hills CC (r.)
Arkansas
R. T. Jones
North Hills CC [now Norwood Hills](East and West courses)
Missouri
W. E. Stiles, J. R. Van Kleek
North Hills CC
North Carolina
G. W. Cobb
North Hills CC (New site)
New York
R. T. Jones
North Hills Muni
Pennsylvania
E. B. Ault
North Island Naval Air Station GC
California
J. L. Daray
North Jersey CC (r.)
New Jersey
W. J. Travis

North Jersey CC (r.)
New Jersey
H. Purdy
North Jersey CC (r.)
New Jersey
N. T. Psiahas
North Jersey CC (r.)
New Jersey
R. T. Jones
North Kent GC
Michigan
K. W. Bowen
North Lake Ranch GC
Texas
L. Howard
Northland CC
Minnesota
D. J. Ross
Northland CC (r.)
Minnesota
D. Herfort
Northmoor CC
Illinois
D. J. Ross
Northmoor CC (r.)
Illinois
K. Killian, R. Nugent
Northmoore GC
North Carolina
J. P. Gibson
North Oaks CC
Minnesota
S. Thompson
North Olmstead CC
Ohio
(Earl Yesberger)
North Park GC (r.)
Pennsylvania
X. G. Hassenplug
North Park Muni
Michigan
(George A. Ferry)
North Port Charlotte, CC of
Florida
C. F. Ankrom
Northport CC
New York
D. Emmet
North Port GC
Florida
(Leroy Phillips)
North Ranch CC
California
T. G. Robinson
North Redoubt Club (now Garrison GC)
New York
L. S. "Dick" Wilson
North Ridge CC
California
W. F. and W. P. Bell
North Ridge CC (Lakes and Oaks courses)
North Carolina
E. Hamm
North River Shores CC
Florida
A. M. Young
North River Yacht & CC
Alabama
R. Kirby, G. Player
North Rockland GC
New York
D. W. Gordon
North Salem Links (9, n.l.e.)
Massachusetts
R. White
North Shore CC
Illinois
H. S. Colt, C. H. Alison, A. Mackenzie

North Shore CC
Missouri
R. Foulis
North Shore CC (27)
Missouri
H. G. Herpel
North Shore CC (r.27)
Missouri
C. H. Adams
North Shore CC
Washington
A. Smith
North Shore CC (n.l.e.)
Wisconsin
W. B. Langford
North Shore CC (New site; 27)
Wisconsin
D. Gill
North Shore GC
Michigan
A. H. Jolly
North Shore GC
England
J. Braid
North Shore GC (r.)
New Zealand
J.D. Harris, P.W. Thomson, M. Wolveridge
North Shore Towers GC
New York
F. Duane
Northstar at Tahoe GC
California
R. M. Graves
Northumberland GC (r.)
England
H. S. Colt
Northumberland GC (r.)
England
J. Braid
Northumberland GC
Nova Scotia, Canada
C. E. Robinson
Northwest GC
Ireland
E. Hackett
Northway Heights G&CC
New York
A. Craig
Northwest Mississippi Jr. College GC
Mississippi
(John Frazier)
Northwest Park GC
Maryland
E. B. Ault
Northwest Park Muni
Oklahoma
A. J. Jackson
Northwood Club
California
W.R. Hunter, A. Mackenzie
Northwood Club
Georgia
W. C. Byrd
Northwood Club
Texas
W. Diddel
Northwood Club (r.)
Texas
R. Plummer
Northwood Club (r.)
Texas
M. H. Ferguson
Northwood CC (r.)
Mississippi
E. B. Ault
Northwood G&CC
Ontario, Canada
S. Thompson

Northwood GC
California
A. Mackenzie
Northwood GC
England
T. Dunn
North Woodmere GC
New York
D. W. Gordon
Northwoods CC
Georgia
W. C. Byrd
North Worcestershire
England
J. Braid
Norway Point GC (r.)
Ontario, Canada
S. Thompson
Norwich Inn GC [now Norwich Muni]
Connecticut
D. J. Ross
Norwich Muni
England
F. G. Hawtree
Norwood CC
Massachusetts
S. Mitchell
Norwood CC
New Jersey
A. W. Tillinghast
Norwood GC
Indiana
H. Purdy
Norwood Hills CC [formerly North Hills
    CC](East and West courses)
Missouri
W. E. Stiles, J. R. Van Kleek
Notre Dame University GC
Indiana
K. Killian, R. Nugent
Nottingham GC (r.)
Pennsylvania
E. B. Ault
Nottingham GC
England
W. Park, Jr.
Notts GC
England
W. Park, Jr.
Notts GC (a. bunkers)
England
J. H. Taylor
Notts GC (r.)
England
T. Williamson
Noyac G&CC
New York
W. F. Mitchell
N.T.C. Great Lakes GC (a.9)
Illinois
K. Killian, R. Nugent
Nubbins Ridge
Tennessee
A. G. McKay
Neuman Park GC (a. 9)
Ohio
J. Kidwell, M. Hurdzan
Nuevo Andelucia GC (Las Brisas, Los
    Naranjos and 18 hole Par 3 course)
Spain
R. T. Jones
Nuevo Vallarta
Mexico
E. B. Seay, A. Palmer
Nuneaton Works
England
T. Williamson

Nuns Island GC
Province of Québec, Canada
H. Watson
Nuremore GC (r.)
Ireland
E. Hackett
Oahu CC
Hawaii
(Alex Bell)

Oakbourne CC
Louisiana
L. S. "Dick" Wilson
Oakbourne CC (r.)
Louisiana
B. J. Riviere
Oak Brook Muni
Illinois
E. L. and R. B. Packard
Oak Cliff CC
Texas
J. P. Maxwell
Oak Creek CC
Arizona
R. T. Jones
Oakcrest CC (9)
Maryland
E. B. Ault, A. Jamison
Oakdale
England
A. Mackenzie
Oakdale CC (9)
California
R. E. Baldock
Oakdale G&CC (Original 18)
Ontario, Canada
S. Thompson
Oakdale G&CC (a.9)
Ontario, Canada
C. E. Robinson
Oakdale GC
South Carolina
R. Robertson
Oakfield CC
Nova Scotia, Canada
C. E. Robinson
Oak Forest CC
Texas
B. Martindale
Oak Harbor G&TC
Minnesota
(Emile F. Perret)
Oak Hill CC
Massachusetts
D. J. Ross
Oak Hill CC (a.9)
Massachusetts
W. E. Stiles, J. R. Van Kleek
Oak Hill CC (r.5)
Massachusetts
G. S. Cornish, W. G. Robinson
Oak Hill CC
Nebraska
(Robert Popp)
Oak Hill CC (West and East courses)
New York
D. J. Ross
Oak Hill CC (r. East course)
New York
R. T. Jones
Oak Hill CC (r. a. 3 East course)
New York
G. and T. Fazio
Oak Hill GC
Indiana
W. Diddel
Oak Hill GC
New Jersey
W. F. and D. W. Gordon

Oak Hill GC
Texas
L. Howard
Oak Hills CC
Connecticut
A. H. Tull
Oak Hills CC
Texas
A. W. Tillinghast
Oak Hills CC (r.6,a.5)
Texas
J. Finger
Oak Hills CC (r.)
Texas
R. Kirby, G. Player
Oak Hills CC
Virginia
R. P. Hines
Oak Hills CC
Japan
R. T. Jones
Oak Hills GC
Wisconsin
R. A. Anderson
Oak Hollow GC
North Carolina
P. Dye
Oakhurst CC
Ohio
J. Kidwell
Oakhurst Links (9; n.l.e.)
West Virginia
(G. Grant, L. Torrin)
Oak Island GC
North Carolina
G. W. Cobb
Oakland CC (9)
Maryland
E. B. Ault
Oakland Greens GC (a.9)
Ontario, Canada
C. E. Robinson
Oakland Hills CC (South course)
Michigan
D. J. Ross
Oakland Hills CC (North course) (r.)
Michigan
R. T. Jones
Oakland Hills CC (r. South course)
Michigan
R. T. Jones
Oak Lane CC
Connecticut
G. S. Cornish
Oaklawn Par 3 GC
Illinois
W. B. Langford
Oakley CC
Massachusetts
D. J. Ross
Oak Meadow G&TC
Indiana
K. Killian, R. Nugent
Oakmont CC, Santa Rosa (36)
California
T. G. Robinson
Oakmont CC Glendale
California
M. Behr
Oakmont CC
Pennsylvania
H. C. and W. C. Fownes
Oakmont CC (r.)
Pennsylvania
R. T. Jones
Oakmont CC (r.)
Pennsylvania
E. B. Seay, A. Palmer

Oak Mountain State Park GC
Alabama
E. Stone
Oak Park CC (r.)
Illinois
E. B. Dearie, Jr.
Oak Ridge CC
Florida
H. Schmeisser
Oak Ridge CC
Massachusetts
G. and T. Fazio
Oakridge CC
Utah
W. F. Bell, W. H. Neff
Oak Ridge GC
California
B. Stamps
Oak Ridge CC (1980)
Texas
J. Kidwell, M. Hurdzan
Oak Ridge Muni at Brockton [now D. W.
    Field GC]
Massachusetts
W. E. Stiles, J. R. Van Kleek
(The) Oaks CC
Oklahoma
A. W. Tillinghast
Oak Tree CC
California
T. G. Robinson
Oak Tree CC [formerly Oakwood CC]
Ohio
E. B. Ault
Oak Tree CC
Oklahoma
P. Dye
Oak Tree CC
Pennsylvania
E. B. Ault
Oak Tree G&CC
Oklahoma
P. Dye
Oak Tree GC
Oklahoma
P. Dye (across the road from the course
    above)
Oakville GC (r.)
Ontario, Canada
C. E. Robinson
Oakwood CC
Illinois
P. Dye
Oakwood CC (9)
Ohio
(Arthur Boggs)
Oakwood CC (a. 9)
Ohio
T. Bendelow
Oakwood CC (r.6)
Ohio
G. S. Alves
Oakwood CC [now Oak Tree](r.)
Ohio
E. B. Ault
Oakwood CC
Oklahoma
P. D. and J. P. Maxwell
Oakwood Park GC
Wisconsin
E. L. Packard
Oarai GC
Japan
K. Fujita
Oberau GC
West Germany
D. Harradine
Oberfranken GC
West Germany
B. Von Limburger

O. B. Keeler Memorial GC [now Pine Tree CC]
Georgia
C. H. Adams
Obregon, CC
Mexico
P. Clifford
Obrien Estate GC at Plattsburgh
New York
H. Watson
Ocala GC (9; n.l.e.)
Florida
J. D. Dunn
Ocala Muni (Course #1)
Florida
W. F. Gordon
Ocean Acres GC
New Jersey
H. Purdy
Ocean City CC (9)
Maryland
R. Roberts
Ocean City CC
New Jersey
W. Park, Jr.
Ocean City G&YC
Maryland
W. F. and D. W. Gordon
Ocean Forest CC [now Pine Lakes International]
South Carolina
R. White
Ocean Golf Links (18 par 3)
Florida
W. Amick
Ocean Isle Beach GC
South Carolina
R. F. Breeden
Ocean Palms CC
Florida
F. Bolton
Ocean Pines G&CC
Maryland
R. T. Jones, R. L. Jones
Ocean Reef Club (Dolphin course)
Florida
M. Mahannah
Ocean Reef Club (r. Dolphin course; a. Harbour course)
Florida
R. Von Hagge, B. Devlin
Ocean Shores GC
Australia
R. Von Hagge, B. Devlin
Oceanside CC
California
W. H. Johnson
Oceanside Muni
California
(Richard Bigler)
Ocean Trail GC
Florida
G. Fazio
Ockbrook GC (r.)
England
T. Williamson
Oconto GC
Michigan
A. H. Jolly
Ocotillo Park GC (Original 9)
New Mexico
W. D. Cantrell
Ocotillo Park GC (a.9)
New Mexico
M. H. Ferguson
Odawara CC
Japan
R. Kirby, A. L. Davis

O'Donnell GC (1948)
California
J.W. Dawson
Odowara Gotenba
Japan
R. Kirby, G. Player
Offut AFB (Capehart GC)
Nebraska
R. T. Jones
Oglebay Park Par 3 GC
West Virginia
W. F. and D. W. Gordon
Oglebay Park Speidel GC
West Virginia
R. T. Jones
Ohio State University GC (Scarlet and Grey courses)
Ohio
A. Mackenzie, P. D. Maxwell
Ohio University GC (a.9)
Ohio
J. Kidwell
Ohnuma GC
Japan
R. T. Jones, Jr.
Ojai Valley Inn & CC
California
G. C. Thomas, Jr., W. P. Bell
Ojai Valley Inn & CC (r.)
California
W. F. Bell
Okanagon Park Par 3 GC
British Columbia, Canada
W. G. Robinson
Okeechobee G&CC
Florida
M. Mahannah
Oklahoma City G&CC
Oklahoma
P. D. Maxwell
Oklahoma City G&CC (r.)
Oklahoma
A. W. Tillinghast
Oklahoma City G&CC (r.)
Oklahoma
J P. Maxwell
Oklahoma City G&CC (r.)
Oklahoma
D. R. Sechrest
Old Baldy Club
Wyoming
H. B. Hughes
Old Channel Trail GC
Michigan
W. B. and G. H. Matthews
Old Country Club (n.l.e.)
New York
W. J. Travis
Old Country Club (r.; n.l.e.)
New York
D. Emmet
(The) Old Course, St. Andrews (r.)
Scotland
A. Robertson
(The) Old Course, St. Andrews (r.)
Scotland
T. Morris
Olde Hickory GC (9)
Pennsylvania
E. B. Ault
Old Elm Club
Illinois
D.J. Ross, H.S. Colt
Old Elm GC
Texas
W. D. Cantrell

Olde Mill GC
Virginia
E. Maples
Oldenburgescher GC
West Germany
B. Von Limburger
Old Flatbush CC (9; n.l.e.)
New York
M. J. McCarthy, Sr.
Old Landing GC
Delaware
R. Roberts
Old Lyme GC (r.)
Connecticut
W. F. Mitchell
Old Meadowbrook CC
New York
D. Emmet
Old (Auld) Newbury CC
Massachusetts
(Fred Pearson)
Old (Auld) Newbury CC (r.)
Massachusetts
M. L. Francis
Old Oakland GC
Indiana
C. E. Maddox
Old Oaks CC
New York
C. H. Alison
Old Oaks CC (r.)
New York
W. F. Mitchell
Old Oaks CC (r.6)
New York
F. Duane
Old Paradise Club [now Plantation Hotel CC]
Florida
M. Mahannah
Old Ranch CC
California
T. G. Robinson
Old Spanish Fort CC
Alabama
J. L. Daray
Old Tappan GC
New Jersey
H. Purdy
Old Town CC (9)
Georgia
A. L. Davis
Old Warson CC
Missouri
R. T. Jones
Old Wayne GC
Illinois
C. E. Maddox
Old Westbury CC
New York
W. F. Mitchell
Old Westbury CC (r.2)
New York
F. Duane
Old York Road CC (r.)
Pennsylvania
A. W. Tillinghast
Ole Monterey CC
Virginia
F. A. Findlay
Olgiata GC (27)
Italy
C. K. Cotton, J. J. F. Pennink
Olivas Park Muni
California
W. F. Bell
Olive Glen GC
Wyoming
R. E. Baldock

Olmos Basin GC
Texas
G. Hoffman
Olmstead AFB GC
Pennsylvania
E. B. Ault
Olomana Golf Links
Hawaii
R. E. Baldock
Olympia Fields CC (Courses #1 and #3; n.l.e.)
Illinois
T. Bendelow
Olympia Fields CC (South course)
Illinois
W. Watson
Olympia Fields CC (North course)
Illinois
W. Park, Jr.
Olympia G&CC (a.9)
Washington
F. Federspiel
Olympia Spa & CC
Alabama
R. A. Simmons
Olympic Club (Lake course, formerly Lakeside G&CC)
California
W. Reid
Olympic Club (r. Lakeside course
California
S. Whiting
Olympic Club (Ocean course)
California
W. Watson
Olympic Club (r. Lakeside course)
California
R. T. Jones
Olympic G&CC
Illinois
C. D. Wagstaff
Olympic Hills GC
Minnesota
C. E. Maddox
Omaha CC
Nebraska
W. B. Langford, T. J. Moreau
Omaha CC (r.)
Nebraska
P. D. Maxwell
100 Mile House GC
British Columbia, Canada
S. Leonard, P. Tattersfield
Oneida CC
New York
W. E. Harries
Oneida CC
Wisconsin
S. F. Pelchar
Oneota CC (r.9,a.9)
Iowa
D. Herfort
1001 Ranch GC (r.)
California
R. E. Baldock
Onion Creek CC
Texas
J. N. Demaret
Onondaga CC
New York
S. Thompson
Onondaga CC (r.)
New York
H. Purdy
Ontario GC (Original 9)
New York
(George Swatt)

Ontario Muni
Oregon
R.E. Baldock
Ontario National GC
California
W. H. Tucker, Jr.
Ontario National Par 3 GC
California
W. H. Tucker, Jr.
On Top of the World GC
Florida
C. Adams
Onwentsia Club (a. 9)
Illinois
H.J. Tweedie, H.J. Whigham and Foulis Brothers
Onwentsia Club (Original 9)
Illinois
J. and R. Foulis
Onwentsia Club (r.)
Illinois
K. Killian, R. Nugent
Operman CC (Dublin Sports Club)
Ireland
E. Hackett
Oporto GC (r.)
Portugal
P. M. Ross
Oppersdorf Estate GC
Germany
C. S. Butchart
Oquirrah Hills Muni
Utah
J. M. Riley
Orange Blossom GC
Florida
R. Garl
Orange Brook CC (r.9,a.9, Course #2)
Florida
R. F. Lawrence
Orange County GC (a.3)
New York
A. Zikorus
Orange Hills GC (a.9)
Connecticut
G. S. Cornish
Orange Tree CC [formerly Century CC]
Arizona
L. M. Hughes
Orange Tree CC
Florida
R. A. Simmons
Orange Tree GC (r.)
Arizona
G. A. Panks
Orchard Beach G&CC
Ontario, Canada
S. Thompson
Orchard Hills CC (Original 9)
Ohio
R. A. Anderson
Orchard Hills CC (r.9,a.9)
Ohio
A. Hills
Orchard Hills G&CC
Illinois
R. B. Harris
Orchard Hills G&CC
Washington
(William Sander)
Orchard Lake CC
Michigan
W. Reid, W. Connellan
Orchard Ridge CC (r.)
Indiana
C. E. Maddox
Orchards GC
Massachusetts
D. J. Ross

282

Oregon CC (r.)
Illinois
C. D. Wagstaff

Orgill CC
Tennessee
J. P. Maxwell

Orillia GC
Ontario, Canada
R. Moote

Orinda CC
California
W. Watson

Oriole G&TC (Margate course and Oriole Exec. course)
Florida
W. H. Dietsch, Jr.

Oriole G&TC (Delray)
Florida
W. H. Dietsch Jr.

Oristo G&RC
South Carolina
T. Jackson

Orkil Farms Muni [now Simsbury Farms]
Connecticut
G. S. Cornish, W. G. Robinsin

Orlando, CC of (r.)
Florida
R. T. Jones

Orleans GC
Vermont
(Alex Reid)

Ormesson GC
France
J. D. Harris

Ormond Beach CC
Florida
W. Diddel

Ormond GC
Florida
A. Findlay

Ormskirk GC
England
(H. H. Hilton)

Orono Muni
Minnesota
(Leo J. Feser)

Oronoque Village GC
Connecticut
D. Muirhead

Oro Valley G&CC
Arizona
R. B. Harris

Oro Valley G&CC (r.)
Arizona
D. Bennett

Orsett GC
England
J. Braid, J. R. Stutt

Osage Hills [now Greenbrier Hills CC]
Missouri
C. D. Wagstaff

Osage Hills CC [now Sand Springs Muni]
Oklahoma
F. Farley

Osawatomie Muni (a.9)
Kansas
C. Mendenhall

Osceola Muni
Florida
(Bill Melhorn)

Oshawa GC (r.)
Ontario, Canada
S. Thompson

Oshawa GC (r.)
Ontario, Canada
C. E. Robinson

Osiris CC
New York
F. Duane

Oso Beach GC
Texas
J. Bredemus

Ostwestfallen-Lippe, Golf und Landclub
West Germany
B. Von Limburger

Oswego CC (Original 9)
New York
A. W. Tillinghast

Oswego CC (a.9)
New York
G. S. Cornish, W. G. Robinson

Oswego Lake CC
Oregon
H. C. Egan

Oswego Lake CC (r.)
Oregon
R. M. Graves

Oswestry GC
England
J. Braid, J. R. Stutt

Otesega Hotel GC (Leatherstocking)
New York
D. Emmet

Othello G&CC (9)
Washington
(Melvin A. Hueston)

Otis AFB GC
Massachusetts
R. E. Baldock

Ottawa CC
Kansas
H. Robb, Sr.

Ottawa GC (n.l.e.)
Ontario, Canada
W. F. Davis

Ottawa GC at Hull, Royal (r.)
Province of Québec, Canada
H. Watson

Ottawa Hunt & Motor Club
Ontario, Canada
W. Park, Jr.

Ottawa Park GC (r.)
Ohio
A. Hills

Otter Creek GC
Indiana
R. T. Jones

Otterkill G&CC
New York
W. F. Mitchell

Otto Kahn Estate GC
New York
C. B. Macdonald, S. J. Raynor

Ottumwa G&CC (a.9)
Iowa
C. H. Adams

Oughterard GC
Ireland
E. Hackett

Overbrook CC
Pennsylvania
J. B. McGovern, X. G. Hassenplug

Overgaard GC(9)
Arizona
M. Coggins

Overlake G&CC
Washington
A. V. Macan

Overlake G&CC (r.)
Washington
D. Muirhead

Overland Park Muni (a.9)
Colorado
W. F. Bell

Overland Park Muni (27)
Kansas
F. Farley

Overpeck County GC
New Jersey
N. T. Psiahas

Owensboro CC (r.)
Kentucky
J. L. Lee

Owensboro Muni
Kentucky
A. G. McKay

Owen Sound GC
Ontario, Canada
S. Thompson

Owen Sound GC (r.)
Ontario, Canada
R. Moote

Oxbow CC
Florida
(Leroy Phillips)

Oxbow CC (r.)
Florida
A. Hills

Oxbow CC
North Dakota
R. T. Jones, Sr. and Jr.

Oxbow G&CC
Ohio
J. Kidwell

Oxford G&CC
Ontario, Canada
C. E. Robinson

Oxford G&RC
Massachusetts
P.A. Wogan

Oxhey
England
H. S. Colt

Oxnard Muni [now Silver K GC]
California
W. F. Bell

Oxney
England
H. Vardon

Oxon Run GC (9)
Washington, D.C.
R. P. Hines

Oxton
England
J. J. F. Pennink

Oyster Harbors Club
Massachusetts
D. J. Ross

Oyster Reef GC
South Carolina
R. L. Jones

Ozark G&CC
Alabama
R. Garl

Ozaukee CC
Wisconsin
W. B. Langford, T. J. Moreau

Ozaukee CC (r.)
Wisconsin
D. Gill

Pacific Grove Muni (Original 9)
California
H. C. Egan

Pacific Grove Muni (a.9)
California
J. F. Neville

Pacific Harbor G&CC
Fiji
R. T. Jones, Sr. and Jr.

Pacific Palisades Par 3 GC
Hawaii
W. Wilkinson

Palm Springs Ranch CC

Packachaug Hills CC
Massachusetts
O. E. Smith

Packanack Lake CC
New Jersey
G. S. Cornish

Paddock CC
Missouri
H. G. Herpel

Padova, GC
Italy
J. D. Harris

Paducah, CC of
Kentucky
R. T. Jones

Paganica G&CC
Kansas
L. I. Johnson

Page Belcher Muni
Oklahoma
L. Howard

Pagosa Pines GC
Colorado
(Johnny Bulla)

Paint Branch GC
Maryland
E. B. Ault

Pajaro Valley CC
California
R. M. Graves

Pala Mesa GC (r.)
California
V. C. Rossen

Pala Mesa GC
California
W. H. Johnson

Palatine Hills GC
Illinois
E. L. Packard

Pali Muni
Hawaii
W. G. Wilkinson

Pallanza GC
Italy
F. G. Hawtree

Palma Ceia G&CC
Florida
T. Bendelow

Palma Ceia G&CC (r.)
Florida
D. J. Ross

Palma Ceia G&CC (r.)
Florida
M. Mahannah

Palm-Aire CC (Palms course)
Florida
W. F. Mitchell

Palm-Aire CC (Sabals and Pines courses)
Florida
R. Von Hagge, B. Devlin

Palm-Aire CC (Cypress and Oaks courses)
Florida
G. and T. Fazio

Palm Aire CC of Sarasota [formerly De-Soto Lake G&CC]
Florida
L. S. "Dick" Wilson

Palm Aire West CC [formerly DeSoto Lakes G&CC](r.)
Florida
R. A. Anderson

Palma Real GC [formerly Ixtapa-Zihuatawejo]
Mexico
R. T. Jones, Sr. and Jr.

Palmares GC
Portugal
J. J. F. Pennink

Palmas Del Mar GC
Puerto Rico
R. Kirby, G. Player, A. L. Davis

Palma Sola CC
Florida
R. A. Anderson

Palm Beach CC (9) [now Breakers GC]
Florida
A. Findlay

Palm Beach CC
Florida
D. J. Ross

Palm Beach Gardens [formerly PGA National; now J. D. MacArthur GC]
Florida
L. S. "Dick" Wilson

Palm Beach Gardens [formerly PGA National; now J.D. MacArthur GC](r.; a.18)
Florida
J. L. Lee

Palm Beach G&CC, Royal (36)
Florida
M. Mahannah

Palm Beach Lakes GC
Florida
W. F. Mitchell

Palm Beach National CC
Florida
J. P. Gibson

Palm Beach National CC (r.)
Florida
J. L. Lee

Palm Beach Par 3 GC
Florida
L. S. "Dick" Wilson

Palm Beach Polo & CC [formerly Wellington CC]
Florida
G. and T. Fazio

Palmbrook Sun City CC
Arizona
J. Hardin, G. Nash

Palm Coast GC (Original course)
Florida
W. W. Amick

Palm Coast GC (a.18)
Florida
E. B. Seay, A. Palmer

Palm Desert Greens G&CC
California
T. G. Robinson

Palmer Hills GC
Iowa
W. J. Spear

Palmetto CC
Louisiana
P. D. Maxwell

Palmetto CC (Original 9)
South Carolina
H. C. Leeds

Palmetto CC (r.)
South Carolina
A. Mackenzie

Palmetto Dunes GC (Jones course)
South Carolina
R. T. Jones

Palmetto Dunes GC (Fazio course)
South Carolina
G. and T. Fazio

Palmetto GC
Florida
L. S. "Dick" Wilson

Palmetto Pine CC
Florida
A. Hills

Palm Meadows GC
California
W. F. Bell
Palm River CC
Florida
B. W. Zink
Palm Springs CC
California
(Paul Addessi)
Palm Springs Ranch GC (r. 9, a. 9)
California
L. M. Hughes
Palm Verba CC
California
D. Kent
Palm View Muni
Texas
R. Plummer
Palo Alto Hills GC
California
C. Glasson
Palo Alto Hills GC (r.)
California
R. M. Graves
Palo Alto Muni
California
W. F. Bell
Palo Alto Muni (r.)
California
R. T. Jones, Jr.
Palolo GC
Hawaii
(Alex Bell)
Palos Verdes CC
California
M. Behr
Palos Verdes CC (r.)
California
D. W. Kent
Palos Verdes CC (r.)
California
T. G. Robinson
Pals, Golf de
Spain
F. W. Hawtree
Panama CC
Florida
D. J. Ross
Panama, Club de Golf (New site)
Panama
B. J. Riviere
Panama City Beach GC [now Hilton G&RC]
Florida
W. W. Amick
Panorama CC (27)
Texas
(Jack B. Miller)
Panorama G&CC [now Rio Rancho]
New Mexico
D. Muirhead
Panoramo Village Par 3 GC
California
H. M. and D. A. Rainville
Panshanger
England
J. D. Harris
Panther Valley CC
New Jersey
R. T. Jones, R. L. Jones
Papago Muni
Arizona
W. F. Bell
Paradise Hills GC
New Mexico
R. F. Lawrence
Paradise Island GC [formerly Arawak GC]
Bahamas
L. S. "Dick" Wilson

Paradise Park GC (r.)
Jamaica
R. Moote
Paradise Pines GC
California
R. E. Baldock
Paradise Point GC (Course #1)
North Carolina
F. A. Findlay
Paradise Point GC (Course #2)
North Carolina
G. W. Cobb
Paradise Valley CC
Arizona
L. M. Hughes
Paradise Valley CC
Nevada
C. Glasson
Paradise Valley CC
Wyoming
H. B. Hughes
Paradise Valley GC (27)
Colorado
H. B. Hughes
Paradise Valley Park Exec. GC
Arizona
M. Coggins
Paradise Village GC [now Mummy Mountain GC]
Arizona
P. and R. Dye
Paraparaumu Beach GC
New Zealand
A. Russell
Parcwood GC (now Villa Du Parc)
Wisconsin
D. Gill
Paris Landing State Park GC
Tennessee
B. J. Wihry
Pariso Springs CC (9)
California
R. E. Baldock
Park Carleton, Golf du
Province of Québec, Canada
W. F. Mitchell
Park City GC (Original 9)
Utah
W. H. Neff
Park City GC (r.9,a.9)
Utah
J. P. Maxwell
Park CC
New York
H. S. Colt
Park CC (r.)
New York
W. J. Travis
Park County GC
Indiana
W. Diddel
Park District GC (East St. Louis)
Illinois
J. A. Roseman
Park District of Highland Park (r. 5, 1977)
Illinois
K. Killian, R. Nugent
Park District GC (Fallsburgh)
New York
W. F. Mitchell
Parkersburg CC (r.)
West Virginia
E. B. Ault
Park Forest GC
Illinois
H. Collis
Park Hills CC (r.)
Kansas
E. L. Bell

Park Hills CC
Pennsylvania
J. G. Harrison
Park Hills CC (r.)
Pennsylvania
F. Garbin
Park Hills GC (East and West courses)
Illinois
C. D. Wagstaff
Park Lake GC
Illinois
C. D. Wagstaff
Park Meadows GC
Utah
J. Nicklaus
Parknasilla GC (r.)
Ireland
E. Hackett
Park Place GC
Illinois
W. J. Spear
Park Ridge CC
Illinois
H. J. Tweedie
Park Ridge CC (r.)
Illinois
D. Gill
Park Ridge CC (r.3)
Illinois
K. Killian, R. Nugent
Parkstone GC (Original course)
England
W. Park, Jr.
Parkstone GC (r.)
England
J. Braid, J. R. Stutt
Parkstone GC (r.)
England
J. H. Stutt
Parkview GC
Ontario, Canada
C. E. Robinson
Parkview Manor GC (Hershey)
Pennsylvania
M. J. McCarthy, Sr.
Parkview Muni (Original 9)
Illinois
F. Macdonald, C. E. Maddox
Parkview Muni (r.9,a.9)
Illinois
R. B. Harris
Parrin AFB GC
Texas
J. Finger
Parris Island GC
South Carolina
F. A. Findlay
Parsen's Island GC
Michigan
W. Reid, W. Connellan
Pasadena CC
Florida
W. Stiles, J. Van Kleek, W. Hagen
Pasadena CC (r.)
Florida
W. H. Dietsch, Jr.
Pasadena Ellington GC
Texas
B. J. Riviere
Pasadena GC
California
M. Behr
Pasadena GC (r.)
California
G. O'Neill
Pasadena GC (r.)
California
W. P. Bell

Pasatiempo GC
California
A. Mackenzie
Pasatiempo GC (r.)
California
P.W. Thomson, M. Wolveridge, R. Fream
Pasco Muni (r.; a.12)
Washington
R. M. Graves
Pasco Muni
Washington
R. E. Baldock
Paso Robles G&CC
California
B. Stamps
Passaic County GC (a.9)
New Jersey
A. H. Tull
Patriots Point
South Carolina
W. C. Byrd
(The) Patterson Club
Connecticut
R. T. Jones
(The) Patterson Club (r.1)
Connecticut
F. Duane
Patton Brook Exec. GC
Connecticut
G. S. Cornish, W. G. Robinson
Patty Jewett GC (a.18)
Colorado
J. P. Maxwell
Patuxent Naval Air Station GC (r.)
Virginia
R. F. Loving
Paul Block Private GC
Connecticut
W. E. Stiles, J. R. Van Kleek
Paul Harney GC
Massachusetts
P. Harney
Paul Smith's GC
New York
S. Dunn
Paul's Valley G&CC
Oklahoma
R. C. Dunning
Paul's Valley Muni (9)
Oklahoma
R. C. Dunning
Pauma Valley CC
California
R. T. Jones
Pautipaug CC
Connecticut
G. S. Cornish
Pawnee Prairie Muni
Kansas
R. C. Dunning
Pawpaw CC
South Carolina
R. Breeden
Pawtucket GC
Rhode Island
W. Park, Jr.
Pawtuckett GC
North Carolina
R. F. Breeden
Peaceful Valley CC
Colorado
D. Bennett
Peace Portal GC (r.)
British Columbia, Canada
S. Leonard, P. Tattersfield
Peach Tree CC
California
R. E. Baldock

Peachtree GC
Georgia
R. T. Jones, "Bobby" Jones, Jr.
Peachtree GC (r.)
Georgia
J. Finger
Pearl CC [formerly Francis Brown CC]
Hawaii
(Akiro Sato)
Pebble Beach Golf Links
California
J. F. Neville, D. Grant
Pebble Beach Golf Links (r.)
California
A. Mackenzie, R. Hunter
Pebble Beach Golf Links (r.)
California
H. C. Egan
Pebble Brook CC (9)
Georgia
A. L. Davis, R. Kirby
Pebble Brook CC
Ohio
B. W. Zink
Pebble Creek GC
Ohio
W. F. Mitchell
Pebble Creek GC
South Carolina
T. Jackson
Pecan Hollow GC
Texas
B. Martindale
Pecan Plantation GC
Texas
L. Howard
Pecan Valley CC
Texas
J. P. Maxwell
Pecan Valley Muni [formerly Woodlawn Park](27)
Texas
R. Plummer
Pecan Valley Muni (a.9)
Texas
D. Bennett
Peckets GC
New Hampshire
R. M. Barton
Pedernales CC
Texas
L. Howard
Pedley Farms GC [later Arlington CC; now Victoria GC]
California
C. Maud
Pedley Par 3 GC (18)
California
W. H. Johnson
Pedrena GC, Real
Spain
H. S. Colt, J. S. F. Morrison
Peek 'N Peak Resort
New York
F. Garbin
Peel (Isle of Man)
England
J. Braid
Pelham Bay Park GC (Original 9)
New York
L. E. Van Etten
Pelham Bay Park GC (Split Rock course)
New York
T. Winton

Pelham CC (r.)
Georgia
H. C. Moore, Sr.
Pelham CC (n.l.e.)
New York
L. E. Van Etten
Pelham CC (a.9; n.l.e.)
New York
T. Bendelow
Pelham CC (New site)
New York
D. Emmet
Pelham CC (r.)
New York
A. H. Tull
Pelican Bay Club
Florida
W. W. Amick
Pelican Bay, Club at
Florida
A. Hills
Pelican GC
Florida
D. J. Ross
Pembroke CC
Massachusetts
P. A. Wogan
Pembroke Lakes GC (27)
Florida
H. Watson
Penderbrook GC
Virginia
E. B. Ault
Penfield CC
New York
A. Craig
Penina GC (27)
Portugal
H. Cotton
Peninsula C GC (r.)
Australia
P.W. Thomson, M. Wolveridge
Peninsula G&CC [formerly Beresford CC]
California
D. J. Ross
Peninsula Park GC
Ontario, Canada
S. Thompson
Peninsula State Park GC
Wisconsin
E. L. Packard
Penmar Exec. GC (9)
California
D. Kent
Penn Hills Club at Bradford (r.9,a.9)
Pennsylvania
L. S. "Dick" Wilson
Pennhurst CC
Pennsylvania
O. E. Smith
Penn Oaks CC
Pennsylvania
R. Roberts
Penn State University GC (Blue course)
Pennsylvania
W. Park, Jr.
Penn State University GC (r. Blue course; a. White course)
Pennsylvania
J. G. Harrison, F. Garbin
Pennsylvania National G&CC
Pennsylvania
E. B. Ault
Pennyrile State Park GC
Kentucky
E. L. Packard

Penobscot Valley CC
Maine
D. J. Ross
Pen-Park Muni (9)
Virginia
R. F. Loving
Penticton G&CC (Original 9)
British Columbia, Canada
A. V. Macan
Penticton G&CC (a.9)
British Columbia, Canada
N. Woods
Peoria, CC of
Illinois
(F.M. Birks)
Pepper Pike Club
Ohio
W. S. Flynn
Pepper Tree CC [now Corona National GC]
California
L. M. Hughes
Pequabuc CC (a.3)
Connecticut
G. S. Cornish, W. G. Robinson
Perdido Bay CC
Florida
W. W. Amick
Perranporth
England
J. Braid
Perry CC
Georgia
(Sid Clarke)
Perry Park CC
Colorado
R. N. Phelps
Persimmon Hill CC
South Carolina
F. Bolton
Peterborough G&CC (r.)
Ontario, Canada
S. Thompson
Peterborough Milton
England
J. Braid
Peter Hay Par 3 at Pebble Beach
California
(Leonard Feliciano)
Peter Pan GC
California
J. D. Dunn
Petersborough Milton GC
England
J. Braid
Petersburg, CC of (n.l.e.)
Virginia
D. J. Ross
Petersburg, CC of (New site)
Virginia
E. B. Ault
Peterson Fields GC
Colorado
R. N. Phelps
Petrifying Springs GC
Wisconsin
J. A. Roseman
Petworth
Great Britain
T. Dunn
Pevero GC
Sardinia (Italy)
R. T. Jones
Phalen Park GC
Minnesota
D. Herfort
Pharaoh's CC
Texas
R. Plummer

Pheasant Ridge GC
Iowa
(Paul Fjare)
Pheasant Run CC
Ontario, Canada
R. and C. Muylaert
Pheasant Run Lodge GC
Illinois
W. Maddox
Pheasant Valley CC
Indiana
R. A. Anderson
Phenix City Muni
Alabama
(Lester Lawrence)
Philadelphia CC [now Bala CC]
Pennsylvania
"Young" W. Dunn
Philadelphia CC (Spring Mill course)
Pennsylvania
W. S. Flynn
Philadelphia CC (r. Spring Mill course)
Pennsylvania
P. D. Maxwell
Philadelphia Cricket Club
Pennsylvania
D. J. Ross
Philadelphia Cricket Club
Pennsylvania
A. W. Tillinghast
Philippines CC
Philippines
R. E. Baldock
Phillipsburg CC
Pennsylvania
F. A. Findlay
Philmont CC (South course)
Pennsylvania
W. Park, Jr.
Philmont CC (North course)
Pennsylvania
W. S. Flynn
Philmont CC (r. North course)
Pennsylvania
W. F. and D. W. Gordon
Phoenician Resort GC (1981)
Arizona
A.J. Snyder
Phoenix CC
Arizona
H. Collis
Picatinny Arsenal G&TC
New Jersey
E. F. Wogan
Pichaco Hills CC
New Mexico
J. Finger
Pichlarn, Schloss GC
Austria
B. Von Limburger
Pickens County CC (r.)
South Carolina
R. A. Renaud
Pickwick CC [now Glenview Naval Air Station GC]
Illinois
J. A. Roseman, Sr.
Pickwick Landing State Park GC
Tennessee
B. J. Wihry
Pico Rivera Muni
California
W. F. Bell
Piedmont Crescent CC
North Carolina
E. Maples
Piencourt, Normandie
France
J. H. Stutt

Pierre CC
South Dakota
C. E. Maddox
Pierre-Marques, Club de Golf
Mexico
P. Clifford
Pike Creek Valley CC
Delaware
E. B. Ault
Pike Fold GC
England
(E. W. Phillips)
Pike Run CC (r.)
Pennsylvania
J. G. Harrison
Pilgrim's Harbour GC
Connecticut
A. H. Tull
Pilot Knob Park GC
North Carolina
E. Hamm
Pilot Mountain CC
North Carolina
E. Hamm
Pima CC
Arizona
W. F. Bell
Pinawa CC
Manitoba, Canada
H. Watson
Pine Acres CC
Pennsylvania
J. G. Harrison
Pine Beach East GC
Minnesota
J. Dalgleish
Pine Beach Par 3 GC (9)
Minnesota
(Jim Madden)
Pine Beach West GC
Minnesota
(Jim Madden)
Pine Bluff CC (Original 9)
Arkansas
H. C. Hackbarth
Pine Bluff CC (r.9,a.9)
Arkansas
J. Finger
Pine Brook CC
Massachusetts
W. E. Stiles, J. R. Van Kleek
Pine Brook CC
North Carolina
E. Maples
Pine Burr CC
Mississippi
E. Stone
Pine Creek CC
Alabama
G. W. Cobb
Pinecrest CC
Texas
J. P. Maxwell
Pine Crest CC (Course #2)
Virginia
A. Jamison
Pine Crest G&CC
Illinois
E. G. Lockie
Pinecrest GC
Texas
B. J. Riviere
Pine Forest CC (27), Houston
Texas
B. J. Riviere

Pine Forest CC (r. 9), Houston (n.1.e.)
Texas
R. Plummer
Pine Forest CC, Bastrop
Texas
B. Martindale
Pine Grove CC (a.9)
Michigan
E. L. Packard
Pinegrove G&CC (27)
Province of Québec, Canada
H. Watson
Pine Harbor Champions G&CC
Alabama
J. H. Williams, Sr.
Pine Haven CC
New York
(James Thomson)
Pine Hill GC
Connecticut
E. Pyle
Pine Hills CC
Mississippi
G. Curtis
Pine Hills GC
Louisiana
G. Curtis
Pine Hills GC (r.)
Louisiana
B. J. Riviere
Pine Hills GC (Carrol)
Ohio
J. Kidwell
Pine Hills GC (Cleveland)
Ohio
H. D. Paddock, Sr.
Pine Hollow CC
New York
W. F. Mitchell
Pinehurst CC (27)
Colorado
J. P. Maxwell
Pinehurst CC (Original #1 course)
North Carolina
J. W. Tufts, L. Culver, L. Tufts
Pinehurst CC (r. Course #1; a. Courses #2, #3 and #4)
North Carolina
D. J. Ross
Pinehurst CC (Course #4)
North Carolina
R. S. Tufts
Pinehurst CC (Course #5)
North Carolina
E. Maples, R. S. Tufts
Pinehurst CC (r. Courses #4 and #5)
North Carolina
R. T. Jones
Pinehurst CC (Course #6)
North Carolina
G. and T. Fazio
Pinehurst CC (r. Course #2)
North Carolina
P. V. Tufts
Pinehurst CC
Texas
D. J. Ross
Pine Island CC
North Carolina
M. Mahannah
Pine Island GC [formerly Marsh Island GC]
Mississippi
P. Dye

Pine Isle Resort Hotel GC
Georgia
R. Kirby, G. Player, A. L. Davis
Pineknoll CC
Georgia
W. W. Amick
Pine Lake CC
Michigan
W. Park, Jr.
Pine Lake CC
Michigan
E. W. Way
Pine Lake CC (Original 9)
North Carolina
E. Hamm
Pine Lake CC (a.9)
North Carolina
J. P. Gibson
Pine Lake GC (a. 2nd 9)
Ontario, Canada
C. E. Robinson
Pine Lake Par 3 GC
Nebraska
R. Watson
Pine Lakes GC
North Carolina
R. White
Pine Lakes International GC [formerly Ocean Forest GC]
South Carolina
R. White
Pine Lakes Par 3 GC (18)
Florida
A. Hills
Pineland GC
South Carolina
E. Hamm
Pineland Plantation Golf & Hunt Club
South Carolina
R. F. Breeden
Pine Mountain Lake Club
California
W. F. Bell
Pine Needles Lodge & CC
North Carolina
D. J. Ross
Pine Oaks GC (9)
Massachusetts
G. S. Cornish, W. G. Robinson
Pine Oaks Muni
Tennessee
A. G. McKay
Pine Orchard CC
Connecticut
R. D. Pryde
Pine Orchard CC (r.4)
Connecticut
A. Zikorus
Pine Ridge CC
Ohio
H. D. Paddock Sr.
Pine Ridge CC
South Carolina
R. F. Breeden
Pine Ridge CC at Newcastle
New York
A. H. Tull
Pine Ridge G&CC (Original course)
Manitoba, Canada
H. S. Colt
Pine Ridge G&CC (New course)
Manitoba, Canada
S. Thompson
Pine Ridge G&CC (r.)
Manitoba, Canada
C. E. Robinson

Pine Ridge GC (Round Up Muni)
Montana
F. Hummel
Pine Ridge Muni
Maryland
C. Hook
Pine River CC
Michigan
W. B. and G. H. Matthews
Pinery CC (27)
Colorado
(David Bingaman)
Pines CC
West Virginia
E. B. Ault
Pines GC at Emerson
New Jersey
E. V. Ternyey
Pines Hotel CC (9)
New York
R. T. Jones
Pines Hotel GC at Digby
Nova Scotia, Canada
S. Thompson
Pines Par 3 GC at Hollywood
Florida
H. Schmeisser
Pinetop CC
Arizona
M. Coggins
Pinetop Lakes Exec. GC
Arizona
M. Coggins
Pine Tree CC
Connecticut
A. H. Tull
Pine Tree CC
Florida
L. S. "Dick" Wilson
Pine Tree CC
Georgia
C. H. Adams
Pine Tree G&CC
Alabama
G. W. Cobb
Pine Tree GC
North Carolina
R. F. Breeden
Pine Tree GC
North Carolina
E. Hamm
Pine Trees Par 3 GC (Santa Ana)
California
H. M. and D. A. Rainville
Pine Valley GC
New Jersey
G. A. Crump, H. S. Colt
Pine Valley GC (Completion of 4 holes)
New Jersey
H. I. and A. Wilson
Pine Valley GC (r.)
New Jersey
W. S. Flynn
Pine Valley GC (r. several greens)
New Jersey
P. D. Maxwell
Pine Valley GC
Ontario, Canada
H. Watson
Pine View G&CC [formerly Maccleny G&CC]
Florida
W. W. Amick

Pineview GC
Ontario, Canada
H. Watson
Pinewood CC
Arizona
L. M. Hughes
Pinewood GC
Texas
L. Howard
Piney Branch G&CC
Maryland
E. B. Ault
Piney Point CC
North Carolina
J. P. Gibson
Piney Point Par 3 GC
Texas
J. Finger
Pinnacle Peak CC
Arizona
(Dick Turner)
Pinner Hill GC
England
F. G. Hawtree
Pioneers Park GC
Nebraska
W. H. Tucker, Sr.
Pipe O' Peace GC
Illinois
J. Foulis
Pipers Landing GC
Florida
J.L. Lee
Pipestem State Park GC
West Virginia
G. S. Cornish, W. G. Robinson
Pipestem State Park Par 3 GC
West Virginia
G. S. Cornish, W. G. Robinson
Piping Rock Club
New York
C. B. Macdonald
Piqua CC (a.9)
Ohio
J. Kidwell
Piramides, Club de Golf
Mexico
P. Clifford
Pistaqua Hills CC
Illinois
H. Collis
Pitlochry GC
Scotland
W. Fernie
Pitlochry GC (r.)
Scotland
C. K. Hutchison
Pitman GC
New Jersey
A. Findlay
Pittsburgh Field Club (Original course)
Pennsylvania
A. Findlay
Pittsburgh Field Club (r.)
Pennsylvania
W. Park, Jr.
Pittsburgh Field Club (r.)
Pennsylvania
D. J. Ross
Pittsburgh Field Club (r.)
Pennsylvania
A. W. Tillinghast
Pittsburgh Field Club (r.)
Pennsylvania
R. T. Jones
Pittsburgh Field Club (r.)
Pennsylvania
X. G. Hassenplug

Pittsburgh GC (9)
California
A. Mackenzie, W. R. Hunter
Pittsfield CC
Massachusetts
D. J. Ross
Pittsfield CC (r.)
Massachusetts
W. E. Stiles, J. R. Van Kleek
Placid Lakes Inn & CC
Florida
F. Murray
Plainfield CC
New Jersey
D. J. Ross
Plainfield CC (Short nine)
New Jersey
(Marty O'Loughlin)
Pla-Mor GC
Arkansas
H. C. Hackbarth
Plandome CC
New York
O. E. Smith
Plantation CC, Fort Lauderdale
Florida
R. F. Lawrence
Plantation G&CC, Venice
Florida
R. Garl
Plantation GC (r.)
Idaho
R. M. Graves
Plantation Hotel CC [formerly Old Paradise Club]
Florida
M. Mahannah
Plantation Pines Par 3 GC
South Carolina
G. and T. Fazio
Platteview CC
Nebraska
E. L. Packard
Plattsburgh AFB GC
New York
A. Zikorus
Plausawa Valley CC
New Hampshire
W. F. Mitchell
Playa Dorado GC
Dominican Republic
R. T. Jones
Playboy Club GC (27)
New Jersey
G. and T. Fazio
Playboy Club GC (Brute course)
Wisconsin
R. B. Harris
Playboy Club GC (Briar Patch course)
Wisconsin
P. Dye, J. Nicklaus
Playland Park Golf Center
Indiana
W. J. Spear
Pleasant Hill GC
Ohio
J. Kidwell
Pleasant Valley CC (27)
Arkansas
J. Finger
Pleasant Valley CC
Hawaii
F. Duane
Pleasant Valley CC
Massachusetts
D. Hoenig

Pleasant Valley CC (9)
New Jersey
F. Duane
Pleasant Valley CC
Pennsylvania
E. F. Loeffler, J. McGlynn
Pleasant Valley CC (r.)
Pennsylvania
X. G. Hassenplug
Pleasant Valley CC (9)
West Virginia
(Horace Smith)
Pleasant Valley GC
Ohio
J. Kidwell
Pleasant View CC
Pennsylvania
E. B. Ault, A. Jamison
Pleasant View CC (r.)
Pennsylvania
P. Erath
Pleasant View Lodge
New York
F. Duane
Pleasant Vue GC (r.18,a.9)
Ohio
F. Garbin
Plencourt GC
France
J. H. Stutt
Plettenberg Bay
South Africa
F. W. Hawtree
P. L. London
England
F. W. Hawtree
Plum Hollow G&CC
Michigan
W. Reid, W. Connellan
Plum Hollow GC (r.)
Michigan
W. B. and G. H. Matthew
Plum Hollow GC (r.)
Michigan
W. K. Newcomb
Plum Tree National GC
Illinois
J. L. Lee
Plymouth CC
Massachusetts
D. J. Ross
Plymouth CC
New Hampshire
R. M. Barton
Plymouth CC (r.)
Pennsylvania
W. S. Flynn
Pocantico Hills [formerly John D. Rockefeller Estate GC](9)
New York
W. S. Flynn
Pocasset GC
Massachusetts
D. J. Ross
Poco Diablo Par 3 GC at Sedona
Arizona
A. J. Snyder
Pocono Farms CC
Pennsylvania
A. Wall
Pocono Manor GC (West course)
Pennsylvania
G. Fazio
Pohick Bay GC
Virginia
G. W. Cobb, J. B. LaFoy

Poinciana CC, Royal (North and South courses)
Florida
D. L. Wallace
Poinciana G&RC
Florida
R. Von Hagge, B. Devlin
Point Aquarius CC
Texas
B. J. Riviere
Point Aquarius Hotel & CC (Alabama International; East and West courses)
Alabama
R. T. Jones, R. L. Jones
Point Grey G&CC (r.)
British Columbia, Canada
G. S. Cornish, W. G. Robinson
Point Judith CC (r.)
Rhode Island
D. J. Ross
Point Judith CC (r.9)
Rhode Island
G. S. Cornish, W. G. Robinson
Point Loma GC
California
T. Bendelow
Point Mallard Park GC
Alabama
(C.W. Graves)
Point North GC
Montana
T. J. Wirth, D. Bennett
Point O' Woods Exec. GC (9)
Florida
(Walter Pursley)
Point O' Woods G&CC
Michigan
R. T. Jones
Point West GC (9)
Florida
A. L. Davis
Pokegama CC (Original 9)
Minnesota
(C. V. Anderson)
Pokegama CC (a.9)
Minnesota
(Jack Melville)
Pokemouche, Club de Golf
New Brunswick, Canada
H. and J. Watson
Pok-ta-pok GC (Cancun Resort)
Mexico
R. T. Jones, Jr.
Poland CC
Ohio
L. Macomber
Poland Springs CC
Maine
A. H. Fenn
Polk County GC
Nebraska
H. W. Glissmann
Pomona National CC [formerly Pomona Valley CC]
California
W. P. Bell
Pomonok CC
New York
D. Emmet
Pompano Beach CC (Palms course)
Florida
R. F. Lawrence
Pompano Beach CC (r. Palms course; a. Pines course)
Florida
R. Von Hagge

Pompano Park Exec. GC
Florida
F. Murray
Pompey Hills GC
New York
H. Purdy
Ponca City CC
Oklahoma
P. D. Maxwell
Ponca City CC (r.)
Oklahoma
D. R. Sechrest
Ponca City Muni
Oklahoma
A. J. Jackson
Ponce de Leon GC (Original 9; n.l.e.)
Florida
A. Findlay
Ponce de Leon GC [formerly St. Augustine Links]
Florida
D. J. Ross
Ponce de Leon GC (r.; a.2)
Florida
W. C. Byrd
Ponce GC
Puerto Rico
A. H. Tull
Pond a River GC
Indiana
R. D. Beard
Ponderosa CC
Ohio
H. D. Fieldhouse
Ponderosa Muni
California
R. E. Baldock
Ponderosa Par 3 GC
Idaho
(Ernest Schneiter)
Pondok Indah GC
Indonesia
R. T. Jones, Jr.
Poniente, Club de Golf
Spain
J. Gancedo
Ponkapoag CC (27)
Massachusetts
D. J. Ross
Ponkapoag CC (a.9)
Massachusetts
W. F. Mitchell
Ponte Vedra Club (Old course)
Florida
H. B. Strong
Ponte Vedra Club (r. Old course; a. Lagoon course (9)
Florida
R. T. Jones
Ponte Vedra Club (a.9, Lagoon course)
Florida
J. L. Lee
Pontiac CC
Michigan
E. W. Way
Pont St. Maxence GC
France
W. Reid
Pope AFB GC (9)
North Carolina
G. W. Cobb, J. B. LaFoy
Poplar Bluff Muni
Missouri
E. B. Ault

Poplar Forest GC
Virginia
K. Killian, R. Nugent
Poquoy Brook GC
Massachusetts
G. S. Cornish
Porches Bluff
South Carolina
W. C. Byrd
Portage CC
Ohio
W. Langford
Portage CC (r.)
Ohio
G. S. Cornish, W. G. Robinson
Portage La Prairie GC (r.9,a.9)
Manitoba, Canada
C. E. Robinson
Portage Yacht & CC
Florida
C. H. Adams
Portales CC
New Mexico
W. H. Tucker, Sr.
Port Alfred, Club de Golf (r.)
Province of Québec, Canada
H. Watson
Port Alfred GC, Royal (r.)
South Africa
S. V. Hotchkin
Port Arthur CC
Texas
R. Plummer
Port Charlotte CC
Florida
M. Mahannah, D. Wallace
Port Charlotte CC (r.)
Florida
C. F. Ankrom
Port Cherry Hills CC
Pennsylvania
P. Erath
Port Colborne GC (r.)
Ontario, Canada
R. Moote
Port Columbus GC
Ohio
J Kidwell
Port Elizabeth GC
South Africa
S. V. Hotchkin
Porter Valley CC
California
T. G. Robinson
Porthcawl GC, Royal (n.l.e.)
Wales
(Charles Gibson)
Porthcawl GC, Royal (r.)
Wales
H. S. Colt
Porthcawl GC, Royal (r.)
Wales
F. G. Hawtree
Porthcawl GC, Royal
Wales
J. Braid
Porthcawl GC, Royal (r.)
Wales
T. C. Simpson
Porthcawl GC, Royal (r.)
Wales
C. K. Cotton
Port Huenume GC
California
J. L. Daray
Porthmadog CG
Wales
J. Braid

Port Jervis CC
New York
A. W. Tillinghast
Portland CC
Maine
D. J. Ross
Portland CC (r.)
Maine
R. T. Jones
Portland GC
Connecticut
G. S. Cornish, W. G. Robinson
Portland GC
Oregon
(Donald Junor)
Portland GC (r.)
Oregon
R. T. Jones
Port Ludlow GC
Washington
R. M. Graves
Porthmadog
Wales
J. Braid
Port Malabar GC
Florida
C. F. Ankrom
Portmarnock GC
Ireland
(George Ross, W. L. Pickeman)
Portmarnock GC (r.)
Ireland
F. G. Hawtree
Portmarnock GC (a. 3rd 9)
Ireland
F. W. Hawtree
Portmarnock GC (r.)
Ireland
E. Hackett
Porto Carras, Links of
Greece
G. S. Cornish, W. G. Robinson
Port Royal GC
Bermuda
R. T. Jones
Port Royal Plantation (Barony and Robber's Row courses)
South Carolina
G. W. Cobb
Portrush GC, Royal (Dunluce and Valley courses)
Northern Ireland
H. S. Colt
Portrush GC, Royal (r. Dunluce and Valley courses)
Northern Ireland
J. S. F. Morrison, H. S. Colt
Portsdown Hill GC
England
F. W. Hawtree
Portsmouth AFB GC (r.)
New Hampshire
A. Zikorus
Portsmouth CC
New Hampshire
R. T. Jones
Portsmouth CC
Ohio
D. J. Ross
Port Sunlight GC
England
F. W. Hawtree
Portumna GC (r.)
Ireland
E. Hackett
Possum Trot GC
South Carolina
R. F. Breeden

Potomac Club
West Virginia
A.M. Pulley
Potowatomi Tribal GC
Oklahoma
D. R. Sechrest
Potowomat CC (a.9)
Rhode Island
W. Johnson
Poughkeepsie Muni (r.)
New York
W. F. Mitchell
Poult Wood Muni
England
F. W. Hawtree
Powder Horn Par 3 GC (n.1.e.)
Massachusetts
G. S. Cornish
Powder River CC
Montana
F. Hummel
Powell Muni
Wyoming
T. J. Wirth
Powelton GC (6)
New York (J
(J. Taylor)
Powelton GC (r. 6, a. 12)
New York
D. Emmet
Powelton GC (r.)
New York
R. T. Jones
Powfoot
Scotland
J. Braid
Poxebogue CC
New York
A. H. Tull
Prague GC
Czechoslovakia
J. J. F. Pennink
Prairie Creek GC
Michigan
W. K. Newcomb
Prairie Dog GC (9)
Kansas
F. Hummel
Prairie Dunes CC (Original 9)
Kansas
P. D. Maxwell
Prairie Dunes CC (a.9)
Kansas
J. P. Maxwell
Prairiewood GC
North Dakota
R.M. Phelps, B. Benz
Prairiewood GC [now Moccasin Creek]
South Dakota
C. E. Maddox
Pratt GC (r.)
Kansas
E. L. Bell
Prattville CC [now Rolling Green CC]
Alabama
R. A. Anderson
Preakness Hills CC
New Jersey
W. H. Tucker Sr.
Preakness Valley Park GC
New Jersey
F. Duane
Prenton
England
F. W. Hawtree
Prescott CC
Arizona
M. Coggins
President CC (North and South courses)
Florida
W. F. Mitchell

Presidents GC [formerly Wollaston CC](r.)
Massachusetts
G. and T. Fazio
Presidio GC (r.)
California
R. Johnstone
Presidio GC (r.)
California
D. Muirhead
Presidio GC (r.)
California
R. M. Graves
Prestbury GC
England
H. S. Colt, J. S. F. Morrison
Preston CC (9)
West Virginia
E. B. Ault
Preston Grange GC (Royal Musselburgh)
Scotland
J. Braid
Preston Trail CC
Texas
R. Plummer
Prestonwood CC
Texas
R. Plummer, (Byron Nelson)
Prestonwood CC (r.)
Texas
J. Finger
Prestwick, Club of
Indiana
R. A. Simmons
Prestwick CC
Illinois
E. L. Packard
Prestwick GC
Scotland
T. Morris
Prestwick GC (r.; a.4)
Scotland
J. Braid, J. R. Stutt
Prestwick St. Cuthbert
Scotland
J. H. Stutt
Prestwick St. Nicholas
Scotland
C. Hunter
Pretty Acres GC
Louisiana
(Louis Prima)
Prien GC
Germany
D. Harradine
Prieure, Golf de
France
F. W. Hawtree
Prince George CC
British Columbia, Canada
E. Brown
Prince George's G&CC [formerly Beaver Dam CC]
Maryland
D. J. Ross
Prince George's G&CC (New course)
Maryland
E. B. Seay, A. Palmer
Prince's GC, Sandwich (Original course)
England
(Charles Hutchings, Percy Montagu Lucas)
Prince's GC, Sandwich (r. Blue course; a. Red course)
England
J. S. F. Morrison, G. Campbell

Prince's GC, Sandwich (r.)
England
C. K. Hutchison
Princess, Acapulco
Mexico
T. G. Robinson
Princess Southampton (Original Par 3)
Bermuda
A. H. Tull
Princess Southampton (r. into Exec. GC)
Bermuda
T. G. Robinson
Princeton CC
Minnesota
W. H. Kidd, Sr.
Princeton CC
New Jersey
W. F. and D. W. Gordon
Princeton Hills Golf Academy
New Jersey
E. V. Ternyey
Princeville Makai GC (27)
Hawaii
R. T. Jones, Jr.
PGA Resort Community GC (PGA National Complex, Championship and Haig and Squire courses)
Florida
G. and T. Fazio
Prospect CC
Connecticut
A. Zikorus
Prospect Hill
Maryland
G. W. Cobb
Prouts Neck GC (r.9,a.9)
Maine
W. E. Stiles, J. R. Van Kleek
Pruneridge Farms Exec. GC
California
J. Fleming
Pruneridge Farms GC (r.)
California
R. T. Jones, Jr.
Pryor Muni
Oklahoma
(Hugh Bancroft)
Puckerbrush CC
Ohio
R. A. Anderson
Puerto Azul GC
Philippines
R. Kirby, G. Player
Puerto de Hierro, Real Club de la
Spain
H. S. Colt, C. H. Alison
Puerto de Hierro, Real Club de la (r.)
Spain
T. C. Simpson
Puerto de Hierro, Real Club de la (r.)
Spain
H. Cotton
Puerto de Hierro, Real Club de la (a.18)
Spain
J. D. Harris
Puerto del Sol Muni (9, 1978)
New Mexico
A.J. Snyder
Pukalini CC
Hawaii
R. E. Baldock
Punderson State Park GC
Ohio
J. Kidwell
Punta Borinquen CC [formerly Ramey AFB GC]
Puerto Rico
A. Zikorus

Punta Gorda GC (r.)
Florida
D. J. Ross
Punta Gorda GC (r.)
Florida
R. A. Anderson
Punta Gorda Isles G&CC (36)
Florida
R. Garl
Punta Rojja GC
Spain
J. D. Harris
Punxsutawney CC
Pennsylvania
J. G. Harrison
Purchase CC [now Old Oaks CC]
New York
C. H. Alison
Purdue University GC (North and South courses)
Indiana
W. Diddel
Purley Downs GC
England
S. V. Hotchkin
Purple Hawk CC
Minnesota
D. Herfort
Purple Sage GC
Wyoming
J. M. Riley
Purple Sage Muni
Idaho
A. V. Macan
Putnam CC
New York
W. F. Mitchell
Putterham Meadows Muni
Massachusetts
W. E. Stiles, J. R. Van Kleek
Putterham Meadows Muni (r.2)
Massachusetts
P. A. Wogan
Pwllheli (Original 9)
Wales
T. Morris
Pwllheli (a.9)
Wales
J. Braid
Pyecomb GC (r.)
England
F. W. Hawtree
Pyle and Kenfig GC
Wales
P. M. Ross
Pyle and Kenfig GC (r.)
Wales
J. H. Stutt
Pyma Valley GC (9)
Ohio
(J. Thomas Francis)
Pype Hayes' Muni (Birmingham Corp.)
England
F. G. Hawtree

Quabog CC (r.2)
Massachusetts
G. S. Cornish, W. G. Robinson
Quail Creek G&CC
Florida
A. Hills
Quail Creek G&CC
Oklahoma
F. Farley
Quail Creek GC
Iowa
L. I. Johnson

Quail Creek GC
South Carolina
E. Hamm
Quail Hollow CC
North Carolina
G. W. Cobb
Quail Hollow CC (r.)
North Carolina
T. Jackson
Quail Hollow Inn & CC
Ohio
R. Von Hagge, B. Devlin
Quail Lake CC
California
D. Muirhead
Quail Ridge CC (North and South courses)
Florida
J. L. Lee
Quail Ridge CC
North Carolina
(Mike Souchak)
Quail Run, Sun City
Arizona
J. Hardin, G. Nash
Quail Valley CC (Original 27)
Texas
(Jack B. Miller)
Quail Valley CC (a.27)
Texas
B. J. Riviere
Quaker Hill CC
New York
R. T. Jones
Quaker Hill CC (r.)
New York
W. F. Mitchell
Quaker Meadows GC (27)
North Carolina
R. F. Breeden
Quaker Ridge CC (orig 9)
New York
J. D. Dunn
Quaker Ridge GC (r. 9, a. 9)
New York
A. W. Tillinghast
Quaker Ridge CC (r.)
New York
R.T. Jones, F. Duane
Quarry Hill Par 3 GC
Vermont
(Walter Barcomb)
Quebec GC, Royal (18)
Province of Québec, Canada
W. Park, Jr.
Quebec GC, Royal (18)
Province of Québec, Canada
H. Watson
Quebec GC, Royal (r.36)
Province of Québec, Canada
H. and J. Watson
Quechee Lakes CC (Highland and Lakeland courses)
Vermont
G. S. Cornish, W. G. Robinson
Queensboro Links
New York
D. Emmet, A. H. Tull
Queensland GC, Royal
Australia
A. Mackenzie
Queens Park Exec. GC (9)
Bermuda
D. Gordon

Queens Park GC
England
J. H. Taylor
Queens Park GC (r.)
England
J. Braid
Queretaro CC
Mexico
P. Clifford
Quidnesset CC
Rhode Island
G. S. Cornish, W. G. Robinson
Quilchena G&CC
British Columbia, Canada
D. Muirhead
Quilchena G&CC (r.6)
British Columbia, Canada
G. S. Cornish, W. G. Robinson
Quimper, Golf de
France
F. W. Hawtree
Quinnatisset CC (a.9)
Connecticut
G. S. Cornish, W. G. Robinson
Quintado de Lago, Club de
Portugal
W. F. Mitchell
Quonset Naval Air Station GC [now Kingstown Muni]
Rhode Island
W. Johnson

Raccoon Run GC
South Carolina
E. Hamm
Racebrook CC
Connecticut
R. D. Pryde
Racebrook CC (r.2)
Connecticut
A. Zikorus
Rackham Park Muni
Michigan
D. J. Ross
Racine CC
Wisconsin
J. A. Roseman
Racine CC (r.)
Wisconsin
D. Gill
Racing Club of France at La Boulie
France
S. Dunn
Racing Club of France at La Boulie
France
W. Park, Jr.
Racing Club of France at La Boulie
France
W. Reid
Radcliffe-on-Trent (r.)
England
T. Williamson
Radcliffe-on-Trent (r.)
England
J. J. F. Pennink
Raddison Greens CC
New York
R. T. Jones
Radley Run CC
Pennsylvania
A. H. Tull
Radnor Valley CC
Pennsylvania
L. S. "Dick" Wilson, X. G. Hassenplug

288

Radnor Valley CC (r.4,a.14)
Pennsylvania
W. F. and D. W. Gordon
Radrick Farm GC
Michigan
P. Dye
RAF Cranwell GC
England
S. V. Hotchkin
Ragaz Spa GC
Switzerland
D. Harradine
(The) Rail GC
Illinois
R. T. Jones
Rainbow Bay GC [formerly Edgewater CC]
Mississippi
J. L. Daray
Rainbow Bay GC (r.12,a.6)
Mississippi
E. Stone
Rainbow Canyon Golf Resort
California
V. C. Rosen
Rainbow End G&CC
Florida
J. L. Lee
Rainelle CC (r.9)
West Virginia
G. W. Cobb, J. B. LaFoy
Rain Tree GC (North and South courses)
North Carolina
R. F. Breeden
Raisin River CC (Original 18 and Exec. course)
Michigan
C. E. Maddox
Ralara GC
Canary Islands
T. Dunn
Raleigh CC
North Carolina
D. J. Ross
Raleigh Golf Association
North Carolina
G. W. Cobb
Ralph G. Cover GC
Maryland
E. B. Ault
Ramblewood GC
New Jersey
E. B. Ault
Ramey AFB [now Punta Borinquen CC]
Puerto Rico
A. Zikorus
Ramsey G&CC (a. 9)
New Jersey
H. Purdy
Ramsey GC (Huntingdonshire)
England
J. Braid
Ramsey GC (Huntingdonshire)
England
J. H. Stutt
Ramsey GC (Isle of Man)
England
J. Braid, J. R. Stutt
(The) Ranch at Roaring Fork Exec. GC (9)
Colorado
M. Coggins
(The) Ranch at Westminster GC
Colorado
R.M. Phelps

Ranch at Carefree GC
Arizona
P. and R. Dye
Ranchitos, Club de Golf
Mexico
P. Clifford
Ranchland Hills GC (Original 9)
Texas
R. Plummer
Ranchland Hills GC (a.9)
Texas
R. Plummer
Rancho Bernardo GC (Oaks and Exec. courses)
California
T. G. Robinson
Rancho Bernardo Inn & GC (West course)
California
W. F. Bell
Rancho California Golf Resort [now Rainbow Canyon]
California
V. C. Rossen
Rancho Canada GC (East and West courses)
California
R. D. Putnam
Rancho GC (n.l.e.)
California
M. Behr
Rancho Duarte GC
California
W.F. Bell
Rancho Las Palmas GC (27)
California
T.G. Robinson
Rancho Murieta GC (North course)
California
B. Stamps
Rancho Murieta GC (South course)
California
T. G. Robinson
Rancho Park Muni (27)
California
W. P. Bell, W. H. Johnson
Rancho San Joaquin CC
California
W. F. Bell
Rancho San Joaquin GC
California
R. M. Graves
Rancho Santa Fe CC
California
M. Behr
Rancho Santa Fe CC (r.)
California
H. M. and D. A. Rainville
Rancho Viejo CC (El Angel and El Diablo courses)
Texas
(Dennis Arp)
Randall Oaks GC
Illinois
W. J. Spear
Randers GC
Denmark
C. K. Cotton
Randolph Field GC (Original 9)
Texas
J. P. and P. D. Maxwell
Randolph Field GC (r.9,a.9)
Texas
J. Finger
Randolph Muni (South course)
Arizona
W. P. Bell
Randolph Muni (North course)
Arizona
W. F. Bell

Randolph Muni (r. North course)
Arizona
P. Dye
Range End GC
Pennsylvania
J. G. Harrison
Ransom Oaks CC
New York
R. T. Jones
Raquette Lake GC
New York
S. Dunn
Raritan Arsenal GC (r.)
New Jersey
H. Purdy
Raritan Valley CC (r.)
New Jersey
D. W. Gordon
Rarotongo GC
Rarotongo
P.W. Thomson, M. Wolveridge
Ratcliffe-on-Trent
England
T. Williamson
Rathfarnham GC (r.)
Ireland
E. Hackett
Rattle Run G&TC
Michigan
(Lou Powers)
Ravenna GC
Ohio
E. B. Ault
Ravenneaux CC (Gold and Orange courses)
Texas
R. Von Hagge, B. Devlin
Ravines GC
Florida
R. Garl
Ravinia Green CC
Illinois
E. L. Packard
Ravisloe CC
Illinois
W. B. Langford, T. J. Moreau
Ravisloe CC (r.)
Illinois
D. J. Ross
Ravisloe CC
Illinois
R. White
Rawiga CC
Ohio
E. L. Packard
Rayburn Country GC (Original 9)
Texas
B. J. Riviere
Rayburn Country GC (a.9)
Texas
R. T. Jones, R. L. Jones
Rayne's Park GC
England
T. Dunn
Reading CC
Pennsylvania
F. A. Findlay
Real Automovil GC
Spain
J. Arana
Real Club de Golf "El Prat"
Spain
J. Arana
Real Club de la Puerto de Hierro
Spain
H. S. Colt, C. H. Alison
Real Club de la Puerto de Hierro (r.)
Spain
T. C. Simpson

Real Club de la Puerto de Hierro (r.)
Spain
H. Cotton
Real Club de la Puerto de Hierro (a.18)
Spain
J. D. Harris
Real GC
Spain
C. H. Alison
Real GC de San Sebastian
Spain
T. C. Simpson
Real Pedrena GC
Spain
H. S. Colt, J. S. F. Morrison
Real Sociedad de Golf Neguri "La Galea"
Spain
J. Arana
Real Sociedad Hipica Espanola Club de Campo
Spain
J. Arana
Reames G&CC (a.9)
Oregon
R. E. Baldock
Rebsamen Park Muni
Arkansas
H. C. Hackbarth
Recreation GC (9)
Oklahoma
F. Farley
Recreation Park GC
California
W.P. Bell
Red Apple Inn & CC
Arkansas
G. Panks
Red Apple Inn & CC (a. 2nd 9)
Arkansas
G.A. Panks
Redbourn GC
England
(J. Day)
Red Butte CC
Wyoming
F. Hummel
Red Deer G&CC (r.)
Alberta, Canada
W. G. Robinson
Redding CC (Original 9)
Connecticut
E. Ryder
Redding CC (a.9)
Connecticut
R. L. Jones
Reddish Vale
England
A. Mackenzie
Redford Muni
Michigan
D. J. Ross
Red Fox CC
North Carolina
E. Maples
Red Hill CC (Original 9)
California
G. C. Thomas, Jr.
Red Hill CC (a.9)
California
W. P. Bell
Red Hill CC (r.)
California
H. M. and D. A. Rainville
Red Hill CC (r.)
Massachusetts
W. F. Mitchell, A. Zikorus

Red Hook GC (r.)
New York
A. H. Tull
Regional Park Muni
Oklahoma
F. Farley
Redlands G&CC
Florida
R. F. Lawrence
Redmond Golf Links
Washington
A. Smith
Red Oaks CC
Texas
L. Howard
Red Oaks GC
Michigan
(Robert W. Bills, Donald G. Childs)
Red River CC
Michigan
W. Park, Jr.
Red Run CC
Michigan
E. F. Loeffler, J. McGlynn
Red Wing CC (r.)
Minnesota
D. Herfort
Red Wing Lake GC
Virginia
G. W. Cobb
Redwoods G&CC
Washington
(Dale Nolte)
Red Wood Meadows GC
Alberta, Canada
S. Leonard, P. Tattersfield
Reedsburg CC
Wisconsin
K. Killian, R. Nugent
Reeves Par 3 GC (9)
Ohio
J. Kidwell
Regensburg GC
West Germany
D. Harradine
Regina GC (r.)
Saskatchewan, Canada
C. E. Robinson
Rehobeth Beach CC
Delaware
F. Murray, R. Roberts
Rehoboth GC
Massachusetts
G. S. Cornish, W. G. Robinson
Reina Cristina GC
Spain
J. Arana
Rend Lake GC
Illinois
E. L. and R. B. Packard
Renishaw GC (r.)
England
T. Williamson
Reno Brookside CC
Nevada
R. E. Baldock
Reno CC
Nevada
L. M. Hughes
Renwood CC
Illinois
W. J. Spear
Restigouche G&CC (a.9)
New Brunswick, Canada
C. E. Robinson

Reston South CC
Virginia
E. B. Ault
Retford GC
England
T. Williamson
Retreat G&CC
Virginia
R. F. Loving
Reynold's Park GC
North Carolina
P. D. Maxwell
Reynold's Park GC (r.)
North Carolina
E. Maples
Rheden, Schloss GC
West Germany
B. Von Limburger
Rhinelander CC
Wisconsin
C. E. Maddox, F. Macdonald
Rhinelander CC (a.9)
Wisconsin
H. Collis
Rhode Island CC
Rhode Island
D. J. Ross
Rhode Island CC (r.1)
Rhode Island
G. S. Cornish
Rhodes GC (Rodos)
Greece
D. Harradine
R. H. Storrer Estate at Woodbridge
Ontario, Canada
H. Watson
Rhuddlan GC
Wales
F. G. Hawtree
Rhyl GC
Wales
J. Braid
Rib Mountain Lodge
Wisconsin
E. L. Packard
Richards-Gebaur AFB GC
Missouri
R. E. Baldock
Richelieu Valley CC (Red and Blue courses)
Province of Québec, Canada
W. F. and D. W. Gordon
Richland CC
Tennessee
D. J. Ross
Richland CC (r.)
Tennessee
J. Finger
Richmond CC
British Columbia, Canada
A. V. Macan
Richmond County CC (r.)
New York
R. White
Richmond County CC (r.4)
New York
F. Duane
Richmond GC (Original course)
England
T. Dunn
Richmond GC (r.)
England
W. Park, Jr.
Richmond Hill G&CC
Ontario, Canada
C. E. Robinson

Richmond Park GC (Princes and Dukes courses)
England
F.G. Hawtree, J.H. Taylor
Richmond Pines CC
North Carolina
D. J. Ross
Richter Memorial GC
Connecticut
E. Ryder
Richview G&CC
Ontario, Canada
C. E. Robinson
Ricklinghausen GC
Germany
D. Harradine
Rickmansworth Muni (r.)
England
F. G. Hawtree, J. H. Taylor
Riddell's Bay G&CC
Bermuda
D. Emmet
Ridder's GC (a.9)
Massachusetts
G. S. Cornish
Rideau Valley CC
Ontario, Canada
H. Watson
Rideau View G&CC (a.9)
Ontario, Canada
C. E. Robinson
Ridge CC
Illinois
H. J. Tweedie
Ridge CC (r.)
Illinois
K. Killian, R. Nugent
Ridgefield Muni
Connecticut
G. and T. Fazio
Ridgelea GC (North course)
Texas
J. Bredemus
Ridgelea GC (r. North course; a. South course)
Texas
R. Plummer
Ridge Manor CC (Original 9)
Florida
H. Schmeisser
Ridge Manor CC (a.9)
Florida
W. Ogg
Ridge Mark CC
California
(Richard Bigler)
Ridgemoor CC (r.)
Illinois
E. B. Dearie, Jr.
Ridgemoor CC (r.)
Illinois
E.L. Packard
Ridgeway CC (r.9)
New York
F. Duane
Ridgeway CC (n.l.e.)
Tennessee
W. B. Langford, T. J. Moreau
Ridgeway CC (New site)
Tennessee
E. Maples
Ridgewood CC (r.)
Connecticut
R. T. Jones
Ridgewood CC (r.; n.l.e.)
New Jersey
D. J. Ross

Ridgewood CC (New site)
New Jersey
A. W. Tillinghast
Ridgewood CC (r.)
Texas
R. Plummer
Ridgewood Muni (n.l.e.)
Ohio
G. S. Alves
Riding Mountain GC (r. 9, a. 9)
Manitoba, Canada
(A.W. Creed)
Ried Park GC (North and South courses)
Ohio
J. Kidwell
Rio Bravo GC
California
R.M. Graves
Rio Del Mar GC [formerly Aptos Seascape](r.)
California
B. Stamps
Rio Hondo CC
California
J. D. Dunn
Riomar CC (a.9)
Florida
E. E. Smith
Riomar CC (original 9)
Florida
H. Strong
Rio Mar GC
Puerto Rico
G. and T. Fazio
Rio Pinar CC (27)
Florida
M. Mahannah
Rio Rancho G&CC [formerly Panorama G&CC]
New Mexico
D. Muirhead
Rio Rico G&CC
Arizona
R. T. Jones
Rio Salado Muni
Arizona
T. G. Robinson
Rio Seco, Club de Golf
Mexico
P. Clifford
Rio Verde CC (Original 9 of Quail Run course and Original 9 of 2nd 18)
Arizona
F. Bolton
Rio Verde CC (a.9 to Quail Run course and a.9 to 2nd 18)
Arizona
M. Coggins, J. Hardin, G. Nash
Rio Vista GC
Ontario, Canada
S. Thompson
Ripon GC
England
G. Lowe
Risebridge GC
England
F. W. Hawtree
Rittswood CC
Pennsylvania
J. G. Harrison, F. Garbin
Riudosa CC
New Mexico
R. Plummer
River Bend CC (r.)
Texas
B. J. Riviere
River Bend CC
Virginia
E. B. Ault, A. Jamison

River Bend Exec. GC
Florida
G. and T. Fazio
Riverbend GC [formerly Grand Forks CC](r.)
North Dakota
R. B. Harris
Riverbend GC
Ohio
R. B. Harris
River Bend GC
Pennsylvania
X. G. Hassenplug
Riverbend GC
Texas
J. P. Maxwell
Riverchase CC
Alabama
J. L. Lee
Rivercliff GC
Arkansas
E. Stone
River Crest CC (r.)
Texas
R. Plummer
Riverdale CC
New York
O. E. Smith
Riverdale GC [formerly Riverside Park GC]
Arkansas
H. C. Hackbarth
Riverdale GC (9)
Montana
(George Schneiter)
River Forest GC
Illinois
E. B. Dearie, Jr.
River Forest GC (r.)
Illinois
E.L. Packard
River Greens GC
Ohio
J. Kidwell
River Green South GC
Florida
J. Kidwell
Riverhill GC
Texas
J. Finger
River Hills CC [now Knollwood CC]
Texas
P. D. Maxwell
River Hills Plantation GC
South Carolina
W. C. Byrd
River Island GC
California
R. E. Baldock
River Island GC
Wisconsin
E. L. Packard
Riverlake CC
Texas
J. P. Maxwell
Rivermont G&CC
Georgia
J. L. Lee
River North G&CC
Georgia
R. Kirby, G. Player, A. L. Davis
River Oaks GC (Formerly Merrywood G&CC)
Missouri
(Larry Runyon, Mike Malyn)
River Oaks CC
New York
D. Muirhead

River Oaks CC
Texas
D. J. Ross
River Oaks CC (r.)
Texas
R. Plummer
River Oaks CC (r.)
Texas
J. Finger
Riveroaks CC
Wisconsin
D. Gill
River Oaks GC (9)
Georgia
A. L. Davis
River Oaks GC
Illinois
K. Killian, R. Nugent
River Plantation GC
Texas
B. J. Riviere
River Ranch CC
Florida
J. L. Lee
River Road GC
Maryland
E. B. Ault, A. Jamison
Riverside (Portland Muni; Original 18)
Maine
W. E. Stiles
Riverside (Portland Muni; r.18)
Maine
W. F. Mitchell
Riverside (Portland Muni; a.9)
Maine
G. S. Cornish, W. G. Robinson
Riverside CC (r.)
Massachusetts
W. F. Mitchell
Riverside CC
Michigan
A. H. Jolly
Riverside CC
Michigan
W. B. and G. H. Matthews
Riverside CC (a.9)
Montana
R. N. Phelps, B. Benz
Riverside CC (r.)
Oregon
W. F. Bell
Riverside CC
Texas
R. Plummer
Riverside CC
Utah
W. F. Bell, W. H. Neff
Riverside G&CC (9)
California
R. M. Graves
Riverside G&CC (a.9)
California
W. F. Bell
Riverside G&CC
Georgia
C. H. Adams
Riverside G&CC (r.)
New Brunswick, Canada
D. J. Ross
Riverside G&CC (r.)
New Brunswick, Canada
C. E. Robinson
Riverside G&CC
Saskatchewan, Canada
W. Kinnear
Riverside G&CC (r.)
Saskatchewan, Canada
W. G. Robinson

Riverside Golf & Polo Club
California
C. Maud

Riverside GC
California
J. Fleming

Riverside GC (Herndon; r.9,a.9)
California
W. P. Bell

Riverside GC (r.)
Illinois
W. B. Langford

Riverside GC
Montana
T. J. Wirth

Riverside GC
New York
E. L. Packard

Riverside GC
Texas
G. A. Hoffman

Riverside GC (Ogden)
Utah
(Ernest Schneiter)

Riverside Inn & CC
Pennsylvania
(William Baird)

Riverside Muni (Original 9)
Texas
R. Plummer

Riverside Muni
Wisconsin
R. B. Harris

Riverside Muni at Jackson
Mississippi
E. Stone

Riverton CC
New Jersey
D. J. Ross

Riverton CC (a.9)
Wyoming
R. N. Phelps, B. Benz

Riverton GC (South course)
New York
E. B. Ault

River Valley GC
Pennsylvania
G. S. Cornish

Riverview City GC
Michigan
W. K. Newcomb

Riverview CC
Connecticut
A. Zikorus

Riverview CC [now Hidden Lakes CC]
Kansas
F. Farley

Riverview CC
Missouri
R. Foulis

Riverview CC (r.)
Tennessee
A. G. McKay

Riverview Muni (9)
Colorado
F. Hummel

Riverview Muni
Michigan
A. Hills

Riverview Muni
North Dakota
L. I. Johnson

Riverview Sun City
Arizona
J. Hardin, G. Nash

Riverwood Muni
North Dakota
L. I. Johnson

Riviera Africaine GC
Ivory Coast (Africa)
A. L. Davis, R. Kirby

Riviera CC
California
G. C. Thomas, Jr., W. P. Bell

Riviera CC (r.)
Florida
L. S. "Dick" Wilson

Riviere du Loup CC (r.9,a.9)
Province of Québec, Canada
H. Watson

Road Runner Dunes Muni (9)
California
L. M. Hughes

Roanoke CC (a. 9)
North Carolina
E. Maples

Roanoke CC (new site)
Virginia
E. Maples

Roanoke CC (r.) (n.i.e.)
Virginia
A. W. Tillinghast

Roaring Gap G&CC
North Carolina
D. J. Ross

Robber's Roost GC
South Carolina
R. F. Breeden

Robert Black Exec. Muni
Illinois
K. Killian, R. Nugent

Robert Van Patten GC
New York
(Andrew Farina)

Robinhead Lakes GC
Mississippi
E. D. Guy

Robin Hood GC
England
H. S. Colt

Robins AFB GC (r.)
Georgia
A. L. Davis

Rob Roy GC
Illinois
E. B. Dearie, Jr.

Robstown CC
Texas
W. D. Cantrell

Roca Llisa GC (9)
Island of Ibiza, Spain
F. W. Hawtree

Rochdale GC
England
J. J. F. Pennink

Rochefort en Yvelines GC
France
D. Harradine

Rochefort, Golf de
France
F. W. Hawtree

Rochelle CC (r.9,a.9)
Illinois
D. Gill

Rochester CC (a.9)
New Hampshire
P. A. Wogan

Rochester CC (r.)
New Hampshire
M. L. Francis

Rochester, CC of
New York
D. J. Ross

Rochester, CC of (a.3)
New York
R. T. Jones

Rochester G&CC
Minnesota
A. W. Tillinghast

Rochford Hundred
England
F. G. Hawtree

Rockleigh-Bergen County GC
New Jersey
W. F. and D. W. Gordon

Rockaway CC
New Jersey
G. Low

Rockaway Hunting Club
New York
T. Bendelow

Rockaway Hunting Club (r.)
New York
A. W. Tillinghast

Rockaway River CC (r.)
New Jersey
H. Purdy

Rock Barn GC
North Carolina
R. F. Breeden

Rock Creek Park GC (r.)
Washington, D.C.
W. S. Flynn

Rockdale CC
Texas
L. Howard

Rocket City GC
Florida
R. A. Anderson

Rockford CC
Illinois
H. J. Tweedie

Rockford CC (r.)
Illinois
C. D. Wagstaff

Rock Hill CC
South Carolina
J. P. Gibson

Rock Hill CC (original 9)
South Carolina
A. W. Tillinghast

Rock Hill G&CC
New York
F. Duane

Rock Island Arsenal GC (r.)
Illinois
D. Gill

Rockland County CC (r.)
New York
A. H. Tull

Rockland Par 3 GC
Massachusetts
P. A. Wogan

Rockledge CC
Florida
R. A. Anderson

Rockedge Muni (r.9,a.9)
Connecticut
O. E. Smith, A. Zikorus

Rockledge Muni (r.)
Connecticut
W. F. Mitchell

Rockleigh GC (r. Bergen course)
New Jersey
R. T. Jones

Rockleigh GC (r. Rockleigh course and a.
9 to Bergen course)
New Jersey
W. F. and D. W. Gordon

Rockport GC (r.2)
Massachusetts
P. A. Wogan

Rockrimmon CC (Original 9)
Connecticut
R. T. Jones

Rockrimmon CC (a.9)
Connecticut
O. E. Smith, A. Zikorus

Rock River CC
Illinois
W. J. Spear

Rock River Hills GC
Wisconsin
H. D. Fieldhouse

Rock Spring CC (r.)
New Jersey
H. Purdy

Rockville CC (r.1)
New York
F. Duane

Rockwell College GC
Ireland
E. Hackett

Rockwood Hall GC (n.i.e.)
New York
D. Emmet, A. H. Tull

Rockwood Hall GC
New York
W. S. Flynn

Rockwood Muni
Texas
J. Bredemus

Rockwood Muni (r.27)
Texas
R. Plummer

Rockwood Park GC (a. 3)
New Brunswick, Canada
W.G. and J.F. Robinson

Rocky Bayou CC
Florida
W. W. Amick

Rocky Point GC (a. 3rd 9)
Florida
D. L. Wallace

Rocky Point GC
Maryland
R. Roberts

Rocky Ridge CC
Vermont
(Walter Barcomb)

Rodos (Rhodes) GC
Greece
D. Harradine

Roebuck CC
Alabama
J. L. Daray

Rogers Park GC (r.)
Florida
R. Garl

Rogue River GC
Michigan
W. K. Bowen

Rogue Valley CC (Original 9)
Oregon
H. C. Egan

Rogue Valley CC (r.9,a.9)
Oregon
W. P. Bell

Rohnert Park Muni
California
R. E. Baldock

Rolland Road GC
Maryland
W. Park, Jr.

Rolling Acres CC
Pennsylvania
J. G. Harrison

Rolling Green CC [formerly Prattville
    CC]
Alabama
R. A. Anderson

Rolling Green CC
Illinois
W. Diddel

Rolling Green CC (r.)
Illinois
D. Gill

Rolling Green CC
Pennsylvania
W. S. Flynn

Rolling Green CC (9)
Wyoming
H. B. Hughes

Rolling Green G&CC
Florida
R. A. Anderson

Rolling Green G&CC (a.9)
Florida
W. H. Dietsch

Rolling Greens CC
Minnesota
C. E. Maddox

Rolling Greens CC
New Jersey
N. T. Psiahas

Rolling Hills CC
California
T. G. Robinson

Rolling Hills CC [now Applewood CC]
Colorado
J. P. Maxwell

Rolling Hills CC (new site)
Colorado
J. P. Maxwell

Rolling Hills CC
Connecticut
A. H. Tull

Rolling Hills CC (Davie; a. 9)
Florida
W. H. Dietsch

Rolling Hills CC (Ft. Lauderdale)
Florida
W. F. Mitchell

Rolling Hills CC (r.)
Kansas
F. Farley

Rolling Hills CC
Mississippi
G. Curtis

Rolling Hills CC
North Carolina
G. W. Cobb

Rolling Hills CC [formerly Indian Hills
    CC]
Oklahoma
P. D. Maxwell

Rolling Hills CC (r.)
Oklahoma
F. Farley

Rolling Hills CC
Pennsylvania
J. G. Harrison

Rolling Hills CC
Texas
R. Plummer

Rolling Hills Exec. GC (Tempe; 9)
Arizona
M. Coggins

Rolling Hills Exec. GC (Tucson)
Arizona
W. F. Bell

291

Rolling Hills Exec. GC
Washington
(Donald Hogan)
Rolling Hills GC [now Applewood GC]
Colorado
J. P. Maxwell
Rolling Hills Golf Estates
Michigan
W. K. Bowen
Rolling Hills Par 3 GC (n.l.e.)
Massachusetts
R. Armacost
Rolling Meadows GC
Kansas
R. Watson
Rolling Rock Creek GC
Pennsylvania
D. J. Ross
Roman Hills GC
Texas
B. J. Riviere
Roman Nose State Park GC (9)
Oklahoma
F. Farley
Romford
England
J. Braid
Romsey
England
J. J. F. Pennink, C. Lawrie
Rondout GC at Accord
New York
H. Purdy
Rookery Park at Lowestoft
England
C. D. Lawrie
Roosevelt GC (Griffith Park System)
California
W. H. Johnson
Roosevelt Muni
Utah
J. B. Williams
Rosapenna GC
Ireland
T. Morris
Rosapenna GC (r.)
Ireland
H. S. Colt
Roscommon GC (r.)
Ireland
E. Hackett
Roscrea GC (r.; a.9)
Ireland
E. Hackett
Roseburg CC (r.9,a.9)
Oregon
G. Baird
Rosedale CC (r.)
Ontario, Canada
D. J. Ross
Rosedale GC (r.)
Ontario, Canada
H. Watson
Rose Hall (Half Moon Hotel)
Jamaica
R. T. Jones
Rose Hall (Hotel Intercontinental)
Jamaica
(Henry C. Smedley)
Roseland G&CC
Ontario, Canada
D. J. Ross
Roselle CC
New Jersey
S. J. Raynor
Rosemont CC (a.9)
Ohio
E. L. Packard

Rosemont GC
Florida
L. Clifton
Rosemount GC (r.)
Scotland
J. R. Stutt
Resendail GC
Holland
J. J. F. Pennink
Rose Park GC (Original 9)
Utah
J. M. Riley
Rose Park GC (a.9)
Utah
W. F. Bell
Roseville CC
California
J. Fleming
Ross Hill Muni
Virginia
L. Howard
Rosslare (r.)
Ireland
J. H. Stutt
Rossmere G&CC
Manitoba, Canada
N. Woods
Rossmoor GC (Walnut Creek; a. Exec.
GC)
California
H. M. and D. A. Rainville
Rossmoor GC (Walnut Creek; a.9)
California
R. M. Graves
Rossmoor Leisure World GC
Arizona
J. Hardin, G. Nash
Rossmoor Leisure World GC
California
D. Muirhead
Rossmoor Leisure World GC
Maryland
D. Muirhead
Rossmoor Leisure World GC
New Jersey
D. Muirhead
Rossmore GC (r.)
Ireland
E. Hackett
Ross on Wye GC
England
C. K. Cotton, J. J. F. Pennink
Ross Rogers Muni
Texas
L. Howard
Rosswood CC
Arkansas
A. H. Tull
Rothchild (Baron Edward) Estate GC
France
T. C. Simpson
Rothchild (Baron Henry) Estate GC
France
T. C. Simpson
Rothesay (Island of Bute)
Scotland
J. Braid
Rothley Park GC
England
T. Williamson
Rotorua GC (18 puls Par 3)
New Zealand
(C. H. Redhead)
Rotunda CC
Florida
(James Petrides)
Rouen GC
France
W. Park, Jr.

Rougemont (Comte de) Estate GC
France
T. C. Simpson
Rough River State Park
Kentucky
B. J. Wihry
Round Hill CC
Connecticut
W. J. Travis
Round Hill CC (r.)
Connecticut
R. T. Jones
Round Hill G&CC (r.)
California
R. M. Graves
Round Hill G&CC
California
L. M. Hughes
Round Meadow CC
Virginia
J. P. Gibson
Round Up Muni (Pine Ridge GC, 9)
Montana
F. Hummel
Routenburn GC
Scotland
J. Braid
Rowlands Castle
England
H. S. Colt
Rowley CC
Massachusetts
P. A. Wogan
Roxboro CC (a.9)
North Carolina
E. Maples
Roxborough Park GC (now Arrowhead
GC)
Colorado
R. T. Jones, Sr. and Jr.
Roxbury Run GC
New York
H. Purdy
Roxiticus CC
New Jersey
H. Purdy
Royal Aberdeen GC (Ladies course)
Scotland
J. J. F. Pennink
Royal Adelaide GC
Australia
(C.L. Gardiner)
Royal Adelaide GC (r.)
Australia
P.W. Thomson, M. Wolveridge
Royal Adelaide GC (r.)
Australia
A. Mackenzie
Royal Aeroclub de Zaragoza
Spain
F. W. Hawtree
Royal Air Force Cranwell GC
England
S. V. Hotchkin
Royal and Ancient GC of St. Andrews
Scotland
See St. Andrews
Royal Antwerp GC
Belgium
W. Park, Jr.
Royal Antwerp GC (r.18,a.9)
Belgium
T. C. Simpson, P. M. Ross
Royal Automobile GC
England
W. H. Fowler
Royal Belfast GC
Northern Ireland
H. S. Colt

Royal Belgique GC (1904)
Belgium
W. Reid
Royal Belgique GC (r.)
Belgium
T. C. Simpson
Royal Birkdale (Original course)
England
G. Lowe
Royal Birkdale GC (r.)
England
F. G. Hawtree, J. H. Taylor
Royal Birkdale GC (r.)
England
F. W. Hawtree
Royal Blackheath GC (r.)
England
"Old" W. Dunn
Royal Blackheath GC (New course)
England
J. Braid
Royal Burgess of Edinburgh (Original
course) (n.i.e.)
Scotland
T. Morris
Royal Burgess of Edinburgh (r.)
Scotland
J. Braid
Royal Calcutta GC (r. Old course)
India
P. Thomson
Royal Canberra GC
Australia
J. D. Harris
Royal Canberra GC (r.)
Australia
P.W. Thomson, M. Wolveridge
Royal Cinque Ports (Deal; Original 9)
England
T. Dunn
Royal Cinque Ports (Deal; r.)
England
G. Campbell
Royal Colwood G&CC (r.)
British Columbia
A. V. Macan
Royal County Down (Original course)
Northern Ireland
T. Morris
Royal County Down (r.)
Northern Ireland
S. Dunn
Royal County Down (r.)
Northern Ireland
H. Vardon
Royal Cromer
England
J. Braid
Royal Dornoch [then Dornoch] GC
Scotland
T. Morris
Royal Dornoch GC (r.9,a.9)
Scotland
J. Sutherland
Royal Dornoch GC (r.)
Scotland
J. Sutherland, J. H. Taylor
Royal Dornoch GC (r.; a.4)
Scotland
G. Duncan
Royal Downs Exec. GC
Ontario, Canada
R. and C. Muylaert
Royal Dublin GC (r.)
Ireland
H. S. Colt
Royal Dublin GC (r.)
Ireland
G. Campbell

Royal Eastbourne GC
England
H. G. Hutchinson (C. Mayhewe)
Royal Eastbourne GC (r.)
England
J. H. Stutt
Royal Fagnes GC
Belgium
T. C. Simpson, P. M. Ross
Royal GC du Sart Tilman
Belgium
T. C. Simpson
Royal GC Les Buttes Blanches (r.)
Belgium
F. W. Hawtree
Royal Golf Rabat (Red, Blue and Green
courses; 45)
Morocco
R. T. Jones
Royal Green GC
Utah
(Keith Downs)
Royal Guernsey CC (r.)
Channel Islands
P. M. Ross
Royal Hong Kong (Old course)
Hong Kong
(Captain H. N. Dumbleton, R.E.)
Royal Hong Kong (New course)
Hong Kong
(L. S. Greenhill)
Royal Hong Kong (Eden course)
Hong Kong
J. D. Harris, M. Wolveridge
Royal Johannesburg GC (West course
South Africa
L. B. Waters
Royal Johnnesburg GC (East course)
South Africa
R. G. Grimsdell
Royal Johannesburg GC (r.)
South Africa
R. Kirby, G. Player
Royal Kaanapali GC (North course)
Hawaii
R. T. Jones
Royal Kaanapali GC (South course)
Hawaii
A. J. Snyder
Royal Liverpool GC (Hoylake; Original
course)
England
R. Chambers, G. Morris
Royal Liverpool GC (Hoylake) (r. 9, a.9)
England
J. Braid
Royal Liverpool GC (Hoylake; r.)
England
H. S. Colt
Royal Liverpool GC (Hoylake; r.)
England
J. J. F. Pennink
Royal Lytham & St. Annes GC (Original
course)
England
G. Lowe
Royal Lytham & St. Annes GC (r.)
England
H. S. Colt
Royal Lytham & St. Annes GC (r.)
England
W. H. Fowler
Royal Lytham & St. Annes GC (r.)
England
T. C. Simpson
Royal Lytham & St. Annes GC (r.)
England
C. K. Cotton, J. J. F. Pennink

Royal Lytham Short Course
England
C. D. Lawrie
Royal Madrid GC (n. i. e.)
Spain
H. S. Colt
Royal Madrid GC
Spain
T. C. Simpson
Royal Madrid GC
Spain
J.D. Harris, M. Wolveridge
Royal Melbourne GC (West course)
Australia
A. Mackenzie
Royal Melbourne GC (East course)
Australia
A. Russell
Royal Melbourne GC (r. East and West courses)
Australia
L. S. "Dick" Wilson
Royal Mid Surrey [then Mid Surrey]
England
T. Dunn
Royal Mid Surrey (r.)
England
J. H. Taylor
Royal Mid Surrey (r.)
England
R. Beale
Royal Mid Surrey Ladies Course (r.)
England
J. H. Taylor
Royal Montreal (Dixie; n.l.e.)
Province of Québec, Canada
"Young" W. Dunn
Royal Montreal (Dixie; 36; n.l.e.)
Province of Québec, Canada
W. Park, Jr.
Royal Montreal (Dixie; r. South; n.l.e.)
Province of Québec, Canada
H. S. Colt
Royal Montreal GC (Isle Bizard; Blue, Red and Green courses
Province of Québec, Canada
L. S. "Dick" Wilson
Royal Musselburgh GC (Preston Grange)
Scotland
J. Braid
Royal Musselburgh GC (Preston Grange; r.)
Scotland
M. Park II
Royal North Devon GC (Westward Ho!; Original course)
England
T. Morris
Royal North Devon GC (Westward Ho!; r.)
England
W. H. Fowler
Royal Oak G&CC
Florida
L. S. "Dick" Wilson, R. Von Hagge
Royal Oak GC
Michigan
W. B. and G. H. Matthews
Royal Oaks CC
North Carolina
E. Hamm
Royal Oaks CC
Texas
D. January, B. Martindale

Royal Oaks CC
Washington
F. Federspiel
Royal Oaks CC (r.)
Washington
T. G. Robinson
Royal Oaks GC
California
R. M. Graves
Royal Oaks GC
Georgia
R. Kirby, A. L. Davis
Royal Ottawa GC at Hull (r. 9, a. 27)
Province of Québec, Canada
H. Watson
Royal Ottawa GC at Hull (r.)
Province of Québec, Canada
C. E. Robinson
Royal Palm Beach G&CC (36)
Florida
M. Mahannah
Royal Palms Exec. Club (9)
Arizona
D. Gill
Royal Palm Yacht & CC
Florida
R. T. Jones
Royal Pines CC (Pines and Marsh courses)
South Carolina
(Walter Rodgers)
Royal Poinciana CC (North and South courses)
Florida
D. L. Wallace
Royal Port Alfred GC (r.)
South Africa
S. V. Hotchkin
Royal Porthcawl GC (n.l.e.)
Wales
(Charles Gibson)
Royal Porthcawl GC (r.)
Wales
H. S. Colt
Royal Porthcawl GC (r.)
Wales
F. G. Hawtree
Royal Porthcawl GC (new site)
Wales
J. Braid
Royal Porthcawl GC (r.)
Wales
T. C. Simpson
Royal Porthcawl GC (r.)
Wales
C. K. Cotton
Royal Portrush GC (Dunluce and Valley courses; 36)
Northern Ireland
H. S. Colt
Royal Portrush GC (r. Dunluce and Valley courses)
Northern Ireland
J. S. F. Morrison, H. S. Colt
Royal Quebec GC (a. 9)
Canada
W. Park, Jr.
Royal Quebec GC (a.18)
Province of Québec, Canada
H. Watson
Royal Quebec GC (r.)
Province of Québec, Canada
H. and J. Watson
Royal Queensland GC
Australia
A. Mackenzie
Royal St. David's GC (r.)
Wales
F. W. Hawtree

Royal St. Georges [formerly St. Georges]
England
(W. Laidlaw Purves)
Royal St. Georges (r.)
England
A. Mackenzie
Royal St. Georges (r.)
England
J. J. F. Pennink
Royal St. Kitts GC
St. Kitts
J.D. Harris, M. Wolveridge, R. Fream
Royal Salisbury GC
Zimbabwe (Rhodesia)
L. B. Waters
Royal Salisbury GC (r.2)
Zimbabwe (Rhodesia)
F. W. Hawtree
Royal Scot GC
Wisconsin
D. Herfort
Royal Selangor GC (r. Old Course)
Malaysia
H. S. Colt
Royal Selangor GC (new course)
Malaysia
J. J. F. Pennink
Royal Sydney GC
Australia
(S. R. Robbie)
Royal Sydney GC (r.)
Australia
A. Mackenzie
Royal Sydney GC (r.)
Australia
P. W. Thomson, M. Wolveridge
Royal Tara (r.)
Ireland
E. Hackett
Royal Troon
Scotland
See Troon
Royal Waterloo GC (36; n.l.e.)
Belgium
H. S. Colt
Royal Waterloo GC (New courses)
Belgium
F. W. Hawtree
Royal West Norfolk GC
England
H. G. Hutchinson
Royal West Norfolk GC (r.)
England
C. K. Hutchison
Royal Wimbledon GC (n.l.e.)
England
T. Dunn
Royal Wimbledon GC (New site)
England
H. S. Colt
Royal Wimbledon GC (r.)
England
C. D. Lawrie
Royal Worlington and New Market
England
T. Dunn
Royal Worlington and New Market (r.)
England
S. V. Hotchkin
Royal York GC [now St. Georges]
Ontario, Canada
S. Thompson
Royal Zoute GC
Belgium
H. S. Colt
Roy Rogers Par 3 GC
California
W. H. Johnson

Rozella Ford GC
Indiana
W. Diddel
Ruby View Muni
Nevada
A. J. Snyder
Ruidoso (Alto)
New Mexico
M. Coggins
Ruislip and Northwood Muni
England
F. G. Hawtree
Ruma CC
Zimbabwe (Rhodesia)
(George Waterman), L. B. Waters
Runaway Bay GC
Jamaica
J. D. Harris
Runaway Brook GC [now International GC]
Massachusetts
G. S. Cornish
Rungsted GC
Denmark
(Major C. A. Mackenzie)
Running Hills CC
Maine
G. S. Cornish, W. G. Robinson
Rushcliffe GC
England
T. Williamson
Rushcliffe GC
England
J.J.F. Pennink
Rushden and District GC
England
(C. Catlow)
Rushden GC
England
T. Williamson
Rush GC (r.)
Ireland
E. Hackett
Rusley GC (r.)
New Zealand
J.D. Harris, P.W. Thomson, M. Wolveridge
Rutgers University GC (r. 9, a. 9)
New Jersey
H. Purdy
Ruth Lake CC
Illinois
W. B. Langford, T. J. Moreau
Ruth Lake CC (r.)
Illinois
E.L. Packard
Ruth Park GC
Missouri
R. B. Harris
Rutland CC (r.9,a.9)
Vermont
W. E. Stiles, J. R. Van Kleek
Ryde GC on Isle of Wright (r.)
England
J. H. Stutt
Rye GC (Original course)
England
H. S. Colt
Rye GC (r.)
England
G. Campbell
Rye GC (a.9)
England
J. J. F. Pennink

Sabah G&CC
East Malaysia
R. M. Graves
Sabal Palms CC
Florida
F. Murray

Sacramento GC
California
A. Mackenzie
Sadaquada GC (r.)
New York
W. F. Mitchell
Saddlebrook G&TC
Florida
(Dean Refram)
Saddlebrook G&TC (a. 9)
Florida
E.B. Seay, A. Palmer
Saddle Hill CC
Massachusetts
W. F. Mitchell
Safari Inn Par 3 GC
Florida
(Carl H. Anderson)
Saffron Walden
England
H. Vardon
Sagamore GC
New York
D. J. Ross
Sahalee CC (27)
Washington
T. G. Robinson
Saham
Great Britain
T. Dunn
Sahara/Nevada CC
Nevada
B. Stamps
Sailfish Point
Florida
J. Nicklaus
Sail Ho! Par 3 GC
California
J. Daray
Saint Albans CC
New York
W. Park, Jr.
Saint Albans CC
New York
A. W. Tillinghast
Saint Andrews (The Old Course; r.)
Scotland
A. Robertson
St. Andrews (The Old Course; r.)
Scotland
T. Morris
St. Andrews (The New Course)
Scotland
T. Morris
St. Andrews (The Eden Course)
Scotland
H. S. Colt
St. Andrews (The Jubilee Course)
Scotland
W. Auchterlonie
St. Andrews by the Sea (Algonquin Hotel course)
New Brunswick, Canada
D. J. Ross
St. Andrews CC
Province of Québec, Canada
H. B. Strong
St. Andrews G&CC (Courses #1 and #2)
Illinois
E. B. Dearie, Jr.
St. Andrews G&CC (r. Courses #1 and #2)
Illinois
J. L. Lee
St. Andrews GC (n.l.e.)
California
N. Macbeth
St. Andrews GC (n.l.e.)
Missouri
J. Dalgleish

293

St. Andrews GC (Toronto; 27; n.l.e.)
Ontario, Canada
S. Thompson
St. Andrews GC
Japan
D. Muirhead, J. Nicklaus
St. Andrews GC (Original course)
Trinidad
H. S. Colt
St. Andrews GC (New site)
Trinidad
J.D. Harris, M. Wolveridge, R. Fream
St. Andrews GC on the Hudson (one version)
New York
W. H. Tucker, Sr.
St. Andrews GC on the Hudson (r.)
New York
J. Braid
St. Andrews GC on the Hudson (r.)
New York
J. Nicklaus
St. Andrews South GC
Florida
R. Fream
St. Annes GC (r.)
Ireland
E. Hackett
St. Ann GC
Missouri
A. Linkogel
St. Augustine CC (Original 9)
Florida
A. Findlay
St. Augustine Links (36)
Florida
D. J. Ross
St. Augustine Shores CC (Exec.)
(John Denton)
St. Austell
England
J. Braid
St. Bernard CC
Ohio
(Earl Yesberger)
St. Boswells
Scotland
W. Park, Jr.
St. Catherines G&CC
Ontario, Canada
S. Thompson
St. Catherines G&CC (r.)
Ontario, Canada
C. E. Robinson
St. Catherines Muni
Ontario, Canada
R. and C. Muylaert
St. Charles CC (r.)
Illinois
D. Gill
St. Charles CC (r.)
Illinois
R. T. Jones
St. Charles CC (South 9)
Manitoba, Canada
D. J. Ross
St. Charles CC (North 9)
Manitoba, Canada
A. Mackenzie
St. Charles CC (West 9)
Manitoba, Canada
N. Woods
St. Charles CC (r.2)
Manitoba, Canada
C. E. Robinson
St. Charles Muni
Missouri
A. Linkogel

St. Clair CC (n.l.e.)
Pennsylvania
T. Bendelow
St. Clair CC
Pennsylvania
W. F. Gordon
St. Clair CC (r.)
Pennsylvania
J. G. Harrison
St. Clair CC (a. 3rd 9)
Pennsylvania
J. L. Lee
St. Clair Shores CC
Michigan
W. B. and G. H. Matthews
St. Cloud GC (Yellow course)
France
H. S. Colt
St. Cuthbert, Prestwick
Scotland
J. H. Stutt
St. Davids GC
Pennsylvania
D. J. Ross
St. Davids GC (r.)
Pennsylvania
A. W. Tillinghast
St. Davis GC, Royal (r.)
Wales
F. W. Hawtree
St. Delnial GC
Wales
J. Braid
St. Elmo GC
Illinois
W. J. Spear
Ste. Anne Beaupre, Club de Golf
Province of Québec, Canada
H. Watson
Ste. Marguerite GC on Sept Isles
Province of Québec, Canada
H. Watson
Ste. Marie, Club de Golf
Province of Québec, Canada
H. Watson
Ste. Marie de Beauce GC
Province of Québec, Canada
H. Watson
St. Enodoc GC
England
J. Braid
St. Eurach GC
Germany
D. Harradine
St. Francoise, Golf Internationale de
Guadeloupe
R. T. Jones
St. Georges G&CC
New York
D. Emmet
St. Georges G&CC (Original course)
Ontario, Canada
H. S. Colt
St. Georges GC [formerly Royal York]
Ontario, Canada
S. Thompson
St. Georges G&CC (r.)
Ontario, Canada
C. E. Robinson
St. Georges GC
Province of Québec, Canada
H. Watson
St. Georges GC, Royal
England
H. S. Colt, J. S. F. Morrison, H. Cotton
(W. Laidlaw Purves)
St. Georges GC, Royal (r.)
England
A. Mackenzie

St. Georges GC, Royal (r.)
England
J. J. F. Pennink
St. Georges Hill (1st and 2nd 18's)
England
H. S. Colt
St. Georges Hill (r.)
England
J. H. Stutt
St. Georges Hotel GC (r.)
Bermuda
D. Emmet
St. James GC
Jamaica
W. B. Langford
St. Johnsbury CC
Vermont
W. Park, Jr.
St. Joseph CC (r.)
Missouri
R. C. Dunning
St. Joseph's Bay CC
Florida
W. W. Amick
St. Kitts GC, Royal
St. Kitts
J. D. Harris
St. Knuds GC
Denmark
C. K. Cotton, J. J. F. Pennink
St. Laurent, Club de Golf
Province of Québec, Canada
H. Watson
St. Lawrence University GC (Original 9)
New York
D. Emmet
St. Lawrence University GC (a.12)
New York
G. S. Cornish, W. G. Robinson
St. Louis CC (n.l.e.)
Missouri
J. Foulis
St. Louis CC (New site)
Missouri
C. B. Macdonald
St. Louis CC (r.)
Missouri
R. T. Jones
St. Luc, Club de Golf
Province of Québec, Canada
H. Watson
St. Luc, Club de Golf
Province of Québec, Canada
J. Watson
St. Lucie CC [now Sandpiper CC] (Sinners course)
Florida
M. Mahannah
St. Lucie CC [now Sandpiper CC] (Saints course)
Florida
D. L. Wallace
St. Lucie River CC
Florida
W. B. Langford, T. J. Moreau
St. Marys GC
West Virginia
X. G. Hassenplug
St. Mellion G&CC
England
J. H. Stutt
St. Mellons GC
Wales
H. S. Colt, J. S. F. Morrison, H. Cotton
St. Michel, Club de Golf
Province of Québec, Canada
H. Watson

St. Michaels GC
Australia
(Clement Glancey)
St. Nicholas Prestwick
Scotland
C. Hunter
St. Nom La Breteche, Golf de (36)
France
F. W. Hawtree
St. Patrick, Club de Golf
Province of Québec, Canada
H. and J. Watson
St. Petersburg CC
Florida
A. W. Tillinghast
St. Pierre (36)
Wales
C. K. Cotton, J. J. F. Pennink
St. Poswells
Great Britain
W. Park, Jr.
St. Samson, Golf de
France
F. W. Hawtree
St. Simons Island Club
Georgia
J. L. Lee
St. Thomas G&CC (a.9)
Ontario, Canada
C. E. Robinson
Sakonnet GC
Rhode Island
D. J. Ross
Salem CC
Massachusetts
D. J. Ross
Salem CC (9)
Missouri
F. Farley
Salem CC
New York
E. Ryder, (V. Carlson)
Salem GC (a.9)
Ohio
R. A. Simmons
Salem Hills GC
Michigan
W. B. and G. H. Matthews
Salina CC
Kansas
(John Eberhardt)
Salina Muni
Kansas
F. Farley
Salinas CC
California
J. Fleming
Salinas Fairways GC
California
J. Fleming
Salisbury CC (r.)
Virginia
E. B. Ault
Salisbury, CC of (Original 9)
North Carolina
D. J. Ross
Salisbury GC, Royal
Zimbabwe (Rhodesia)
L. B. Waters
Salisbury GC, Royal (r.2)
Zimbabwe (Rhodesia)
F. W. Hawtree
Salisbury Golf Links [now Eisenhower Park GC, Red course]
New York
D. Emmet

Salishan Golf Links
Oregon
F. Federspiel
Salmon Brook CC (r.)
Connecticut
O. E. Smith
Salt Fork State Park
Ohio
J. Kidwell
Salt Lake city, CC of (r.)
Utah
R. Plummer
Salt Lake City, CC of
Utah
H. Lamb
Salt Lake City, CC of (r.)
Utah
W. P. Bell
Salt Lake City, CC of (r.9)
Utah
W. H. Neff
Salton City CC
California
W. F. Bell
Salzborg Property GC at Morin Heights
Province of Québec, Canada
H. Watson
Sam Snead All-American Exec. GC (San Diego)(27)
California
R. T. Jones
Sam Snead All-American Exec. GC (Colton)
California
R. T. Jones
Sam Snead All-American GC ,
Florida
R. T. Jones
San Andres de Llavaneras, Club de Golf (Original 9)
Spain
J. P. Gannon
San Andres de Llavaneras, Club de Golf (r.)
Spain
F. W. Hawtree
San Andres GC
Argentina
M. Park II
San Andres GC
Colombia
S. Thompson
San Angelo CC
Texas
W. D. Cantrell
San Antonio CC (r.)
Texas
J. Finger
San Antonio Shores GC
Mexico
R. E. Baldock
San Bernardino CC (r.5)
California
R. M. Pulley
San Carlos, Club de Golf (Toluca)
Mexico
P. Clifford
San Carlos CC
Mexico
P. and R. Dye
San Carlos Park G&CC
Florida
J. E. O'Connor, Jr.
San Clemente Muni (original 9)
California
W. P. Bell

294

San Clemente Muni (r.9,a.9)
California
W. F. Bell
Sandalfoot Cove G&CC (27)
Florida
R. Von Hagge, B. Devlin
San Dar Acres GC
Ohio
J. Kidwell, M. Hurdzan
Sandbridge GC (now Virginia Beach GC)
Virginia
R. L. Jones
Sand Cliff Club
Bahamas
G. and T. Fazio
Sand Creek Club
Indiana
K. Killian, R. Nugent
Sand Creek Park GC
Idaho
W. F. Bell
Sandestin GC
Florida
T. Jackson
Sandia Mountain Par 3 GC
New Mexico
R. D. Putnam
San Diego CC
California
W. P. Bell
San Diego CC (r.)
California
H. M. and D. A. Rainville
San Diego Country Estates
California
T. G. Robinson
San Diego Naval Base GC (27)
California
J. Daray
Sandiway GC
England
(Edward "Ted" Ray, S. Collins)
Sandinay GC (r.)
England
H. S. Colt
Sandinay GC (r.3)
England
F. W. Hawtree
Sandown Park GC
England
(J. Jacobs, J. Corey)
Sandpiper CC [formerly St. Lucie CC]
  (Sinners course)
Florida
M. Mahannah
Sandpiper CC [formerly St. Lucie CC]
  (Saints course)
Florida
D. L. Wallace
Sandpiper CC [formerly St. Lucie CC]
  (Par 3 course)
Florida
C. F. Ankrom
Sandpiper CC (Wilderness course, 9)
Florida
(Leroy Phillips)
Sandpiper Golf Links
California
W. F. Bell
Sandringham GC
Australia
A. Mackenzie
Sands Point GC (r.)
New York
R. T. Jones, F. Duane

Sand Springs Muni [formerly Osage Hills
  CC]
Oklahoma
F. Farley
Sandwell GC (r.)
England
H. S. Colt
Sandy Brae CC
West Virginia
E. B. Ault
Sandy Burr CC
Massachusetts
D. J. Ross
Sandy Hollow GC
Illinois
T. Bendelow
Sandy Hollow GC (r.)
Illinois
D. Gill
Sandy Hollow Muni
Illinois
C. D. Wagstaff
Sandy Lane Hotel & CC
Barbados
(Robertson Ward)
Sandy Lodge CC
England
H. S. Colt, H. Vardon
Sandy Ridge GC
Michigan
W. B. and G. H. Matthews
Sandy Ridge GC
North Carolina
E. Hamm
San Francisco GC
California
A. W. Tillinghast
San Gabriel CC
California
N. Macbeth
San Gabriel CC (r.)
California
W. P. Bell
San Gabriel CC (r.)
California
R. T. Jones, Sr. and Jr.
San Gaspar, Club de Golf
Mexico
P. Clifford
San Geronimo National GC
California
A. V. Macan
San Gil CC
Mexico
P. and R. Dye
San Gorgio Par 3 GC
California
W. H. Johnson
San Isidro GC
Mexico
L. M. Hughes
San Joaquin CC
California
R. E. Baldock
San Joaquin CC (r.)
California
R. D. Putnam
San Jose CC
Florida
D. J. Ross
San Jose CC (r.)
Florida
E. B. Seay
San Jose G&CC
California
T. Nicoll

San Jose G&CC (r.)
California
R. M. Graves
San Jose Muni
California
R. M. Graves
San Juan Hills CC
California
H. M. and D. A. Rainville
Sankaty Head GC
Massachusetts
D. J. Ross, E. F. Wogan
San Luis Bay Inn & CC (Original 9)
California
D. Muirhead
San Luis Bay Inn & CC (a.9)
California
(Olin Dutra)
San Luis, Club de Golf
Mexico
P. Clifford
San Luis Obispo CC
California
B. Stamps
San Luis Rey CC
California
W. F. Bell
San Marcos Hotel & Club
Arizona
H. Collis
San Marcos Hotel & Club (r.)
Arizona
R. F. Lawrence
San Marino GC
Michigan
W. B. and G. H. Matthews
San Miguel GC (The Azores)
Portugal
P. M. Ross
San Pedro Community Hotel Par 3 GC
California
W. P. Bell
San Pedro CC
California
W. P. Bell
San Pedro CC (Original 9)
Mexico
W. Smith
San Ramon CC
California
C. Glasson
Sanrizuka GC
Japan
K. Fujita
San Sebastian, Real GC de
Spain
T. C. Simpson
Santa Ana Canyon CC
California
L. M. Hughes
Santa Ana CC (r.)
California
D. Muirhead
Santa Ana CC (r.)
California
H. M. and D. A. Rainville
Santa Anna CC (r.)
California
R. W. Fream
Santa Anita, Club de Golf
Mexico
L. M. Hughes
Santa Anna CC (r.)
California
R. W. Fream

Santa Barbara Community GC
California
L. M. Hughes
Santa Cruz CC [formerly Kino Springs]
Arizona
R. F. Lawrence
Santa Cruz Park Muni
Arizona
A. J. Snyder
Santa Maria GC (r.)
California
R. E. Baldock
Santa Maria GC
Colombia
M. Mahannah
Santa Rosa CC
California
J. Fleming
Santa Rose CC (r.)
California
R. T. Jones, Jr.
Santa Rosa Exec. GC
Florida
R. A. Anderson
Santa Rosa GC (r.)
California
R. T. Jones, Jr.
Santa Rosa Muni
California
W. P. Bell
Santa Rosa Shores CC
Florida
W. W. Amick
Santa Teresa CC
New Mexico
D. Bennett
Santee-Cooper Club (Old and New
  courses)
South Carolina
G. W. Cobb
Santiago, Club
Mexico
L. M. Hughes
Santiam GC
Oregon
F. Federspiel
Santo Ponsa, Club de Golf (r.)
Spain
J. Gancedo
San Vicente CC
California
T. G. Robinson
Sao Fernando GC at Sao Paulo (r.)
Brazil
A. Serra
Sao Paulo GC (r.)
Brazil
S. Thompson
Sapphire Valley CC
North Carolina
G. W. Cobb
Sapona CC
North Carolina
E. Maples
Sapphire Valley CC
North Carolina
G. W. Cobb
Sappora GC (2 courses)
Japan
R. T. Jones, Jr.
Sara Bay CC (r.)
Florida
J. L. Lee
Saranac GC
Pennsylvania
P. Erath

Saranac Inn
New York
S. Dunn
Sarasota, CC of
Florida
R. Von Hagge, B. Devlin
Sarasota GC
Florida
(Wynn Treadway)
Sarasota Muni
Florida
L. L. Marshall
Saratoga CC
California
R. M. Graves
Saratoga Spa GC (r.; a.9)
New York
W. F. Mitchell
Sarinia Golf & Curling Club (r.)
Ontario, Canada
C. E. Robinson
Sart-Tilman, Royal GC du
Belgium
T. C. Simpson
Saskatoon CC
Saskatchewan, Canada
W. Kinnear
Saskatoon GC (27)
Michigan
M. DeVries
Saticoy CC
California
W. F. Bell
Saticoy Public Links [formerly Ventura
  CC]
California
G. C. Thomas, Jr.
Saucon Valley CC (Saucon course)
Pennsylvania
H. B. Strong
Saucon Valley CC (r. Saucon course)
Pennsylvania
P. D. Maxwell
Saucon Valley CC (r. Saucon course; a.
  Grace, Junior (6) and Weyhill
  courses)
Pennsylvania
W. F. and D. W. Gordon
Saugatuck CC
Michigan
(George B. Ferry)
Sault St. Marie GC (r.)
Ontario, Canada
S. Thompson
Saunton GC (n.l.e.)
England
T. Dunn
Saunton GC (East)
England
W. H. Fowler
Saunton GC (West)
England
C. K. Cotton, J. J. F. Pennink
Saunton GC (west course)
England
J. F. Pennink
Savannah GC (r.)
Georgia
G. W. Cobb
Savannah Inn & CC
Georgia
D. J. Ross
Savannah Inn & CC (r.)
Georgia
W. C. Byrd

Savannah Muni (36)
Georgia
D. J. Ross
Sawgrass GC
Florida
E. B. Seay
Sawgrass GC (r.)
Florida
G. Dickinson
Sawgrass GC (r.)
Florida
E. B. Seay
Saw Mill Creek GC
Ohio
G. and T. Fazio
Sawyer AFB GC
Michigan
R. E. Baldock
Saxon Woods GC
New York
T. Winton
Sayville CC
New York
H. B. Strong
Scarboro G&CC (r.)
Ontario, Canada
A. W. Tillinghast
Scarboro G&CC (r.)
Ontario, Canada
S. Thompson
Scarborough GC
England
J. R. Stutt
Scarborough on Hudson (r.)
New York
A. W. Tillinghast
Scarborough on Hudson (r.)
New York
T. Winton
Scarborough Southcliff GC
England
J. Braid, A. Mackenzie
Scarlett Woods GC
Ontario, Canada
H. Watson
Scarsdale CC (Original 9)
New York
"Young" W. Dunn
Scarsdale GC (r. 9, a. 9)
New York
A. W. Tillinghast
Scarsdale GC (r.)
New York
L. S. "Dick" Wilson
Scarsdale GC (r.)
New York
R. T. Jones
Scarsdale GC (r.4)
New York
F. Duane
Scenic Hills
Florida
C. H. Adams
Schenectady CC
New York
D. Emmet
Schilling AFB GC (n.l.e.)
Kansas
L. Howard
Schloss Anholt GC
West Germany
B. Von Limburger
Schloss Fuschl Par 3 GC
Austria
B. Von Limburger

Schloss Myllendonk GC
West Germany
B. Von Limburger
Schloss Pichlarn GC
Austria
B. Von Limburger
Schloss Rheden GC
West Germany
B. Von Limburger
Schoenenberg GC
Switzerland
D. Harradine
Schroon Lake CC
New York
S. Dunn
Schuss Mountain GC
Michigan
K. W. Bowen
Schuyler Meadows GC
New York
D. Emmet, A. H. Tull
Scilly Islands GC (Isles of Scilly)
England
H. G. Hutchinson
Sciota CC
Ohio
D. J. Ross
Scioto CC (r.)
Ohio
L. S. "Dick" Wilson
Scona Lodge GC
Tennessee
R. T. Jones
Scotch Meadow GC
North Carolina
R. F. Breeden
Scott County GC (9)
Kansas
H. Hughes, R. Watson
Scottish Tourist Board Courses (r. several)
Scotland
J. H. Stutt
Scott Lake CC
Michigan
W. B. and G. H. Matthews
Scott Park Muni
New Mexico
A. J. Snyder
Scottsbluff CC (New site)
Nebraska
F. Hummel
Scottsdale CC
Arizona
L. M. Hughes
Scranton, CC of
Pennsylvania
W. J. Travis
Scranton, CC of (a.9)
Pennsylvania
A. Wall
Scranton Muni (Mt. Cobb Muni)
Pennsylvania
J. G. Harrison
Scraptoft GC
England
T. Williamson
Scunthorpe GC
England
F. W. Hawtree
Sea and Air Exec. GC
California
J. Daray
Seabrook Island GC (Crooked Oaks)
South Carolina
R.T. Jones

Seabrook Island GC (Original 18)
South Carolina
W. C. Byrd
Seacroft GC
England
T. Dunn
Seacroft GC (r.)
England
W. Reid
Seacroft GC (r.)
England
G. Campbell
Seaford
Great Britain
W. Park, Jr.
Seaford CC
Delaware
A. H. Tull
Seaford GC (r.)
England
W. Park, Jr.
Seaford GC (r.)
England
T. Dunn
Seaford GC (r.)
England
J. H. Taylor
Seaford GC (r.)
England
J. S. F. Morrison
Seaford Head GC
England
(Thompson of Felixstowe)
Seaforth GC
Ontario, Canada
H. Watson
Sea-Gull GC
South Carolina
E. Hamm
Sea Island GC (Plantation 9)
Georgia
W. J. Travis
Sea Island GC (r. Plantation 9, a. Seaside 9)
Georgia
H. S. Colt, C. H. Alison
Sea Island GC (r.; a. Retreat 9)
Georgia
L. S. "Dick" Wilson
Sea Island GC (r. Plantation and Seaside 9's)
Georgia
R. T. Jones
Sea Island GC (r. Seaside 9, a. Marshside 9)
Georgia
J. L. Lee
Seamountain Ninole GC
Hawaii
A. J. Snyder
Sea Palms CC (Original 18)
Georgia
G. W. Cobb
Sea Palms CC (a.9)
Georgia
T. Jackson
Sea Pines (Club course)
South Carolina
F. Duane, A. Palmer
Sea Pines (Harbour Town GC)
South Carolina
P. Dye, J. Nicklaus
Sea Pines (Dolphin Head GC)
South Carolina
R. Kirby, G. Player, A. L. Davis

Sea Pines Plantation (Ocean and Seamarsh courses)
South Carolina
G. W. Cobb
Sea Ranch GC
California
R. M. Graves
Seascale (Original 9)
England
W. Campbell
Seascale (a.9)
England
G. Lowe
Seascape G&RC
Florida
(Robert Logan)
Seascape G&RC (r.)
Florida
J. L. Lee
Seascape GC
North Carolina
J. P. Gibson
Seascape GC
North Carolina
A. Wall
Seattle GC
Washington
R. Johnstone
Seattle GC (r.)
Washington
A. V. Macan
Seattle GC (r.)
Washington
T. G. Robinson
Seaview GC (Bay course)
New Jersey
D. J. Ross
Seaview GC (Original 9, Pines course)
New Jersey
W. S. Flynn
Seaview GC (r. Bay course)
New Jersey
A. W. Tillinghast
Seaview CC (r.9 of Bay course; a.9 to Pines course)
New Jersey
W. F. and D. W. Gordon
Seaview GC (r.9,a.9)
Nova Scotia, Canada
C. E. Robinson
Seawane Club
New York
D. Emmet, A. H. Tull
Seawane Club (r.)
New York
F. Duane
Sebring Shores Par 3 GC
Florida
H. Schmeisser
Sedgefield GC (36)
North Carolina
D. J. Ross
Sedgefield GC (r.)
North Carolina
E. Hamm
Sedgefield GC (r.)
North Carolina
W. C. Byrd
Seefeld Wildmoos GC
Austria
D. Harradine
Segregansett CC (a.9)
Massachusetts
G. S. Cornish, W. G. Robinson

Seguin CC (9)
Texas
J. Bredemus
Seguin CC (a.9)
Texas
R. Plummer
Sehoy Plantation (9)
Alabama
E. and D. Maples
Seigniory Club [now Le Chateau Montebello]
Province of Québec, Canada
S. Thompson
Selangor GC, Royal (r.)
Malaysia
H. S. Colt
Selangor GC, Royal (r.)
Malaysia
J. J. F. Pennink
Seldson Park GC
England
F. G. Hawtree, J. H. Taylor
Selkirk GC (a.9)
Manitoba, Canada
J. A. Thompson
Selkirk GC
Scotland
W. Park, Jr.
Selma Valley
California
R. E. Baldock
Selva Marina CC
Florida
E. E. Smith
Seminary GC (r.)
Illinois
J. L. Lee
Seminole GC
Florida
D. J. Ross
Seminole GC (Florida State University)
Florida
R. A. Anderson
Seminole GC (Florida State University; r.3,a.9)
Florida
W. W. Amick
Seminole Lake G&CC
Florida
C. H. Adams
Seneca GC at Louisville
Kentucky
B. J. Wihry
Seneca Muni GC
Kentucky
A. G. McKay
Sene Valley GC
England
H. Cotton
Senneville CC
Province of Québec, Canada
W. Park, Jr.
Sentosa GC
Singapore
J. J. F. Pennink
Sentosa Island (New course)
Singapore
P.W. Thomson, M. Wolveridge, R. Fream
Sentry International (H.Q.) GC
Wisconsin
R. T. Jones, Jr.
Sepulveda Muni (Balboa and Encino courses)
California
W. P. Bell, W. H. Johnson
Sequin CC (a. 2nd 9)
Texas
R. Plummer

Sequoyah CC (r.)
California
R. M. Graves
Sequoyah State Park GC
Oklahoma
F. Farley
Seraincourt, Golf de
France
F. W. Hawtree
Serlby Park
England
T. Williamson
Seth Hughes Par 3 GC
Oklahoma
F. Farley
Seven Hills CC
California
H. M. and D. A. Rainville
Seven Hills GC
Ohio
W. K. Newcomb
Seven Lakes CC
California
T. G. Robinson
Seven Lakes Exec. GC
Florida
E. E. Smith
Seven Lakes GC
North Carolina
P. V. Tufts
Sevenoaks
England
T. Dunn
Seven Oaks GC
Pennsylvania
X. G. Hassenplug
Seven Oaks GC (Colgate University GC)
New York
R. T. Jones
Seven Rivers CC
Florida
W. W. Amick
Seven Springs G&CC
Florida
(James King)
Seven Springs G&CC (a.18)
Florida
R. Garl
Seven Springs Resort GC
Pennsylvania
X. G. Hassenplug
76 Falls CC (9)
Kentucky
(Harold England)
Seward CC (9)
Nebraska
H. W. Glissmann
Sewickley Heights GC
Pennsylvania
J. G. Harrison, F. Garbin
Seyoy Plantation
Alabama
D. and E. Maples
Shackamaxon G&CC
New Jersey
A. W. Tillinghast
Shadow Lake G&RC (27)
New York
A. Craig
Shadow Moss G&TC
South Carolina
R. F. Breeden
Shadow Ridge CC
California
H. and D. Rainville
Shady Hills GC
Indiana
W. Diddel
Shady Lawn GC
Illinois
R. A. Anderson

Shady Oaks CC, Fort Worth
Texas
R, T. Jones
Shady Oaks GC, Baird
Texas
L. Howard
Shady Oaks GC
Texas
R. Plummer
Shaganappi Muni (27)
Alberta, Canada
(Neil Little)
Shaker Farms CC
Massachusetts
G. S. Cornish
Shaker Heights CC
Ohio
D. J. Ross
Shaker Run
Ohio
A. Hills
Shamanah GC
Idaho
R. Von Hagge, B. Devlin
Sham-Na-Pum GC
Washington
(Melvin A. Hueston)
Shangri La CC
Oklahoma
D. R. Sechrest
Shangri-La Minorca GC
Spain
J. D. Harris
Shanklin and Sandown on Isle of Wight (r.)
England
J. H. Stutt
Shannon G&CC
Bahamas
J. L. Lee
Shannon Green
Virginia
E. B. Ault
Shannopin CC
Pennsylvania
E. F. Loeffler, J. McGlynn
Shanty Creek Lodge GC
Michigan
W. Diddel
(The) Sharon Club
Ohio
G. W. Cobb
Sharon CC (r.)
Massachusetts
W. E. Stiles, J. R. Van Kleek
Sharon Heights G&CC
California
J. Fleming
Sharon Woods CC
Ohio
W. Diddel
Sharp Park Muni
California
A. Mackenzie
Sharpstown CC
Texas
R. Plummer
Sharpstown CC (r.)
Texas
B. J. Riviere
Shattuck CC (9)
Oklahoma
F. Farley
Shaughnessy Heights Club (Original site)
British Columbia, Canada
A. V. Macan
Shaughnessy GC (New site)
British Columbia, Canada
A. V. Macan

Shawinigan G&CC
Province of Québec, Canada
H. Watson
Shawnee CC
Delaware
E. B. Ault, A. Jamison
Shawnee CC [now Tomahawk Hills CC]
Kansas
H. Robb, Sr.
Shawnee CC, Topeka
Kansas
D. J. Ross
Shawnee CC (r.), Topeka
Kansas
C. Mendenhall
Shawnee CC (Shawnee on Delaware)
Pennsylvania
A. W. Tillinghast
Shawnee CC (Shawnee on Delaware; r.; a.9)
Pennsylvania
W. Diddel
Shawnee Hills GC
Ohio
B. W. Zink
Shawnee Lookout GC
Ohio
J. Kidwell, M. Hurdzan
Shawnee Muni
Kentucky
A. G. McKay
Shawnee Muni
West Virginia
R. Kirby, G. Player
Shawnee Slopes GC
Alberta, Canada
(Peter Olynyk, Ernest Tate)
Shawnee Slopes GC (r.)
Alberta, Canada
R. Moote
Shawnee State Park GC (a.9)
Ohio
J. Kidwell, M. Hurdzan
Sheaffer Memorial Park GC
Iowa
C. D. Wagstaff
Sheerness GC
England
W. Park, Jr.
Sheffield and District GC
England
T. Dunn
Shelby Green GC
Illinois
K. Killian, R. Nugent
Shelbyville CC (a.4)
Kentucky
B. J. Wihry
Shelbyville CC
Tennessee
R. A. Anderson
Shelbyville GC
Michigan
A. M. Young
Shelridge CC
New York
X. G. Hassenplug
Shenandoah CC
Virginia
F. Findlay
Shenandoah G&CC
Michigan
W. B. and G. H. Matthews
Shenandoah Valley GC
Virginia
R. F. Loving
Shenecosset GC
Connecticut
D. J. Ross
Shenvallee (Lodge) GC (r.9,a.9)
Virginia
E. B. Ault

Sheoah GC, Florida, R. Von Hagge, B. Devlin, is now Big Cypress GC
Florida
R. Von Hagge, B. Devlin
Shepard Hill CC (a.9)
New York
G. S. Cornish, W. G. Robinson
Sheraton Moloka (Kaluakol)
Hawaii
T. G. Robinson
Sheraton Motor Inn GC (Fredericksburg)
Virginia
E. B. Ault
Sheraton-Picaso (now Hershey Poconos)
Pennsylvania
G. S. Cornish, W. G. Robinson
Sherbrooke G&CC
Florida
R. Von Hagge, B. Devlin
Sheridan (Kendrick) Muni (a.9)
Wyoming
F. Hummel
Sheridan Park GC
New York
W. E. Harries
Sheridan Park GC (r.)
New York
A.R. Tryon
Sherborn
England
J. Braid
Sherill Park Muni
Texas
L. Howard
Sheringham GC (9)
England
T. Dunn
Sherwood Forest GC
California
R. E. Baldock
Sherwood Forest GC (r.)
England
J. Braid
Sherwood Forest GC (r.)
England
T. Williamson
Sherwood G&CC
Florida
W. W. Amick
Sherwood Hills GC
Utah
(Mark D. Ballif)
Shetland (Dale GC)
Scotland
F. Middleton
Shifferdecker CC (r. 9, a. 9)
Missouri
E. L. Bell
Shifnal GC
England
J. J. F. Pennink
Shimotsuki CC
Japan
E. B. Seay, A. Palmer
Shinnecock Hills GC (Original and Ladies courses)
New York
"Young" W. Dunn
Shinnecock Hills GC (New course)
New York
W. S. Flynn
Shipyard Plantation (Hilton Head GC)
South Carolina
G. W. Cobb
Shireoaks
Great Britain
T. Dunn
Shirkey CC
Missouri
C. Mendenhall

Shiskine GC on Arran (12)
Scotland
W. Park, Jr.
Shiun CC
Japan
K. Fujita
Shizuoke CC
Japan
K. Fujita
Shoaf Park GC
Indiana
H. Purdy
Shoal Canyon Park Exec. GC
California
W. F. Bell
Shoal Creek GC
Alabama
J. Nicklaus
Shooter's Hill GC
England
W. Park, Jr.
Shoreacres CC (r.)
Illinois
S.J. Raynor
Shore Acres GC (r.)
Florida
H. Schmeisser
Shorecliffs CC (Estrella GC)
California
J. B. Williams
Shoreham GC
England
G. Campbell
Shoreline Park Muni
California
R. T. Jones, Jr.
(The) Shores CC
Texas
R. Plummer
Shorewood CC
New York
W. E. Harries
Short Hills CC (r.)
Illinois
E.L. Packard
Show Low CC
Arizona
A. J. Snyder
Shreveport CC (r.)
Louisiana
L. Howard
Shreveport CC (r.9,a.3)
Louisiana
J. Finger
Shrewsbury GC
England
J. J. F. Pennink
Shrine GC [now Hillcrest CC]
Nebraska
W. H. Tucker, Sr.
Shuttlemeadow CC
Connecticut
W. Park, Jr.
Sibu (Sarawak)
Malaysia
J. J. F. Pennink
Sickleholme GC (r.)
England
T. Williamson
Sidmouth
England
J. H. Taylor
Sidney G&CC (r.)
Ohio
H. Purdy
Siegen-Olpe GC
West Germany
B. Von Limbuger

Sierra Blanca CC
Texas
W. D. Cantrell
Sierra Estrella GC
Arizona
R. F. Lawrence
Sierra Sky Ranch (9)
California
R. E. Baldock
Sierra View GC (Original 9)
California
J. Fleming
Sierra View GC (a.9)
California
R. E. Baldock
Signal Hill CC at Armonk
New York
O. E. Smith
Signal Point Club
Michigan
R. B. Harris
Signal Point CC
Montana
N. Woods
Siler City CC
North Carolina
E. Maples
Silloth on Solway GC
England
W. Park, Jr.
Silverado CC (North course)
California
T. B. Harmon, J. Dawson
Silverado CC (r. North course; a. South course)
California
R. T. Jones, Sr. and Jr.
Silverbell Muni
Arizona
A. J. Snyder
Silver Creek GC (9)
California
W. H. Johnson
Silver K GC
California
W. F. Bell
Silver Lake CC
Ohio
E. L. Packard
Silver Lake G&CC
Florida
E. E. Smith
Silver Lake GC [formerly Euclid Hills CC](North course)
Illinois
L. Macomber
Silver Lake GC (South course)
Illinois
C. E. Maddox, F. MacDonald
Silverlake School GC
Pennsylvania
F. Garbin
Silver Lakes GC
California
T. G. Robinson
Silver Mine GC
Connecticut
(John E. Warner, Jr)
Silver Mine CC
Connecticut
A. H. Tull
Silver Pine Exec. GC (9)
Florida
L. Clifton
Silver Spring CC (r.)
Connecticut
A. H. Tull
Silver Springs CC
Connecticut
R. White

Silver Spring Exec. GC
Pennsylvania
G. Fazio
Silver Spring G&CC (n.l.e.)
Florida
S. Dunn
Silverspring G&CC
Alberta, Canada
R. N. Phelps, C. Muret
Silver Spring GC [formerly Indian Springs CC](r.)
Maryland
E. B. Ault
Silver Spring Shores G&CC
Florida
D. Muirhead
Silver Springs Resort GC
Pennsylvania
X. G. Hassenplug
Sim Park Muni (r.)
Kansas
R. C. Dunning
Simsbury Farms Muni
Connecticut
G. S. Cornish, W. G. Robinson
Singapore Island GC (Bukit course)
Singapore
J. Braid
Singapore Island GC (r. Bukit course)
Singapore
J. J. F. Pennink
Singapore Island GC (r. Island course)
Singapore
J. J. F. Pennink, C. K. Cotton
Singapore Island GC (New course)
Singapore
J. D. Harris, J. J. F. Pennink
Singapore Island GC (Sime course)
Singapore
J. J. F. Pennink
Singing Hills CC (Willow Glen course)
California
W. P. Bell, W. H. Johnson
Singing Hills CC (Oak and Pine Glen courses)
California
C. B. Hollingsworth
Singletree GC
Colorado
(Bob Cupp)
Sinking Valley CC
Pennsylvania
E. B. Ault
Sinton Muni
Texas
H. B. Hughes, R. Watson
Sippihaw CC (formerly Fuquay Varina CC) (Original 9)
North Carolina
C. D. Wagstaff
Sippihaw CC (a. 2nd 9)
North Carolina
E. Hamm
Sitges GC (a.9)
Spain
F. W. Hawtree
Sitwell Park GC
England
A. Mackenzie
Siwanoy CC
New York
D. J. Ross
Siwanoy CC (r.)
New York
T. Winton

Siwanoy CC (r.)
New York
R. T. Jones
Skaneatelas GC (a.9)
New York
H. Purdy
Skenandoa Club
New York
R. D. Bailey
Skerries GC
Ireland
E. Hackett
Skibo Castle GC
Scotland
J. Sutherland
Skidaway Island (Marshwood at The Landings)
Georgia
F. Duane, A. Palmer
Skidaway Island (The Landings)
Georgia
E. B. Seay, A. Palmer
Skips
England
J. J. F. Pennink
Skokie CC (r.)
Illinois
D. J. Ross
Skokie CC (r.)
Illinois
W. B. Langford, T. J. Moreau
Skokie CC (r.)
Illinois
K. Killian, R. Nugent
Sky-Bryce Resort GC
Virginia
E. B. Ault
Skycenter CC
Alabama
R. E. Baldock
Sky Lake GC
North Carolina
W. W. Amick
Skyland GC
Colorado
R.T. Jones, Jr.
Skyline CC
Alabama
C. H. Adams
Skyline CC (a.9)
Alabama
E. Stone
Skyline CC
Arizona
(Guy Greene)
Skyline CC
Texas
(L. Wesley Flatt)
Skyline GC (Greens only)
Massachusetts
R. Armacost
Skyline GC (r. 18,a.9)
West Virginia
F. Garbin
Sky Links GC
California
W. F. Bell
Skytop Club
Pennsylvania
R. White
Sky Valley CC
Georgia
W. R. Watts
Sky Valley GC (r.)
Indiana
G. Kern
Skywater CC
Georgia
W. Stiles, J. Van Kleek (J. Kirkwood)

Skyway GC (27)
South Carolina
R. T. Jones, R. L. Jones
Skywest Public GC
California
R. E. Baldock
Slade Valley (r.)
Ireland
E. Hackett
Sleaford GC
England
T. Williamson
Sleeping Giant GC
Connecticut
R. M. Barton
Sleeping Giant GC (r.)
Connecticut
W. F. Mitchell
Sleepy Hole GC
Virginia
R. F. Breeden
Sleepy Hollow CC
New York
C. B. Macdonald
Sleepy Hollow CC (r.)
New York
T. Winton
Sleepy Hollow CC (r.)
New York
A. W. Tillinghast
Sleepy Hollow CC (r.)
New York
R. T. Jones
Sleepy Hollow GC
Kentucky
(Harold England)
Slengingford GC
Great Britain
T. Dunn
Sligo Creek GC
Maryland
E. B. Ault, A. Jamison
Smiley's Sportland Par 3 GC (n.l.e.)
Kansas
E. L. Bell
Smithfield CC
North Carolina
E. Maples
Smith-Richardson GC
Connecticut
M. and H. Purdy
Smithville Lakes Muni
Missouri
E. B. Ault
Snapfinger Woods GC (27)
Georgia
J. L. Lee
Snee Farm CC
South Carolina
G. W. Cobb
Snowmass at Aspen (Original 9)
Colorado
J. P. Maxwell
Snowmass at Aspen (a.9)
Colorado
J. N. Cochran
Snowmass at Aspen (r.18)
Colorado
E.B. Seay, A. Palmer
Snyder Park GC (r.)
Ohio
J. Kidwell
Sobhu CC (r.)
Japan
R. T. Jones
Sobobo Springs CC
California
D. Muirhead

Societe Africaine Du Tourisme, Resort Development, Cabo Negro
Morocco
F. W. Hawtree
Soco Gap
South Carolina
W. C. Byrd
Sodus Point GC (r. Original 9)
New York
R. T. Jones
Sodegaura CC
Japan
(Ichisuke Izumi)
Sodus Point GC (r.9,a.9)
New York
G. S. Cornish, W. G. Robinson
Solent Meadows
England
J. H. Stutt
Sombrero CC
Florida
(Carl H. Anderson)
Somers CC (r.9,a.9)
New York
A. Zikorus
Somerset CC (r.)
Minnesota
S. Thompson
Somerset CC (r.)
Minnesota
R. B. Harris
Somerset CC (r.)
Minnesota
G W. Cobb, J. B. LaFoy
Somerset CC (r.)
Minnesota
G. S. Cornish, W. G. Robinson
Somerset CC (r.)
Pennsylvania
F. Garbin
Somerset Hills CC
New Jersey
A. W. Tillinghast
Sonning GC (r.)
England
F. G. Hawtree
Sonny Guy Muni
Mississippi
E. D. Guy
Sonoma National GC
California
S. Whiting (probably with W. Watson)
Son Vida GC of Majorca
Spain
F. W. Hawtree
Soparovan CC (9)
Nevada
R. E. Baldock
Sorel Tracy GC (r.6,a.9)
Province of Québec, Canada
J. Watson
Sorrento GC (r.)
Australia
P.W. Thomson, M. Wolveridge
Sorrento Shores
Florida
R. A. Anderson
Sotogrande CC
Texas
L. Howard
Sotogrande GC (Old, New and Par 3 courses)
Spain
R. T. Jones
Soule Park GC
California
W. F. Bell

298

Sound Shore GC
New York
F. Duane

Sousis Valley GC
North Dakota
W. J. Spear

Southampton
England
W. Park, Jr.

Southampton Corporation Muni (27)
England
F. G. Hawtree

Southampton CC (r.)
New York
W. F. Mitchell

Southampton Princess (Original Par 3)
Bermuda
A. H. Tull

Southampton Princess (r. to Exec. length course)
Bermuda
T. C. Robinson

South Bend CC
Indiana
G. O'Neill

South Boston CC
Virginia
F. A. Findlay

South Boston CC (r.9,a.18)
Virginia
E. Hamm

South Carolina, CC of
South Carolina
E. Maples

Southcliffe and Canwick
England
F. W. Hawtree

Southdown at Shoreham GC
England
S. V. Hotchkin, C. K. Hutchison, G. Campbell

Southern GC
Victoria, Australia
P.W. Thomson, M. Wolveridge

Southern GC (r.)
Australia
P.W. Thomson, M. Wolveridge

Southerndown GC (Original course)
Wales
W. Fernie

Southerndown GC
Wales
W. Park, Jr.

Southerndown GC (r.)
Wales
W. H. Fowler

Southerndown GC (r.)
Wales
H. S. Colt

Southerness GC
Scotland
P. M. Ross

Southern Hills CC
Oklahoma
P. D. Maxwell

Southern Hills CC (r.)
Oklahoma
R. T. Jones

Southern Hills CC (r.)
Oklahoma
G. and T. Fazio

Southern Hills GC
Ohio
R. A. Anderson

Southern Hills GC
South Dakota
R. N. Phelps, B. Benz

Southern International Corp. Par 3 GC
Florida
W. H. Dietsch, Jr.

Southern Manor GC
Florida
W. F. Mitchell

Southern Pines CC (36)
North Carolina
D. J. Ross

Southern Pines CC (r.)
North Carolina
W. F. Mitchell

Southfields GC
England
H. S. Colt

South Forks CC (r. 3)
New York
F. Duane

South Gate Par 3 GC
California
W. H. Johnson

South Herts GC
England
W. Park, Jr.

South Herts GC
England
H. Vardon

South Herts GC (r.)
England
J. H. Stutt

South Hill CC
Virginia
F. Findlay

South Hills CC
California
W. P. Bell

South Hills CC (r.)
California
D. Muirhead

South Hills GC
Pennsylvania
W. F. and D. W. Gordon

South Hills GC (r.)
Pennsylvania
E. B. Ault

Southmoor CC [formerly Cypress Creek CC]
Alabama
E. Stone

Southmoor GC
Michigan
W. B. and G. H. Matthews

Southmore CC (r.)
Pennsylvania
W. F. Gordon

South Muskoka Curling & GC
Ontario, Canada
C. E. Robinson

South Ocean Beach Hotel GC
Bahamas
J. L. Lee

South Park GC (r.)
Pennsylvania
X. G. Hassenplug

South Pine Creek (Fairfield Muni Par 3)
Connecticut
G. S. Cornish, W. G. Robinson

Southport and Ainsdale GC (r.)
England
J. Braid

Southport GC
Australia
J. D. Harris

Southridge CC
Florida
D. L. Wallace

South Rockland GC
New York
D. W. Gordon

South Seas Plantation CC on Captiva Island
Florida
E. E. Smith

South Sherwood Forest GC
Maryland
H. B. Strong

South Shore CC
Massachusetts
W. E. Stiles, J. R. Van Kleek

South Suburban GC
Colorado
R. N. Phelps, B. Benz

Southview CC (r.7)
Minnesota
R. N. Phelps

South Wales G&RC
Virginia
E. B. Ault

Southwell GC
England
T. Williamson

Southwest Park Muni
Oklahoma
A. J. Jackson

Southwinds CC
Kansas
D. R. Sechrest

Southwood G&CC
Manitoba, Canada
S. Thompson

Southwood G&CC (r.)
Manitoba, Canada
J. A. Thompson

Southwood GC
England
J. D. Harris

Spa GC
Northern Ireland
(R. R. Bell, A. Mathers)

Spangdahlem GC (U. S. Army Base)
West Germany
B. Von Limburger

Spanish Wells CC (9)
Florida
W. Maddox

Spanish Wells Plantation GC (9)
South Carolina
G. W. Cobb

Sparrows Point CC (Bethlehem Steel; 27)
Maryland
W. F. and D. W. Gordon

Spartansburg CC (r.9,a.9)
South Carolina
G. W. Cobb

Speedway 500 GC
Indiana
W. Diddel

Speidel Park GC (Oglebay Park)
West Virginia
R. T. Jones

Spencer G&CC
Iowa
D. Gill

Spessard Holland Golf Park Exec. GC
Florida
E. B. Seay, A. Palmer

Spokane CC (Original 9)
Washington
(Jim Barnes)

Spook Hill GC
Arizona
M. Coggins

Spook Rock GC
New York
F. Duane

Spooky Brook
New Jersey
E. B. Ault

Spooncreek GC (9)
Virginia
E. Hamm

Sportsman G&CC (East and West courses)
Illinois
E. B. Dearie, Jr.

Sportsman GC
Pennsylvania
J. G. Harrison, F. Garbin

Sportsman Muni (r.)
Illinois
K. Killian, R. Nugent

Spotswood CC
Virginia
E. B. Ault

Spotswood CC
Virginia
F. A. Findlay

Spotswood CC (a.9)
Virginia
A. G. McKay

Spotswood GC Exec. (9)
Virginia
R. T. Jones

Sprain Brook GC (27)
New York
T. Winton

Springbrook GC
Illinois
E. L. and R. B. Packard

Spring Creek G&CC (Original 9)
California
J. Fleming

Spring Creek Exec. GC (9)
Pennsylvania
M. J. McCarthy Sr.

Spring Creek GC (a.9)
Illinois
K. Killian, R. Nugent

Springdale CC (r.)
New Jersey
W. S. Flynn

Springfield CC (r.)
Massachusetts
W. F. Mitchell

Springfield CC
Ohio
D. J. Ross

Springfield G&CC
Virginia
E. B. Ault, A. Jamison

Springfield Oaks
Michigan
M. DeVries

Springhaven Club (r.)
Pennsylvania
W. S. Flynn

Spring Haven Par 3 GC
Rhode Island
P. A. Wogan

Spring Hill CC [now Azalea City CC]
Alabama
R. B. Harris

Spring Hill CC
Georgia
W. C. Byrd

Spring Hill CC
Ohio
J. G. Harrison

Spring Hill G&CC
Florida
D. L. Wallace

Springhill GC (a.9)
Colorado
R. N. Phelps, B. Benz

Spring Hill Muni
Colorado
R. N. Phelps, B. Benz

Spring Lake CC (a.9)
Illinois
E. L. Packard

Spring Lake CC [formerly Spring Valley CC]
Kentucky
C.R. Blankenship

Spring Lake CC (r.)
Michigan
W. K. Newcomb

Springlake CC (r.)
New Jersey
W. S. Flynn

Springlake CC (Original 9)
South Carolina
F. Bolton

Springlake CC (a.9)
South Carolina
R. A. Renaud

Spring Lake G&CC
Florida
F.J. Duane

Spring Lake G&CC
New Jersey
G. C. Thomas, Jr.

Spring Lake G&CC (r.)
New Jersey
A. W. Tillinghast

Spring Lake GC
Texas
L. Howard

Spring Lake Par 3 GC
South Carolina
F. Bolton

Spring Lakes GC (36)
Ontario, Canada
R. and C. Muylaert

Spring Meadows CC
Michigan
E. L. Packard

(The) Springs Club
California
D. Muirhead

(The) Springs GC
Wisconsin
R. T. Jones

Springs Mill GC (9)
South Carolina
G. W. Cobb

Spring Tree Exec. GC
Florida
W. H. Dietsch, Jr.

Spring Vale GC
Ohio
J.G. Harrison

Spring Valley CC [now Spring Lake CC]
Kentucky
C.R. Blankenship

Spring Valley CC
Ohio
H. D. Paddock, Sr.

Spring Valley CC
Massachusetts
G. S. Cornish, S. Mitchell

Spring Valley CC
South Carolina
G. W. Cobb

Spring Valley GC
Michigan
W. K. Bowen

Spring Valley GC
Wisconsin
R. A. Anderson

Spring Valley Lake GC
California
R. T. Jones, Sr. and Jr.

Spruce Creek GC
Florida
W. W. Amick

Spruce Grove GC
Alberta, Canada
W.G. Robinson

Spruce Needles GC
Ontario, Canada
H. Watson

Spruce Pine CC
North Carolina
(Ross Taylor)

Spyglass Hill Golf Links
California
R. T. Jones

Squaw Creek CC
Texas
R. Plummer

Squires GC
Pennsylvania
G. Fazio

Squires Par 3 GC
California
W. H. Johnson

Stairmore GC
Great Britain
T. Dunn

Stallion Springs G&CC (Horse Thief)
California
R. E. Baldock

(The) Standard Club
Georgia
R. T. Jones

(The) Standard Club (a.1 hole)
Georgia
A. L. Davis

Standard club (Original 9)
Kentucky
R. B. Harris

Standard Club (a.9)
Kentucky
E. L. Packard

Standing Stone GC
Pennsylvania
G. S. Cornish, W. G. Robinson

Stanford University GC
California
W. P. Bell

Stanford University GC (r.)
California
R. T. Jones, Sr. and Jr.

Stanhope G&CC
Prince Edward Island, Canada
C. E. Robinson

Stanley GC (New Britain Muni; a. 9)
Connecticut
O. E. Smith, A. Zikorus

Stanley GC (New Britain Mui; r.27)
Connecticut
G. S. Cornish, W. C. Robinson

Stanly County CC (r.)
North Carolina
E. Maples

Stannum GC
Sweden
J. J. F. Pennink

Stansbury Park CC
Utah
W. H. Neff

Stanton Heights CC
Pennsylvania
T. Bendelow

Stanton on the Wolds GC
England
T. Williamson

Stanwich Club
Connecticut
W. F. and D. W. Gordon

Stardust CC [formerly Mission Valley CC]
California
L. M. Hughes

Stardust CC (r.)
California
T. G. Robinson

Star Fort National GC
South Carolina
G. W. Cobb

Star Haven GC (3 holes)
Iowa
C. D. Wagstaff

Star Hill G&CC
North Carolina
(Russell T. Burney)

Starke G&CC
Florida
R. A. Anderson

Starmount Forest CC [formerly Starmount GC]
North Carolina
P. D. Maxwell

Starmount Forest CC (r.)
North Carolina
G. W. Cobb

Starr Hollow Club
Texas
J. Finger

Statesville CC
North Carolina
A. G. McKay

Staunton, CC of
Virginia
D. W. Gordon

Staunton GC
England
T. Dunn

Stavenger GC
Norway
(Fred Smith)

Stead AFB GC
Nevada
R. E. Baldock

Steamboat Village GC
Colorado
R. T. Jones, Sr. and Jr.

Steed and Evans GC (9)
Ontario, Canada
R. and C. Muylaert

Steiermarischer GC
Austria
B. Von Limburger

Steinback Fly Inn GC
Manitoba, Canada
C. E. Robinson

Stepaside GC
Ireland
E. Hackett (1981)

Stephen F. Austin GC (r.)
Texas
B. J. Riviere

Sterling CC
Colorado
H. B. Hughes

Sterling Farms GC (Stanford Muni)
Connecticut
G. S. Cornish, W. G. Robinson

Sterling Park Par 3 GC
Virginia
E. B. Ault

Steubenville CC (r.9,a.9)
Ohio
F. Garbin

Stevens Point CC
Wisconsin
E. L. Packard

Stevensville G&CC
New York
W. F. Mitchell

Stewart Port
Northern Ireland
W. Park, Jr.

Still Meadow CC (r.)
Ohio
W. Diddel

Stillwater CC (a.9)
Minnesota
P. Coates

Stillwater G&CC
Oklahoma
D. R. Sechrest

Still Waters CC
Alabama
G. W. Cobb

Stinchcombe Hill GC
England
J. Braid

Stirling GC
Scotland
T. Morris

Stirling GC (r.)
Scotland
H. Cotton

Stockdale CC (Original 9)
California
A. J. Snyder

Stockdale CC (a. 9)
California
R. M. Graves

Stockgrove GC
England
F. G. Hawtree

Stockholm GC (New site)
Sweden
H. S. Colt, J. S. F. Morrison

Stocksfield
England
J. J. F. Pennink

Stockton G&CC (r.)
California
R. M. Graves

Stockwood Park
British Isles
J. J. F. Pennink

Stoke Rochford GC
England
S. V. Hotchkin

Stokes Poges GC
England
H. S. Colt

Stone Bridge Exec. GC [now Nautical Inn]
Arizona
R. F. Lawrence

Stonebridge GC
Tennessee
G. W. Cobb

Stoneham GC
England
W. Park, Jr.

Stonehaven GC
Scotland
G. Duncan

Stonehenge
Virginia
E. B. Ault

Stonehenge GC
Illinois
C. E. Maddox

Stone Mountain Park GC
Georgia
R. T. Jones

Stoneridge CC
California
T.G. Robinson

Stones River CC (r.9)
Tennessee
A. L. Davis

Stoney Creek GC
Ohio
J. Kidwell

Stony Brae GC
Massachusetts
W. E. Stiles, J. R. Van Kleek

Stony Brook GC
Connecticut
A. Zikorus

Stony Creek GC
Michigan
R. D. Beard

Stonycroft Hills CC (r.)
Michigan
W. B. and G. H. Matthews

Stony Ford GC
New York
H. Purdy

Stony Home
England
J. J. F. Pennink

Stornoway (Isle of Lewis) (r.)
Scotland
J. R. Stutt

Stornoway (Isle of Lewis)
Scotland
J. J. F. Pennink

Stow Acres CC (r.9,a.27)
Massachusetts
G. S. Cornish, W. G. Robinson

Stowe CC
Vermont
W. F. Mitchell

Stowe School GC
British Isles
J. J. F. Pennink

Strabane GC
Ireland
E. Hackett

Stranorlor GC
Ireland
E. Hackett

Strantaer
Scotland
J. Braid

Strasbourg
France
D. Harradine

Strathcona Exec. GC
Ontario, Canada
C. E. Robinson

Strathlene GC
Scotland
(George E. Smith)

Strathroy CC (9)
Ontario, Canada
R. and C. Muylaert

Stratton Mountain Golf Academy
Vermont
G. S. Cornish, W. G. Robinson

Stratton Mountain GC
Vermont
G. S. Cornish, W. G. Robinson

Streetsville Glen GC
Ontario, Canada
R. and D. Moote

Stuart Yacht & CC
Florida
(Charles P. Martin)

Studeley Royal Park
England
G. Lowe

Stumpy Lake GC
Virginia
R. T. Jones

Sturgeon Point GC
Ontario, Canada
C. E. Robinson

Sturgeon Valley G&CC (a.12)
Alberta, Canada
W. G. Robinson

Subic Bay GC
Philippines
W. G. Wilkinson

Suburban CC (r.)
Maryland
R. T. Jones

Suburban CC (r.)
Maryland
E. B. Ault

Sudden Valley CC
Washington
T. G. Robinson

Suffield CC
Connecticut
O. E. Smith

Suffolk County CC
New York
S. J. Raynor

Suffolk GC
Virginia
R. F. Breeden

Sugar Bush CC
Ohio
H. D. Paddock, Sr.

Sugarbush GC
Vermont
R. T. Jones, F. Duane

Sugar Creek CC (27)
Texas
R. T. Jones, R. L. Jones

Sugar Creek G&CC
Ohio
K. Killian, R. Nugent

Sugar Hill GC
New Hampshire
R. M. Barton

Sugar Hills GC
Kansas
H. D. Fieldhouse

Sugar Hollow Exec. GC
North Carolina
F. Duane

Sugar Isle GC (9)
Ohio
J. Kidwell

Sugarloaf GC
Pennsylvania
G. S. Cornish, W. G. Robinson

Sugarloaf Mountain GC
Michigan
C. D. Wagstaff

Sugar Mill CC
Florida
J. L. Lee

Sugarmill Wood G&CC
Florida
R. Garl

Sugar Springs GC
Michigan
W. B. and G. H. Matthews
Sullivan CC [now Timberlake GC](9)
Illinois
R. B. Harris
Sulphur Hills CC (9)
Oklahoma
F. Farley
Sumatra
Indonesia
J. J. F. Pennink
(Old) Summerlea GC at Lachine (27)
Province of Québec, Canada
W. Park, Jr.
(New) Summerlea GC (Dorion and Cascades courses; 36)
Province of Québec, Canada
G. S. Cornish
Summertrea GC
Indiana
W. B. and G. H. Matthews
Summit CC (9)
Pennsylvania
E. B. Ault
Summit GC at Lake Holiday
Virginia
R. Watson
Summit Hills CC (r. 10, a. 1, 1980)
Kentucky
J. Kidwell, M. Hurdzan
Summit Par 3 GC
New Jersey
H. Purdy
Summer Heights GC
Ontario, Canada
H. Watson
Sun and Fun Par 3 GC
Illinois
G. E. Maddox
Sun City (Lakes East and Lakes West)
Arizona
J. Hardin, G. Nash
Sun City Centre G&CC (Original 9, South course)
Florida
M. Coggins
Sun City CC
Arizona
J. Hardin, G. Nash
Sun City CC
California
M. Coggins
Sun City Exec. GC
California
J. Hardin, G. Nash
Sun City GC (North)
Arizona
M. Coggins
Sun City GC (South)
Arizona
M. Coggins
Sun City GC (Willowbrook and Willowcreek)
Arizona
J.Hardin, G. Nash, G. and T. Fazio
Sun City GC
Florida
M. Mahannah
Sun City, Lakes East (Sun City CC; Lakes West; Lakes East; Palmbrook CC; Riverview; Willowbrook; Willowcreek; Quail Run; Union Hills CC)
Arizona
J. Hardin, G. Nash (c. Webb Staff)
Sun City Lake West
Arizona
M. Coggins

Sun City West (Briarwood CC; Hillcrest GC; Pebblebrook GC; Stardust GC)
Arizona
J. Hardin, G. Nash (c. Webb Staff)
Suncrest CC (a.9)
Pennsylvania
J. G. Harrison
Suncrest CC (r.)
Pennsylvania
F. Garbin
Sundance GC
Washington
(Dale Knott)
Sundowner GC
Kentucky
W. H. Way
Sundown GC
Iowa
E. B. Ault
Sundridge Park
England
W. Park, Jr.
Suneagles CC
New Jersey
S. Dunn
Sunflower Hills GC
Kansas
E. L. and R. B. Packard
Sun Harbours
Texas
W. C. Byrd
Sunken Gardens Muni
California
C. Glasson
Sunken Meadow Park GC
New York
A. H. Tull
Sunkist CC
Mississippi
R. Robertson
Sun Lakes CC
Arizona
See Sun City Lakes East
Sunland GC
Washington
A. V. Macan
Sunland Village Exec. GC (9)
Arizona
J. Hardin, G. Nash
Sunland Village GC
Arizona
M. Coggins
Sun Meadow CC [now Chigger Creek CC]
Texas
B. J. Riviere
Sunnbrook CC
Michigan
W. Reid, W. Connellan
Sunnehanna CC
Pennsylvania
A. W. Tillinghast
Sunningdale GC (Original 9)
New Hampshire
G. S. Cornish
Sunningdale GC (Original course)
England
W. Park, Jr.
Sunningdale GC (r. Old course, a. New course)
England
H. S. Colt
Sunningdale GC (r.)
England
C. H. Alison
Sunningdale GC (r. New course)
England
J. S. F. Morrison
Sunningdale GC (r.)
New York
A.W. Tillinghast

Sunningdale GC (r. New course)
England
T. C. Simpson
Sunningdale GC
Ontario, Canada
S. Thompson
Sunningdale GC (a.18)
Ontario, Canada
C. E. Robinson
Sun 'N Lake Exec. GC of Lake Placid
Florida
W. R. Watts
Sun 'N Lake of Sebring
Florida
W. R. Watts
Sunny Breeze Palms GC
Florida
R. A. Anderson
Sunnybrook CC
Michigan
W. B. Matthews
Sunnybrook CC (now Flourtown CC)
Pennsylvania
D. J. Ross
Sunnybrook CC (r.)
Pennsylvania
P. D. Maxwell
Sunnybrook CC (New site)
Pennsylvania
W. F. and D. W. Gordon
Sunnycrest CC (27)
New York
A. Craig
Sunny Hill CC (r.18,a.9)
New York
H. Purdy
Sunnyhill GC
Ohio
F. Garbin
Sunny Jim GC [now Medford Village]
New Jersey
W. F. Gordon
Sunnyside CC
California
W. P. Bell
Sunnyside CC (r.)
California
R. D. Putnam
Sunnyside CC
Iowa
E. L. Packard
Sunnyside CC
Texas
(Bruce Littell)
Sunnyvale Muni GC
California
C. Glasson
Sunol Valley GC (Cypress and Palms courses)
California
C. Glasson
Sunport Muni (r.9)
New Mexico
A. J. Snyder
Sunport Par 3 GC
New Mexico
R. F. Lawrence
Sunrise CC
Florida
W. R. Watts
Sunrise GC (Nellis AFB)
Nevada
T. G. Robinson
Sunrise CC at Rancho Mirage
California
T. G. Robinson

Sunrise National GC
Florida
R. A. Anderson
Sun River CC (Original 18)
Oregon
F. Federspiel
Sun River CC (Fairway Crest course)
Oregon
R. T. Jones, Jr.
Sunset Canyon Par 3 GC at Burbank (n.l.e.)
California
W. Watson
Sunset CC
Georgia
H. C. Moore
Sunset CC (r.)
Illinois
D. Gill
Sunset CC
Missouri
R. Foulis
Sunset CC
Oklahoma
R. C. Dunning
Sunset Dunes Par 3 GC
California
R. T. Jones
Sunset Golf Centre Par 3 GC
Ontario, Canada
R. and C. Muylaert
Sunset GC
Florida
D. J. Ross
Sunset GC (Hollywood; 9)
Florida
R. F. Lawrence
Sunset Hills CC (9)
Georgia
R. T. Jones
Sunset Hills CC (a.9)
Illinois
E. L. Packard
Sunset Hills Exec. GC
California
W. F. Bell
Sunset Hills GC
California
T. G. Robinson
Sunset Park GC (n.l.e.)
New York
T. Bendelow
Sunset Ridge CC
Illinois
W. Diddel
Sunset Ridge CC (r.)
Illinois
C. D. Wagstaff
Sunset Valley GC
New Jersey
H. Purdy
Suntree GC (Original 18)
Florida
E. Ryder
Suntree GC (a.18)
Florida
E. B. Seay, A. Palmer
Sun Valley GC
Idaho
W. P. Bell
Sun Valley GC (r.)
Idaho
G. Von Elm
Sun Valley GC (r.)
Idaho
R. T. Jones, Jr.

Sun Valley GC (r.)
Kentucky
B. J. Wihry
Sun Valley GC (Route plan)
Massachusetts
W. Johnson
Sun Valley GC
Massachusetts
G. S. Cornish
Sun Valley Par 3 GC
Iowa
L. I. Johnson
Surbiton GC
England
T. Dunn
Surfer's Paradise GC
Australia
S. Morpeth
Surf GC
South Carolina
G. W. Cobb
Surrey Hills GC
Oklahoma
F. Farley
Susquehanna Valley CC (r.)
Pennsylvania
W. F. Gordon
Sussex Pines CC
Delaware
E. B. Ault
Sutton-on-sea GC
England
S. V. Hotchkin
Sutton-on-Sea GC (r.)
England
T. Williamson
Suwannee River Valley CC (9)
Florida
J. L. Lee
Swain Fields GC
Ohio
W. Diddel
Swakopmund CC
Namibia
(S.W. Africa)
R. L. Jones
Swallows Nest GC (9)
Washington
R. E. Baldock
Swallows Nest Par 3 GC
California
R. E. Baldock
Swan Creek CC
Maryland
F. Murray, R. Roberts
Swan Hills GC
Illinois
W. J. Spear
Swan Lake CC (r.)
Tennessee
B. J. Wihry
Swannanoa GC
Virginia
F. A. Findlay
Swansea GC
Massachusetts
G. S. Cornish
Swartkop CC
South Africa
R.G. Grimsdell
Swartz Creek Muni
Michigan
(Fred A. Ellis)
Sweetwater Creek CC
Florida
R. Garl

Sweetwater GC
Utah
W. H. Neff
Sweetwater Oaks CC
Florida
L. Clifton
Swenson Park Muni (Original 9)
California
J. Fleming
Swenson Park Muni (a.9)
California
R. M. Graves
Swinford (r.)
Ireland
E. Hackett
Swinley Forest GC
England
H. S. Colt
Swinton Park GC
England
J. Braid
Swinton Park GC
England
F. G. Hawtree
Swope Park GC (Course #1)
Missouri
J. Dalgleish
Swope Park GC (r. Course #1)
Missouri
A. W. Tillinghast
Sycamore Creek CC (r.)
Ohio
A. Hills
Sycamore GC
New York
F. Duane
Sycamore Hills CC
Illinois
G. Kern
Sydney GC (r.)
Nova Scotia, Canada
S. Thompson
Sydney GC, Royal
Australia
(S. R. Robbie)
Sydney GC, Royal(r.)
Australia
A. Mackenzie
Sylvania CC
Ohio
W. Park, Jr.
Sylvania CC (r.6)
Ohio
G. S. Alves

Tabachines Club de Golf (Los Tabachine CC)
Mexico
P. Clifford
Table Rock GC
Ohio
J. Kidwell, M. Hurdzan
Taboada GC
New Mexico
D. Bennett
Taconic CC
Massachusetts
W. E. Stiles, J. R. Van Kleek
Tadmarton Heath GC
England
C. K. Hutchison, H. Vardon
Tahoe Donner GC
California
J. B. Williams
Tailor's Ocean Links (n.l.e.)
Rhode Island
S. J. Raynor
Tain GC
Scotland
T. Morris

Tain GC (r.)
Scotland
J. Sutherland
Taiwan G&CC
Taiwan
R. and S. Akaboshi
Takaha Royal CC
Japan
P.W. Thomson, M. Wolveridge
Takakurayama GC
Japan
R. T. Jones, Jr.
Tallgrass CC
Kansas
A. Hills
Tall Oaks CC
Ohio
R. B. Harris
Tall Pines GC
California
R. E. Baldock
Tall Pines Inn GC
New Jersey
W. F. and D. W. Gordon
Tall Timber CC
British Columbia, Canada
S. Leonard, P. Tattersfield
Tall Timbers CC
New York
F. Duane
Tall Wood CC
Connecticut
(Michael Ovian)
Tally Mountain Club
Georgia
J. L. Lee
Tamarac CC
Florida
L. S. "Dick" Wilson
Tamarack CC
New York
C. H. Banks
Tamarack CC
Pennsylvania
J. G. Harrison, F. Garbin
Tamarack GC (27)
New Jersey
H. Purdy
Tamarisk CC
California
W. P. Bell
Tamarisk CC (r.)
California
T. G. Robinson
Tamarron Inn CC
Colorado
A. Hills
Tamcrest CC (9)
New Jersey
F. Duane
Tamiment CC
Pennsylvania
R. T. Jones
Tammy Brook CC
New Jersey
R. T. Jones
Tam O Shanter CC
Illinois
C. D. Wagstaff
Tam O' Shanter CC (r.; n.l.e.)
Illinois
W. B. Langford
Tam O Shanter CC (Courses #1 and #2)
Ohio
L. Macomber
Tam O Shanter GC (r.)
Michigan
W. Reid, W. Connellan

Tam O Shanter GC (r.)
New York
R. T. Jones
Tam O' Shanter GC
Washington
A. Smith
Tam O' Shanter Muni
Ontario, Canada
H. Watson
Tampa Bay GC
Florida
J. D. Dunn
Tampa Palas GC
Florida
A. Hills
Tampico CC
Mexico
J. Bredemus
Tamworth GC
England
J. R. Stutt
Tandragee (a.9)
Northern Ireland
F. W. Hawtree
Tandridge GC
England
H. S. Colt
Tanforan Exec. GC
California
J. Fleming
Tangier GC
Morocco
J. J. F. Pennink
Tanglewood CC, (Chagrin Falls)
Ohio
W. F. Mitchell
Tanglewood GC (Delaware)
Ohio
J. Kidwell
Tanglewood Manor GC
Pennsylvania
(Chester Ruby)
Tanglewood On Texoma GC
Texas
F. Farley
Tanglewood Park GC (East, West and Par 3 courses)
North Carolina
R. T. Jones
Tanjong Penggerahg GC
Malaysia
R. T. Jones, Jr.
Tannenhauf GC
Ohio
J. G. Harrison
Tanoan GC
New Mexico
R. Von Hagge, B. Devlin
Tansi Resort GC
Tennessee
R. A. Renaud
Tantallon CC
Washington, D. C.
T. G. Robinson
Tan-Tar-A Resort GC
Missouri
R. Von Hagge, B. Devlin
Tapton Park
England
G. Duncan
Tara Hilis Muni (9)
Nebraska
R. Watson
Tara, Royal (r.)
Ireland
E. Hackett
Tarbot GC
Scotland
J. Sutherland

Tarkio CC
Missouri
C. Mendenhall
Tarpon Lake Village GC
Florida
L. L. Marshall
Tarpon Springs GC
Florida
W. E. Stiles, J. R. Van Kleek
Tarpon Springs GC (r.)
Florida
M. Mahannah
Tarpon Woods GC
Florida
L. L. Marshall
Tarry Brae CC
New York
W. F. Mitchell
Tartan Park CC
Minnesota
D. Herfort
Tascosa CC
Texas
W. D. Cantrell
Tashua Knolls GC (Trumbull Muni)
Connecticut
A. Zikorus
Tasmania GC
Tasmania, Australia
(Al Howard)
Tasmanian CC Casino
Tasmania, Australia
P.W. Thomson, M. Wolveridge
Tatnuck CC
Massachusetts
D. J. Ross
Tatnuck CC (r.4)
Massachusetts
G. S. Cornish, W. G. Robinson
Taughannock G&CC
New York
(Wester White)
Tavares Cove Exec. GC
Florida
W. Mitchell
Tavistock CC
New Jersey
A. Findlay
Tavistock CC (r.)
New Jersey
J. G. Harrison
Tavistock CC (r.)
New Jersey
R. T. Jones
Tazewell County CC
Virginia
D. and E. Maples
Tchefuncta CC (a.9)
Louisiana
J. L. Lee
Tchefuncta CC
Louisiana
J. L. Daray
Teaford Lake GC
California
R. E. Baldock
Teamsters CG
Missouri
H.Herpel
Tecolote Canyon Exec. GC
California
R. T. Jones
Tedesco CC (r.)
Massachusetts
E. F. Wogan
Ted Makalena GC
Hawaii
R. E. Baldock

Teeside GC
England
(C. Robertson)
Tega Cay CC (Trade Wind and South Wind courses)
South Carolina
W. B. Lewis, Jr.
Tegernseler GC
West Germany
D. Harradine
Teignmouth GC
England
H. S. Colt
Tejas GC
Texas
J. Finger
Telemark GC
Wisconsin
(Art Johnson)
Telford New Town GC
England
J.D.Harris, P.W. Thomson, M. Wolveridge
Tempe Muni
Arizona
A. J. Snyder
Temple CC
Texas
R. Plummer
Temple CC (a.9)
Texas
B. J. Riviere
Temple GC
England
W. Park, Jr., (J. Temple)
Temple GC (r.)
England
H. Cotton
Temple Hills CC (27)
Tennessee
L. Howard
Tenanah Lake House at Roscoe
New York
A. H. Tull
Tenison Park Muni (West course)
Texas
J. Bredemus
Tenison Park Muni (East course)
Texas
R. Plummer
Tennwood GC
Texas
R. Plummer
Tennwood GC (a.18)
Texas
G. and T. Fazio
Tequesta CC
Florida
L. S. "Dick" Wilson
Teresopolis GC
Brazil
S. Thompson
Terrapin Hills GC
Alabama
J. H. Williams, Sr.
Terrebone, Club de Golf
Province of Québec, Canada
J. Watson
Terre Du Lac G&CC
Missouri
R. A. Anderson
Terrell CC
Texas
R. Plummer
Terri Pines CC
Alabama
T. Jackson
Terverun
Belgium
S. Dunn

Teugega CC
New York
D. J. Ross

Teugega CC (r.)
New York
W. F. Mitchell

Tewkesbury Park G&CC
England
J. J. F. Pennink

Texarkana CC
Arkansas
W. B. Langford, T. J. Moreau

Texarkana CC (r.)
Arkansas
L. Howard

Texas A & M University GC
Texas
R. Plummer

Texas A & M University GC (r.)
Texas
(Bruce Littell)

Texas National GC
Texas
(Jack B. Miller)

The Country Club
(See Country Club)

Thendara CC (Original 9)
New York
D. J. Ross

Thendara CC (a.9)
New York
W. E. Harries

Thendara CC (r.1)
New York
G. S. Cornish, W. G. Robinson

Theodore Wirth Muni (Original 9)
Minnesota
(Charles Erickson)

Theodore Wirth Muni (a.9)
Minnesota
E. L. Packard

Thetford GC
England
(C.H. Mayo)

Thetford GC (r.)
England
J. Braid

Thetford GC (r.)
England
P.M. Ross

Thetford Mines Golf & Curling Club (r.9,a.9)
Province of Québec, Canada
H. and J. Watson

Theydon Bois GC (Original 9)
England
J. Braid

Theydon Bois GC (a.9)
England
F. W. Hawtree

Thistledown GC (9)
Ontario, Canada
R. and C. Muylaert

Thomas County CC
Georgia
W. C. Byrd

Thomas Memorial GC (9)
Massachusetts
W. B. Hatch

Thompson Raceway GC
Connecticut
D. Hoening

Thomson Club
Massachusetts
G. S. Cornish

Thomson CC (r.)
Georgia
R.A. Renaud

Thornapple CC
Ohio
J. Kidwell

Thorngate CC [formerly Vernon Ridge CC](r.)
Illinois
R. B. Harris

Thornhill GC (r.)
Ontario, Canada
S. Thompson

Thornhill GC(r.)
Ontario, Canada
H. Watson

Thornhill GC (r.)
Ontario, Canada
C. E. Robinson

Thorn Spring GC (r.9,a.9)
Virginia
F. Garbin

Thorny Lea GC
Massachusetts
W. E. Stiles, J. R. Van Kleek

Thorpeness GC
England
J. Braid

Thorpe Wood
England
P. Alliss, D. Thomas

Thousand Islands Club
New York
S. J. Raynor

Thousand Oaks CC [now Los Robles Green CC]
California
R. E. Baldock

Thousand Oaks CC
Florida
W. W. Amick

Three Lakes CC
Japan
P.W. Thomson, M. Wolveridge

Three Pines CC
South Carolina
W. W. Amick

Thunderbird CC
California
L. M. Hughes

Thunderbird CC (r.)
California
H. Purdy

Thunderbird CC (r.)
California
T.G. Robinson

Thunderbird CC (r.)
California
H. M. and D. A. Rainville

Thunderbird CC
Illinois
D. Gill

Thunderbird Par 3 GC
Massachusetts
G. S. Cornish

Thunder Ridge CC
New York
A. Craig

Thurles (r.)
Ireland
E. Hackett

Thurloona GC (27)
New South Wales, Australia
P.W. Thomson, M. Wolveridge

Thurrock
British Isles
J. J. F. Pennink

Ticonderoga GC
New York
S. Dunn

Tides CC
Florida
D. Gill

(The) Tides Inn CC (Original 9 of Tartan course)
Virginia
G. Campbell

(The) Tides Inn CC (2nd 9 of Tartan course and Golden Eagle course)
Virginia
G. W. Cobb

Tidewater GC
Maine
P. A. Wogan

Tierra Del Sol GC
California
R. Von Hagge, B. Devlin

Tierra Verde GC
Florida
F. Murray

Tifton GC at Darlington
South Carolina
R. Robertson

Tiger Point GC
Florida
W. W. Amick

Tijeras Arroya GC at Kirkland AFB
New Mexico
R. D. Putnam

Tijuana CC [formerly Agua Caliente]
Mexico
W. P. Bell

Timaru GC (r.)
New Zealand
P.W. Thomson, M. Wolveridge

Timber Creek CC
Texas
G. R. Baird

Timberlake GC [formerly Sullivan CC](9)
Illinois
R. B. Harris

Timberlane GC
Louisiana
R. T. Jones

Timberlin GC (Berlin Muni)
Connecticut
A. Zikorus

Timberlink GC
Pennsylvania
X. G. Hassenplug

Timber Oaks GC
Michigan
R. Garl

Timber Point GC
New York
H. S. Colt, C. H. Alison

Timber Point Park GC
New York
W. F. Mitchell

Timber Ridge CC
Wisconsin
E. L. and R. B. Packard

Timmendorferstrand GC (2 courses)
West Germany
B. Von Limburger

Timpanogos Muni
Utah
J. M. Riley

Timuquana CC
Florida
D. J. Ross

Timuquana CC (r.)
Florida
G. W. Cobb

Timuquana CC (r.)
Florida
D. W. Gordon

Tinker AFB GC
Oklahoma
F. Farley

Tinley Park Muni
Illinois
K. Killian, R. Nugent

Tinsley Park
England
F. W. Hawtree

Tioga GC
New York
H. Purdy

Tippecanoe CC
Indiana
J. A. Roseman

Tipton Muni
Indiana
W. Diddel

Tipworth
England
T. Williamson

Titirangi GC
New Zealand
(F. G. Hood, Gilbert Martin)

Titirangi GC (r.)
New Zealand
A. Mackenzie

Tiverton GC
England
J. Braid

Tiverton GC
England
J. R. Stutt

Tizeras Arroya GC (Kirkland AFB)
New Mexico
R. D. Putnam

Tobago GC (Mt. Irvine Bay Hotel)
Tobago
J. D. Harris

Toftrees CC
Pennsylvania
E. B. Ault

Tokatee CC
Oregon
T. G. Robinson

Tokuyara CC
Japan
P.W. Thomson, M. Wolveridge

Tokyo CC
Japan
C. H. Alison

Toledo CC
Ohio
W. Park, Jr.

Toledo CC (r.)
Ohio
R. B. Harris

Toledo CC (r.)
Ohio
A. Hills

Tomahawk CC
Ohio
B. W. Zink

Tomahawk Hills CC [formerly Shawnee CC]
Kansas
H. Robb, Sr.

Tomahawk Hills GC (9)
Indiana
G. Kern

Tomahawk Lake GC [formerly Homestead Mine](9)
South Dakota
L. M. Hughes

Tommy Bolt's Golden Tee
Florida
R. A. Anderson

Tomoka Oaks CC
Florida
J. P. Gibson

Tomoko Inn GC
Florida
L. Clifton

Tooele GC
Utah
J. M. Riley

Toorresdale CC
Pennsylvania
W. Campbell

Tooting Bec Club
England
T. Dunn

Tooting Bec Club
England
W. Park, Jr.

Topeka CC (9; n.l.e.)
Kansas
T. Bendelow

Topeka CC (r.9,a.9)
Kansas
P. D. Maxwell

Topeka CC (r.)
Kansas
C. Mendenhall

Topeka Public GC
Kansas
W. Leonard, L. C. McClellan

Topsail CC
North Carolina
(Russell T. Burney)

Tor Hill CC
Saskatchewan, Canada
J. A. Thompson

Torey Pines Resort GC
New Hampshire
(Dick Tremblay)

Toronto Board of Trade GC (36)
Ontario, Canada
H. Watson

Toronto Board of Trade GC (r.9,a.9)
Ontario, Canada
A. Hills

Toronto GC
Ontario, Canada
H. S. Colt

Toronto GC (r.)
Ontario, Canada
H. Watson

Toronto Hunt Club
Ontario, Canada
W. Park, Jr.

Torquay GC
England
J. Braid, J. R. Stutt

Torrance House
Scotland
F. W. Hawtree

Torreon, CC
Mexico
P. Clifford

Torrequebrado
Spain
J. Gancedo

Torresdale CC (Original 18)
Pennsylvania
W. Campbell

Torresdale Frankford CC
Pennsylvania
D. J. Ross

Torrey Pines GC (North and South courses)
California
W. P. and W. F. Bell

Torrey Pines GC (r. North and South courses)
California
H. M. and D. A. Rainville

Torrington CC
Connecticut
O. E. Smith

Torwoodlee GC
Scotland
W. Park, Jr.

Totteridge
Great Britain
W. Park, Jr.

303

Toulouse, Golf de (a.9)
France
F. W. Hawtree
Touquet, GC du (45)
France
H. S. Colt
Touquet, GC du (r. Forest and Sea courses)
France
P. M. Ross
Tournament Players Club
Florida
P. Dye
Tovarich Hills GC
U.S.S.R.
R. T. Jones, Sr. and Jr.
Tower GC (Bahama Princess, Grand Bahamas Island)
Bahamas
L. S. "Dick" Wilson
Tower Hill GC
England
(Sam Chisholm)
Tower Tee
Missouri
R. A. Anderson
Town and Country Club (r.)
Minnesota
R. Foulis
Town and Country GC
Ohio
E. B. Ault
Towson G&CC (Eagles Nest)
Maryland
G. S. Cornish, W. G. Robinson
Toy Town Tavern GC
Massachusetts
D. J. Ross
Trabolgan GC
Ireland
E. Hackett
Tracy CC
California
R. E. Baldock
Tracy Park G&CC
England
(G. Aitken)
Trafalgar G&CC
Ontario, Canada
C. E. Robinson
Tralee GC (r.)
Ireland
E. Hackett
Tramore GC
Ireland
W. Park, Jr.
Traverse City CC
Michigan
W. B. Matthews
Travis AFB GC [now Cypress Lakes GC]
California
J. Finger
Travis Pointe CC
Michigan
W. K. Newcomb
Treasure Cay GC
Bahamas
L. S. "Dick" Wilson
Treasure Island Exec. GC
Texas
W. D. Cantrell
Treasure Lake G&CC
Georgia
W. C. Byrd
Trehaven GC
Ontario, Canada
R. Moote

Trent GC (9)
Ontario, Canada
R. and C. Muylaert
Trentham GC
England
T. Williamson
Tres Vidas, En La Playa (West and East courses)
Mexico
R. T. Jones
Trevose G&CC (27)
England
H. S. Colt
Trevòse G&CC (r. 27)
England
G. Campbell
Triangle D'Or, Club de Golf
Province of Québec, Canada
H. Watson
Tri-City GC
Utah
J. B. Williams
Tri County GC
Indiana
R. D. Beard
Trim Tullamore GC (r.)
Ireland
E. Hackett
Triple A CC (r.)
Missouri
R. Foulis
Tripoli
Libya
J. J. F. Pennink
Tri-Way GC
Missouri
J. P. Maxwell
Troia GC
Portugal
R. T. Jones
Troon GC (Original 5 holes)
Scotland
C. Hunter
Troon GC (now Royal Troon)
Scotland
W. Fernie
Troon GC, Royal (r.)
Scotland
J. Braid
Troon Portland GC
Scotland
W. Fernie
(The) Trophy Club (Creek and Oaks courses)
Texas
J. L. Lee, (Ben Hogan)
Tropicana CC
Nevada
B. Stamps
Trosper Park GC
Oklahoma
A. J. Jackson
Trout Lake CC
Wisconsin
F. MacDonald, C. E. Maddox
Troy CC (r.9,a.9)
Ohio
J. Kidwell, M. Hurdzan
Trull Brook GC
Massachusetts
G. S. Cornish
Trumbull CC (r.)
Ohio
W. K. Newcomb
Trumbull Muni (now Tashua Knolls CC)
Connecticut
A. Zikorus

Truro GC (r.)
Nova Scotia, Canada
S. Thompson
Truro GC (r.9,a.9)
Nova Scotia, Canada
C. E. Robinson
Truro GC
England
J. Braid, J. R. Stutt
T.R.W. GC [formerly J. D. Wright Rec. GC](27)
Ohio
P. and R. Dye
Tryall Golf & Beach Club
Jamaica
R. Plummer
Tsawwassen CC
British Columbia, Canada
N. Woods
Tuam GC
Ireland
E. Hackett
Tubac Valley CC
Arizona
R. F. Lawrence
Tuckaway CC
Wisconsin
K. Killian, R. Nugent
Tucson CC
Arizona
W. P. Bell
Tucson CC (r.)
Arizona
A. J. Snyder
Tucson Estates (West Par 3 and East Exec. courses)
Arizona
R. F. Lawrence
Tucson GC (North and South courses)
Arizona
W. P. Bell
Tucson National GC (r.)
Arizona
R. B. Harris
Tucson National GC (r.)
Arizona
R. F. Lawrence
Tucson National GC (r.)
Arizona
R. Von Hagge, B. Devlin
Tulare CC
California
R. E. Baldock
Tullatin CC
Oregon
(George Junor)
Tullahoma CC (9)
Tennessee
(Bubber Johnson)
Tulsa CC
Oklahoma
A. W. Tillinghast
Tulsa CC (r.)
Oklahoma
P. D. Maxwell
Tumble Brook CC (Original 9)
Connecticut
W. Park, Jr.
Tumble Brook CC (a.9)
Connecticut
O. E. Smith, W. F. Mitchell
Tumble Brook CC (a.9)
Connecticut
G. and T. Fazio
Tumblebrook GC
Wisconsin
E. L. Packard
Tumwater Valley GC
Washington
R. R. Goss, Glen Proctor

Tunxis Plantation CC (27)
Connecticut
A. Zikorus
Tupelo CC (New site)
Mississippi
(John Frazier)
Tupper Lake GC
New York
D. J. Ross
Tura Beach CC
New South Wales, Australia
P.W. Thomson, M. Wolveridge
Turf and Surf GC
Florida
C. H. Adams
Turf Valley CC (North and South courses)
Maryland
E. B. Ault, A. Jamison
Turin Highland CC
New York
W. E. Harries
Turkey Creek CC
Indiana
F. MacDonald, C. E. Maddox
Turkey Creek G&CC
Florida
(Ward Northrup)
Turkey Run GC
Indiana
G. Kern
Turlock G&CC
California
R. E. Baldock
Turnberry CC
Illinois
E. L. Packard
Turnberry Hotel GC (Original Ailsa and Arran courses; n.l.e.)
Scotland
W. Fernie
Turnberry Hotel GC (r. Ailsa and Arran courses)
Scotland
C. K. Hutchison
Turnberry Hotel GC (r. Ailsa course)
Scotland
P. M. Ross
Turnberry Hotel GC (r. Arran course)
Scotland
J. Alexander
Turnberry Hotel GC (r.) Ailsa course
Scotland
P. Alliss, D. Thomas
Turnberry Isle GC (formerly Aventura CC) (North and South courses)
Florida
R. T. Jones, R. L. Jones
Turner AFB GC
Georgia
H. C. Moore
Turnhouse GC
Scotland
W. Park, Jr.
Turnhouse GC
Scotland
J. Braid
Turtle Cove GC
Georgia
W. J. Spear
Turtle Creek Club
Florida
J. L. Lee
Turtle Point G&CC
Alabama
R. T. Jones
Tuscarora CC
New York
S. Dunn

Tuscarora GC
Virginia
E. Hamm
Tuscawilla CC
Florida
J. L. Lee
Tuxedo Muni
Manitoba, Canada
(A.W. Creed)
Tuxedo Park (Original course; n.l.e.)
New York
(Henry Hewett)
Tuxedo Park (r. Original course;n.l.e)
New York
W. S. Flynn
Tuxedo Park Club (New site)
New York
R. T. Jones
Twain Harte Exec GC
California
C. Glasson
Twenty-Nine Palms Marine Base GC
California
D. W. Kent
Twenty-Nine Palms Muni
California
L. M. Hughes
Twickenham
England
J. J. F. Pennink, C. D. Lawrie
Twiggs Memorial (Providence Muni)
Rhode Island
D. J. Ross
Twilight Par 3 GC
Colorado
H. B. Hughes
Twin Creek CC
Georgia
A. L. Davis
Twin Falls State Park GC (9)
West Virginia
G. S. Cornish, W. G. Robinson
Twin Falls State Park GC (a.9)
West Virginia
G. Cobb, J. LaFoy
Twin Hills CC
Massachusetts
A. Zikorus
Twin Hills CC (r. 9, a. 9)
Missouri
E. L. Bell
Twin Hills G&CC
Oklahoma
P. D. Maxwell
Twin Hills G&Cc (r.)
Oklahoma
D. R. Sechrest
Twin Hills GC
New York
A. Craig
Twin Lakes CC
Idaho
(Ed Hunnicutt)
Twin Lakes CC (Kent)
Ohio
G. S. Alves
Twin Lakes CC [now Norman CC](9)
Oklahoma
F. Farley
Twin Lakes CC
Washington
A. Smith
Twin Lakes GC
Arkansas
C. B. Hollingsworth
Twin Lakes GC (Mansfield)
Ohio
J. Kidwell

Twin Lakes GC
Pennsylvania
D. W. Gordon
Twin Lakes Par 3 GC
California
W. H. Johnson
Twin Oaks CC
Missouri
F. Farley
Twin Oaks GC
Michigan
W. K. Bowen
Twin Oaks Par 3 GC
North Carolina
E. Maples
Twin Orchards CC (n.l.e.)
Illinois
W. B. Langford, T. J. Moreau
Twin Orchards CC (36)
Illinois
C. D. Wagstaff
Twin Orchards CC (r.)
Illinois
E. B. Dearie, Jr.
Twin Peaks Muni
Colorado
F. Hummel
Twin Pines G&CC
Missouri
(Dewitt "Maury" Bell)
Twin Ponds Par 3 at Crystal Lake
Illinois
C. D. Wagstaff
Twin Run GC
Ohio
W. Diddel
Twin Valley CC
North Carolina
R. Kirby G. Player
Two Bridges GC
New Jersey
N. T. Psiahas
Two Rivers Muni
Tennessee
L. Howard
Tyandaca Muni
Ontario, Canada
C. E. Robinson
Tygart's Valley CC (r.)
West Virginia
J. G. Harrison
Tylney Park GC
England
(W. Wiltshire)
Tyndal AFB GC (Original 9)
Florida
R. E. Baldock
Tyndal AFB GC (a.9)
Florida
J. L. Lee
Tynemouth GC
England
W. Park, Jr.
Tyneside GC
England
H. S. Colt
Tyoga CC
Pennsylvania
E. B. Ault
Tyrone CC
Pennsylvania
E. B. Ault
Tyrone Hills GC
Michigan
W. B. Matthews

Ulm-Do GC
West Germany
B. Von Limburger

Ulverston
England
A. Herd
Ulzama, Club de Golf
Spain
J. Arana
Unicorn CC
Massachusetts
W. E. Stiles, J. R. Van Kleek
Union CC
Ohio
W. K. Newcomb
Union Hills CC (Sun City)
Arizona
J. Hardin, G. Nash
Union League G&CC (n.l.e.)
California
A. MacKenzie
Uniontown CC
Pennsylvania
E. F. Loeffler, J. McGlynn
Unionville Fairways Par 3 GC
Ontario, Canada
R. and C. Muylaert
United Shoe CC (r.)
Massachusetts
E. F. Wogan
U.S. Air Force Academy (Blue course)
Colorado
R. T. Jones
U.S. Air Force Academy (Silver course)
Colorado
F. Hummel
U.S. Military Academy
New York
R. T. Jones
U.S. Naval Academy GC (r.)
Maryland
W. S. Flynn
U.S. Veteran's Hospital GC (Encino; 9)
California
W. H. Johnson
U.S. Veteran's Hospital GC (San Fer-
    nando; 9)
California
W. H. Johnson
U.S. Veteran's Hospital GC
New Jersey
R. T. Jones
University Heights GC
Ohio
G. S. Alves
University of Alabama GC (Original 9)
Alabama
J.H. Williams, Sr., (T. Nicol)
University of Florida GC (r.)
Florida
R. Garl
University of Georgia GC
Georgia
R. T. Jones
University of Idaho GC (Original 9)
Idaho
(Francis L. James)
University of Idaho GC (r.9,a.9)
Idaho
R. E. Baldock
University of Illinois GC (Orange and
    Blue courses)
Illinois
C. D. Wagstaff
University of Iowa GC (Finkbine course)
Iowa
R. B. Harris
University of Maryland GC
Maryland
G. W. Cobb

University of Michigan GC
Michigan
A. Mackenzie, P. D. Maxwell
University of Minnesota GC
Minnesota
S. J. Raynor
University of Mississippi GC
Mississippi
E. D. Guy
University of Missouri (A. L. Gustin, Jr.
    Memorial GC)
Missouri
F. Farley
University of New Mexico (North course
    plus 9 par 3)
New Mexico
W.H. Tucker, Sr.
University of N.M. GC (south)
New Mexico
R. F. Lawrence
University of Oklahoma GC
Oklahoma
J. P. and P. D. Maxwell
University of Southern Mississippi GC
Mississippi
E. D. Guy
University of South Florida GC
Florida
W. F. Mitchell
University of the Philippines
Philippines
(Francisco D. Santana)
University Park CC
Florida
F. Murray
University Park GC
Michigan
W. B. and G. H. Matthews
University Village GC at Galeta
California
H. M. and D. A. Rainville
Upper Canada CC at Oakville
Ontario, Canada
H. Watson
Upper Canada GC at Morrisburg (Chrys-
    ler Farm Park)
Ontario, Canada
C. E. Robinson
Upper Landsdowne CC
Ohio
J. Kidwell
Upper Maine Line CC
Pennsylvania
W. F. and D. W. Gordon
Upper Montclair CC (r.)
New Jersey
A. W. Tillinghast
Upper Montclair CC (New site, 27)
New Jersey
R. T. Jones
Upton-By-Chester GC
England
(W. Davis)
Upton G&CC
Jamaica
(John S. Collier)
Upton G&CC (r.)
Jamaica
H. Watson
Urban Par 3 GC
Illinois
E. L. Packard
Urbana CC
Illinois
T. Bendelow

Urban Hills CC
Illinois
E. L. Packard
Urban Par 3 GC
Illinois
E. L. Packard
Uruguay, GC de
Uruguay
A. Mackenzie
Utrecht GC
Holland
H. S. Colt, J. S. F. Morrison, C. H. Alison

Vail GC
Colorado
J. P. Maxwell
Valbonne GC
France
D. Harradine
Valcros, Golf de
France
F. W. Hawtree
Vale Lobo GC (27)
Portugal
H. Cotton
Valdosta CC
Georgia
J. L. Lee
Valencia GC
California
R. T. Jones
Val Halla CC
Maine
P. A. Wogan
Valle Alto GC
Mexico
L. M. Hughes
Valle Arriba GC
Venezuela
(James B. Wilson)
Valle de Parc, Club de Golf
Province of Québec, Canada
H. Watson
Valle Oaks GC
Florida
R. Garl
Vallescondido, Club de Golf
Mexico
P. Clifford
Valle Vista CC
Indiana
R. A. Simmons
Valley Brook CC (Pittsburgh)
Pennsylvania
J. G. Harrison
Valley Brook CC (McMurrah) (27)
Pennsylvania
F. Garbin
Valley Brook CC (r.)
Pennsylvania
R. T. Jones
Valleybrook G&CC
Tennessee
C. H. Adams
Valley Club of Montecito
California
A. Mackenzie, W. R. Hunter
Valley CC
Arizona
D. Gill
Valley CC
Colorado
W. F. Bell

Valley CC (9)
Nebraska
(William Kubley)
Valley CC
Philippines
S. Inouye
Valley CC on Ledgemont (a.9)
Rhode Island
G. S. Cornish
Valley Forge Veteran's Administration
    GC
Pennsylvania
A. H. Tull
Valley Garden GC
California
R. E. Baldock
Valley Green Exec. GC (9)
Illinois
R. B. Harris
Valley Green GC
Pennsylvania
X. G. Hassenplug
Valley Heights GC (r.)
Pennsylvania
J. G. Harrison
Valley Hi CC
Colorado
H. B. Hughes
Valley High Par 3 GC
Minnesota
H. D. Fieldhouse
Valley Inn & CC (r.)
Texas
J. Finger
Valley International CC (r.; a. Par 3
    course)
Texas
(Dennis Arp)
Valley Oaks GC
Iowa
R. B. Harris
Valley Springs GC
Maryland
R. Roberts
Valley Verde CC
California
D. W. Kent
Valley View GC
Indiana
C. R. Blankenship
Valley View GC
Montana
T. J. Wirth
Valley View GC (Omaha; n.l.e.)
Nebraska
J. Dalgleish
Valley View GC (Central City; 9)
Nebraska
H. W. Glissmann
Valley View GC (Fremont; 9)
Nebraska
H. W. Glissmann
Valley View GC (Lancster)
Ohio
H. D. Paddock, Sr.
Valley View Muni (r.)
New York
R. T. Jones
Vallromas, Club de Golf
Spain
F. W. Hawtree
Val Morin GC (r.)
Province of Québec, Canada
H. Watson
Val Niegette GC
Province of Québec, Canada
J. Watson

Valparaiso CC (n.l.e.)
Florida
W. B. Langford, T. J. Moreau
Valparaiso CC (r.9,a.9)
Indiana
J. R. Darrah
Valparaiso GC
Argentina
(John Anderson)
Van Buren GC
Iowa
L. I. Johnson
Van Buskirk Park Muni (a.9)
California
R. M. Graves
Van Cortlandt Park GC
New York
T. Bendelow
Van Cortlandt Park GC (r.)
New York
W. F. Mitchell
Vancouver GC (r.)
British Columbia, Canada
C. E. Robinson
Vancouver GC (r.)
British Columbia, Canada
W. G. Robinson
Vancouver Muni
Washington
F. Federspiel
Vandenberg AFB GC
California
R.E. Baldock
Vanderbilt Estate, GC, Manhasset (9)
New York
D. Emmet
Van Zandt CC
Texas
L. Howard
Varese GC
Italy
D. Harradine
Vaudreuil, Golf de
France
F. W. Hawtree
Vaughan Valley Exec. GC
Ontario, Canada
R. and C. Muylaert
Veenker Memorial GC (Iowa State
   University)
Iowa
P. D. Maxwell
Velleaire GC
Ohio
H. D. Paddock, Sr.
Venanco Trails GC
Pennsylvania
J. G. Harrison
Vendera Beach CC
Cuba
H. B. Strong
Venezuela Golf & Yacht Club
Venezuela
J. R. Van Kleek
Venice CC
Florida
(Carl H. Anderson)
Venice East Exec. GC
Florida
R. A. Anderson
Venice Golf Club
Italy
C. K. Cotton
Venohara GC
Japan
R. T. Jones, Jr.
Ventnor (Isle of Wight)
England
T. Dunn

Ventnor (Isle of Wight)
England
J. H. Stutt
Ventura CC [now Saticoy Public Links]
California
G. C. Thomas, Jr.
Ventura Muni
California
W. F. Bell
Ventura Y&CC
Texas
(Bruce Littell)
Vermillion Hills CC
Illinois
E. L. Packard
Vernon Hills CC
New York
D. Emmet, A. H. Tull
Vernonia CC (9)
Oregon
(George Junor)
Vernon Ridge CC [now Thorngate CC](r.)
Illinois
R. B. Harris
Vero Beach CC
Florida
H. B. Strong
Vesper CC (r.9,a.9)
Massachusetts
D. J. Ross
Vesper CC (r.)
Massachusetts
M. L. Francis
Vesper Hills CC
New York
G. S. Cornish, W. G. Robinson
Vestal Hills CC (former course n.l.e.)(r.)
New York
R. T. Jones
Vestal Hills CC (new site)
New York
G. S. Cornish
Vestavia CC (r.)
Alabama
G. W. Cobb
Veterans Memorial GC
Massachusetts
G. S. Cornish
V. F. W. GC (9)
Pennsylvania
J. G. Harrison, F. Garbin
V. F. W. GC. (a.9)
Pennsylvania
E. B. Ault
Via Verde CC
California
L. M. Hughes
Victor Hills GC (9)
New York
A. Craig
Victoria GC [formerly Pedley Farms GC,
   also Arlington GC](Original course)
California
C. E. Maud
Victoria GC (r.9,a.9)
California
M. H. Behr
Victoria GC (r.)
California
W. H. Johnson
Victoria GC
Texas
G. A. Hoffman
Victoria GC
Australia
A. Mackenzie
Victoria GC (r.)
Australia
P. Thompson, M. Wolveridge

Victoria GC (r.)
British Columbia, Canada
A. V. Macan
Victoria Muni
California
W. F. Bell
Victoria Park Golf Centre (36)
Ontario, Canada
R. and C. Muylaert
Victoriaville, Club de Golf (r.9,a.9)
Province of Québec, Canada
H. Watson
Victory Hills CC
Kansas
J. Dalgleish
Vidago, Club de Golf de
Portugal
P. M. Ross
Vielles Forge, Club de Golf
Province of Québec, Canada
H. Watson
Vielles Forge, Club de Golf (a.9)
Province of Québec, Canada
H. and J. Watson
Vienna GC
Austria
W. Park, Jr.
Vilamoura (CdG Vilamoura)
Portugal
J. J. F. Pennink
Vilamoura (CdG Dom Pedro)
Portugal
J. J. F. Pennink
Villa Del Ray CC
Florida
(Frank Batto)
Villa de Paz GC (a.9)
Arizona
J. Hardin, G. Nash
Villa D'Este GC
Italy
J. P. Gannon
Villa Du Parc CC
Wisconsin
D. Gill
Village CC
Texas
J. P. Maxwell
(The) Village Course (Kapalua GC)
Hawaii
E. B. Seay, A. Palmer
Village Green CC
Illinois
W. B. Langford
Village Green CC [now Kentucky Dam
   State Park GC]
Kentucky
H. Purdy
Village Green GC
New York
M. and H. Purdy
Village Green GC
Ohio
(J. Thomas Francis)
Village Green Par 3 GC (Bradenton; 9)
Florida
W. B. Lewis, Jr.
Village Green Par 3 GC (Sarasota; 9)
Florida
W. B. Lewis, Jr.
Village Greens GC
Kansas
C. R. Blankenship
Village Greens GC (a.9)
Kansas
L. C. McClellan
Village Links GC
Illinois
D. Gill

Village Nine GC
Florida
A. Hills
Village of Oak Creek CC
Arizona
R. T. Jones, Sr. and Jr.
(The) Villages G&CC
California
R. M. Graves
Villages of America CC
Ohio
E. B. Ault
Villa Monterey GC (Original 9)
Arizona
M. Coggins
Villa Olivia CC (r. 7, 1975)
Illinois
K. Killian, R. Nugent
Villa Real GC
Cuba
L. S. "Dick" Wilson
Vincennes GC
Indiana
C. E. Maddox
Vinita CC (r.)
Oklahoma
F. Farley
Vinoy Park Club
Florida
D. Gill
(The) Vintage CC
California
G. and T. Fazio
Virginia Beach GC
Virginia
R. L. Jones
Virginia CC (r.)
California
W. P. Bell
Virginia, CC of (Westhampton course)
Virginia
H. N. Barker
Virginia, CC of (r. James River course)
Virginia
G. O'Neill
Virginia, CC of (r. James River and
   Westhampton courses)
Virginia
F. A. Findlay
Virginia, CC of (James River course)
Virginia
W. S. Flynn
Virginia, CC of (Tuckahoe course) (a. 9)
Virginia
E. B. Ault
Virginia GC
Ireland
(Hession and Gallagher)
Virginia Hot Springs G&TC
Virginia
See (The) Homestead
Visalia CC (r.)
California
D. Muirhead
Viscaya CC [formerly North Dade CC]
Florida
F. Murray
Vista Chica Par 3 GC
California
(Terry E. Van Gorder)
Visalia Plaza GC
California
R. D. Putnam
Vista Hills GC
Texas
R. Von Hagge, B. Devlin
Vista Royale GC
Florida
A. Hills
Vista Valencia Exec. GC
California
(Terry E. Van Gorder)

Vista Valley CC
California
T. G. Robinson
Vivary Park at Taunton
England
J. H. Stutt
Voisins, Golf de
France
T. C. Simpson
Volcano G&CC (r.9,a.9)
Hawaii
A. J. Snyder
Voyager Village GC
Wisconsin
W. J. Spear
V. P. I. GC (9)
Virginia
R. F. Loving

Wabash CC (a.9)
Michigan
A. Hills
Wabeek CC
Michigan
P. and R. Dye, J. Nicklaus
Waccabuc CC (r.)
New York
A. H. Tull
Wachusset CC
Massachusetts
D. J. Ross
Wack Wack GC (East and West courses)
Philippines
(James Black)
Wack Wack GC (r. East course)
Philippines
R. Kirby, G. Player
Waco Muni
Texas
R. Plummer
Waddesden Manor
Great Britain
T. Dunn
Wadena GC (r.9,a.9)
Minnesota
D. Herfort
Wagon Wheel
Illinois
E. L. Packard
Wahalla CC [now Willows CC]
New York
W. F. Mitchell
Wahconah CC (Original 9)
Massachusetts
W. E. Stiles, J. R. Van Kleek
Wahconah CC (a.9)
Massachusetts
G. S. Cornish, R. Armacost
Waialae CC
Hawaii
S. J. Raynor, C. H. Banks
Waialae CC (r.)
Hawaii
R.E. Baldock
Waikoloa Village GC (36)
Hawaii
R. T. Jones, Sr. and Jr.
Wailea GC (Blue and Orange courses)
Hawaii
A. J. Snyder
Wailua
Hawaii
(T. Shirai)
Wairakei GC
New Zealand
J.D. Harris, M. Wolveridge
Wakaya Island GC
Fiji
R. T. Jones, Jr.

Wake Forest CC
North Carolina
E. Hamm
Wakonda Club
Iowa
W. B. Langford, T. J. Moreau
Waldemere Hotel GC
New York
W. F. Mitchell
Walden G&TC
Ohio
W. F. Mitchell
Walden on Conroe CC
Texas
R. Von Hagge, B. Devlin
Walden Lake CC
Florida
(Bob Cupp)
Waldkirchen GC
Germany
D. Harradine
Wallasey Corporation Pitch and Putt
England
F. G. Hawtree
Wallasey GC
England
T. Norris
Wallasey GC (r.)
England
J. Braid
Wallasey GC (r.)
England
(Harold Hilton)
Walled Lake CC
Michigan
H. Collis
Wallingford CC (r.6)
Connecticut
A. Zikorus
Wallsend GC
England
(G. Snowball)
Walnut Creek CC
North Carolina
E. Maples
Walnut Creek CC
Texas
D. January, B. Martindale
Walnut Creek Muni
California
R. M. Graves
Walnut Grove GC
Indiana
W. Diddel
Walnut Hills CC
Michigan
J. A. Roseman
Walnut Hills CC (r.3)
Michigan
W. B. and G. H. Matthews
Walnut Hills CC
Missouri
F. Farley
Walnut Hills CC
Ohio
J. G. Harrison
Walnut Hills CC
Texas
P. D. Maxwell
Walpole CC (Former 9)
Massachusetts
E. F. Wogan
Walpole CC (New course)
Massachusetts
A. Zikorus
Walsall
England
A. Mackenzie
Walt Disney World Exec. GC (Wee Links; 6 holes)
Florida
R. Garl

Walt Disney World GC (Palm, Lake Buena Vista and Magnolia courses)
Florida
J. L. Lee
Walton Hall
England
J. J. F. Pennink
Walton Heath GC (Old and New courses)
England
W. H. Fowler
Walton-on-Thames
England
T. Dunn
Wampanoag CC
Connecticut
D. J. Ross
Wampatuck CC
Massachusetts
G. S. Cornish
Wanago CC (r.)
Pennsylvania
A. W. Tillinghast
Wannamoisett CC (Original course; n.l.e.)
Rhode Island
W. Campbell
Wannamoisett CC (New site)
Rhode Island
D. J. Ross
Wantage Golf Centre Par 3 GC
New Jersey
N. T. Psiahas
Wareham GC
Massachusetts
G. S. Cornish
Warm Springs Par 3 GC (Fremont; 9)
California
J. Fleming
Warm Springs Resort
California
H. M. and D. A. Rainville
Warner Robins AFB GC
Georgia
H. C. Moore
Warner Springs Resort
California
H. M. and D. A. Rainville
Warrenbrook CC
New Jersey
H. Purdy
Warren GC
Pennsylvania
C. E. Robinson
Warren Park GC (Exec. 9, 1978)
Illinois
K. Killian, R. Nugent
Warrenton CC
Virginia
R. P. Hines
Warren Valley CC
Michigan
D. J. Ross
Warrington
England
J. J. F. Pennink
Warrington G&CC
Pennsylvania
W. F. and D. W. Gordon
Warriors Path GC
Tennessee
G. W. Cobb
Warsash CC
England
S. V. Hotchkin, C. K. Hutchison, G. Campbell
Warwick CC (Original 9)
Rhode Island
D. J. Ross

Warwick CC (a.9)
Rhode Island
G. S. Cornish
Warwick CC
Virginia
W. F. and D. W. Gordon
Warwick Golf Centre
England
(D. G. Dunkley)
Warwick Hills Club
Michigan
J. G. Harrison
Warwick Hills Club (r.)
Michigan
J. L. Lee
Wasatch State Park GC
Utah
W. H. Neff
Wausau CC
Wisconsin
E. L. Packard
Wascana G&CC (r.)
Saskatchewan, Canada
C. E. Robinson
Washington CC (r.)
Connecticut
A. Zikorus
Washington CC
Ohio
(George Sargent)
Washington G&CC
Virginia
D. J. Ross
Washington G&CC (r. 3)
Virginia
A.M. Pulley
Washington G&CC
Virginia
(Admiral P.M. Rixey)
Washington G&CC (r.)
Virginia
F. Findlay
Washington G&CC (r.)
Viginia
W.S. Flynn
Washington G&CC (r.)
Virginia
A. Jamison
Washingtonian CC (36)
Maryland
R. Roberts
Washington New Town GC
England
J.D. Harris, P.W. Thomson, M. Wolveridge
Washington Park CC
Illinois
H. J. Tweedie
Washington Park Muni (9)
Wisconsin
T. Bendelow
Washington State University GC (9)
Washington
R. M. Graves
Washington Y&CC
North Carolina
E. Hamm
Washtenaw CC
Michigan
D. J. Ross
Washtenaw CC (r. 9, a. 9)
Michigan
W. B. and G. H. Matthews
Waskesiu GC
Saskatchewan, Canada
S. Thompson
Waskesiu GC (r.)
Saskatchewan, Canada
C. E. Robinson

Waterbury, CC of
Connecticut
D. J. Ross
Waterford GC
Ireland
W. Park, Jr.
Waterford GC (r.)
Ireland
J. Braid
Waterford GC (r.)
Ireland
E. Hackett
Waterford Park
West Virginia
X. G. Hassenplug
Watergap CC
Pennsylvania
R. White
Waterloo GC, Royal (36)
Belgium H. S. Colt
Waterloo GC, Royal
Belgium
F. W. Hawtree
Waterton National Park GC
Alberta, Canada
S. Thompson
Watertown CC (a.9)
Connecticut
G. S. Cornish, W. G. Robinson
Watertown CC (a.9)
Wisconsin
E. L. Packard
Waterville CC (Original 9)
Maine
O. E. Smith
Waterville CC (a.9)
Maine
G. S. Cornish, W. G. Robinson
Waterwood National GC
Texas
P. and R. Dye
Watsonville CC (27)
California
T. B. Harmon
Watsonville CC (27)
California
T. B. Harmon
Waubeeka Springs Golf Links
Massachussets
R. Armacost
Waubeek GC
Michigan
P. Dye, J. Nicklaus
Waukegan Willow CC
Illinois
L. Macomber
Waumbek Inn & CC
New Hampshire
R. M. Barton
Wausau CC
Wisconin
E. L. Packard
Waveland GC
Illinois
J. A. Roseman
Waveland Muni (r.)
Iowa
P. Coates
Wave Oak CC
Pennsylvania
J. G. Harrison
Waverley CC (r.)
Oregon
H. C. Egan
Waverley CC (r.)
Oregon
A. V. Macan
Waverly GC (a.9)
Iowa
R.M. Phelps

Wawasee GC
Indiana
W. Diddel
Wawashkamo GC (Mackinac Island)
Michigan
(Alex Smith)
Wawenock GC
Maine
W. E. Stiles, J. R. Van Kleek
Wawona Hotel GC
California
A. Mackenzie
Wayland CC (r.)
Massachusetts
W. F. Mitchell
Wayne CC
Nebraska
H. B. Hughes, R. Watson
Wayne CC (n.l.e.)
New Jersey
R. T. Jones
Wayne County Road Commission (r.)
Michigan
W. B. and G. H. Matthews
Wayne Golf Centre
New Jersey
N. T. Psiahas
Wayne Recreation Association GC
New York
E. L. Packard
Wayne Public Exec GC
Washington
A. Smith
Waynesboro CC (9)
Georgia
G. W. Cobb
Waynesboro CC
Mississippi
E. Stone
Waynesborough CC, Paoli
Pennsylvania
G. Fazio
Waynesboro CC (9), Waynesboro
Pennsylvania
E. B. Ault
Waynesville CC
North Carolina
(John Drake)
Wayzata CC
Minnesota
R. B. Harris
W. B. Homes Exec. GC
Florida
W. H. Dietch, Jr.
Weatherwax GC (36)
Ohio
A. Hills
Webb AFB GC
Texas
W. D. Cantrell
Webb Brook GC
Massachusetts
W. F. Mitchell
Webb Hill CC
Texas
L. Howard
Weber Park Par 3 GC (9)
Illinois
K. Killian, R. Nugent
Webhannett CC
Maine
E. F. Wogan
Webhannett CC (r.4)
Maine
G. S. Cornish
Webster GC [now Happy Acres]
New York
J. G. Harrison

Wedgefield Plantation GC
South Carolina
J. P. Gibson
Wedgewood CC
North Carolina
E. B. Ault
Wedgewood GC
Illinois
E. L. Packard
Wedgewood GC
Pennsylvania
W. F. and D. W. Gordon
Wee Burn CC
Connecticut
D. Emmet
Wee Burn CC (r.3)
Connecticut
G. S. Cornish, W. G. Robinson
Weequahic CC (Original 9)
New Jersey
G. Low
Weequahic CC (a. 9)
New Jersey
H. Purdy
Weidenbruck-Gutersloh GC
West Germany
B. Von Limburger
Weir Park GC
England
J. Braid
Wekiva GC
Florida
R. Von Hagge, B. Devlin
Welbech Abbey
Great Britain
T. Dunn
Welcombe Hotel GC
England
T. J. A. McAuley
Weld GC
Massachusetts
W. E. Stiles, J. R. Van Kleek
Welland CC [formerly Lookout Point CC]
Ontario, Canada
W. J. Travis
Wellesley CC (Original 9)
Massachusetts
D. J. Ross
Wellesley CC (r.)
Massachusetts
W. E. Stiles, J. R. Van Kleek
Wellesley CC (a.12)
Massachusetts
G. S. Cornish
Wellingborough GC
England
T. Williamson
Wellingborough GC (9)
England
F. W. Hawtree
Wellington CC [now Palm Beach Golf and Polo Club]
Florida
G. and T. Fazio
Wellington GC
Florida
R. Von Hagge, B. Devlin
Wellington GC
New Zealand
(J. S. Watson)
Wellman CC
South Carolina
E. Maples
Wells Muni (1975)
Nevada
A.J. Snyder
Wellshire GC
Colorado
D. J. Ross

Wells-next-the-Sea (approach and putt)
England
F. W. Hawtree
Welshpool GC
Wales
J. Braid, J. R. Stutt
Welwyn Garden City
England
F. W. Hawtree
Wembley
England
W. Park, Jr.
Wenatchee CC (a.9)
Washington
A. V. Macan
Wentworth-by-the-Sea (Original 9)
New Hampshire
D. J. Ross
Wentworth-by-the-Sea (a.9)
New Hampshire
G. S. Cornish, W. G. Robinson
Wentworth GC (East and West courses)
England
H. S. Colt, C. H. Alison, J. S. F. Morrison
Wentworth GC on Ille Perrot
Province of Québec, Canada
H. Watson
Wentworth GC "Short Course" (9)
England
C. K. Cotton
Wentworth Hall GC
New Hampshire
W. E. Stiles
Wepaug CC (r.)
Connecticut
A. Zikorus
Wesselman Park GC (9)
Indiana
E. B. Ault
West Bend CC (Original 9)
Wisconsin
W. B. Langford, T. J. Moreau
West Bend CC (a.9)
Wisconsin
D. Gill
West Branch GC (a.9)
Michigan
W. K. Newcomb
West Briar CC [now Westwood CC]
Virginia
A. H. Tull
Westbrook CC
New York
"Young" W. Dunn
Westbury GC
Oklahoma
D. January, B. Martindale
Westchester CC (36)
New York
W. J. Travis
Westchester CC (r.)
New York
W. S. Flynn
Westchester CC (r. 36 greens)
New York
T. Winton
Westchester CC (r.)
New York
A. H. Tull
Westchester CC (r.)
New York
J Finger
West Delta Park GC
Oregon
R. T. Jones, Sr. and Jr.
West End Exec. GC at Gainesville
Florida
J. E. O'Connor, Jr.

Western Area GC
Maryland
E. B. Ault
Western Gailes GC (Original course)
Scotland
W. Park, Jr.
Western Gailes GC (r.)
Scotland
F. W. Hawtree
Western G&CC
Michigan
D.J. Ross
Western Greens GC
Michigan
M. DeVries
Western Hills CC
California
H. M. and D. A. Rainville
Western Hills GC
Arkansas
H. C. Hackbarth
Western Hills GC
Texas
L. Howard
Western Illinois University GC (Original 9)
Illinois
R. B. Harris
Western Illinois University GC (a.9)
Illinois
K. Killian, R. Nugent
Western Park Muni
England
F. W. Hawtree
Western Turnpike GC
New York
(James Thomson)
Western Village GC
Oklahoma
F. Farley
Westfield CC (original 9)
Ohio
(Nelson Monical)
Westfield CC (r.9,a.27)
Ohio
G. S. Cornish, W. G. Robinson
Westfield G&CC (r.9,a.9)
New Brunswick, Canada
C. E. Robinson
Westhampton CC
New York
C. H. Banks
West Herts GC
England
T. Morris
West Herts GC
England
H. Vardon
West Herts GC (r.)
England
A. Mackenzie
Westhill (Aberdeen)
Scotland
J. J. F. Pennink
Westhill (Hampshire)
England
C. D. Lawrie
Westhill (Surrey)
England
W. Park, Jr.
West Hill CC
New York
H. Purdy
West Hills CC
Ohio
L. Macomber
West Hills Muni (n.l.e.)
Oregon
H. C. Egan

West Hove
England
J. Braid
West Kent GC
England
W. H. Fowler
Westlake CC (36)
California
T. G. Robinson
West Lake CC
Georgia
E. Maples
West Lancashire GC (r.)
England
C. K. Cotton
Westland Hills GC
Utah
W. H. Neff
West Middlesex GC
England
W. Park, Jr.
West Middlesex GC
England
F. G. Hawtree
Westminister GC (Original 9)
Massachusetts
M. L. Francis
Westmoor GC (r.; a.9)
Wisconsin
D. Gill
Westmoreland CC
Illinois
J. A. Roseman, Sr.
Westmoreland CC (r.)
Illinois
W. B. Langford, T. J. Moreau
Westmoreland CC (r.)
Illinois
A. W. Tillinghast
Westmoreland CC (r.)
Illinois
W. Diddel
Westmoreland CC (Verona; n.l.e.)
Pennsylvania
E. F. Loeffler, J. McGlynn
Westmoreland CC (Export; a. 12)
Pennsylvania
J. Finger
Westmoreland CC (Export)
Pennsylvania
X. G. Hassenplug, L. S. "Dick" Wilson
Westmoreland CC (Export; r.)
Pennsylvania
R. T. Jones
Westmoreland CC (r.a.12)
Pennsylvania
J. Finger
Westmoreland CC (Export; r.3)
Pennsylvania
F. Garbin
Westmoreland G&CC
Missouri
E. L. and R. B. Packard
Westmount G&CC (r.)
Ontario, Canada
C. E. Robinson
West Norfolk GC, Royal
England
H. C. Hutchinson
West Norfolk GC , Royal (r.)
England
C. K. Hutchison
Weston CC
Ontario, Canada
W. Park, Jr.

Weston GC
Massachusetts
D. J. Ross
Weston GC (a.2)
Massachusetts
G. S. Cornish
Westonbirt GC
England
(Monty Hearn)
Weston-Super-Mare
England
T. Dunn
Weston-Super-Mare (r.)
England
A. Mackenzie
West Orange GC
Florida
L. Clifton
West Orange Muni [formerly Mountain Ridge CC](Original 9; n.l.e.)
New Jersey
D. Hunter
West Ottawa GC
Michigan
W. B. and G. H. Matthews
Westover AFB GC [now Ludlow Muni]
Massachusetts
O. E. Smith, A. Zikorus
West Palm Beach CC
Florida
L. S. "Dick" Wilson
West Plains CC
Missouri
M. H. Ferguson
West Point (U.S. Military Academy) GC
New York
R. T. Jones
West Port CC
North Carolina
J. P. Gibson
Westport GC
New York
T. Winton
Westport GC
Ireland
F. W. Hawtree
West Runton GC (r.)
England
T. Williamson
West Shore G&CC
Michigan
(George B. Ferry)
West Surrey GC
England
W. H. Fowler
West Sussex GC
England
G. Campbell, S. Hotchkin, C. Hutchison
Westview CC (Original 9)
Florida
L. S. "Dick" Wilson
Westview CC (a.9)
Florida
M. Mahannah
Westview CC
Wisconsin
E. L. Packard
Westview GC (r.)
Ontario, Canada
R. and D. Moote
West View Park GC (9)
Wyoming
F. Hummel
West Village GC
Illinois
D. Bennett
Westward Ho! CC
California
(John Gurley and Hoagy Carmichael)

308

Westward Ho! (n.l.e.)
Illinois
H. J. Tweedie
Westward Ho! (r.)
Illinois
(Stewart Gardner)
Westward Ho! (Royal North Devon)
England
T. Morris
Westward Ho! (Royal North Devon; r.)
England
W. H. Fowler
Westward Ho! CC
South Dakota
E. L. Packard
West Went GC
England
J. F. Abercromby
West Wilmette Illuminated Par 3 GC
Illinois
J. A. Roseman, Sr.
West Wiltshire
England
J. H. Taylor
West Wiltshire (r.)
England
(Huggett & Coles)
West Winds GC (George AFB; 9)
California
R. E. Baldock
West Winds GC
Florida
J. L. Lee
Westwood CC
Missouri
H. D. Paddock, Sr.
Westwood CC (r.)
Missouri
M. H. Ferguson
Westwood CC
New Jersey
(Horace W. Smith)
Westwood CC
New York
W. E. Harries
Westwood CC (r.)
New York
G. S. Cornish
Westwood CC
Ohio
C. H. Alison
Westwood CC (r. 2, 1981)
Ohio
J. Kidwell, M. Hurdzan
Westwood CC
Texas
J. Finger
Westwood CC [formerly West Briar CC]
Virginia
A. H. Tull
Westwood GC
Georgia
(Charles W. Graves)
Westwood GC
Iowa
D. Gill
Westwood GC
Nebraska
H. W. Glissmann
Westwood Muni
Oklahoma
F. Farley
Westwoods Exec. GC
Connecticut
G. S. Cornish
Westwood Shores GC
Texas
(Carlton Gipson)

Wethersfield CC (Original course)
Connecticut
R. D. Pryde
Wethersfield CC (r.)
Connecticut
R. J. Ross
Wethersfield CC (r.1)
Connecticut
G. S. Cornish, W. G. Robinson
Wewoka Muni
Oklahoma
F. Farley
Wexford GC
Ireland
J. H. Stutt
Whaling City (New Bedford Muni; Original 9)
Massachusetts
D. J. Ross
Whaling City (New Bedford Muni; r. Original 9)
Massachusetts
W. F. Mitchell
Whaling City (New Bedford Muni; a.9)
Massachusetts
S. Mitchell
Wheatland CC (9)
Wyoming
F. Hummel
Wheatley GC
England
G. Duncan
Wheatley GC
England
A. Mackenzie
Wheatley Hills CC (r.)
New York
D. Emmet, A. H. Tull
Whetstone River GC
Ohio
R. LaConte, E. McAnlis
Whiffletree Hill GC
Michigan
A. M. Young
Whippoorwill CC (9)
New Hampshire
M. L. Francis
Whippoorwill CC
New York
D. J. Ross
Whippoorwill GC (r.)
New York
C. H. Banks
Whirlpool GC
Ontario, Canada
S. Thompson
Whirlpool GC (r)
Ontario, Canada
C. E. Robinson
Whiskey Creek Exec. GC
Florida
W. B. Lewis, Jr.
Whispering Hills
Florida
R. A. Anderson
Whispering Hills GC
New York
A. Craig
Whispering Lakes Par 3 GC
Florida
G. A. Pattison, Jr.
Whispering Palms CC (27)
California
H. M. and D. A. Rainville
Whispering Pines (East and West courses)
North Carolina
E. Maples

Whispering Pines CC (South course)
North Carolina
D. and E. Maples
Whispering Willows GC
Michigan
M. DeVries
Whistler Mountain GC
British Columbia
E. B. Seay, A. Palmer
Whitby GC (r.)
England
J. H. Stutt
White Barn GC
Utah
(Keith Downs)
White Bear Yacht Club (r.)
Minnesota
D. Herfort
White Beeches CC
New Jersey
W. J. Travis
White Beeches CC (r.)
New Jersey
A. H. Tull, W. F. Mitchell
White Birch Hills GC
Michigan
W. B. Matthews
White Bluffs of Whitney GC
Texas
L. Howard
White Cliffs GC
Massachusetts
G. S. Cornish
White Craigs
Scotland
W. Fernie
White Deer CC
Pennsylvania
(Kenneth J. Polakowski)
Whiteface Inn GC
New York
J. R. Van Kleek
Whitehaven CC
Tennessee
(John Frazier)
Whitehead GC
Northern Ireland
(A. B. Armstrong)
White Lakes CC
Kansas
H. Robb, Sr.
Whiteman AFB GC
Missouri
E. L. Packard
White Manor CC (New site)
Pennsylvania
W. F. and D. W. Gordon
Whitemarsh Valley CC [formerly Mount Airy CC]
Pennsylvania
G.C. Thomas, Jr. (Sam Heebner)
Whitemarsh Valley CC (r.)
Pennsylvania
W. S. Flynn
Whitemarsh Valley CC (r.)
Pennsylvania
D. J. Ross
White Mountain CC (Original 9)
Arizona
(Arthur A. Snyder)
White Mountain CC (South 9)
Arizona
A. J. Snyder
White Mountain CC (Cold Springs GC)
New Hampshire
G. S. Cornish, W. G. Robinson
White Mountain Muni
Wyoming
(Brauer and Associates)

White Path GC
Georgia
W. C. Byrd
White Pines CC
Illinois
J. L. Daray
White Pines GC (9)
Nevada
R. E. Baldock
White Plains GC
Maryland
J. P. Gibson
White Sands GC
New Mexico
L. Howard
Whitesbridge CC
California
R. E. Baldock
Whitewebb Muni (Enfield U.D.C.)
England
F. G. Hawtree
Whitford CC
Pennsylvania
W. F. and D. W. Gordon
Whitinsville CC
Massachusetts
D. J. Ross
Whitlock G&CC
Province of Québec, Canada
W. Park, Jr
Whitlock G&CC (r.18,a.9)
Province of Québec, Canada
H. Watson
Whitnall Muni
Wisconsin
G. Hansen
Whitney Estates
New York
C. B. Macdonald
Whitney Farms CC
Connecticut
H. and M. Purdy
Whit Sand Bay
England
W. Fernie
Whittier Narrows GC (27)
California
W. F. Bell
Wianno CC
Massachusetts
(Leonard Biles)
Wicham
Great Britain
T. Dunn
Wichita CC [now MacDonald Park] (Original course)
Kansas
J. Dalgleish
Wichita CC (r.)
Kansas
P.D. Maxwell
Wichita CC (r.)
Kansas
O. E. Smith
Wichita CC (New site)
Kansas
W. Diddel
Wichita Falls GC (r.)
Texas
R. Plummer
Wickenburg CC
Arizona
W. P. Bell
Wicklow GC (r.)
Ireland
E. Hackett
Widow Maker GC
South Carolina
R. F. Breeden

Wien GC
Austria
(M. C. Noskowski)
Wigan GC
England
J. J. F. Pennink
(The) Wigwam (Goodyear Park); (Blue and Gold courses)
Arizona
R. T. Jones
(The) Wigwam (Goodyear Park); West course)
Arizona
J. Hardin, G. Nash, R. F. Lawrence
Wigwam CC (r. 9, a. 9) (n.l.e.)
Arizona
A. J. Snyder
Wik-Auf-For GC
Germany
J. J. F. Pennink
Wikiup G&TC (9)
California
C. Glasson
Wilbraham CC
Massachusetts
W. Ogg, (Archibald Donald)
Wilcox Oaks CC
California
T. B. Harmon
Wildcat Cliffs CC
North Carolina
G. W. Cobb
Wildcat Run CC
Florida
E. B. Seay, A. Palmer
Wild Coast Holiday Inn GC
Transkei, South Africa
R.T. Jones, Jr.
Wildcreek GC
Nevada
R.M. Phelps, B. Benz
Wild Dunes GC [formerly Isle of Palms]
South Carolina
G. and T. Fazio
Wilderness CC
Florida
A. Hills
Wilderness Gardens GC [now Lazy H GC]
California
R. E. Baldock
Wilderness GC
England
J. Braid
Wilderness Valley GC
Michigan
W. B. and G. H. Matthews
Wildflower CC
Florida
L. Marshall
Wildflower GC (1975)
Missouri
K. Killian, R. Nugent
Wildwood CC
Florida
R. Garl
Wildwood CC
Kentucky
W. Diddel
Wildwood CC
New Jersey
W. E. Stiles, J. R. Van Kleek
Wildwood CC [formerly Hampton GC]
New York
F. Duane
Wildwood CC (Rush)
New York
A. Craig

Wildwood CC
North Carolina
E. Hamm
Wildwood CC (r.)
Ohio
A. Hills
Wildwood CC
Pennsylvania
E. F. Loeffler, J. McGlynn
Wildwood CC (r.)
Pennsylvania
W. F. and D. W. Gordon
Wildwood CC (r.2)
Pennsylvania
F. Garbin
Wildwood CC
South Carolina
R. F. Breeden
Wildwood CC
Texas
L. Howard
Wildwood GC
Ohio
A. Hills
Wildwood GC (r.)
Ohio
J. Kidwell, M. Hurdzan
Wildwood Muni (9)
Nebraska
(Robert Popp)
Wilkes Barre Muni
Pennsylvania
G. S. Cornish, W. G. Robinson
Willard CC
Ohio
R. LaConte, E. McAnlis
Willard GC
Ohio
H. D. Paddock, Sr.
William Sahm Park GC [formerly North Eastway]
Indiana
P. Dye
Williamsburg Colony Inn Par 3 GC (9)
Virginia
R. F. Loving
Williamsburg CC
Virginia
F. A. Findlay
Williamsburg CC (New site)
Virginia
W. F. and D. W. Gordon
Williamsburg Inn and Golden Horseshoe GC
Virginia
R. T. Jones
Williamson Creek Muni
Texas
J. Finger
Williamsport CC (r.)
Pennsylvania
A. W. Tillinghast
Williamsport CC (r.)
Pennsylvania
D. W. Gordon
Williamstown CC (9)
North Carolina
E. Hamm
Williamwood GC
Scotland
F. G. Hawtree
Willingboro CC
New Jersey
R. T. Jones
Willingdon GC
England
J. H. Taylor
Willingdon GC (r.)
England
A. Mackenzie

Willmar Exec. GC (a.9)
Minnesota
R. A. Anderson
Willowbrook CC
Alabama
L. Howard
Willow Brook CC
Florida
D. L. Wallace
Willowbrook CC
Pennsylvania
J. G. Harrison
Willow Brook CC
Texas
R. Plummer
Willow Brook CC (r.)
Texas
J. Finger
Willowbrook GC
New Jersey
W. F. and D. W. Gordon
Willow Brook, Sun City
Arizona
J. Hardin, G. Nash, G. and T. Fazio
Willow Creek CC
Utah
H. B. Hughes
Willow Creek CC (r.)
Utah
W. H. Neff
Willow Creek CC
Virginia
(Charles Schaelstock)
Willow Creek GC (a.9)
Iowa
R. N. Phelps
Willow Creek GC
North Carolina
W. C. Byrd
Willow Creek GC (Boone)
North Carolina
T. Jackson
Willow Creek, Sun City
Arizona
J. Hardin, G. Nash, G. and T. Fazio
Willowdale CC at Buffalo (9)
New York
O.E. Smith
Willowdale GC
Maine
E. F. Wogan
Willow GC (Huron-Clinton Metro Park)
Michigan
W. K. Newcomb
Willow Grove GC
Ohio
(George B. Ferry)
Willow Haven CC
North Carolina
G. W. Cobb
Willow Lakes G&CC
Florida
F. Bolton
Willow Lakes GC (a.18)
Florida
L. Clifton
Willow Muni
Michigan
W. K. Newcomb
Willow Oaks CC
Virginia
W. F. and D. W. Gordon
Willow Park CC
Alberta, Canada
N. Woods

Willow Park GC
California
R. E. Baldock
Willow Point G&CC
Alabama
(Thomas H. Nicol)
Willow Run GC
Ohio
J. Kidwell
Willows CC [formerly Wahalla CC]
New York
W. F. Mitchell
Willow Springs CC
Missouri
F. Farley
Willow Springs G&CC
Utah
R. B. Hughes
Willow Springs GC
Texas
(Vernon Schmidt)
Wilmette GC
Illinois
J. A. Roseman, Sr.
Wilmette Park GC
Illinois
J. A. Roseman, Sr.
Wilmette Park GC (r.)
Illinois
K. Killian, R. Nugent
Wilmington CC (North course)
Delaware
L. S. "Dick" Wilson
Wilmington CC (South course)
Delaware
R. T. Jones
Wilmington CC (n.l.e.)
Vermont
R. M. Barton
Wilmington Muni
North Carolina
D. J. Ross
Wilshire CC
California
N. Macbeth
Wilson CC
North Carolina
W. C. Byrd
Wilson Exec. GC
Ohio
J. Kidwell
Wilton Grove CC
New Jersey
A. W. Tillinghast
Wiltwyck CC
New York
R. T. Jones
Wimbledon
England
W. Park, Jr
Wimbledon (London Scottish)
England
"Old" W. Dunn
Wimbledon (London Scottish; r.)
England
T. Dunn
Wimbledon GC, Royal (r.)
England
H. S. Colt
Wimbledon GC, Royal (r.)
England
C. D. Lawrie
Winchester CC
Massachusetts
D. J. Ross
Winchester GC
Virginia
E. B. Ault

Windber GC
Pennsylvania
J. G. Harrison
Windbrook CC [formerly Mirror Lake CC](r.7,a.9)
Missouri
R. N. Phelps
Winchester CC
Virginia
F. Findlay
Windcrest GC
Texas
G. A. Hoffman
Windermere G&CC
Alberta, Canada
C. E. Robinson, (A. Olynyk)
Windermere GC
England
G. Lowe
Windham CC (a. 9)
New York
H. Purdy
Winding Creek GC
Michigan
W. B. and G. H. Matthews
Winding Hollow CC
Ohio
R. T. Jones
Windlesham Moor GC
England
T. C. Simpson
Windmill GC
Ohio
E. B. Ault
Windmill Hill GC
England
H. Cotton
Windsor Forest CC (9)
Georgia
G. W. Cobb
Windsor Gardens Exec. GC (9)
Colorado
H. B. Hughes
Windsor GC (r.)
Manitoba, Canada
J. A. Thompson
Windward Hills G&CC
Guam
W. F. Bell
Windyhill GC
Scotland
H. Cotton
Win Dyke CC (East course)
Tennessee
(John Frazier)
Win Dyke CC (West course)
Tennessee
W. W. Amick
Winewood GC
Florida
E. L. and R. B. Packard
Winged Foot (East and West courses)
New York
A. W. Tillinghast
Winged Foot (r. East and West courses)
New York
R. T. Jones
Winged Foot (r.3, West course)
New York
L. S. "Dick" Wilson
Winged Foot (r. West course)
New York
G. and T. Fazio
Winged Pheasant CC
New York
A. Craig
Winnemucca Muni
Nevada
R. E. Baldock

Winnesucket CC (a.9)
Rhode Island
G. S. Cornish, S. Mitchell
Winnetka Park GC
Illinois
C. D. Wagstaff
Winnetka Park GC (a. 9 Par 3)
Illinois
W. B. Langford
Winnetka Park GC (a. 18 Par 3)
Illinois
C. D. Wagstaff
Winnipeg GC (n.l.e.)
Manitoba, Canada
W. Park, Jr.
Winnipeg Hunt Club (n.l.e.)
Manitoba, Canada
W. Park, Jr.
Winona GC (9)
Minnesota
B. Knight
Winslow Muni
Arizona
G. A. Panks
Winslow Muni (9, 1980)
Arizona
A.J. Snyder
Winston Lake Par 3 GC
North Carolina
E. Maples
Winter Creek GC (a.9)
Michigan
W. B. and G. H. Matthews
Winter Hill
England
J. J. F. Pennink
Winter Park GC (9; n.l.e.)
Florida
J. D. Dunn
Winter Pines Exec. GC
Florida
L. Clifton
Winter Springs CC
Florida
J. L. Lee
Winters Run GC
Maryland
R. F. Loving
Winterwood GC
Nevada
L. S. "Dick" Wilson
Winthrop GC (r.)
Massachusetts
W. F. Mitchell, A. Zikorus
Winton CC
Virginia
E. B. Ault
Wittem G&CC (9)
Holland
F. W. Hawtree
Wittenberg GC
East Germany
B. Von Limburger, K. Hoffmann
Woburn (Duke's course)
England
J.J.F. Pennink, C.D. Laurie
Woburn (Dutchess course)
England
C. D. Lawrie, D. M. A. Steel
Woking GC
England
T. Dunn
Woking GC (r.)
England
J. Low, S. Paton
Wolf Creek GC
Kansas
M. H. Ferguson

310

Wolf Hollow CC
Pennsylvania
R. White

Wolf Laurel CC
North Carolina
W. B. Lewis

Wollaston CC (n.l.e.)
Massachusetts
G. Wright

Wollaston CC (r.)
Massachusetts
W. E. Stiles, J. R. Van Kleek

Wollaston CC (r.)
Massachusetts
W. F. Mitchell

Wollaston CC [now President's GC](r.)
Massachusetts
G. and T. Fazio

Wollaston CC (New site)
Massachusetts
G. and T. Fazio

Wollaton Park GC
England
T. Williamson

Wolverhampton GC (r.)
England
H. Cotton

Wolverine GC
Michigan
W. B. and G. H. Matthews

Woman's CC
Illinois
S. F. Pelchar

Womens National GC [now Glen Head CC]
New York
D. Emmet

Woman's National GC (r.)
New York
W. S. Flynn

Woodbine Downs GC
Ontario, Canada
H. Watson

Woodbranch CC
South Carolina
G. W. Cobb

Woodbridge CC
Connecticut
O. E. Smith

Woodbridge CC
North Carolina
J. P. Gibson

Woodbridge G&CC
California
B. Stamps

Woodbridge GC (a.9)
England
F. W. Hawtree

Woodbrook GC
Ireland
F. W. Hawtree

Woodcreek CC (Original and Cypress Creek courses)
Texas
(Bruce Littell)

Woodcreek CC (a. Brookollow course)
Texas
L. Howard

Woodcrest CC
New Jersey
W. S. Flynn

(The) Woodcrest CC
New York
W. F. Mitchell

Woodcrest CC (r.)
New York
F. Duane

Woodcrest CC
Texas
D. January, (B. Martindale)

Woodcrest Par 3 GC (r.)
Florida
R. A. Anderson

Woodhall Spa
England
H. Vardon

Woodhall Spa (r.)
England
H. S. Colt

Woodhall Spa (r.)
England
S. V. Hotchkin, C. K. Hutchison

Woodhaven CC
Connecticut
A. Zikorus

Woodhaven CC
Texas
L. Howard

Woodhill CC
Minnesota
D. J. Ross

Woodhill CC (r.)
Minnesota
G. S. Cornish, W. G. Robinson

Woodholme CC
Maryland
H. B. Strong

Woodholme CC (r.)
Maryland
H. B. Strong

Woodholme CC (r.)
Maryland
E. B. Ault

Woodlake CC
New Jersey
E. L. Packard

Woodlake CC [formerly Lake Surf CC]
North Carolina
E. and D. Maples

Woodlake CC
Texas
D. Muirhead

(The) Woodland CC (East and West courses)
Florida
R. Von Hagge, B. Devlin

Woodland CC (r.)
Massachusetts
D. J. Ross

Woodland CC (r.18)
Massachusetts
G. S. Cornish

Woodland CC
Rhode Island
G. S. Cornish

Woodland CC (r.)
West Virginia
J. G. Harrison

Woodland GC
Indiana
W. Diddel

Woodland GC (9)
Ohio
J. Kidwell, M. Hurdzan

Woodland Hills CC
California
W. P. Bell

Woodland Hills GC
Texas
D. January, (B. Martindale)

Woodland Manor GC
England
F. G. Hawtree

(The) Woodlands CC (West course)
Texas
J. L. Lee

(The) Woodlands CC (East course)
Texas
R. Von Hagge, B. Devlin

Woodlawn CC
Virginia
R. Roberts

Woodlawn GC
Oklahoma
F. Farley

Woodlawn Park Muni [now Pecan Valley Muni](27)
Texas
R. Plummer

Woodward Muni
Oklahoma
R. C. Dunning

Woodmere CC (r.)
New York
R. T. Jones

Woodmont CC
Colorado
J. P. Maxwell

Woodmont CC (Cypress and Pines courses)
Florida
R. Von Hagge, B. Devlin

Woodmont CC (r.)
Maryland
W. S. Flynn

Woodmont CC (a.9)
Tennessee
E. B. Ault

Woodmont CC at Bethesda
Maryland
A. H. Tull

Woodmont CC at Rockville (27)
Maryland
A. H. Tull

Woods Hole GC
Massachusetts
T. Winton

Woods Hole GC (r.)
Massachusetts
W. E. Stiles, J. R. Van Kleek

Woodson Bend GC
Kentucky
D. Bennett, J. F. Robinson

Woodson Park GC
Oklahoma
A. J. Jackson

Woodstock CC
New York
W. E. Stiles

Woodstock CC (Original 9)
Vermont
W. H. Tucker, Sr.

Woodstock CC (r.9,a.9)
Vermont
W. E. Stiles, J. R. Van Kleek

Woodstock CC (Existing course)
Vermont
R. T. Jones

Woodward Muni
Oklahoma
R. C. Dunning

Woodway CC
Connecticut
W. Park, Jr.

Woodway CC (r.1)
Connecticut
A. Zikorus

Woodway CC (r.5, a. ponds)
Connecticut
G. S. Cornish, W. G. Robinson

Woolacombe Bay Hotel (approach and putt)
England
F. G. Hawtree

Woonsocket CC [formerly Winnesucket CC](a.9)
Rhode Island
G. S. Cornish, S. Mitchell

Wooster CC (a.9)
Ohio
W. K. Newcomb

Worcester CC
Massachusetts
D. J. Ross

Worcester CC (r.2)
Massachusetts
G. S. Cornish

Worcester G&CC
England
A. Mackenzie

Worcestershire GC
England
A. Mackenzie

Workington
England
J. Braid

Worksop GC
England
T. Williamson

World of Golf (a. 19, 1979)
Kentucky
J. Kidwell, M. Hurdzan

World of Resorts, Inn GC
Texas
L. Howard

Worlingham GC
England
T. Dunn

Worlington and Newmarket, Royal
England
T. Dunn

Worlington and Newmarket, Royal (r.)
England
S. V. Hotchkin

Worplesdon GC
England
W. Park, Jr.

Worplesdon GC (R.)
England
J. F. Abercromby

Worplesdon GC
England
H. S. Colt

Worsley Muni
England
F. W. Hawtree

Worthing GC (Upper and Lower courses)
England
H. S. Colt

Wray CC
Colorado
F. Hummel

Wright Patterson AFB GC
Ohio
W. Diddel

Wright Patterson AFB GC (r.9,a.9)
Ohio
A. G. McKay

Wright Patterson AFB GC (a.9)
Ohio
E. L. Packard

Wright Patterson AFB GC (r.)
Ohio
J. Kidwell

Wuppertal GC (r.)
Germany
B. Von Limburger

Wyandot Muni (n.l.e)
Ohio
D. J. Ross

Wyckoff Park CC [formerly Mt. Tom] (Original course)
Massachusetts
D. J. Ross

Wyckoff Park CC [formerly Mt. Tom] (New course)
Massachusetts
A. Zikorus

Wykagyl CC
New York
L. E. Van Etten

Wykagyl CC (r.)
New York
R. White

Wykagyl CC (r.)
New York
A. W. Tillinghast

Wykagyl CC (r.)
New York
D. J. Ross

Wykagyl CC (r.)
New York
H. Purdy

Wyke Green GC
England
F. G. Hawtree

Wyndemere Par 3 G&CC
Florida
A. Hills

Wyndhurst Club
Massachusetts
W. E. Stiles, J. R. Van Kleek

Wynding Brook CC [formerly Atzinachson CC](a.2)
Pennsylvania
E. V. Ternyey

Wyndwyck CC
Michigan
A. Hills

Wyoming Valley CC
Pennsylvania
A. W. Tillinghast

Wytheville CC (9)
Virginia
F. Findlay

Yacht Exec. GC
Florida
C. H. Adams

Yadkin CC
North Carolina
E. Hamm

Yadkinville CC
North Carolina
E. Hamm

Yahara Hills (East and West courses)
Wisconsin
K. Killian, R. Nugent

Yahata CC
Japan
K. Fujita

Yahnundasis GC
New York
W. J. Travis

Yahnundasis GC (r.5)
New York
W. F. and D. W. Gordon

Yakima CC
Washington
A. V. Macan

Yakima CC (r.)
Washington
T. G. Robinson

311

Yale University GC
Connecticut
C. B. Macdonald, S. J. Raynor, C. Banks

Yarra Yarra GC
Australia
A. Mackenzie, A. Russell

Yeaman's Hall Club
South Carolina
S. J. Raynor

Yellowstone G&CC
Montana
R. T. Jones

Yelverton
England
W. H. Fowler

Yolo Fliers Club
California
R. E. Baldock

Yomiuri CC (Nishinomiym; 36)
Japan
S. Inouye

Yomiuri CC (Tokyo)
Japan
S. Inouye

Yorba Linda CC
California
H. M. and D. A. Rainville

York, CC of
Pennsylvania
D. J. Ross

York, CC of (r.)
Pennsylvania
W. S. Flynn

York Downs G&CC (Original course)
Ontario, Canada
C. H. Alison

York Downs G&CC (r. Original course)
Ontario, Canada
S. Thompson

York Downs G&CC (New site; 27)
Ontario, Canada
G. S. Cornish, W. G. Robinson

York G&CC
Maine
D. J. Ross

York GC, Royal [now St. Georges]
Ontario, Canada
S. Thompson

York Temple GC (r.)
Ohio
J. Kidwell, M. Hurdzan

Yorktown CC (r.)
Virginia
W. S. Flynn

Yosemite Lakes CC
California
R. E. Baldock

Youghioghenny CC
Pennsylvania
W. Park, Jr.

Youngstown CC
Ohio
D. J. Ross

Youngstown CC (r.2)
Ohio
G. S. Cornish, W. G. Robinson

Yowani CC
Australia
(Al Howard)

Yucaipa Valley CC
California
W. F. Bell

Yuma East
Arizona
W. K. Bowen

Yuma G&CC
Arizona
W. F. and W. P. Bell

Zanesville CC (r.)
Ohio
O. E. Smith

Zapata Falls GC
Colorado
R. Von Hagge, B. Devlin

Zaragoza GC
Spain
F. W. Hawtree

Z Boaz GC
Texas
J. Bredemus

Z Boaz GC (r.)
Texas
R. Plummer

Zellwood Station
Florida
W. Maddox

Zintel Canyon GC
Washington
R. W. Fream

Zion Park District GC
Illinois
E. L. Packard

Zoar Village GC
Ohio
G. S. Cornish, W. G. Robinson

Zollner GC (Tri State College)
Indiana
R. D. Beard

Zoute GC, Royal
Belgium
H. S. Colt

Zumikon-Zuerich
Switzerland
D. Harradine

Zumikon-Zuerich (r.)
Switzerland
D. Harradine

Zurich GC
Switzerland
T. Williamson

Zurich GC (r.)
Switzerland
T. C. Simpson

Zurich-Hittnau G&CC
Switzerland
B. Von Limburger

Zur Vahr GC (Garlstedter course)
West Germany
B. Von Limburger

With some 20,000 links and courses in existence around the world, there are many layouts yet to be identified and included in the master list. This compilation is an ongoing project. The authors welcome additions, deletions and corrections so that an even more accurate and complete listing can be prepared.

ARCHITECTS' ASSOCIATIONS

The American Society of Golf Course Architects, founded by thirteen men in 1947, was the first professional organization of course designers in America. Robert Bruce Harris was elected the first president while Donald Ross served as honorary president. An earlier organization, the International Society of Golf Architects, had existed in Great Britain in the 1920s but disbanded during World War II.

Qualifications for membership in the ASGCA included experience (six years on the job) and accomplishemnt (responsibility for five finished designs). Consequently membership grew slowly. But over the years, the majority of prominent course architects in North America became members.

Critics of the ASGCA claimed it perpetuated only its own membership, not the art or practice of design. Perhaps, like any professional organization, the ASGCA in the beginning did concentrate on membership affairs; and its first few annual meetings were get-togethers at golf resorts for a few days of camaraderie and golf. But by the early 1950s the group was undertaking serious discussions of issues pertinent to course design and issuing public policy statements on some issues.

For example, in 1953 the ASGCA resolved some basic standards for course architecture, favoring strategic design, the placement of hazards to provide minimum interference to high handicap golfers and green bunkering that didn't sacrifice the need for accuracy in the name of easy maintenance. The next year it publicized the membership's opposition to a federal tax on club memberships.

In 1956 the ASGCA stated its opposition to the rapid rise in use of motorized golf carts, feeling they damaged courses, compromised design and maintenance, and diminished much of the charm of the game in terms of reduced exercise and companionship. The Society urged the use of golf carts only by those with a medical need. It was a parting shot on a controversy that would last many more years.

Still, despite public positions and promotion of the profession through articles, advertisements and appearances, the Society remained a once-a-year activity for most members until 1970, the year of E. Lawrence Packard's presidency.

The public relations firm of Selz, Seabolt, Inc. of Chicago was retained to conduct full-time relations for the Society, and one of its staff members was named executive director of the ASGCA. He was Paul Fullmer, a Notre Dame graduate in journalism who happened to be married to the daughter of course architect Percy Clifford. Fullmer, who remained as the executive director of the ASGCA throughout the seventies assisted in the institution of a number of dynamic changes under the direction of Packard and subsequent presidents.

Committees were formed to address the problems and challenges of course design:

· The Foundation Committee under chairman E. L. Packard collected funds to establish a research project directed by Dr. Albert E. Dudek of the University of Florida on the effect of heavy metals in waste water used for irrigation. In 1978 this committee also cosponsored the first conference on the use of waste water for turfgrass irrigation.

· The Environmental Committee, chaired by Philip Wogan, a graduate biologist, prepared a widely circulated White Paper on the impact of golf courses and their construction on the environment.

· The Design Committee, chaired by Edmund Ault, prepared comprehensive design standards for consideration by members.

· The Professional Development Committee, cochaired by David Gill and Dr. Michael Hurdzan, organized seminars at annual meetings and devised a limited form of certification for course architects.

· The Hall of Fame Committee, chaired by Roger Rulewich, established a display showing the history of course architecture at the Hall of Fame, Pinehurst, North Carolina.

· The Awards Committee, chaired by Albert Zikorus, initiated an annual Donald Ross Award for outstanding contributions to golf and its architecture. Recipients subsequently included Robert Trent Jones, a founding member of the Society; Herbert Warren Wind, noted writer; Herb and Joe Graffis, founders of the National Golf Foundation; Joe Dey, former director of the USGA and PGA tour commissioner; and Gerald H. Micklem, former captain of the Royal and Ancient, president of the English Golf Union and chairman of the Rules Committee of the Royal and Ancient. The award to Micklem was presented at Gleneagles, Scotland, during the Society's pilgrimage in 1980 to Dornoch, the home of Donald Ross.

The American Society of Golf Course Architects has exerted a powerful, if subtle, influence upon the profession of course design in North America and on public perceptions of the field. A counterpart was created in Britain in 1970 with the formation of the British Association of Golf Course Architects. Philip Mackenzie Ross was its first president.

BIBLIOGRAPHY

Bibliography 1

Several are out of print but are obtainable at libraries or through a "search."

Baron, Harry. *Golf Resorts of the U.S.A.* New York: The New American Library, 1967.

Bartlett, Michael, and Roberts, Tony. *The Golf Book.* New York: Arbor House, 1980.

Bauer, Aleck. *Hazards, Those Essential Elements in a Golf Course Without which the Game Would Be Tame and Uninteresting.* Chicago: Toby Rubovits, 1913.

Braid, James. *Advanced Golf.* London: Methuen, 1908.

Browning, Robert. *A History of Golf.* New York: E. P. Dutton, 1955.

Clark, Robert. *Golf: A Royal and Ancient Game.* London: Macmillan, 1899.

Colt, H. S., and Alison, C. H. *Some Essays on Golf Course Architecture.* New York: Charles Scribner's Sons, 1920.

Colville, George M. *Five Open Champions and The Musselburgh Golf Story.* Musselburgh, Scotland: Colville Books, 1980.

Cornish, G. S., and Robinson, W. G. *Golf Course Design, An Introduction.* Amherst: Cornish-Robinson. Distributed by National Golf Foundation, North Palm Beach, Florida. 1975, Reprinted 1979.

Cousins, Geoffrey. *Golf in Britain.* London: Routledge and Kegan Paul, 1975.

Darwin, Bernard. *James Braid.* London: Hodder and Stoughton, 1952.

———. *The Golf Courses of the British Isles.* London: Duckworth & Co., 1910.

Darwin, Bernard; Campbell, Sir Guy; and others. *A History of Golf in Britain.* London: Cassel and Co. Ltd., 1952.

Davis, William H., and Editors of *Golf Digest. Great Golf Courses of the World.* Norwalk, Conn.: Golf Digest, 1974.

Dawson, Taylor. *St. Andrews, Cradle of Golf.* London: A. S. Barnes & Co., 1976.

Dobereiner, Peter. *The Glorious World of Golf.* New York: McGraw-Hill, 1973.

Evan, Webster. *Encyclopedia of Golf.* New York: St. Martin's Press, 1971.

Everard, H. S. C. *A History of the Royal and Ancient Golf Club, St. Andrews from 1754–1900.* Edinburgh: William Blackwood, 1907.

Finger, Joseph S. *The Business End of Building or Rebuilding a Golf Course.* Houston: Joseph S. Finger Assoc. 1972. Distributed by National Golf Foundation, North Palm Beach, Florida.

Gill, Garrett D. *Golf Course Design and Construction Standards.* College Station, Texas: Texas A & M University, 1977.

Graffis, Herb. *Esquire's World of Golf—What Every Golfer Must Know.* New York: Esquire, Inc. in association with Trident Press, 1933; revised 1965.

———. *The P.G.A.* New York: Thomas Y. Crowell, 1975.

Grant, Donald. *Donald Ross of Pinehurst and Royal Dornoch.* Golspie, Scotland: The Sutherland Press, 1973.

Grimsley, Will. *Golf—Its History, People & Events.* Englewood Cliffs, N.J.: Prentice-Hall, 1966.

Hamilton, E. A., Preston, C., and Laney, A. *Golfing America.* Garden City, New York: Doubleday and Co., Inc., 1958.

Henderson, I. T., and Stirk, D. I. *Golf in the Making.* London: Henderson and Stirk, Ltd., 1979.

Huggins, Percy, ed. *The Golfer's Handbook 1971.* Glasgow: The Golfer's Handbook, 1971. Printed annually.

Hunter, Robert. *The Links.* New York, London: Charles Scribner's Sons, 1926.

Hutchinson, Horace G. *Fifty Years of Golf.* New York: Charles Scribner's Sons, 1919.

———. *Golf.* Badminton Series. London: Longmans, Green & Co., 1895 and other years.

———, ed. *Golf Greens and Greenkeeping.* London: George Newnes and Country Life, 1906.

Jenkins, Dan. *The Best 18 Golf Holes in America.* New York: Delacorte Press, 1966.

Jones, Rees L., and Rando, Guy L. *Golf Course Developments.* Washington, D.C.: Urban Land Institute Technical Bulletin 70, 1974.

Jones, Robert Tyre. *Golf Is My Game.* Garden City, New York: Doubleday and Co., Inc., 1960.

Kavanagh, L. V. *History of Golf in Canada.* Ontario: Fitzhenry & Whiteside Ltd., 1973.

Leach, Henry. *Great Golfers in the Making* (By 34 Famous Players). Philadelphia: George W. Jacobs & Co., 1907.

Low, John L. *Concerning Golf.* London: Hodder and Stoughton Ltd., 1903.

Macdonald, Charles Blair. *Scotland's Gift—Golf.* New York, London: Charles Scribner's Sons, 1928.

Mackenzie, Dr. A. *Golf Architecture.* London: Simpkin, Marshall, Hamilton, Kent & Co., Ltd., 1920.

Mahoney, Jack. *The Golf History of New England.* Framingham, Mass.: New England Golf, Wellesly Press, Inc., 1973.

Martin, H. B. *Fifty Years of American Golf.* 2nd ed. New York: Argosty-Antiquarian Ltd., 1966.

McCormack, Mark H. *The Wonderful World of Professional Golf.* New York: Atheneum, 1973.

Miller, Dick. *America's Greatest Golfing Resorts.* Indianapolis, N.Y.: Bobbs-Merrill, 1977.

Montague, W. K. *The Golf of Our Fathers.* Grand Rapids, Minnesota: Grand Rapids Herald Review, 1952.

Mulvoy, Mark, and Spander, Art. *Golf: The Passion and the Challenge.* New York: Rutledge Books for Prentice Hall, 1977.

Murdoch, Joseph F. *The Library of Golf* 1743–1966. Detroit: Gale Research Co., 1968. Supplement 1978.

Murdoch, Joseph F., and Seagle, Janet. *Golf, A Guide to Information Sources.* Detroit: Gale Research Co., 1979.

Park, Wiliam, Jr. *The Art of Putting.* Edinburgh: James J. Gray, 1920.

———. *The Game of Golf.* London: Longmans, Green & Co., 1896.

Pennink, Frank. *Golfer's Companion.* London: Cassell, 1962.

Price, Charles, ed. *The American Golfer.* New York: Random House, 1964.

Price, Charles. *The World of Golf.* New York: Random House, 1962.

Robertson, James K. *St. Andrews—Home of Golf.* St. Andrews, Fife, Scotland: J & G Innes, Ltd., 1967.

Ryde, P.; Steel, D. M. A.; and Wind, H. W. *Encyclopedia of Golf.* New York: Viking Press, 1975.

Scharff, Robert, and Editors of *Golf Magazine. Encyclopedia of Golf.* New York: Harper & Row, 1970.

Scott, Tom. *The Concise Dictionary of Golf.* New York: Mayflower Books, 1978.

Scott, Tom, ed. *A. A. Guide to Golf in Great Britain.* London: Octopus Books, 1977.

Simpson, Tom. *The Game of Golf.* Vol. IX. The Lonsdale Library, New York: A. S. Barnes, revised 1951.

Sorenson, Gary L. *The Architecture of Golf.* College Station, Texas: By the Author, Department of Environmental Design, Texas A & M, 1976.

Steel, Donald. *Golf Facts and Feats.* London: Guinnes Superlatives Ltd., 1980.,

———. *The Golf Course Guide.* Glasgow, London: Collins with Daily Telegraph, revised 1980.

Steel, Donald; Ryde, Peter; and Wind, Herbert Warren. *The Shell International Encyclopedia of Golf.* London: E. Bury Press and Pelham Books, 1975.

Sutton, Martin, ed. *The Book of the Links.* London: W. H. Smith & Son, 1912.

Sutton, Martin A. F., ed. *Golf Course Design, Construction and Upkeep.* Reading, England: Sutton and Sons, Ltd., 1950.

Thomas, George C., Jr. *Golf Architecture in America—Its Strategy and Construction.* Los Angeles: The Times-Mirror Press, 1927.

Ward-Thomas, Pat. *The Royal and Ancient.* Edinburgh: Scottish Academic Press, 1980.

Ward-Thomas, Pat, and others. *The World Atlas of Golf.* New York: Random House, 1976.

314

Wethered, H. N., and Simpson, T. *The Architectural Side of Golf.* London: Longmans, Green & Co., 1929.

Wild, Roland. *Golf, The Loneliest Game.* Vancouver: Mitchell Press, Ltd., 1969.

Wind, Herbert Warren, ed. *The Complete Golfer.* New York: Simon & Schuster, 1954.

Wind, Herbert Warren. *The Story of American Golf.* New York: Alfred A. Knopf, 1975, 3rd edition.

Bibliography 2
Selected Articles in Periodicals
(*Denotes an article on one or more golf course architects)

Bartlett, Michael. "A Short Look at a Lot of Golf History." *Golf Journal,* January/February 1977.

———. "A Tradition in the Balance." *Golf Journal,* March 1977.

Brown, Cal. "How to be an Armchair Golf Architect." *Golf Digest,* November/December 1972.

Brown, Gwilyn S., "Golf's Battling Architects" (Dick Wilson and R. T. Jones) *Sports Illustrated* July 2, 1962.

Cornish, Geoffrey S. "Golf at the Town Dump." *Parks and Recreation,* May 1977.

*Dann, Mike. "Donald Ross, Giant in Golf." *Golf World,* November 29 and December 6, 1974.

Dunn, Tom. "Random Notes by Tom Dunn" *Professional Golfer,* April and May 1969.

Edmonson, Jolee. "Short Course, Long Future." *Golf Magazine,* February 1977.

English, John P. "Dorset's Claim as Oldest Club." *Golf Journal,* September 1965.

Finegan, James. "Emerald Golf—Golf in Ireland." *Golf Journal,* January/February 1977.

*Goodner, Ross. "Joe Lee's Course Designs are Challenging But Fun." *Golf Digest,* February 1981.

*Hannigan, Frank. "Golf's Forgotten Genius" (A. W. Tillinghast). *Golf Journal,* May 1974.

Hawtree, Frederick W. "British Golf Course Architecture." *Golf Superintendent,* January 1975.

Hurdzan, Michael J. "Designers Forum." *Golf Business,* 1979, 1980.

———. "So You Want to be a Golf Course Architect." *Golf Business,* March 1980.

Jenkins, Dan, "The Course that Jack Built" *Sports Illustrated, Oct. 14, 1974.*

Jonah, Kathy. "Is Your Course Designed for Women?" *Golf Digest,* May 1976.

Jones, Rees. "Hazards." *Golf Magazine,* November 1978.

Jones, Robert Trent. "The Rise and Fall of Penal Architecture." *Golf Journal,* April 1974.

*Lacerda, John. "He Drives Golfers Crazy on Purpose" (Stanley Thompson). *Saturday Evening Post,* June 8, 1946.

Levy, Joseph. "A Recreation Renaissance." *Parks and Recreation,* December 1977.

Littler, Frank. "The Sun Never Sets—Golf Around the World." *Golf Journal,* March 1977.

Packard, E. Lawrence. "Golf Course Design Principles." *Golf Superintendent,* August 1970.

*Palmer, Arnold. "A Good Golf Course Should Challenge the Mind" (Edwin Seay). *Golf Magazine,* May 1976.

*Pearson, David. "You Aren't Playing the Course, You're Playing the Designer." *Esquire,* April 1969.

*Peper, George. "Jack's Other Career." *Golf Magazine,* March 1981.

"Robert Trent Jones." *Golf Magazine,* February 1976.

*Saltzstein, Rob. "Letting Nature Make a Course (Alister Mackenzie). *Golf Journal,* April 1977.

Seay, Edwin B. "Master Planning for Golf Course Construction." *Golf Journal,* July 1977.

Seitz, Nick. "The Changing State of the Game." *Golf Digest,* June 1979.

*Shecter, Leonard. "The Jones Idea of a Golf Course." *The New York Times Magazine,* July 7, 1968.

Simpson, Tom. "John's Principles of Golf Architecture Stand Up." *Golfdom,* May 1955. Reprinted from *Golf Monthly,* Edinburgh.

*Sommers, Robert. "Charles Blair Macdonald." *Golf Journal,* June 1975.

Tatum, Frank D., Jr. "The Decline of Design." *Golf Journal,* May 1976.

"The United States Golf Association—A Group Tradition." *Golf Journal,* January/February 1976.

Weiss, Don. "In the Beginning." *Golf Journal,* March 1977.

Wind, Herbert Warren. "A Calling for Correct Proportions." *Golf Journal,* July 1977.

———. "Changing Golf Scene." *Golf Digest,* March, April and May 1972.

———. "Linksland and Meadowland." *The New Yorker,* August 4, 1951.

———. "North to the Links of Dornoch." *The New Yorker,* June 6, 1964.

———. "Pete Dye: Improving on Mother Nature." *Golf Digest,* May and June 1978.

———. "The Masters." *Sports Illustrated,* April 4, 1955.

———. "Understanding Golf Course Architecture." *Golf Digest,* November, December 1966.

———. "Watson, Weather and Muirfield." *The New Yorker,* August 11, 1980.

Bibliography 3
Sources of Related Publications

1. Two periodicals no longer in circulation with which golf architects Max Behr, Walter Travis and A. W. Tillinghast were associated contain articles on course design and can be found in libraries. They are:

    American Golfer
    Golf Illustrated

2. *National Golf Foundation Publications:* The National Golf Foundation, Inc., 200 Castlewood Drive, North Palm Beach, Florida 33408, Don A. Rossi, Executive Director and Harry Eckhoff, Director of Information Services, is the nation's clearinghouse for golf information. The Foundation has many publications on course development, several of which contain historical material.

3. *The Golf Development Council,* 3 The Quadrant, Richmond, Surrey, England T.W. 91BY. The Secretary, W. D. Hughes, offers services in Great Britain similar to those of the NGF in the United States.

4. *The American Society of Golf Course Architects,* 221 North LaSalle Street, Chicago, Illinois 60601, Paul Fullmer, Executive Secretary, distributes publications on golf course development.

5. *Bibliographies:*
    Murdoch, Joseph F. *The Library of Golf* 1743–1966. Detroit: Gale Research Co., 1968. Supplement 1978.
    Murdoch, Joseph F., and Seagle, Janet. *Golf, A Guide to Information Sources.* Detroit: Gale Research Co.,1979.

6. *Turfgrass Science:*
    Beard, James B. *Turfgrass Science and Culture.* Englewood Cliffs, N.J.: Prentice-Hall, 1973.
    Daniel, W. H. and Freeborg, R. P. *Turf Managers Handbook.* Cleveland, Ohio: The Harvest Publishing Co., 1979.
    Hanson, A. A., and Juska, F. V., ed. *Turfgrass Science.* Madison, Wisc.: American Society of Agronomy, 1969.
    Madison, John H. *Practical Turfgrass Management.* New York: Van Nostrand-Reinhold Co., 1971.
    ———. *Principles of Turfgrass Culture.* New York: Van Nostrand-Reinhold Co., 1971.
    Musser, Burton H. *Turf Management.* McGraw-Hill, 1950 and 1962.
    Piper, C. V., and Oakley, R. A. *Turf for Golf Courses.* New York: The Macmillan Co., 1917 and 1929.

ACKNOWLEDGMENTS

The authors are gratified by the immense assistance so many persons gave them. It seems almost as though the world of golf yearned to contribute to a history of course architecture, a subject never written on at length before.

Nearly every course architect in North America responded to our requests for information about themselves, as did every colleague we reached in Great Britain, Ireland and on the continent of Europe. Descendants of architects now deceased also responded, as did friends and strangers, golf course superintendents, professional golfers and others in the business world of golf.

Six names stand out as links to the publisher: William G. Robinson, course architect and associate of Cornish for many years, who prepared several of the sketches and urged that the manuscript be prepared; Naomi H. Gillison of West Vancouver, Canada, who persuaded us to persevere; Dr. T. T. Kozlowski of the University of Wisconsin, who persuaded us to find a publisher; Kathryn R. Buckheit of Amherst, Massachusetts, who rearranged many passages and typed the manuscript; Richard Bartholomae of Manchester, Vermont, who instructed us in methods of finding a publisher; and finally, Heinz Eller of New York, who found a firm whose staff was filled with golfers deeply interested in the subject.

We must remark on the help Cameron Dunn, retired professional of the Carlisle Country Club, Pennsylvania, gave us in providing otherwise unavailable information concerning his ancestors, the Dunns of Musselburgh and Royal Blackheath, who were pioneer designers on both sides of the Atlantic.

Here is a partial list of those whose help we should acknowledge. Included with the list are those members of the American Society of Golf Course Architects (ASGCA) and the British Association of Golf Course Architects (BAGCA) who researched material and checked innumerable points for us in addition to furnishing the information on themselves that appears in the biographies and appendix:

J. W. L. Adams, Henley on Thames, England (author of "Willie Park, Jr. and His Family," unpublished paper)
Robert Alves, North Olmstead, Ohio (brother of Grange Alves)
William W. Amick, ASGCA
Don B. Austin, Texas A & M University
Charles J. Backus, Springfield, Massachusetts
Paul Barratt, CC of New Bedford, Massachusetts
Ted M. Bishop, Phil Harris GC, Indiana
Norman Blackburn, Burbank, California
Richard C. Blake, Woodstock CC, Vermont
Elmer C. Border, El Cabellero CC, California
Jean Bryant, director Ralph W. Miller Golf Library, City of Industry, California
Orin E. Burley, Wharton School of Business, Pennsylvania
John Campbell, Foxhill GC, Surrey, England
Elmer O. Cappers, The Country Club, Massachusetts
William P. Carey, Florida State Golf Association
Steven Carlson, San Jose CC, California
Percy Clifford, ASGCA
George M. Colville, Musselburgh, Scotland (author of 5 Open Champions and the Musselburgh Golf Story)
Martin J. Connelly, Wykagyl CC, New York
Henry Cotton, Penina, Portugal
Sidney T. Cox, Ives Hill GC, New York
John Cronin, Cocheco GC, New Hampshire
Allan J. Cump, Amherst, Massachusetts
Jack Daray, Jr., El Cajon, California (son of Jack Daray)
J. B. Devany, Jr., Allen Park, Michigan
James Diorio, Manchester CC, New Hampshire
Mrs. Gordon Dunn, Lake Placid, New York (daughter-in-law of Seymour Dunn)
Harry C. Eckhoff, The National Golf Foundation
Ashton G. Eldredge, Huntington CC, Long Island, New York
William Emerson, The Chevy Chase Club, Maryland
Peter Engelhart, Berkeley, California (grandson of Max Behr)
Daniel England, The Pittsfield CC, Massachusetts
John English, Eastward Ho!, Massachusetts
Gerald Faubel, Saginaw CC, Michigan
David Fearis, The CC of Peoria, Illinois
G. Ward Fenley, The Albuquerque (New Mexico) Journal
John Fleming, Olympic CC, California (son of Jack Fleming)
Marjorie M. Ford, librarian, Ralph W. Miller Golf Library, City of Industry, California
Ronald J. Foulis, Washington, D.C. (son of Robert Foulis)
Paul Fullmer, ASGCA
Mrs. F. Paul Gardner, Indian Wells, California (daughter of George C. Thomas)
Miss Holly Gleason, Shaker Heights, Ohio
David W. Gordon, ASGCA
(the late) William F. Gordon, ASGCA
David Gourlay, Thornhill G&CC, Ontario, Canada
Herb Graffis, golf writer and former editor Golfdom, Florida
Donald Grant, Royal Dornoch GC, Scotland
Robert Grant, Braeburn CC, Massachusetts
Dr. Fred V. Grau, turfgrass scientist, Maryland
Robert M. Graves, ASGCA
Bryan G. Griffiths, Great Britain
Harland C. Hackbarth, Ft. Worth, Texas (son of Herman C. Hackbarth)
Joseph Hadwick, CC/Lincoln, Nebraska

Brinley M. Hall, The Myopia Hunt Club, Massachusetts
J. Kennedy Hamill, Adventures in Golf, New Hampshire
Robert E. Hanna, Northern California Golf Association
William Harding, The Kittansett Club, Massachusetts
John C. Harper II, Pennsylvania State University
Frederick W. Hawtree, BAGCA
Martin Hawtree, BAGCA
C. Thomas Hebert, Riviera CC, California
Bruce Herd, Ft. Myers, Florida
Aimee L. Herpel, University City, Missouri (widow of Homer Herpel)
Cyril Hewertson, O.B.E., Walton Heath GC, England
Dr. Thomas K. Hitch, Waialae CC, Hawaii
Arthur T. "Red" Hoffman of R.T. Jones Inc.
Donald Hogan, Seattle, Washington
Edward Horton, Westchester CC, New York
Howard C. Hosmer, Locust Hill CC, New York
Neil S. Hotchkin, Woodhall Spa GC, England (son of S. V. Hotchkin)
Henry B. Hughes, Denver, Colorado
W. D. Hughes, The Golf Development Council, England
Dr. Michael Hurdzan, ASGCA
Arthur Jackson, Oklahoma City, Oklahoma
William Johnson, Hanover CC, New Hampshire
A. H. Jolly, Jr., San Diego, California (son of Jack Jolly)
Harvey Junor, Portland GC, Oregon
Jack Kidwell, ASGCA
Ms. M. S. Kinney, Flossmoor CC, Illinois
Mrs. Joseph M. Lagerman, Jr., Pennsylvania (daughter of architect William Flynn)
Thomas Langford, Chicago, Illinois (son of William B. Langford)
William Lansdowne, The CC of Scranton, Pennsylvania
John P. LaPoint, The National Golf Foundation
Joseph L. Lee, Boynton Beach, Florida
James R. Lefevre, formerly The Royal Montreal, now Capilano G&CC, West Vancouver, British Columbia, Canada
James Lipe, Ann Arbor, Michigan
Bertram Lippincott, Jamestown, Rhode Island
Karl Litten, Miami, Florida
R. F. Loving, ASGCA
Melvin B. Lucas, The Piping Rock Club, Long Island, New York
Norman Macbeth, Jr., Spring Valley, New York (son of Norman Macbeth)
Neil C. H. Mackenzie, Town Clerk, St. Andrews, Fife, Scotland
H. G. MacPherson, Secretary, Royal Liverpool GC, England
Ted R. Maddock, The CC of Pittsfield, Massachusetts
Edward D. Magee, Jr., manager, Pine Valley GC, New Jersey
Dan Maples, ASGCA
Palmer Maples, The Golf Course Superintendents Association of America
Charles Martineau, The Whippoorwill Club, New York
Frank McGuiness, formerly The Lake Placid Club, New York
John C. McHose, Esq., Wilshire CC, California
Eleanora F. Miller, Colorado Springs, Colorado (daughter of Robert Foulis)
Robert Miller, Interlachen CC, Minnesota
Philip Mitchell, The Edison Club, New York
Harvey Moelter, St. Paul, Minnesota
Hugh Moore, Jr., professional, Brunswick CC, Georgia (son of Hugh Moore)
Sherwood Moore, formerly Woodway CC, Connecticut, now Winged Foot GC, New York
Rodney A. Morgan, Dartmouth College
George Morris, formerly Colonial CC, Pennsylvania (grandson of George Morris, brother of "Old Tom")
Harold Nathanson, The Plymouth CC, Massachusetts
W. H. Neale, The Connecticut Golf Association
Gary L. Nelson, Lee Park GC, North Dakota
(the late) Jack Neville
Paul J. O'Leary, Ekwanok GC, Vermont
Albert William Olsen, Jr., The Hotchkiss School, Connecticut
Warren Orlick, professional, Tam O'Shanter GC, Michigan
A. W. Patterson, Gulph Mills CC, Pennsylvania
David Patterson, Adventures in Golf, England
Ralph Plummer, ASGCA
Tom Rader, Sup't Shoreacres, Illinois
Alexander M. Radko, USGA Green Section
Fred Reese, Hot Springs G&TC, Virginia
W. H. Richardson, Royal Melbourne GC, Australia
David A. Root, Gary CC, Indiana
Warren Roseman, Glenview, Illinois (Son of Joseph Roseman)
Roger G. Rulewich, ASGCA
Leon St. Pierre, Longmeadow CC, Massachusetts
Chester Sawtelle, Sawtelle Brothers, Massachusetts
Janet Seagle, USGA
Charles H. Seaver, Pebble Beach, California
Edwin B. Seay, ASGCA
Brian Silva, Lake City Community College, Florida

316

Arthur A. Snyder, retired superintendent, Arizona
Jack Snyder, ASGCA
Frank Socash, Elmira CC, New York
D. M. A. Steel, BAGCA
(the late) Leonard Strong (brother of Herbert Strong)
Mrs. Leonard Strong, Center Valley, Pennsylvania
J. Hamilton Stutt, BAGCA
E. Clinton Swift, Jr., Golf Photography International
Frederick Swochuck, The Lake Placid Club, New York
George Thompson, The Columbia CC, Maryland

Alfred Tull, ASGCA
Mrs. C. D. Wagstaff, Boca Raton, Florida (widow of C. D. Wagstaff)
Edward Weeks, The Myopia Hunt Club, Massachusetts
Gordon Whitaker, British Transport Hotels
Roland Wild, The Vancouver Daily Province, British Columbia, Canada
Robert Williams, Bob-O-Link GC, Illinois
Katherine Cameron Winton, Bronxville, New York (daughter of Tom Winton)
Philip Wogan, ASGCA
Richard Wynn, The Wildwood Park GC, Iowa
Joan Zmistowski, West Palm Beach, Florida (daughter of Wilfrid Reid)

Photograph and Drawing Credits

The photographs of the renowned BRIAN MORGAN, official photographer for a host of British Opens and the 1981 United States Open, and the drawings of the talented course architect and artist WILLIAM G. ROBINSON of Calgary, Alberta, were a boundless help in illustrating the authors' thoughts. Special thanks are also due to the photographers listed below.

The authors are not unmindful that a number of persons generously provided wonderful illustrations that could not be used because of lack of space. Among these were Janet Seagle of the U.S.G.A., golf architects Robert Muir Graves and Richard Phelps and course superintendents Bruce Cadenelli (Hollywood G.C.), Edward Horton (Westchester C.C.), John O'Connell (Blue Rock G.C.), Tom Rader (Shore Acres G.C.) and Charles Tadge (Mayfield C.C.).

Photo Credits

ex-excluding
t-top
c-center
b-bottom
l-left
r-right

ASGCA (Paul Fullmer); 153
Cornish, Carol Burr; 42-43, 50 (t), 51, 54-55, 58-59 (ex bl), 78 (b), 82, 84 (tr),
91 (t), 94, 103 (tr, cr), 106-107 (ex cl, bl), 115 (b), 118 (t), 126-127, 136-137
deGarmo, John; 25 (t,b), 85 (b), 90, 91 (b)
Dickinson, Lawrence S.; 84-85 (t)
Dunn, Mrs. Gordon; 46 (cr)
Hemmer, John (Givens Memorial Library); 58 (bl), 70-71
Hawtree, Fred W.; 114-115 (ex br)
Jones, R.T. (Jones, Rulewich, Hoffman); 22, 96-97, 110-111 (bl)
Kelsey Airviews (Richard C. Kelsey); 34-35
Loft, Mara; 40 (bl), 56-57, 134-135
Mahoney, James; Cover Photo
Morgan, Brian (Golf Photography Int.); Jacket Photo, 6-7, 9, 10-11, 14-15, 17, 18, 23,
24, 26-27, 30-31, 37, 40 (ex bl), 52-53, 62-63, 65, 68-69, 72-73, 75 (t), 80-81, 98-99,
102-103 (ex tr, cr), 110-111 (tc & tr), 118 (b), 122-123, 148-149, 154-155
Robinson, William; 20, 21 (c,b), 29 (t), 83 (tr, cr, br), 128-133, 138-147
St. Pierre, Leon; 75 (b)
Silva, Brian; 78 (t), 86-87, 151
Steel, Donald; 19 (b)
Whitten, Ronald; 19 (t), 21 (t), 29 (b), 33, 45, 46 (ex cr), 48, 50 (b), 84 (b), 89,
93, 95, 106 (bl, cl), 109, 110-111 (br), 112-113, 119, 120-121, 124-125

INDEX

(Numbers in italics indicate illustrations of the named subject)

318

319